STUDY GUIDE
to accompany
McConnell and Brue
MICROECONOMICS

STUDY GUIDE
to accompany
McConnell and Brue
MICROECONOMICS

Sixteenth Edition

WILLIAM B. WALSTAD
PROFESSOR OF ECONOMICS
UNIVERSITY OF NEBRASKA–LINCOLN

ROBERT C. BINGHAM
LATE PROFESSOR OF ECONOMICS
KENT STATE UNIVERSITY

 McGraw Hill Irwin

Boston Burr Ridge, IL Dubuque, IA Madison, WI New York
San Francisco St. Louis Bangkok Bogotá Caracas Kuala Lumpur
Lisbon London Madrid Mexico City Milan Montreal New Delhi
Santiago Seoul Singapore Sydney Taipei Toronto

McGraw-Hill
Irwin

Study Guide to Accompany Microeconomics
Principles, Problems, and Policies

ISBN 0-07-288472-X

Editorial director: Robin Zwettler
Publisher: Gary Burke
Sponsoring editor: Lucille Sutton
Developmental editor: Erin Strathmann
Marketing manager: Martin Quinn
Project manager: Jean Lou Hess
Production supervisor: Rose Hepburn
Director of design: Keith McPherson
Editorial coordinator: Karen Minnich
Editorial assistant: Rebecca Hicks
Compositor: TechBooks
Typeface: Helvetica
Printer: Quebecor World Dubuque, Inc.

http://www.mhhe.com

About the Authors

William B. Walstad is a professor of economics at the University of Nebraska–Lincoln, where he directs the National Center for Research in Economic Education. He received his Ph.D. degree from the University of Minnesota. Professor Walstad has been honored with a Distinguished Teaching Award at Nebraska. He also received the Henry H. Villard Research Award for his published research in economic education. He is the chair of the Committee on Economic Education of the American Economic Association. He coedited *Teaching Undergraduate Economics: A Handbook for Instructors* (McGraw-Hill) and serves as an associate editor of the *Journal of Economic Education*.

Robert C. Bingham was an undergraduate student at DePauw University and obtained M.A. and Ph.D. degrees from Northwestern University. He taught at the University of Nebraska–Lincoln, where he was a colleague of Professor McConnell before moving to Kent State University, from which he retired in 1985. He was the author of several other study guides and supplements for the principles of economics courses.

To
Tammie, Laura, Kristin, Eileen, Clara, and Martha

Contents

How to Use the Study Guide to Learn Economics

This *Study Guide* is designed to help you read and understand Campbell R. McConnell and Stanley L. Brue's textbook, *Microeconomics,* sixteenth edition. If used properly, a study guide can be a great aid to you for what is probably your first course in economics.

No one pretends that the study of economics is easy, but it can be made easier. Of course, a study guide will not do your work for you, and its use is no substitute for reading the text. You must be willing to read the text, spend time on the subject, and work at learning if you wish to understand economics.

Many students do read their text and work hard on their economics course and still fail to learn the subject. This occurs because principles of economics is a new subject for these students, and they have had no previous experience in learning economics. They want to learn but do not know just how to go about it. Here is where the *Study Guide* can help. Let's first see what the *Study Guide* contains and then how to use it.

■ WHAT THE STUDY GUIDE IS

This *Study Guide* contains 25 chapters to support your learning of each of the 25 textbook chapters in *Microeconomics*. There are also two more *Study Guide* chapters that support the two **Bonus Web Chapters** for *Microeconomics*. In addition, the *Study Guide* has a **glossary** and answers to each end-of-chapter **Key Question** in your textbook. This *Study Guide* should give you a complete set of resources to advance your learning of principles of economics.

Each *Study Guide* chapter has 11 sections to give you complete coverage of the textbook material in each chapter. The first five sections identify and explain the basic content and concepts in each chapter.

1. An **introduction** explains what is in the chapter of the text and how it is related to material in earlier and later chapters. It points out topics to which you should give special attention and reemphasizes difficult or important principles and facts.

2. A **checklist** tells you the things you should be able to do when you have finished the chapter.

3. A **chapter outline** shows how the chapter is organized and summarizes briefly the essential points made in the chapter.

4. Selected **hints and tips** for each chapter help you master the material and make connections with any previous discussion of a topic.

5. A list of the **important terms** in the chapter points out what you must be able to define in order to understand the material in the chapter. A definition of each term is in the glossary at the end of the *Study Guide*.

The next six sections of the *Study Guide* allow you to **self-test** your understanding of the chapter material.

6. Fill-in questions (short-answer and list questions) help you learn and remember the important generalizations and facts in the chapter.

7. True–false questions test your understanding of the material in the chapter.

8. Multiple-choice questions also give you a chance to check your knowledge of the chapter content and prepare for this type of course examination.

9. Problems help you learn and understand economic concepts by requiring different skills—drawing a graph, completing a table, or finding relationships—to solve the problems.

10. Short answer and **essay questions** can be used as a self-test, to identify important questions in the chapter and to prepare for examinations.

11. Answers to fill-in questions, problems and projects, true–false questions, and multiple-choice questions are found at the end of each chapter. References to the specific pages in the textbook for each true–false, multiple-choice, and short answer or essay question are also provided.

■ HOW TO STUDY AND LEARN WITH THE HELP OF THE *STUDY GUIDE*

1. *Read and outline.* For best results, quickly read the introduction, outline, list of terms, and checklist in the *Study Guide* before you read the chapter in *Microeconomics*. Then read the chapter in the text slowly, keeping one eye on the *Study Guide* outline and the list of terms. Highlight the chapter as you read it by identifying the *major and minor* points and by placing *Study Guide* outline numbers or letters (such as I or A or 1 or a) in the margins. When you have completed the chapter, you will have the chapter highlighted, and the *Study Guide* outline will serve as a handy set of notes on the chapter.

2. *Review and reread.* After you have read the chapter in the text once, return to the introduction, outline, and list of terms in the *Study Guide*. Reread the introduction and outline. Does everything there make sense? If not, go back to the text and reread the topics that you do not remember well or that still confuse you. Look at the outline. Try to recall each of the minor topics or points that were contained in the text under each of the major points in the outline. When you come to the list of terms, go over them one by one. *Define or explain each to yourself and then look for the definition of the term either in the text chapter or in the glossa*ry. Compare your own definition or explanation with that in the *text or glossary.* The quick way to find the definition of a term in the text is to look in the text index for the page(s) in which that term or concept is mentioned. Make any necessary correction or change in your own definition or explanation.

3. Test and check answers. When you have done the above reading and review, you will have a good idea of what is in the text chapter. Now complete the self-test sections of the *Study Guide* to check your understanding.

In doing the self-test, start with the *fill-in, true–false, multiple-choice,* and *problems* sections. Tackle each of these four sections one at a time, using the following procedures: (1) answer as many self-test items as you can without looking in the text or in the answer section of the *Study Guide*; (2) check the text for whatever help you need in answering the items; and (3) consult the answer section of the *Study Guide* for the correct answers and reread any section of the text for which you missed items.

The self-test items in these four sections are not equally difficult. Some will be easy to answer and others will be harder. Do not expect to get them all correct the first time. Some are designed to pinpoint material of importance that you will probably miss the first time you read the text and answering them will get you to read the text again with more insight and understanding.

The *short answer and essay questions* cover the major points in the chapter. For some of the easier questions, all you may do is mentally outline your answer. For the more difficult questions, you may want to write out a brief outline of the answer or a full answer. Do not avoid the difficult questions just because they are more work. Answering these questions is often the most valuable work you can do toward acquiring an understanding of economic relationships and principles.

Although no answers are given in the *Study Guide* to the short answer and essay questions, the answer section does list text page references for each question. You are *strongly* encouraged to read those text pages for an explanation of the question or for better insight into the question content.

4. Double check. Before you turn to the next chapter in the text and *Study Guide,* return to the checklist. If you cannot honestly check off each item in the list, you have not learned what the authors of the text and of this *Study Guide* hoped you would learn.

■ BONUS WEB CHAPTERS FOR *MICROECONOMICS*

The *Study Guide* includes chapters to cover the textbook material in the two web-based chapters for *Microeconomics*: Applications and Extensions of Supply and Demand Analysis (Chapter 3W) and Transition Economies:

Russia and China (Chapter 26W). These chapters are available for students at www.mcconnell16.com.

■ GLOSSARY

All of the important terms and concepts in *Microeconomics* are defined and described in the glossary. It is included in the *Study Guide* for easy reference when you see a term or concept you do not know. It will also aid your work on self-test items in the *Study Guide*.

■ ANSWERS TO KEY QUESTIONS IN *ECONOMICS*

Your textbook has end-of-chapter questions that you can work on to further your understanding of economics. Some of these questions are designated as **Key Questions** because they cover important material. The answer to each Key Question is provided in the final part of the *Study Guide*. It is highly recommended that you try to complete these questions for each textbook chapter and then check the correct answers in the *Study Guide*.

■ SOME FINAL WORDS

Perhaps the method of using the *Study Guide* outlined above seems like a lot of work. It is! Study and learning necessarily entail work on your part. This is a fact you must accept if you are to learn economics.

After you have used the *Study Guide* to study three or four chapters, you will find that some sections are more valuable to you than others. Let your own experience determine how you will use it. But do not discontinue use of the *Study Guide* after three or four chapters merely because you are not sure whether it is helping you. **Stick with it.**

■ ACKNOWLEDGMENTS

The late Professor Robert Bingham prepared the first 10 editions of the *Study Guide* to serve as a valuable instructional aid for students. Although Professor Bingham did not participate directly in this revision, his work remains a major contribution.

I also want to acknowledge the other help I received. Campbell McConnell and Stanley Brue offered many insightful comments on the *Study Guide* and encouraged my work. I have also received valuable suggestions and help over the years from Kevin Clark, Loretta Fairchild, Joyce Gleason, Richard Harmstone, Ralph Lewis, Peter Kerr, Ken Rebeck, Dave Rosenbaum, Casey Snyder, Mary Stevenson, and Joshua Stull. Students in my principles of economics classes at the University of Nebraska–Lincoln continue to give me feedback that has improved the *Study Guide* with each edition. Sharon Nemeth has been of invaluable assistance in preparing and proofing the manuscript. Lucille Sutton and Erin Strathmann at McGraw-Hill provided great editorial and production support. In spite of the contributions from others, all responsibility for errors and omissions are mine. And as one final note, users of the *Study Guide* are encouraged to send me comments or suggestions at any time.

William B. Walstad

STUDY GUIDE
to accompany
McConnell and Brue
MICROECONOMICS

CHAPTER 1

The Nature and Method of Economics

Chapter 1 introduces you to economics—the study of how people decide how to use scarce productive resources to satisfy material wants. The purpose of this chapter is to explain the nature of the subject and to describe the methods that economists use to study economic questions.

The first section of the chapter describes the three key features of the *economic perspective.* This perspective first recognizes that all choices involve costs and that these costs must be involved in an economic decision. The economic perspective also incorporates the view that to achieve a goal, people make decisions that reflect their rational self-interest. The third feature considers that people compare marginal benefits against marginal costs when making decisions and will choose the situation where the marginal benefit is greater than the marginal cost. You will develop a better understanding of these features and the meaning of the economic perspective as you read about the economic issues in this book.

As you begin your study of economics, you might be wondering if the work you will do to learn the chapter material is worthwhile. It most certainly is. Knowledge of economics is important because it is essential for well-informed citizenship and has many practical applications to professional and personal decisions.

Economics relies heavily on the scientific method to develop theories and principles to explain the likely effects from human events and behavior. A central part of the economic methodology section focuses on *theoretical economics.* It involves gathering data, creating models, and making generalizations. In essence, economic theories and principles (and related terms such as hypotheses, laws, and models) are generalizations. They are imprecise statements and subject to exceptions because economists cannot easily conduct controlled laboratory experiments to test the validity of the generalizations. Economic theories and principles are simplifications—approximations of a complex world—for analyzing problems and for finding solutions to these problems.

Policy economics develops recommended actions (policies) for addressing an economic problem or advancing an economic goal. It involves stating the goal, considering the policy options, and evaluating the likely outcome. The analysis is based on economic theories and principles, but the choice of an economic policy often depends on the value judgments and weights given to different economic goals. In making a policy recommendation, we move from *economic theory* and *positive economics,* which investigates what is, to *normative economics,* which incorporates subjective views of what ought to be. Many of the apparent disagreements among economists are over normative policy issues and involve deciding which economic goals for our economy are most important in making the case for a policy solution.

Both theoretical economics and policy economics are conducted at two levels. Studies in *macroeconomics* focus on the whole economy, or large segments of it, and investigate such issues as how to increase economic growth, control inflation, or maintain full employment. Studies in *microeconomics* target specific units in the economy, and conduct research on such questions as how prices and output are determined for particular products and how consumers will react to price changes.

Clear thinking about economic questions requires that beginning students avoid many pitfalls. Errors of commission and omission can occur from bias, loaded terminology, imprecise definitions, fallacies of composition, and causation fallacies. Awareness of these pitfalls will help you think more objectively about the economic issues you will read about throughout this book.

■ CHECKLIST

When you have studied this chapter you should be able to

☐ Write a formal definition of economics.
☐ Describe the three key features of the economic perspective.
☐ Give applications of the economic perspective.
☐ Give two good reasons for studying economics.
☐ Identify the elements of the scientific method.
☐ Describe theoretical economics.
☐ Distinguish among hypotheses, theories, principles, laws, and models.
☐ Discuss how economic principles are generalizations and abstractions.
☐ Explain the "other things equal" (*ceteris paribus*) assumption and its use in economics.
☐ Define policy economics.
☐ List three steps in economic policymaking.
☐ Identify eight economic goals widely accepted in the United States and many other nations.
☐ Discuss the conflicting or complementary nature of economic goals.
☐ Distinguish between macroeconomics and microeconomics.

☐ Give examples of positive and normative economics.
☐ Identify the five pitfalls to objective thinking when given examples.

■ CHAPTER OUTLINE

1. Economics is concerned with the efficient use of limited productive resources to achieve the maximum satisfaction of economic wants.

2. The *economic perspective* has three interrelated features.
   a. It recognizes that scarcity requires choice and all choices entail a cost.
   b. It views people as rational decision makers who make choices based on their self-interests.
   c. It uses marginal analysis to assess how the marginal costs of a decision compare with the marginal benefits.

3. Citizens in a democracy must understand elementary economics to comprehend the present-day problems of their society and to make intelligent decisions when they vote. Economics is an academic rather than a vocational subject, but a knowledge of it is valuable to business executives, consumers, and workers.

4. Economic methodology relies on the scientific method and includes both theoretical economics and policy economics.
   a. *Theoretical economics* is the gathering and analysis of relevant facts to derive economic principles.
   (1) Hypotheses are propositions that are tested and used to develop economic theories. Highly reliable theories are called principles or laws. Theories, principles, and laws are meaningful statements about economic behavior or the economy that can be used to predict the likely outcome from an economic action or event. Models are created when several economic principles are used to explain or describe reality.
   (2) Each principle or theory is a generalization that shows a tendency or average effect.
   (3) The "other-things-equal" (*ceteris paribus*) assumption is used to limit the influence of other factors when making a generalization.
   (4) Economic principles and theories are abstractions from reality.
   (5) Many economic principles or models can be illustrated graphically.
   b. *Policy economics* is the use of economic principles to develop a course of action to solve economic problems.
   (1) The three steps in creating economic policy are stating the goal, considering the options, and evaluating the results.
   (2) Eight major economic goals are considered important in the United States and many other nations: economic growth, full employment, economic efficiency, price-level stability, economic freedom, economic security, an equitable distribution of income, and a balance of trade. Economic goals can be complementary, or they can conflict and require tradeoffs. The interpretation of economic goals and the setting of priorities can be difficult and cause problems in economic policymaking.

5. Economic analysis is conducted at two levels, and might be positive or normative.
   a. *Macroeconomics* looks at the entire economy or its major aggregates or sectors, such as households, businesses, or government.
   b. *Microeconomics* studies the economic behavior of individuals, particular markets, firms, or industries.
   c. *Positive economics* focuses on facts and is concerned with what is, or the scientific analysis of economic behavior.
   d. *Normative economics* suggests what ought to be and answers policy questions based on value judgments. Most disagreements among economists involve normative economics.

6. Sound reasoning in the study and use of economic principles requires strict application of the rules of logic, in which personal emotions are irrelevant, if not detrimental. The pitfalls beginning students encounter when studying and applying economic principles include the following:
   a. Bias of preconceived beliefs not warranted by facts.
   b. Loaded terminology or the use of terms in a way that appeals to emotion and leads to a nonobjective analysis of the issues.
   c. The definition of terms by economists in ways that may not be the same as the ways in which these terms are more commonly used.
   d. The fallacy of composition or the assumption that what is true of the part is necessarily true of the whole.
   e. Two causation fallacies confuse cause and effect.
   (1) The "after this, therefore because of this fallacy" (*post hoc, ergo propter hoc*) is the mistaken belief that when one event precedes another, the first event is the cause of the second.
   (2) The other fallacy is to confuse correlation with causation. Two factors may be related, but that does not mean that one factor caused the other.

■ HINTS AND TIPS

1. The economic perspective presented in the first section of the chapter has three features related to decision making: scarcity and the necessity of choice, rational self-interest in decision making, and marginal analysis of the costs and benefits of decisions. Although these features may seem strange to you at first, they are central to the economic thinking used to examine decisions and problems throughout the book.

2. The chapter introduces important pairs of terms: theoretical economics and policy economics; microeconomics and macroeconomics; and positive economics and normative economics. Make sure you understand what each pair means.

3. Sound reasoning about economic problems is difficult and requires that you be able to recognize the major pitfalls—loaded terminology, inaccurate definitions, fallacy of composition, *post hoc* fallacy, and confusing correlation with causation. One way to remember these pitfalls is to associate each one with a practical example.

■ **IMPORTANT TERMS**

Note: See Glossary in the back of the book for definitions of terms.

economics	tradeoffs
economic perspective	macroeconomics
utility	aggregate
marginal analysis	microeconomics
scientific method	positive economics
theoretical economics	normative economics
principles	fallacy of composition
generalizations	"after this, therefore because of this" fallacy (*post hoc, ergo propter hoc*)
"other-things-equal" assumption (*ceteris paribus*)	
policy economics	

SELF-TEST

■ **FILL-IN QUESTIONS**

1. Economics is the study of the efficient use of (unlimited, limited) _____ resources to achieve (minimum, maximum) _____ satisfaction of economic wants.

2. The economic perspective recognizes that (resources, scarcity) _____ requires choice and that choice has an opportunity (benefit, cost) _____. "There is no such thing as a free lunch" in economics because scarce resources have (unlimited, alternative) _____ uses.

3. The economic perspective also assumes that people make choices based on their self-interest and that they are (irrational, rational) _____. It also is based on comparisons of the (extreme, marginal) _____ costs and benefits of an economic decision.

4. An understanding of economics is essential if we are to be well-informed (citizens, technicians) _____, and such an understanding has many personal and professional applications even though it is (a vocational, an academic) _____ and not _____ subject.

5. Economics relies on the (model, scientific) _____ method. It involves the gathering of (facts, theories) _____, and the formulation of (data, hypotheses) _____. These are then tested to develop (facts, theories) _____.

6. The systematic arranging of facts, the interpretation of them, and the drawing of conclusions based on them is called (policy, theoretical) _____ economics.

7. Statements about economic behavior that enable the prediction of the likely effects of certain actions are economic (facts, theories) _____. The most reliable of these, those with strong predictive accuracy, are called (hypotheses, principles) _____. Sometimes they are also called (policies, laws) _____. Simplified representations of how markets or the economy works based on combinations of economic principles are called (policies, models) _____.

8. Economic principles are often imprecise quantitative statements or (fallacies, generalizations) _____ about people's economic behavior, and they necessarily involve (abstractions, distractions) _____ from reality to simplify complex situations.

9. When economists assume that other factors are held constant and do not change when studying an economic relationship, they are using the (*post hoc,* other-things-equal) _____ assumption.

10. The formulation of recommended solutions or remedies for economic problems is referred to as (theoretical, policy) _____ economics.

11. The three steps in the formulation of economic policy are (1) stating the economic (theory, goal) _____, (2) determining the policy (results, options) _____, and (3) implementing and evaluating policy (assumptions, effectiveness) _____.

12. Eight widely accepted economic goals in the United States and many nations are

a. _____
b. _____
c. _____
d. _____
e. _____
f. _____
g. _____
h. _____

13. Increases in economic growth that promote full employment would be an example of a set of (conflicting, complementary) _____ economic goals. Efforts to achieve an equitable distribution of income that at the same time reduce economic efficiency would be an example of a set of (conflicting, complementary) _____ economic goals, indicating that there are (tradeoffs, laws) _____ among economic goals.

14. The study of the total output of the economy or the general level of prices is the subject of (microeconomics, macroeconomics) _____, whereas the study of output in a particular industry or of a particular product is the subject of _____.

15. The collection of specific units that are being added and treated as if they were one unit is an (assumption, aggregate) _____.

16. Two different types of statements can be made about economic topics. A (positive, normative) _____ statement explains what is, by offering a scientific proposition about economic behavior that is based on economic theory and facts, but a _____ statement includes a value judgment about an economic policy or the economy that suggests what ought to be. Many of the reported disagreements among economists usually involve (positive, normative) _____ statements.

17. Holding a preconceived notion, such as thinking that corporate profits are always excessive, is an example of (an aggregate, a bias) _____ pitfall in sound economic thinking.

18. Pitfalls to sound economic thinking can also occur because terminology is (theoretical, loaded) _____ and definitions used by the public are based on (common, scientific) _____ usage.

19. The statement that "What is good for the individual is also good for the group" may not be correct because of the fallacy of (complexity, composition) _____.

20. The person who believes that "washing a car will cause it to rain tomorrow" is expressing an ("other-things-equal," "after this, therefore because of this") _____ fallacy.

■ TRUE–FALSE QUESTIONS

Circle T if the statement is true, F if it is false.

1. Economics is the social science concerned with the efficient use of scarce resources to achieve the maximum satisfaction of economic wants.   **T F**

2. From the economic perspective, "there is no such thing as a free lunch."   **T F**

3. Rational self-interest is the same thing as being selfish.   **T F**

4. The economic perspective views individuals or institutions as making rational choices based on the marginal analysis of the costs and benefits of decisions.   **T F**

5. Economics is academic and of little value because it does not teach the student how to earn a living.   **T F**

6. The scientific method involves the observation of real-world data, the formulation of hypotheses based on the data, and the testing of those hypotheses to develop theories.   **T F**

7. Systematically arranging facts, interpreting them, and using them to derive economic principles is called economic analysis.   **T F**

8. Economic principles enable us to predict the economic consequences of many human actions.   **T F**

9. The most reliable economic theories are often called economic principles or laws.   **T F**

10. An economic model is simply an adding up of economic facts about an economic event.   **T F**

11. The "other-things-equal" or *ceteris paribus* assumption is made to simplify the reasoning process.   **T F**

12. Economic principles, or theories, are abstractions.   **T F**

13. The first step in the formulation of an economic policy, the statement of goals, may be occasion for disagreement because different people may have different and conflicting goals to be achieved.   **T F**

14. Determining the policy options requires a detailed assessment of the benefits, costs, and political feasibility of alternative policies.   **T F**

15. One of the widely (although not universally) accepted economic goals of people in the United States is an equitable distribution of income.   **T F**

16. A tradeoff is a situation in which some of one economic goal is sacrificed to obtain some of another economic goal.   **T F**

17. Macroeconomic analysis is concerned with the economic activity of specific firms or industries.   **T F**

18. Microeconomic analysis is concerned with the performance of the economy as a whole or its major aggregates.   **T F**

19. The statement that "the legal minimum wage should be raised to give working people a decent income" is an example of a normative statement.   **T F**

20. When value judgments are made about the economy or economic policy, this is called positive economics.   **T F**

21. The belief that lending money is always superior to borrowing money is an example of a bias in sound reasoning about economic issues.   **T F**

22. The fallacy of composition would be calling profits "excessive" or an unemployed worker "lazy."   **T F**

23. If you speak of "capital" to most people, they understand that you are referring to money. The economist, therefore, is obligated to use the term "capital" to mean money. **T F**

24. The *post hoc, ergo propter hoc* fallacy is the belief that "what is true for the individual or part of a group is necessarily true for the group or whole." **T F**

25. A person who concludes that more education increases income may be confusing correlation with causation. **T F**

■ **MULTIPLE-CHOICE QUESTIONS**

Circle the letter that corresponds to the best answer.

1. What statement would best complete a short definition of economics? "Economics is the study of
(a) how businesses produce goods and services"
(b) the efficient use of scarce productive resources"
(c) the equitable distribution of society's income and wealth"
(d) the printing and circulation of money throughout the economy"

2. The idea in economics that "there is no such thing as a free lunch" means that
(a) the marginal benefit of such a lunch is greater than its marginal cost
(b) businesses cannot increase their market share by offering free lunches
(c) scarce resources have alternative uses or opportunity costs
(d) consumers are irrational when they ask for a free lunch

3. A major feature of the economic perspective is
(a) equating rational self-interest with selfishness
(b) comparing marginal benefits with marginal costs
(c) the validity of normative economics for decision making
(d) the recognition of the abundance of economic resources

4. From the economic perspective, when a business decides to employ more workers, the business decision maker has most likely concluded that the marginal
(a) costs of employing more workers have decreased
(b) benefits of employing more workers have increased
(c) benefits of employing more workers are greater than the marginal costs
(d) costs of employing more workers are not opportunity costs for the business because more workers are needed to increase production

5. Economic analysis that derives economic principles about how individuals behave or institutions act is called
(a) policy economics
(b) macroeconomics
(c) normative economics
(d) theoretical economics

6. The combination of economic theories or principles into a simplified representation of reality is referred to as an economic
(a) fact
(b) law
(c) model
(d) hypothesis

7. From the perspective of economists, which of the following would offer the highest degree of confidence for explaining economic behavior
(a) an assumption
(b) a speculation
(c) a correlation
(d) a principle

8. When economists state that "consumer spending rises when personal income increases," this is an example of
(a) a generalization
(b) loaded terminology
(c) a normative statement
(d) a fallacy of composition

9. Another term for the assumption that "other things equal" is
(a) *ceteris paribus*
(b) the correlation fallacy
(c) the fallacy of composition
(d) *post hoc, ergo propter hoc*

10. An economic principle states that the lower the price of a product, the greater the quantity consumers will wish to purchase. This principle is based on the critical assumption that
(a) economic analysis is normative
(b) the whole is not greater than the sum of the parts
(c) economic goals are complementary and not conflicting
(d) there are no other important changes affecting the demand for the product

11. The three basic steps in economic policymaking are
(a) gather facts, make abstractions, show findings
(b) state the goal, determine the options, evaluate results
(c) create the theory, analyze assumptions, derive conclusions
(d) form hypotheses, simplify the model, assume other things are equal

12. The production of more goods and services and the development of a higher standard of living would be associated with what economic goal?
(a) economic security
(b) economic freedom
(c) economic growth
(d) full employment

13. Which economic goal is associated with the idea that we want to get the maximum benefit at the minimum cost from the limited productive resources available?
(a) economic security
(b) economic freedom
(c) economic growth
(d) economic efficiency

14. Which economic goal would be most abstract and difficult to measure?
- **(a)** full employment
- **(b)** economic efficiency
- **(c)** economic freedom
- **(d)** price-level stability

15. To say that two economic goals are conflicting means
- **(a)** it is impossible to quantify both goals
- **(b)** there is a tradeoff in the achievement of the two goals
- **(c)** the two goals are not fully accepted as important economic goals
- **(d)** the attainment of one goal also results in the attainment of the other goal

16. If economic growth tends to produce a more equitable distribution of income among people in a nation, this relationship between the two economic goals appears to be
- **(a)** deductive
- **(b)** conflicting
- **(c)** complementary
- **(d)** mutually exclusive

17. When we look at the whole economy or its major aggregates, our analysis would be at the level of
- **(a)** microeconomics
- **(b)** macroeconomics
- **(c)** positive economics
- **(d)** normative economics

18. Which would be studied in microeconomics?
- **(a)** the output of the entire U.S. economy
- **(b)** the general level of prices in the U.S. economy
- **(c)** the output and price of wheat in the United States
- **(d)** the total number of workers employed in the United States

19. Which is a normative economic statement?
- **(a)** The consumer price index rose 1.2% last month.
- **(b)** The unemployment rate of 6.8% is too high.
- **(c)** The average rate of interest on loans is 4.6%.
- **(d)** The economy grew at an annual rate of 3.6%.

20. Sandra states that "there is a high correlation between consumption and income." Arthur replies that the correlation occurs because "people consume too much of their income and don't save enough."
- **(a)** Both Sandra's and Arthur's statements are positive.
- **(b)** Both Sandra's and Arthur's statements are normative.
- **(c)** Sandra's statement is positive and Arthur's statement is normative.
- **(d)** Sandra's statement is normative and Arthur's statement is positive.

21. What pitfall to sound reasoning is reflected in a person's view that corporate profits are always excessive?
- **(a)** bias
- **(b)** definition
- **(c)** the fallacy of composition
- **(d)** confusing correlation and causation

22. During World War II, the United States used price controls to prevent inflation; some people said this was "a fascist and arbitrary restriction of economic freedom," while others said it was "a necessary and democratic means of preventing ruinous inflation." Both labels are examples of
- **(a)** economic bias
- **(b)** loaded terminology
- **(c)** the fallacy of composition
- **(d)** the misuse of commonsense definitions

23. If a farmer grows a larger crop one year, he or she will likely receive more income. Therefore, to reason that if all farmers grew larger crops one year they will likely receive more income is an example of
- **(a)** the after this, therefore because of this fallacy
- **(b)** the fallacy of composition
- **(c)** using loaded terminology
- **(d)** economic bias

24. The government increases its expenditures for road construction equipment, and later the average price of this equipment falls. The belief that the lowered price was the result of the increase in government expenditures is an example of
- **(a)** the after this, therefore because of this fallacy
- **(b)** the fallacy of composition
- **(c)** using loaded terminology
- **(d)** imprecise definition

25. You observe that more education is associated with more income and conclude that more income leads to more education. This would be an example of
- **(a)** the fallacy of composition
- **(b)** confusing correlation and causation
- **(c)** using the other-things-equal assumption
- **(d)** the after this, therefore because of this fallacy

■ PROBLEMS

1. Use the appropriate number to match the terms with the phrase.

1. economics	5. microeconomics
2. theoretical economics	6. positive economics
3. policy economics	7. normative economics
4. macroeconomics	8. marginal analysis

a. The formulation of courses of action to bring about desired economic outcomes or to prevent undesired occurrences. _____

b. The attempt to establish scientific statements about economic behavior; a concern with "what is" rather than "what ought to be." _____

c. Part of economics that involves value judgments about what the economy should be like or the way the economic world should be. _____

d. Social science concerned with the efficient use of scarce resources to achieve maximum satisfaction of human material wants. _____

e. Part of economics concerned with the whole economy or its major sectors. _____

f. The comparison of additional benefits and additional costs. _____

THE NATURE AND METHOD OF ECONOMICS 7

g. Deriving economic principles from relevant economic facts. _____

h. Part of economics concerned with the economic behavior of individual units such as households, firms, and industries (particular markets). _____

2. News report: "The worldwide demand for wheat from the United States increased and caused the price of wheat in the United States to rise." This is a *specific* instance of a more *general* economic principle. Of which economic *generalization* is this a particular example? _____

_____

_____

3. Following is a list of economic statements. Indicate in the space to the right of each statement whether it is positive (**P**) or normative (**N**). Then, in the last four lines below, write two of your own examples of positive economic statements and two examples of normative economic statements.

a. New York City should control the rental price of apartments. _____

b. Consumer prices rose at an annual rate of 2% last year. _____

c. Most people who are unemployed are just too lazy to work. _____

d. Generally, if you lower the price of a product, people will buy more of that product. _____

e. The profits of drug companies are too large and ought to be used to conduct research on new medicines. _____

f. Government should do more to help the poor. _____

g. _____ P

h. _____ P

i. _____ N

j. _____ N

4. Following are five statements. Each is an example of one of the pitfalls frequently encountered in the study of economics. Indicate in the space following each statement the type of pitfall involved.

a. "Investment in stocks and bonds is the only way to build real capital assets." _____

b. "An unemployed worker can find a job if the worker looks diligently and conscientiously for employment; therefore, all unemployed workers can find employment if they are diligent and conscientious in looking for a job."

_____

c. McConnell: "Regulation of public utilities in the United States is an immoral and unconscionable interference with the divine right of private property and, as you know, there is no private property in the socialist nations." **Brue:** "It is far from that. You know perfectly well that it is an attempt to limit the unmitigated

avarice of mammoth corporations in order, as the Constitution commands, to promote the general welfare of a democratic America." _____

_____

d. "The stock market crash of 1929 was followed by and resulted in 10 years of depression." _____

_____

e. "Be neither a borrower nor lender of money." _____

_____

■ **SHORT ANSWER AND ESSAY QUESTIONS**

1. Define economics in both a less and a more sophisticated way. In your latter definition, explain the meaning of "resources" and "wants."

2. What are the three interrelated features of the economic perspective?

3. What is the economic meaning of the statement "There is no such thing as a free lunch"?

4. What is the difference between rational self-interest and selfishness?

5. How do economists use marginal analysis?

6. What are the principal reasons for studying economics?

7. What are the elements of the scientific method?

8. Define and explain the relationships between economic theory and policy economics.

9. What are the differences and similarities between hypotheses, theories, principles, laws, and models?

10. What is a "laboratory experiment under controlled conditions"? Does the science of economics have any kind of laboratory? Why do economists use the "other-things-equal" assumption?

11. Why are economic principles and models necessarily generalized and abstract?

12. What does it mean to say that economic principles can be used for prediction?

13. What procedure should be followed in formulating sound economic policies?

14. Of the eight economic goals listed in the text, which one would you rank first, second, third, and so on? Would you add any other goals to this list? If the goals of full employment and price-level stability were conflicting, which goal would you prefer? Why? If goals of economic growth and an equitable distribution of income were conflicting, which would you prefer? Why?

15. How can the concept "tradeoffs" be applied to the discussion of economic goals? Give an example.

16. Explain the difference between macroeconomics and microeconomics.

17. Why do economists disagree?

18. What are some current examples of positive economic statements and normative economic statements?

19. Explain each of the following terms:
   (a) fallacy of composition
   (b) loaded terminology
   (c) the *post hoc, ergo propter hoc* fallacy

20. Use an example to describe how correlation differs from causation.

ANSWERS

Chapter 1 The Nature and Method of Economics

FILL-IN QUESTIONS

1. limited, maximum
2. scarcity, cost, alternative
3. rational, marginal
4. citizens, an academic, a vocational
5. scientific, facts, hypotheses, theories
6. theoretical
7. theories, principles, laws, models
8. generalizations, abstractions
9. other-things-equal (or *ceteris paribus*)
10. policy
11. goal, options, effectiveness
12. *a.* economic growth; *b.* full employment; *c.* economic efficiency; *d.* price stability; *e.* economic freedom; *f.* equitable distribution of income; *g.* economic security; *h.* balance of trade (*any order for a–h*)
13. complementary, conflicting, tradeoffs
14. macroeconomics, microeconomics
15. aggregate
16. positive, normative, normative
17. bias
18. loaded, common
19. composition
20. "after this, therefore because of this"

TRUE–FALSE QUESTIONS

1. T, p. 3	**8.** T, pp. 6–7	**15.** T, p. 9	**22.** F, p. 11
2. T, p. 3	**9.** T, pp. 6–7	**16.** T, p. 9	**23.** F, p. 11
3. F, p. 4	**10.** F, pp. 6–7	**17.** F, pp. 9–10	**24.** F, p. 11
4. T, pp. 4–5	**11.** T, pp. 7–8	**18.** F, pp. 9–10	**25.** T, pp. 11–12
5. F, p. 5	**12.** T, p. 8	**19.** T, p. 10	
6. T, p. 6	**13.** T, pp. 8–9	**20.** F, p. 10	
7. F, p. 6	**14.** T, p. 8	**21.** T, p. 10	

MULTIPLE-CHOICE QUESTIONS

1. b, p. 3	**8.** a, p. 7	**15.** b, p. 9	**22.** b, p. 10–11
2. c, pp. 3–4	**9.** a, pp. 7–8	**16.** c, p. 9	**23.** b, p. 11
3. b, pp. 4–5	**10.** d, pp. 7–8	**17.** b, p. 9	**24.** a, p. 11
4. c, pp. 4–5	**11.** b, p. 8	**18.** c, p. 9–10	**25.** b, pp. 11–12
5. d, p. 6	**12.** c, p. 8	**19.** b, p. 10	
6. c, p. 7	**13.** d, p. 9	**20.** c, p. 10	
7. d, p. 7	**14.** c, p. 9	**21.** a, pp. 10–11	

PROBLEMS

1. *a.* 3; *b.* 6; *c.* 7; *d.* 1; *e.* 4; *f.* 8; *g.* 2; *h.* 5
2. An increase in the demand for an economic good will cause the price of that good to rise.
3. *a.* N; *b.* P; *c.* N; *d.* P; *e.* N; *f.* N
4. *a.* definitions; *b.* the fallacy of composition; *c.* loaded terminology; *d.* the after this, therefore because of this fallacy; *e.* bias

SHORT ANSWER AND ESSAY QUESTIONS

1. p. 3	**6.** pp. 5–6	**11.** pp. 7–8	**16.** pp. 9–10
2. pp. 3–4	**7.** p. 6	**12.** pp. 7–8	**17.** p. 10
3. pp. 3–4	**8.** pp. 6–9	**13.** pp. 8–9	**18.** p. 10
4. p. 4	**9.** pp. 6–8	**14.** pp. 8–9	**19.** pp. 10–11
5. p. 4	**10.** pp. 7–8	**15.** p. 9	**20.** pp. 11–12

Graphs and Their Meaning

This appendix introduces graphing in economics. Graphs help illustrate and simplify the economic theories and models presented throughout this book. The old saying that "a picture is worth 1000 words" applies to economics; graphs are the way that economists "picture" relationships between economic variables.

You must master the basics of graphing if these "pictures" are to be of any help to you. This appendix explains how to achieve that mastery. It shows you how to construct a graph from a table with data of two variables, such as income and consumption.

Economists usually, but not always, place the *independent variable* (income) on the horizontal axis and the *dependent variable* (consumption) on the vertical axis of the graph. Once the data points are plotted and a line drawn to connect the plotted points, you can determine whether there is a *direct* or an *inverse relationship* between the variables. Identifying direct and inverse relationships between variables is an essential skill used repeatedly in this book.

Information from data in graphs and tables can be written in an equation. This work involves determining the *slope* and *intercept* from a straight line in a graph or data in a table. Using values for the slope and intercept, you can write a *linear equation* that will enable you to calculate what the dependent variable would be for a given level of the independent variable.

Some graphs used in the book are *nonlinear*. With *nonlinear curves,* the slope of the line is no longer constant throughout but varies as one moves along the curve. This slope can be estimated at a point by determining the slope of a straight line that is drawn tangent to the curve at that point. Similar calculations can be made for other points to see how the slope changes along the curve.

■ **APPENDIX CHECKLIST**

After you have studied this appendix you should be able to

☐ Explain why economists use graphs.
☐ Construct a graph of two variables using the numerical data from a table.
☐ Make a table with two variables from data on a graph.
☐ Distinguish between a direct and an inverse relationship when given data on two variables.
☐ Identify dependent and independent variables in economic examples and graphs.
☐ Describe how economists use the other-things-equal (*ceteris paribus*) assumption in graphing two variables.

☐ Calculate the slope of a straight line between two points when given the tabular data, and indicate whether the slope is positive or negative.
☐ Describe how slopes are affected by the choice of the units of measurement for either variable.
☐ Explain how slopes are related to marginal analysis.
☐ Graph infinite or zero slopes and explain their meaning.
☐ Determine the vertical intercept for a straight line in a graph with two variables.
☐ Write a linear equation using the slope of a line and the vertical intercept; when given a value for the independent variable, determine a value for the dependent variable.
☐ Estimate the slope of a nonlinear curve at a point using a line that is tangent to the curve at that point.

■ **APPENDIX OUTLINE**

1. Graphs illustrate the relationship between variables and give economists and students another way, in addition to verbal explanation, of understanding economic phenomena. Graphs are aids in describing economic theories and models.

2. The construction of a simple graph involves plotting the numerical data of two variables from a table.
  a. Each graph has a *horizontal axis* and a *vertical axis* that can be labeled for each variable and then scaled for the range of the data points that will be measured on the axis.
  b. Data points are plotted on the graph by drawing perpendiculars from the scaled points on the two axes to the place on the graph where the perpendiculars intersect.
  c. A line or curve can then be drawn to connect the points plotted on the graph. If the graph is a straight line, it is *linear.*

3. A graph provides information about relationships between variables.
  a. An upward-sloping line to the right on a graph indicates that there is a positive or *direct relationship* between two variables: an increase in one is associated with an increase in the other; a decrease in one is associated with a decrease in the other.
  b. A downward-sloping line to the right means that there is a negative or *inverse relationship* between the two variables: an increase in one is associated with a decrease in the other; a decrease in one is associated with an increase in the other.

4. Economists are often concerned with determining cause and effect in economic events.

    a. A *dependent variable* changes (increases or decreases) because of a change in another variable.

    b. An *independent variable* produces or "causes" the change in the dependent variable.

    c. In a graph, mathematicians place an independent variable on the horizontal axis and a dependent variable on the vertical axis; economists are more arbitrary about which variable is placed on an axis.

5. Economic graphs are simplifications of economic relationships. When graphs are plotted, usually an implicit assumption is made that all other factors are being held constant. This "other-things-equal" or *ceteris paribus* assumption is used to simplify the analysis so the study can focus on the two variables of interest.

6. The *slope of a straight line* in a two-variable graph is the ratio of the vertical change to the horizontal change between two points.

    a. A *positive* slope indicates that the relationship between the two variables is *direct*.

    b. A *negative* slope indicates that there is an *inverse* relationship between the two variables.

    c. Slopes are affected by the *measurement units* for either variable.

    d. Slopes measure *marginal* changes.

    e. Slopes can be *infinite* (line parallel to vertical axis) or *zero* (line parallel to horizontal axis).

7. The *vertical intercept* of a straight line in a two-variable graph is the point where the line intersects the vertical axis of the graph.

8. The slope and intercept of a straight line can be expressed in the form of a *linear equation,* which is written as $y = a + bx$. Once the values for the intercept (**a**) and the slope (**b**) are calculated, then given any value of the independent variable (**x**), the value of the dependent variable (**y**) can be determined.

9. The slope of a straight line is constant, but the slope of a *nonlinear curve* changes throughout. To estimate the slope of a nonlinear curve at a point, the slope of a line tangent to the curve at that point is calculated.

■ HINTS AND TIPS

1. This appendix will help you understand the graphs and problems presented throughout the book. Do not skip reading the appendix or working on the self-test questions and problems in this *Study Guide*. The time you invest now will pay off in improved understanding in later chapters. Graphing is a basic skill for economic analysis.

2. Positive and negative relationships in graphs often confuse students. To overcome this confusion, draw a two-variable graph with a positive slope and another two-variable graph with a negative slope. In each graph, show what happens to the value of one variable when there is a change in the value of the other variable.

3. A straight line in a two-variable graph can be expressed in an equation. Make sure you know how to interpret each part of the linear equation.

■ IMPORTANT TERMS

vertical axis	independent variable
horizontal axis	slope of a straight line
direct (positive) relationship	vertical intercept
inverse (negative) relationship	nonlinear curve
dependent variable	tangent

SELF-TEST

■ FILL-IN QUESTIONS

1. The relationship between two economic variables can be visualized with the aid of a two-dimensional (graph, matrix) _____, which has (a horizontal, an inverse) _____ axis and a (vertical, direct) _____ axis.

2. Customarily, the (dependent, independent) _____ variable is placed on the horizontal axis and the _____ is placed on the vertical axis. The _____ variable is said to change because of a change in the _____ variables.

3. The vertical and horizontal (scales, ranges) _____ of the graph are calibrated to reflect the _____ of values in the table of data points on which the graph is based.

4. The graph of a straight line that slopes downward to the right indicates that there is (a direct, an inverse) _____ relationship between the two variables. A graph of a straight line that slopes upward to the right tells us that the relationship is (direct, inverse) _____. When the value of one variable increases and the value of the other variable increases, then the relationship is _____; when the value of one increases, while the other decreases, the relationship is _____.

5. When interpreting an economic graph, the "cause" or the "source" is the (dependent, independent) _____ variable and the "effect" or "outcome" is the _____ variable.

6. Other variables, beyond the two in a two-dimensional graph, that might affect the economic relationship are assumed to be (changing, held constant) _____. This assumption is also referred to as the "other-things-equal" assumption or as (*post hoc, ceteris paribus*) _____.

7. The slope of a straight line between two points is defined as the ratio of the (vertical, horizontal) _____ change to the _____ change.

8. When two variables move in the same direction, the slope will be (negative, positive) _____; when the variables move in opposite directions, the slope will be _____.

9. The slope of a line will be affected by the (units of measurement, vertical intercept) _____.

10. The concept of a slope is important to economists because it reflects the (marginal, total) _____ change in one variable on another variable.

11. A graph of a line with an infinite slope is (horizontal, vertical) _____, while a graph of a line with a zero slope is _____.

12. The point at which the slope of the line meets the vertical axis is called the vertical (tangent, intercept) _____.

13. We can express the graph of a straight line with a linear equation that can be written as $y = a + bx$.

  a. a is the (slope, intercept) _____ and b is the _____.

  b. y is the (dependent, independent) _____ variable and x is the _____ variable.
  c. If a were 2, b were 4, and x were 5, then y would be _____. If the value of x changed to 7, then y would be _____. If the value of x changed to 3, then y would be _____.

14. The slope of a (straight line, nonlinear curve) _____ is constant throughout; the slope of a _____ varies from point to point.

15. An estimate of the slope of a nonlinear curve at a certain point can be made by calculating the slope of a straight line that is (tangent, perpendicular) _____ to the point on the curve.

■ **TRUE–FALSE QUESTIONS**

Circle T if the statement is true, F if it is false.

1. Economists design graphs to confuse people. **T F**

2. If the straight line on a two-variable graph slopes downward to the right, then there is a positive relationship between the two variables. **T F**

3. A variable that changes as a consequence of a change in another variable is considered a dependent variable. **T F**

4. Economists always put the independent variable on the horizontal axis and the dependent variable on the vertical axis of a two-variable graph. **T F**

5. *Ceteris paribus* means that other variables are changing at the same time. **T F**

6. In the ratio for the calculation of the slope of a straight line, the vertical change is in the numerator and the horizontal change is in the denominator. **T F**

7. If the slope of the linear relationship between consumption and income was .90, then it tells us that for every $1 increase in income there will be a $.90 increase in consumption. **T F**

8. The slope of a straight line in a two-variable graph will *not* be affected by the choice of the units for either variable. **T F**

9. The slopes of lines measure marginal changes. **T F**

10. Assume in a graph that price is on the vertical axis and quantity is on the horizontal axis. The absence of a relationship between price and quantity would be a straight line parallel to the horizontal axis. **T F**

11. A line with an infinite slope in a two-variable graph is parallel to the horizontal axis. **T F**

12. In a two-variable graph, income is graphed on the vertical axis and the quantity of snow is graphed on the horizontal axis. If income was independent of the quantity of snow, then this independence would be represented by a line parallel to the horizontal axis. **T F**

13. If a linear equation is $y = 10 + 5x$, the vertical intercept is 5. **T F**

14. When a line is tangent to a nonlinear curve, then it intersects the curve at a particular point. **T F**

15. If the slope of a straight line on a two-variable (x, y) graph were .5 and the vertical intercept were 5, then a value of 10 for x would mean that y is also 10. **T F**

16. A slope of -4 for a straight line in a two-variable graph indicates that there is an inverse relationship between the two variables. **T F**

17. If x is an independent variable and y is a dependent variable, then a change in y results in a change in x. **T F**

18. An upward slope for a straight line that is tangent to a nonlinear curve indicates that the slope of the nonlinear curve at that point is positive. **T F**

19. If one pair of x, y points was (13, 10) and the other pair was (8, 20), then the slope of the straight line between the two sets of points in the two-variable graph, with x on the horizontal axis and y on the vertical axis, would be 2. **T F**

20. When the value of *x* is 2, a value of 10 for *y* would be calculated from a linear equation of *y* = −2 + 6*x*.

T   F

■ **MULTIPLE-CHOICE QUESTIONS**

Circle the letter that corresponds to the best answer.

1. If an increase in one variable is associated with a decrease in another variable, then we can conclude that the variables are
(a) nonlinear
(b) directly related
(c) inversely related
(d) positively related

2. The ratio of the absolute vertical change to the absolute horizontal change between two points of a straight line is the
(a) slope
(b) vertical intercept
(c) horizontal intercept
(d) point of tangency

3. There are two sets of *x, y* points on a straight line in a two-variable graph, with *y* on the vertical axis and *x* on the horizontal axis. If one set of points was (0, 5) and the other set (5, 20), the linear equation for the line would be
(a) *y* = 5*x*
(b) *y* = 5 + 3*x*
(c) *y* = 5 + 15*x*
(d) *y* = 5 + .33*x*

4. In a two-variable graph of data on the price and quantity of a product, economists place
(a) price on the horizontal axis because it is the independent variable and quantity on the vertical axis because it is the dependent variable
(b) price on the vertical axis because it is the dependent variable and quantity on the horizontal axis because it is the independent variable
(c) price on the vertical axis even though it is the independent variable and quantity on the horizontal axis even though it is the dependent variable
(d) price on the horizontal axis even though it is the dependent variable and quantity on the vertical axis even though it is the independent variable

5. In a two-dimensional graph of the relationship between two economic variables, an assumption is usually made that
(a) both variables are linear
(b) both variables are nonlinear
(c) other variables are held constant
(d) other variables are permitted to change

6. If the slope of a straight line is zero, then the straight line is
(a) vertical
(b) horizontal
(c) upward sloping
(d) downward sloping

Questions 7, 8, 9, and 10 are based on the following four data sets. In each set, the independent variable is in the left column and the dependent variable is in the right column.

(1)		(2)		(3)		(4)	
A	B	C	D	E	F	G	H
0	1	0	12	4	5	0	4
3	2	5	8	6	10	1	3
6	3	10	4	8	15	2	2
9	4	15	0	10	20	3	1

7. There is an inverse relationship between the independent and dependent variable in data sets
(a) 1 and 4
(b) 2 and 3
(c) 1 and 3
(d) 2 and 4

8. The vertical intercept is 4 in data set
(a) 1
(b) 2
(c) 3
(d) 4

9. The linear equation for data set 1 is
(a) *B* = 3*A*
(b) *B* = 1 + 3*A*
(c) *B* = 1 + .33*A*
(d) *A* = 1 + .33*B*

10. The linear equation for data set 2 is
(a) *C* = 12 − 1.25*D*
(b) *D* = 12 + 1.25*C*
(c) *D* = 12 − .80*C*
(d) *C* = 12 − .80*D*

Answer Questions 11, 12, 13, and 14 on the basis of the following diagram.

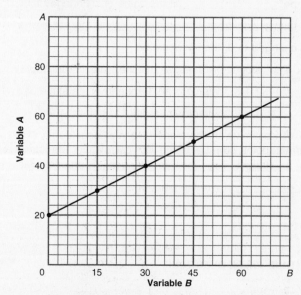

11. The variables *A* and *B* are:
(a) positively related
(b) negatively related
(c) indirectly related
(d) nonlinear

12. The slope of the line is
  (a) .33
  (b) .67
  (c) 1.50
  (d) 3.00

13. The vertical intercept is
  (a) 80
  (b) 60
  (c) 40
  (d) 20

14. The linear equation for the slope of the line is
  (a) $A = 20 + .33B$
  (b) $B = 20 + .33A$
  (c) $A = 20 + .67B$
  (d) $B = 20 + .67A$

Answer Questions 15, 16, and 17 on the basis of the following diagram.

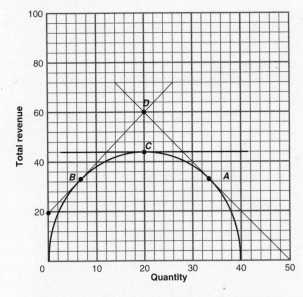

15. The slope of the line tangent to the curve at point **A** is
  (a) 2
  (b) −2
  (c) −1.5
  (d) −0.5

16. The slope of the line tangent to the curve at point **B** is
  (a) −2
  (b) 2
  (c) 3
  (d) 0.5

17. The slope of the line tangent to the curve at point **C** is
  (a) −1
  (b) 1
  (c) 0
  (d) undefined

18. Assume that the relationship between concert ticket prices and attendance is expressed in the equation $P =$ $25 - 1.25Q$, where **P** equals ticket price and **Q** equals concert attendance in thousands of people. On the basis of this equation, it can be said that
  (a) more people will attend the concert when the price is high compared to when the price is low
  (b) if 12,000 people attended the concert, then the ticket price was $10
  (c) if 18,000 people attended the concert, then entry into the concert was free
  (d) an increase in ticket price by $5 reduces concert attendance by 1000 people

19. If you know that the equation relating consumption (**C**) to income (**Y**) is $C = \$7,500 + .2Y$, then
  (a) consumption is inversely related to income
  (b) consumption is the independent variable and income is the dependent variable
  (c) if income is $15,000, then consumption is $10,500
  (d) if consumption is $30,000, then income is $10,000

20. If the dependent variable changes by 22 units when the independent variable changes by 12 units, then the slope of the line is
  (a) 0.56
  (b) 1.83
  (c) 2.00
  (d) 3.27

■ **PROBLEMS**

1. Following are three tables for making graphs. On the graphs, plot the economic relationships contained in each table. Be sure to label each axis of the graph and indicate the unit measurement and scale used on each axis.
  a. Use the table at the top of the next page to graph national income on the horizontal axis and consumption expenditures on the vertical axis below; connect the seven points and label the curve "Consumption." The relationship between income and consumption

is (a direct, an inverse) _____ one and the consumption curve is (an up-, a down-)

_____ sloping curve.

National income, billions of dollars	Consumption expenditures, billions of dollars
$ 600	$ 600
700	640
800	780
900	870
1000	960
1100	1050
1200	1140

b. Use the next table to graph investment expenditures on the horizontal axis and the rate of interest on the vertical axis; connect the seven points and label the curve "Investment." The relationship between the rate of interest and investment expenditures is (a direct, an inverse) _____ one and the investment curve is (an up-, a down-) _____ sloping curve.

Rate of interest, %	Investment expenditures, billions of dollars
8	$220
7	280
6	330
5	370
4	400
3	420
2	430

0

c. Use the next table to graph average salary on the horizontal axis and wine consumption on the vertical axis; connect the seven points.

Average salary, U.S. college professors	Annual per capita wine consumption in liters
$62,000	11.5
63,000	11.6
64,000	11.7
65,000	11.8
66,000	11.9
67,000	22.0
68,000	22.1

0

(1) The average salary of a college professor and wine consumption (are, are not) _____ correlated. The higher average salary (is, is not) _____ the *cause* of the greater consumption of wine.

(2) The relationship between the two variables may be purely (coincidental, planned) _____; or, both the higher salaries and the greater consumption of wine may be the result of the higher (taxes, incomes) _____.

2. This question is based on the following graph.

a. Construct a table for points **A–I** from the data shown in the graph.

b. According to economists, price is the (independent, dependent) _____ variable and quantity is the _____ variable.

c. Write a linear equation that summarizes the data.

3. The following three sets of data each show the relationship between an independent variable and a dependent variable. For each set, the independent variable is in the left column and the dependent variable is in the right column.

(1)		(2)		(3)	
A	**B**	**C**	**D**	**E**	**F**
00	10	0	100	0	20
10	30	10	75	50	40
20	50	20	50	100	60
30	70	30	25	150	80
40	90	40	0	200	100

a. Write an equation that summarizes the data for each of the sets (1), (2), and (3).
b. State whether each data set shows a positive or an inverse relationship between the two variables.
c. Plot data sets 1 and 2 on the following graph. Use the same horizontal scale for both sets of independent variables and the same vertical scale for both sets of dependent variables.

0

4. This problem is based on the following graph.

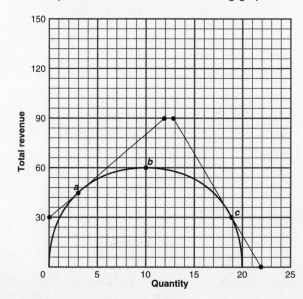

a. The slope of the straight line through point **a** is?
b. The slope of the straight line through point **b** is?
c. The slope of the straight line through point **c** is?

■ **SHORT ANSWER AND ESSAY QUESTIONS**

1. Why do economists use graphs in their work?

2. Give two examples of a graph that illustrates the relationship between two economic variables.

3. What does the slope tell you about a straight line? How would you interpret a slope of 4? A slope of −2? A slope of .5? A slope of −.25?

4. If the vertical intercept increases in value but the slope of a straight line stays the same, what happens to the graph of the line? If the vertical intercept decreases in value, what will happen to the line?

5. How do you interpret a vertical line on a two-variable graph? How do you interpret a horizontal line?

6. When you know that the price and quantity of a product are inversely related, what does this tell you about the slope of a line? What do you know about the slope when the two variables are positively related?

7. Which variable is the dependent and which is the independent in the following economic statement: "A decrease in business taxes had a positive effect on investment spending."

8. How do you tell the difference between a dependent and independent variable when examining economic relationships?

9. Why is an assumption made that all other variables are held constant when we construct a two-variable graph of the price and quantity of a product?

10. How do mathematicians and economists differ at times in how they construct two-dimensional graphs? Give an example.

11. How is the slope of a straight line in a two-variable graph affected by the choice of the units for either variable? Explain and give an example.

12. What is the relationship between the slopes of lines and marginal analysis?

13. Describe a case in which a straight line in a two-variable graph would have an infinite slope and a case in which the slope of a line would be zero.

14. If you know that the equation relating consumption (C) to income (Y) is $C = 10,000 + 5Y$, then what would consumption be when income is $5000? Construct an income-consumption table for five different levels of income.

15. How do the slopes of a straight line and a nonlinear curve differ? How do you estimate the slope of a nonlinear curve?

ANSWERS

Appendix to Chapter 1 Graphs and Their Meaning

FILL-IN QUESTIONS

1. graph, a horizontal, vertical
2. independent, dependent, dependent, independent
3. scales, ranges
4. an inverse, direct, direct, inverse
5. independent, dependent
6. held constant, *ceteris paribus*
7. vertical, horizontal
8. positive, negative
9. units of measurement
10. marginal
11. vertical, horizontal
12. intercept
13. *a.* intercept, slope; *b.* dependent, independent; *c.* 22, 30, 14
14. straight line, nonlinear curve
15. tangent

TRUE–FALSE QUESTIONS

1. F, p. 15	**6.** T, p. 17	**11.** F, pp. 17–18	**16.** T, p. 17
2. F, p. 16	**7.** T, pp. 17–18	**12.** T, pp. 17–18	**17.** F, pp. 16–17
3. T, p. 16	**8.** F, p. 17	**13.** F, p. 18	**18.** T, pp. 18–19
4. F, p. 16	**9.** T, p. 17	**14.** F, p. 19	**19.** F, p. 17
5. F, p. 17	**10.** T, pp. 17–18	**15.** T, p. 18	**20.** T, p. 18

MULTIPLE-CHOICE QUESTIONS

1. c, p. 16	**6.** b, pp. 17–18	**11.** a, p. 16	**16.** b, pp. 18–19
2. a, p. 17	**7.** d, p. 16	**12.** b, p. 17	**17.** c, pp. 18–19
3. b, p. 18	**8.** d, p. 18	**13.** d, p. 18	**18.** b, p. 18
4. c, p. 16	**9.** c, p. 18	**14.** c, p. 18	**19.** c, p. 18
5. c, p. 17	**10.** c, p. 18	**15.** b, pp. 18–19	**20.** b, p. 17

PROBLEMS

1. *a.* direct, up-; *b.* inverse, down-; *c.* (1) are, is not; (2) coincidental, incomes (standard of living, or similar answer)
2. *a. table below; b.* independent, dependent; *c.* $P = 4.00 - .25Q$

Point	Price	Quantity
A	$4.00	0
B	3.50	2
C	3.00	4
D	2.50	6
E	2.00	8
F	1.50	10
G	1.00	12
H	.50	14
I	.00	16

3. *a.* (1) $B = 10 + 2A$; (2) $D = 100 - 2.5C$; (3) $F = 20 + .4E$; *b.* (1) positive; (2) inverse; (3) positive
4. *a.* 5; *b.* 0; *c.* −10

SHORT ANSWER AND ESSAY QUESTIONS

1. p. 15	**5.** pp. 17–18	**9.** p. 17	**13.** pp. 17–18
2. pp. 15–16	**6.** p. 16	**10.** p. 16	**14.** p. 18
3. pp. 17–18	**7.** p. 16	**11.** p. 17	**15.** pp. 18–19
4. pp. 17–18	**8.** p. 16	**12.** p. 17	

CHAPTER 2

The Economizing Problem

Chapter 2 explains that the central problem of economics is based on two fundamental facts. First, individuals and institutions have unlimited economic wants. The main purpose of economic activity is to satisfy these wants. Second, economic resources are limited or scarce. It is these resources—land, capital, labor, and entrepreneurial ability—that are used to produce the goods and services that ultimately satisfy these economic wants. The **economizing problem** for both individuals and institutions arises from this continual struggle to decide how best to use limited productive resources to satisfy insatiable economic wants.

Economics is called the science of efficiency. To understand what efficiency means, however, you must first define its two characteristics: **full employment** and **full production.** Full employment means that all productive resources available to the economy are being used. Full production requires that two types of efficiency—allocative and productive—are being achieved. **Allocative efficiency** means that resources are being devoted to the production of the goods and services society most highly values. **Productive efficiency** entails producing this optimal product mix in the least costly way.

The **production possibilities curve** is used in this chapter's tables and graphs to discuss the major concerns of economics. The production possibilities model is a valuable device for illustrating the meaning of many concepts defined in the chapter—scarcity, choice, tradeoffs, opportunity cost, allocative and productive efficiency, unemployment, economic growth, and international trade. It can also be applied to many real economic situations, as you will learn from the examples in the text. This basic economic model is the first and one of the most important ones presented in the text that you will be using to understand the economic world.

Every economy needs to develop an **economic system** to respond to the economizing problem of limited resources and unlimited wants. The two basic types of systems are the *market system* and the *command system*. In the market system there is extensive private ownership of resources and the use of markets and prices to coordinate and direct economic activity. In the command system, there is extensive public ownership of resources and the use of central planning for most economic decision making in the economy. Chapters 3 through 6 explain in greater detail how the U.S. economy uses the market system to respond to the economizing problem.

The **circular flow model** (or diagram) is a device that illustrates for a capitalistic economy the relationship between households and businesses, the flow of money and economic goods and services between households and businesses, their dual role as buyers and sellers, and the two basic types of markets essential to the capitalistic process.

■ **CHECKLIST**

When you have studied this chapter you should be able to

☐ Explain the economizing problem in terms of economic wants and resources.
☐ Identify four types of economic resources.
☐ Describe the resource payments made in return for each economic resource.
☐ Write a definition of economics that incorporates the relationship between resources and wants.
☐ Explain why full employment and full production are necessary for the efficient use of resources.
☐ Distinguish between allocative efficiency and productive efficiency.
☐ State the four assumptions made when a production possibilities table or curve is constructed.
☐ Construct a production possibilities curve when you are given the appropriate data.
☐ Define opportunity cost and utilize a production possibilities curve to explain the concept.
☐ Show how the law of increasing opportunity cost is reflected in the shape of the production possibilities curve.
☐ Explain the economic rationale for the law of increasing opportunity cost.
☐ Use marginal analysis to define allocative efficiency.
☐ Explain how allocative efficiency determines the optimal point on a production possibilities curve.
☐ Use a production possibilities curve to illustrate unemployment and productive inefficiency.
☐ Use the production possibilities curve to illustrate economic growth.
☐ Explain how international trade affects a nation's production possibilities curve.
☐ Give examples and applications of the production possibilities model.
☐ Compare and contrast the market system (capitalism) with the command system (socialism).
☐ Draw the circular flow model, correctly labeling the two markets and the real and money flows between the two sectors in this simplified economy.

■ **CHAPTER OUTLINE**

1. The study of economics rests on the bases of two facts:
a. Society's material wants are unlimited.
b. The economic resources that are the ultimate means of satisfying these wants are scarce in relation to the wants.
(1) Economic resources are classified as land, capital, labor, and entrepreneurial ability. They are called *factors of production.*
(2) The payments received by those who provide the economy with these four resources are in the form of rental income, interest income, wages, and profits, respectively.
(3) Because these resources are scarce (or limited), the output that the economy is able to produce is also limited.

2. Economics, then, is the study of how society's scarce resources are used (administered) to obtain the greatest satisfaction of its economic wants. To be efficient in the use of its resources, an economy must achieve both full employment and full production.
a. *Full employment* means that the economy is using all available resources.
b. *Full production* means that all resources used for production should contribute to the maximum satisfaction of society's economic wants. Full production implies that there is
(1) *productive efficiency,* in which the goods and services society desires are being produced in the least costly way.
(2) *allocative efficiency,* in which resources are devoted to the production of goods and services society most highly values.
c. The *production possibilities table* indicates the alternative combinations of goods and services an economy is capable of producing when it has achieved full employment and productive efficiency.
(1) The four assumptions usually made when a production possibilities table is constructed are that full employment and productive efficiency, fixed resources, fixed technology, and two products are being considered.
(2) The table illustrates the fundamental choice every economy must make: what quantity of each good it must sacrifice to obtain more of another good.
d. The data in the production possibilities table can be plotted on a graph to obtain a production possibilities curve.
e. The opportunity cost of producing an additional unit of one product is the amount of other products that are sacrificed. The *law of increasing opportunity costs* reflects that the opportunity cost of producing an additional unit of a product (the marginal opportunity cost) increases as more of that product is produced.
(1) The law of increasing opportunity costs results in a production possibilities curve that is concave (from the origin).
(2) The opportunity cost of producing an additional unit of a product increases as more of the product is produced because resources are not completely adaptable to alternative uses.
f. Allocative efficiency means that resources are devoted to the optimal product mix for society. This optimal mix is determined by assessing marginal costs and benefits.
(1) The marginal-cost curve for a product rises because of the law of increasing opportunity costs; the marginal-benefit curve falls because the consumption of a product yields less and less satisfaction.
(2) There will be *underallocation* of resources to production of a product when the marginal benefit is greater than the marginal cost, and *overallocation* when the marginal cost is greater than the marginal benefit.
(3) Allocative efficiency is achieved when the marginal cost of a product equals the marginal benefit of a product.

3. Different outcomes will occur when assumptions underlying the production possibilities model are relaxed.
a. *Unemployment.* The economy may be operating at a point inside the production possibilities curve if the assumption of full employment and productive efficiency no longer holds. In this case, there will be an unemployment of resources and production will not occur in the least costly way.
b. *Economic Growth.* The production possibilities curve can move outward if the assumption of fixed resources or the assumption of no technological change is dropped.
(1) Economic growth can occur when there is an expansion in the quantity and quality of resources.
(2) It can increase when there is technological advancement.
(3) The combination of goods and services an economy chooses to produce today helps determine its production possibilities in the future.
c. *Trade.* International specialization and trade allow a nation to obtain more goods and services than is indicated by its production possibilities curve. The effect on production possibilities is similar to an increase in economic growth.

4. There are many real-world examples and applications of the production possibilities model.
a. Events leading to unemployment and productive inefficiency may cause nations to operate inside their production possibilities curves. Examples would be the Great Depression in the United States, recessions in different nations, and policies of racial, ethnic, or religious discrimination.
b. It illustrates tradeoffs and opportunity costs. Controversies over the use of land (for wilderness or production) or decisions over how public funds should be spent (for more criminal justice or more education) are two applications.
c. The curves can shift. The increase in the number of women in the workforce over the past four decades and their increased productivity have shifted the curve outward for the United States. Similarly, recent advances in technology have shifted the curve outward for the United States.

5. An *economic system* is a set of institutions and a coordinating mechanism to respond to the economizing problem.

    a. The *market system* (capitalism) has extensive private ownership of resources and uses markets and prices to coordinate and direct economic activity. In pure (*laissez-faire*) capitalism there is a limited government role in the economy. In a capitalist economy such as the United States, government plays a large role, but the two characteristics of the market system—private property and markets—dominate.

    b. The *command system* (also called *socialism* or *communism*) is based primarily on extensive public ownership of resources and the use of central planning for most economic decision making. There used to be many examples of command economies (e.g., Soviet Union), but today there are few (e.g., Cuba, North Korea). Most former socialistic nations have been or are being transformed into capitalistic and market-oriented economies.

6. The circular flow model is a device used to clarify the relationships between households and business firms in a market economy. In resource markets, households sell and firms buy resources, and in product markets, the firms sell and households buy products. Households use the incomes they obtain from selling resources to purchase the goods and services produced by the firms, and in the economy there is a real flow of resources and products and a money flow of incomes and expenditures.

■ HINTS AND TIPS

1. Chapter 2 presents many economic definitions and classifications. Spend time learning these definitions now because they will be used in later chapters, and you must know them if you are to understand what follows.

2. The production possibilities graph is a simple and extremely useful economic model. Practice your understanding of it by using it to explain the following economic concepts: scarcity, choice, opportunity cost, the law of increasing opportunity costs, full employment, full production, productive efficiency, allocative efficiency, unemployment, and economic growth.

3. Opportunity cost is always measured in terms of a forgone alternative. From a production possibilities table, you can easily calculate how many units of one product you forgo when you get another unit of a product.

4. In the section on the law of increasing opportunity costs, note the distinction made between two types. The *marginal* opportunity cost measures what is given up to obtain an additional unit. Note too that the size of one unit can vary (e.g., 2 to 3 or 200 to 300). The *total* opportunity cost measures what is given up to obtain a specific number of units (e.g., 3 or 300 units). Review Quick Quiz 2–1 in the text.

■ IMPORTANT TERMS

economizing problem
economic resources
land
capital
investment
labor
entrepreneurial ability
factors of production
full employment
full production
productive efficiency
allocative efficiency
consumer goods
capital goods
production possibilities table
production possibilities curve
opportunity cost
law of increasing opportunity costs
economic growth
economic system
market system
capitalism
command system
resource market
product market
circular flow model

SELF-TEST

■ FILL-IN QUESTIONS

1. The economizing problem arises because society's economic wants are (limited, unlimited) _____ and its economic resources are _____.

2. Consumers want to obtain goods and services that provide satisfaction, or what economists call (resources, utility) "_____." Some wants that meet this objective are considered (capital goods, necessities) _____, while others are considered (investment goods, luxuries) _____.

3. The four types of resources are

    a. _____

    b. _____

    c. _____

    d. _____

4. Both consumer goods and capital goods satisfy human economic wants. The consumer goods satisfy these wants (directly, indirectly) _____, and the capital goods satisfy them _____.

5. The income individuals receive from supplying land or natural resources is (interest, rental) _____ income, whereas the income received from supplying capital goods is _____ income. The income received by individuals who supply labor is (wage, profit) _____ income; the income received from entrepreneurial ability is _____ income.

6. Economics is the social science concerned with the problem of using (unlimited, scarce) _____ resources to attain the maximum fulfillment of society's _____ economic wants.

7. Economic efficiency requires full (employment, allocation) _____ so that all available resources can be used and that there be full (production, distribution) _____ so that the employed resources contribute to the maximum satisfaction of material wants.

8. Full production implies that two types of efficiency are achieved: Resources are devoted to the production of the mix of goods and services society most wants, or there is (allocative, productive) _____ efficiency, and the goods and services will be produced in the least costly way, or there will be _____ efficiency.

9. When a production possibilities table or curve is constructed, four assumptions are made:

a. _____

b. _____

c. _____

d. _____

10. In a two-product world, the quantity of the other good or service an economy must give up to produce more housing is the opportunity (benefit, cost) _____ of producing the additional housing.

11. The law of increasing opportunity costs explains why the production possibilities curve is (convex, concave) _____ from the origin. The economic rationale for the law is that economic resources (are, are not) _____ completely adaptable to alternative uses.

12. Allocative efficiency is determined by assessing the marginal costs and benefits of the output from the allocation of resources to production.

a. The marginal cost curve for a product rises because of increasing (satisfaction, opportunity costs) _____, and the marginal benefit curve falls because of less _____ from the additional consumption of a product.

b. When the marginal benefit is greater than the marginal cost, there will be (over, under) _____-allocation of resources to the production of a product, but when the marginal cost is greater than the marginal benefit, there will be an _____-allocation.

c. Optimal allocation of resources occurs when the marginal costs of the product output are (greater than, less than, equal to) _____ the marginal benefits.

13. Following is a production possibilities curve for capital goods and consumer goods.

a. If the economy moves from point **A** to point **B,** it will produce (more, fewer) _____ capital goods and (more, fewer) _____ consumer goods.

b. If the economy is producing at point **X,** some resources in the economy are either (not available, unemployed) _____ or (underemployed, overemployed) _____.

c. If the economy moves from point **X** to point **B** (more, fewer) _____ capital goods and (more, fewer) _____ consumer goods will be produced.

d. If the economy is to produce at point **Y,** there must be (unemployment, economic growth) _____. This can occur because of a resource supply (decrease, increase) _____ or a technological (decline, improvement) _____.

14. Technological advances can shift a nation's production possibilities curve (inward, outward) _____ because the effects lead to (economic growth, unemployment) _____.

15. The more an economy consumes its current production, the (more, less) _____ it will be capable of producing in future years if other things are equal.

16. International specialization and trade enable a nation to obtain (more, less) _____ of a desired good at _____ sacrifice of some other good. The output gains from greater international specialization and trade are the equivalent to economic (growth, decline) _____.

17. The institutional arrangements and coordinating mechanisms used to respond to the economic problem are called (*laissez-faire* capitalism, an economic system) _____.

18. In capitalism, property resources are primarily (publicly, privately) _____ owned. The means used to direct and coordinate economic activity (is central planning, are markets and prices) _____.

19. In a command economy, property resources are primarily (publicly, privately) _____ owned. The coordinating device(s) in this economic system (is central planning, are markets and prices) _____.

20. In the circular flow model,

a. Households are buyers and businesses are sellers in (product, resource) _____ markets, and businesses are buyers and households are sellers in _____ markets.

b. The flow of economic resources and finished goods and services is the (money, real) _____ flow, and the flow of income and expenditures is the _____ flow.

■ **TRUE–FALSE QUESTIONS**

Circle T if the statement is true, F if it is false.

1. The conflict between the scarce economic wants of society and its unlimited economic resources gives rise to the economizing problem. **T F**

2. The wants with which economics is concerned include only those wants that can be satisfied by goods and services. **T F**

3. Money is a resource and is classified as "capital." **T F**

4. From the economist's perspective, investment refers to the production and purchase of capital goods. **T F**

5. The payment to entrepreneurial ability is interest income. **T F**

6. Resources are scarce because society's material wants are unlimited and productive resources are limited. **T F**

7. Economic efficiency requires that there be both full employment of resources and full production. **T F**

8. Allocative efficiency means that goods and services are being produced by society in the least costly way. **T F**

9. Only allocative efficiency is necessary for there to be full production. **T F**

10. Given full employment and full production, it is not possible for an economy capable of producing just two goods to increase its production of both at any one point in time. **T F**

11. The opportunity cost of producing antipollution devices is the other goods and services the economy is unable to produce because it has decided to produce these devices. **T F**

12. The opportunity cost of producing a good tends to increase as more of it is produced because resources less suitable to its production must be employed. **T F**

13. Drawing a production possibilities curve concave to the origin is the geometric way of stating the law of increasing opportunity costs. **T F**

14. Economic rationale for the law of increasing opportunity cost is that economic resources are fully adaptable to alternative uses. **T F**

15. Allocative efficiency is determined by assessing the marginal costs and benefits of the output from the allocation of resources to production. **T F**

16. The marginal-cost curve for a product rises because of increasing satisfaction from the consumption of the product. **T F**

17. Economic growth means an increase in the production of goods and services, and is shown by a movement of the production possibilities curve outward and to the right. **T F**

18. The more capital goods an economy produces today, the greater will be the total output of all goods it can produce in the future, other things being equal. **T F**

19. International specialization and trade permit an economy to overcome the limits imposed by domestic production possibilities and have the same effect on the economy as having more and better resources. **T F**

20. The elimination of widespread discrimination based on race, ethnicity, or religion in an economy would move it from a point inside its production possibilities curve toward a point on its curve. **T F**

21. Pure capitalism is also called *laissez-faire* capitalism. **T F**

22. A command economy is characterized by the private ownership of resources and the use of markets and prices to coordinate and direct economic activity. **T F**

23. Russia and most nations in Eastern Europe have been transforming their economies from a command to market system since the demise of the former Soviet Union. **T F**

24. In the circular flow model, households function on the buying side of the resource and product markets. **T F**

25. In the circular flow model, there is a *real flow* of economic resources and finished goods and services and a *money flow* of income and consumption expenditures. **T F**

■ **MULTIPLE-CHOICE QUESTIONS**

Circle the letter that corresponds to the best answer.

1. Which is the correct match of an economic resource and payment for that resource?
(a) land and wages

(b) labor and interest income
(c) capital and rental income
(d) entrepreneurial ability and profit

2. An "innovator" is defined as an entrepreneur who
(a) makes basic policy decisions in a business firm
(b) combines factors of production to produce a good or service
(c) invents a new product or process for producing a product
(d) introduces new products on the market or employs a new method to produce a product

3. An economy is efficient when it has achieved
(a) full employment
(b) full production
(c) either full employment or full production
(d) both full employment and full production

4. Allocative and productive efficiency are conditions that best characterize
(a) full employment
(b) full production
(c) traditional economies
(d) command economies

5. When a production possibilities schedule is written (or a production possibilities curve is drawn) in this chapter, four assumptions are made. Which is one of those assumptions?
(a) More than two products are produced.
(b) The state of technology changes.
(c) The economy has both full employment and full production.
(d) The quantities of all resources available to the economy are variable, not fixed.

Answer Questions 6, 7, 8, and 9 based on the following graph for an economy.

6. At point **A** on the production possibilities curve in the above illustration,
(a) wheat production is inefficient
(b) tractor production is inefficient
(c) the economy is employing all its resources
(d) the economy is not employing all its resources

7. Unemployment and productive inefficiency would best be represented in the graph by point
(a) *A*
(b) *B*
(c) *C*
(d) *D*

8. The choice of point **B** over point **A** as the optimal product mix for society would be based on
(a) productive efficiency
(b) full employment of resources
(c) the law of increasing opportunity costs
(d) a comparison of marginal costs and benefits

9. Economic growth could be represented by
(a) a movement from point **A** to point **B**
(b) a movement from point **B** to point **A**
(c) a shift in the production possibilities curve out to point **C**
(d) a shift in the production possibilities curve out to point **D**

10. The production possibilities curve is
(a) concave
(b) convex
(c) linear
(d) positive

11. What is the economic rationale for the law of increasing opportunity cost?
(a) Full production and full employment of resources have not been achieved.
(b) Economic resources are not completely adaptable to alternative uses.
(c) Economic growth is being limited by the pace of technological advancement.
(d) An economy's present choice of output is determined by fixed technology and fixed resources.

12. If there is an increase in the resources available within the economy,
(a) more goods and services will be produced in the economy
(b) the economy will be capable of producing more goods and services
(c) the standard of living in the economy will rise
(d) the technological efficiency of the economy will improve

13. If the production possibilities curve *on the next page* moves from position **A** to position **B**, then
(a) the economy has increased the efficiency with which it produces wheat
(b) the economy has increased the efficiency with which it produces tractors
(c) the economy has put previously idle resources to work
(d) the economy has gone from full employment to less than full employment

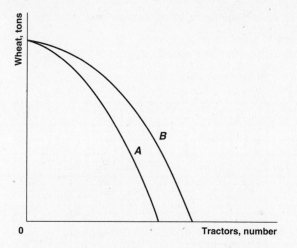

14. Which would be the best example of allocative efficiency? When society devoted resources to the production of
(a) slide rules instead of handheld calculators
(b) horse-drawn carriages instead of automobiles
(c) computers with word processors instead of typewriters
(d) long-playing records instead of compact discs

15. Which situation would most likely shift the production possibilities curve for a nation in an outward direction?
(a) deterioration in product quality
(b) reductions in the supply of resources
(c) increases in technological advances
(d) rising levels of discrimination

16. The opportunity cost of a new public stadium is the
(a) money cost of hiring guards and staff for the new stadium
(b) cost of constructing the new stadium in a future year
(c) change in the real estate tax rate to pay off the new stadium
(d) other goods and services that must be sacrificed to construct the new stadium

17. Which situation would most likely cause a nation's production possibilities curve to shift inward?
(a) investing more resources in new plants and equipment
(b) eliminating discrimination based on race and ethnic background
(c) increasing international trade or incurring a trade deficit
(d) going to war with another nation and suffering a major defeat

18. The combination of products in society's production possibilities table that is the most valued or optimal is determined
(a) at the midpoint of the production possibilities table
(b) at the endpoint of the production possibilities table
(c) where the marginal benefits equal marginal costs
(d) where the opportunity costs are maximized

19. The underallocation of resources by society to the production of a product means that the
(a) marginal benefit is greater than the marginal cost
(b) marginal benefit is less than the marginal cost
(c) opportunity cost of production is rising
(d) consumption of the product is falling

Answer Questions 20, 21, and 22 on the basis of the data given in the following production possibilities table.

	Production possibilities (alternatives)					
	A	B	C	D	E	F
Capital goods	100	95	85	70	50	0
Consumer goods	0	100	180	240	280	300

20. The choice of alternative **B** compared with alternative **D** would tend to promote
(a) a slower rate of economic growth
(b) a faster rate of economic growth
(c) increased consumption in the present
(d) central economic planning

21. If the economy is producing at production alternative **D,** the opportunity cost of 40 more units of consumer goods is about
(a) 5 units of capital goods
(b) 10 units of capital goods
(c) 15 units of capital goods
(d) 20 units of capital goods

22. In the table, the law of increasing opportunity costs is suggested by the fact that
(a) greater and greater quantities of consumer goods must be given up to get more capital goods
(b) smaller and smaller quantities of consumer goods must be given up to get more capital goods
(c) capital goods are relatively more scarce than consumer goods
(d) the production possibilities curve will eventually shift outward as the economy expands

23. The private ownership of property resources and use of markets and prices to direct and coordinate economic activity is characteristic of
(a) capitalism
(b) communism
(c) socialism
(d) a command economy

24. The two kinds of markets found in the circular flow model are
(a) real and money markets
(b) real and socialist markets
(c) money and command markets
(d) product and resource markets

25. In the circular flow model, businesses
(a) buy products and resources
(b) sell products and resources
(c) buy products and sell resources
(d) sell products and buy resources

■ PROBLEMS

1. Following is a list of resources. Indicate in the space to the right of each whether the resource is land (**LD**), capital (**C**), labor (**LR**), entrepreneurial ability (**EA**), or some combination of these resources.

   a. Fishing grounds in the North Atlantic   _____

   b. A computer in a retail store   _____

   c. Uranium deposits in Canada   _____

   d. An irrigation ditch in Nebraska   _____

   e. Bill Gates in his work in starting Microsoft   _____

   f. The oxygen breathed by human beings   _____

   g. An IBM plant in Rochester, Minnesota   _____

   h. The food on the shelf of a grocery store   _____

   i. A machine in an auto plant   _____

   j. A person who creates new computer software and uses it to start a successful business   _____

   k. A carpenter building a house   _____

2. Following is a production possibilities table for two products, corn and cars. The table is constructed using the usual assumptions. Corn is measured in units of 100,000 bushels and cars in units of 100,000.

Combination	Corn	Cars
A	0	7
B	7	6
C	13	5
D	18	4
E	22	3
F	25	2
G	27	1
H	28	0

   a. Follow the general rules for making graphs (see the appendix to Chapter 1); plot the data from the table on the graph in the next column to obtain a production possibilities curve. Place corn on the vertical axis and cars on the horizontal axis.

   b. Fill in the following table showing the opportunity cost per unit of producing the 1st through the 7th car unit in terms of corn units.

Cars	Cost of production
1st	_____
2nd	_____
3rd	_____
4th	_____
5th	_____
6th	_____
7th	_____

   c. What is the *marginal* opportunity cost of the 3rd car unit in terms of units of corn? _____

   d. What is the *total* opportunity cost of producing 6 car units in terms of units of corn? _____

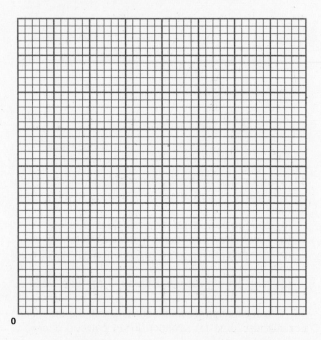

0

3. The following graph is a production possibilities curve. Draw on this graph

   a. a production possibilities curve that indicates greater efficiency in the production of good **A**

   b. a production possibilities curve that indicates greater efficiency in the production of good **B**

   c. a production possibilities curve that indicates an increase in the resources available to the economy

4. Following is a list of 12 economic goods. Indicate in the space to the right of each good whether it is a consumer good (**CON**), a capital good (**CAP**), or that it depends (**DEP**) on who is using it and for what purpose.

   a. An automobile   _____

   b. A tractor   _____

c. A taxicab   _____

d. A house   _____

e. A factory building   _____

f. An office building   _____

g. An ironing board   _____

h. A refrigerator   _____

i. A telephone   _____

j. A quart of a soft drink   _____

k. A cash register   _____

l. A screwdriver   _____

5. In the circular flow diagram below, the upper pair of flows (*a* and *b*) represents the resource market and the lower pair (*c* and *d*) the product market.

Supply labels or explanations for each of the four flows:

a. _____

b. _____

c. _____

d. _____

■ SHORT ANSWER AND ESSAY QUESTIONS

1. Explain what the term "economizing problem" means. Why are resources scarce?

2. In what sense are economic wants satiable or insatiable?

3. What are the four economic resources? How is each resource defined?

4. What is the income each economic resource earns?

5. When is a society economically efficient? What does "full production" mean, and how does it differ from "full employment"?

6. Explain why full production implies both allocative efficiency and productive efficiency.

7. What four assumptions are made in drawing a production possibilities curve or schedule?

8. What is opportunity cost? Give an example.

9. What is the law of increasing opportunity cost? Why do costs increase?

10. What determines the optimal product mix for society's production possibilities?

11. How can unemployment be illustrated with the production possibilities curve?

12. What will be the effect of increasing resource supplies on production possibilities?

13. Describe how technological advances will affect the production possibilities curve.

14. Explain the tradeoff between goods for the present and goods for the future and the effect of this tradeoff on economic growth.

15. What qualification does international specialization and trade make for the interpretation of production possibilities?

16. Give examples of how tradeoffs and opportunity costs can be illustrated by the production possibilities curve.

17. Give examples of shifts in the production possibilities curve.

18. The market system and the command system differ in two important ways. Compare and contrast the two economic systems.

19. In the circular flow model, what are the two markets? What roles do households play and what roles do businesses play in each market?

20. In the circular flow model, what are the income flows? What are the expenditure flows?

ANSWERS

Chapter 2 The Economizing Problem

FILL-IN QUESTIONS

1. unlimited, limited
2. utility, necessities, luxuries
3 *a.* land or natural resources, *b.* capital, *c.* labor, *d.* entrepreneurial ability
4. directly, indirectly
5. rental, interest, wage, profit
6. scarce, unlimited
7. employment, production
8. allocative, productive
9. *a.* there is full employment and productive efficiency; *b.* the available supplies of the factors of production are fixed; *c.* technology does not change during the course of the analysis; *d.* the economy produces only two products (any order for *a–d*)
10. cost
11. concave, are not
12. *a.* opportunity costs, satisfaction; *b.* under, over; *c.* equal to
13. *a.* fewer, more; *b.* unemployed, underemployed; *c.* more, more; *d.* economic growth, increase, improvement
14. outward, economic growth
15. less
16. more, less, growth
17. an economic system
18. privately, are markets and prices
19. publicly, is central planning
20. *a.* product, resource; *b.* real, money

TRUE–FALSE QUESTIONS

1. F, pp. 22–23 **8.** F, p. 24 **15.** T, pp. 27–28 **22.** F, pp. 33–34
2. T, pp. 22–23 **9.** F, p. 24 **16.** F, pp. 27–28 **23.** T, pp. 33–34
3. F, p. 23 **10.** T, pp. 25–27 **17.** T, pp. 29–30 **24.** F, pp. 34–35
4. T, p. 23 **11.** T, p. 27 **18.** T, pp. 30–31 **25.** T, pp. 34–35
5. F, pp. 23–24 **12.** T, p. 27 **19.** T, p. 31
6. T, p. 24 **13.** T, p. 27 **20.** T, p. 32
7. T, p. 24 **14.** F, p. 27 **21.** T, p. 33

MULTIPLE-CHOICE QUESTIONS

1. d, pp. 23–24 **8.** d, pp. 27–28 **15.** c, pp. 29–30 **22.** a, p. 27
2. d, pp. 23–24 **9.** d, pp. 29–30 **16.** d, p. 27 **23.** a, p. 33
3. d, p. 24 **10.** a, p. 27 **17.** d, pp. 32–33 **24.** d, pp. 34–35
4. b, p. 24 **11.** b, p. 27 **18.** c, pp. 27–28 **25.** d, pp. 34–35
5. c, p. 25 **12.** b, p. 29 **19.** a, pp. 27–28
6. c, pp. 26–27 **13.** b, pp. 29–31 **20.** b, pp. 30–31
7. c, p. 29 **14.** c, pp. 27–28 **21.** d, p. 27

PROBLEMS

1. *a.* LD; *b.* C; *c.* LD; *d.* C; *e.* EA; *f.* LD; *g.* C; *h.* C; *i.* C; *j.* EA; *k.* LR
2. *b.* 1, 2, 3, 4, 5, 6, 7 units of corn; *c.* 3; *d.* 21
3. *a.* curve will shift outward along good A axis but stay at the same point on good B axis; *b.* curve will shift outward along good B axis but stay at the same point on good A axis; *c.* entire curve will shift outward
4. *a.* DEP; *b.* CAP; *c.* CAP; *d.* DEP; *e.* CAP; *f.* CAP; *g.* DEP; *h.* DEP; *i.* DEP; *j.* DEP; *k.* CAP; *l.* DEP
5. *a.* money income payments (wages, rent, interest, and profit); *b.* services or resources (land, labor, capital, and entrepreneurial ability); *c.* goods and services; *d.* expenditures for goods and services

SHORT ANSWER AND ESSAY QUESTIONS

1. pp. 22–24 **6.** p. 24 **11.** p. 29 **16.** p. 32
2. pp. 22–23 **7.** p. 25 **12.** p. 29 **17.** pp. 32–33
3. p. 23 **8.** p. 27 **13.** pp. 29–30 **18.** pp. 33–34
4. p. 24 **9.** p. 27 **14.** pp. 30–31 **19.** pp. 34–35
5. p. 24 **10.** pp. 27–28 **15.** p. 31 **20.** pp. 34–35

CHAPTER 3

Individual Markets: Demand and Supply

Chapter 3 introduces you to the most fundamental tools of economic analysis: demand and supply. To progress successfully into the later chapters, it is essential that you understand what is meant by demand and supply and how to use these powerful tools.

Demand and supply are simply "boxes" or categories into which all the forces and factors that affect the price and the quantity of a good bought and sold in a competitive market are placed. Demand and supply determine price and quantity exchange, and it is necessary to see *why* and *how* they do this.

Many students never learn to *define* demand and supply. They never learn (1) what an increase or decrease in demand or supply means, (2) the important distinctions between "demand" and "quantity demanded" and between "supply" and "quantity supplied," and (3) the equally important distinctions between a change in demand and a change in quantity demanded, and between a change in supply and a change in quantity supplied.

Having learned these, however, it is no great trick to comprehend the so-called laws of demand and supply. The equilibrium price—that is, the price that will tend to prevail in the market as long as demand and supply do not change—is simply the price at which **quantity demanded** and **quantity supplied** are equal. The quantity bought and sold in the market (the equilibrium quantity) is the quantity demanded and supplied at the equilibrium price. If you can determine the equilibrium price and quantity under one set of demand and supply conditions, you can determine them under any other set.

This chapter includes a brief examination of the factors that determine demand and supply and the ways in which changes in these determinants will affect and cause changes in demand and supply. A graphic method is used in this analysis to illustrate demand and supply, equilibrium price and quantity, changes in demand and supply, and the resulting changes in equilibrium price and quantity. The **demand curve** and the **supply curve** are graphic (or geometric) representations of the same data contained in the schedules of demand and supply.

The application section at the end of the chapter explains government-set prices. When the government sets a legal price in a competitive market, it creates a **price ceiling** or **price floor**. This prevents supply and demand from determining the equilibrium price and quantity of a product that will be provided by a competitive market. As you will learn, the economic consequence of a price ceiling is that it will result in a persistent shortage of the product. An example of a price ceiling would be price controls on apartment rents. A price floor will result in a persistent surplus of a product, and the example given for it is price supports for an agricultural product.

You will use supply and demand over and over. It will turn out to be as important to you in economics as jet propulsion is to the pilot of an airplane: You can't get off the ground without it.

■ CHECKLIST

When you have studied this chapter you should be able to

☐ Define a market.

☐ Define demand and state the law of demand.

☐ Graph the demand curve when you are given a demand schedule.

☐ Explain the difference between individual demand and market demand.

☐ List the major determinants of demand and explain how each one shifts the demand curve.

☐ Distinguish between change in demand and change in the quantity demanded.

☐ Define supply and state the law of supply.

☐ Graph the supply curve when you are given a supply schedule.

☐ List the major determinants of supply and explain how each shifts the supply curve.

☐ Distinguish between change in supply and change in the quantity supplied.

☐ Define surplus and shortage.

☐ Describe how the equilibrium price and quantity are determined in a competitive market.

☐ Determine, when you are given the demand for and the supply of a good, the equilibrium price and the equilibrium quantity.

☐ Predict the effects of changes in demand and supply on equilibrium price and equilibrium quantity and on the prices of substitute and complementary goods.

☐ Explain the meaning of the rationing function of prices.

☐ Explain why violations of the "other-things-equal" assumption may cause confusion about the validity of the laws of demand and supply.

☐ Explain the economic effects of a government-set price ceiling on product price and quantity in a competitive market and give an example.

☐ Describe the economic consequences of a government-set price floor on product price and quantity in a competitive market and supply an example.

■ CHAPTER OUTLINE

1. A market is any institution or mechanism that brings together buyers ("demanders") and sellers ("suppliers") of a particular good or service. This chapter assumes that markets are highly competitive.

2. *Demand* is a schedule of prices and the quantities that buyers would purchase at each of these prices during a selected period of time.

  a. As price rises, other things being equal, buyers will purchase smaller quantities, and as price falls they will purchase larger quantities; this is the law of demand.

  b. The demand curve is a graphic representation of demand and the law of demand.

  c. Market (or total) demand for a good is a summation of the demands of all individuals in the market for that good.

  d. The demand for a good depends on the tastes, income, and expectations of buyers; the number of buyers in the market; and the prices of related goods.

  e. A change (increase or decrease) in the entire demand schedule and the demand curve is referred to as a *change in demand.* It is the result of a change in one or more of the determinants of demand. For example, an *increase* in the demand for a good may result from an increase in:

  (1) *tastes or preferences* for the good;

  (2) *the number of buyers* (for the good);

  (3) *income* if it is a normal good, but if it is a normal good, it may result from a decrease in income;

  (4) *the price of a related good*, but if they are complements, it may result from a decrease in the price of a related good; and

  (5) *expectations* of a price increase or a rise in income.

  f. A change in demand and a change in the quantity demanded are *not* the same thing.

3. *Supply* is a schedule of prices and the quantities that sellers will sell at each of these prices during some period of time.

  a. The supply schedule shows, other things equal, that as the price of the good rises, larger quantities will be offered for sale, and as the price of the good falls, smaller quantities will be offered for sale.

  b. The supply curve is a graphic representation of supply and the law of supply; the market supply of a good is the sum of the supplies of all sellers of the good.

  c. The supply of a good depends on the techniques used to produce it, the prices of the resources employed in its production, the extent to which it is taxed or subsidized, the prices of other goods that might be produced, the price expectations of sellers, and the number of sellers of the product.

  d. A change (increase or decrease) in the entire supply schedule and the supply curve is referred to as a *change in supply.* It is the result of a change in one or more of the determinants of supply. For example, an increase in supply for a good may result from:

(1) a decrease in the *prices of resources* used to make it;

(2) an improvement in the *technology* to produce it;

(3) a fall in *taxes* on it, or an increase in *subsidies* for it;

(4) a decline in the *prices of other goods* that could be produced by firms making it;

(5) an increase or decrease (depending on the market in question) in *expectations* of its higher future prices; and

(6) an increase in the number of sellers of it.

  e. A change in supply must be distinguished from a change in quantity supplied.

4. The *market* or *equilibrium price* of a product is that price at which quantity demanded and quantity supplied are equal; the quantity exchanged in the market (the equilibrium quantity) is equal to the quantity demanded and supplied at the equilibrium price.

  a. If the price of a product is above the market equilibrium price, there will be a *surplus* or *excess supply.* In this case, the quantity demanded is less than the quantity supplied at that price.

  b. If the price of a product is below the market equilibrium price, there will be a *shortage* or *excess demand.* In this case, the quantity demanded is greater than the quantity supplied at that price.

  c. The rationing function of prices is the elimination of surpluses and shortages of a product.

  d. A change in demand, supply, or both changes both the equilibrium price and the equilibrium quantity in specific ways. (See #4 in "Hints and Tips" section.)

  e. When demand and supply schedules (or curves) are drawn up, it is assumed that all the nonprice determinants of demand and supply remain unchanged. This assumption is often stated as "other-things-equal."

5. Supply and demand analysis has many important applications to *government-set prices.*

  a. A price ceiling set by government prevents price from performing its rationing function in a market system. It creates a shortage (quantity demanded is greater than the quantity supplied) at the government-set price.

(1) Another rationing method must be found, so government often steps in and establishes one. But all rationing systems have problems because they exclude someone.

(2) Also, a government-set price creates an illegal *black market* for those who want to buy and sell above the government-set price.

(3) One example of a legal price ceiling that creates a shortage would be rent control established in some cities to restrain apartment rents.

  b. A *price floor* is a minimum price set by government for the sale of a product or resource. It creates a surplus (quantity supplied is greater than the quantity demanded) at the fixed price. The surplus may induce the government to increase demand or decrease supply to eliminate the surplus. The use of price floors has often been applied to several agricultural products.

■ HINTS AND TIPS

1. This chapter is the most important one in the book. Make sure you spend extra time on it and master the material. If you do, your long-term payoff will be a much easier understanding of the applications in later chapters.

2. One mistake students often make is to confuse **change in demand** with **change in quantity demanded.** A change in demand causes the entire demand curve to *shift,* whereas a change in quantity demanded is simply a *movement* along an existing demand curve.

3. It is strongly recommended that you draw supply and demand graphs as you work on supply and demand problems so you can see a picture of what happens when demand shifts, supply shifts, or both demand and supply shift.

4. Make a chart and related graphs that show the eight possible outcomes from changes in demand and supply. Figure 3–6 in the text illustrates the *four single shift* outcomes:

(1) **D↑: P↑, Q↑**   (3) **S↑: P↓, Q↑**
(2) **D↓: P↓, Q↓**   (4) **S↓: P↑, Q↓**

Four shift combinations are described in Table 3–9 of the text. Make a figure to illustrate each combination.

(1) **S↑, D↓: P↓, Q?**   (3) **S↑, D↑: P?, Q↑**
(2) **S↓, D↑: P↑, Q?**   (4) **S↓, D↓: P?, Q↓**

5. Make sure you understand the "other-things-equal" assumption described at the end of the chapter. It will help you understand why the law of demand is not violated even if the price and quantity of a product increase over time.

6. Practice always helps in understanding graphs. Without looking at the textbook, draw a supply and demand graph with a **price ceiling** below the equilibrium price and show the resulting shortage in the market for a product. Then, draw a supply and demand graph with a **price floor** above the equilibrium price and show the resulting surplus. Explain to yourself what the graphs show. Check your graphs and your explanations by referring to textbook Figures 3–7 and 3–8 and the related explanations.

■ IMPORTANT TERMS

market	change in quantity demanded
demand	quantity demanded
demand schedule	individual demand
law of demand	total or market demand
diminishing marginal utility	supply
income effect	supply schedule
substitution effect	law of supply
demand curve	quantity supplied
determinants of demand	supply curve
normal good	determinants of supply
inferior good	change in supply
substitute goods	change in quantity supplied
complementary goods	surplus
change in demand	shortage

equilibrium price	price ceiling
equilibrium quantity	price floor
rationing function of prices	

SELF-TEST

■ FILL-IN QUESTIONS

1. A market is the institution or mechanism that brings together buyers or (demanders, suppliers) _____ and sellers or _____ of a particular good or service.

2. The relationship between price and quantity in the demand schedule is (a direct, an inverse) _____ relationship; in the supply schedule the relationship is _____ one.

3. The added satisfaction or pleasure a consumer obtains from additional units of a product decreases as the consumer's consumption of the product increases. This phenomenon is called diminishing marginal (equilibrium, utility) _____.

4. A consumer tends to buy more of a product as its price falls because
a. The purchasing power of the consumer is increased and the consumer tends to buy more of this product (and of other products); this is called the (income, substitution) _____ effect;
b. The product becomes less expensive relative to similar products and the consumer tends to buy more of the original product and less of the similar products, which is called the _____ effect.

5. When demand or supply is graphed, price is placed on the (horizontal, vertical) _____ axis and quantity on the _____ axis.

6. The change from an individual to a market demand schedule involves (adding, multiplying) _____ the quantities demanded by each consumer at the various possible (incomes, prices) _____.

7. When the price of one product and the demand for another product are directly related, the two products are called (substitutes, complements) _____; however, when the price of one product and the demand for another product are inversely related, the two products are called _____.

8. When a consumer demand schedule or curve is drawn up, it is assumed that five factors that determine demand are fixed and constant. These five determinants of consumer demand are

a. _____

b. _____

c. _____

d. _____

e. _____

9. A decrease in demand means that consumers will buy (larger, smaller) _____ quantities at every price, or will pay (more, less) _____ for the same quantities.

10. A change in income or in the price of another product will result in a change in the (demand for, quantity demanded of) _____ the given product, while a change in the price of the given product will result in a change in the _____ the given product.

11. An increase in supply means that producers will make and be willing to sell (larger, smaller) _____ quantities at every price, or will accept (more, less) _____ for the same quantities.

12. A change in resource prices or the prices of other goods that could be produced will result in a change in the (supply, quantity supplied) _____ of the given product, but a change in the price of the given product will result in a change in the _____.

13. The fundamental factors that determine the supply of any commodity in the product market are

a. _____

b. _____

c. _____

d. _____

e. _____

f. _____

14. If quantity demanded is greater than quantity supplied, price is (above, below) _below_ the equilibrium price, and the (shortage, surplus) _Shortage_ will cause the price to (rise, fall) _Rise_. If quantity demanded is less than the quantity supplied, price is (above, below) _above_ the equilibrium price, and the (shortage, surplus) _Surplus_ will cause the price to (rise, fall) _fall_.

15. The equilibrium price of a product is the price at which quantity demanded is (greater than, equal to) _____ quantity supplied, and there (is, is not) _____ a surplus or a shortage at that price.

16. In the space next to **a–h**, indicate the effect [*increase* (+), *decrease* (−), or *indeterminate* (?)] on equilibrium price (**P**) and equilibrium quantity (**Q**) of each of these changes in demand and/or supply.

                                                        P   **Q**

a. Increase in demand, supply constant ____ ____

b. Increase in supply, demand constant ____ ____

c. Decrease in demand, supply constant ____ ____

d. Decrease in supply, demand constant ____ ____

e. Increase in demand, increase in supply ____ ____

f. Increase in demand, decrease in supply ____ ____

g. Decrease in demand, decrease in supply ____ ____

h. Decrease in demand, increase in supply ____ ____

17. If supply and demand establish a price for a good so that there is no shortage or surplus of the product, then price is successfully performing its (utility, rationing) _____ function. The price that is set is a market-(changing, clearing) _____ price.

18. To assume that all the determinants of demand and supply do not change is to employ the (marginal utility, other-things-equal) _____ assumption.

19. A price ceiling is the (minimum, maximum) _____ legal price a seller may charge for a product or service, whereas a price floor is the _____ legal price set by government.

20. If a price ceiling is below the market equilibrium price, a (surplus, shortage) _____ will arise in a competitive market, and if a price floor is above the market equilibrium price, a (surplus, shortage) _____ will arise in a competitive market.

■ **TRUE–FALSE QUESTIONS**

Circle T if the statement is true, F if it is false.

1. A market is any arrangement that brings together the buyers and sellers of a particular good or service. **T F**

2. Demand is the amount of a good or service that a buyer will purchase at a particular price. **T F**

3. The law of demand states that as price increases, other things being equal, the quantity of the product demanded increases. **T F**

4. The law of diminishing marginal utility is one explanation of why there is an inverse relationship between price and quantity demanded. **T F**

5. The substitution effect suggests that, at a lower price, you have the incentive to substitute the more expensive product for similar products which are relatively less expensive.　**T　F**

6. There is no difference between individual demand schedules and the market demand schedule for a product.　**T　F**

7. In graphing supply and demand schedules, supply is put on the horizontal axis and demand on the vertical axis.　**T　F**

8. If price falls, there will be an increase in demand.　**T　F**

9. If consumer tastes or preferences for a product decrease, the demand for the product will tend to decrease.　**T　F**

10. An increase in income will tend to increase the demand for a product.　**T　F**

11. When two products are substitute goods, the price of one and the demand for the other will tend to move in the same direction.　**T　F**

12. If two goods are complementary, an increase in the price of one will tend to increase the demand for the other.　**T　F**

13. A change in the quantity demanded means that there has been a change in demand.　**T　F**

14. Supply is a schedule that shows the amounts of a product a producer can make in a limited time period.　**T　F**

15. An increase in resource prices will tend to decrease supply.　**T　F**

16. A government subsidy for the production of a product will tend to decrease supply.　**T　F**

17. An increase in the prices of other goods that could be made by producers will tend to decrease the supply of the current good that the producer is making.　**T　F**

18. A change in supply means that there is a movement along an existing supply curve.　**T　F**

19. A surplus indicates that the quantity demanded is less than the quantity supplied at that price.　**T　F**

20. If the market price of a product is below its equilibrium price, the market price will tend to rise because demand will decrease and supply will increase.　**T　F**

21. The rationing function of prices is the elimination of shortages and surpluses.　**T　F**

22. If the supply of a product increases and demand decreases, the equilibrium price and quantity will increase.　**T　F**

23. If the demand for a product increases and the supply of the product decreases, the equilibrium price will increase and equilibrium quantity will be indeterminant.　**T　F**

24. Economists often make the assumption of other things equal to hold constant the effects of other factors when examining the relationship between prices and quantities demanded and supplied.　**T　F**

25. A price ceiling set by government below the competitive market price of a product will result in a surplus.　**T　F**

■ **MULTIPLE-CHOICE QUESTIONS**

Circle the letter that corresponds to the best answer.

1. The markets examined in this chapter
  (a) sell nonstandard or differentiated products
  (b) have buyers cooperating to determine prices
  (c) are controlled by a single producer
  (d) are highly competitive

2. A schedule that shows the various amounts of a product consumers are willing and able to purchase at each price in a series of possible prices during a specified period of time is called
  (a) supply
  (b) demand
  (c) quantity supplied
  (d) quantity demanded

3. The reason for the law of demand can best be explained in terms of
  (a) supply
  (b) complementary goods
  (c) the rationing function of prices
  (d) diminishing marginal utility

4. Assume that the price of video game players falls. What will most likely happen to the equilibrium price and quantity of video games, assuming this market is competitive?
  (a) Price will increase; quantity will decrease.
  (b) Price will decrease; quantity will increase.
  (c) Price will decrease; quantity will decrease.
  (d) Price will increase; quantity will increase.

5. Given the following individuals' demand schedules for product X, and assuming these are the only three consumers of X, which set of prices and output levels below will be on the market demand curve for this product?

Price X	Consumer 1 Q_{dx}	Consumer 2 Q_{dx}	Consumer 3 Q_{dx}
$5	1	2	0
4	2	4	0
3	3	6	1
2	4	8	2
1	5	10	3

  (a) ($5, 2); ($1, 10)
  (b) ($5, 3); ($1, 18)
  (c) ($4, 6); ($2, 12)
  (d) ($4, 0); ($1, 3)

6. Which factor will decrease the demand for a product?
   (a) a favorable change in consumer tastes
   (b) an increase in the price of a substitute good
   (c) a decrease in the price of a complementary good
   (d) a decrease in the number of buyers

7. The income of a consumer decreases and the consumer's demand for a particular good increases. It can be concluded that the good is
   (a) normal
   (b) inferior
   (c) a substitute
   (d) a complement

8. Which of the following could cause a decrease in consumer demand for product X?
   (a) a decrease in consumer income
   (b) an increase in the prices of goods that are good substitutes for product X
   (c) an increase in the price that consumers expect will prevail for product X in the future
   (d) a decrease in the supply of product X

9. If two goods are substitutes for each other, an increase in the price of one will necessarily
   (a) decrease the demand for the other
   (b) increase the demand for the other
   (c) decrease the quantity demanded of the other
   (d) increase the quantity demanded of the other

10. If two products, A and B, are complements, then
   (a) an increase in the price of A will decrease the demand for B
   (b) an increase in the price of A will increase the demand for B
   (c) an increase in the price of A will have no significant effect on the price of B
   (d) a decrease in the price of A will decrease the demand for B

11. If two products, X and Y, are independent goods, then
   (a) an increase in the price of X will significantly increase the demand for Y
   (b) an increase in the price of Y will significantly increase the demand for X
   (c) an increase in the price of Y will have no significant effect on the demand for X
   (d) a decrease in the price of X will significantly increase the demand for Y

12. The law of supply states that, other things being constant, as price increases
   (a) supply increases
   (b) supply decreases
   (c) quantity supplied increases
   (d) quantity supplied decreases

13. If the supply curve moves from S_1 to S_2 on the graph in the next column, there has been
   (a) an increase in supply
   (b) a decrease in supply
   (c) an increase in quantity supplied
   (d) a decrease in quantity supplied

14. A decrease in the supply of a product would most likely be caused by
   (a) an increase in business taxes
   (b) an increase in consumer incomes
   (c) a decrease in resource costs for production
   (d) a decrease in the price of a complementary good

15. If the quantity supplied of a product is greater than the quantity demanded for a product, then
   (a) there is a shortage of the product
   (b) there is a surplus of the product
   (c) the product is a normal good
   (d) the product is an inferior good

16. If the price of a product is below the equilibrium price, the result will be
   (a) a surplus of the good
   (b) a shortage of the good
   (c) a decrease in the supply of the good
   (d) an increase in the demand for the good

Answer Questions 17, 18, and 19 on the basis of the data in the the following table. Consider the following supply and demand schedules for bushels of corn.

Price	Quantity demanded	Quantity supplied
$20	395	200
22	375	250
24	350	290
26	320	320
28	280	345
30	235	365

17. The equilibrium price in this market is
   (a) $22
   (b) $24
   (c) $26
   (d) $28

18. An increase in the cost of labor lowers the quantity supplied by 65 bushels at each price. The new equilibrium price would be
   (a) $22
   (b) $24
   (c) $26
   (d) $28

19. If the quantity demanded at each price increases by 130 bushels, then the new equilibrium quantity will be
   (a) 290
   (b) 320
   (c) 345
   (d) 365

20. A decrease in supply and a decrease in demand will
(a) increase price and decrease the quantity exchanged
(b) decrease price and increase the quantity exchanged
(c) increase price and affect the quantity exchanged in an indeterminate way
(d) affect price in an indeterminate way and decrease the quantity exchanged

21. An increase in demand and a decrease in supply will
(a) increase price and increase the quantity exchanged
(b) decrease price and decrease the quantity exchanged
(c) increase price and the effect upon quantity exchanged will be indeterminate
(d) decrease price and the effect upon quantity exchanged will be indeterminate

22. An increase in supply and an increase in demand will
(a) increase price and increase the quantity exchanged
(b) decrease price and increase the quantity exchanged
(c) affect price in an indeterminate way and decrease the quantity exchanged
(d) affect price in an indeterminate way and increase the quantity exchanged

23. A cold spell in Florida devastates the orange crop. As a result, California oranges command a higher price. Which of the following statements best explains the situation?
(a) The supply of Florida oranges decreases, causing the supply of California oranges to increase and their price to increase.
(b) The supply of Florida oranges decreases, causing their price to increase and the demand for California oranges to increase.
(c) The supply of Florida oranges decreases, causing the supply of California oranges to decrease and their price to increase.
(d) The demand for Florida oranges decreases, causing a greater demand for California oranges and an increase in their price.

Answer Questions 24, 25, 26, and 27 based on the following graph showing the market supply and demand for a product.

24. Assume that the market is initially in equilibrium where D_1 and S_1 intersect. If there is an increase in the number of buyers, then the new equilibrium would most likely be at point
(a) W
(b) X
(c) Y
(d) Z

25. Assume that the equilibrium price and quantity in the market are P_2 and Q_2. Which factor would cause the equilibrium price and quantity to shift to P_1 and Q_3?
(a) an increase in product price
(b) an increase in demand
(c) an increase in supply
(d) a decrease in quantity

26. What would cause a shift in the equilibrium price and quantity from point Z to point X?
(a) a decrease in production costs and more favorable consumer tastes for the product
(b) an increase in the number of suppliers and an increase in consumer incomes
(c) an increase in production costs and decrease in consumer incomes
(d) an improvement in production technology and decrease in the price of a substitute good

27. Assume that the market is initially in equilibrium where D_1 and S_1 intersect. If consumer incomes increased and the technology for making the product improved, then new equilibrium would most likely be at
(a) P_1 and Q_1
(b) P_2 and Q_2
(c) P_1 and Q_3
(d) P_3 and Q_1

28. The demand curve and its inverse relationship between price and quantity demanded is based on the assumption of
(a) other things equal
(b) changing expectations
(c) complementary goods
(d) increasing marginal utility

Questions 29 and 30 relate to the following table that shows a hypothetical supply and demand schedule for a product.

Quantity demanded (pounds)	Price (per pound)	Quantity supplied (pounds)
200	$4.40	800
250	4.20	700
300	4.00	600
350	3.80	500
400	3.60	400
450	3.40	300
500	3.20	200

29. A shortage of 150 pounds of the product will occur if a government-set price is established at
(a) $3.20
(b) $3.40
(c) $3.80
(d) $4.00

30. If a price floor set by the government is established at $4.20, there will be a

(a) surplus of 300 pounds
(b) shortage of 300 pounds
(c) surplus of 450 pounds
(d) shortage of 450 pounds

■ **PROBLEMS**

1. Using the demand schedule that follows, plot the demand curve on the graph below the schedule. Label the axes and indicate for each axis the units being used to measure price and quantity.

Price	Quantity demanded, 1000 bushels of soybeans
$7.20	10
7.00	15
6.80	20
6.60	25
6.40	30
6.20	35

0

a. Plot the following supply schedule on the same graph.

Price	Quantity supplied, 1000 bushels of soybeans
$7.20	40
7.00	35
6.80	30
6.60	25
6.40	20
6.20	15

b. The equilibrium price of soybeans will be $_____.
c. How many thousand bushels of soybeans will be exchanged at this price? _____

d. Indicate clearly on the graph the equilibrium price and quantity by drawing lines from the intersection of the supply and demand curves to the price and quantity axes.
e. If the Federal government supported a price of $7.00 per bushel there would be a (shortage, surplus) _____ of _____ bushels of soybeans.

2. The demand schedules of three individuals (Ellie, Sam, and Lynn) for loaves of bread are shown in the following table. Assuming there are only three buyers of bread, determine and graph the total or market demand schedule for bread.

Price	Quantity demanded, loaves of bread			Total
	Ellie	Sam	Lynn	
$1.50	1	4	0	____
1.40	3	5	1	____
1.30	6	6	5	____
1.20	10	7	10	____
1.10	15	8	16	____

3. Following is a demand schedule for bushels of apples. In columns 3 and 4 insert *any* new figures for quantity that represent in column 3 an increase in demand and in column 4 a decrease in demand.

(1) Price	(2) Quantity demanded	(3) Demand increases	(4) Demand decreases
$6.00	400	____	____
5.90	500	____	____
5.80	600	____	____
5.70	700	____	____
5.60	800	____	____
5.50	900	____	____

4. Assume that O'Rourke has, when his income is $100 per week, the demand schedule for good A shown in columns 1 and 2 of the following table and the demand schedule for good B shown in columns 4 and 5. Assume that the prices of A and B are $.80 and $5, respectively.

Demand for A (per week)			Demand for B (per week)		
(1) Price	(2) Quantity demanded	(3) Quantity demanded	(4) Price	(5) Quantity demanded	(6) Quantity demanded
$.90	10	0	$5.00	4	7
.85	20	10	4.50	5	8
.80	30	20	4.00	6	9
.75	40	30	3.50	7	10
.70	50	40	3.00	8	11
.65	60	50	2.50	9	12
.60	70	60	2.00	10	13

a. How much A will O'Rourke buy? _____

How much B? _____

b. Suppose that as a consequence of a $10 increase in O'Rourke's weekly income, the quantities demanded of A become those shown in column 3 and the quantities demanded of B become those shown in column 6.

(1) How much A will he now buy? _____

How much B? _____

(2) Good A is (normal, inferior) _____.

(3) Good B is _____.

5. The market demand for good X is shown in columns 1 and 2 of the following table. Assume the price of X to be $2 and constant.

(1) Price	(2) Quantity demanded	(3) Quantity demanded	(4) Quantity demanded
$2.40	1,600	1,500	1,700
2.30	1,650	1,550	1,750
2.20	1,750	1,650	1,850
2.10	1,900	1,800	2,000
2.00	2,100	2,000	2,200
1.90	2,350	2,250	2,450
1.80	2,650	2,550	2,750

a. If as the price of good Y rises from $1.25 to $1.35, the quantities demanded of good X become those shown in column 3, it can be concluded that X and Y are (substitute, complementary) _____ goods.

b. If as the price of good Y rises from $1.25 to $1.35, the quantities of good X become those shown in column 4, it can be concluded that X and Y are _____

_____ goods.

6. In a local market for hamburger on a given date, each of 300 identical sellers of hamburger has the following supply schedule.

(1) Price	(2) Quantity supplied— one seller, lbs	(3) Quantity supplied— all sellers, lbs
$2.05	150	_____
2.00	110	_____
1.95	75	_____
1.90	45	_____
1.85	20	_____
1.80	0	_____

a. In column 3 construct the market supply schedule for hamburger.

b. Following is the market demand schedule for hamburger on the same date and in the same local market as that given above.

Price	Quantity demanded, lbs
$2.05	28,000
2.00	31,000
1.95	36,000
1.90	42,000
1.85	49,000
1.80	57,000

If the Federal government sets a price on hamburger of $1.90 a pound, the result would be a (shortage, surplus) _____ of _____ pounds of hamburger in this market.

7. Each of the following events would tend to increase or decrease either the demand for or the supply of computer games and, as a result, will increase or decrease the price of these games. In the first blank indicate the effect on demand or supply (increase, decrease); in the second blank, indicate the effect on price (increase, decrease). Assume that the market for computer games is a competitive one.

a. It becomes known that an electronics store is going to have a sale on these games 3 months from now.

_____ ;

_____

b. The workers who produce the games go on strike for over 2 months. _____ ; _____

c. The workers in the industry receive a $2 an hour wage increase. _____ ; _____

d. The average price of movie tickets (a substitute) increases. _____ ; _____

e. The price of business software, a product also supplied by the computer software producers, rises.

_____ ; _____

f. It is announced by a private research institute that children who play computer games also improve their grades in school. _____ ; _____

g. Because of the use of mass production techniques, the amount of labor necessary to produce a game decreases._____ ; _____

h. The price of computers decreases. _____ ;

_____

i. The average consumer believes that a shortage of games is developing in the economy. _____ ;

_____

j. The Federal government imposes a $5 tax per game on the manufacturers of computer games.

_____ ; _____

■ **SHORT ANSWER AND ESSAY QUESTIONS**

1. Define demand and the law of demand.

2. Use the diminishing marginal utility concept to explain why the quantity demanded of a product will tend to rise when the price of the product falls.

3. In past decades, the price of coffee in the United States rose significantly as a result of bad weather in coffee-producing regions. Use the income effect and the substitution effect concepts to explain why the quantity of coffee demanded in the United States significantly decreased.

4. What is the difference between individual demand and market demand? What is the relationship between these two types of demand?

5. Explain the difference between an increase in demand and an increase in the quantity demanded.

6. What are the factors that cause a change in demand? Use supply and demand graphs to illustrate what happens to price and quantity when demand increases.

7. How are inferior and normal (or superior) goods defined? What is the relationship between these goods and changes in income?

8. Why does the effect of a change in the price of related goods depend on whether a good is a substitute or complement? What are substitutes and complements?

9. A newspaper reports that "Blue jeans have become even more popular and are now the standard clothing that people wear for both play and work." How will this change affect the demand for blue jeans? What will happen to the price and quantity of blue jeans sold in the market? Explain and use a supply and demand graph to illustrate your answer.

10. Compare and contrast the supply schedule with the demand schedule.

11. Supply does not remain constant for long because the factors that determine supply change. What are these factors? How do changes in them affect supply?

12. Explain the difference between an increase in supply and an increase in the quantity supplied.

13. Describe and illustrate with a supply and demand graph the effect of an increase in supply on price and quantity. Do the same for a decrease in supply.

14. The U.S. Congress passes a law that raises the excise tax on gasoline by $1 per gallon. What effect will this change have on the demand and supply of gasoline? What will happen to gasoline prices and quantity? Explain and use a supply and demand graph to illustrate your answer.

15. What is the relationship between the price of a product and a shortage of the product? What is the relationship between the price of a product and a surplus of the product?

16. Given the demand for and the supply of a commodity, what price will be the equilibrium price of this commodity? Explain why this price will tend to prevail in the market and why higher (lower) prices, if they do exist temporarily, will tend to fall (rise).

17. Analyze the following quotation and explain the fallacies contained in it: "An increase in demand will cause price to rise; with a rise in price, supply will increase and the increase in supply will push price down. Therefore, an increase in demand results in little change in price because supply will increase also."

18. Suppose an industry sells 2000 units of a product at $10 per unit one year, 3000 units at $12 the next year, and 4000 units at $14 the third year. Is this evidence that the law of demand is violated? Explain.

19. What are the consequences of a price ceiling for a product if it is set below the equilibrium price? Illustrate your answer with a graph.

20. What are the economic problems with price floors? How have they been used by government?

ANSWERS

Chapter 3 Individual Markets: Demand and Supply

FILL-IN QUESTIONS

1. demanders, suppliers
2. an inverse, a direct
3. utility
4. *a.* income; *b.* substitution
5. vertical, horizontal
6. adding, prices
7. substitutes, complements
8. *a.* the tastes or preferences of consumers; *b.* the number of consumers in the market; *c.* the money income of consumers; *d.* the prices of related goods; *e.* consumer expectations with respect to future prices, product availability, and income (any order for *a–e*)
9. smaller, less
10. demand for, quantity demanded of
11. larger, less
12. supply, quantity supplied
13. *a.* the technology of production; *b.* resource prices; *c.* taxes and subsidies; *d.* prices of other goods; *e.* price expectations; *f.* the number of sellers in the market (any order for *a–f*)
14. below, shortage, rise, above, surplus, fall
15. equal to, is not
16. *a.* +, +; *b.* −, +; *c.* −, −; *d.* +, −; *e.* ?, +; *f.* +, ?; *g.* ?, −; *h.* −, ?
17. rationing, clearing
18. other-things-equal
19. maximum, minimum
20. shortage, surplus

TRUE–FALSE QUESTIONS

1. T, p. 39	**10.** T, p. 43	**19.** T, p. 48
2. F, pp. 40; 44–45	**11.** T, p. 44	**20.** F, pp. 48–49
3. F, p. 40	**12.** F, p. 44	**21.** T, p. 50
4. T, p. 40	**13.** F, pp. 44–45	**22.** F, pp. 50–52
5. F, pp. 40–41	**14.** F, p. 45	**23.** T, pp. 50–52
6. F, pp. 41–42	**15.** T, pp. 46–47	**24.** T, p. 52
7. F, p. 42	**16.** F, p. 47	**25.** F, pp. 52–53
8. F, pp. 42–44	**17.** T, p. 47	
9. T, p. 43	**18.** F, pp. 47–48	

MULTIPLE-CHOICE QUESTIONS

1. d, p. 39   **11.** c, p. 44   **21.** c, p. 51
2. b, p. 40   **12.** c, p. 45   **22.** d, p. 52
3. d, pp. 40–41 **13.** a, p. 46   **23.** b, p. 51
4. d, pp. 44; 50 **14.** a, pp. 46–47 **24.** c, pp. 43; 50
5. b, pp. 41–42 **15.** b, p. 48   **25.** c, p. 50
6. d, pp. 43–44 **16.** b, p. 48   **26.** c, pp. 43–44; 46–47; 51
7. b, p. 43   **17.** c, p. 49   **27.** c, pp. 43–44; 46–47; 52
8. a, p. 44   **18.** d, pp. 47; 50 **28.** a, p. 52
9. b, p. 44   **19.** d, pp. 45; 50 **29.** b, p. 53
10. a, p. 44   **20.** d, p. 52   **30.** c, p. 54

PROBLEMS

1. *a.* graph; *b.* 6.60; *c.* 25,000; *d.* graph; *e.* surplus, 20,000
2. Total: 5, 9, 17, 27, 39
3. Each quantity in column 3 is greater than in column 2, and each quantity in column 4 is less than in column 2.
4. *a.* 30, 4; *b.* (1) 20, 7; (2) inferior; (3) normal (superior)

5. *a.* complementary; *b.* substitute
6. *a.* 45,000; 33,000; 22,500; 13,500; 6,000; 0; *b.* shortage, 28,500
7. *a.* decrease demand, decrease price; *b.* decrease supply, increase price; *c.* decrease supply, increase price; *d.* increase demand, increase price; *e.* decrease supply, increase price; *f.* increase demand, increase price; *g.* increase supply, decrease price; *h.* increase demand, increase price; *i.* increase demand, increase price; *j.* decrease supply, increase price

SHORT ANSWER AND ESSAY QUESTIONS

1. p. 40   **8.** p. 44   **15.** p. 48
2. p. 40   **9.** pp. 43; 50   **16.** pp. 48–50
3. p. 41   **10.** pp. 40; 45 **17.** pp. 50–51
4. pp. 41–42   **11.** pp. 46–47   **18.** pp. 50–51
5. pp. 44–45   **12.** pp. 47–48   **19.** pp. 52–53
6. pp. 43–44   **13.** pp. 46; 50–51 **20.** pp. 54–55
7. p. 43   **14.** pp. 47; 50–51

Applications and Extensions of Supply and Demand Analysis

Note: This bonus web chapter is available at the textbook website: www.mcconnell16.com. Go to Chapter 3W at the Student Center.

Chapter 3 Web has two basic purposes. It offers you numerous real-world applications of supply and demand analysis. It also uses supply and demand analysis to provide new insights into the allocation of common resources and economic efficiency.

The first section of the chapter gives you more examples of the effects of *changes in supply and demand* on price and quantity. You will first read about simple changes in which either the demand curve changes or the supply curve changes, but not both. These simple changes result in predictable effects on the price and quantity of a product, such as lettuce or American flags. Then you are given examples, using pink salmon, gasoline, and sushi, of complex changes. In these cases, there is a simultaneous shift in supply and demand. Here the effect of changes in supply and demand on price and quantity will be less certain and will depend on the direction and extent of the changes.

The chapter then extends your understanding of what happens in markets if *pre-set prices* are above or below the equilibrium price. You have already learned that when the government intervenes in a competitive market and sets the price below equilibrium (a price ceiling), it creates a shortage of a product. Similarly, when government sets a price above the equilibrium price (a price floor), it will result in a surplus. As you will learn, shortages and surpluses can also occur in competitive markets when sellers set the price in advance of sales and that pre-set price turns out to be below or above the equilibrium or actual price. The examples given in the text are ticket prices for sporting events that are priced too low or too high by the sellers, resulting in shortages and surpluses.

The third section of the chapter introduces you to a new concept, *nonpriced goods.* These goods or resources are ones that are owned in common by society, such as wildlife, fish, public water, and public land. Although there are no competitive markets or prices, supply and demand analysis can provide insights about the effective use and management of these resources. As you will read, this analysis can explain the plight of buffalo since the 1800s. The text also discusses the alternative methods government uses to ration scarce resources that do not have a market price.

Supply and demand analysis is also used to enhance your understanding of *economic efficiency* in the fourth section of the chapter. This extension requires an explanation of the concepts of *consumer and producer surplus.* Consumer surplus is the difference between the maximum price consumers are willing to pay for a product and the actual price. Producer surplus is the difference between the minimum price producers are willing to accept for a product and the actual price. The chapter also revisits the concept of *allocative efficiency* and explains that it is achieved when the combination of consumer and producer surplus is at a maximum.

Supply and demand analysis is one of the most important means for improving your understanding of the economic world. If you master its use, it will help you explain many events and outcomes in everyday life. This chapter helps you achieve that mastery and understanding.

■ CHECKLIST

When you have studied this chapter you should be able to

☐ Explain and graph the effect of an increase in the supply of a product (lettuce) on its equilibrium price and quantity.

☐ Describe and graph the effect of an increase in the demand for a product (American flags) on its equilibrium price and quantity.

☐ Discuss and graph the effects of an increase in the supply of and a decrease in demand for a product (pink salmon) on its equilibrium price and quantity.

☐ Predict and graph the effects of a decrease in the supply of and an increase in the demand for a product (gasoline) on its equilibrium price and quantity.

☐ Explain and graph the effects of an equal increase in the supply of and demand for a product (sushi) on its equilibrium price and quantity.

☐ Discuss and graph how a seller price for a service (Olympic figure skating finals) that is set below the equilibrium price will result in a shortage.

☐ Describe and graph how a seller price for a service (Olympic curling preliminaries) that is set above the equilibrium price will result in a surplus.

☐ Define and give examples of nonpriced goods.

☐ Describe and graph the supply and demand conditions that will result in a shortage of a nonpriced good.

☐ Explain and graph the supply and demand conditions that will result in a surplus of a nonpriced good.

☐ Define consumer surplus and give a graphical example.

☐ Define producer surplus and give a graphical example.

☐ Use consumer surplus and producer surplus to explain how allocative efficiency is achieved in a competitive market.

☐ List the three conditions for achieving allocative efficiency at a quantity level in a competitive market.
☐ Use a supply and demand graph to illustrate efficiency losses when the quantity is greater or less than its equilibrium in a competitive market.

■ CHAPTER OUTLINE

1. ***Changes in supply and demand*** result in changes in the equilibrium price and quantity. The simplest cases are ones where demand changes and supply remains constant, or where supply changes and demand remains constant. More complex cases involve simultaneous changes in supply and demand.

   a. *Supply increase.* In a competitive market for lettuce, if a severe freeze destroys a portion of the lettuce crop, then the supply of lettuce will decrease. The decrease in the supply of lettuce, with demand constant, will increase the equilibrium price and decrease the equilibrium quantity.

   b. *Demand increase.* In a competitive market for American flags, an increase in patriotism will increase the demand for flags. This increase in demand, with supply remaining the same, will increase the equilibrium price and quantity of flags.

   c. *Supply increase and demand decrease.* Over the years, improved fishing techniques and technology contributed to an increase in the supply of pink salmon. Also, an increase in consumer incomes and a lowering of the price of substitute fish contributed to reducing the demand for pink salmon. As a result the price of pink salmon fell. The equilibrium quantity could have increased, decreased, or stayed the same. In this case, the increase in supply was greater than the decrease in demand, so the equilibrium quantity increased.

   d. *Demand increase and supply decrease.* An increase in the price of oil, a resource used to produce gasoline, resulted in a decrease in the supply of gasoline. At the same time, rising incomes and a stronger economy created a greater demand for gasoline. This decrease in supply and increase in demand increased the equilibrium price. The equilibrium quantity could have increased, decreased, or stayed the same. In this case, the decrease in supply was less than the increase in demand, so the equilibrium quantity increased.

   e. *Demand increase and supply increase.* An increase in the taste for sushi among U.S. consumers resulted in an increase in the demand for this product. At the same time, there was an increase in the number of sushi bars and other food outlets that provide sushi, thus increasing its supply. This increase in both demand and supply increased the equilibrium quantity of sushi. The equilibrium price could have increased, decreased, or stayed the same. In this case, the increase in demand was the same as the increase in supply, so the equilibrium price remained the same.

2. ***Pre-set prices*** that are set by the seller below or above the equilibrium price can produce shortages and surpluses.

   a. If a price is set below the equilibrium price by a seller, then at that pre-set price the quantity demanded is greater than the quantity supplied, resulting in a ***shortage.*** This situation is typical of the market for tickets to Olympic figure skating finals. The shortage of tickets at the pre-set price creates a secondary market (*black market*) for tickets in which buyers bid for tickets held by the initial purchaser. The ticket scalping drives up the price of tickets.

   b. If a price is set above the equilibrium price by a seller, then at that pre-set price the quantity demanded is less than the quantity supplied, resulting in a ***surplus.*** This situation is typical of the market for tickets to Olympic curling preliminaries at which there are many empty seats.

3. ***Nonpriced goods*** (or resources) are ones that are owned in common by society and available for public use. The prices of these goods are essentially zero because they are not bought and sold in markets. Yet, supply and demand analysis can be applied to explain events and situations involving these nonpriced goods.

   a. When the demand for a nonpriced good is less than the supply of the good at each and every price across the demand and supply curves, the price of the good will be zero. In this case, the demand and supply curves do not intersect at any positive price. This situation occurred with the buffalo in the pre-railroad era in the United States.

   b. With the advent of the railroad and greater hunting of buffalo, the demand for buffalo increased. In graphical terms, the demand curve now intersected the supply curve at a positive equilibrium price, and this price for buffalo would have prevailed if there had been a market. But buffalo was a nonpriced good, so it had a zero price, and at this price a shortage arose. This shortage grew progressively worse as the supply curve shifted left because the buffalo population could not be sustained. Nonpriced goods often get overused.

   c. When price is not used as a rationing device, other types of rationing allocate scarce resources. In the case of nonpriced goods such as wildlife or fish sought by hunters or fishers, licenses or quantity limits are used to decrease demand so that it is balanced with the sustainable supply. In some cases, nonpriced goods such as buffalo are being converted to privately owned goods that can be bought and sold in competitive markets.

4. In market transactions, consumers can obtain a beneficial surplus and so can producers.

   a. ***Consumer surplus*** is the difference between the maximum price consumers are willing to pay for a product and the actual (equilibrium) price paid. Graphically, it is the triangular area bounded by the portion of the vertical axis between the equilibrium price and the demand curve intersection, the portion of the demand curve above the equilibrium price, and the horizontal line at the equilibrium price from the vertical axis to the demand curve. Price and consumer surplus are inversely (negatively) related: Higher prices reduce it and lower prices increase it.

b. *Producer surplus* is the difference between the minimum price producers are willing to accept for a product and the actual (equilibrium) price received. Graphically, it is the triangular area bounded by the portion of the vertical axis between the equilibrium price and the supply curve intersection, the portion of the supply curve below the equilibrium price, and the horizontal line at the equilibrium price from the vertical axis to the supply curve. Price and producer surplus are directly (positively) related: Higher prices increase it and lower prices decrease it.

c. The equilibrium quantity shown by the intersection of demand and supply curves reflects *economic efficiency*.

(1) *Productive efficiency* is achieved because production costs are minimized at each quantity level of output.

(2) *Allocative efficiency* is achieved at the equilibrium quantity of output because three conditions are satisfied: Marginal benefit equals marginal cost; maximum willingness to pay equals minimum acceptable price; and the combination of the consumer and producer surplus is at a maximum.

d. If quantity is less than or greater than the equilibrium or most efficient level, there are **efficiency losses.** The efficiency losses reduce the maximum possible size of the combined consumer and producer surplus.

■ **HINTS AND TIPS**

1. This web chapter offers applications and extensions of Chapter 3 in the textbook, so check your understanding of the corresponding text and web sections: (a) Review the text Chapter 3 section on "Changes in Supply, Demand, and Equilibrium" (pp. 50–52) before reading the web Chapter 3 section on "Changes in Supply and Demand"; and (b) review the text Chapter 3 section on "Application: Government-Set Prices" (pp. 52–55) before reading the web Chapter 3 section on "Pre-Set Prices."

2. Correct terminology is important for mastering supply and demand analysis. You must remember the distinction between a change in demand and a change in quantity demanded or a change in supply and a change in quantity supplied. Consider the case of a single shift in demand with supply staying the same. As the demand curve increases along the existing supply curve, it increases the quantity supplied, but it does not increase supply (which would be a shift in the entire supply curve).

3. The newest concepts in the chapter are those related to consumer surplus and producer surplus. The term "surplus" should not be confused with the previous use related to pre-set prices (when quantity supplied is greater than quantity demanded at a pre-set price). What the consumer surplus refers to is the extra utility or satisfaction that consumers get when they do not have to pay the price they were willing to pay and pay the lower equilibrium price. The producer surplus arises when producers receive an equilibrium price that is above the minimum price that they consider acceptable to selling the product.

4. The concept of allocative efficiency using marginal benefit and marginal cost was first presented in the text, Chapter 2 (pp. 27–28). Review your understanding of this concept in Chapter 2 before reading the web Chapter 3 section on "Efficiency Revisited."

■ **IMPORTANT TERMS**

nonpriced goods	producer surplus
consumer surplus	efficiency losses

SELF-TEST

■ **FILL-IN QUESTIONS**

1. A decrease in the supply of lettuce will result in an equilibrium price that (increases, decreases) _____ and an equilibrium quantity that _____.

2. An increase in the demand for American flags will result in an equilibrium price that (increases, decreases) _____ and an equilibrium quantity that _____.

3. An increase in the supply of pink salmon that is greater than the decrease in the demand for pink salmon will result in an equilibrium price that (increases, decreases, stays the same) _____ and an equilibrium quantity that _____.

4. An increase in the demand for gasoline that is greater than the decrease in the supply of gasoline will result in an equilibrium price that (increases, decreases, stays the same) _____ and an equilibrium quantity that _____.

5. An increase in the demand for sushi that is equal to the increase in the supply of sushi will result in an equilibrium price that (increases, decreases, stays the same) _____ and an equilibrium quantity that _____.

6. If government sets a legal price for a product, a shortage would arise from a price (ceiling, floor) _____ and a surplus would arise from a price _____.

7. If a pre-set price is set by the seller below the equilibrium price it will create a (surplus, shortage) _____, but if a pre-set price is set by the seller above the equilibrium price it will create a _____.

8. A market for tickets to popular sporting events in which buyers bid for tickets held by initial purchasers is referred to as a (primary, secondary) _____ market. In these markets, ticket (destruction, scalping) _____ occurs.

9. Nonpriced goods are resources that are (privately owned, owned in common) _____ and available for taking on (private, public) _____ lands.

10. At a zero price for a nonpriced good, where the quantity available (quantity supplied) is greater than the quantity demanded, there will be a (shortage, surplus) _____, but when the quantity available (quantity supplied) is less than the quantity demanded, there will be a _____.

11. A significant increase in the demand for a nonpriced good will lead to (under-, over-) _____ consumption of the good and (an increase, a decrease) _____ in the sustainable supply of the good.

12. The alternative to using prices and markets to ration nonpriced goods such as fish and game on public lands is to use (scalping, licenses) _____ or set (bonuses, limits) _____ on the number that can be taken.

13. A consumer surplus is the difference between the actual price and the (minimum, maximum) _____ price a consumer is (or consumers are) willing to pay for a product. In most markets, consumers individually or collectively gain more total utility or satisfaction when the actual or equilibrium price they have to pay for a product is (less, more) _____ than what they would have been willing to pay to obtain the product.

14. Consumer surplus and price are (positively, negatively) _____ related. This means that higher prices (increase, decrease) _____ consumer surplus and lower prices _____ it.

15. A producer surplus is the difference between the actual or equilibrium price and the (minimum, maximum) _____ acceptable price a producer is (or producers are) willing to accept in exchange for a product. In most markets, sellers individually or collectively benefit when they sell their product at an actual or equilibrium price that is (less, more) _____ than what they would have been willing to receive in exchange for the product.

16. Producer surplus and price are (positively, negatively) _____ related. This means that higher prices (increase, decrease) _____ producer surplus and lower prices _____ it.

17. When competition forces producers to use the best techniques and combinations of resources to make a product, then (allocative, productive) _____ efficiency is being achieved. When the correct or optimal quantity of output of a product is being produced relative to the other goods and services, then _____ efficiency is being achieved.

18. Points on the demand curve measure the marginal (cost, benefit) _____ of a product whereas points on the supply curve measure the marginal _____ of a product.

19. Allocative efficiency occurs at quantity levels where marginal benefit is (greater than, less than, equal to) _____ marginal cost, maximum willingness to pay by consumers is _____ the minimum acceptable price for producers, and the combined consumer and producer surplus is at a (minimum, maximum) _____.

20. When there is overproduction of a product, there are efficiency (gains, losses) _____ and when there is underproduction there are efficiency _____. In both cases, the combined consumer and producer surplus is (greater than, less than) _____ the maximum that would occur at the efficient quantity of output.

■ **TRUE–FALSE QUESTIONS**

Circle T if the statement is true, F if it is false.

1. An increase in the supply of lettuce decreases its equilibrium price and increases its equilibrium quantity. **T F**

2. A decrease in the demand for an American flag increases its equilibrium price and decreases its equilibrium quantity. **T F**

3. When demand for American flags increases, there is an increase in the quantity supplied as the equilibrium price rises, but no increase in supply. **T F**

4. In the market for pink salmon, the reason that the equilibrium quantity increased was that the increase in supply was greater than the decrease in demand. **T F**

5. In the market for gasoline, the reason that the equilibrium quantity increased was that the increase in demand was less than the decrease in supply. **T F**

6. In the market for sushi, an equal increase in supply and demand will increase the equilibrium price, but have no effect on the equilibrium quantity. **T F**

7. If the government sets a price ceiling below what would be the competitive market price of a product, a shortage of the product will develop. **T F**

8. A price floor set by government will increase the equilibrium price and quantity in a market. **T F**

9. If a seller pre-sets a price that turns out to be below the actual equilibrium price, a shortage will develop in the market. **T F**

10. Ticket scalping often occurs in markets where there is a surplus of tickets. **T F**

11. If a sporting event is not sold out, this indicates that the ticket prices for the event were pre-set above the actual equilibrium price. **T F**

12. A nonpriced good is one that is owned in common by society and available for the taking on public lands. **T F**

13. An example of a nonpriced good is cattle that are raised on a cattle ranch. **T F**

14. A nonpriced good has a zero price because demand is less than supply regardless of the price. **T F**

15. Assume that a downsloping demand curve intersects a vertical supply curve. A leftward shift in the supply curve will result in a surplus of a product. **T F**

16. Ways that government rations nonpriced goods are to use licenses and set quantity limits. **T F**

17. Consumer surplus is the difference between the minimum and maximum price a consumer is willing to pay for a good. **T F**

18. Consumer surplus is a utility surplus that reflects a gain in total utility or satisfaction. **T F**

19. Consumer surplus and price are directly or positively related. **T F**

20. The higher the equilibrium price, the greater the amount of consumer surplus. **T F**

21. Producer surplus is the difference between the actual price a producer receives for a product and the minimum price the producer would have been willing to accept for the product. **T F**

22. The higher the actual price, the less the amount of producer surplus. **T F**

23. Competitive markets produce equilibrium prices and quantities that minimize the sum of consumer and producer surpluses. **T F**

24. One of the three conditions for allocative efficiency is that the maximum willingness to pay by consumers is equal to the minimum acceptable price for producers. **T F**

25. Efficiency losses are increases in the combined consumer and producer surplus. **T F**

■ **MULTIPLE-CHOICE QUESTIONS**

Circle the letter that corresponds to the best answer.

1. Bad weather in coffee-producing regions of the world devastated the coffee crop. As a result, coffee prices increased worldwide. Which of the following statements best explains the situation?
  (a) the demand for coffee increased
  (b) the supply of coffee decreased
  (c) the demand for coffee increased and the supply of coffee increased
  (d) the demand for coffee decreased and the supply of coffee decreased

2. Assume that the supply of tomatoes in a competitive market increases. What will most likely happen to the equilibrium price and quantity of tomatoes?
  (a) price will increase; quantity will decrease
  (b) price will decrease; quantity will increase
  (c) price will decrease; quantity will decrease
  (d) price will increase; quantity will increase

3. Assume that the demand for security services increases in a competitive market. What will most likely happen to the equilibrium price and quantity of security services?
  (a) price will increase; quantity will decrease
  (b) price will decrease; quantity will increase
  (c) price will decrease; quantity will decrease
  (d) price will increase; quantity will increase

4. A decrease in the demand for hamburger is more than offset by an increase in its supply. As a result the equilibrium price will
  (a) increase and the equilibrium quantity will decrease
  (b) increase and the equilibrium quantity will increase
  (c) decrease and the equilibrium quantity will decrease
  (d) decrease and the equilibrium quantity will increase

5. A decrease in the supply of oil is more than offset by an increase in its demand. As a result, the equilibrium price will
  (a) increase and the equilibrium quantity will decrease
  (b) increase and the equilibrium quantity will increase
  (c) decrease and the equilibrium quantity will decrease
  (d) decrease and the equilibrium quantity will increase

6. What will happen to the equilibrium quantity and price of a product in a competitive market when there is an equal increase in demand and supply?
  (a) equilibrium quantity and price will both increase
  (b) equilibrium quantity and price will both decrease
  (c) equilibrium quantity will increase and equilibrium price will stay the same
  (d) equilibrium quantity will stay the same and equilibrium price will increase

7. What will happen to the equilibrium quantity and price of a product in a competitive market when the decrease in demand exactly offsets the increase in supply?
  (a) equilibrium quantity will increase and equilibrium price will decrease

(b) equilibrium quantity will decrease and equilibrium price will increase

(c) equilibrium quantity will increase and equilibrium price will stay the same

(d) equilibrium quantity will stay the same and equilibrium price will decrease

8. Which of the following is a correct statement?
  (a) price ceilings increase supply
  (b) price ceilings create shortages
  (c) price floors create shortages
  (d) price floors increase demand

9. If a seller sets a price for a product that turns out to be below the equilibrium price, then there will be a
  (a) shortage of the product
  (b) surplus of the product
  (c) price floor for a product
  (d) a zero price for the product

10. A surplus means that
  (a) demand for a product is greater than the supply
  (b) supply of the product is greater than the demand
  (c) quantity demanded is less than the quantity supplied at that price
  (d) quantity demanded is greater than the quantity supplied at that price

Answer Questions 11, 12, and 13 based on the following graph showing the market supply and demand for a product.

Quantity (in thousands)

11. Given this market, if a seller pre-sets the price at $10, then this action results in a
  (a) surplus of 10,000 units
  (b) surplus of 80,000 units
  (c) shortage of 10,000 units
  (d) shortage of 80,000 units

12. Given this market, if a seller pre-sets the price at $30, then this action results in a
  (a) surplus of 10,000 units
  (b) surplus of 60,000 units
  (c) surplus of 70,000 units
  (d) shortage of 10,000 units

13. What price will eliminate a surplus or shortage in this market?
  (a) $0
  (b) $10
  (c) $20
  (d) $30

14. A market for tickets in which buyers bid for tickets held by initial purchasers rather than the original seller is a
  (a) primary market
  (b) secondary market
  (c) pre-set market
  (d) surplus market

15. What are resources called that are owned in common by society and available for the taking on public land?
  (a) consumer surplus
  (b) producer surplus
  (c) nonpriced goods
  (d) priced goods

16. A supply and demand graph of the "market" for buffalo in the pre-railroad era would show that
  (a) quantity demanded equaled quantity supplied
  (b) quantity demanded was greater than quantity supplied
  (c) demand was less than supply, so there was a zero price
  (d) supply was less than demand, so there was a zero price

17. A supply and demand graph of the "market" for buffalo in the post-railroad era would show that at a zero price
  (a) the supply curve was horizontal
  (b) the demand curve was vertical
  (c) quantity demanded was less than quantity supplied
  (d) quantity demanded was greater than quantity supplied

18. Why does government often ration the use of public resources such as fishing and hunting by using licenses and setting limits on quantities or seasons?
  (a) to increase the supply of these nonpriced goods
  (b) to increase the demand for these nonpriced goods
  (c) to decrease the demand for these nonpriced goods
  (d) to decrease the supply of these nonpriced goods

19. The difference between the maximum price a consumer is (or consumers are) willing to pay for a product and the actual price is consumer
  (a) sovereignty
  (b) demand
  (c) surplus
  (d) utility

20. Katie is willing to pay $50 for a product and Tom is willing to pay $40. The actual price that they have to pay is $30. What is the amount of the consumer surplus for Katie and Tom combined?
  (a) $30
  (b) $40
  (c) $50
  (d) $60

21. Given the demand curve, the consumer surplus is
(a) increased by higher prices and decreased by lower prices
(b) decreased by higher prices and increased by lower prices
(c) increased by higher prices but not affected by lower prices
(d) decreased by lower prices, but not affected by higher prices

22. The difference between the actual price that a producer receives (or producers receive) and the minimum acceptable price is producer
(a) cost
(b) wealth
(c) surplus
(d) investment

23. The minimum acceptable price for a product that Juan is willing to receive is $20. It is $15 for Carlos. The actual price they receive is $25. What is the amount of the producer surplus for Juan and Carlos combined?
(a) $10
(b) $15
(c) $20
(d) $25

24. When the combined consumer and producer surplus is at a maximum for a product,
(a) the quantity supplied is greater than the quantity demanded
(b) the market finds alternative ways to ration the product
(c) the market is allocatively efficient
(d) the product is a nonpriced good

25. When the output is greater than the optimal level of output for a product there are efficiency
(a) gains from the underproduction of the product
(b) losses from the underproduction of the product
(c) gains from the overproduction of the product
(d) losses from the overproduction of the product

■ **PROBLEMS**

1. The existing demand and supply schedules are given in columns 1, 2, and 3 of the following table.

Demand and Supply Schedules			New Demand and Supply Schedules		
(1)	(2) Quantity	(3) Quantity	(4)	(5) Quantity	(6) Quantity
Price	demanded	supplied	Price	demanded	supplied
$5.00	10	50	$5.00	___	___
4.00	20	40	4.00	___	___
3.00	30	30	3.00	___	___
2.00	40	20	2.00	___	___
1.00	50	10	1.00	___	___

a. Now the demand *increases* by 10 units at each price and supply *decreases* by 10 units. Enter the new amounts for quantity demanded and quantity supplied in columns 5 and 6.

b. What was the old equilibrium price? _____
What will be the new equilibrium price? _____

c. What was the old equilibrium quantity? _____
What will be the new equilibrium quantity? _____

2. The demand and supply schedules for a certain product are those given in the following table. Answer the related questions.

Quantity demanded	Price	Quantity supplied
12,000	$10	18,000
13,000	9	17,000
14,000	8	16,000
15,000	7	15,000
16,000	6	14,000
17,000	5	13,000
18,000	4	12,000

a. The equilibrium price of the product is $_____
and the equilibrium quantity is _____.

b. If a seller established a pre-set price of $5 on this product, there would be a (shortage, surplus) _____ of _____ units.

c. If a seller established a pre-set price of $8, there would be a (shortage, surplus) _____ of _____ units.

3. Given the following information, calculate the consumer surplus for each individual A to F.

(1) Person	(2) Maximum price willing to pay	(3) Actual price (equilibrium price)	(4) Consumer surplus
A	$25	$12	$_____
B	23	12	_____
C	18	12	_____
D	16	12	_____
E	13	12	_____
F	12	12	_____

4. Given the following information, calculate the producer surplus for each producer A to F.

(1) Person	(2) Maximum acceptable price	(3) Actual price (equilibrium price)	(4) Producer surplus
A	$4	$12	$_____
B	5	12	_____
C	7	12	_____
D	9	12	_____
E	10	12	_____
F	12	12	_____

5. Answer this question based on the following graph showing the market supply and demand for a product. Assume that the output level is Q_1.

a. The area of consumer surplus would be shown by the area _____.

b. The area of producer surplus would be shown by the area _____.

c. The area that maximizes the combined consumer and producer surplus is _____.

d. If the output level is now Q_2, then there are efficiency losses shown by area _____.

e. If the output level is now Q_3, then there are efficiency losses shown by area _____.

■ **SHORT ANSWER AND ESSAY QUESTIONS**

1. Explain, using a supply and demand graph, how a freeze in a vegetable crop will affect the equilibrium price and quantity.

2. In a competitive market, if the supply of a product decreases and demand remains the same, what happens to the quantity demanded?

3. When there are single shifts in the supply or demand curve, you can predict the effects on both equilibrium price and quantity. When there are simultaneous shifts in demand and supply you can make only one prediction of the effects with any certainty. Why?

4. You observe that the equilibrium price has decreased and the equilibrium quantity has increased. What supply and demand conditions would best explain this outcome?

5. If the increase in the demand for gasoline outweighs the decrease in the supply of gasoline, what is the most likely effect on the equilibrium price and quantity? Explain and show your answer with a graph.

6. You observe that the equilibrium quantity has increased but the equilibrium price has stayed the same. What supply and demand conditions would best explain this outcome?

7. What are price ceilings and price floors?

8. What are the consequences if a seller sets a price below the actual equilibrium price?

9. Why do secondary markets arise? Give examples of such markets.

10. Explain, using a supply and demand graph, the situation that arises when there are many unsold tickets to an event. Why does this occur?

11. What are the differences in the characteristics of non-priced and market goods? Give examples of each type.

12. Discuss the plight of the American bison since the 1800s using supply and demand analysis. How did the conditions for the buffalo change from the pre-railroad era to the post-railroad era?

13. What rationing mechanisms are typically used by society to limit consumption of nonpriced goods?

14. Explain using an example how a nonpriced good could be converted to a positively priced good in a private market.

15. How is the consumer surplus related to utility or satisfaction? Explain, using a supply and demand graph.

16. What is the nature of the relationship between prices and consumer surplus?

17. Define, using a supply and demand graph, the meaning of producer surplus.

18. Compare and contrast the relationship between price and consumer surplus and price and producer surplus.

19. Explain the three conditions that exist when there is allocative efficiency.

20. Use consumer and producer surplus to describe efficiency losses in a competitive market. Provide a supply and demand graph to show such losses.

ANSWERS

Chapter 3 Web: Applications and Extensions of Supply and Demand Analysis

FILL-IN QUESTIONS

1. increases, decreases
2. increases, increases
3. decreases, increases
4. increases, increases
5. stays the same, increases
6. ceiling, floor
7. shortage, surplus
8. secondary, scalping
9. owned in common, public
10. surplus, shortage
11. over-, a decrease
12. licenses, limits
13. maximum, less
14. negatively, decrease, increase
15. minimum, more
16. positively, increase, decrease
17. productive, allocative

18. benefit, cost
19. equal to, equal to, maximum
20. losses, losses, less than
Note: Page numbers refer to Chapter 3 Web of the textbook that is available at www.mcconnell16.com.

TRUE–FALSE QUESTIONS

1. T, pp. 2–3	**8.** F, p. 5	**15.** F, p. 7	**22.** F, p. 10
2. F, p. 3	**9.** T, p. 5	**16.** T, p. 8	**23.** F, p. 10
3. T, p. 3	**10.** F, p. 5	**17.** F, p. 8	**24.** T, p. 10
4. T, pp. 3–4	**11.** T, pp. 5–6	**18.** T, pp. 8–9	**25.** F, pp. 10–11
5. F, p. 4	**12.** T, p. 7	**19.** F, p. 9	
6. F, pp. 4–5	**13.** F, pp. 7–8	**20.** F, p. 9	
7. T, p. 5	**14.** T, p. 7	**21.** T, p. 9	

MULTIPLE-CHOICE QUESTIONS

1. b, p. 2	**8.** b, p. 5	**15.** c, p. 7	**22.** c, pp. 9–10
2. b, pp. 2–3	**9.** a, p. 5	**16.** c, p. 7	**23.** b, p. 10
3. d, p. 3	**10.** c, p. 5	**17.** d, pp. 7–8	**24.** c, p. 11
4. d, pp. 3–4	**11.** c, p. 5	**18.** c, p. 8	**25.** d, pp. 11–12
5. b, p. 4	**12.** a, pp. 5–6	**19.** c, pp. 8–9	
6. c, pp. 4–5	**13.** c, pp. 5–6	**20.** a, p. 9	
7. d, pp. 4–5	**14.** b, p. 5	**21.** b, p. 9	

PROBLEMS

1. *a.* column 5 (quantity demanded): 20, 30, 40, 50, 60; column 6 (quantity supplied): 40, 30, 20, 10, 0; *b.* $3.00, $4.00; *c.* 30, 30
2. *a.* $7, 15,000; *b.* shortage, 4000; *c.* surplus, 2000
3. 13, 11, 6, 4, 1, 0
4. 8, 7, 5, 3, 2, 0
5. *a.* abc; *b.* 0ac; *c.* 0bc; *d.* efc; *e.* ghc

SHORT ANSWER AND ESSAY QUESTIONS

1. p. 2	**6.** pp. 4–5	**11.** p. 7	**16.** p. 9
2. p. 2	**7.** p. 5	**12.** pp. 7–8	**17.** p. 9
3. pp. 3–5	**8.** p. 5	**13.** p. 8	**18.** pp. 9–10
4. pp. 3–4	**9.** p. 5	**14.** p. 8	**19.** pp. 10–11
5. p. 4	**10.** p. 6	**15.** pp. 8–9	**20.** pp. 11–12

CHAPTER 4

The Market System

Chapter 4 describes the major characteristics of the market system and offers a detailed explanation of how it works. The first part describes the *ideological* and *institutional* characteristics of the market system. In this system, most of the resources are owned as private property by citizens, who are free to use them as they wish in their own self-interest. Prices and markets express the self-interests of resource owners, consumers, and business firms. Competition regulates self-interest—to prevent the self-interest of any person or any group from working to the disadvantage of the economy and to make self-interests work for the benefit of the entire economy. Government plays an active, but limited, role in a market economy.

Three other characteristics are also found in a market economy. They are the employment of large amounts of *capital goods,* the development of *specialization,* and the *use of money.* Economies use capital goods and engage in specialization because this is a more efficient use of their resources; it results in larger total output and the greater satisfaction of wants. When workers, business firms, and regions within an economy specialize, they become dependent on each other for the goods and services they do not produce for themselves and they must engage in trade. Trade is made more convenient by using money as a medium of exchange.

The second part of Chapter 4 describes the operation of the market system. There are *Four Fundamental Questions* that any economic system must answer in its attempt to use its scarce resources to satisfy its material wants. The four questions or problems are: (1) What will be produced? (2) How will the output be produced? (3) Who is to receive the output? (4) Can the system adapt to change?

The explanation of how the market system finds answers to the Four Fundamental Questions is only an approximation—a simplified version or model—of the methods actually employed by the U.S. economy and other market economies. Yet this simple model, like all good models, contains enough realism to be truthful and is general enough to be understandable. If the aims of this chapter are accomplished, you can begin to understand the market system and methods our economy uses to solve the economizing problem presented in Chapter 2.

■ CHECKLIST

When you have studied this chapter you should be able to

☐ Identify the nine important characteristics of the market system.

☐ Describe the significance of property rights in the market system.

☐ Distinguish between freedom of enterprise and freedom of choice.

☐ Explain why self-interest is a driving force of the market system.

☐ Identify two features of competition.

☐ Explain the roles of markets and prices.

☐ Explain why the market system relies on technology and capital goods, and also why the production of capital goods entails roundabout production.

☐ Discuss how two types of specialization improve efficiency in the market system.

☐ Describe the advantages of money over barter for the exchange of goods and services in a market economy.

☐ Describe the size and role of government in the market system.

☐ List the Four Fundamental Questions to answer about the operation of a market economy.

☐ Explain how a market system determines what goods and services will be produced.

☐ Distinguish between normal profit and economic profit.

☐ Predict what will happen to the price charged by and the output of an expanding and a declining industry, and explain why these events will occur.

☐ Explain how consumer sovereignty and dollar votes work in a market economy.

☐ Describe market restraints on economic freedom.

☐ Explain how goods and services will be produced in a market system.

☐ Find the least costly combination of resources needed for production when given the technological data and the prices of the resources.

☐ Explain how a market system determines who will get the goods and services it produces.

☐ Describe the guiding function of prices to accommodate change in the market system.

☐ Explain how the market system initiates change by fostering technological advances and capital accumulation.
☐ State how the "invisible hand" in the market system tends to promote public or social interests.
☐ List three virtues of the market system.

■ CHAPTER OUTLINE

1. The market system has the following nine characteristics:

a. Private individuals and organizations own and control their property resources by means of the institution of private property.

b. These individuals and organizations possess both the freedom of enterprise and the freedom of choice.

c. Each of them is motivated largely by self-interest.

d. Competition is based on the independent actions of buyers and sellers. They have the freedom to enter or leave markets. This competition spreads economic power and limits its potential abuse.

e. Markets and prices are used to communicate and coordinate the decisions of buyers and sellers.

f. The market system employs complicated and advanced methods of production, new technology, and large amounts of capital equipment to produce goods and services efficiently.

g. It is a highly specialized economy. Human and geographic specializations increase the productive efficiency of the economy.

h. It uses money exclusively to facilitate trade and specialization.

i. Government has an active but limited role.

2. The system of prices and markets and households' and business firms' choices furnish the market economy with answers to **Four Fundamental Questions.**

a. *What goods and services will be produced?* The demands of consumers for products and the desires of business firms to maximize their profits determine what and how much of each product is produced and its price.

b. *How will the goods and services be produced?* The desires of business firms to maximize profits by keeping their costs of production as low as possible guide them to use the most efficient techniques of production and determine their demands for various resources; competition forces them to use the most efficient techniques and ensures that only the most efficient will be able to stay in business.

c. *Who will get the goods and services that are produced?* With resource prices determined, the money income of each household is determined; and with product prices determined, the quantity of goods and services these money incomes will buy is determined.

d. *How will the market system accommodate change?* The market system is able to accommodate itself to changes in consumer tastes, technology, and resource supplies.

(1) The desires of business firms for maximum profits and competition lead the economy to make the appropriate adjustments in the way it uses its resources.

(2) Competition and the desire to increase profits promote better techniques of production and capital accumulation.

3. Competition in the economy compels firms seeking to promote their own interests to promote (as though led by an "invisible hand") the best interests of society as a whole.

a. Competition results in an allocation of resources appropriate to consumer wants, production by the most efficient means, and the lowest possible prices.

b. Three noteworthy merits of the market system are
(1) The *efficient* use of resources
(2) The *incentive* the system provides for productive activity
(3) The personal *freedom* allowed participants as consumers, producers, workers, or investors.

■ HINTS AND TIPS

1. The first section of the chapter describes nine characteristics and institutions of a market system. After reading the section, check your understanding by listing the nine points and writing a short explanation of each one.

2. The section on the "Market System at Work" is both the most important and the most difficult part of the chapter. A market economy must answer *Four Fundamental Questions.* Detailed answers to the four questions are given in this section of the chapter. If you examine each one individually and in the order in which it is presented, you will more easily understand how the market system works. (Actually, the market system finds the answers simultaneously, but make your learning easier for now by considering them one by one.)

3. Be sure to understand the *importance* and *role* of each of the following in the operation of the market system: (1) the guiding function of prices, (2) the profit motive of business firms, (3) the entry into and exodus of firms from industries, (4) the meaning of competition, and (5) consumer sovereignty.

■ IMPORTANT TERMS

private property	economic cost
freedom of choice	normal profit
freedom of enterprise	economic profit
self-interest	expanding industry
competition	declining industry
roundabout production	consumer sovereignty
specialization	dollar votes
division of labor	derived demand
medium of exchange	guiding function of prices
barter	creative destruction
money	"invisible hand"
Four Fundamental Questions	

SELF-TEST

■ FILL-IN QUESTIONS

1. The ownership of property resources by private individuals and organizations is the institution of private (resources, property) _____. The freedom of private businesses to obtain resources and use them to produce goods and services is the freedom of (choice, enterprise) _____, while the freedom to dispose of property or money as a person sees fit is the freedom of _____.

2. Self-interest means that each economic unit attempts to do what is best for itself, but this might lead to an abuse of power in a market economy if it were not directed and constrained by (government, competition) _____. Self-interest and selfishness (are, are not) _____ the same thing in a market economy.

3. Broadly defined, competition is present if two conditions prevail; these two conditions are

a. _____

_____

b. _____

_____

4. In a capitalist economy, individual buyers communicate their demands and individual sellers communicate their supplies in the system of (markets, prices) _____, and the outcomes from economic decisions are a set of product and resource _____ that are determined by demand and supply.

5. Market economies make extensive use of capital goods and engage in roundabout production because it is more (efficient, inefficient) _____ than direct production; they practice specialization and the division of labor because the self-sufficient producer or worker tends to be an _____ one.

6. In market economies money functions chiefly as a medium of (commerce, exchange) _____. Barter between two individuals will take place only if there is a coincidence of (resources, wants) _____.

7. In a market system, government is active, but is assigned (a limited, an extensive) _____ role.

8. List the Four Fundamental Questions every economy must answer.

a. _____

b. _____

c. _____

d. _____

9. A *normal profit* (is, is not) _____ an economic cost because it is a payment that (must, need not) _____ be paid to (workers, entrepreneurs) _____, but an *economic profit* (is, is not) _____ an economic cost because it (must, need not) _____ be paid to them to secure and retain the resources needed by the firm.

10. Pure or economic profit is equal to the total (revenue, cost) _____ of a firm less its total _____.

11. Business firms tend to produce those products from which they can obtain at least a(n) (economic, normal) _____ profit and a maximum _____ profit.

12. If firms in an industry are obtaining economic profits, firms will (enter, leave) _____ the industry; the price of the industry's product will (rise, fall) _____; the industry will employ (more, fewer) _____ resources and produce a (larger, smaller) _____ output; and the industry's economic profits will (increase, decrease) _____ until they are equal to (zero, infinity) _____.

13. Consumers vote with their dollars for the production of a good or service when they (sell, buy) _____ it, and because of this, consumers are said to be (dependent, sovereign) _____ in a market economy. The buying decisions of consumers (restrain, expand) _____ the freedom of firms and resource suppliers.

14. Firms are interested in obtaining the largest economic profits possible, so they try to produce a product in the (most, least) _____ costly way. The most efficient production techniques depend on the available (income, technology) _____ and the (prices, quotas) _____ of needed resources.

15. The market system determines how the total output of the economy will be distributed among its households by determining the (incomes, expenditures) _____ of each household and by determining the (prices, quality) _____ for each good and service produced.

16. In market economies, change is almost continuous in consumer (preferences, resources)

_____, in the supplies of _____, and in technology. To make the appropriate adjustments to these changes, a market economy allows price to perform its (monopoly, guiding) _____ function.

17. The market system fosters technological change. The incentive for a firm to be the first to use a new and improved technique of production or to produce a new and better product is a greater economic (profit, loss) _____, and the incentive for other firms to follow its lead is the avoidance of _____.

18. Technological advance will require additional (capital, consumer) _____ goods, so the entrepreneur uses profit obtained from the sale of _____ goods to acquire (capital, consumer) _____ goods.

19. A market system promotes (unity, disunity) _____ between private and public interests. Firms and resource suppliers seem to be guided by (a visible, an invisible) _____ hand to allocate the economy's resources efficiently.

20. The two *economic* arguments for a market system are that it promotes (public, efficient) _____ use of resources and that it uses (incentives, government) _____ for directing economic activity. The major *noneconomic* argument for the market system is that it allows for personal (wealth, freedom) _____.

■ TRUE–FALSE QUESTIONS

Circle T if the statement is true, F if it is false.

1. In a market system, the government owns most of the property resources (land and capital).   **T   F**

2. Property rights encourage investment, innovation, exchange, maintenance of property, and economic growth.   **T   F**

3. The freedom of business firms to produce a particular consumer good is always limited by the desires of consumers for that good.   **T   F**

4. The pursuit of economic self-interest is the same thing as selfishness.   **T   F**

5. When a market is competitive, the individual sellers of a product are unable to reduce the supply of the product and control its price.   **T   F**

6. The market system is an organizing mechanism and also a communication network.   **T   F**

7. The employment of capital to produce goods and services requires that there be "roundabout" production and it is more efficient than "direct" production.   **T   F**

8. Increasing the amount of specialization in an economy generally leads to the more efficient use of its resources.   **T   F**

9. One way human specialization can be achieved is through a division of labor in productive activity.   **T   F**

10. Money is a device for facilitating the exchange of goods and services.   **T   F**

11. "Coincidence of wants" means that two persons want to acquire the same good or service.   **T   F**

12. Shells may serve as money if sellers are generally willing to accept them as money.   **T   F**

13. One of the Four Fundamental Questions is who will control the output.   **T   F**

14. Business firms try to maximize their normal profits.   **T   F**

15. Industries in which economic profits are earned by the firms in the industry will attract the entry of new firms.   **T   F**

16. If firms have sufficient time to enter industries, the economic profits of an industry will tend to disappear.   **T   F**

17. Business firms are only free to produce whatever they want in any way they wish if they do not want to maximize profits or to minimize losses.   **T   F**

18. The derived demand of a resource depends on the demands for the products the resource produces.   **T   F**

19. Resources will tend to be used in those industries capable of earning normal or economic profits.   **T   F**

20. Economic efficiency requires that a given output of a good or service be produced in the least costly way.   **T   F**

21. If the market price of resource A decreases, firms will tend to employ smaller quantities of resource A.   **T   F**

22. Changes in the tastes of consumers are reflected in changes in consumer demand for products.   **T   F**

23. The incentive that the market system provides to induce technological improvement is the opportunity for economic profits.   **T   F**

24. The tendency for individuals pursuing their own self-interests to bring about results that are in the best interest of society as a whole is often called the "invisible hand."   **T   F**

25. A basic economic argument for the market system is that it promotes an efficient use of resources.   **T   F**

■ MULTIPLE-CHOICE QUESTIONS

Circle the letter that corresponds to the best answer.

1. Which is one of the main characteristics of the market system?
(a) central economic planning

(b) limits on freedom of choice

(c) the right to own private property

(d) an expanded role for government in the economy

2. In the market system, freedom of enterprise means that

(a) businesses are free to produce products that consumers want

(b) consumers are free to buy goods and services that they want

(c) resources are distributed freely to businesses that want them

(d) government is free to direct the actions of businesses

3. The maximization of profit tends to be the driving force in the economic decision making of

(a) entrepreneurs

(b) workers

(c) consumers

(d) legislators

4. How do consumers typically express self-interest?

(a) by minimizing their economic losses

(b) by maximizing their economic profits

(c) by seeking the lowest price for a product

(d) by seeking jobs with the highest wages and benefits

5. Which is a characteristic of competition as economists see it?

(a) a few sellers of all products

(b) the widespread diffusion of economic power

(c) a small number of buyers in product markets

(d) the relatively difficult entry into and exit from industries by producers

6. To decide how to use its scarce resources to satisfy economic wants, capitalism relies on

(a) central planning

(b) monopoly power

(c) markets and prices

(d) command and control

7. The market system is a method of

(a) communicating and coordinating the decisions of consumers, producers, and resource suppliers

(b) making economic decisions by central planning

(c) promoting productive efficiency, but not allocative efficiency

(d) promoting allocative efficiency, but not productive efficiency

8. What is roundabout production?

(a) the division of labor that results from specialization in the production of a good or service

(b) the production and use of capital goods to help make consumer goods

(c) the production of a good and service and the payment for it with money

(d) the production of a consumer good and its sale to consumers

9. When workers specialize in various tasks to produce a commodity, the situation is referred to as

(a) a coincidence of wants

(b) roundabout production

(c) freedom of choice

(d) division of labor

10. In what way does human specialization contribute to an economy's output?

(a) It serves as consumer sovereignty.

(b) It is a process of creative destruction.

(c) It acts like an "invisible hand."

(d) It fosters learning by doing.

11. Which is a prerequisite of specialization?

(a) having a convenient means of exchanging goods

(b) letting government create a plan for the economy

(c) deciding who will get the goods and services in an economy

(d) market restraints on freedom

12. In the market system, the role of government is best described as

(a) nonexistent

(b) significant

(c) extensive

(d) limited

13. Which best defines economic costs?

(a) the difference between economic profit and normal profit

(b) total payments made to secure and retain needed resources

(c) the demand for resources minus the supply of resources

(d) the total revenue plus the total losses of the firm

14. If a business's total economic cost of producing 10,000 units of a product is $750,000 and this output is sold to consumers for $1,000,000, then the firm would earn

(a) a normal profit of $750,000

(b) an economic profit of $750,000

(c) an economic profit of $250,000

(d) a normal profit of $1,750,000

15. If less-than-normal profits are being earned by the firms in an industry, the consequences will be that

(a) lower-priced resources will be drawn into the industry

(b) firms will leave the industry, causing the price of the industry's product to fall

(c) firms will leave the industry, causing the price of the industry's product to rise

(d) the price of the industry's product will fall and thereby cause the demand for the product to increase

16. Which would necessarily result, sooner or later, from a decrease in consumer demand for a product?

(a) a decrease in the profits of firms in the industry

(b) an increase in the output of the industry

(c) an increase in the supply of the product

(d) an increase in the prices of resources employed by the firms in the industry

17. The demand for resources is
  (a) increased when the price of resources falls
  (b) most influenced by the size of government in a capitalist economy
  (c) derived from the demand for the products made with the resources
  (d) decreased when the product that the resources produce becomes popular

Answer Questions 18, 19, and 20 on the basis of the following information.

Suppose 50 units of product X can be produced by employing just labor and capital in the four ways shown below. Assume the prices of labor and capital are $5 and $4, respectively.

	A	B	C	D
Labor	1	2	3	4
Capital	5	3	2	1

18. Which technique is economically most efficient in producing product X?
  (a) A
  (b) B
  (c) C
  (d) D

19. If the price of product X is $1, the firm will realize
  (a) an economic profit of $28
  (b) an economic profit of $27
  (c) an economic profit of $26
  (d) an economic profit of $25

20. Now assume that the price of labor falls to $3 and the price of capital rises to $5. Which technique is economically most efficient in producing product X?
  (a) A
  (b) B
  (c) C
  (d) D

21. Which is the primary factor determining the share of the total output of the economy received by a household?
  (a) the tastes of the household
  (b) the medium of exchange used by the household
  (c) the prices at which the household sells its resources
  (d) ethical considerations in the operation of a market economy

22. If an increase in the demand for a product and a rise in its price cause an increase in the quantity supplied, the size of the industry, and the resources used for production, price is successfully performing its
  (a) guiding function
  (b) roundabout function
  (c) division-of-labor function
  (d) medium-of-exchange function

23. The advent of personal computers and word processing software that eliminated the market for electric typewriters would be an example of

  (a) creative destruction
  (b) the "invisible hand"
  (c) derived demand
  (d) specialization

24. In the market system, if one firm introduces a new and better method of production that enhances the firm's economic profits, other firms will be forced to adopt the new method to
  (a) increase derived demand
  (b) follow rules for roundabout production
  (c) avoid economic losses or bankruptcy
  (d) specialize and divide the labor in an efficient way

25. The chief economic virtue of the competitive market system is that it
  (a) allows extensive personal freedom
  (b) efficiently allocates resources
  (c) provides an equitable distribution of income
  (d) eliminates the need for decision making

■ PROBLEMS

1. Use the appropriate number to match the term with the phrase.

1. invisible hand	5. consumer sovereignty
2. coincidence of wants	6. derived demand
3. division of labor	7. specialization
4. guiding function of prices	8. roundabout production

a. The construction and use of capital goods to aid in the production of consumer goods. _____
b. The ability of price changes to bring about changes in the quantities of products and resources demanded and supplied. _____
c. Using the resources of an individual, a firm, a region, or a nation to produce one (or a few) goods and services.

_____
d. The tendency of firms and resource suppliers seeking to further their own self-interest while also promoting the interests of society in a market economy. _____
e. The demand for a resource that depends on the demand for the product it can be used to produce. _____
f. Splitting the work required to produce a product into a number of different tasks that are performed by different workers. _____
g. A situation in which the product the first trader wants to sell is the same as that the second trader wants to buy, and the product the second trader wants to sell is the same as the product the first trader wants to buy. _____
h. Determination by consumers of the types and quantities of goods and services that will be produced in a market economy. _____

2. Assume that a firm can produce product A, product B, *or* product C with the resources it currently employs.

These resources cost the firm a total of $50 per week. Assume, for the purposes of the problem, that the firm's employment of resources cannot be changed. Their market prices, and the quantities of A, B, and C these resources will produce per week are given below. Compute the firm's profit when it produces A, B, or C, and enter these profits in the table below.

Product	Market price	Output	Economic profit
A	$7.00	8	$_____
B	4.50	10	_____
C	.25	240	_____

a. Which product will the firm produce? _____

b. If the price of A rose to $8, the firm would _____

_____

(Hint: You will have to recompute the firm's profit from the production of A.)

c. If the firm were producing A and selling it at a price of $8, what would tend to happen to the number of firms producing A? _____

_____

3. Suppose that a firm can produce 100 units of product X by combining labor, land, capital, and entrepreneurial ability in three different ways. If it can hire labor at $2 per unit, land at $3 per unit, capital at $5 per unit, and entrepreneurship at $10 per unit, and if the amounts of the resources required by the three methods of producing 100 units of product X are indicated in the table, answer the following questions.

	Method		
Resource	1	2	3
Labor	8	13	10
Land	4	3	3
Capital	4	2	4
Entrepreneurship	1	1	1

a. Which method is the least expensive way of producing 100 units of X? _____

b. If X sells for 70 cents per unit, what is the economic profit of the firm? $_____

c. If the price of labor should rise from $2 to $3 per unit and if the price of X is 70 cents,
(1) the firm's use of

labor would change from _____ to _____

land would change from _____ to _____

capital would change from _____ to _____
entrepreneurship would not change
(2) the firm's economic profit would change from

$_____ to $_____

■ SHORT ANSWER AND ESSAY QUESTIONS

1. Explain the major characteristics — institutions and assumptions — embodied in a market system.

2. What do each of the following seek if they pursue their own self-interest: consumers, resource owners, and business firms?

3. Explain what economists mean by competition. For a market to be competitive, why is it important that there be buyers and sellers and easy entry and exit?

4. What are the advantages of indirect or roundabout production?

5. How does an economy benefit from specialization and the division of labor?

6. Give an example of how specialization can benefit two separate and diversely endowed geographic regions.

7. What is money? What important function does it perform? Explain how money performs this function and how it overcomes the disadvantages associated with barter.

8. For an item to be useful as money, what is its necessary major characteristic? Can you think of other characteristics that might be favorable?

9. What are the Four Fundamental Questions?

10. In what way do the desires of entrepreneurs to obtain economic profits and avoid losses make consumer sovereignty effective?

11. Why is the ability of firms to enter industries that are prosperous important to the effective functioning of competition?

12. Explain in detail how an increase in the consumer demand for a product will result in more of the product being produced and more resources being allocated to its production.

13. To what extent are firms "free" to produce what they wish by methods that they choose? Do resource owners have freedom to use their resources as they wish?

14. How can the market system adapt to change? How is it done?

15. What is the guiding function of price? Explain how it works.

16. Explain how the market system provides a strong incentive for technological advance.

17. What is "creative destruction"? Give some examples of it.

18. Who "votes" for the production of capital goods, why do they "vote" for capital goods production, and where do they obtain the dollars needed to cast these "votes"?

19. An "invisible hand operates to identify private and public interests." What are private interests and what is the public interest? What is it that leads the economy to operate as if it were directed by an invisible hand?

20. Describe three virtues of the market system.

ANSWERS

Chapter 4 The Market System

FILL-IN QUESTIONS

1. property, enterprise, choice
2. competition, are not
3. *a.* independently acting buyers and sellers operating in markets; *b.* freedom of buyers and sellers to enter or leave these markets
4. markets, prices
5. efficient, inefficient
6. exchange, wants
7. a limited
8. *a.* What goods and services will be produced? *b.* How will the goods and services be produced? *c.* Who will get the goods and services? *d.* How will the system accommodate change?
9. is, must, entrepreneurs, is not, need not
10. revenue, cost
11. normal, economic
12. enter, fall, more, larger, decrease, zero
13. buy, sovereign, restrain
14. least, technology, prices
15. incomes, prices
16. preferences, resources, guiding
17. profit, losses
18. capital, consumer, capital
19. unity, an invisible
20. efficient, incentives, freedom

TRUE–FALSE QUESTIONS

1. F, p. 60	8. T, p. 63	15. T, pp. 65–66	22. T, pp. 67–68
2. T, p. 60	9. T, p. 63	16. T, pp. 65–66	23. T, pp. 68–69
3. T, p. 61	10. T, pp. 63–64	17. T, pp. 66–67	24. T, p. 69
4. F, p. 61	11. F, p. 63	18. T, pp. 66–67	25. T, p. 69
5. T, p. 62	12. T, pp. 63–64	19. T, pp. 66–67	
6. T, p. 62	13. F, p. 65	20. T, p. 67	
7. T, pp. 62–63	14. F, p. 65	21. F, pp. 67–68	

MULTIPLE-CHOICE QUESTIONS

1. c, p. 60	8. b, p. 63	15. c, p. 66	22. a, p. 68
2. a, p. 61	9. d, p. 63	16. a, p. 66	23. a, pp. 68–69
3. a, p. 61	10. d, p. 63	17. c, pp. 66–67	24. c, pp. 68–69
4. c, p. 61	11. a, p. 63	18. b, p. 67	25. b, p. 69
5. b, p. 62	12. d, p. 64	19. a, pp. 65; 67	
6. c, p. 62	13. b, p. 65	20. d, p. 67	
7. a, p. 62	14. c, p. 65	21. c, pp. 67–68	

PROBLEMS

1. *a.* 8; *b.* 4; *c.* 7; *d.* 1; *e.* 6; *f.* 3; *g.* 2; *h.* 5
2. $6, −$5, $10; *a.* C; *b.* produce A and have an economic profit of $14; *c.* it would increase
3. *a.* method 2; *b.* 15; *c.* (1) 13, 8; 3, 4; 2, 4; (2) 15, 4

SHORT ANSWER AND ESSAY QUESTIONS

1. pp. 60–64	6. p. 63	11. pp. 65–66	16. pp. 68–69
2. p. 61	7. pp. 63–64	12. p. 66	17. pp. 68–69
3. p. 62	8. pp. 63–64	13. pp. 66–67	18. p. 69
4. pp. 62–63	9. p. 65	14. pp. 68–69	19. p. 69
5. p. 63	10. pp. 65–66	15. p. 68	20. p. 69

CHAPTER 5

The U.S. Economy: Private and Public Sectors

The U.S. economy is divided into a private sector and a public sector. The first half of Chapter 5 discusses the private sector—the characteristics of millions of households and business firms. The second half of Chapter 5 describes the public sector—the functions and financing of the Federal, state, and local governments. Learning about these two sectors will give you the basic facts and framework you need for understanding the U.S. economy.

Chapter 5 begins with an examination of the **households** of the economy. Two different distributions of household income are examined. The way in which the total personal income received by all U.S. households is divided among the five types of earned income is called the *functional distribution of income.* The way in which the total personal income received by all households is distributed among the various income classes is called the *personal distribution of income.* Households dispose of the income they receive by spending money on *personal consumption expenditures,* paying *personal taxes,* or allocating funds to *personal saving.*

Businesses in the United States are also a focus of the chapter. It is apparent that what most characterizes U.S. businesses is the differences among firms in size and legal form, as well as in the products they produce. You should note the distinctions between a *proprietorship,* a *partnership,* and a *corporation* and the major advantages and disadvantages of each business form. You will also learn about the principal–agent problem with corporations that can arise from the separation of ownership (the principals) and management (the agents).

Chapter 5 also introduces you to the five basic functions performed by the **government** in the U.S. economy. The chapter does not attempt to list all the specific ways in which government affects the behavior of the economy: Instead, it provides a general classification of the five functions that government performs.

The chapter also returns to the **circular flow model** first presented in Chapter 2. The model has now been modified to include government along with business and household sectors. This addition changes the real and monetary flows in the model.

The facts of **government finance** in the United States are presented in the final sections of Chapter 5. The organization of the discussion is relatively simple. First, the trends for taxes collected and expenditures made by all levels of government—Federal, state, and local—are examined. Second, an explanation is given for the major items on which the Federal government spends its income, the principal taxes it levies to obtain its income,

and the relative importance of these taxes. Third, the chapter closes with a look at the major expenditures and taxes of the state and local governments.

■ CHECKLIST

When you have studied this chapter you should be able to

☐ Define and distinguish between a functional and a personal distribution of income.
☐ State the five sources of personal income in the functional distribution.
☐ List the three uses to which households put their personal incomes and state the relative size of each.
☐ Distinguish among durable goods, nondurable goods, and services in personal consumption expenditures.
☐ Give definitions for a plant, a firm, and an industry.
☐ List the three legal forms of business enterprise.
☐ Report the relative importance of each of the legal forms of business enterprise in the U.S. economy.
☐ State the advantages and disadvantages of the three legal forms of business enterprise.
☐ Identify two hybrid structures for corporations.
☐ Explain the principal–agent problem as it applies to corporations.
☐ List the five economic functions of government in the United States.
☐ Give examples of how government provides the legal framework for the economy.
☐ Define monopoly and explain why government wishes to prevent monopoly and to maintain competition in the economy.
☐ Explain why government redistributes income and list the three principal policies it uses for this purpose.
☐ Define spillover cost and spillover benefit.
☐ Explain why a competitive market fails to allocate resources efficiently when there are spillover costs and benefits.
☐ List two actions government can take to reduce spillover costs.
☐ List three actions government can take to encourage spillover benefits.
☐ Give definitions of a public good and a quasi-public good.
☐ Explain how the government reallocates resources from the production of private goods to the production of public or quasi-public goods.
☐ Describe the stabilization role of government and the two main economic problems it is designed to address.

☐ Explain the qualifications to government's role in the economy.

☐ Draw the circular flow model that includes businesses, households, and government, labeling all the flows and illustrating the role of government.

☐ Explain the difference between government purchases and transfer payments and the effect of each on the composition of national output.

☐ Identify the four largest categories of Federal expenditures.

☐ List the three main sources of Federal tax revenues.

☐ Define and explain the differences between marginal and average tax rates.

☐ Identify the major expenditures by state and local governments.

☐ Describe how state and local governments raise tax revenue.

■ **CHAPTER OUTLINE**

1. *Households* play a dual role in the economy. They supply the economy with resources, and they purchase the greatest share of the goods and services produced by the economy. They obtain their personal incomes in exchange for the resources they furnish the economy and from the transfer payments they receive from government.

   a. The *functional distribution of income* indicates the way in which total personal income is divided among the five sources of earned income (wages and salaries, proprietors' income, corporate profits, interest, and rents).

   b. The *personal distribution of income* indicates the way in which total personal income is divided among households in different income classes.

2. Households use their incomes to purchase consumer goods, pay taxes, and accumulate savings.

   a. *Personal taxes* constitute a deduction from a household's personal income; what remains after taxes can be either saved or spent.

   b. *Saving* is what a household does not spend of its after-tax income.

   c. Households make *personal consumption expenditures* for durable goods, nondurable goods, and services.

3. The *businesses* of the U.S. economy consist of three major types of entities. A *plant* is a physical structure that produces a product. A *business firm* is an organization that owns and operates plants. (Multiplant firms may be horizontally or vertically integrated, or they may be conglomerates.) An *industry* is a group of firms producing the same or similar goods or services.

4. The three principal *legal forms* of business firms are the *proprietorship, partnership,* and *corporation.*

   a. Each has special characteristics and advantages and disadvantages.

   (1) The *proprietorship* is easy to form, lets the owner be boss, and allows for great freedom. Disadvantages are lack of access to large amounts of financial capital, difficulty of managerial specialization, and the owner's *unlimited liability.*

   (2) The *partnership* is also easy to form and allows for more access to financial capital and permits more managerial specialization. Potential disadvantages are that partners may disagree, there are still limits to financial capital or managerial specialization, continuity of the firm over time is a problem, and partners face unlimited liability.

   (3) The *corporation* can raise financial capital through the sale of stocks and bonds, has *limited liability* for owners, can become large in size, and has an independent life. Chief disadvantages of the corporation are the double taxation of some corporate income, potential for abuse of this legal entity, and legal or regulatory expenses.

   (4) There are also "hybrid" business structures such as the *limited liability company* (LLC) or the *S corporation* that give the advantage of corporations to one or relatively few owners.

   b. Large corporations are a major feature of the U.S. economy. They are also subject to a *principal–agent problem* that arises from the separation of ownership (by stockholders) and control (by corporate executives). This problem can sometimes be overcome by aligning the interests of executives with those of stockholders through stock payment plans.

5. *Government* performs five economic functions.

   a. The first of these functions is to provide the **legal framework and services** that contribute to the effective operation of the market economy.

   b. The second function of government is to **maintain competition** and the control of *monopoly* through regulation and antitrust laws.

   c. Government performs its third function when it **redistributes income** to reduce income inequality. The policies and programs it uses to achieve this objective are transfer payments, market interventions (changing market prices), and taxation.

   d. When government **reallocates resources** it performs its fourth function.

   (1) It reallocates resources to take into account spillovers or externalities.

      (a) Spillover costs are production or consumption costs paid for by a third party without compensation.

      (b) Spillover costs can be discouraged by legislation or specific taxes.

      (c) Spillover benefits are outcomes that benefit third parties without these parties paying for the benefits.

      (d) Spillover benefits can be encouraged by subsidizing consumers, subsidizing producers, or by having government provide the goods (when the benefits are extremely large).

   (2) Government also provides public goods. These goods have the characteristic of *nonrivalry* (benefits are not reduced by consumption) and *nonexcludability* (people cannot be excluded from the benefits).

   (3) Quasi-public goods (e.g., education) are divisible and subject to the exclusion principle, but they often have large spillover benefits, so they are provided by government.

(4) Government levies taxes and uses tax revenues to reallocate income and resources from private uses to public ones (for providing public and quasi-public goods).

e. The fifth function of government is **stabilization** of the economy by controlling inflation and reducing unemployment.

f. The economic role of government is conducted in the context of politics. This process can lead to imperfect and inefficient outcomes.

6. *A* **circular flow model** that includes the public sector as well as business firms and households in the private sector of the economy reveals that government purchases public goods from private businesses, collects taxes from and makes transfer payments to these firms, purchases labor services from households, collects taxes from and makes transfer payments to these households, and can alter the distribution of income, reallocate resources, and change the level of economic activity by affecting the real and monetary flows in the diagram.

7. **Government finance** is important in the economy. Government spending consists of *purchases* of goods and services and *transfer payments,* but they have different effects on the economy. Purchases are exhaustive because they directly use the economy's resources, while transfers are nonexhaustive. Total government spending is equal to about one-third of domestic output.

8. For the **Federal government,**
a. most spending goes for pensions and income security, national defense, health care, or interest on the public debt.
b. the major sources of revenue are personal income taxes, payroll taxes, and corporate income taxes.

9. For other levels of government,
a. **state governments** depend largely on sales, excise, and personal income taxes, and they spend their revenues on public welfare, education, health care, and highways.
b. **local governments** rely heavily on property taxes; they spend much of the revenue on education.

■ HINTS AND TIPS

1. This chapter is a long one, so do not try to learn everything at once. Break the chapter into its three natural parts and work on each one separately. The first part describes features of the private sector. The second part explains the functions of government. The third part looks at government finance.

2. There are many descriptive statistics about the private and public sectors. Avoid memorizing these statistics. Instead, look for the trends and generalizations that these statistics illustrate about the private or public sector. For example, the discussion of government finance describes recent trends in government expenditures and taxes and indicates the relative importance of taxes and expenditures at each level of government.

■ IMPORTANT TERMS

functional distribution of income	double taxation
personal distribution of income	principal–agent problem
personal taxes	monopoly
personal saving	spillover costs
personal consumption	spillover benefits
expenditures	public goods
durable good	free-rider problem
nondurable good	quasi-public goods
services	government purchases
plant	transfer payment
firm	personal income tax
industry	marginal tax rate
sole proprietorship	average tax rate
partnership	payroll tax
corporation	corporate income tax
stocks	sales tax
bonds	excise tax
limited liability	property tax

SELF-TEST

■ FILL-IN QUESTIONS

1. There are approximately 109 million (businesses, households) _____ in the United States. They play a dual role in the economy because they (sell, buy) _____ their resources and _____ most of the total output of the economy.

2. The largest single source of income in the United States is (corporate profits, wages and salaries) _____. It is equal to about (30, 70) _____% of total income.

3. In the United States the poorest (1, 20) _____% of all families receive about 4% of total personal income, and the richest (1, 20) _____% of these families receive about 50% of total personal income.

4. The total income of households is disposed of in three ways: personal _____, personal _____, and personal _____.

5. Households use about 13% of their total income to pay for personal (taxes, consumption expenditures) _____ and about 84% for personal _____.

6. If a product has an expected life of 3 years or more it is a (durable, nondurable) _____ good, whereas if it has an expected life of less than 3 years it is a _____ good.

7. There are millions of business (firms, industries) _____ in the United States. The legal form of the great majority of them is the (sole proprietorship, partnership, corporation) _____, but the legal form that produces almost 90% of the sales of the U.S. economy is the _____.

8. Shares of ownership of corporations are called (stocks, bonds) _____, whereas promises by corporations to repay a loan, usually at a fixed rate of interest, are _____.

9. The liabilities of a sole proprietor and of partners are (limited, unlimited) _____, but the liabilities of stockholders in a corporation are _____.

10. The separation of ownership and control in a corporation may create a (free-rider, principal–agent) _____ problem. In this case, stockholders would be the (riders, principals, agents) _____ and managers would be the _____.

11. List the five economic functions of government.

a. _____

b. _____

c. _____

d. _____

e. _____

12. To control monopoly, the U.S. government has created commissions to (tax, regulate) _____ natural monopolies, and in cases at the local level, government has become an (agent, owner) _____. Government has also enacted (trust, antitrust) _____ laws to maintain competition.

13. The market system, because it is an impersonal mechanism, results in an (equal, unequal) _____ distribution of income. To redistribute income from the upper- to the lower-income groups, the government has provided (transfer, tax) _____ payments, engaged in (military, market) _____ intervention, and used the (income, sales) _____ tax to raise much of its revenues.

14. Government frequently reallocates resources when it finds instances of (market, public) _____ failure. The two major cases of such failure occur when the competitive market system either

a. _____ ;

b. _____

_____

15. Competitive markets bring about an efficient allocation of resources only if there are no (private, spillover) _____ costs or benefits in the consumption and production of a good or service.

16. There is an externality whenever some of the costs of producing a product accrue to people other than the (seller, buyer) _____ or some of the benefits from consuming a product accrue to people other than the _____.

17. a. What two things can government do to make the market reflect spillover costs?

(1) _____

(2) _____

b. What three things can government do to make the market reflect spillover benefits?

(1) _____

(2) _____

(3) _____

18. One characteristic of a public good is (rivalry, nonrivalry) _____ and the other characteristic of a public good is (excludability, nonexcludability) _____. A private firm will not find it profitable to produce a public good because there is a (free-rider, principal–agent) _____ problem.

19. To reallocate resources from the production of private to the production of public and quasi-public goods, government reduces the demand for private goods by (taxing, subsidizing) _____ consumers and then uses the (profits, tax revenue) _____ to buy public or quasi-public goods.

20. To stabilize the economy with less than full employment, government may try to increase total spending by (increasing, decreasing) _____ its expenditures for public goods and services by (increasing, decreasing) _____ taxes, or by (raising, lowering) _____ interest rates. When there are inflationary pressures, the government may try to decrease total spending by (decreasing, increasing) _____ its expenditures for public goods and services, by _____ taxes, or by (raising, lowering) _____ interest rates.

21. An examination of government finance reveals that **a.** since 1960 government *purchases* of goods and services as a percentage of total output (increased, decreased) _____,

b. but government *transfer payments* as a percentage of domestic output since 1960 has (increased, decreased) _____,

c. and the tax revenues required to finance total government spending (purchases plus transfer payments) are today about (30, 70) _____% of domestic output.

d. Government transfer payments are (exhaustive, nonexhaustive) _____, whereas government purchases of goods and services are _____ because they absorb resources.

22. The most important source of revenue for the Federal government is the (personal income, payroll) _____ tax; next in importance is the _____ tax. The three largest categories of Federal expenditures ranked by budget size are (health, national defense, pensions and income security) _____,

_____, and _____.

23. Federal income tax rates are progressive, which means that people with (lower, higher) _____ incomes pay a larger percentage of that income as taxes than do persons with _____ incomes. The tax rate paid on an additional unit of income is the (average, marginal) _____ tax rate, while the total tax paid divided by the total taxable income is the _____ tax rate.

24. Many state governments rely primarily on (property, sales and excise) _____ taxes and (personal, corporate) _____ income taxes for their revenue, which they spend mostly on (national defense, public welfare) _____ and (interest, education) _____.

25. At local levels of government the single most important source of revenue is the (income, property) _____ tax and the single most important expenditure is for (public safety, education) _____.

■ **TRUE–FALSE QUESTIONS**

Circle T if the statement is true, F if it is false.

1. The personal distribution of income describes the manner in which society's total personal income is divided among wages and salaries, corporate profits, proprietors' income, interest, and rents. **T F**

2. Personal taxes have risen in relative terms since World War II. **T F**

3. Most of the personal saving in the U.S. economy is done by those households in the top 10% of its income receivers. **T F**

4. *Dissaving* means that personal consumption expenditures exceed after-tax income. **T F**

5. A durable good is defined as a good that has an expected life of 3 years or more. **T F**

6. A plant is defined as a group of firms under a single management. **T F**

7. An industry is a group of firms that produce the same or nearly the same products. **T F**

8. Limited liability refers to the fact that all members of a partnership are liable for the debts incurred by one another. **T F**

9. The corporate form of organization is the least used by firms in the United States. **T F**

10. The corporation in the United States has a tax advantage over other legal forms of business organization. **T F**

11. Whether a business firm should incorporate or not depends chiefly on the amount of money capital it must have to finance the enterprise. **T F**

12. A limited liability company is like an ordinary partnership for tax purposes, but like a corporation in matters of liability. **T F**

13. Bonds are shares of ownership in a corporation. **T F**

14. When the interests of the principals are the same as those of agents, there is a free-rider problem. **T F**

15. When the Federal government provides for a monetary system, it is doing so primarily to maintain competition. **T F**

16. Transfer payments are one means government uses to redistribute income. **T F**

17. If demand and supply reflected all the benefits and costs of producing a product, there would be efficient resource use. **T F**

18. When there are spillover costs, more resources are allocated to the production of the product and more is produced than is efficient. **T F**

19. One way for government to correct for spillover costs from a product is to increase its demand. **T F**

20. When there are spillover benefits from a product, there will be an overallocation of resources for its production. **T F**

21. One way for government to correct spillover benefits from a product is to subsidize consumers of the product. **T F**

22. Nonexcludability means government provides public goods so as to exclude private businesses from providing them. **T F**

23. Obtaining the benefits of private goods requires that they be purchased; obtaining benefits from public goods requires only that they be produced. **T F**

24. Government provides homeland defense services because these services have public benefits and because private producers of such services experience the free-rider problem. **T F**

25. When the Federal government takes actions to control unemployment or inflation it is performing the allocative function of government. **T F**

26. Government purchases of goods and services are called nonexhaustive expenditures and government transfer payments are called exhaustive expenditures. **T F**

27. When a government levies taxes and uses the tax revenue to make transfer payments, it shifts resources from the production of private goods to the production of public goods. **T F**

28. The chief source of revenue for the Federal government is the corporate income tax. **T F**

29. If the marginal tax rate is higher than the average tax rate, the average tax rate will fall as income rises. **T F**

30. Property taxes are the largest percentage of the total revenues of local governments. **T F**

■ **MULTIPLE-CHOICE QUESTIONS**

Circle the letter that corresponds to the best answer.

1. The functional distribution for the United States shows that the largest part of the nation's income is
(a) wages and salaries
(b) proprietors' income
(c) corporate profits
(d) interest and rents

2. The part of after-tax income which is not consumed is defined as
(a) saving
(b) capital investment
(c) wages and salaries
(d) nondurable goods expenditure

3. If personal consumption expenditures were 80% of income and personal taxes were 8% of income, then personal savings would be
(a) 8% of income
(b) 10% of income
(c) 12% of income
(d) 88% of income

4. Consumer products that have expected lives of three years or more are
(a) durable goods
(b) nondurable goods
(c) quasi-public goods
(d) services

5. A firm owns and operates a farm growing wheat, a flour-milling plant, and a plant that bakes and sells bakery products. This firm would best be described as
(a) a horizontally integrated firm
(b) a vertically integrated firm
(c) a conglomerate
(d) a monopoly

6. Limited liability is associated with
(a) sole proprietorships
(b) partnerships
(c) free-riders
(d) corporations

7. Which form of business can most effectively raise money capital?
(a) corporation
(b) partnership
(c) proprietorship
(d) households

8. The separation of ownership and control in a corporation may create
(a) a principal–agent problem
(b) a free-rider problem
(c) a monopoly
(d) limited liability

9. One major means that government uses to deal with a monopoly is to
(a) increase the demand for its product
(b) decrease the supply of its product
(c) stabilize incomes
(d) regulate the firm

10. Government redistributes income through
(a) limited liability
(b) conglomerates
(c) transfer payments
(d) sole proprietorships

11. To redistribute income from high-income to low-income households, government might
(a) increase transfer payments to high-income and decrease transfer payments to low-income households
(b) increase the taxes paid by high-income and increase the transfer payments to low-income households
(c) increase the taxes paid by low-income and decrease the taxes paid by high-income households
(d) decrease the taxes paid by high-income and decrease the transfer payments to low-income households

12. Which is the best example of a good or service providing the economy with a spillover cost?
(a) a textbook
(b) an automobile
(c) a business suit
(d) an audit of a business firm's books

13. Which economic situation would result in overallocation of resources to the production of a good?
(a) spillover benefits
(b) spillover costs

(c) a free-rider program

(d) inflation

14. How does government correct for spillover benefits?

(a) by taxing consumers

(b) by taxing producers

(c) by subsidizing producers

(d) by separating ownership from control

15. Which is characteristic of public goods?

(a) nonrivalry

(b) excludability

(c) limited liability

(d) spillover costs

16. There is a free-rider problem when people

(a) are willing to pay for what they want

(b) are not willing to pay for what they want

(c) benefit from a good without paying for its cost

(d) want to buy more than is available for purchase in the market

17. Quasi-public goods are goods and services

(a) that are indivisible

(b) that have large spillover costs

(c) that have large spillover benefits

(d) that would not be produced by private producers through the market system

18. In the circular flow model, government provides goods and services and receives net taxes from

(a) colleges and universities

(b) businesses and households

(c) resource and product markets

(d) foreign nations and corporations

19. Which accounts for the largest percentage of all Federal expenditures?

(a) income security

(b) national defense

(c) interest on the public debt

(d) veterans' services

20. Which is the largest source of the tax revenues of the Federal government?

(a) sales and excise taxes

(b) property taxes

(c) payroll taxes

(d) personal income taxes

21. A tax that would most likely alter consumer expenditures on a particular product would be

(a) an excise tax

(b) a payroll tax

(c) a personal income tax

(d) a corporate income tax

22. Which pair represents the chief source of income and the most important type of expenditure of *state* governments?

(a) personal income tax and expenditures for hospitals

(b) personal income tax and expenditures for highways

(c) sales and excise taxes and expenditures for education

(d) sales and excise taxes and expenditures for public safety

23. Which pair represents the chief source of income and the most important type of expenditure of local governments?

(a) property tax and expenditures for highways

(b) property tax and expenditures for education

(c) sales and excise taxes and expenditures for public welfare

(d) sales and excise taxes and expenditures for police, fire, safety, and general government

Questions 24 and 25 are based on the tax table given below. [Note: total tax is for the highest income in that tax bracket.]

Taxable income	Total tax
$ 0	$ 0
30,000	5,000
70,000	15,000
150,000	42,000

24. The marginal tax rate at the $70,000 level of taxable income is

(a) 16.6%

(b) 21.4

(c) 25.0

(d) 28.0

25. The average tax rate at the $150,000 level of taxable income is

(a) 21.4%

(b) 28.0

(c) 31.5

(d) 33.8

■ **PROBLEMS**

1. The following table shows the functional distribution of total income in the United States in a recent year.

	Billions of dollars
Wages and salaries	$4,703
Proprietors' income	545
Corporate profits	804
Interest	450
Rents	148
Total income	6,650

Of the total income about _____% were wages and salaries, and about _____% were corporate profits.

2. Indicate in the space to the right of **a–i** whether these business characteristics are associated with the proprietorship (**PRO**), partnership (**PART**), corporation (**CORP**), two of these, or all three of these legal forms.

a. Red tape and legal expense in obtaining a charter for the firm _____

b. Unlimited liability _____

c. No specialized management _____

d. Has a life independent of its owner(s) _____

e. Double taxation of income _____

f. Greatest ability to acquire funds for the expansion of the firm _____

g. Permits some but not a great degree of specialized management _____

h. Possibility of an unresolved disagreement among several owners of the firm over courses of action

_____

i. The potential for the separation of ownership and control of the business _____

3. Following is a list of various government activities. Indicate in the space to the right of each into which of the five classes of government functions the activity falls. If it falls under more than one of the functions, indicate this.

a. Maintaining an army _____

b. Providing for a system of unemployment compensation _____

c. Establishment of the Federal Reserve Banks _____

_____

d. Providing medical care for government employees _____

e. Establishment of an Antitrust Division in the Department of Justice _____

f. Making it a crime to sell stocks and bonds under false pretenses _____

g. Providing low-cost lunches to school children _____

_____

h. Taxation of beer and wine _____

_____

i. Regulation of organized stock, bond, and commodity markets _____

j. Setting tax *rates* higher for larger incomes than for smaller ones _____

4. The following circular flow diagram includes business firms, households, and the government (the public sector). Also shown are the product and resource markets.

a. Supply a label or an explanation for each of the 12 flows in the model:

(1) _____

(2) _____

(3) _____

(4) _____

(5) _____

(6) _____

(7) _____

(8) _____

(9) _____

(10) _____

(11) _____

(12) _____

b. If government wished to

(1) expand output and employment in the economy, it would increase expenditure flows _____ or _____, decrease net tax flows _____ or _____, or do both;

(2) increase the production of public goods and decrease the production of private goods in the economy, it would increase flows _____ and _____ or _____;

(3) redistribute income from high-income to low-income households, it would (increase, decrease) _____ the net taxes (taxes minus transfers) paid by the former and _____ the net taxes paid by the latter in flow _____.

5. In the following table are several levels of taxable income and hypothetical marginal tax rates for each $1000 increase in income.

Taxable income	Marginal tax rate, %	Tax	Average tax rate, %
$1500		$300	20
2500	22	520	20.8
3500	25	_____	_____
4500	29	_____	_____
5500	34	_____	_____
6500	40	_____	_____

a. At the four income levels compute the tax and the average tax rate.

b. As the marginal tax rate

(1) increases, the average tax rate (increases, decreases, remains constant) _____

_____.

(2) decreases, the average tax rate _____.

c. This tax is (progressive, regressive) _____ because the average tax rate increases as income (decreases, increases) _____.

■ **SHORT ANSWER AND ESSAY QUESTIONS**

1. Explain the difference between a functional and a personal distribution of income. Rank the five types of earned income in the order of their size.

2. Describe how saving and personal consumption vary across income levels. Which group is most likely to *dissave*?

3. The purchase of what type of consumer goods is largely postponable? Why is this? How is it possible for a family's personal consumption expenditures to exceed its after-tax income?

4. What is the difference between a plant and a firm? Between a firm and an industry?

5. What are the principal advantages and disadvantages of each type of the three legal forms of business organization?

6. Which of the disadvantages of the proprietorship and partnership accounts for the formation of corporations? Explain why it is important.

7. Describe the two different hybrid structures for business.

8. Explain what "separation of ownership and control" of the modern corporation means. What problem does this separation create for stockholders and managers?

9. How does government provide a legal framework and services for the effective operation of the economy?

10. What does the government do to maintain competition?

11. Why does the market system provide some people with lower incomes than it provides others?

12. What is meant by a spillover in general and by a spillover cost and a spillover benefit in particular?

13. How does the existence of spillover costs and benefits affect the allocation of resources and the prices of products?

14. What methods does government use to
(a) redistribute income?
(b) reallocate resources to take account of spillover costs?
(c) reallocate resources to take account of spillover benefits?

15. Distinguish between a private and a public good. Include in your answer an explanation of rivalry, excludability, and the free-rider problem.

16. What basic method does government in the United States use to reallocate resources away from the production of private goods and toward the production of public and quasi-public goods?

17. What is the stability function of government? What are the two economic problems that this function addresses?

18. How does politics affect the economic role of government in the economy?

19. In a circular flow diagram that includes not only business firms and households but also government (or the public sector), what are the four flows of money into or out of the government sector of the economy? Using this diagram, explain how government redistributes income, reallocates resources from the private to the public sector, and stabilizes the economy.

20. What is the present size of government spending and taxation in the U.S. economy?

21. Government expenditures fall into two broad classes: expenditures for goods and services and transfer payments. Explain the difference between these, and give examples of expenditures that fall into each of the two classes.

22. Explain precisely the difference between the marginal tax rate and the average tax rate.

23. Explain how the Federal personal income tax enables the Federal government to perform some of its economic functions.

24. Explain in detail the differences that exist among Federal and state governments in the taxes on which they primarily rely for their revenues and the major purposes for which they use these revenues.

25. What are tax revenue sources and expenditures at the local level?

ANSWERS

Chapter 5 The U.S. Economy: Private and Public Sectors

FILL-IN QUESTIONS

1. households, sell, buy
2. wages and salaries, 70
3. 20, 20
4. consumption, saving, taxes (any order)
5. taxes, consumption expenditures
6. durable, nondurable
7. firms, sole proprietorship, corporation
8. stocks, bonds
9. unlimited, limited
10. principal–agent, principals, agents
11. *a.* provide legal foundation; *b.* maintain competition; *c.* redistribute income; *d.* reallocate resources; *e.* stabilize the economy (any order for *a–e*)
12. regulate, owner, antitrust
13. unequal, transfer, market, income
14. market; *a.* produces the "wrong" amounts of certain goods and services; *b.* fails to allocate any resources to the production of certain goods and services whose production is economically justified
15. spillover
16. seller, buyer

17. *a.* (1) enact legislation, (2) pass special taxes; *b.* (1) subsidize consumers, (2) subsidize suppliers, (3) government financing or production of the product
18. nonrivalry, excludability, free-rider
19. taxing, tax revenue
20. increasing, decreasing, lowering, decreasing, increasing, raising
21. *a.* decreased; *b.* increased; *c.* 30; *d.* nonexhaustive, exhaustive
22. personal income, payroll, pensions and income security, national defense, health
23. higher, lower, marginal, average
24. sales and excise, personal, public welfare, education
25. property, education

TRUE–FALSE QUESTIONS

1. F, pp. 73–74	**9.** F, pp. 76–77	**17.** T, p. 80	**25.** F, pp. 82–83
2. T, p. 74	**10.** F, pp. 77–78	**18.** T, p. 80	**26.** F, p. 84
3. T, p. 74	**11.** T, pp. 77–78	**19.** F, pp. 80–81	**27.** F, pp. 84–85
4. T, p. 74	**12.** T, pp. 77–78	**20.** F, p. 81	**28.** F, pp. 85–86
5. T, p. 75	**13.** F, p. 77	**21.** T, p. 81	**29.** F, p. 86
6. F, p. 75	**14.** F, p. 78	**22.** F, p. 81	**30.** T, p. 87
7. T, p. 76	**15.** F, p. 79	**23.** T, p. 81	
8. F, p. 77	**16.** T, pp. 79–80	**24.** T, p. 81	

MULTIPLE-CHOICE QUESTIONS

1. a, p. 73	**8.** a, p. 78	**15.** a, p. 81	**22.** c, p. 87
2. a, p. 74	**9.** d, p. 79	**16.** c, pp. 81–82	**23.** b, p. 87
3. c, pp. 74–75	**10.** c, pp. 79–80	**17.** c, p. 82	**24.** c, p. 86
4. a, p. 75	**11.** b, pp. 79–80	**18.** b, pp. 83–84	**25.** b, p. 86
5. b, p. 76	**12.** b, p. 80	**19.** a, pp. 85–86	
6. d, p. 77	**13.** b, pp. 80–81	**20.** d, p. 86	
7. a, pp. 77–78	**14.** c, p. 81	**21.** a, p. 87	

PROBLEMS

1. 71, 12
2. *a.* CORP; *b.* PRO and PART; *c.* PRO; *d.* CORP; *e.* CORP; *f.* CORP; *g.* PART; *h.* PART; *i.* CORP
3. *a.* reallocates resources; *b.* redistributes income; *c.* provides a legal foundation and stabilizes the economy; *d.* reallocates resources; *e.* maintains competition; *f.* provides a legal foundation and maintains competition; *g.* redistributes income; *h.* reallocates resources; *i.* provides a legal foundation; *j.* redistributes income
4. *a.* (1) businesses pay costs for resources that become money income for households; (2) households provide resources to businesses; (3) household expenditures become receipts for businesses; (4) businesses provide goods and services to households; (5) government spends money in product market; (6) government receives goods and services from product market; (7) government spends money in resource market; (8) government receives resources from resource market; (9) government provides goods and services to households; (10) government provides goods and services to businesses; (11) businesses pay net taxes to government; (12) households pay net taxes to government; *b.* (1) 5, 7 (either order), 11, 12 (either order); (2) 9, 10, 11 (any order); (3) increase, decrease, 12
5. *a.* tax: $770, 1,060, 1,400, 1,800; average tax rate: 22%, 23.6%, 25.5%, 27.7%; *b.* (1) increases, (2) decreases; *c.* progressive, increases

SHORT ANSWER AND ESSAY QUESTIONS

1. pp. 73–74	**8.** p. 78	**15.** p. 81	**22.** p. 86
2. pp. 74–75	**9.** p. 79	**16.** pp. 81–82	**23.** pp. 85–86
3. p. 75	**10.** p. 79	**17.** pp. 82–83	**24.** pp. 85–87
4. pp. 76–77	**11.** pp. 79–80	**18.** p. 83	**25.** p. 87
5. pp. 76–78	**12.** pp. 80–81	**19.** p. 83	
6. pp. 76–78	**13.** pp. 80–81	**20.** pp. 84–85	
7. p. 78	**14.** pp. 79–80	**21.** p. 84	

CHAPTER 6

The United States in the Global Economy

The United States is linked to the global economy in many ways. As you will learn in the first section of Chapter 6, there are four types of *economic flows* among nations: trade; resource; information and technology; and financial.

The second section explains *why international trade is important* to the United States. In *relative* terms, other nations have exports and imports that are a larger percentage of their GDPs because they often have a small domestic market and a limited resource base. By contrast, the exports and imports of the United States account for a smaller percentage of its GDP because it has a larger domestic market and a more abundant resource base. In *absolute* terms, however, the United States is the world's largest trading nation. Most of the trade is with other industrially advanced nations such as Canada, Japan, and Germany. This volume of trade has grown over the years with expansion of the global economy, the rise of multinational corporations, and the emergence of new trading nations.

In the third section, you learn about the principle of *comparative advantage,* which is the basis for all trade between individuals, regions, and nations. A nation, for example, will specialize in the production of a product for which it has a lower domestic opportunity cost and trade to obtain those products for which its domestic opportunity cost is higher. Thus, specialization and trade increase productivity within a nation and increase a nation's output and standard of living.

Trading in a global economy requires a *foreign exchange market* in which national currencies are exchanged, as you discover in the fourth section. This market is competitive, so the principles of supply and demand that you read about in Chapter 3 apply to it. Changes in supply and demand for currency will affect the price of a national currency. When the U.S. dollar price of another currency has increased, the value of the U.S. dollar has *depreciated* relative to the other currency. Conversely, when the U.S. dollar price of another currency has decreased, the value of the U.S. dollar has *appreciated* in value relative to the other currency.

Government can affect international trade in many ways, as you learn in the fifth section. Governments can impose protective tariffs, import quotas, and nontariff barriers, or they can foster exports through subsidies. The reasons for the interventions are difficult to explain given the strong economic rationale for free trade based on the principle of comparative advantage. Nevertheless, public misunderstanding of the gains from trade, or political considerations designed to protect domestic industries, often lead to government policies that create trade barriers and distort the free flow of products between nations, thus increasing costs for society.

The sixth section discusses *multilateral agreements* among nations and the creation of *free-trade zones* that have been designed to reduce trade barriers and increase world trade. In the United States, the process of gradual tariff reduction began with the Reciprocal Trade Agreements Act of 1934. Since 1947, worldwide multilateral negotiations to reduce trade barriers have been conducted through the General Agreement on Tariffs and Trade (GATT). The Uruguay Round of GATT negotiations established the World Trade Organization (WTO) as GATT's successor. Trade negotiations under the WTO continue in the Doha Round that began in 2001.

The other major development has been the formation of free-trade zones. The European Union (EU), which was originally started in 1958 as the Common Market, is now a trading bloc of 25 European nations. A major accomplishment of the EU, in addition to the reduction of trade barriers among member nations, was the establishment of a common currency (the *euro*) that in 2003 was used by 12 nations. The United States, Canada, and Mexico also established a free-trade zone in 1993 through the North American Free Trade Agreement (NAFTA).

The final section of the chapter briefly explores the issue of the effects of *increased competition in the global economy.* Global competition has certainly changed production practices and employment in U.S. industry. Many U.S. firms have adapted to the changes by increasing productivity to reduce costs, improving product quality, and expanding export markets. Although some firms have failed and domestic jobs have been lost, the benefits of free trade to the economy in the form of lower prices, greater economic efficiency, and a wider variety of products far outweigh any losses.

■ CHECKLIST

When you have studied this chapter you should be able to

☐ Identify the four main categories of economic flows linking nations.

☐ Explain the importance of international trade to the U.S. economy in terms of volume, dependence, trade patterns, and financial linkages.

☐ Describe several factors that have facilitated the rapid growth of international trade since World War II.

☐ Identify the key participating nations in international trade.

☐ Explain the basic principle of comparative advantage based on an individual example.

☐ Compute the comparative costs of production from production possibilities data when you are given an example with cost data for two countries.

☐ Determine which of two countries has a comparative advantage in an example.

☐ Indicate the range in which the terms of trade will be found in an example.

☐ Show the gains from specialization and trade in an example.

☐ Define the main characteristics of the foreign exchange market.

☐ Demonstrate how supply and demand analysis applies to the foreign exchange market.

☐ Distinguish between the appreciation and depreciation of a currency.

☐ Identify four means by which governments interfere with free trade.

☐ Discuss two reasons why governments intervene in international trade.

☐ Give estimates of the cost to society from trade restrictions.

☐ List the major features of the Reciprocal Trade Agreements Act and the General Agreement on Tariffs and Trade (GATT).

☐ Identify the major provisions of the Uruguay round of GATT negotiations.

☐ Describe the World Trade Organization (WTO).

☐ Describe the history, goals, and results from the European Union (EU).

☐ Explain what the euro is and expectations for it.

☐ Explain the features and significance of the North American Free Trade Agreement (NAFTA).

☐ Discuss the effects on increased competition in the global economy on U.S. firms, workers, and consumers.

■ **CHAPTER OUTLINE**

1. Four main categories of *economic flows* link nations: goods and services flows, capital and labor flows, information and technology flows, and financial flows.

2. *Trade is important* and thus warrants special attention.

   a. Although the relative importance of international trade to the United States is less than it is for other nations, it is still vital.

   (1) Exports and imports are about 11–16% of GDP, and the United States is the largest trading nation in the world.

   (2) The U.S. economy depends on international trade for vital raw materials and a variety of finished products.

   (3) There are some patterns in U.S. trade: Most are with industrially advanced nations, with Canada being the largest trade partner; overall imports exceed exports, but the deficits are greatest with Japan, China, and OPEC countries.

   (4) International trade must be financed, and, in the case of the United States, large trade deficits have required the selling of business ownership (securities) to companies in other nations.

   b. Factors facilitating trade since World War II include improvements in transportation and communications technology, and a general decline in tariffs.

   c. The major participants in international trade are the United States, Japan, and the nations of western Europe. Newer participants include many Asian economies—Hong Kong (now part of China), Singapore, South Korea, Taiwan, Malaysia, and Indonesia. China has also emerged as a major trading nation in this region. The collapse of communism in the former Soviet Union and the nations of Eastern Europe significantly changed trade patterns in that region, opened these nations to market forces, and increased international trade.

3. International trade policies have changed over the years with the development of *multilateral agreements* and *free-trade* zones.

   a. United States trade policy has been significantly affected by the *Reciprocal Trade Agreements Act* of 1934. Until 1934, the United States steadily increased tariff rates to protect private interest groups, but since the passage of the 1934 act, tariff rates have been substantially reduced. This act gave the President the authority to negotiate with foreign nations and included *most-favored-nation (MFN) status* clauses.

   b. The *General Agreement on Tariffs and Trade* (GATT) began in 1947. GATT provided equal treatment of all member nations and sought to reduce tariffs and eliminate import quotas by multilateral negotiations. The Uruguay Round of GATT negotiations started in 1986 and was completed in 1993. The major provisions, which will be phased in through 2005, reduce tariffs on products, cut restrictive rules applying to services, phase out quotas on textiles and apparel, and decrease subsidies for agriculture.

   c. The *World Trade Organization* (WTO) was the successor to GATT. It oversees trade agreements and provides a forum for trade negotiations, the latest of which is the *Doha Round*. The WTO works to expand trade and reduce protectionism, but the outcomes can be controversial.

   d. The *European Union* (EU) is an example of a regional free-trade zone or trade bloc among 25 western European nations. It abolished tariffs among member nations and developed common policies on various economic issues, such as the tariffs on goods to and from nonmember nations. The EU has produced freer trade and increased economies of scale for production in its member nations, but such a trading bloc creates trade frictions with nonmember nations like the United States. Many of the EU nations share a common currency—the *euro*.

   e. In 1993, *The North American Free Trade Agreement* (NAFTA) created a free-trade zone covering the United States, Mexico, and Canada. Critics of this agreement fear job losses and the potential for abuse by other nations using Mexico as a base for production. Defenders cite the mutual advantages from freer trade and the fact that increased worldwide investment in Mexico will stimulate growth in that nation and trade with the United States.

4. Increased international trade has resulted in more *global competition.* Most U.S. firms have been able to meet the competitive challenge by lowering production costs, improving products, or using new technology. Some firms and industries have had difficulty remaining competitive and continue to lose market share and employment. Overall, increased trade has produced substantial benefits for U.S. consumers (lower prices and more products) and enabled the nation to make more efficient use of its scarce resources.

■ **HINTS AND TIPS**

1. Comparative advantage is directly related to the opportunity cost concept and production possibilities you learned about in Chapter 2.

    a. A nation has a comparative advantage in the production of a product when it can produce the product at a lower domestic opportunity cost than can a trading partner. A nation will specialize in the production of a product for which it is the low (opportunity) cost producer.

    b. When production possibilities schedules for two nations that trade two products have a constant cost ratio, you can reduce the complicated production possibilities schedules to a 2 × 2 table. Put the two products in the two columns and the two nations in the two rows of the matrix. In each cell of the matrix put the *maximum* of each product that can be produced by that row's nation. Then for each nation, divide the maximum of one product into the maximum amount of the other product to get the domestic opportunity cost of one product in terms of the other.

    c. This last point can be illustrated with an example from problem 2 in this study guide chapter. Lilliput can produce a *maximum* of 40 pounds of apples or 20 pounds of bananas. Brobdingnag can produce a *maximum* of 75 pounds of apples or 25 pounds of bananas. The 2 × 2 matrix would look like this:

	Apples	Bananas
Lilliput	40	20
Brobdingnag	75	25

For Lilliput, the domestic opportunity cost of producing 1 pound of apples is .5 pound of bananas. In Brobdingnag, the domestic opportunity cost of producing 1 pound of apples is .33 pound of bananas. Brobdingnag is the lower (opportunity) cost producer of apples and will specialize in the production of that product. Lilliput is the lower (opportunity) cost producer of bananas, because producing 1 pound of bananas requires giving up 2 pounds of apples, whereas in Brobdingnag producing 1 pound of bananas requires giving up 3 pounds of apples.

2. Foreign exchange rates often confuse students because they can be expressed in two ways: the U.S. dollar price of a unit of foreign currency ($1.56 for 1 British pound), or the amount of foreign currency that can be purchased by one U.S. dollar ($1 can purchase .64 British pound). If you know the exchange rate in one way, you can easily calculate it the other way. Using the information from the first way, dividing $1.56 into 1 British pound gives you the British pound price for 1 U.S. dollar (1/1.56 = .64 of a British pound). Using information from the second way, dividing .64 of a British pound into 1 U.S. dollar gives you the dollar price of a British pound (1/.64 = 1.56). Both ways may be used, although one way may be used more often than the other. Rates for British pounds or Canadian dollars are usually expressed the first way, in terms of U.S. dollars. Rates for the Swiss franc, Japanese yen, or European euro are expressed the second way, per U.S. dollar.

■ **IMPORTANT TERMS**

multinational corporations	most-favored-nation clauses
comparative advantage	General Agreement on Tariffs and Trade (GATT)
terms of trade	
foreign exchange market	World Trade Organization (WTO)
exchange rates	
depreciation	European Union (EU)
appreciation	trade bloc
protective tariffs	euro
import quotas	North American Free Trade Agreement (NAFTA)
nontariff barriers	
export subsidies	
Smoot-Hawley Tariff Act	
Reciprocal Trade Agreements Act	

SELF-TEST

■ **FILL-IN QUESTIONS**

1. List the four major economic flows among nations.

    a. _____

    b. _____

    c. _____

    d. _____

2. The importance of international trade varies by nation. Nations in which exports account for a relatively high percentage of GDP tend to have a (limited, diversified) _____ resource base and domestic market, whereas nations in which exports account for a lower percentage of GDP tend to have a _____ resource base and domestic market. An example of a higher exporting nation would be the (United States, Netherlands) _____, and a lower exporting nation would be the _____ .

3. In relative terms, the imports and exports of the United States amounted to about (11–16, 31–36) _____% of the economy's GDP in 2002. In absolute terms, the United States is the world's (smallest, largest) _____ trading nation.

4. The bulk of the trade of the United States is with (less-developed, industrially advanced) _____ nations. The largest trading partner for the United States is (Canada, Japan) _____. The United States has a large trade deficit with (Canada, Japan) _____.

5. Factors that have helped increase the growth of world trade since World War II include improvement in _____ and _____ technology and a general decline in _____.

6. The top participants in international trade include the _____, _____, and the nations of western Europe. These participants serve as the headquarters for most (national, multinational) _____ corporations and dominate world trade. The economies of Singapore, South Korea, and Taiwan have (increased, decreased) _____ their share of the world trade in recent decades. Another major trading nation in Asia is (China, Thailand) _____.

7. Specialization and trade (increase, decrease) _____ the productivity of a nation's resources and _____ total output more than would be the case without them.

8. When one nation has a lower opportunity cost of producing a product relative to another nation it has a (nontariff barrier, comparative advantage) _____ _____. The amount of one product that must be given up to obtain 1 unit of another product is the (foreign exchange, opportunity cost) _____.

9. When the dollar price of foreign currency increases, there has been a(n) (appreciation, depreciation) _____ in the the value of the dollar. When the dollar price of foreign currency decreases, there has been a(n) _____ in the value of the dollar. For example, if the dollar price of a euro decreases from $1.00 = 1 euro to $0.90 = 1 euro, then it means that there has been a(n) (appreciation, depreciation) _____ in the value of the dollar; but if the dollar price of a euro increases from $0.95 = 1 euro to $1.05 = 1 euro, then it means that there has been a(n) _____ in the value of the dollar.

10. In the market for Japanese yen, an increase in the (demand for, supply of) _____ yen will decrease the dollar price of yen, while an increase in the _____ yen will increase the dollar price of yen. If the dollar price of the yen increases, then Japanese goods imported into the United States will be (more, less) _____ expensive.

11. The major government policies that restrict trade include
 a. excise taxes or duties on imported goods that are called _____,
 b. limits on the quantities or total value of specific items that may be imported, referred to as _____,
 c. licensing requirements, unreasonable standards, and red tape for a product, which are _____,
 d. government payments to domestic producers of export goods, known as _____.

12. Governments may intervene in trade between nations because they mistakenly think of (exports, imports) _____ as helpful and _____ as harmful for a national economy. In fact, there are important gains from trade in the form of the extra output obtained from abroad. Trade makes it possible to obtain (exports, imports) _____ at a lower cost than would be the case if they were produced using domestic resources, and the earnings from _____ help a nation pay for these lower cost (exports, imports) _____.

13. Another reason why governments interfere with free trade is based on (private, political) _____ considerations. Groups and industries seek protection from foreign competition through (GATT, tariffs) _____ and import (quotas, subsidies) _____, or other kinds of trade restrictions. The costs of trade protectionism are (clear to, hidden from) _____ consumers in the protected product so there is little opposition to demands for protectionism.

14. Tariffs and quotas (benefit, cost) _____ domestic firms in the protected industries, but _____ domestic consumers in the form of (lower, higher) _____ prices than would be the case if there were free trade. They also (benefit, cost) _____ domestic firms that use the protected goods as inputs in their production processes.

15. Until 1934, the trend of tariff rates in the United States was (upward, downward) _____. The trend has been (upward, downward) _____ since the 1934 passage of the (Smoot-Hawley Tariff, Reciprocal Trade Agreements) _____ Act. This act empowered the President to lower (tariffs, quotas) _____ by up to 50% in return for a reduction in foreign restrictions on U.S. goods and incorporated (quotas, most-favored-nation) _____ clauses in U.S. trade agreements.

16. The three cardinal principles established in the General Agreement on Tariffs and Trade of 1947 are

a. _____

b. _____

c. _____

17. The major provisions of the Uruguay Round of (NAFTA, GATT) _____ negotiations include (exchange rate, tariff) _____ reductions, coverage of legal, financial, and other (goods, services) _____ cuts in agricultural (import quotas, subsidies) _____, and protection of (collective, intellectual) _____ property against piracy. It also created the successor to GATT, called the (Reciprocal, World) _____ Trade Organization.

18. An example of a free-trade zone or trade bloc is the (Western, European) _____ Union.

a. The specific aims of the EU were the abolition of (capital and labor, tariffs and quotas) _____, the establishment of (common, different) _____ tariffs on goods imported from outside the EU, the (restricted, free) _____ movement of capital and labor within the EU, and common policies on other matters.

b. The EU created (small, large) _____ markets and stimulated production that has allowed industries to achieve (higher, lower) _____ costs. The economic effects of the EU on nonmember nations such as the United States are mixed because economic growth in the EU causes U.S. exports to the EU to (decrease, increase) _____ while the tariff barriers cause U.S. exports to _____.

c. The common currency of many of the member nations of the EU is called the (peso, euro) _____.

19. The North American Free Trade Agreement (NAFTA) formed a trade (barrier, bloc) _____ among the United States, Canada, and Mexico. This agreement eliminated (terms of trade, tariffs) _____ among the nations. Critics in the United States said that it would (increase, decrease) _____ jobs, but the evidence shows a(n) _____ in jobs and total output since its passage.

20. Many U.S. firms can (monopolize, compete) _____ and be successful in the global economy; however, some firms that benefited from past trade protection may find it difficult to adjust to global (control, competition) _____ and may go out of business.

■ **TRUE–FALSE QUESTIONS**

Circle T if the statement is true, F if it is false.

1. For the United States, the volume of international trade has been increasing relatively but not absolutely. **T F**

2. The U.S. economy's share of world trade has decreased since 1950. **T F**

3. The United States exports and imports goods and services with a dollar value greater than any other nation in the world. **T F**

4. The United States is dependent on trade for certain commodities that cannot be obtained in domestic markets. **T F**

5. Canada is the most important trading partner for the United States in terms of the volume of exports and imports. **T F**

6. If a person, firm, or region has a comparative advantage in the production of a particular commodity, it should specialize in the production of that commodity. **T F**

7. If one nation has a comparative advantage in the production of a commodity over another nation, then it has a higher opportunity cost of production relative to the other nation. **T F**

8. The economic effects of specialization and trade between nations are similar to increasing the quantity of resources or to achieving technological progress. **T F**

9. The interaction of the demand for, and supply of, Japanese yen will establish the dollar price of Japanese yen. **T F**

10. An increase in incomes in the United States would tend to cause the dollar price of the Japanese yen to fall. **T F**

11. When the dollar price of another nation's currency increases, there has been an appreciation in the value of the dollar. **T F**

12. When the dollar depreciates relative to the value of the currencies of the trading partners of the United States, then goods imported into the United States will tend to become more expensive. **T F**

13. Export subsidies are government payments to reduce the price of a product to buyers from other nations. **T F**

14. Nontariff barriers include excise taxes or duties placed on imported goods. **T F**

15. Through world trade, an economy can reach a point beyond its domestic production possibilities curve.　　**T　F**

16. One reason that trade restrictions get public support is that the alleged benefits of the restrictions are often immediate and clear-cut, but the adverse affects are often obscure and dispersed over the economy.　　**T　F**

17. Tariffs and quotas benefit domestic firms in the protected industries and also help domestic consumers by lowering the prices for those products.　　**T　F**

18. The Smoot-Hawley Tariff Act of 1930 reduced tariffs in the United States to the lowest level ever in an attempt to pull the nation out of the Great Depression.　　**T　F**

19. If the United States concludes a tariff agreement that lowers the tariff rates on goods imported from another nation, the lower tariff rates are then applied to those goods when they are imported from other nations with most-favored-nation (MFN) status.　　**T　F**

20. The World Trade Organization (WTO) is the world's major advocate for trade protectionism.　　**T　F**

21. The members of the European Union (EU) have experienced freer trade since it was formed.　　**T　F**

22. The economic integration of nations creates larger markets for firms within the nations that integrate and makes it possible for these firms and their customers to benefit from the economies of large-scale (mass) production.　　**T　F**

23. The formation of the European Union (EU) may make it more difficult for U.S. firms to compete for European customers with firms located within the Union.　　**T　F**

24. The 1993 North American Free Trade Agreement (NAFTA) includes all Central American nations.　　**T　F**

25. Major U.S. firms are unable to compete in global markets without significant protection from foreign competition.　　**T　F**

■ MULTIPLE-CHOICE QUESTIONS

Circle the letter that corresponds to the best answer.

1. Which nation is the world's leading trading nation in terms of absolute volumes of imports and exports?
   (a) Japan
   (b) China
   (c) Germany
   (d) United States

2. Which nation is our most important trading partner in terms of the quantity of trade volume?
   (a) Japan
   (b) Canada
   (c) Germany
   (d) United Kingdom

3. Which of the following is true?
   (a) Exports as a percentage of GDP are greatest in the United States.

   (b) The United States is almost totally dependent on other nations for aircraft, machine tools, and coal.
   (c) Most of the exports and imports trade of the United States is with industrially advanced nations.
   (d) The United States has a trade surplus with Japan.

4. How is most of the trade deficit financed by a nation such as the United States?
   (a) by buying securities or assets from other nations
   (b) by selling securities or assets to other nations
   (c) by borrowing from the Federal government
   (d) by lending to the Federal government

5. Which is one way the United States finances its trade deficit?
   (a) by lending to foreigners
   (b) by selling real assets to foreigners
   (c) by purchasing real assets from foreigners
   (d) by passing protective tariffs on foreign products

6. Which factor has greatly facilitated international trade since World War II?
   (a) greater import quotas
   (b) expanded export subsidies
   (c) increased nontariff barriers
   (d) improved communications

7. Which industrializing nation would be considered one of the new participants in international trade?
   (a) Canada
   (b) Sweden
   (c) Japan
   (d) China

8. Why do nations specialize and engage in trade?
   (a) to protect multinational corporations
   (b) to increase output and income
   (c) to improve communications
   (d) to control other nations

Answer Questions 9, 10, 11, and 12 on the basis of the data given for two regions, Slobovia and Utopia, which have the following production possibilities tables.

SLOBOVIA PRODUCTION POSSIBILITIES TABLE

Product	Production alternatives					
	A	B	C	D	E	F
Cams	1,500	1,200	900	600	300	0
Widgets	0	100	200	300	400	500

UTOPIA PRODUCTION POSSIBILITIES TABLE

Product	Production alternatives				
	A	B	C	D	E
Cams	4,000	3,000	2,000	1,000	0
Widgets	0	200	400	600	800

9. In Slobovia, the comparative cost of
   (a) 1 cam is 3 widgets
   (b) 1 widget is .33 of a cam
   (c) 1 cam is .33 of a widget
   (d) 3 widgets is 1 cam

10. Which of the following statements is *not* true?
(a) Slobovia should specialize in the production of widgets.
(b) Slobovia has a comparative advantage in the production of widgets.
(c) Utopia should specialize in the production of widgets.
(d) Utopia has a comparative advantage in the production of cams.

11. The terms of trade will be
(a) greater than 7 cams for 1 widget
(b) between 7 cams for 1 widget and 5 cams for 1 widget
(c) between 5 cams for 1 widget and 3 cams for 1 widget
(d) less than 3 cams for 1 widget

12. Assume that if Slobovia did not specialize it would produce alternative C and that if Utopia did not specialize it would select alternative B. The gains from specialization are
(a) 100 cams and 100 widgets
(b) 200 cams and 200 widgets
(c) 400 cams and 500 widgets
(d) 500 cams and 400 widgets

13. If the dollar–yen exchange rate is $1 for 110 yen, then a Sony VCR priced at 27,500 yen would cost a U.S. consumer
(a) $200
(b) $250
(c) $275
(d) $300

14. If the equilibrium exchange rate changes so that the dollar price of Japanese yen increases
(a) the dollar has appreciated in value
(b) the dollar has depreciated in value
(c) U.S. citizens will be able to buy more Japanese goods
(d) Japanese citizens will be able to buy fewer U.S. goods

15. A decrease in the United States demand for Japanese goods will
(a) increase the demand for Japanese yen and increase the dollar price of yen
(b) increase the demand for Japanese yen but decrease the dollar price of yen
(c) decrease the demand for Japanese yen and decrease the dollar price of yen
(d) decrease the demand for Japanese yen but increase the dollar price of yen

16. If the exchange rate for one United States dollar changes from 1.0 euro to 1.1 euros, then there has been
(a) an appreciation in the value of the euro
(b) a depreciation in the value of the dollar
(c) a depreciation in the value of the euro
(d) an increase in the price of the euro

17. Which of the following is designed to restrict trade?
(a) GATT
(b) NAFTA
(c) import quotas
(d) multinational corporations

18. Why do governments often intervene in international trade?
(a) to expand a nation's production possibilities
(b) to improve the position of multinational corporations
(c) to protect domestic industries from foreign competition
(d) to increase revenue from tariff duties and excise taxes

19. Tariffs and quotas in a nation benefit domestic
(a) consumers and foreign producers of the protected product
(b) consumers and producers of the protected product
(c) producers of the protected product, but harm domestic consumers of the product
(d) producers and foreign producers of the product

20. Which one of the following specifically empowered the President of the United States to reduce tariff rates up to 50% if other nations would reduce their tariffs on American goods?
(a) the Smoot-Hawley Tariff Act of 1930
(b) the Reciprocal Trade Agreements Act of 1934
(c) the General Agreement on Tariffs and Trade of 1947
(d) North American Free Trade Agreement of 1993

21. Which of the following is characteristic of the General Agreement on Tariffs and Trade? Nations signing the agreement were committed to
(a) the expansion of import quotas
(b) the establishment of a world customs union
(c) the reciprocal increase in tariffs by negotiation
(d) the nondiscriminatory treatment of all member nations

22. One important outcome from the Uruguay Round of GATT was
(a) an increase in tariff barriers on services
(b) establishment of the World Trade Organization
(c) removal of voluntary export restraints in manufacturing
(d) abolishment of patent, copyright, and trademark protection

23. One of the potential problems with the European Union is that
(a) an unregulated free flow of labor and capital may reduce productivity
(b) economies of large-scale production may increase consumer prices
(c) tariffs may reduce trade with nonmember nations
(d) governments may have difficulty covering the shortfall from the elimination of duties and taxes

24. An example of the formation of a trade bloc would be the
(a) Smoot-Hawley Tariff Act
(b) North American Free Trade Agreement
(c) Reciprocal Trade Agreements Act
(d) General Agreement on Tariffs and Trade

25. The increase in global competition has resulted in:
- **(a)** greater inefficiency among U.S. producers
- **(b)** lower quality in the production of goods
- **(c)** the inability of most U.S. firms to compete
- **(d)** lower prices for many consumer goods and services

■ **PROBLEMS**

1. The following problem will help you understand the principle of comparative advantage and the benefits of specialization. A tailor named Hart has the production possibilities table for trousers and jackets as given. He chooses production alternative D.

HART'S PRODUCTION POSSIBILITIES TABLE

Product	Production alternatives					
	A	B	C	D	E	F
Trousers	75	60	45	30	15	0
Jackets	0	10	20	30	40	50

Another tailor, Schaffner, has the following production possibilities table and produces production alternative E.

SCHAFFNER'S PRODUCTION POSSIBILITIES TABLE

Product	Production alternatives						
	A	B	C	D	E	F	G
Trousers	60	50	40	30	20	10	0
Jackets	0	5	10	15	20	25	30

a. To Hart,

(1) the cost of one pair of trousers is _____ jackets

(2) the cost of one jacket is _____ pairs of trousers

b. To Schaffner,

(1) the cost of one pair of trousers is _____ jackets

(2) the cost of one jacket is _____ pairs of trousers

c. If Hart and Schaffner were to form a partnership to make suits,

(1) _____ should specialize in the making of trousers because he can make a pair of trousers at the cost of _____ of a jacket while it costs his partner _____ of a jacket to make a pair of trousers.

(2) _____ should specialize in the making of jackets because he can make a jacket at the cost of _____ pairs of trousers while it costs his partner _____ pairs of trousers to make a jacket.

d. Without specialization, Hart and Schaffner were able to make 50 pairs of trousers and 50 jackets. If each specializes completely in the item in the production in which he has a comparative advantage, their combined production will be _____ pairs of trousers and _____ jackets. Thus the gain from specialization is _____

_____.

e. When Hart and Schaffner come to divide the income of the partnership between them, the manufacture of a pair of trousers should be treated as the equivalent of from _____ to _____ jackets (or a jacket should be treated as the equivalent of from _____ to _____ pairs of trousers).

2. The countries of Lilliput and Brobdingnag have the production possibilities tables for apples and bananas shown below.

Note that the costs of producing apples and bananas are constant in both countries.

LILLIPUT PRODUCTION POSSIBILITIES TABLE

Product (lbs)	Production alternatives					
	A	B	C	D	E	F
Apples	40	32	24	16	8	0
Bananas	0	4	8	12	16	20

BROBDINGNAG PRODUCTION POSSIBILITIES TABLE

Product (lbs)	Production alternatives					
	A	B	C	D	E	F
Apples	75	60	45	30	15	0
Bananas	0	5	10	15	20	25

a. In Lilliput the cost of producing

(1) 8 apples is _____ bananas

(2) 1 apple is _____ bananas

b. In Brobdingnag the cost of producing

(1) 15 apples is _____ bananas

(2) 1 apple is _____ bananas

c. In Lilliput the cost of producing

(1) 4 bananas is _____ apples

(2) 1 banana is _____ apples

d. In Brobdingnag the cost of producing

(1) 5 bananas is _____ apples

(2) 1 banana is _____ apples

e. The cost of producing 1 apple is lower in the country of _____ and the cost of producing 1 banana is lower in the country of _____.

f. Lilliput has a comparative advantage in the production of _____ and Brobdingnag has a comparative advantage in the production of

_____.

g. The information in this problem is not sufficient to determine the exact terms of trade, but the terms of trade will be greater than _____ apples for 1 banana and less than _____ apples for 1 banana. Put another way, the terms of trade will be between _____ bananas for 1 apple and _____ bananas for 1 apple.

h. If neither nation could specialize, each would produce production alternative C. The combined production of apples in the two countries would be _____ apples and the combined production of bananas would be _____ bananas.

(1) If each nation specializes in producing the fruit for which it has a comparative advantage, their combined production will be _____ apples and _____ bananas.

(2) Their gain from specialization will be _____ apples and _____ bananas.

3. Use the following table that shows 10 different currencies and how much of each currency can be purchased with a U.S. dollar.

Currency per U.S. $				
Country	Currency	Year 1	Year 2	A or D
Brazil	Real	0.85	0.91	_____
Britain	Pound	0.65	0.59	_____
Canada	Dollar	1.41	1.51	_____
Switzerland	Franc	1.33	1.19	_____
Germany	Euro	1.58	1.69	_____
India	Rupee	31.39	34.55	_____
Japan	Yen	100.15	110.23	_____
Mexico	Peso	4.65	5.09	_____
Norway	Krone	6.88	6.49	_____
Thailand	Bhat	25.12	23.22	_____

a. In the far right column of the table, indicate whether the U.S. dollar has appreciated (**A**) or depreciated (**D**) from year 1 to year 2.

b. In year 1, a U.S. dollar would purchase _____ Swiss francs, but in year 2, it would purchase _____ Swiss francs. The U.S. dollar has (appreciated, depreciated) _____ against the Swiss franc from year 1 to year 2.

c. In year 1, a U.S. dollar would purchase _____ Japanese yen, but in year 2, it would purchase _____ Japanese yen. The U.S. dollar has (appreciated, depreciated) _____ against the Japanese yen from year 1 to year 2.

4. This problem asks you to calculate prices based on exchange rates. Use the data in the table for Problem 3 to answer the following items.

a. Using the exchange rates shown for year 1, what would be the U.S. dollar cost for the following products?
(1) Japanese television costing 30,000 yen.

$_____

(2) Swiss scarf costing 200 francs. $_____

(3) Thai artwork costing 3,768 bhats. $_____

(4) German auto costing 79,000 euros. $_____

(5) Mexican silver bracelet costing 1,376 pesos.

$_____

b. Using the exchange rates shown for year 2, what would be the U.S. dollar cost of the following products?
(1) Japanese television costing 30,000 yen.

$_____

(2) Swiss scarf costing 200 francs. $_____

(3) Thai artwork costing 3,768 bhats. $_____

(4) German auto costing 79,000 euros. $_____

(5) Mexican silver bracelet costing 1,376 pesos.

$_____

c. Indicate whether the U.S. dollar cost of each product in 4b has increased (+) or decreased (−) from year 1 to year 2. _____ _____ _____ _____ _____

d. What is the relationship between your answers in 4c to the ones you gave for the corresponding nations in 3a?
(1) When the U.S. dollar *appreciates* in value against a foreign currency, the U.S. dollar cost of a product from that nation will (increase, decrease) _____.
(2) When the U.S. dollar *depreciates* in value against a foreign currency, the U.S. dollar cost of a product from that nation will (increase, decrease) _____.

■ **SHORT ANSWER AND ESSAY QUESTIONS**

1. Describe the four major economic flows that link the United States to other nations.

2. In relative and absolute terms, how large is the volume of the international trade of the United States? What has happened to these figures over the past 40 or so years?

3. What are the principal exports and imports of the U.S. economy? What commodities used in the economy come almost entirely from abroad, and what American industries sell large percentages of their outputs abroad?

4. Which nations are the principal trading partners of the United States? How much of this trade is with the industrially advanced nations and how much of it is with the developing nations of the world?

5. Give several factors that have facilitated trade since World War II.

6. Who are the major participants in international trade? Describe the relative influence of the key players.

7. Use an example of two individuals to describe the basic principle of comparative advantage.

8. What is meant by comparative cost and comparative advantage?

9. Explain how comparative advantage determines the terms of trade between nations.

10. What is the gain for a nation that results from specialization in the production of products for which there is a comparative advantage?

11. Describe the characteristics of a foreign exchange market and of exchange rates. Why is an exchange rate an unusual price?

12. Illustrate with a supply and demand graph how equilibrium is determined in a dollar–yen market. Be sure to label axes and curves.

13. Why might an appreciation of the value of the U.S. dollar relative to the Japanese yen depress the U.S. economy and stimulate the Japanese economy? Why might a government intervene in the foreign exchange market and try to increase or decrease the value of its currency?

14. What are the major trade impediments and subsidies? How do they restrict international trade?

15. Why do governments intervene in international trade and develop restrictive trade policies?

16. What is the cost to society from trade protectionism? Who benefits and who is hurt by trade protectionism?

17. What was the Smoot-Hawley Tariff Act of 1930? What international trade problems are illustrated by this act?

18. Explain the basic provisions of the Reciprocal Trade Agreements Act of 1934.

19. What were the cardinal principles contained in the General Agreement on Tariffs and Trade (GATT)? What were the basic provisions and important results of the Uruguay Round of GATT negotiations?

20. Describe the purpose of the World Trade Organization (WTO). Why is it controversial?

21. What is the European Union? What has it achieved?

22. Discuss the potential effects of the European Union on the trade of the United States.

23. What is the euro and what are its likely economic effects?

24. What is the North American Free Trade Agreement (NAFTA)? What do its critics and defenders say about the agreement?

25. Evaluate the effects of increased global competition on U.S. firms, workers, and consumers.

ANSWERS

Chapter 6 The United States in the Global Economy

FILL-IN QUESTIONS

1. *a.* goods and services flows (trade flows); *b.* capital and labor flows (resource flows); *c.* information and technology flows; *d.* financial flows (any order for *a–d*)
2. limited, diversified, Netherlands, United States
3. 11–16, largest
4. industrially advanced, Canada, Japan
5. transportation, communications (any order), tariffs
6. United States, Japan (any order), multinational, increased, China
7. increase, increase
8. comparative advantage, opportunity cost

9. depreciation, appreciation, appreciation, depreciation
10. supply of, demand for, more
11. *a.* protective tariffs; *b.* import quotas; *c.* nontariff barriers; *d.* export subsidies
12. exports, imports, imports, exports, imports
13. political, tariffs, quotas, hidden from
14. benefit, cost, higher, cost
15. upward, downward, Reciprocal Trade Agreements, tariffs, most-favored-nation
16. *a.* equal, nondiscriminatory treatment of all member nations; *b.* reduction of tariffs by multilateral negotiations; *c.* elimination of import quotas
17. GATT, tariff, services, subsidies, intellectual, World
18. European; *a.* tariffs and quotas, common, free; *b.* large, lower, increase, decrease; *c.* euro
19. bloc, tariffs, decrease, increase
20. compete, competition

TRUE–FALSE QUESTIONS

1. F, p. 92	**10.** F, pp. 100–101	**19.** T, pp. 103–104
2. T, p. 92	**11.** F, pp. 100–101	**20.** F, p. 104
3. T, p. 92	**12.** T, pp. 100–101	**21.** T, pp. 104–105
4. T, pp. 92–93	**13.** T, p. 102	**22.** T, p. 105
5. T, p. 94	**14.** F, p. 102	**23.** T, p. 105
6. T, pp. 97–99	**15.** T, p. 102	**24.** F, p. 105
7. F, pp. 97–99	**16.** T, p. 102	**25.** F, pp. 106–107
8. T, pp. 98–99	**17.** F, pp. 102–103	
9. T, pp. 99–100	**18.** F, p. 103	

MULTIPLE-CHOICE QUESTIONS

1. d, p. 92	**10.** c, pp. 97–98	**19.** c, pp. 101–102
2. b, p. 94	**11.** c, p. 98	**20.** b, pp. 103–104
3. c, p. 94	**12.** a, pp. 98–99	**21.** d, p. 104
4. b, p. 94	**13.** b, p. 99	**22.** b, p. 104
5. b, p. 94	**14.** b, pp. 100–101	**23.** c, p. 105
6. d, pp. 95–96	**15.** c, pp. 100–101	**24.** b, p. 105
7. d, p. 95	**16.** c, pp. 100–101	**25.** d, pp. 106–107
8. b, p. 96	**17.** c, p. 102	
9. c, pp. 97–98	**18.** c, p. 102	

PROBLEMS

1. *a.* (1) .67, (2) 1.5; *b.* (1) .5, (2) 2; *c.* (1) Schaffner, .5, .67; (2) Hart, 1.5, 2; *d.* 60, 50, 10 pairs of trousers; *e.* .5, .67, 1.5, 2
2. *a.* (1) 4, (2) .5; *b.* (1) 5, (2) .33; *c.* (1) 8, (2) 2; *d.* (1) 15, (2) 3; *e.* Brobdingnag, Lilliput; *f.* bananas, apples; *g.* 2, 3, .33, .5; *h.* 69, 18, (1) 75, 20, (2) 6, 2
3. *a.* A, D, A, D, A, A, A, A, D, D; *b.* 1.33, 1.19, depreciated; *c.* 100.15, 110.23, appreciated
4. *a.* (1) 299.55 (2) 150.38 (3) 150 (4) 50,000 (5) 295.91; *b.* (1) 272.16 (2) 168.07 (3) 162.27 (4) 46,745.56 (5) 270.33; *c.* (1) − (2) + (3) + (4) − (5)−; *d.* (1) decrease (2) increase

SHORT ANSWER AND ESSAY QUESTIONS

1. pp. 91–92	**10.** pp. 98–99	**19.** p. 104
2. p. 92	**11.** pp. 99–100	**20.** p. 104
3. pp. 92–93	**12.** pp. 100–101	**21.** pp. 104–105
4. p. 94	**13.** pp. 100–101	**22.** p. 105
5. p. 95	**14.** pp. 101–102	**23.** p. 105
6. pp. 95–96	**15.** p. 102	**24.** p. 105
7. pp. 96–97	**16.** pp. 102–103	**25.** pp. 106–107
8. pp. 97–98	**17.** p. 103	
9. p. 98	**18.** pp. 103–104	

CHAPTER 7

Elasticity of Demand and Supply

Chapter 7 is basically a continuation of Chapter 3, as you might have guessed from the chapter title. In the earlier part of the book, you needed only an elementary knowledge of supply and demand. Now the economic principles, problems, and policies to be studied require a more detailed discussion of supply and demand. Therefore, before you start reading Chapter 7, you are urged—you would be commanded if this were possible—to read and study Chapter 3 again. It is absolutely essential that you master Chapter 3 before reading Chapter 7.

The concept of *price elasticity of demand,* to which the major portion of Chapter 7 is devoted, is of great importance for studying the material found in the remainder of the text. You must understand (1) what price elasticity measures; (2) how the price-elasticity formula is applied to measure the price elasticity of demand; (3) the difference between price elastic, price inelastic, and unit elasticity; (4) how total revenue varies by the type of price elasticity of demand; (5) the meaning of perfect price elasticity and of perfect price inelasticity of demand; (6) the four major determinants of price elasticity of demand; and (7) the practical application of the concept to many economic issues.

When you have become thoroughly acquainted with the concept of price elasticity of demand, you will find that you have very little trouble understanding the *price elasticity of supply.* The transition requires no more than the substitution of the words "quantity supplied" for the words "quantity demanded." You should concentrate your attention on the meaning of price elasticity of supply and how it is affected by time. Several examples are provided to show how it affects the prices of many products.

The chapter also introduces you to two other elasticity concepts. The *cross elasticity of demand* measures the sensitivity of a change in the quantity demanded for one product due to a change in the price of another product. This concept is especially important in identifying substitute, complementary, or independent goods. The *income elasticity of demand* assesses the change in the quantity demanded of a product resulting from a change in consumer incomes. It is useful for categorizing products as superior, normal, or inferior.

The concepts of demand and supply, which have been expanded in this chapter to include discussion of elasticity and price ceilings and price floors, are the foundations of the next 10 chapters in the text. If you master the topics in this chapter, you will be prepared to understand the material in the chapters that follow.

■ CHECKLIST

When you have studied this chapter you should be able to

☐ Define price elasticity of demand and compute its coefficient when you are given the demand data.
☐ State two reasons why the formula for price elasticity of demand uses percentages rather than absolute amounts in measuring consumer responsiveness.
☐ Explain the meaning of elastic, inelastic, and unit elasticity as they relate to demand.
☐ Define and illustrate graphically the price elasticity of demand concepts of perfectly elastic and perfectly inelastic.
☐ State the midpoint formula for price elasticity of demand and explain how it refines the original formula for price elasticity.
☐ Describe the relationship between price elasticity of demand and the price range for most demand curves.
☐ Explain why the slope of the demand curve is not a sound basis for judging price elasticity.
☐ Apply the total-revenue test to determine whether demand is elastic, inelastic, or unit elastic.
☐ Illustrate graphically the relationship between price elasticity of demand and total revenue.
☐ List the four major determinants of the price elasticity of demand, and explain how each determinant affects price elasticity.
☐ Describe several applications of the concept of price elasticity of demand.
☐ Define the price elasticity of supply and compute its coefficient when given the relevant data.
☐ Explain the effect of time (short run and long run) on price elasticity of supply.
☐ Describe several applications of price elasticity of supply.
☐ Define cross elasticity of demand and compute its coefficient when given relevant data.
☐ Cite applications of cross elasticity of demand and income elasticity of demand.
☐ Define income elasticity of demand and compute its coefficient when given relevant data.

■ CHAPTER OUTLINE

1. *Price elasticity of demand* is a measure of the responsiveness or sensitivity of quantity demanded to changes in the price of a product. When quantity demanded is relatively responsive to a price change, demand is said to be *elastic.* When quantity demanded is relatively unresponsive to a price change, demand is said to be *inelastic.*

   a. The exact degree of elasticity can be measured by using a formula to compute the elasticity coefficient.

   (1) The changes in quantity demanded and in price are comparisons of consumer responsiveness to price changes of different products.

   (2) Because price and quantity demanded are inversely related to each other, the price elasticity of demand coefficient is a negative number, but economists ignore the minus sign in front of the coefficient and focus their attention on its absolute value.

   b. The coefficient of price elasticity has several interpretations.

   (1) Demand is *elastic* when the percentage change in quantity is greater than the percentage change in price. The elasticity coefficient is greater than 1.

   (2) Demand is *inelastic* when the percentage change in quantity is less than the percentage change in price. The elasticity coefficient is less than 1.

   (3) Demand is *unit elastic* when the percentage change in quantity is equal to the percentage change in price. The elasticity coefficient is equal to 1.

   (4) *Perfectly inelastic demand* means that a change in price results in no change in quantity demanded of a product, whereas *perfectly elastic demand* means that a small change in price causes buyers to purchase all they desire of a product.

   c. A midpoint formula calculates price elasticity across a price and quantity range to overcome the problem of selecting the reference points for price and quantity. In this formula, the average of the two quantities and the average of the two prices are used as reference points.

   d. Note several points about the graph of the demand curve and price elasticity of demand.

   (1) It is not the same at all prices, and demand is typically elastic at higher and inelastic at lower prices.

   (2) It cannot be judged from the slope of the demand curve.

   e. *Total revenue* changes when price changes. The *total-revenue test* shows that when demand is:

   (1) *elastic,* a decrease in price will increase total revenue and an increase in price will decrease total revenue.

   (2) *inelastic,* a decrease in price will decrease total revenue and an increase in price will increase total revenue.

   (3) *unit elastic,* an increase or decrease in price will not affect total revenue.

   f. The relationship between price elasticity of demand and total revenue can be shown by graphing demand and total revenue, one above the other. In this case, the horizontal axis for each graph uses the same quantity scale. The vertical axis for demand represents price. The vertical axis for the total revenue graph measures total revenue.

   (1) When demand is price elastic, as price declines and quantity increases along the demand curve, total revenue increases in the total revenue graph.

   (2) Conversely, when demand is price inelastic, as price declines and quantity increases along the demand curve, total revenue decreases.

   (3) When demand is unit elastic, as price and quantity change along the demand curve, total revenue remains the same.

   g. The price elasticity of demand for a product depends on the number of good substitutes for the product, its relative importance in the consumer's budget, whether it is a necessity or a luxury, and the period of time under consideration.

   h. Price elasticity of demand has practical applications to public policy and business decisions. The concept is relevant to bumper crops in agriculture, decriminalization of illegal drugs, and minimum wage laws.

2. **Price elasticity of supply** is a measure of the sensitivity of quantity supplied to changes in the price of a product.

   a. There are both a general formula and a midpoint formula that are similar to those for the price elasticity of demand, but "quantity supplied" replaces "quantity demanded." This means that the elasticity of supply is the percentage change in quantity supplied of a product divided by its percentage change in the price of the product. There is a midpoint formula that is an average of quantities and prices and is used for calculating the elasticity of supply across quantity or price ranges. The price elasticity of supply depends primarily on the amount of time sellers have to adjust to a price change. The easier and faster suppliers can respond to changes in price, the greater the price elasticity of supply.

   b. In the *market period,* there is too little time for producers to change output in response to a change in price. As a consequence supply is perfectly inelastic. Graphically, this means that the supply curve is vertical at that market level of output.

   c. In the *short run,* producers have less flexibility to change output in response to a change in price because they have fixed inputs that they cannot change. They have only a limited control over the range in which they can vary their output. As a consequence, supply is *price inelastic* in the short run.

   d. In the *long run,* producers can make adjustments to all inputs to vary production. As a consequence, supply is *price elastic* in the long run. There is no total-revenue test for price elasticity of supply because price and total revenue move in the same direction regardless of the degree of price elasticity of supply.

   e. Price elasticity of supply has many practical applications for explaining price volatility. The concept is relevant to the pricing of antiques and gold, for which the supply is perfectly inelastic.

3. Two other elasticity concepts are important.

   a. The *cross elasticity of demand* measures the degree to which the quantity demanded of one product is affected by a change in the price of another product; cross elasticities of demand are positive for substitute goods, negative for complementary goods, and essentially zero for independent goods.

b. The *income elasticity of demand* measures the effect of a change in income on the quantity demanded of a product; income elasticities of demand are positive for normal or superior goods, and negative for inferior goods.

■ HINTS AND TIPS

1. This chapter is an extension of the material presented in Chapter 3. Be sure you thoroughly review the contents and exercises in Chapter 3 before you do the self-test exercises for this chapter.

2. You should *not judge* the price elasticity of demand based on the slope of the demand curve unless it is horizontal (*perfectly elastic*) or vertical (*perfectly inelastic*). Remember that elasticity varies from elastic to inelastic along a downsloping, linear demand curve. The price elasticity equals 1 at the midpoint of a downsloping linear demand curve.

3. Master the *total-revenue test* for assessing the price elasticity of demand (review Table 7.2). For many problems, the total-revenue test is easier to use than the midpoint formula for identifying the type of elasticity (elastic, inelastic, unit), and the test has many practical applications.

4. Do not just memorize the elasticity formulas in this chapter. Instead, work on understanding what they mean and how they are used for economic decisions. The elasticity formulas simply measure the *responsiveness* of a percentage change in *quantity* to a percentage change in some other characteristic (price or income). The elasticity formulas each have a similar structure: A percentage change in some type of *quantity* (demanded, supplied) is divided by a percentage change in the other variable. The price elasticity of demand measures the responsiveness of a percentage change in *quantity demanded* for a product to a percentage change in its *price*. The cross elasticity of demand measures the percentage change in the *quantity demanded of product X* to a percentage change in the *price of product Y*. The income elasticity of demand is the percentage change in *quantity demanded* for a product to a percentage change in *income*. The price elasticity of supply is the percentage change in the *quantity supplied* of a product to a percentage change in its *price*.

SELF-TEST

■ IMPORTANT TERMS

price elasticity of demand	total-revenue test
elastic demand	price elasticity of supply
inelastic demand	market period
unit elasticity	short run
perfectly inelastic demand	long run
perfectly elastic demand	cross elasticity of demand
total revenue	income elasticity of demand

■ FILL-IN QUESTIONS

1. The present chapter begins the study of (macro, micro) _____ economics. This requires an analysis of the (revenues, markets) _____ and how (actions, prices) _____ are determined in them.

2. If a relatively large change in price results in a relatively small change in quantity demanded, demand is (elastic, inelastic) _____. If a relatively small change in price results in a relatively large change in quantity demanded, demand is (elastic, inelastic) _____.

3. The price elasticity formula is based on (absolute amounts, percentages) _____ because it avoids the problems caused by the arbitrary choice of units and permits meaningful comparisons of consumer (responsiveness, incomes) _____ to changes in the prices of different products.

4. If a change in price causes no change in quantity demanded, demand is perfectly (elastic, inelastic) _____ and the demand curve is (horizontal, vertical) _____. If an extremely small change in price causes an extremely large change in quantity demanded, demand is perfectly (elastic, inelastic) _____ and the demand curve is (horizontal, vertical) _____.

5. The midpoint formula for the price elasticity of demand uses the (total, average) _____ of the two quantities as a reference point in calculating the percentage change in quantity and the (total, average) _____ of the two prices as a reference point in calculating the percentage change in price.

6. Two characteristics of the price elasticity of a linear demand curve are that elasticity (is constant, varies) _____ over the different price ranges, and that the slope is (a sound, an unsound) _____ basis for judging its elasticity.

7. Assume the price of a product declines.
a. When demand is inelastic; the loss of revenue due to the lower price is (less, greater) _____ than the gain in revenue due to the greater quantity demanded.
b. When demand is elastic; the loss of revenue due to the lower price is (less, greater) _____ than the gain in revenue due to the greater quantity demanded.
c. When demand is unit elastic; the loss of revenue due to the lower price (exceeds, is equal to)

_____ the gain in revenue due to the greater quantity demanded.

8. If demand is elastic, price and total revenue are (directly, inversely) _____ related, but if demand is inelastic, price and total revenue are (directly, inversely) _____ related.

9. Complete the following summary table.

If demand is	The elasticity coefficient is	If price rises, total revenue will	If price falls, total revenue will
Elastic	_____	_____	_____
Inelastic	_____	_____	_____
Unit elastic	_____	_____	_____

10. What are the four most important determinants of the price elasticity of demand?

a._____

b._____

c._____

d._____

11. The demand for most farm products is highly (elastic, inelastic) _____, which means that large crop yields will most likely (increase, decrease) _____ the total revenue of farmers.

12. Governments often tax products such as liquor, gasoline, and cigarettes because the price elasticity of the demand is (elastic, inelastic) _____. A higher tax on such products will (increase, decrease) _____ tax revenue.

13. The price elasticity of supply measures the percentage change in (price, quantity supplied) _____ divided by the percentage change in _____. If the percentage change in quantity was 30 percent and the percentage change in price was 40 percent, then the elasticity of supply would be (.75, 1.33) _____ and supply would be (elastic, inelastic) _____.

14. The most important factor affecting the price elasticity of supply is (revenue, time) _____. It is easier to shift resources to alternative uses when there is (more, less) _____ time.

15. In the immediate market period, the price elasticity of supply will be perfectly (elastic, inelastic) _____ and the supply curve will be (horizontal, vertical) _____.

16. Typically, in the short run the price elasticity of supply is (more, less) _____ elastic but in the long run the price elasticity of supply is _____ elastic.

17. There is a total-revenue test for the elasticity of (demand, supply) _____. There is no total-revenue test for the elasticity of (demand, supply) _____ because regardless of the degree of elasticity, price and total revenue are (directly, indirectly) _____ related.

18. The measure of the sensitivity of the consumption of one product given a change in the price of another product is the (cross, income) _____ elasticity of demand, while the measure of the responsiveness of consumer purchases to changes in income is the _____ elasticity of demand.

19. When the cross elasticity of demand is positive, two products are (complements, substitutes, independent) _____, but when the cross elasticity of demand is negative, they are _____; a zero cross elasticity suggests that two products are _____.

20. If consumers increase purchases of a product as consumer incomes increase, then a good is classified as (inferior, normal or superior) _____, but if consumers decrease purchases of a product as consumer incomes increase, then a good is classified as _____.

■ **TRUE–FALSE QUESTIONS**

Circle T if the statement is true, F if it is false.

1. If the percentage change in price is greater than the percentage change in quantity demanded, the price elasticity coefficient is greater than 1.　　**T F**

2. If the quantity demanded for a product increases from 100 to 150 units when the price decreases from $14 to $10 using the midpoint formula, the price elasticity of demand for this product in this price range is 1.2.　**T F**

3. A product with a price elasticity of demand equal to 1.5 is described as price inelastic.　　**T F**

4. The flatness or steepness of a demand curve is based on absolute changes in price and quantity, while elasticity is based on relative or percentage changes in price and quantity.　　**T F**

5. Demand tends to be inelastic at higher prices and elastic at lower prices.　　**T F**

6. Price elasticity of demand and the slope of the demand curve are two different things.　　**T F**

7. If the price of a product increases from $5 to $6 and the quantity demanded decreases from 45 to 25, then according to the total-revenue test, the product is price inelastic in this price range.   T F

8. Total revenue will not change when price changes if the price elasticity of demand is unitary.   T F

9. When the absolute value of the price elasticity coefficient is greater than 1 and the price of the product decreases, then the total revenue will increase.   T F

10. In general, the larger the number of substitute goods that are available, the less the price elasticity of demand.   T F

11. Other things equal, the higher the price of a good relative to consumers' incomes, the greater the price elasticity of demand.   T F

12. Other things equal, the higher the price of a good relative to the longer the time period the purchase is considered, the greater the price elasticity of demand. T F

13. The more that a good is considered to be a "luxury" rather than a "necessity," the less the price elasticity of demand.   T F

14. Studies indicate that the short-run demand for gasoline is price elastic, while the long-run response is price inelastic.   T F

15. The demand for most agricultural products is price inelastic. Consequently, an increase in supply will reduce the total income of producers of agricultural products.   T F

16. A state government seeking to increase its excise-tax revenues is more likely to increase the tax rate on restaurant meals than on gasoline.   T F

17. The degree of price elasticity of supply depends on how easily and quickly producers can shift resources between alternative uses.   T F

18. If an increase in product price results in no change in the quantity supplied, supply is perfectly elastic. T F

19. The market period is a time so short that producers cannot respond to a change in demand and price. T F

20. The price elasticity of supply will tend to be more elastic in the long run.   T F

21. There is a total revenue test for the elasticity of supply.   T F

22. For a complementary good, the coefficient of the cross elasticity of demand is positive.   T F

23. Cross elasticity of demand is measured by the percentage change in quantity demanded over the percentage change in income.   T F

24. A negative cross elasticity of demand for two goods indicates that they are complements.   T F

25. Inferior goods have a positive income elasticity of demand.   T F

■ **MULTIPLE-CHOICE QUESTIONS**

Circle the letter that corresponds to the best answer.

1. If, when the price of a product rises from $1.50 to $2, the quantity demanded of the product decreases from 1000 to 900, the price elasticity of demand coefficient, using the midpoint formula, is
(a) 3.00
(b) 2.71
(c) 0.37
(d) 0.33

2. If a 1% fall in the price of a product causes the quantity demanded of the product to increase by 2%, demand is
(a) inelastic
(b) elastic
(c) unit elastic
(d) perfectly elastic

3. In the following diagram, D_1 is a
(a) perfectly elastic demand curve
(b) perfectly inelastic demand curve
(c) unit elastic demand curve
(d) long-run demand curve

4. Compared to the lower-right portion, the upper-left portion of most demand curves tends to be
(a) more inelastic
(b) more elastic
(c) unit elastic
(d) perfectly inelastic

5. In which range of the demand schedule is demand price inelastic?

Price	Quantity demanded
$11	50
9	100
7	200
5	300
3	400

(a) $11–$9
(b) $9–$7
(c) $7–$5
(d) $5–$3

6. If a business increased the price of its product from $7 to $8 when the price elasticity of demand was inelastic, then
(a) total revenues decreased
(b) total revenues increased
(c) total revenues remain unchanged
(d) total revenues were perfectly inelastic

7. You are the sales manager for a pizza company and have been informed that the price elasticity of demand for your most popular pizza is greater than 1. To increase total revenues, you should
(a) increase the price of the pizza
(b) decrease the price of the pizza
(c) hold pizza prices constant
(d) decrease demand for your pizza

8. Assume Amanda Herman finds that her total spending on compact discs remains the same after the price of compact discs falls, other things equal. Which of the following is true about Amanda's demand for compact discs with this price change?
(a) It is unit price elastic.
(b) It is perfectly price elastic.
(c) It is perfectly price inelastic.
(d) It increased in response to the price change.

Questions 9, 10, and 11 are based on the following graph.

9. If price is P_3, then total revenue is measured by the area
(a) $0P_3 CQ_3$
(b) $0P_3 BQ_2$
(c) $0P_3 BQ_3$
(d) $0P_3 CQ_2$

10. If price falls from P_2 to P_1, then in this price range demand is
(a) relatively inelastic because the loss in total revenue (areas 3 + 6 + 8) is greater than the gain in total revenue (area 10)
(b) relatively elastic because the loss in total revenue (areas 3 + 6 + 8) is greater than the gain in total revenue (area 10)
(c) relatively inelastic because the loss in total revenue (area 10) is less than the gain in total revenue (areas 3 + 6 + 8)

(d) relatively inelastic because the loss in total revenue (areas 4 + 7 + 9 + 10) is greater than the gain in total revenue (areas 3 + 6 + 8)

11. As price falls from P_4 to P_3, you know that demand is
(a) elastic because total revenue decreased from $0P_4 AQ_1$ to $0P_3 BQ_2$
(b) inelastic because total revenue decreased from $0P_3 BQ_2$ to $0P_4 AQ_1$
(c) elastic because total revenue increased from $0P_4 AQ_1$ to $0P_3 BQ_2$
(d) inelastic because total revenue decreased from $0P_4 AQ_1$ to $0P_3 BQ_2$

12. Which product is most likely to be the most price elastic?
(a) bread
(b) clothing
(c) restaurant meals
(d) local telephone service

13. Which is characteristic of a product whose demand is elastic?
(a) The price elasticity coefficient is less than 1.
(b) Total revenue decreases if price decreases.
(c) Buyers are relatively insensitive to price changes.
(d) The percentage change in quantity is greater than the percentage change in price.

14. The demand for Nike basketball shoes is more price elastic than the demand for basketball shoes as a whole. This is best explained by the fact that
(a) Nike basketball shoes are a luxury good, not a necessity
(b) Nike basketball shoes are the best made and widely advertised
(c) there are more complements for Nike basketball shoes than for basketball shoes as a whole
(d) there are more substitutes for Nike basketball shoes than for basketball shoes as a whole

15. Which is characteristic of a good whose demand is inelastic?
(a) There are a large number of good substitutes for the good for consumers.
(b) The buyer spends a small percentage of total income on the good.
(c) The good is regarded by consumers as a luxury.
(d) The period of time for which demand is given is relatively long.

16. From a time perspective, the demand for most products is
(a) less elastic in the short run and unit elastic in the long run
(b) less elastic in the long run and unit elastic in the short run
(c) more elastic in the short run than in the long run
(d) more elastic in the long run than in the short run

17. If a 5% fall in the price of a commodity causes quantity supplied to decrease by 8%, supply is
(a) inelastic

(b) unit elastic
(c) elastic
(d) perfectly inelastic

18. In the following diagram, what is the price elasticity of supply between points **A** and **C**?
   (a) 1.33
   (b) 1.67
   (c) 1.85
   (d) 2.46

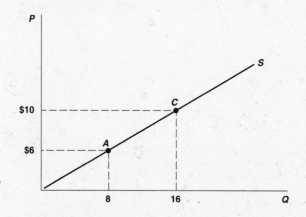

19. If supply is inelastic and demand decreases, the total revenue of sellers will
   (a) increase
   (b) decrease
   (c) decrease only if demand is elastic
   (d) increase only if demand is inelastic

20. The chief determinant of the price elasticity of supply of a product is
   (a) the number of good substitutes the product has
   (b) the length of time sellers have to adjust to a change in price
   (c) whether the product is a luxury or a necessity
   (d) whether the product is a durable or a nondurable good

21. A study shows that the coefficient of the cross elasticity of Coke and Sprite is negative. This information indicates that Coke and Sprite are
   (a) normal goods
   (b) complementary goods
   (c) substitute goods
   (d) independent goods

22. If a 5% increase in the price of one good results in a decrease of 2% in the quantity demanded of another good, then it can be concluded that the two goods are
   (a) complements
   (b) substitutes
   (c) independent
   (d) normal

23. Most goods can be classified as *normal* goods rather than inferior goods. The definition of a normal good means that

(a) the percentage change in consumer income is greater than the percentage change in price of the normal good
(b) the percentage change in quantity demanded of the normal good is greater than the percentage change in consumer income
(c) as consumer income increases, consumer purchases of a normal good increase
(d) the income elasticity of demand is negative

24. Based on the information in the table, which product would be an inferior good?

Product	% change in income	% change in quantity demanded
A	−10	+10
B	+10	+10
C	+5	+5
D	−5	−5

   (a) Product A
   (b) Product B
   (c) Product C
   (d) Product D

25. For which product is the income elasticity of demand most likely to be negative?
   (a) automobiles
   (b) bus tickets
   (c) computers
   (d) tennis rackets

■ **PROBLEMS**

1. Complete the following table, using the demand data given, by computing total revenue at each of the seven prices and the six price elasticity coefficients between each of the seven prices, and indicate whether demand is elastic, inelastic, or unit elastic between each of the seven prices.

Price	Quantity demanded	Total revenue	Elasticity coefficient	Character of demand
$1.00	300	$ _____		
.90	400	_____	_____	_____
.80	500	_____	_____	_____
.70	600	_____	_____	_____
.60	700	_____	_____	_____
.50	800	_____	_____	_____
.40	900	_____	_____	_____

2. Use the data from the table for this problem. On the *first* of the two following graphs, plot the demand curve (price and quantity demanded) and indicate the elastic, inelastic, and unit elastic portions of the demand curve. On the *second* graph, plot the total revenue on the vertical axis and the quantity demanded on the horizontal axis. (*Note:* The scale for quantity demanded that you plot on the horizontal axis of each graph should be the same.)

0

0

a. As price decreases from $1.00 to $0.70, demand is

(elastic, inelastic, unit elastic) _____ and total revenue (increases, decreases, remains the

same) _____.
b. As price decreases from $0.70 to $0.60, demand is

(elastic, inelastic, unit elastic) _____ and total revenue (increases, decreases, remains the

same) _____.
c. As price decreases from $0.60 to $0.40, demand is

(elastic, inelastic, unit elastic) _____ and total revenue (increases, decreases, remains the

same) _____.

3. Using the supply data in the following schedule, complete the table by computing the six price elasticity of supply coefficients between each of the seven prices, and indicate whether supply is elastic, inelastic, or unit elastic.

Price	Quantity demanded	Elasticity coefficient	Character of supply
$1.00	800		
.90	700	___	___
.80	600	___	___
.70	500	___	___
.60	400	___	___
.50	300	___	___
.40	200	___	___

4. The following graph shows three different supply curves (S_1, S_2, and S_3) for a product bought and sold in a competitive market.

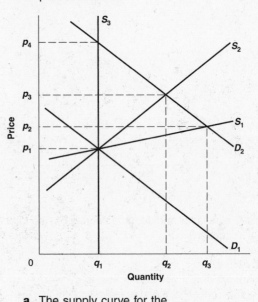

a. The supply curve for the

(1) market period is the one labeled _____.

(2) short run is the one labeled _____.

(3) long run is the one labeled _____.
b. No matter what the period of time under consideration, if the demand for the product were D_1, the equilibrium price of the product would be

_____ and the equilibrium quantity would

be _____.
(1) If demand were to increase to D_2 in the market period the equilibrium price would increase to

_____ and the equilibrium quantity would

be _____.
(2) In the short run the price of the product would in-

crease to _____ and the quantity would

increase to _____.
(3) In the long run the price of the product would be

_____ and the quantity would be

_____.

c. The longer the period of time allowed to sellers to adjust their outputs, the (more, less)

_____ elastic is the supply of the product.

d. The more elastic the supply of a product, the (greater, less) _____ the effect on equilibrium price and the _____ the effect on equilibrium quantity of an increase in demand.

5. For the following three cases, use a midpoint formula to calculate the coefficient for the cross elasticity of demand and identify the relationship between the two goods (complement, substitute, or independent).

a. The quantity demanded for good A increases from 300 to 400 as the price of good B increases from $1 to $2. Coefficient: _____ Relationship: _____

b. The quantity demanded for good J decreases from 2000 to 1500 as the price of good K increases from $10 to $15. Coefficient: _____ Relationship: _____

c. The quantity demanded for good X increases from 100 to 101 units as the price of good Y increases from $8 to $15. Coefficient: _____ Relationship: _____

6. Use the information in the following table to identify the income characteristic of each product A–E using the following labels: **N** = normal (or superior), **I** = inferior.

Product	% change in income	% change in quantity demanded	Income type (N or I)
A	10	10	_____
B	1	15	_____
C	5	−12	_____
D	5	−2	_____
E	10	1	_____

■ SHORT ANSWER AND ESSAY QUESTIONS

1. Define and explain the price elasticity of demand in terms of the relationship between the relative (percentage) change in quantity demanded and the relative (percentage) change in price. Use the elasticity coefficient in your explanation.

2. What is meant by perfectly elastic demand? By perfectly inelastic demand? What does the demand curve look like when demand is perfectly elastic and when it is perfectly inelastic?

3. In computing the price elasticity coefficient, it usually makes a considerable difference whether the higher price and lower quantity or the lower price and higher quantity are used as points of reference. What have economists done to eliminate the confusion that would arise if the price elasticity of demand coefficient varied and depended upon whether a price rise or fall were being considered?

4. Demand seldom has the same elasticity at all prices. What is the relationship between the price of most products and the price elasticity of demand for them?

5. Define and explain the price elasticity of demand in terms of the change in total revenue when price changes.

6. What is the relationship—if there is one—between the price elasticity of demand and the slope of the demand curve?

7. When the price of a product declines, the quantity demanded of it increases. When demand is elastic, total revenue is greater at the lower price, but when demand is inelastic, total revenue is smaller. Explain why total revenue will sometimes increase and why it will sometimes decrease.

8. Explain the effect of the number of substitutes on the price elasticity of demand.

9. Why does the price elasticity of demand differ based on the price of a good as a proportion of household income? Give examples.

10. Is the quantity demanded for necessities more or less responsive to a change in price? Explain using examples.

11. What role does time play in affecting the elasticity of demand?

12. How do opponents of the decriminalization of illegal drugs use elasticity to make their arguments?

13. Explain what determines the price elasticity of supply of an economic good or service.

14. Explain the distinction between the intermediate market period, the short run, and the long run.

15. Why is there no total revenue test for the elasticity of supply?

16. Discuss the supply and demand conditions for antiques. Why are antique prices so high?

17. Use the concepts of the elasticity of supply to explain the volatility of gold prices.

18. How can goods be classified as complementary, substitute, or independent? On what basis is this judgment made?

19. Give definitions of a normal good and an inferior good. Illustrate each definition with an example.

20. What are two examples of insights that income elasticity of demand coefficients provide about the economy?

ANSWERS

Chapter 7 Elasticity of Demand and Supply

FILL-IN QUESTIONS

1. micro, markets, prices
2. inelastic, elastic
3. percentages, responsiveness
4. inelastic, vertical, elastic, horizontal
5. average, average
6. varies, an unsound
7. *a.* greater; *b.* less; *c.* is equal to
8. inversely, directly
9. Elastic: greater than 1, decrease, increase; Inelastic: less than 1, increase, decrease; Unit elastic: equal to 1, remain constant, remain constant

10. *a.* The number of good substitute products; *b.* The relative importance of the product in the total budget of the buyer; *c.* Whether the good is a necessity or a luxury; *d.* The period of time in which demand is being considered (any order *a–d*)
11. inelastic, decrease
12. inelastic, increase
13. quantity supplied, price, .75, inelastic
14. time, more
15. inelastic, vertical
16. less, more
17. demand, supply, directly
18. cross, income
19. substitutes, complements, independent
20. normal or superior, inferior

TRUE–FALSE QUESTIONS

1. F, pp. 112–113
2. T, pp. 114–115
3. F, p. 113
4. T, p. 115
5. F, pp. 115–116
6. T, p. 115
7. F, pp. 116–117
8. T, p. 117
9. T, pp. 116–117
10. F, p. 118
11. T, p. 118
12. T, p. 118
13. F, p. 118
14. F, p. 119
15. T, p. 119
16. F, pp. 119–120
17. T, p. 121
18. F, p. 121
19. T, p. 121
20. T, p. 122
21. F, p. 122
22. F, p. 123
23. F, p. 123
24. T, p. 123
25. F, p. 124

MULTIPLE-CHOICE QUESTIONS

1. c, pp. 114–115
2. b, p. 113
3. b, p. 114
4. b, p. 115
5. d, pp. 115–116
6. b, pp. 116–117
7. b, pp. 116–117
8. a, p. 117
9. b, pp. 116–117
10. a, pp. 116–117
11. c, pp. 116–117
12. c, pp. 118–119
13. d, p. 118
14. d, p. 118
15. b, p. 118
16. d, pp. 118–119
17. c, pp. 120–121
18. a, pp. 120–121
19. b, p. 122
20. b, pp. 121–122
21. b, p. 123
22. a, p. 123
23. c, p. 124
24. a, p. 124
25. b, p. 124

PROBLEMS

1. Total revenue: $300, 360, 400, 420, 420, 400, 360; Elasticity coefficient: 2.71, 1.89, 1.36, 1, 0.73, 0.53; Character of demand: elastic, elastic, elastic, unit elastic, inelastic, inelastic
2. *a.* elastic, increases; *b.* unit elastic, remains the same; *c.* inelastic, decreases
3. Elasticity coefficient: 1.27, 1.31, 1.36, 1.44, 1.57, 1.8; Character of supply: elastic, elastic, elastic, elastic, elastic, elastic
4. *a.* (1) S_3; (2) S_2; (3) S_1; *b.* p_1, q_1; (1) p_4, q_1; (2) p_3, q_2; (3) p_2, q_3; *c.* more; *d.* less, greater
5. *a.* 43, substitute; *b.* −.71, complement; *c.* .02, independent
6. N, N, I, I, N

SHORT ANSWER AND ESSAY QUESTIONS

1. pp. 112–113
2. pp. 112–113
3. pp. 114–115
4. p. 115
5. pp. 116–117
6. p. 115
7. pp. 116–117
8. p. 118
9. p. 118
10. p. 118
11. pp. 118–119
12. p. 124
13. p. 121
14. pp. 121–122
15. p. 122
16. p. 122
17. pp. 122–123
18. p. 124
19. p. 125
20. p. 125

CHAPTER 8

Consumer Behavior and Utility Maximization

Previous chapters explained that consumers typically buy more of a product as its price decreases and less of a product as its price increases. Chapter 8 looks behind this law of demand to explain why consumers behave this way.

Two explanations for the law of demand are presented. The first explanation is a general and simple one based on *income effects* and *substitution effects.* From this perspective, a change in the price of a product changes the amount consumed because of a change in the real income and a change in the price of this good relative to other products that could be purchased. The other explanation is more detailed and abstract because it is based on the concept of *marginal utility.* In this view, the additional satisfaction (or marginal utility) that a consumer obtains from the consumption of each additional unit of a product will tend to decline; therefore a consumer will have an incentive to purchase additional units of a product only if its price falls. (A third explanation of consumer demand that is more complete than the first two is based on the use of indifference curves; this more complex topic is discussed in the appendix to the chapter.)

Most of this chapter presents the *marginal-utility* view of consumer behavior. This explanation requires that you first understand the concepts and assumptions on which this theory of consumer behavior rests, and second, do some rigorous reasoning using these concepts and assumptions. It is an exercise in logic, but be sure that you follow the reasoning. To help you, several problems are provided so that you can work things out for yourself.

No one believes that consumers actually perform these mental gymnastics before they spend their incomes or make purchases. But we study the marginal-utility approach to consumer behavior because the consumers behave as if they made their purchases on the basis of very fine calculations. Thus, this approach explains what we do in fact observe and makes it possible for us to predict with a good deal of precision how consumers will react to changes in their incomes and the prices of products.

The final section of the chapter describes how the theory of consumer behavior can be used to explain many economic events in the real world. The five applications discussed are the takeover by compact discs of the market for recorded music, the water-diamond paradox, the value of time in consumption, the reasons for increased consumer purchases of medical care, and the economic effects of cash and noncash gifts. Be sure you understand how consumer theory is used to explain these five phenomena.

■ CHECKLIST

When you have studied this chapter you should be able to

☐ Define and distinguish between the income and the substitution effects of a price change.
☐ Use the income and the substitution effects to explain why a consumer will buy more of a product when its price falls and less of a product when its price rises.
☐ Define utility, marginal utility, and total utility.
☐ Describe the law of diminishing marginal utility.
☐ Explain the relationship of the law of diminishing marginal utility to demand and elasticity.
☐ List four dimensions of the typical consumer's situation.
☐ State the utility-maximizing rule.
☐ When you are given the utility and price data, use the utility-maximizing rule to determine how consumers would spend their fixed incomes.
☐ Explain how a consumer decides between an optimal and an inferior solution to a utility-maximization problem.
☐ Give an algebraic restatement of the utility-maximizing rule based on an example using two products, A and B.
☐ Derive a consumer's demand for a product from utility, income, and price data.
☐ Explain how the income and substitution effects are involved in utility maximization and the deriving of the demand curve for a product.
☐ Give examples of how consumer theory can be used to explain such economic situations as the
    (1) popularity of DVDs and DVD players,
    (2) diamond-water paradox,
    (3) value of time in consumption,
    (4) consumer purchases of medical care, and
    (5) tradeoffs between cash and noncash gifts.

■ CHAPTER OUTLINE

1. The *law of consumer demand* can be explained in two ways.
    a. The first explanation is the income and substitution effects
    (1) The *income effect* is the impact that a change in the price of a product has on a consumer's real income and thus the quantity demanded of that product. Consumers buy more of a product when its price falls because their real income will increase, and thus they can afford to buy more (if the product is a normal good).

(2) The **substitution effect** is the impact that a change in the price of a product has on how expensive it is relative to other products, and thus the quantity demanded of that product. Consumers buy more of a product when its price falls because the product is now less expensive compared to other products.

b. The second explanation is based on the **law of diminishing marginal utility** that describes how consumers will spend their income.

(1) **Utility** is subjective and difficult to quantify. For the purposes of this chapter it will be assumed that utility is the satisfaction or pleasure a person gets from consuming a product. It will be measured in hypothetical units called *utils*.

(2) **Total utility** is the total amount of satisfaction that a consumer obtains from consuming a product. **Marginal utility** is the extra satisfaction that a consumer obtains from consuming an additional or extra unit of a product. The principle that the marginal utility of a product falls as a consumer uses (consumes) additional units of a product is the law of diminishing marginal utility.

(3) Marginal utility, demand, and elasticity are related. If marginal utility falls sharply as additional units of a product are consumed, then demand is *inelastic*. If marginal utility falls slowly as additional units of a product are consumed, then demand is *elastic*.

2. The **law of diminishing marginal utility** is the basis of the theory that explains how consumers will spend their incomes for particular goods and services.

a. It is assumed that the typical consumer is rational, knows marginal-utility schedules for the various goods available, has a limited money income to spend, and must pay a price to acquire each of the goods that yields utility.

b. Given these assumptions, the consumer maximizes the total utility obtained when the marginal utility of the last dollar spent on each product is the same for all products (the **utility-maximizing rule**).

c. A numerical example is used to illustrate the rule using two products, A and B, and assuming that all money income is spent on one of the two products. In making the decision, the rational consumer must compare the extra or marginal utility from each product with its added cost (as measured by its price). Thus, marginal utility is compared on a per-dollar basis.

d. The allocation rule states that consumers will maximize their satisfaction when they allocate their money income so that the last dollar spent on each product yields the same marginal utility. In the two-product case, this can be stated algebraically as

$$\frac{\text{Marginal utility of A}}{\text{Price of A}} = \frac{\text{Marginal utility of B}}{\text{Price of B}}$$

Total utility is a maximum when the marginal utility of the last unit of a product purchased divided by its price is the same for all products.

3. The utility-maximizing rule can be applied to determine the amount of the product the consumer will purchase at different prices with income, tastes, and the prices of other products remaining constant.

a. The numerical example that is used is based on one price for a product. If the price of the product falls, it is possible to use the utility-maximizing rule to determine how much more of the product the consumer will purchase. Based on this exercise it is possible to show the inverse relationship between price and quantity demanded as shown by a demand curve.

b. Utility maximization can also be understood in terms of the income and substitution effects to explain the law of demand. As the price of a product drops, a consumer increases the amounts purchased to restore equilibrium following the utility-maximizing rule. The change can be viewed as the consumer substituting more of the now less-expensive product for another product and having more real income to spend.

4. Five of the many **applications** and **extensions** of consumer theory for the real world are discussed in this chapter.

a. DVDs have gained popularity among consumers relative to videocassettes (VCs) because many consumers have concluded that DVDs have a higher ratio of marginal utility to price than the ratio for VCs.

b. Diamonds are high in price, but of limited usefulness, while water is low in price, but essential for life. This diamond-water paradox is explained by distinguishing between marginal and total utility. Water is low in price because it is generally in plentiful supply and thus has low marginal utility. Diamonds are high in price because they are relatively scarce and thus have high marginal utility. Water, however, is considered more useful than diamonds because it has much greater total utility.

c. The facts that consumption takes time and time is a scarce resource can be included in the marginal-utility theory. The full price of any consumer good or service is equal to its market price plus the value of time taken to consume it (i.e., the income the consumer could have earned had he or she used that time for work).

d. Expenditures on medical care have increased because of its financing through insurance. Under this system, the consumer does not pay the full price of medical care services and thus has an incentive to consume more than would be the case if the consumer paid the full price.

e. Cash gifts tend to be more efficient for consumers because they are more likely to match consumer preferences and increase the total utility compared to non-cash gifts that restrict consumer choice.

■ **HINTS AND TIPS**

1. Remember that a change in the price of a good has both an **income effect** and a **substitution effect**. For most products, a price decrease gives consumers more income to spend on that product and other products, so the quantity demanded for that product increases. The three steps in the logic for typical product A are (1) $P_A\downarrow$, (2) income$\uparrow$, and (3) $Q_{dA}\uparrow$. A price decrease also makes product A more attractive to buy relative to its substitutes, so the demand for these substitutes decreases and the quantity demanded for product A increases. Again, there are three steps in the logic: (1) $P_A\downarrow$, (2) demand for substitutes$\downarrow$, and (3) $Q_{dA}\uparrow$. In both cases, the end result is the same: $Q_{dA}\uparrow$. Practice your understanding by showing the logic for an increase in the price of product A.

2. *Utility* is simply an abstraction useful for explaining consumer behavior. Do not become overly concerned with the precise measurement of utility or satisfaction. What you should focus on is the relative comparison of the additional satisfaction (marginal utility) from a dollar spent on one good to the additional satisfaction obtained from a dollar spent on another good. The choice of producing more additional utility satisfaction from one good than the other will maximize consumer satisfaction. Thus, you just need to know which good won the contest, not the final score (how much additional utility was added).

3. Master the difference between marginal utility and total utility. Once you think you understand the difference, use the concepts to explain to someone the diamond-water paradox at the end of the chapter.

■ IMPORTANT TERMS

income effect

substitution effect

utility

total utility

marginal utility

law of diminishing marginal utility

rational behavior

budget constraint

utility-maximizing rule

SELF-TEST

■ FILL-IN QUESTIONS

1. The law of demand can be explained in terms of income and (complements, substitution) _____ effects or by the law of (increasing, diminishing) _____ marginal utility.

2. A fall in the price of a product tends to (increase, decrease) _____ a consumer's real income, and a rise in its price tends to _____ real income. This is called the (substitution, income) _____ effect.

3. When the price of a product increases, the product becomes relatively (more, less) _____ expensive than it was and the prices of other products become relatively (higher, lower) _____ than they were; the consumer will therefore buy (less, more) _____ of the product in question and _____ of the other products. This is called the (substitution, income) _____ effect.

4. The overall satisfaction a consumer gets from consuming a good or service is (marginal, total) _____ utility, but the extra or additional satisfaction that a consumer gets from a good or service is (marginal, total) _____ utility. Utility is (an objective, a subjective) _____ concept and (is, is not) _____ the same thing as usefulness.

5. The law of diminishing marginal utility states that marginal utility will (increase, decrease) _____ as a consumer increases the quantity consumed of a product.

6. A graph of total utility and marginal utility shows that when total utility is increasing, marginal utility is (positive, negative) _____, and when total utility is at a maximum, marginal utility is at (a maximum, zero, a minimum) _____.

7. Assuming all other things equal, if the marginal utility of a product decreases rapidly as additional units are consumed, then demand is likely to be (elastic, inelastic) _____, but if marginal utility decreases slowly as consumption increases, then it suggests that demand is _____.

8. The marginal-utility theory of consumer behavior assumes that the consumer is (wealthy, rational) _____ and has certain (preferences, discounts) _____ for various goods.

9. A consumer cannot buy every good and service desired because income is (subsidized, limited) _____ and goods and services are (unlimited, scarce) _____ in relation to the demand for them; thus they have (prices, quantities) _____ attached to them.

10. When the consumer is maximizing the utility the consumer's income will obtain, the ratio of the marginal utility of the (first, last) _____ unit purchased of a product to its price is (the same, greater than) _____ for all the products bought.

11. If the marginal utility of the last dollar spent on one product is greater than the marginal utility of the last dollar spent on another product, the consumer should (increase, decrease) _____ purchases of the first and _____ purchases of the second product.

12. Assume there are only two products, X and Y, that a consumer can purchase with a fixed income. The consumer is maximizing utility algebraically when:

a. _____   c. _____
b. _____ = d. _____

13. In deriving a consumer's demand for a particular product, the two factors (other than the preferences or tastes of the consumer) that are held constant are

a._____

b._____

14. The utility-maximizing rule and the demand curve are logically (consistent, inconsistent) _____. Because marginal utility declines, a lower price is needed to get the consumer to buy (less, more) _____ of a particular product.

15. When consumer preferences changed from video-cassette tapes to DVDs, and the prices of DVD players (increased, decreased) _____ significantly, this led to (increased, decreased) _____ purchases of DVDs.

16. Water is low in price because its (total, marginal) _____ utility is low, while diamonds are high in price because their _____ utility is high. Water, however, is more useful than diamonds because the (total, marginal) _____ utility of water is much greater than the _____ utility of diamonds.

17. The theory of consumer behavior has been generalized to account for (supply, time) _____. This is a valuable economic resource because it is (limited, unlimited) _____. Its value is (greater than, equal to) _____ the income that can be earned with it. The full price to the consumer of any product is, therefore, the market (time, price) _____ plus the value of the consumption _____.

18. With health insurance coverage, the price consumers pay for health care services is less than the "true" value or opportunity (benefit, cost) _____. The lower price to consumers encourages them to consume (more, less) _____ health care services.

19. A comparison of food consumption at an all-you-can-eat buffet with a pay-per-item cafeteria would show that people tend to eat (less, more) _____ at the buffet because the marginal utility of an extra food item is (positive, zero) _____ while its price is _____.

20. Noncash gifts are (less, more) _____ preferred than cash gifts because they yield (less, more) _____ total utility to consumers.

■ TRUE–FALSE QUESTIONS

Circle T if the statement is true, F if it is false.

1. An increase in the real income of a consumer will result from an increase in the price of a product the consumer is buying.   **T F**

2. The income and substitution effects will induce the consumer to buy more of normal good Z when the price of Z increases.   **T F**

3. Utility and usefulness are not synonymous.   **T F**

4. Marginal utility is the change in total utility from consuming one more unit of a product.   **T F**

5. Because utility cannot actually be measured, the marginal-utility theory cannot really explain how consumers will behave.   **T F**

6. A consumer's demand curve for a product is downsloping because total utility decreases as more of the product is consumed.   **T F**

7. If total utility is increasing, then marginal utility is positive and may be either increasing or decreasing.   **T F**

8. There is a significant, positive relationship between the rate of decrease in marginal utility and the price elasticity of demand.   **T F**

9. When marginal utility falls slowly as more of a good is consumed, demand will tend to be inelastic.   **T F**

10. The theory of consumer behavior assumes that consumers act rationally to get the most from their money.   **T F**

11. All consumers are subject to budget constraints.   **T F**

12. To find a consumer's demand for a product, the price of the product is varied while tastes, income, and the prices of other products remain unchanged.   **T F**

13. The theory of consumer behavior assumes that consumers attempt to maximize marginal utility.   **T F**

14. If the marginal utility per dollar spent on product A is greater than the marginal utility per dollar spent on product B, then to maximize utility, the consumer should purchase less of A and more of B.   **T F**

15. When consumers are maximizing total utility, the marginal utilities of the last unit of every product they buy are identical.   **T F**

16. The marginal utility of product X is 15 and its price is $5, while the marginal utility of product Y is 10 and its price is $2. The utility-maximizing rule suggests that there should be *less* consumption of product Y.   **T F**

17. In most cases, a change in incomes will cause a change in the portfolio of goods and services purchased by consumers.   **T F**

18. A fall in the price of DVD players will decrease the demand for DVDs.   **T F**

19. The diamond-water paradox is explained by the fact that the total utility derived from water is low while the total utility derived from diamonds is high. **T F**

20. If a consumer can earn $10 an hour and it takes 2 hours to consume a product, the value of the time required for the consumption of the product is $5. **T F**

21. Paying $300 to fly from one city to another may be cheaper than paying $50 for a bus trip between the two cities when the economic value of time is taken into account. **T F**

22. A decrease in the productivity of labor will tend over time to increase the value of time. **T F**

23. One reason for the increased use of health care services is that consumers pay only part of the full price of the services. **T F**

24. People tend to eat more at an "all-you-can-eat buffet" because the "price" of additional items is zero but the marginal utility for these items is likely to be positive.

T F

25. Noncash gifts add more to total utility than cash gifts.

T F

■ **MULTIPLE-CHOICE QUESTIONS**

Circle the letter that corresponds to the best answer.

1. The reason the substitution effect works to encourage a consumer to buy more of a product when its price decreases is

(a) the real income of the consumer has been increased

(b) the real income of the consumer has been decreased

(c) the product is now relatively less expensive than it was

(d) other products are now relatively less expensive than they were

2. Kristin Hansen buys only two goods, food and clothing. Both are normal goods for Kristin. Suppose the price of food decreases. Kristin's consumption of clothing will

(a) decrease due to the income effect

(b) increase due to the income effect

(c) increase due to the substitution effect

(d) not change due to the substitution effect

3. Which best expresses the law of diminishing marginal utility?

(a) The more a person consumes of a product, the smaller becomes the utility that he receives from its consumption.

(b) The more a person consumes of a product, the smaller becomes the additional utility that she receives as a result of consuming an additional unit of the product.

(c) The less a person consumes of a product, the smaller becomes the utility that she receives from its consumption.

(d) The less a person consumes of a product, the smaller becomes the additional utility that he receives

as a result of consuming an additional unit of the product.

4. Summing the marginal utilities of each unit consumed will determine total

(a) cost

(b) revenue

(c) utility

(d) consumption

The following table shows a hypothetical total utility schedule for a consumer of chocolate candy bars. Use the table to answer Questions 5, 6, and 7.

Number consumed	Total utility
0	0
1	9
2	19
3	27
4	35
5	42
6	42
7	40

5. This consumer begins to experience diminishing marginal utility when he consumes the

(a) first candy bar

(b) second candy bar

(c) third candy bar

(d) fourth candy bar

6. Marginal utility becomes negative with the consumption of the

(a) fourth candy bar

(b) fifth candy bar

(c) sixth candy bar

(d) seventh candy bar

7. Based on the data, you can conclude that the

(a) marginal utility of the fourth unit is 6

(b) marginal utility of the second unit is 27

(c) total utility of 5 units is 42

(d) total utility of 3 units is 55

8. After eating eight chocolate chip cookies, you are offered a ninth cookie. You turn down the cookie. Your refusal indicates that the

(a) marginal utility for chocolate chip cookies is negative

(b) total utility for chocolate chip cookies is negative

(c) marginal utility is positive for the eighth and negative for the ninth cookie

(d) total utility was zero because you ate one cookie and refused the other

9. Other things being equal, demand for a product is likely to be *elastic* if the marginal utility

(a) decreases rapidly as additional units are consumed

(b) decreases slowly as additional units are consumed

(c) increases rapidly as additional units are consumed

(d) increases slowly as additional units are consumed

10. Which is a dimension or assumption of the marginal-utility theory of consumer behavior?

(a) The consumer has a small income.

(b) The consumer is rational.

(c) Goods and services are free.

(d) Goods and services yield continually increasing amounts of marginal utility as the consumer buys more of them.

11. A consumer is making purchases of products A and B such that the marginal utility of product A is 20 and the marginal utility of product B is 30. The price of product A is $10 and the price of product B is $20. The utility-maximizing rule suggests that this consumer should

(a) increase consumption of product B and decrease consumption of product A

(b) increase consumption of product B and increase consumption of product A

(c) increase consumption of product A and decrease consumption of product B

(d) make no change in consumption of A or B

12. Suppose that the prices of A and B are $3 and $2, respectively, that the consumer is spending her entire income and buying 4 units of A and 6 units of B, and that the marginal utility of both the fourth unit of A and the sixth unit of B is 6. It can be concluded that the consumer should buy

(a) more of both A and B

(b) more of A and less of B

(c) less of A and more of B

(d) less of both A and B

13. Robert Woods is maximizing his satisfaction consuming two goods, X and Y. If the marginal utility of X is half that of Y, what is the price of X if the price of Y is $1.00?

(a) $0.50

(b) $1.00

(c) $1.50

(d) $2.00

Answer Questions 14, 15, and 16 based on the following table showing the marginal-utility schedules for goods X and Y for a hypothetical consumer. The price of good X is $1 and the price of good Y is $2. The income of the consumer is $9.

Good X		Good Y	
Quantity	MU	Quantity	MU
1	8	1	10
2	7	2	8
3	6	3	6
4	5	4	4
5	4	5	3
6	3	6	2
7	2	7	1

14. To maximize utility, the consumer will buy

(a) 7X and 1Y

(b) 5X and 2Y

(c) 3X and 3Y

(d) 1X and 4Y

15. When the consumer purchases the utility-maximizing combination of goods X and Y, total utility will be

(a) 36

(b) 45

(c) 48

(d) 52

16. Suppose that the consumer's income increased from $9 to $12. What would be the utility-maximizing combination of goods X and Y?

(a) 5X and 2Y

(b) 6X and 3Y

(c) 2X and 5Y

(d) 4X and 4Y

17. A decrease in the price of product Z will

(a) increase the marginal utility per dollar spent on Z

(b) decrease the marginal utility per dollar spent on Z

(c) decrease the total utility per dollar spent on Z

(d) cause no change in the marginal utility per dollar spent on Z

Answer Questions 18, 19, 20, and 21 on the basis of the following total utility data for products A and B. Assume that the prices of A and B are $6 and $8, respectively, and that consumer income is $36.

Units of A	Total utility	Units of B	Total utility
1	18	1	32
2	30	2	56
3	38	3	72
4	42	4	80
5	44	5	84

18. What is the level of total utility for the consumer in equilibrium?

(a) 86

(b) 102

(c) 108

(d) 120

19. How many units of the two products will the consumer buy?

(a) 1 of A and 4 of B

(b) 2 of A and 2 of B

(c) 2 of A and 3 of B

(d) 3 of A and 4 of B

20. If the price of A decreases to $4, then the utility-maximizing combination of the two products is

(a) 2 of A and 2 of B

(b) 2 of A and 3 of B

(c) 3 of A and 3 of B

(d) 4 of A and 4 of B

21. Which of the following represents the demand curve for A?

(a)		(b)		(c)		(d)	
P	Q_d	P	Q_d	P	Q_d	P	Q_d
$6	1	$6	2	$6	2	$6	2
4	4	4	5	4	3	4	4

22. The price of water is substantially less than the price of diamonds because

(a) the marginal utility of a diamond is significantly less than the marginal utility of a gallon of water

(b) the marginal utility of a diamond is significantly greater than the marginal utility of a gallon of water

(c) the total utility of diamonds is greater than the total utility of water

(d) diamonds have a low marginal utility

23. The full price of a product to a consumer is
(a) its market price
(b) its market price plus the value of its consumption time
(c) its market price less the value of its consumption time
(d) the value of its consumption time less its market price

24. A consumer has two basic choices: rent a DVD movie for $4.00 and spend 2 hours of time watching it or spend $15 for dinner at a restaurant that takes 1 hour of time. If the marginal utilities of the movie and the dinner are the same, and the consumer values time at $15 an hour, the rational consumer will most likely
(a) rent more movies and buy fewer restaurant dinners
(b) buy more restaurant dinners and rent fewer movies
(c) buy fewer restaurant dinners and rent fewer movies
(d) make no change in the consumption of both

25. Compared to cash gifts, noncash gifts are preferred
(a) more because they decrease total utility
(b) more because they increase total utility
(c) less because they increase total utility
(d) less because they decrease total utility

■ **PROBLEMS**

1. Suppose that when the price of bread is $2 per loaf, the Robertson family buys six loaves of bread in a week.
a. When the price of bread falls from $2 to $1.60, the Robertson family will increase its bread consumption to seven loaves.
(1) Measured in terms of bread, the fall in the price of

bread will _____ their real income by

_____ loaves. (*Hint:* How many loaves of bread *could* they now buy without changing the amount they spend on bread?)

(2) Is the Robertsons' demand for bread elastic or

inelastic? _____

b. When the price of bread rises from $2 to $2.40 per loaf, the Robertson family will decrease its bread consumption to four loaves.
(1) Measured in terms of bread, this rise in the price

of bread will _____ their real income by

$_____ loaf.

(2) Is the Robertsons' demand for bread elastic or

inelastic? _____

2. Assume that Harriet Palmer finds only three goods, A, B, and C, for sale and that the amounts of utility that their consumption will yield her are as shown in the table below. Compute the marginal utilities for successive units of A, B, and C and enter them in the appropriate columns.

3. Using the marginal-utility data for goods A, B, and C that you obtained in problem 2, assume that the prices of A, B, and C are $5, $1, and $4, respectively, and that Palmer has an income of $37 to spend.
a. Complete the table on the next page by computing the *marginal utility per dollar* for successive units of A, B, and C.
b. Palmer would *not* buy 4 units of A, 1 unit of B, and

4 units of C because _____.
c. Palmer would *not* buy 6 units of A, 7 units of B, and

4 units of C because _____.
d. When Palmer is maximizing her utility, she will buy

_____ units of A, _____ units

of B, _____ units of C; her total utility will

be _____, and the marginal utility of

the last dollar spent on each good will be

_____.

e. If Palmer's income increased by $1, she would

spend it on good _____, assuming she can buy fractions of a unit of a good, because

_____.

Good A			Good B			Good C		
Quantity	Total utility	Marginal utility	Quantity	Total utility	Marginal utility	Quantity	Total utility	Marginal utility
1	21	___	1	7	___	1	23	___
2	41	___	2	13	___	2	40	___
3	59	___	3	18	___	3	52	___
4	74	___	4	22	___	4	60	___
5	85	___	5	25	___	5	65	___
6	91	___	6	27	___	6	68	___
7	91	___	7	28.2	___	7	70	___

	Good A		Good B		Good C
Quantity	Marginal utility per dollar	Quantity	Marginal utility per dollar	Quantity	Marginal utility per dollar
1	——	1	——	1	——
2	——	2	——	2	——
3	——	3	——	3	——
4	——	4	——	4	——
5	——	5	——	5	——
6	——	6	——	6	——
7	——	7	——	7	——

4. Sam Thompson has an income of $36 to spend each week. The only two goods he is interested in purchasing are H and J. The marginal-utility schedules for these two goods are shown in the table at the bottom of the page.

The price of J does not change from week to week and is $4. The marginal utility per dollar from J is also shown in the table. But the price of H varies from one week to the next. The marginal utilities per dollar from H when the prices of H are $6, $4, $3, $2, and $1.50 are shown in the table.

a. Complete the table below to show how much of H Thompson will buy each week at each of the five possible prices of H.

Price of H	Quantity of H demanded
$6.00	——
4.00	——
3.00	——
2.00	——
1.50	——

b. What is the table you completed in part **a** called?

_____

5. Assume that a consumer can purchase only two goods: R (recreation) and M (material goods). The market price of R is $2 and the market price of M is $1. The consumer spends all her income in such a way that the marginal utility of the last unit of R she buys is 12 and the marginal utility of the last unit of M she buys is 6.

a. If we ignore the time it takes to consume R and M, is the consumer maximizing the total utility she obtains from the two goods? _____

b. Suppose it takes 4 hours to consume each unit of R, 1 hour to consume each unit of M, and the consumer can earn $2 an hour when she works.

(1) The full price of a unit of R is $_____.

(2) The full price of a unit of M is $_____.

c. If we take into account the full price of each of the commodities, is the consumer maximizing her total utility? _____ How do you know this?

_____

d. If the consumer is not maximizing her utility, should she increase her consumption of R or of M? _____ Why should she do this?

_____

e. Will she use more or less of her time for consuming R? _____

■ **SHORT ANSWER AND ESSAY QUESTIONS**

1. Explain, employing the income-effect and substitution-effect concepts, the reasons consumers buy more of a product at a lower price than at a higher price and vice versa.

2. Why is utility a "subjective concept"?

3. How does the subjective nature of utility limit the practical usefulness of the marginal-utility theory of consumer behavior?

4. Define total utility and marginal utility. What is the relationship between total utility and marginal utility?

5. How can the law of diminishing marginal utility be used to explain the law of demand?

	Good H						Good J	
Quantity	MU	MU/$6	MU/$4	MU/$3	MU/$2	MU/$1.50	MU	MU/$4
1	45	7.5	11.25	15	22.5	30	40	10
2	30	5	7.5	20	15	20	36	9
3	20	3.33	5	6.67	10	13.33	32	8
4	15	2.5	3.75	5	7.5	10	28	7
5	12	2	3	4	6	8	24	6
6	10	1.67	2.5	3.33	5	6.67	20	5
7	9	1.5	2.25	3	4.5	6	16	4
8	7.5	1.25	1.88	2.5	3.75	5	12	3

6. What is the relationship of marginal utility to the price elasticity of demand?

7. What essential assumptions are made about consumers and the nature of goods and services in developing the marginal-utility theory of consumer behavior?

8. What is meant by "budget constraint"?

9. When is the consumer in equilibrium and maximizing total utility? Explain why any deviation from this equilibrium will decrease the consumer's total utility.

10. Why must the amounts of extra utility derived from differently priced goods mean that marginal utility must be put on a per-dollar-spent basis? Give an example.

11. How can saving be incorporated into the utility-maximizing analysis?

12. Give and explain an algebraic restatement of the utility-maximizing rule.

13. Using the marginal-utility theory of consumer behavior, explain how an individual's demand schedule for a particular consumer good can be obtained.

14. Why does the demand schedule that is based on the marginal-utility theory almost invariably result in an inverse or negative relationship between price and quantity demanded?

15. What aspects of the theory of consumer behavior explain why consumers started buying DVDs in larger numbers instead of videocassette tapes or long-playing records in the past decade?

16. Why does water have a lower price than diamonds despite the fact that water is more useful than diamonds?

17. Explain how a consumer might determine the value of his or her time. How does the value of time affect the full price the consumer pays for a good or service?

18. What does taking time into account explain that the traditional approach to consumer behavior does not explain?

19. How does the way that we pay for goods and services affect the quantity purchased? Explain by using medical care as an example.

20. Why are noncash gifts less preferred than cash gifts?

ANSWERS

Chapter 8 Consumer Behavior and Utility Maximization

FILL-IN QUESTIONS

1. substitution, diminishing
2. increase, decrease, income
3. more, lower, less, more, substitution
4. total, marginal, a subjective, is not
5. decrease
6. positive, zero
7. inelastic, elastic
8. rational, preferences
9. limited, scarce, prices
10. last, the same
11. increase, decrease
12. *a.* MU of product *X*; *b.* price of *X*; *c.* MU of product *Y*; *d.* price of *Y*
13. *a.* the income of the consumer; *b.* the prices of other products
14. consistent, more
15. decreased, increased
16. marginal, marginal, total, total
17. time, limited, equal to, price, time
18. cost, more
19. more, positive, zero
20. less, less

TRUE–FALSE QUESTIONS

1. F, pp. 128–129	**10.** T, p. 132	**19.** F, p. 136
2. F, pp. 128–129	**11.** T, p. 132	**20.** F, pp. 136–137
3. T, p. 129	**12.** T, p. 132	**21.** T, pp. 136–137
4. T, p. 129	**13.** F, p. 132	**22.** F, pp. 136–137
5. F, p. 129	**14.** F, pp. 132–134	**23.** T, p. 137
6. F, pp. 129–131	**15.** F, p. 134	**24.** T, p. 137
7. T, pp. 129–131	**16.** F, p. 134	**25.** F, p. 137
8. F, p. 131	**17.** T, p. 135	
9. F, p. 131	**18.** F, pp. 135–136	

MULTIPLE-CHOICE QUESTIONS

1. c, p. 129	**10.** b, p. 132	**19.** c, pp. 132–134
2. b, pp. 128–129	**11.** c, pp. 132–134	**20.** c, pp. 134–135
3. b, pp. 129–131	**12.** c, pp. 132–134	**21.** c, pp. 134–135
4. c, pp. 129–131	**13.** a, pp. 132–134	**22.** b, p. 136
5. c, pp. 129–131	**14.** b, pp. 132–134	**23.** b, p. 136
6. d, pp. 129–131	**15.** c, pp. 132–134	**24.** b, pp. 136–137
7. c, pp. 129–131	**16.** b, pp. 134–135	**25.** d, p. 137
8. c, pp. 129–131	**17.** a, pp. 134–135	
9. b, p. 131	**18.** b, pp. 132–134	

PROBLEMS

1. *a.* (1) increase, 1 1/2, (2) inelastic; *b.* (1) decrease, 1, (2) elastic

2. marginal utility of good A: 21, 20, 18, 15, 11, 6, 0; marginal utility of good B: 7, 6, 5, 4, 3, 2, 1.2; marginal utility of good C: 23, 17, 12, 8, 5, 3, 2

3. *a.* marginal utility per dollar of good A: 4.2, 4, 3.6, 3, 2.2, 1.2, 0; marginal utility per dollar of good B: 7, 6, 5, 4, 3, 2, 1.2; marginal utility of good C: 5.75, 4.25, 3, 2, 1.25, .75, .5; *b.* the marginal utility per dollar spent on good B (7) is greater than the marginal utility per dollar spent on good A (3), and the latter is greater than the marginal utility per dollar spent on good C (2); *c.* she would be spending more than her $37 income; *d.* 4, 5, 3, 151, 3; *e.* A, she would obtain the greatest marginal utility for her dollar (2.2)

4. *a.* 2, 3, 4, 6, 8; *b.* the demand schedule (for good H)

5. *a.* yes; *b.* (1) 10, (2) 3; *c.* no, the marginal-utility-to-price ratios are not the same for the two goods; *d.* M, because its MU/P ratio is greater; *e.* less

SHORT ANSWER AND ESSAY QUESTIONS

1. pp. 128–129	**8.** p. 132	**15.** pp. 135–136
2. p. 129	**9.** pp. 132–134	**16.** p. 136
3. p. 129	**10.** pp. 132–134	**17.** pp. 136–137
4. pp. 129–131	**11.** pp. 132–134	**18.** pp. 136–137
5. pp. 129–131	**12.** p. 134	**19.** p. 137
6. p. 131	**13.** pp. 134–135	**20.** p. 137
7. p. 132	**14.** pp. 134–135	

Indifference Curve Analysis

This brief appendix contains the third explanation or approach to the theory of consumer behavior. In it you are introduced first to the **budget line** and then to the **indifference curve.** These two geometrical concepts are then combined to explain when a consumer is purchasing the combination of two products that maximizes the total utility obtainable with his or her income. The last step is to vary the price of one of the products to find the consumer's demand (schedule or curve) for the product.

■ **CHECKLIST**

When you have studied this appendix you should be able to

☐ Describe the concept of a budget line and its characteristics.
☐ Explain how to measure the slope of a budget line and determine the location of the budget line.
☐ Describe the concept of an indifference curve.
☐ State two characteristics of indifference curves.
☐ Explain the meaning of an indifference map.
☐ Given an indifference map, determine which indifference curves bring more or less total utility to consumers.
☐ Use indifference curves to identify which combination of two products maximizes the total utility of consumers.
☐ Derive a consumer's demand for a product using indifference curve analysis.
☐ Compare and contrast the marginal-utility and the indifference curve analyses of consumer behavior.

■ **APPENDIX OUTLINE**

1. A **budget line** shows graphically the different combinations of two products a consumer can purchase with a particular money income. A budget line has a negative slope.
   a. An increase in the money income of the consumer will shift the budget line to the right without affecting its slope. A decrease in money income will shift the budget line to the left.
   b. An increase in the prices of both products shifts the budget line to the left. A decrease in the prices of both products shifts the budget line to the right. An increase (decrease) in the price of the product, the quantity of which is measured horizontally (the price of the other product remaining constant), pivots the budget line around a fixed point on the vertical axis in a clockwise (counterclockwise) direction.

2. An **indifference curve** shows graphically the different combinations of two products that bring a consumer the same total utility.
   a. An indifference curve is downsloping. If the utility is to remain the same when the quantity of one product increases, the quantity of the other product must decrease.
   b. An indifference curve is also convex to the origin. The more a consumer has of one product, the smaller the quantity of a second product he or she is willing to give up to obtain an additional unit of the first product. The slope of an indifference curve is the **marginal rate of substitution** (MRS), the rate at which the consumer will substitute one product for another to remain equally satisfied.
   c. The consumer has an indifference curve for every level of total utility. The nearer a curve is to the origin in this indifference map, the smaller is the utility of the combinations on that curve. The further a curve is from the origin, the larger is the utility of the combinations on that curve.

3. The consumer is in an **equilibrium position,** and purchasing the combination of two products that brings the maximum utility to him, when the budget line is tangent to an indifference curve.

4. In the marginal-utility approach to consumer behavior, it is assumed that utility is measurable, but in the indifference curve approach, it need only be assumed that a consumer can say whether a combination of products has more utility than, less utility than, or the same amount of utility as another combination.

5. The demand (schedule or curve) for one of the products is derived by varying the price of that product and shifting the budget line, holding the price of the other product and the consumer's income constant, and finding the quantity of the product the consumer will purchase at each price when in equilibrium.

■ **HINTS AND TIPS**

1. This appendix simplifies the analysis by limiting consumer choice to just two goods. The **budget line** shows the consumer what it is possible to purchase in the two-good world, given an income. Make sure that you understand what a budget line is. To test your understanding, practice with different income levels and prices. For

example, assume you had an income of $100 to spend for two goods (A and B). Good A costs $10 and Good B costs $5. Draw a budget line to show the possible combinations of A and B that you could purchase.

2. *Indifference curves* and the marginal rate of substitution are perhaps the most difficult concepts to understand in this appendix. Remember that the points on the curve show the possible combinations of two goods for which the consumer is *indifferent,* and thus does not care what combination is chosen. The *marginal rate of substitution* is the rate at which the consumer gives up units of one good for units of another along the indifference curve. This rate will change (diminish) as the consumer moves down an indifference curve because the consumer is less willing to *substitute* one good for the other.

■ **IMPORTANT TERMS**

budget line   indifference map
indifference curve   equilibrium position
marginal rate of substitution (MRS)

SELF-TEST

■ **FILL-IN QUESTIONS**

1. A schedule or curve that shows the various combinations of two products a consumer can buy with a specific (income, feature) _____ is called (a budget, an indifference) _____ line.

2. Given two products X and Y, and a graph with the quantities of X measured horizontally and the quantities of Y measured vertically, the budget line has a slope equal to the ratio of the _____ to the _____.

3. When a consumer's income increases, the budget line shifts to the (left, right) _____, while a decrease in income shifts the budget line to the _____.

4. Given two products, A and B, and a budget line graph with the quantities of A measured horizontally and the quantities of B measured vertically, an increase in the price of A will fan the budget line (outward, inward) _____, and a decrease in the price of A will fan the budget line _____ around a fixed point on the (A, B) _____ axis.

5. (A demand, An indifference) _____ curve shows the various combinations of two products that give a consumer the same total satisfaction or total (cost, utility) _____.

6. An indifference curve slopes (upward, downward) _____ and is (concave, convex) _____ to the origin.

7. The slope of the indifference curve at each point measures the (marginal, total) _____ rate of substitution of the combination represented by that point.

8. The more a consumer has of the first product than the second product, the (greater, smaller) _____ is the quantity of the first product the consumer will give up to obtain an additional unit of the second product. As a result, the marginal rate of substitution (MRS) of the first for the second product (increases, decreases) _____ as a consumer moves from left to right (downward) along an indifference curve.

9. A set of indifference curves reflects different levels of (marginal, total) _____ utility and is called an indifference (plan, map) _____.

10. The farther from the origin an indifference curve lies, the (greater, smaller) _____ the total utility obtained from the combinations of products on that curve.

11. A consumer obtains the greatest attainable total utility or satisfaction when he or she purchases that combination of two products at which his or her budget line is (tangent to, greater than) _____ an indifference curve. At this point the consumer's marginal rate of substitution is equal to the (slope, axis) _____ of the budget line.

12. Were a consumer to purchase a combination of two products that lie on her budget line and at which her budget line is steeper than the indifference curve intersecting that point, she could increase her satisfaction by trading (down, up) _____ her budget line.

13. The marginal-utility approach to consumer behavior requires that we assume utility (is, is not) _____ numerically measurable; the indifference curve approach (does, does not) _____ require that we make this assumption.

14. When quantities of product X are measured along the horizontal axis, a decrease in the price of X
a. fans the budget line (inward, outward) _____ and to the (right, left) _____;
b. puts the consumer, when in equilibrium, on a (higher, lower) _____ indifference curve; and
c. normally induces the consumer to purchase (more, less) _____ of product X.

15. Using indifference curves and different budget lines to determine how much of a particular product an individual consumer will purchase at different prices makes it possible to derive that consumer's (supply, demand) _____ curve or schedule for that product.

■ TRUE–FALSE QUESTIONS

Circle T if the statement is true, F if it is false.

1. The budget line shows all combinations of two products that the consumer can purchase, given money income and the prices of the products.   **T F**

2. The slope of the budget line when quantities of Alpha are measured horizontally and quantities of Beta are measured vertically is equal to the price of Beta divided by the price of Alpha.   **T F**

3. A consumer is unable to purchase any of the combinations of two products which lie below (or to the left) of the consumer's budget line.   **T F**

4. An increase in the money income of a consumer shifts the budget line to the right.   **T F**

5. If a consumer moves from one combination (or point) on an indifference curve to another combination (or point) on the same curve, the total utility obtained by the consumer does not change.   **T F**

6. An indifference curve is concave to the origin.   **T F**

7. The marginal rate of substitution shows the rate, at the margin, at which the consumer is prepared to substitute one good for the other so as to remain equally satisfied.   **T F**

8. The closer to the origin an indifference curve lies, the smaller the total utility a consumer obtains from the combinations of products on that indifference curve.   **T F**

9. On an indifference map, the further from the origin, the lower the level of utility associated with each indifference curve.   **T F**

10. There can be an intersection of consumer indifference curves.   **T F**

11. A consumer maximizes total utility when she or he purchases the combination of the two products at which her or his budget line crosses an indifference curve.   **T F**

12. On an indifference map, the consumer's equilibrium position will be where the slope of the highest attainable indifference curve equals the slope of the budget line.   **T F**

13. It is assumed in the marginal-utility approach to consumer behavior that utility is numerically measurable.   **T F**

14. In both the marginal-utility and indifference curve approaches to consumer behavior, it is assumed that a consumer is able to say whether the total utility obtained from combination A is greater than, equal to, or less than the total utility obtained from combination B.   **T F**

15. A decrease in the price of a product normally enables a consumer to reach a higher indifference curve.   **T F**

■ MULTIPLE-CHOICE QUESTIONS

Circle the letter that corresponds to the best answer.

1. Suppose a consumer has an income of $8, the price of **R** is $1, and the price of **S** is $0.50. Which of the following combinations is on the consumer's budget line?
 (a) 8**R** and 1**S**
 (b) 7**R** and 1**S**
 (c) 6**R** and 6**S**
 (d) 5**R** and 6**S**

2. If a consumer has an income of $100, the price of **U** is $10, and the price of **V** is $20, the maximum quantity of **U** the consumer is able to purchase is
 (a) 5
 (b) 10
 (c) 20
 (d) 30

3. When the income of a consumer is $20, the price of **T** is $5, the price of **Z** is $2, and the quantity of **T** is measured horizontally, the slope of the budget line is
 (a) 0.4
 (b) 2.5
 (c) 4
 (d) 10

4. Assume that everything else remains the same, but there is a decrease in a consumer's money income. The most likely effect is
 (a) an inward shift in the indifference curves because the consumer can now satisfy fewer wants
 (b) an inward shift in the budget line because the consumer can now purchase less of both products
 (c) an increase in the marginal rate of substitution
 (d) no change in the equilibrium of the consumer

5. An indifference curve is a curve that shows the different combinations of two products that
 (a) give a consumer equal marginal utilities
 (b) give a consumer equal total utilities
 (c) cost a consumer equal amounts
 (d) have the same prices

6. In the following schedule for an indifference curve, how much of **G** is the consumer willing to give up to obtain the third unit of **H**?
 (a) 3
 (b) 4
 (c) 5
 (d) 6

Quantity of G	Quantity of H
18	1
12	2
7	3
3	4
0	5

7. The slope of the indifference curve measures the
 (a) slope of the budget line
 (b) total utility of a good
 (c) space on an indifference map
 (d) marginal rate of substitution

8. The marginal rate of substitution
(a) may rise or fall, depending on the slope of the budget line
(b) rises as you move downward along an indifference curve
(c) falls as you move downward along an indifference curve
(d) remains the same along a budget line

9. Which of the following is characteristic of indifference curves?
(a) They are concave to the origin.
(b) They are convex to the origin.
(c) Curves closer to the origin have the highest level of total utility.
(d) Curves closer to the origin have the highest level of marginal utility.

10. To derive the demand curve of a product, the price of the product is varied. For the indifference curve analysis, the
(a) budget line is held constant
(b) money income of the consumer changes
(c) tastes and preferences of the consumer are held constant
(d) prices of other products the consumer might purchase change

Questions 11, 12, 13, and 14 are based on the diagram below.

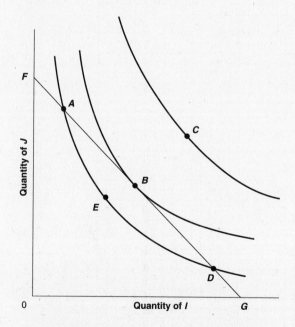

11. The budget line is best represented by line
(a) *AB*
(b) *AD*
(c) *FG*
(d) *DG*

12. Which combination of goods *I* and *J* will the consumer purchase?

(a) *A*
(b) *B*
(c) *C*
(d) *E*

13. Suppose the price of good *I* increases. The budget line will shift
(a) inward around a point on the *J* axis
(b) outward around a point on the *J* axis
(c) inward around a point on the *I* axis
(d) outward around a point on the *I* axis

14. If the consumer chooses the combination of goods *I* and *J* represented by point *E*, then the consumer could
(a) obtain more goods with the available money income
(b) not obtain more goods with the available money income
(c) shift the budget line outward so that it is tangent with point *C*
(d) shift the budget line inward so that it is tangent with point *E*

15. In indifference curve analysis, the consumer will be in equilibrium at the point where the
(a) indifference curve is concave to the origin
(b) budget line crosses the vertical axis
(c) two indifference curves intersect and are tangent to the budget line
(d) budget line is tangent to an indifference curve

16. If a consumer is initially in equilibrium, a decrease in money income will
(a) move the consumer to a new equilibrium on a lower indifference curve
(b) move the consumer to a new equilibrium on a higher indifference curve
(c) make the slope of the consumer's indifference curves steeper
(d) have no effect on the equilibrium position

Questions 17, 18, 19, and 20 are based on the following graph.

17. If the budget line shifts from **BL #1** to **BL #2,** it is because the price of
   (a) *K* increased
   (b) *K* decreased
   (c) *L* increased
   (d) *L* decreased

18. If the budget line shifts from **BL #2** to **BL #1,** it is because the price of
   (a) *K* increased
   (b) *K* decreased
   (c) *L* increased
   (d) *L* decreased

19. When the budget line shifts from **BL #2** to **BL #1,** the consumer will buy
   (a) more of *K* and *L*
   (b) less of *K* and *L*
   (c) more of *K* and less of *L*
   (d) less of *K* and more of *L*

20. Point *C* on indifference curve **IC #3** can be an attainable combination of products *K* and *L,* if
   (a) the price of *K* increases
   (b) the price of *L* increases
   (c) money income increases
   (d) money income decreases

■ **Problems**

1. Following are the schedules for three indifference curves.

Indifference schedule 1		Indifference schedule 2		Indifference schedule 3	
A	B	A	B	A	B
0	28	0	36	0	45
1	21	1	28	1	36
2	15	2	21	2	28
3	10	3	15	3	21
4	6	4	11	4	15
5	3	5	7	5	10
6	1	6	4	6	6
7	0	7	1	7	3
		8	0	8	1
				9	0

a. On the graph below, measure quantities of *A* along the horizontal axis (from 0 to 9) and quantities of *B* along the vertical axis (from 0 to 45).
(1) Plot the 8 combinations of *A* and *B* from indifference schedule 1 and draw through the 8 points a curve which is in no place a straight line. Label this curve **IC #1.**
(2) Do the same for the 9 points in indifference schedule 2 and label it **IC #2.**

(3) Repeat the process for the 10 points in indifference schedule 3 and label the curve **IC #3**.

b. Assume the price of **A** is $12, the price of **B** is $2.40, and a consumer has an income of $72.

(1) Complete the following table to show the quantities of **A** and **B** this consumer is able to purchase.

A	B
0	_____
1	_____
2	_____
3	_____
4	_____
5	_____
6	_____

(2) Plot this budget line on the graph you completed in part **a**.

(3) This budget line has a slope equal to _____.

c. To obtain the greatest satisfaction or utility from his income of $72 this consumer will

(1) purchase _____ units of **A** and _____ of **B**;

(2) and spend $_____ on **A** and $_____ on **B**.

2. Following is a graph with three indifference curves and three budget lines. This consumer has an income of $100, and the price of **Y** remains constant at $5.

a. When the price of **X** is $10, the consumer's budget line is **BL #1** and the consumer

(1) purchases _____ **X** and _____ **Y**;

(2) and spends $_____ on **X** and $_____ on **Y**.

b. If the price of **X** is $6, 2/3 the budget line is **BL #2** and the consumer

(1) purchases _____ **X** and _____ **Y**;

(2) and spends $_____ for **X** and $_____ for **Y**.

c. And when the price of **X** is $5, the consumer has budget line **BL #3** and

(1) buys _____ **X** and _____ **Y**; and

(2) spends $_____ on **X** and $_____ on **Y**.

d. On the following graph, plot the quantities of **X** demanded at the three prices.

e. Between $10 and $5 this consumer's demand for **X** is (elastic, inelastic) _____, and for him products **X** and **Y** are (substitutes, complements) _____.

■ **SHORT ANSWER AND ESSAY QUESTIONS**

1. Why is the slope of the budget line negative?

2. How will each of the following events affect the budget line?
   (a) a decrease in the money income of the consumer
   (b) an increase in the prices of both products
   (c) a decrease in the price of one of the products

3. Explain why the budget line can be called "objective" and an indifference curve "subjective."

4. What is the relationship between an indifference curve and total utility? Between an indifference map and total utility?

5. Why is the slope of an indifference curve negative and convex to the origin?

6. You are given two products, alpha and beta. Why will the utility-maximizing combination of the two products be the one lying on the highest attainable indifference curve?

7. Suppose a consumer purchases a combination of two products that is on her budget line but the budget line is not tangent to an indifference curve at that point. Of which product should the consumer buy more, and of which should she buy less? Why?

8. What is the important difference between the marginal-utility theory and the indifference-curve theory of consumer demand?

9. Explain how the indifference map of a consumer and the budget line are utilized to derive the consumer's demand for one of the products. In deriving demand, what is varied and what is held constant?

10. How does a change in the price of one product shift the budget line and determine a new equilibrium point? Explain and illustrate with a graph.

ANSWERS

Appendix to Chapter 8 Indifference Curve Analysis

FILL-IN QUESTIONS

1. income, a budget
2. price of X, price of Y
3. right, left
4. inward, outward, B
5. An indifference, utility
6. downward, convex
7. marginal
8. greater, decreases
9. total, map
10. greater
11. tangent, slope
12. up
13. is, does not
14. *a.* outward, right; *b.* higher; *c.* more
15. demand

TRUE–FALSE QUESTIONS

1. T, p. 142	**6.** F, pp. 143–144	**11.** F, pp. 144–145
2. F, p. 142	**7.** T, pp. 143–144	**12.** T, pp. 144–145
3. F, p. 142	**8.** T, p. 144	**13.** T, pp. 145–146
4. T, pp. 142–143	**9.** F, p. 144	**14.** T, pp. 145–146
5. T, p. 143	**10.** F, p. 144	**15.** T, p. 146

MULTIPLE-CHOICE QUESTIONS

1. d, p. 142	**8.** c, pp. 143–144	**15.** d, pp. 144–145
2. b, p. 142	**9.** b, pp. 143–144	**16.** a, pp. 142, 388
3. b, p. 142	**10.** c, p. 143	**17.** b, pp. 146–147
4. b, p. 142	**11.** c, p. 142	**18.** a, pp. 146–147
5. b, p. 143	**12.** b, pp. 144–145	**19.** b, pp. 146–147
6. c, pp. 143–144	**13.** a, p. 142	**20.** c, pp. 146–147
7. d, pp. 143–144	**14.** a, pp. 142–143	

PROBLEMS

1. *a.* graph; *b.* (1) 30, 25, 20, 15, 10, 5, 0, (2) graph, (3) −5; *c.* (1) 3, 15, (2) 36, 36
2. *a.* (1) 5, 10, (2) 50, 50; *b.* (1) 12, 4, (2) 80, 20; *c.* (1) 18, 2, (2) 90, 10; *d.* graph; *e.* elastic, substitutes

SHORT ANSWER AND ESSAY QUESTIONS

1. p. 142	**5.** pp. 143–144	**9.** pp. 146–147
2. pp. 142–143	**6.** p. 145	**10.** pp. 146–147
3. p. 143	**7.** pp. 144–145	
4. p. 145	**8.** pp. 144–145	

CHAPTER 9

The Costs of Production

Previous chapters discussed consumer behavior and product demand. This chapter switches to producer behavior and business firms. It explains how a firm's **costs of production** change as the firm's output changes, in the short run and in the long run.

This chapter begins with a definition of cost and profit. You should be somewhat familiar with these terms because they were first introduced in Chapters 2 and 4. The explanation is now more detailed. Several definitions of cost and profit are given in the chapter, so you must know the distinctions if you are to understand the true meaning of **economic cost** and **economic profit.**

The second and third sections of the chapter focus on **short-run** variable relationships and production costs for the firm. You are first introduced to the important **law of diminishing returns,** which defines the relationship between the quantity of resources used by the firm and the output the firm produces in the short run. The chapter discussion then shifts to costs because resource prices are associated with the fixed and variable resources the typical firm uses to produce its output. The three basic types of short-run costs—total, average, and marginal—vary for the firm as the quantity of resources and output changes. The chapter describes the relationship among the various cost curves and how they are shaped by the law of diminishing returns.

The fourth section of the chapter looks at production costs in the **long run.** All resources, and also production costs, are variable in the long run. You will learn that the long-run cost curve for the typical firm is based on the short-run cost curves for firms of different sizes. In the long run, firms can experience **economies of scale** and **diseconomies of scale** that will shape the long-run cost curve for the firm. The chapter concludes with several practical applications of the concept of scale economies.

It is important that you master this material on the costs of production because it sets the foundation for understanding the price and output decisions of a firm operating under different market structures that you will be reading about in the next three chapters.

■ CHECKLIST

When you have studied this chapter you should be able to

☐ Define economic cost in terms of opportunity cost.
☐ Distinguish between an explicit cost and an implicit cost.

☐ Explain the difference between normal profit and economic profit and why the former is a cost and the latter is not a cost.
☐ Distinguish between the short run and the long run in production.
☐ Define total product, marginal product, and average product.
☐ State the law of diminishing returns and explain its rationale.
☐ Compute marginal product and average product to illustrate the law of diminishing returns when you are given the necessary data.
☐ Describe the relationship between marginal product and average product.
☐ Define fixed costs, variable costs, and total cost.
☐ Define average fixed cost, average variable cost, and average total cost.
☐ Explain how average product is related to average variable cost.
☐ Define marginal cost.
☐ Explain how marginal product is related to marginal cost.
☐ Compute and graph average fixed cost, average variable cost, average total cost, and marginal cost when given total-cost data.
☐ Describe the relation of marginal cost to average variable cost and average total cost.
☐ Explain why short-run cost curves shift.
☐ Illustrate the difference between short-run average total cost curves for a firm at different outputs and its long-run average total cost curves.
☐ Describe various possible long-run average total cost curves.
☐ Define and list reasons for the economies and diseconomies of scale.
☐ Explain the concept of minimum efficient scale and its relation to industry structure.
☐ Give examples of short-run costs, economies of scale, and minimum efficient scale in the real world.

■ CHAPTER OUTLINE

1. Resources are scarce and are used to produce many different products. The **economic cost** of using resources to produce a product is an opportunity cost: the value or worth of the resources in its best alternative use.

a. Economic costs can be explicit or implicit. *Explicit costs* are the monetary payments that a firm makes to obtain resources from nonowners of the firm. *Implicit costs* are the monetary payments that would have been paid for self-owned or self-employed resources if they had been used in their next best alternative outside the firm.

b. *Normal profit* is an implicit cost and is the minimum payment that entrepreneurs must receive for performing the entrepreneurial functions for the firm.

c. *Economic,* or pure, *profit* is the revenue a firm receives in excess of all its explicit and implicit economic (opportunity) costs. (The firm's accounting profit is its revenue less only its explicit costs.)

d. A distinction is made between the *short run* and the *long run.* The firm's economic costs vary as the firm's output changes. These costs depend on whether the firm is able to make short-run or long-run changes in its resource use. In the short run, the firm's plant is a fixed resource, but in the long run it is a variable resource. So, in the short run the firm cannot change the size of its plant and can vary its output only by changing the quantities of the variable resources it employs.

2. There are *short-run* relationships between inputs and outputs in the production process.

a. Several product terms need to be defined to show these relationships. *Total product* is the total quantity of output produced. *Marginal product* is the change made in total product from a change in a variable resource input. *Average product,* or productivity, is the total product per unit of resource input.

b. The *law of diminishing returns* determines the manner in which the costs of the firm change as it changes its output in the short run. As more units of a variable resource are added to a fixed resource, beyond some point the marginal product from each additional unit of a variable resource will decline.

(1) There are three phases reflected in a graph of the total product and marginal product curves: increasing, decreasing, and negative marginal returns.

(2) When total product is increasing at an increasing rate, marginal product is rising; when total product is increasing at a decreasing rate, marginal product is falling; and when total product declines, marginal product is negative.

(3) When marginal product is greater than average product, average product rises, and when marginal product is less than average product, average product falls.

3. When input, output, and price information are available, it is possible to calculate *short-run production costs.*

a. The *total cost* is the sum of its fixed costs and variable costs. As output increases,

(1) fixed costs do not change;

(2) at first, the variable costs increase at a decreasing rate, and then increase at an increasing rate;

(3) and at first total costs increase at a decreasing rate and then increase at an increasing rate.

b. *Average costs* consist of *average fixed, average variable,* and *average total costs.* They are equal, respectively, to the firm's fixed, variable, and total costs divided by its output. As output increases,

(1) average fixed cost decreases;

(2) at first, average variable cost decreases and then increases;

(3) and at first, average total cost also decreases and then increases.

c. *Marginal cost* is the extra cost incurred in producing one additional unit of output.

(1) Because the marginal product of the variable resource increases and then decreases (as more of the variable resource is employed to increase output), marginal cost decreases and then increases as output increases.

(2) At the output at which average variable cost is a minimum, average variable cost and marginal cost are equal, and at the output at which average total cost is a minimum, average total cost and marginal cost are equal.

(3) On a graph, marginal cost will always intersect average variable cost at its minimum point and marginal cost will always intersect average total cost at its minimum point. These intersections will always have marginal cost approaching average variable cost and average total cost from below.

d. Changes in either resource prices or technology will cause the cost curves to shift.

4. In the long run, all the resources employed by the firm are variable resources. *Long-run production costs* are all variable costs.

a. As the firm expands its output by increasing the size of its plant, average total cost tends to fall at first because of the *economies of scale,* but as this expansion continues, sooner or later, average total cost begins to rise because of the *diseconomies of scale.*

b. The long-run average total cost curve shows the least average total cost at which any output can be produced after the firm has had time to make all changes in its plant size. Graphically, it is made up of all the points of tangency of the unlimited number of short-run average total cost curves.

c. The economies and diseconomies of scale encountered in the production of different goods are important factors influencing the structure and competitiveness of various industries.

(1) *Economies of scale* (a decline in long-run average total costs) arise because of labor specialization, managerial specialization, efficient capital, and other factors such as spreading the start-up, advertising, or development costs over an increasing level of output.

(2) *Diseconomies of scale* arise primarily from the problems of efficiently managing and coordinating the firm's operations as it becomes a large-scale producer.

(3) *Constant returns to scale* are the range of output where long-run average total cost does not change.

d. Economies and diseconomies of scale can determine the structure in an industry. *Minimum efficient scale (MES)* is the smallest level of output at which a firm can minimize long-run average costs. This concept explains why relatively large and small firms could co-exist in an industry and be viable when there is an extended range of constant returns to scale.

(1) In some industries the long-run average cost curve will decline over a range of output. Given consumer demand, efficient production will be achieved only with a small number of large firms.

(2) If economies of scale extend beyond the market size, the conditions for a **natural monopoly** are produced, which is a rare situation where unit costs are minimized by having a single firm produce a product.

(3) If there are few economies of scale, then there is minimum efficient size at a low level of output and there are many firms in an industry.

5. There are several applications and illustrations of short-run costs, economies of scale, and minimum efficient cost.

a. The rising cost of insurance and security raised short-run average total costs after the terrorists' attacks of September 11, 2001.

b. Economies of scale can be seen in the successful start-up firms such as Intel, Microsoft, or Starbucks.

c. Economies of scale are also exhibited in the Verson stamping machine that makes millions of auto parts per year.

d. A small price can be charged for a newspaper because the fixed costs are spread across a large amount of output, thus achieving economies of scale.

e. Economies of scale are extensive in aircraft production, but modest in concrete mixing, which achieves minimum efficient scale at a low level of output. As a consequence, there are few aircraft factories and many concrete mixing companies.

■ HINTS AND TIPS

1. Many *cost* terms are described in this chapter. Make yourself a glossary so that you can distinguish among them. You need to know what each one means if you are to master the material in the chapter. If you try to learn them in the order in which you encounter them, you will have little difficulty because the later terms build on the earlier ones.

2. Make sure you know the difference between **marginal** and **average** relationships in this chapter. Marginal product (MP) shows the *change* in total output associated with each additional input. Average product (AP) is simply the output per unit of resource input. Marginal cost (MC) shows the change in total cost associated with producing another unit of output. Average cost shows the per-unit cost of producing a level of output.

3. Practice drawing the different sets of **cost curves** used in this chapter: (1) short-run total cost curves, (2) short-run average and marginal cost curves, and (3) long-run cost curves. Also, explain to yourself the relationship between the curves in each set that you draw.

4. In addition to learning *how* the costs of the firm vary as its output varies, be sure to understand *why* the costs vary the way they do. In this connection note that the behavior of short-run costs is the result of the law of diminishing returns and that the behavior of long-run costs is the consequence of economies and diseconomies of scale.

■ IMPORTANT TERMS

economic (opportunity) cost	variable costs
explicit costs	total cost (TC)
implicit costs	average fixed cost (AFC)
normal profit	average variable cost (AVC)
economic profit	average total cost (ATC)
short run	marginal cost (MC)
long run	economies of scale
total product (TP)	diseconomies of scale
marginal product (MP)	constant returns to scale
average product (AP)	minimum efficient scale (MES)
law of diminishing returns	
fixed costs	natural monopoly

SELF-TEST

■ FILL-IN QUESTIONS

1. The value or worth of any resource in its best alternative use is called the (out-of-pocket, opportunity) _____ cost of that resource.

2. The economic cost of producing a product is the amount of money or income the firm must pay or provide to (government, resource suppliers) _____ to attract land, labor, and capital goods away from alternative uses in the economy. The monetary payments, or out-of-pocket payments, are (explicit, implicit) _____ costs, and the costs of self-owned or self-employed resources are _____ costs.

3. Normal profit is a cost because it is the payment that the firm must make to obtain the services of the (workers, entrepreneurs) _____. Accounting profit is equal to the firm's total revenue less its (explicit, implicit) _____ costs. Economic profit is not a cost and is equal to the firm's total (costs, revenues) _____ less its economic _____.

4. In the short run the firm can change its output by changing the quantity of the (fixed, variable) _____ resources it employs, but it cannot change the quantity of the _____ resources. This means that the firm's plant capacity is fixed in the (short, long) _____ run and variable in the _____ run.

5. The law of diminishing returns is that as successive units of a (fixed, variable) _____ resource are added to a _____ resource, beyond some point the (total, marginal) _____ product of the former resource will decrease. The law assumes that all units of input are of (equal, unequal) _____ quality.

6. If the total product increases at an increasing rate, the marginal product is (rising, falling) _____. If it increases at a decreasing rate, the marginal product is (positive, negative, zero) _____, but (rising, falling) _____.

7. If total product is at a maximum, the marginal product is (positive, negative, zero) _____, but if it decreases, the marginal product is _____.

8. If the marginal product of any input exceeds its average product the average product is (rising, falling) _____, but if it is less than its average product the average product is _____. If the marginal product is equal to its average product the average product is at a (minimum, maximum) _____.

9. Those costs that in total do not vary with changes in output are (fixed, variable) _____ costs, but those costs that in total change with the level of output are _____ costs. The sum of fixed and variable costs at each level of output is (marginal, total) _____ cost.

10. The law of diminishing returns explains why a firm's average variable, average total, and marginal cost may at first tend to (increase, decrease) _____ but ultimately _____ as the output of the firm increases.

11. Marginal cost is the increase in (average, total) _____ variable cost or _____ cost that occurs when the firm increases its output by one unit.

12. If marginal cost is less than average variable cost, average variable cost will be (rising, falling, constant) _____ but if average variable cost is less than marginal cost, average variable cost will be _____.

13. Assume that labor is the only variable input in the short run and that the wage rate paid to labor is constant.
a. When the marginal product of labor is rising, the marginal cost of producing a product is (rising, falling) _____.

b. When the average variable cost of producing a product is falling, the average product of labor is (rising, falling) _____.
c. At the output at which marginal cost is at a minimum, the marginal product of labor is at a (minimum, maximum) _____.
d. At the output at which the average product of labor is at a maximum, the average variable cost of producing the product is at a (minimum, maximum) _____.
e. At the output at which the average variable cost is at a minimum, average variable cost and (marginal, total) _____ cost are equal and average product and _____ product are equal.

14. Changes in either resource prices or technology will cause cost curves to (shift, remain unchanged) _____. If average fixed costs increase, then the average fixed costs curve will (shift up, shift down, remain unchanged) _____ and the average total cost curve will _____, but the average variable cost curve will _____ and the marginal cost curve will (shift up, shift down, remain unchanged) _____.

15. If average variable costs increase, then the average variable cost curve will (shift up, shift down, remain unchanged) _____ and the average total cost curve will _____, and the marginal cost curve will (shift up, shift down, remain unchanged) _____, but the average fixed cost curve would _____.

16. The short-run costs of a firm are fixed and variable costs, but in the long run all costs are (fixed, variable) _____. The long-run average total cost of producing a product is equal to the lowest of the short-run costs of producing that product after the firm has had all the time it requires to make the appropriate adjustments in the size of its (workforce, plant) _____.

17. List the three important sources of economies of scale:
a. _____
b. _____
c. _____

18. When the firm experiences diseconomies of scale, it has (higher, lower) _____ average total costs as output increases. Where diseconomies of scale are operative, an increase in all inputs will cause a (greater, less) _____-than-proportionate increase in output. The factor that gives rise to large diseconomies of scale is managerial (specialization, difficulties) _____.

19. The smallest level of output at which a firm can minimize long-run average costs is (maximum, minimum) _____ efficient scale. Relatively large and small firms could coexist in an industry and be equally viable when there is an extended range of (increasing, decreasing, constant) _____ returns to scale.

20. In some industries, the long-run average cost curve will (increase, decrease) _____ over a long range of output and efficient production will be achieved with only a few (small, large) _____ firms. The conditions for a natural monopoly are created when (economies, diseconomies) _____ of scale extend beyond the market's size so that unit costs are minimized by having a single firm produce a product.

■ TRUE–FALSE QUESTIONS

Circle T if the statement is true, F if it is false.

1. The economic costs of a firm are the payments it must make to resource owners to attract their resources from alternative employments. **T F**

2. Economic or pure profit is an explicit cost, while normal profit is an implicit cost. **T F**

3. In the short run the size (or capacity) of a firm's plant is fixed. **T F**

4. The resources employed by a firm are all variable in the long run and all fixed in the short run. **T F**

5. The law of diminishing returns states that as successive amounts of a variable resource are added to a fixed resource, beyond some point total output will diminish. **T F**

6. An assumption of the law of diminishing returns is that all units of variable inputs are of equal quality. **T F**

7. When total product is increasing at a decreasing rate, marginal product is positive and increasing. **T F**

8. When average product is falling, marginal product is greater than average product. **T F**

9. When marginal product is negative, total production (or output) is decreasing. **T F**

10. The larger the output of a firm, the smaller the fixed cost of the firm. **T F**

11. The law of diminishing returns explains why increases in variable costs associated with each 1-unit increase in output become greater and greater after a certain point. **T F**

12. Fixed costs can be controlled or altered in the short run. **T F**

13. Total cost is the sum of fixed and variable costs at each level of output. **T F**

14. Marginal cost is the change in fixed cost divided by the change in output. **T F**

15. The marginal-cost curve intersects the average-total-cost (ATC) curve at the ATC curve's minimum point. **T F**

16. If the fixed cost of a firm increases from one year to the next (because the premium it must pay for the insurance on the buildings it owns has been increased) while its variable-cost schedule remains unchanged, its marginal-cost schedule will also remain unchanged. **T F**

17. Marginal cost is equal to average variable cost at the output at which average variable cost is at a minimum. **T F**

18. When the marginal product of a variable resource increases, the marginal cost of producing the product will decrease, and when marginal product decreases, marginal cost will increase. **T F**

19. If the price of a variable input should increase, the average variable cost, average total cost, and marginal cost curves would all shift upward, but the position of the average fixed cost curve would remain unchanged. **T F**

20. One explanation why the long-run average-total-cost curve of a firm rises after some level of output has been reached is the law of diminishing returns. **T F**

21. If a firm increases all its inputs by 20% and its output increases by 30%, the firm is experiencing economies of scale. **T F**

22. The primary cause of diseconomies of scale is increased specialization of labor. **T F**

23. If a firm has constant returns to scale in the long run, the *total* cost of producing its product does not change when it expands or contracts its output. **T F**

24. Minimum efficient scale occurs at the largest level of output at which a firm can minimize long-run average costs. **T F**

25. The fundamental reason that newspapers have such low prices is the low production costs from economies of scale. **T F**

■ MULTIPLE-CHOICE QUESTIONS

Circle the letter that corresponds to the best answer.

1. Suppose that a firm produces 100,000 units a year and sells them all for $5 each. The explicit costs of production are $350,000 and the implicit costs of production are $100,000. The firm has an accounting profit of
   (a) $200,000 and an economic profit of $25,000
   (b) $150,000 and an economic profit of $50,000
   (c) $125,000 and an economic profit of $75,000
   (d) $100,000 and an economic profit of $50,000

2. Economic profit for a firm is defined as the total revenues of the firm minus its
   (a) accounting profit

(b) explicit costs of production
(c) implicit costs of production
(d) opportunity cost of all inputs

3. Which would best describe the short run for a firm as defined by economists?
(a) The plant capacity for a firm is variable.
(b) The plant capacity for a firm is fixed.
(c) There are diseconomies of scale.
(d) There are economies of scale.

4. Which is most likely to be a long-run adjustment for a firm that manufactures golf carts on an assembly line basis?
(a) an increase in the amount of steel the firm buys
(b) a reduction in the number of shifts of workers from three to two
(c) a change in the production managers of the assembly line
(d) a change from the production of golf carts to motorcycles

5. The change in total product divided by the change in resource input defines
(a) total cost
(b) average cost
(c) average product
(d) marginal product

Use the following table to answer Questions 6 and 7. Assume that the only variable resource used to produce output is labor.

Amount of labor	Amount of output
1	3
2	8
3	12
4	15
5	17
6	18

6. The marginal product of the fourth unit of labor is
(a) 2 units of output
(b) 3 units of output
(c) 4 units of output
(d) 15 units of output

7. When the firm hires four units of labor the average product of labor is
(a) 3 units of output
(b) 3.75 units of output
(c) 4.25 units of output
(d) 15 units of output

8. Because the marginal product of a variable resource initially increases and later decreases as a firm increases its output,
(a) average variable cost decreases at first and then increases
(b) average fixed cost declines as the output of the firm expands
(c) variable cost at first increases by increasing amounts and then increases by decreasing amounts
(d) marginal cost at first increases and then decreases

9. Because the marginal product of a resource at first increases and then decreases as the output of the firm increases,
(a) average fixed cost declines as the output of the firm increases
(b) average variable cost at first increases and then decreases
(c) variable cost at first increases by increasing amounts and then increases by decreasing amounts
(d) total cost at first increases by decreasing amounts and then increases by increasing amounts

For Questions 10, 11, and 12, use the data given in the following table. The fixed cost of the firm is $500, and the firm's total variable cost is indicated in the table.

Output	Total variable cost
1	$ 200
2	360
3	500
4	700
5	1000
6	1800

10. The average variable cost of the firm when 4 units of output are produced is
(a) $175
(b) $200
(c) $300
(d) $700

11. The average total cost of the firm when 4 units of output are being produced is
(a) $175
(b) $200
(c) $300
(d) $700

12. The marginal cost of the sixth unit of output is
(a) $200
(b) $300
(c) $700
(d) $800

13. Marginal cost and average variable cost are equal at the output at which
(a) marginal cost is a minimum
(b) marginal product is a maximum
(c) average product is a maximum
(d) average variable cost is a maximum

14. Average variable cost may be either increasing or decreasing when
(a) marginal cost is decreasing
(b) marginal product is increasing
(c) average fixed cost is decreasing
(d) average total cost is increasing

15. Why does the short-run marginal-cost curve eventually increase for the typical firm?
(a) diseconomies of scale
(b) minimum efficient scale
(c) the law of diminishing returns
(d) economic profit eventually decreases

16. If the price of labor or some other variable resource increased, the
   (a) AVC curve would shift downward
   (b) AFC curve would shift upward
   (c) AFC curve would shift downward
   (d) MC curve would shift upward

Questions 17, 18, 19, and 20 are based on the following figure.

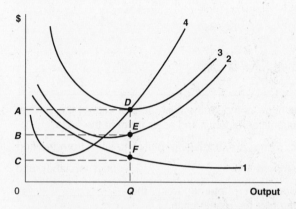

17. In the figure, curves **1, 3,** and **4,** respectively, represent
   (a) average variable cost, marginal cost, and average total cost
   (b) average total cost, average variable cost, and marginal cost
   (c) average fixed cost, average total cost, and marginal cost
   (d) marginal cost, average total cost, and average variable cost

18. At output level *Q,* the average fixed cost is measured by the vertical distance represented by
   (a) *DE*
   (b) *DF*
   (c) *DQ*
   (d) *EF*

19. As output increases beyond the level represented by *Q,*
   (a) marginal product is rising
   (b) marginal product is falling
   (c) total fixed costs are rising
   (d) total costs are falling

20. If the firm is producing at output level *Q,* then the total variable costs of production are represented by area
   (a) 0*QFC*
   (b) 0*QEB*
   (c) 0*QDC*
   (d) *CFEB*

21. At an output of 10,000 units per year, a firm's total variable costs are $50,000 and its average fixed costs are $2. The total costs per year for the firm are
   (a) $50,000
   (b) $60,000
   (c) $70,000
   (d) $80,000

22. A firm has total fixed costs of $4,000 a year. The average variable cost is $3.00 for 2000 units of output. At this level of output, its average total costs are

   (a) $2.50
   (b) $3.00
   (c) $4.50
   (d) $5.00

23. If you know that total fixed cost is $100, total variable cost is $300, and total product is 4 units, then
   (a) marginal cost is $50
   (b) average fixed cost is $45
   (c) average total cost is $125
   (d) average variable cost is $75

24. If the short-run average variable costs of production for a firm are falling, then this indicates that
   (a) average variable costs are above average fixed costs
   (b) marginal costs are below average variable costs
   (c) average fixed costs are constant
   (d) total costs are falling

Answer Questions 25 and 26 using the following table. Three short-run cost schedules are given for three plants of different sizes that a firm might build in the long run.

Plant 1		Plant 2		Plant 3	
Output	ATC	Output	ATC	Output	ATC
10	$10	10	$15	10	$20
20	9	20	10	20	15
30	8	30	7	30	10
40	9	40	10	40	8
50	10	50	14	50	9

25. What is the long-run average cost of producing 40 units of output?
   (a) $7
   (b) $8
   (c) $9
   (d) $10

26. At what output is long-run average cost at a minimum?
   (a) 20
   (b) 30
   (c) 40
   (d) 50

27. If the long-run average total cost curve for a firm is downsloping, then it indicates that there
   (a) is a minimum efficient scale
   (b) are constant returns to scale
   (c) are diseconomies of scale
   (d) are economies of scale

28. Which factor contributes to economies of scale?
   (a) less efficient use of capital goods
   (b) less division of labor and specialization
   (c) greater specialization in management of a firm
   (d) greater difficulty controlling the operations of a firm

29. A firm is encountering constant returns to scale when it increases all of its inputs by 20% and its output increases by
   (a) 10%
   (b) 15%
   (c) 20%
   (d) 25%

30. If economies of scale are limited and diseconomies appear quickly in an industry, then minimum efficient scale occurs at a

(a) high level of output, and there will be a few firms
(b) high level of output, and there will be many firms
(c) low level of output, and there will be few firms
(d) low level of output, and there will be many firms

■ **PROBLEMS**

1. On the following graph, sketch the way in which the average product and the marginal product of a resource change as the firm increases its employment of that resource.

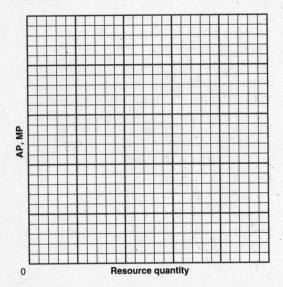

0   **Resource quantity**

2. The table in the next column shows the total production of a firm as the quantity of labor employed increases. The quantities of all other resources employed remain constant.

   a. Compute the marginal products of the first through the eighth units of labor and enter them in the table.

Units of labor	Total production	Marginal product of labor	Average product of labor
0	0		0
1	80	_____	_____
2	200	_____	_____
3	330	_____	_____
4	400	_____	_____
5	450	_____	_____
6	480	_____	_____
7	490	_____	_____
8	480	_____	_____

   b. Now compute the average products of the various quantities of labor and enter them in the table.

   c. There are increasing returns to labor from the first through the _____ units of labor and decreasing returns from the _____ through the eighth units.

   d. When total production is increasing, marginal product is (positive, negative) _____ and when total production is decreasing, marginal product is _____.

   e. When marginal product is greater than average product, then average product will (rise, fall) _____, and when marginal product is less than average product, then average product will _____.

3. On the graph in the first column of the next page, sketch the manner in which fixed cost, variable cost, and total cost change as the output the firm produces in the short run changes.

Quantity of labor employed	Total output	Marginal product of labor	Average product of labor	Total cost	Marginal cost	Average variable cost
0	0	—	—	$_____	—	—
1	5	5	5	_____	$_____	$_____
2	11	6	5.50	_____	_____	_____
3	18	7	6	_____	_____	_____
4	24	6	6	_____	_____	_____
5	29	5	5.80	_____	_____	_____
6	33	4	5.50	_____	_____	_____
7	36	3	5.14	_____	_____	_____
8	38	2	4.75	_____	_____	_____
9	39	1	4.33	_____	_____	_____
10	39	0	3.90	_____		

e. When the average product of labor

(1) increases, the average variable cost (increases, decreases) _____.

(2) decreases, the average variable cost _____.

5. The law of diminishing returns causes a firm's average variable, average total, and marginal cost to decrease at first and then to increase as the output of the firm increases.

Sketch these three cost curves on the following graph in such a way that their proper relationship to each other is shown.

Cost, dollars (y-axis) / *Output* (x-axis) — graph

4. Assume that a firm has a plant of fixed size and that it can vary its output only by varying the amount of labor it employs. The table at the bottom of page 110 shows the relationships between the amount of labor employed, the output of the firm, the marginal product of labor, and the average product of labor.

a. Assume each unit of labor costs the firm $10. Compute the total cost of labor for each quantity of labor the firm might employ, and enter these figures in the table.

b. Now determine the marginal cost of the firm's product as the firm increases its output. Divide the increase in total labor cost by the *increase* in total output to find the marginal cost. Enter these figures in the table.

c. When the marginal product of labor

(1) increases, the marginal cost of the firm's product (increases, decreases) _____.

(2) decreases, the marginal cost of the firm's product _____.

d. If labor is the only variable input, the total labor cost and total variable cost are equal. Find the average variable cost of the firm's product (by dividing the total labor cost by total output) and enter these figures in the table.

6. The table that follows is a schedule of a firm's fixed cost and variable cost.

a. Complete the table by computing total cost, average fixed cost, average total cost, and marginal cost.

b. On the graph at the top of page 112, plot and label fixed cost, variable cost, and total cost.

c. On the graph at the bottom of page 112, plot average fixed cost, average variable cost, average total cost, and marginal cost. Label the four curves.

Output	Total fixed cost	Total variable cost	Total cost	Average fixed cost	Average variable cost	Average total cost	Marginal cost
$ 0	$200	$ 0	$____				
1	200	50	____	$____	$50.00	$____	$____
2	200	90	____		45.00		____
3	200	120	____	____	40.00	____	____
4	200	160	____	____	40.00	____	____
5	200	220	____	____	44.00	____	____
6	200	300	____	____	50.00	____	____
7	200	400	____	____	57.14	____	____
8	200	520	____	____	65.00	____	____
9	200	670	____	____	74.44	____	____
10	200	900	____	____	90.00	____	____

7. Following are the short-run average-cost curves of producing a product with three different sizes of plants, **Plant 1, Plant 2,** and **Plant 3.** Draw the firm's long-run average cost on this graph.

8. Following are the short-run average-total-cost schedules for three plants of different sizes that a firm might build to produce its product. Assume that these are the only possible sizes of plants that the firm might build.

Plant size A		Plant size B		Plant size C	
Output	ATC	Output	ATC	Output	ATC
10	$ 7	10	$17	10	$53
20	6	20	13	20	44
30	5	30	9	30	35
40	4	40	6	40	27
50	5	50	4	50	20
60	7	60	3	60	14
70	10	70	4	70	11
80	14	80	5	80	8
90	19	90	7	90	6
100	25	100	10	100	5
110	32	110	16	110	7
120	40	120	25	120	10

a. Complete the *long-run* average-cost schedule for the firm in the following table.

Output	Average cost	Output	Average cost
10	$_____	70	$_____
20	_____	80	_____
30	_____	90	_____
40	_____	100	_____
50	_____	110	_____
60	_____	120	_____

b. For outputs between

(1) _____ and _____, the firm should build Plant A.

(2) _____ and _____, the firm should build Plant B.

(3) _____ and _____, the firm should build Plant C.

■ **SHORT ANSWER AND ESSAY QUESTIONS**

1. Explain the meaning of the opportunity cost of producing a product and the difference between an explicit cost and an implicit cost. How would you determine the implicit money cost of a resource?

2. What is the difference between normal profit and economic profit? Why is the former an economic cost? How do you define accounting profit?

3. What type of adjustments can a firm make in the long run that it cannot make in the short run? What adjustments can it make in the short run? How long is the short run?

4. Why is the distinction between the short run and the long run important?

5. State precisely the law of diminishing returns. Exactly what is it that diminishes, and why does it diminish?

6. Distinguish between a fixed cost and a variable cost.

7. Why are short-run total costs partly fixed and partly variable costs, and why are long-run costs entirely variable?

8. Why do short-run variable costs increase at first by decreasing amounts and later increase by increasing amounts?

9. How does the behavior of short-run variable costs influence the behavior of short-run total costs?

10. Describe the way in which short-run average fixed cost, average variable cost, average total cost, and marginal cost vary as the output of the firm increases.

11. What are the connections between marginal product and marginal cost, and between average product and average variable cost? How will marginal cost behave as marginal product decreases and increases? How will average variable cost change as average product rises and falls?

12. What are the precise relationships between marginal cost and minimum average variable cost, and between marginal cost and minimum average total cost? Why are these relationships necessarily true?

13. What happens to the average total cost, average variable cost, average fixed cost, and marginal cost curves when the price of a variable input increases or decreases? Describe what other factor can cause short-run cost curves to shift.

14. What does the long-run average-cost curve of a firm show? What relationship is there between long-run average cost and the short-run average-total-cost schedules of the different-sized plants which a firm might build?

15. Why is the long-run average-cost curve of a firm U-shaped?

16. What is meant by economies of scale and by diseconomies of scale?

17. What are factors that contribute to economies of scale?

18. What causes diseconomies of scale?

19. What is minimum efficient scale? How can this concept, combined with economies and diseconomies of scale, be used to describe the number and size of firms in an industry?

20. Describe real examples of short-run costs, economies of scale, and minimum efficient scale.

PROBLEMS

1. See Figure 9.2(b) of the text
2. *a.* 80, 120, 130, 70, 50, 30, 10, −10; *b.* 80, 100, 110, 100, 90, 80, 70, 60; *c.* third, fourth; *d.* positive, negative; *e.* rise, fall
3. See Figure 9.3 of the text
4. *a.* $0, 10, 20, 30, 40, 50, 60, 70, 80, 90, 100; *b.* $2.00, 1.67, 1.43, 1.67, 2.00, 2.50, 3.33, 5.00, 1.00, NA; *c.* (1) decreases, (2) increases; *d.* 2.00, 1.82, 1.67, 1.67, 1.72, 1.82, 1.94, 2.11, 2.31, 2.56; *e.* (1) decreases, (2) increases
5. See Figure 9.5 of the text
6. *a.* see table below; *b.* graph; *c.* graph

ANSWERS

Chapter 9   The Costs of Production

FILL-IN QUESTIONS

1. opportunity
2. resource suppliers, explicit, implicit
3. entrepreneurs, explicit, revenues, costs
4. variable, fixed, short, long
5. variable, fixed, marginal, equal
6. rising, positive, falling
7. zero, negative
8. rising, falling, maximum
9. fixed, variable, total
10. decrease, increase
11. total, total
12. falling, rising
13. *a.* falling; *b.* rising; *c.* maximum; *d.* minimum; *e.* marginal, marginal
14. shift, shift up, shift up, remain unchanged, remain unchanged
15. shift up, shift up, shift up, remain unchanged
16. variable, plant
17. *a.* labor specialization; *b.* managerial specialization; *c.* more efficient use
18. higher, less, difficulties
19. minimum, constant
20. decrease, large, economies

Total cost	Average fixed cost	Average total cost	Marginal cost
$ 200	—	—	—
250	$200.00	$250.00	$ 50
290	100.00	145.00	40
320	66.67	106.67	30
360	50.00	90.00	40
420	40.00	84.00	60
500	33.33	83.33	80
600	28.57	85.71	100
720	25.00	90.00	120
870	22.22	96.67	150
1100	20.00	110.00	230

7. See Figures 9.7 and 9.8 of the text
8. *a.* $7.00, 6.00, 5.00, 4.00, 4.00, 3.00, 4.00, 5.00, 6.00, 5.00, 7.00, 10.00; *b.* (1) 10, 40, (2) 50, 80, (3) 90, 120

SHORT ANSWER AND ESSAY QUESTIONS

1. pp. 148–149	8. pp. 154–158	15. pp. 160–161
2. pp. 149–150	9. pp. 154–158	16. pp. 160–162
3. p. 150	10. pp. 154–158	17. pp. 160–162
4. p. 150	11. pp. 158–159	18. p. 163
5. pp. 151–152	12. pp. 158–159	19. pp. 163–164
6. p. 154	13. p. 159	20. pp. 164–165
7. pp. 154–156	14. pp. 159–160	

TRUE–FALSE QUESTIONS

1. T, pp. 148–149	10. F, p. 154	19. T, pp. 158–159
2. F, pp. 149–150	11. T, pp. 154–155	20. F, pp. 159–161
3. T, p. 150	12. F, p. 154	21. T, pp. 159–160
4. F, p. 150	13. T, p. 154	22. F, p. 163
5. F, pp. 151–152	14. F, p. 156	23. F, p. 163
6. T, pp. 151–152	15. T, p. 157	24. F, pp. 163–164
7. F, pp. 152–154	16. T, pp. 156–159	25. T, pp. 164–165
8. F, pp. 152–154	17. T, pp. 156–159	
9. T, pp. 152–154	18. T, pp. 156–159	

MULTIPLE-CHOICE QUESTIONS

1. b, pp. 148–149	11. c, pp. 154–156	21. c, pp. 154–156
2. d, pp. 149–150	12. d, pp. 154–156	22. d, pp. 154–156
3. b, p. 150	13. c, pp. 155–157	23. d, pp. 154–156
4. d, p. 150	14. c, pp. 155–157	24. b, pp. 155–158
5. d, p. 151	15. c, pp. 156–159	25. b, pp. 159–161
6. b, pp. 151–152	16. d, p. 159	26. b, pp. 159–161
7. b, pp. 151–152	17. c, pp. 156–157	27. d, pp. 160–161
8. a, pp. 151–153	18. a, pp. 155–156	28. c, pp. 160–162
9. d, pp. 151–153	19. b, pp. 157–158	29. c, pp. 160–162
10. a, pp. 154–156	20. b, pp. 155–157	30. d, p. 163

CHAPTER 10

Pure Competition

Chapter 10 is the first of three chapters that bring together the previous discussion of demand and production costs. These chapters examine demand and production costs under four different market structures: pure competition, monopoly, oligopoly, and monopolistic competition. This chapter focuses exclusively on the pure competition market structure, which is characterized by (1) a large number of firms, (2) the selling of a standardized product, (3) firms that are price takers rather than price makers, and (4) ease of entry into and exit from the industry.

The main section of the chapter describes profit maximization for the purely competitive firm in the **short run.** Although two approaches to profit maximization are presented, the one given the greatest emphasis is the **marginal revenue–marginal cost** approach. You will learn the rule that a firm maximizes profit or minimizes losses by producing the output level at which marginal revenue equals marginal cost. Finding this equality provides the answers to the three central questions each firm has to answer: (1) Should we produce? (2) If so, how much output? (3) What profit (or loss) will be realized?

Answers to these questions also give insights about the **short-run supply curve** for the individual firm. The firm will find it profitable to produce at any output level where marginal revenue is greater than marginal costs. The firm will also produce in the short run, but it will experience losses if marginal revenue is less than marginal costs and greater than the minimum of average total cost. You will be shown how to construct the short-run supply curve for the purely competitive firm, given price and output data. The market supply curve for the industry is the sum of all supply curves for individual firms.

This chapter also discusses what happens to competitive firms in the **long run** as equilibrium conditions change. Over time, new firms will enter an industry that is making economic profits and existing firms will exit an industry that is experiencing economic losses, and changing price and output in the industry. Here you will learn that the shape of the **long-run supply curve** is directly affected by whether the industry is one characterized by constant costs, increasing costs, or decreasing costs as output increases.

In the long run, pure competition produces almost ideal conditions for **economic efficiency.** These ideal conditions and their qualifications are discussed in detail near the end of the chapter. A pure competition results in products produced in the least costly way, and thus it is *productively efficient.* Pure competition also allocates resources to firms so that they produce the products most wanted by society, and therefore it is *allocatively efficient.* You will find out that these two efficiency conditions can be expressed in the triple equality: Price (and marginal revenue) = marginal cost = minimum of average total cost.

You must understand the purely competitive model because it is the efficiency standard or norm for evaluating different market structures. You will be using it often for comparison with the pure monopoly model in Chapter 11 and with the models for monopolistic and oligopoly competition in Chapter 12.

■ CHECKLIST

When you have studied this chapter you should be able to

☐ List the five characteristics of each of the four basic market models.
☐ Give examples of industries that reflect the characteristics of the four basic market models.
☐ Describe the major features of pure competition.
☐ Explain why a purely competitive firm is a price taker.
☐ Describe the demand curve for a purely competitive firm.
☐ Explain the relationship between marginal revenue and price in pure competition.
☐ Compute average, total, and marginal revenues when you are given a demand schedule faced by a purely competitive firm.
☐ Use the total-revenue and total-cost approach to determine the output that a purely competitive firm will produce in the short run in the profit-maximizing case.
☐ Use the marginal-revenue and marginal-cost approaches to determine the output that a purely competitive firm will produce in the short run in the profit-maximizing, loss-minimizing, and shutdown cases.
☐ State three characteristics of the MR = MC rule.
☐ Find the firm's short-run supply curve when you are given the firm's short-run cost schedules.
☐ Explain the links among the law of diminishing returns, production costs, and product supply in the short run.
☐ Graph a shift in the firm's short-run supply curve and cite factors that cause the curve to increase or decrease.
☐ Find the industry's short-run supply curve (or schedule) when you are given the typical firm's short-run cost schedules.

□ Determine, under short-run conditions, the price at which the product will sell, the output of the industry, and the output of the individual firm.

□ Describe the basic goal for long-run adjustments in pure competition.

□ Determine, under long-run conditions, the price at which the product will sell, the output of the firm, and the output of the industry.

□ Explain the role played by the entry and exit of firms in a purely competitive industry in achieving equilibrium in the long run.

□ Describe the characteristics and rationale for the long-run supply curve in a constant-cost industry, in an increasing-cost industry, and in a decreasing-cost industry.

□ Distinguish between productive and allocative efficiency.

□ Explain the significance of MR (= *P*) = MC = minimum ATC.

□ Discuss how pure competition makes dynamic adjustments.

■ CHAPTER OUTLINE

1. The price a firm charges for the good or service it produces and its output of that product depend not only on the demand for and the cost of producing it, but on the characteristics of the market (industry) in which it sells the product. The **four market models** are pure competition, pure monopoly, monopolistic competition, and oligopoly. These models are defined by the number of firms, whether the product is standardized or differentiated, the firm's control over price, the conditions for entry into the industry, and degree of nonprice competition.

2. This chapter examines **pure competition,** in which a large number of independent firms, no one of which is able to influence market price by itself, sell a standardized product in a market where firms are free to enter and to leave in the long run. Although pure competition is rare in practice, it is the standard against which the *efficiency* of the economy and other market models can be compared.

3. *Demand* as seen by the purely competitive firm is unique because a firm selling its product cannot influence the price at which the product sells, and therefore is a *price taker.*

　　a. The demand for its product is *perfectly elastic.*

　　b. Average revenue (or price) and marginal revenue are equal and constant at the fixed (equilibrium) market price (**AR = P = MR**). Total revenue increases at a constant rate as the firm increases its output.

　　c. The demand (average revenue) and marginal revenue curves faced by the firm are horizontal and identical at the market price. The total revenue curve has a constant positive slope.

4. The purely competitive firm operating in the **short run** is a price taker that can maximize profits (or minimize losses) only by changing its level of output. Two approaches can be used to determine the optimal level of output for the firm.

　　a. The **total revenue–total cost** approach to profit maximization sets the level of output at that quantity where the difference between total revenue minus total cost is greatest.

　　b. The **marginal revenue–marginal cost** approach to profit maximization basically sets the level of output at the quantity where marginal revenue (or price) equals marginal cost. There are three possible cases to consider when using this approach.

　　(1) The firm will **maximize profits** when MR = MC at an output level where price is greater than average total cost.

　　(2) The firm will **minimize losses** when MR = MC at an output level where price is greater than the minimum average variable cost (but less than average total cost).

　　(3) The firm will **shut down** when MR = MC at an output level where price is less than average variable cost.

5. There is a close relationship between **marginal cost and the supply curve** for the purely competitive firm and industry.

　　a. The **short-run supply curve for the purely competitive firm** is the portion of the marginal-cost curve that lies above average variable cost.

　　b. There are links among the law of diminishing returns, production costs, and product supply. The law of diminishing returns suggests that marginal costs will increase as output expands. The firm must receive more revenue (get higher prices for its products) if it is to expand output.

　　c. Changes in variable inputs will change the marginal-cost or supply curve for the purely competitive firm. For example, an improvement in technology that increases productivity will decrease the marginal-cost curve (shift it downward).

　　d. The **short-run supply curve of the industry** (which is the sum of the supply curves of the individual firms) and the total demand for the product determine the short-run equilibrium price and equilibrium output of the industry. Firms in the industry may be either prosperous or unprosperous in the short run.

6. In the **long run,** the price of a product produced under conditions of pure competition will equal the minimum average total cost (**P = minimum ATC**). The firms in the industry will neither earn economic profits nor suffer economic losses.

　　a. If economic profits are being received in the industry in the short run, firms will enter the industry in the long run (attracted by the profits), increase total supply, and thereby force price down to the minimum average total cost, leaving only a normal profit.

　　b. If losses are being suffered in the industry in the short run, firms will leave the industry in the long run (seeking to avoid losses), reduce total supply, and thereby force price up to the minimum average total cost, leaving only a normal profit.

　　c. If an industry is a **constant-cost industry,** the entry of new firms will not affect the average-total-cost schedules or curves of firms in the industry.

(1) An increase in demand will result in no increase in the long-run equilibrium price, and the industry will be able to supply larger outputs at a constant price.

(2) Graphically, the long-run supply curve in a constant-cost industry is horizontal at the minimum of the average-total-cost curve, indicating that firms make only normal profits, but not economic profits.

d. If an industry is an *increasing-cost industry,* the entry of new firms will raise the average-total-cost schedules or curves of firms in the industry.

(1) An increase in demand will result in an increase in the long-run equilibrium price, and the industry will be able to supply larger outputs only at higher prices.

(2) Graphically, the long-run supply curve in an increasing-cost industry is upsloping at the minimum of the average-total-cost curve, indicating that firms make only normal profits but not economic profits.

e. If an industry is a *decreasing-cost industry,* the entry of new firms will lower the average-total-cost schedules or curves of firms in the industry.

(1) An increase in demand will result in a decrease in the long-run equilibrium price, and the industry will be able to supply larger outputs only at lower prices.

(2) Graphically, the long-run supply curve in a decreasing-cost industry is downsloping at the minimum of the average-total-cost curve, indicating that firms make only normal profits, but not economic profits.

7. In the long run, *competition* and *efficiency* compel the purely competitive firm to produce that output at a price at which marginal revenue, average cost, and marginal cost are equal and average cost is a minimum. An economy in which all industries were purely competitive makes efficient use of its resources.

a. There is *productive efficiency* when the average total cost of producing goods is at a minimum; buyers benefit most from this efficiency when they are charged a price just equal to minimum average total cost (*P = minimum ATC*).

b. There is *allocative efficiency* when goods are produced in such quantities that the total satisfaction obtained from the economy's resources is at a maximum, or when the price of each good is equal to its marginal cost (*P = MC*).

(1) When price is greater than marginal cost, there is an *underallocation* of resources to the production of a product.

(2) When price is less than marginal cost, there is an *overallocation* of resources to the production of a product.

(3) When price is equal to marginal cost, there is efficient allocation of resources to the production of a product.

(4) The purely competitive economy makes dynamic adjustments to changes in demand or supply that restore equilibrium and efficiency.

(5) The "invisible hand" is at work in a competitive market system by organizing the private interests of producers that will help achieve society's interest in the efficient use of scarce resources.

■ **HINTS AND TIPS**

1. The purely competitive model is extremely important for you to master even if examples of it in the real world are rare. The model is the standard against which the other market models—pure monopoly, monopolistic competition, and oligopoly—will be compared for effects on economic efficiency. Spend extra time learning the material in this chapter so you can make model comparisons in later chapters.

2. Make sure that you understand why a purely competitive firm is a *price "taker"* and not a price "maker." The purely competitive firm has no influence over the price of its product and can only make decisions about the level of output.

3. Construct a table for explaining how the purely competitive firm maximizes profits or minimizes losses in the short run. Ask yourself the three questions in the table: (1) Should the firm produce? (2) What quantity should be produced to maximize profits? (3) Will production result in economic profit? Answer the questions using a marginal-revenue–marginal-cost approach. Check your answers against those presented in the text.

4. The average purely competitive firm in long-run equilibrium will not make economic profits. Find out why by following the graphical analysis in Figures 10.8 and 10.9.

5. The triple equality of MR (= P) = MC = minimum ATC is the most important equation in the chapter because it allows you to judge the allocative and productive efficiency of a purely competitive economy. Check your understanding of this triple equality by explaining what happens to productive efficiency when $P >$ minimum ATC, or to allocative efficiency when $P <$ MC or $P >$ MC.

■ **IMPORTANT TERMS**

pure competition	break-even point
pure monopoly	MC = MR rule
monopolistic competition	short-run supply curve
oligopoly	long-run supply curve
imperfect competition	constant-cost industry
price taker	increasing-cost industry
average revenue	decreasing-cost industry
total revenue	productive efficiency
marginal revenue	allocative efficiency

SELF-TEST

■ **FILL-IN QUESTIONS**

1. The four market models examined in this and the next two chapters are

a. _____

b. _____

c. _____

d. _____

2. The four market models differ in terms of the (age, number) _____ of firms in the industry, whether the product is (a consumer good, standardized) _____ or (a producer good, differentiated) _____, and how easy or difficult it is for new firms to (enter, leave) _____ the industry.

3. What are the four specific conditions that characterize pure competition?

a. _____

b. _____

c. _____

d. _____

4. The individual firm in a purely competitive industry is a price (maker, taker) _____ and finds that the demand for its product is perfectly (elastic, inelastic) _____.

5. The firm's demand schedule is also a (cost, revenue) _____ schedule. The price per unit to the seller is (marginal, total, average) _____ revenue; price multiplied by the quantity the firm can sell is _____ revenue; and the extra revenue that results from selling one more unit of output is _____ revenue.

6. In pure competition, product price (rises, falls, is constant) _____ as an individual firm's output increases. Marginal revenue is (less than, greater than, equal to) _____ product price.

7. Economic profit is total revenue (plus, minus) _____ total cost. If the firm is making only a normal profit, total revenue is (greater than, equal to) _____ total cost. In the latter case, this output level is called the (profit, break-even) _____ point by economists.

8. If a purely competitive firm produces any output at all, it will produce that output at which its profit is at a (maximum, minimum) _____ or its loss is at a _____. Or, said another way, the output at which marginal cost is (equal to, greater than) _____ marginal revenue.

9. A firm will be willing to produce at an economic loss in the short run if the price which it receives is greater than its average (fixed, variable, total) _____ cost.

10. In the short run, the individual firm's supply curve in pure competition is that portion of the firm's (total, marginal) _____ cost curve which lies (above, below) _____ the average variable cost curve.

11. The short-run market supply curve is the (average, sum) _____ of the (short-run, long-run) _____ supply curves of all firms in the industry.

12. In the short run in a purely competitive industry, the equilibrium price is the price at which quantity demanded is equal to (average cost, quantity supplied) _____, and the equilibrium quantity is the quantity demanded and _____ at the equilibrium price.

13. In a purely competitive industry, in the short run the number of firms in the industry and the sizes of their plants are (fixed, variable) _____, but in the long run they are _____.

14. When a purely competitive industry is in long-run equilibrium, the price that the firm is paid for its product is equal to (total, average) _____ revenue, and to long-run _____ cost. In this case, the long-run average cost is at a (maximum, minimum) _____.

15. An industry will be in long-run equilibrium when firms are earning (normal, economic) _____ profits, but firms tend to enter an industry if the firms in the industry are earning _____ profits. Firms will tend to leave an industry when they are realizing economic (profits, losses) _____.

16. If the entry of new firms into an industry tends to raise the costs of all firms in the industry, the industry is said to be (a constant-, an increasing-, a decreasing-) _____ cost industry. Its long-run supply curve is (horizontal, downsloping, upsloping) _____.

17. If the entry of new firms into an industry tends to lower costs of all firms in the industry, the industry is said to be (a constant-, an increasing-, a decreasing-) _____ cost industry. Its long-run supply curve is (horizontal, downsloping, upsloping) _____.

18. The purely competitive economy achieves productive efficiency in the long run because price and (total, average) _____ cost are equal and the latter is at a (maximum, minimum) _____.

19. In the long run the purely competitive economy is allocatively efficient because price and (total, marginal) _____ cost are equal.

20. One of the attributes of purely competitive markets is their ability to restore (monopoly, efficiency) _____ when disrupted by changes in the economy. The "invisible hand" also operates in a competitive market system because it (maximizes, minimizes) _____ the profits of individual producers and at the same time the system creates a pattern of resource allocation that _____ consumer satisfaction.

■ TRUE–FALSE QUESTIONS

Circle T if the statement is true, F if it is false.

1. The structures of the markets in which business firms sell their products in the U.S. economy are very similar. **T F**

2. A large number of sellers does not necessarily mean that the industry is purely competitive. **T F**

3. Only in a purely competitive industry do individual firms have no control over the price of their product. **T F**

4. Imperfectly competitive markets are defined as all markets except those that are purely competitive. **T F**

5. One reason for studying the pure competition model is that many industries are almost purely competitive. **T F**

6. The purely competitive firm views an average revenue schedule as identical to its marginal revenue schedule. **T F**

7. The demand curves for firms in a purely competitive industry are perfectly inelastic. **T F**

8. Under purely competitive conditions, the product price charged by the firm increases as output increases. **T F**

9. The purely competitive firm can maximize its economic profit (or minimize its loss) only by adjusting its output. **T F**

10. Economic profit is the difference between total revenue and average revenue. **T F**

11. The break-even point means that the firm is realizing normal profits, but not economic profits. **T F**

12. A purely competitive firm that wishes to produce and not close down will maximize profits or minimize losses at that output at which marginal costs and marginal revenue are equal. **T F**

13. Assuming that the purely competitive firm chooses to produce and not close down, to maximize profits or minimize losses it should produce at that point where price equals average cost. **T F**

14. If a purely competitive firm is producing output less than its profit-maximizing output, marginal revenue is greater than marginal cost. **T F**

15. If, at the profit-maximizing level of output for the purely competitive firm, price exceeds the minimum average variable cost but is less than average total cost, the firm will make a profit. **T F**

16. A purely competitive firm will produce in the short run the output at which marginal cost and marginal revenue are equal provided that the price of the product is greater than its average variable cost of production. **T F**

17. The short-run supply curve of a purely competitive firm tends to slope upward from left to right because of the law of diminishing returns. **T F**

18. If a purely competitive firm is in short-run equilibrium and its marginal cost is greater than its average total cost, firms will leave the industry in the long run. **T F**

19. When firms in a purely competitive industry are earning profits that are less than normal, the supply of the product will tend to decrease in the long run. **T F**

20. The long-run supply curve for a competitive, increasing-cost industry is upsloping. **T F**

21. Pure competition, if it could be achieved in all industries in the economy, would result in the most efficient allocation of resources. **T F**

22. Under conditions of pure competition, firms are forced to employ the most efficient production methods available to survive. **T F**

23. The marginal costs of producing a product are society's measure of the marginal worth of alternative products. **T F**

24. In a purely competitive market, product price measures the marginal benefit, or additional satisfaction, that society obtains from producing additional units of the product. **T F**

25. The operation of the "invisible hand," in which the pursuit of private interests promotes the public or social interests, is a missing feature of pure competition. **T F**

■ MULTIPLE-CHOICE QUESTIONS

Circle the letter that corresponds to the best answer.

1. For which market model are there a very large number of firms?
 (a) monopolistic competition
 (b) oligopoly
 (c) pure monopoly
 (d) pure competition

2. In which market model is the individual seller of a product a price taker?
 (a) pure competition
 (b) pure monopoly

(c) monopolistic competition

(d) oligopoly

3. Which industry comes *closest* to being purely competitive?

(a) wheat

(b) shoes

(c) electricity

(d) automobile

4. In a purely competitive industry,

(a) each existing firm will engage in various forms of nonprice competition

(b) new firms are free to enter and existing firms are able to leave the industry very easily

(c) individual firms have a price policy

(d) each firm produces a differentiated (nonstandardized) product

5. The demand schedule or curve confronted by the individual purely competitive firm is

(a) perfectly inelastic

(b) inelastic but not perfectly inelastic

(c) perfectly elastic

(d) elastic but not perfectly elastic

6. Total revenue for producing 10 units of output is $6. Total revenue for producing 11 units of output is $8. Given this information, the

(a) average revenue for producing 11 units is $2.

(b) average revenue for producing 11 units is $8.

(c) marginal revenue for producing the 11th unit is $2.

(d) marginal revenue for producing the 11th unit is $8.

7. In pure competition, product price is

(a) greater than marginal revenue

(b) equal to marginal revenue

(c) equal to total revenue

(d) greater than total revenue

8. The individual firm's short-run supply curve is that part of its marginal-cost curve lying above its

(a) average total-cost curve

(b) average variable-cost curve

(c) average fixed-cost curve

(d) average revenue curve

9. Which statement is true of a purely competitive industry in short-run equilibrium?

(a) Price is equal to average total cost.

(b) Total quantity demanded is equal to total quantity supplied.

(c) Profits in the industry are equal to zero.

(d) Output is equal to the output at which average total cost is a minimum.

10. Suppose that when 2000 units of output are produced, the marginal cost of the 2001st unit is $5. This amount is equal to the minimum of average total cost, and marginal cost is rising. If the optimal level of output in the short run is 2500 units, then at that level,

(a) marginal cost is greater than $5 and marginal cost is less than average total cost

(b) marginal cost is greater than $5 and marginal cost is greater than average total cost

(c) marginal cost is less than $5 and marginal cost is greater than average total cost

(d) marginal cost is equal to $5 and marginal cost is equal to average total cost

11. The Zebra, Inc., is selling in a purely competitive market. Its output is 250 units, which sell for $2 each. At this level of output, marginal cost is $2 and average variable cost is $2.25. The firm should

(a) produce zero units of output

(b) decrease output to 200 units

(c) continue to produce 250 units

(d) increase output to maximize profits

Questions 12, 13, 14, and 15 are based on the following graph.

12. If the firm is producing at output level 0*n*, the rectangular area ***fecb*** is

(a) total variable cost

(b) total fixed costs

(c) total revenue

(d) total economic profit

13. At the profit-maximizing output, average fixed cost is

(a) *ab*

(b) *ac*

(c) *na*

(d) *nb*

14. At the profit-maximizing output, the total variable costs are equal to the area

(a) 0*fbn*

(b) 0*ecn*

(c) 0*gan*

(d) *gfba*

15. The demand curve for this firm is equal to

(a) **MR**, and the supply curve is the portion of the **MC** curve where output is greater than level *n*

(b) **MR**, and the supply curve is the portion of the **MC** curve where output is greater than level *k*

(c) **MR**, and the supply curve is the portion of the **MC** curve where output is greater than level *h*

(d) **MR**, and the supply curve is the portion of the **ATC** curve where output is greater than level *k*

Answer Questions 16, 17, 18, 19, and 20 on the basis of the following cost data for a firm that is selling in a purely competitive market.

Output	AFC	AVC	ATC	MC
1	$300	$100	$400	$100
2	150	75	225	50
3	100	70	170	60
4	75	73	148	80
5	60	80	140	110
6	50	90	140	140
7	43	103	146	180
8	38	119	156	230
9	33	138	171	290
10	30	160	190	360

16. If the market price for the firm's product is $140, the competitive firm will produce
(a) 5 units at an economic loss of $150
(b) 6 units and break even
(c) 7 units and break even
(d) 8 units at an economic profit of $74

17. If the market price for the firm's product is $290, the competitive firm will produce
(a) 7 units at an economic profit of $238
(b) 8 units at an economic profit of $592
(c) 9 units at an economic profit of $1071
(d) 10 units at an economic profit of $1700

18. If the product price is $179, the *per-unit* economic profit at the profit-maximizing output is
(a) $15
(b) $23
(c) $33
(d) $39

19. The total fixed costs are
(a) $100
(b) $200
(c) $300
(d) $400

Assume there are 100 identical firms in this industry and total or market demand is as shown.

Price	Quantity demanded
$360	600
290	700
230	800
180	900
140	1000
110	1100
80	1200

20. The equilibrium price will be
(a) $140
(b) $180
(c) $230
(d) $290

21. Assume that the market for wheat is purely competitive. Currently, firms growing wheat are experiencing economic losses. In the long run, we can expect this market's
(a) supply curve to increase
(b) demand curve to increase
(c) supply curve to decrease
(d) demand curve to decrease

22. The long-run supply curve under pure competition will be
(a) downsloping in an increasing-cost industry and upsloping in a decreasing-cost industry
(b) horizontal in a constant-cost industry and upsloping in a decreasing-cost industry
(c) horizontal in a constant-cost industry and upsloping in an increasing-cost industry
(d) upsloping in an increasing-cost industry and vertical in a constant-cost industry

23. The long-run supply curve in a constant-cost industry will be
(a) perfectly elastic
(b) perfectly inelastic
(c) unit elastic
(d) income elastic

24. In a decreasing-cost industry, the long-run
(a) demand curve would be perfectly inelastic
(b) demand curve would be perfectly elastic
(c) supply curve would be upsloping
(d) supply curve would be downsloping

25. Increasing-cost industries find that their costs rise as a consequence of an increased demand for the product because of
(a) the diseconomies of scale
(b) diminishing returns
(c) higher resource prices
(d) a decreased supply of the product

26. When a purely competitive industry is in long-run equilibrium, which statement is true?
(a) Firms in the industry are earning normal profits.
(b) Price and long-run average total cost are not equal to each other.
(c) Marginal cost is at its minimum level.
(d) Marginal cost is equal to total revenue.

27. Which triple identity results in the most efficient use of resources?
(a) $P = MC =$ minimum ATC
(b) $P = AR = MR$
(c) $P = MR =$ minimum MC
(d) $TR = MC = MR$

28. An economy is producing the goods most wanted by society when, for each and every good, its
(a) price and average cost are equal
(b) price and marginal cost are equal
(c) marginal revenue and marginal cost are equal
(d) price and marginal revenue are equal

29. If there is an increase in demand for a product in a purely competitive industry, it results in an industry
(a) contraction that will end when the price of the product is greater than its marginal cost
(b) contraction that will end when the price of the product is equal to its marginal cost

(c) expansion that will end when the price of the product is greater than its marginal cost

(d) expansion that will end when the price of the product is equal to its marginal cost

30. The idea of the "invisible hand" operating in the competitive market system means that

(a) there is a unity of private and social interests that promotes efficiency

(b) the industries in this system are described as decreasing-cost industries

(c) there is an overallocation of resources to the production of goods and services

(d) productive efficiency is more important than allocative efficiency

■ **PROBLEMS**

1. Using the following set of terms, complete the following table by inserting the appropriate letter or letters in the blanks.

a. one
b. few
c. many
d. a very large number
e. standardized
f. differentiated
g. some

h. considerable
i. very easy
j. blocked
k. fairly easy
l. fairly difficult
m. none
n. unique

Market characteristics	Pure competition	Pure monopoly	Monopolistic competition	Oligopoly
Number of firms	___	___	___	___
Type of product	___	___	___	___
Control over price	___	___	___	___
Conditions of entry	___	___	___	___
Nonprice competition	___	___	___	___

Market model

2. Following is the demand schedule facing the individual firm.

Price	Quantity demanded	Average revenue	Total revenue	Marginal revenue
$10	0	$___	$___	--
10	1	___	___	$___
10	2	___	___	___
10	3	___	___	___
10	4	___	___	___
10	5	___	___	___
10	6	___	___	___

a. Complete the table by computing average revenue, total revenue, and marginal revenue.

b. Is this firm operating in a market that is purely competitive? _____ How can you tell?

_____

c. The coefficient of the price elasticity of demand is the same between every pair of quantities demanded.

What is it? _____

d. What relationship exists between average revenue and marginal revenue? _____

_____

e. On the first graph on page 123, plot the demand schedule, average revenue, total revenue, and marginal revenue; label each curve.

f. The demand, average-revenue, and marginal-revenue curves are all _____ lines at a price of $_____ across all quantities.

g. The total-revenue curve is an upsloping line with a _____ slope because marginal revenue is _____.

3. Assume that a purely competitive firm has the following schedule of costs.

Output	TFC	TVC	TC
0	$300	$ 0	$ 300
1	300	100	400
2	300	150	450
3	300	210	510
4	300	290	590
5	300	400	700
6	300	540	840
7	300	720	1020
8	300	950	1250
9	300	1240	1540
10	300	1600	1900

a. Complete the following table to show the total revenue and total profit of the firm at each level of output the firm might produce. Assume the market price is $200.

Output	Revenue	Profit
0	$___	$___
1	___	___
2	___	___
3	___	___
4	___	___
5	___	___
6	___	___
7	___	___
8	___	___
9	___	___
10	___	___

Market price = $200

b. At a price of $200, the firm would produce an output of _____ units and earn a profit of $_____.

c. Plot the cost data for total variable cost and total cost on the second graph on page 123. Then plot the total revenue when the price is $200. For this price, indicate the level of output and the economic profit or loss on the graph.

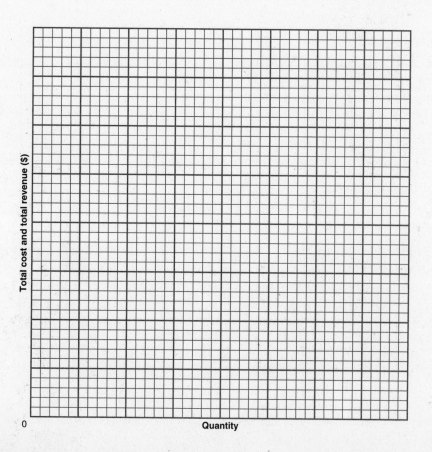

4. Now assume that the same purely competitive firm has the following schedule of average and marginal costs:

Output	AFC	AVC	ATC	MC
1	$300	$100	$400	$100
2	150	75	225	50
3	100	70	170	60
4	75	73	148	80
5	60	80	140	110
6	50	90	140	140
7	43	103	146	180
8	38	119	156	230
9	33	138	171	290
10	30	160	190	360

a. At a price of $55, the firm would produce _____ units of output. At a price of $120, the firm would produce _____ units of output. At a price of $200, the firm would produce _____ units of output. At the $200 price compare your answers to those you gave in problem 3.

b. The *per-unit* economic profit (or loss) is calculated by subtracting _____ at a particular level of output from the product price. This *per-unit* economic profit is then multiplied by the number of units of _____ to determine the economic profit for the competitive firm.

(1) At the product price of $200, the average total costs are $_____, so *per-unit* economic profit is $_____. Multiplying this amount by the number of units of output results in an economic profit of $_____.

(2) At the product price of $120, the average total costs are $_____, so *per-unit* economic losses are $_____. Multiplying this amount by the number of units of output results in an economic loss of $_____.

c. Plot the data for average and marginal cost in the graph below. Then plot each marginal revenue when the price is $55, $120, and $200. For each price, indicate the level of output and the economic profit or loss on the graph.

5. Use the average and marginal cost data in problem 4 in your work on problem 5.

a. In the following table, complete the supply schedule for the competitive firm and state what the economic profit will be at each price.

Price	Quantity supplied	Profit
$360	_____	$_____
290	_____	_____
230	_____	_____
180	_____	_____
140	_____	_____
110	_____	_____
80	_____	_____
60	_____	_____

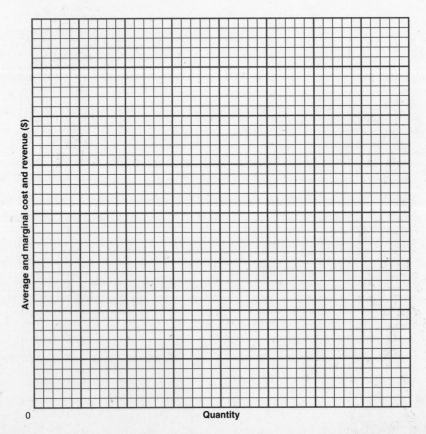

Average and marginal cost and revenue ($)

0   Quantity

b. If there are 100 firms in the industry and all have the same cost schedule,
(1) complete the market supply schedule in the following table.

Quantity demanded	Price	Quantity supplied
400	$360	_____
500	290	_____
600	230	_____
700	180	_____
800	140	_____
900	110	_____
1000	80	_____

(2) Using the demand schedule given in (1):
(*a*) What will the market price of the product be?

$_____

(*b*) What quantity will the individual firm produce?

_____

(*c*) How large will the firm's profit be?

$_____

(*d*) Will firms tend to enter or leave the industry in the long run? _____ Why? _____

_____

6. If the average total costs assumed for the individual firm in problem 4 were long-run average total costs and if the industry were a constant-cost industry,
a. what would be the market price of the product in

the long run? $_____
b. what output would each firm produce when the industry was in long-run equilibrium? _____
c. approximately how many firms would there be in the industry in the long run, given the present demand for the product as shown in the table in **5b**?

_____

d. if the following table were the market demand schedule for the product, how many firms would there

be in the long run in the industry? _____

Price	Quantity demanded
$360	500
290	600
230	700
180	800
140	900
110	1000
80	1100

7. On the following graph, draw a long-run supply curve of
a. a constant-cost industry
b. an increasing-cost industry

0

■ **SHORT ANSWER AND ESSAY QUESTIONS**

1. What are the four market models (or situations) that economists employ, and what are the major characteristics of each type of market?

2. Describe in detail four characteristics of pure competition.

3. If pure competition is so rare in practice, why are students of economics asked to study it?

4. Explain how the firm in a purely competitive industry sees the demand for the product it produces in terms of the
(a) price elasticity of demand,
(b) relationship of average to marginal revenue, and
(c) behavior of total, average, and marginal revenues as the output of the firm increases.

5. Describe the total-revenue–total-cost approach to profit maximization.

6. Compare and contrast the total-revenue–total-cost approach with the marginal-revenue–marginal-cost approach to profit maximization. Are the two approaches consistent?

7. Explain the MR = MC rule and its three characteristics.

8. Why does the purely competitive firm want to maximize total profit but not its per-unit profit?

9. Why is a firm willing to produce at a loss in the short run if the loss is no greater than the fixed costs of the firm?

10. Explain how the short-run supply of an individual firm and of the purely competitive industry are each determined.

11. What determines the equilibrium price and output of a purely competitive industry in the short run? Will economic profits in the industry be positive or negative?

12. Why do the MC = MR rule and MC = *P* rule mean the same thing under conditions of pure competition?

13. What are the important distinctions between the short run and the long run and between equilibrium in the short run and in the long run in a competitive industry?

14. When is the purely competitive industry in long-run equilibrium? What forces the purely competitive firm into this position?

15. What is a constant-cost industry? What is an increasing-cost industry? Under what economic conditions is each likely to be found? What will be the nature of the long-run supply curve in each of these industries?

16. Explain the conditions for productive efficiency in an economy.

17. Describe the conditions for allocative efficiency. Why is it said that a purely competitive economy is an efficient economy?

18. How does a purely competitive economy eliminate an overallocation for resources for the production of a product and correct for an underallocation?

19. Explain how dynamic adjustments are made in pure competition as a result of changes in demand for a product or the supply of a resource.

20. What is the relationship between the "invisible hand" of Adam Smith and efficiency in the competitive market system?

ANSWERS

Chapter 10 Pure Competition

FILL-IN QUESTIONS

1. *a.* pure competition; *b.* pure monopoly; *c.* monopolistic competition; *d.* oligopoly (any order *a–d*)
2. number, standardized, differentiated, enter
3. *a.* a large number of sellers; *b.* a standardized product; *c.* firms are price takers; *d.* free entry and exit of firms
4. taker, elastic
5. revenue, average, total, marginal
6. is constant, equal to
7. minus, equal to, break-even
8. maximum, minimum, equal to
9. variable
10. marginal, above
11. sum, short-run
12. quantity supplied, quantity supplied
13. fixed, variable
14. average, average, minimum
15. normal, economic, losses
16. an increasing-, upsloping
17. a decreasing-, downsloping
18. average, minimum
19. marginal
20. efficiency, maximizes, maximizes

TRUE–FALSE QUESTIONS

1. F, pp. 169–170	10. F, p. 173	19. T, pp. 183–185
2. T, pp. 169–170	11. T, p. 173	20. T, p. 186
3. T, pp. 169–170	12. T, p. 175	21. T, pp. 187–189
4. T, pp. 169–170	13. F, p. 175	22. T, pp. 187–189
5. F, p. 171	14. T, pp. 175–178	23. T, pp. 187–189
6. T, p. 171	15. F, pp. 175–178	24. T, pp. 187–189
7. F, pp. 171–172	16. T, pp. 175–178	25. F, p. 189
8. F, pp. 171–172	17. T, pp. 179–180	
9. T, pp. 172–174	18. F, pp. 183–185	

MULTIPLE-CHOICE QUESTIONS

1. d, pp. 169–170	11. a, pp. 174–178	21. c, pp. 183–185
2. a, pp. 169–170	12. d, pp. 174–178	22. c, pp. 183–186
3. a, pp. 169–170	13. a, pp. 174–178	23. a, pp. 185–186
4. b, pp. 169–170	14. c, pp. 174–178	24. d, pp. 186–187
5. c, p. 171	15. c, pp. 174–178	25. c, p. 186
6. c, pp. 171–172	16. b, pp. 174–178	26. a, pp. 187–189
7. b, pp. 171–172	17. c, pp. 174–178	27. a, pp. 187–189
8. b, pp. 179–180	18. d, pp. 174–178	28. b, pp. 187–189
9. b, pp. 181–182	19. c, pp. 174–178	29. d, pp. 187–189
10. b, pp. 174–178	20. c, pp. 181–182	30. a, p. 189

PROBLEMS

1. Number of firms: d, a, c, b; Type of product: e, n, f, e, or f; Control over price: m, h, g, g; Conditions of entry: i, j, k, l; Nonprice competition: m, g, h, g, or h

2. *a.* Average revenue: all are $10.00; Total revenue: $0, 10.00, 20.00, 30.00, 40.00, 50.00, 60.00; Marginal revenue: all are $10.00; *b.* yes, because price (average revenue) is constant and equal to marginal revenue; *c.* infinity; *d.* they are equal; *e.* see Figure 10.1 of the text for an example; *f.* horizontal, $10; *g.* constant, constant

3. *a.* See following table; *b.* 7, 380; *c.* see Figure 10.2 of the text for an example

	Market price = $200	
Output	Revenue	Profit
0	$ 0	$−300
1	200	−200
2	400	−50
3	600	90
4	800	210
5	1000	300
6	1200	360
7	1400	380
8	1600	350
9	1800	260
10	2000	100

4. *a.* 0, 5, 7 (last answer is the same as 3b); *b.* average total cost, output; (1) $146, ($200 − $146 = $54), ($54 × 7 = $378), (2) $140, ($120 − $140 = −$20), (−$20 × 5 = −$100); *c.* see Figure 10.3 of the text for an example

5. *a.* see following table; *b.* (1) Quantity supplied: 1000, 900, 800, 700, 600, 500, 400, (2) (a) 180, (b) 7, (c) 238, (d) enter, profits in the industry will attract them into the industry

Price	Quantity supplied	Profit
$360	10	$1700
290	9	1071
230	8	592
180	7	238
140	6	0
110	5	−150
80	4	−272
60	0	−300

6. *a.* 140; *b.* 6; *c.* 133 = 800 [the total quantity demanded at $140 divided by 6 (the output of each firm)]; *d.* 150 = 900 divided by 6

7. *a.* The curve is a horizontal line (see Figure 10.10 in the text); *b.* the curve slopes upward (see Figure 10.11 in the text)

SHORT ANSWER AND ESSAY QUESTIONS

1. pp. 169–170
2. pp. 169–170
3. p. 171
4. pp. 171–172
5. pp. 172–173
6. pp. 172–178
7. pp. 174–175
8. pp. 176–178
9. p. 177
10. pp. 179–182
11. pp. 181–182
12. pp. 179–181
13. pp. 181–184
14. pp. 183–187
15. pp. 185–186
16. pp. 187–189
17. p. 188
18. pp. 188–189
19. p. 189
20. p. 189

CHAPTER 11

Pure Monopoly

This chapter looks at the other end of the spectrum and examines pure monopoly, a market structure in which there is a **single seller**. Like pure competition, pure monopoly is rarely found in the U.S. economy, but it is still important. Many government-owned or government-regulated public utilities (electricity, water, natural gas, or cable television) are close to being pure monopolies, and other business firms are near monopolies because they have a large share of a market. Monopolies play a key role in the allocation of resources and the production of goods and services in the economy.

It is possible for a single seller or pure monopolist to dominate an industry if firms are prevented in some way from entering the industry. Factors that restrict firms from entering an industry are referred to as **barriers to entry**. The second section of this chapter is devoted to a description of the more important types of these barriers, such as economies of scale, patents and licenses, control of essential resources, and strategies for product pricing.

The chapter answers certain questions about the pure monopolist, such as what output will the firm produce, what price it will charge, and the amount of profit for the firm. In answering these questions and in comparing pure competition and pure monopoly, note the following:

1. Both the competitive and monopoly firm try to maximize profits by producing the output at which marginal cost and marginal revenue are equal (**MR = MC**).

2. The individual firm in a perfectly competitive industry sees a perfectly price elastic demand for its product at the going market price because it is but one of many firms in the industry, but the monopolist sees a market demand schedule that is less than perfectly price elastic because the **monopolist is the industry**. The purely competitive firm has *only* an output policy and is a price taker, but the monopolist is able to determine the price at which it will sell its product and is a price maker.

3. When demand is perfectly price elastic, price is equal to marginal revenue and is constant, but when demand is less than perfectly price elastic, marginal revenue is less than price and both decrease as the output of the firm increases.

4. Because entry is blocked in the long run, firms cannot enter a monopolistic industry to compete away profits as they can under conditions of pure competition.

This chapter has three other goals that deserve your study time and careful attention. One goal is to evaluate **economic efficiency** under pure monopoly. Here the purely competitive industry that you read about in Chapter 10 serves as the standard for comparison. You will learn that unlike the purely competitive industry, pure monopoly does not result in allocative efficiency. Although the inefficiencies of monopoly are offset or reduced by economies of scale and technological progress, they are reinforced by the presence of X-inefficiency and rent-seeking behavior.

The second goal is to discuss the possible pricing strategies of the pure monopolist. The monopolist may be able to set multiple prices for the same product even when the price differences are not justified by cost differences, a situation called **price discrimination**. This type of pricing power works only under certain conditions, and when it is effective it results in higher profits for the monopolist and also greater output.

The pricing power and inefficiency of the pure monopoly have made it a target for **regulation**. Therefore, the last section of the chapter explains the economic choices a regulatory agency faces when it must determine the maximum price that a public utility will be allowed to charge for its product. Here you will learn about the **socially optimum price** and the **fair-return price** and their effects on efficiency and profits. You will also discover the difficult economic dilemma regulatory officials face as they decide what prices they should permit a monopolist to charge.

■ CHECKLIST

When you have studied this chapter you should be able to

☐ Define pure monopoly based on five characteristics.
☐ Give several examples of monopoly and explain its importance.
☐ List and explain four potential barriers that would prevent or deter the entry of new firms into an industry.
☐ Define a natural monopoly using an average total-cost curve.
☐ Compare the demand curve for the pure monopolist with that of the purely competitive firm.
☐ Compute marginal revenue when you are given the demand for the monopolist's product.
☐ Explain the relationship between the price a monopolist charges and the marginal revenue from the sale of an additional unit of the product.

☐ Explain why the monopolist is a price maker.

☐ Use elasticity to explain the region of the demand curve where the monopolist produces.

☐ State the rule that explains what output the monopolist will produce and the price that will be charged.

☐ Determine the profit-maximizing output and price for the pure monopolist when you are given the demand and cost data.

☐ Explain why there is no supply curve for the pure monopolist.

☐ Counter two popular misconceptions about the price charged and the profit target in pure monopoly.

☐ Explain why monopolists can experience losses.

☐ Compare the economic effects of pure monopoly in terms of price, output, efficiency, and income distribution with a purely competitive industry producing the same product.

☐ Discuss the cost complications caused by economies of scale, X-inefficiency, rent-seeking behavior, and technological advance for pure monopoly and a purely competitive industry.

☐ Describe three general policy options for dealing with the economic inefficiency of monopoly.

☐ Define and give examples of price discrimination.

☐ List three conditions that are necessary for price discrimination.

☐ Explain the economic consequences of price discrimination.

☐ Use graphical analysis to identify the socially optimal price and the fair-return price for the regulated monopoly.

☐ Explain the dilemma of regulation based on a graphical analysis of a regulated monopoly.

■ **CHAPTER OUTLINE**

1. Pure monopoly is a market structure in which a single firm sells a product for which there are no close substitutes. These characteristics make the monopoly firm a **price maker** rather than a price taker, as was the case for the purely competitive firm. Entry into the industry is blocked, and there can be nonprice competition through advertising to influence the demand for the product.

    a. Examples of monopolies typically include regulated public utilities such as firms providing electricity, natural gas, local telephone service, and cable television, but they can also be unregulated, such as the De Beers diamond syndicate.

    b. The study of monopoly is useful for understanding the economic effects of other market structures—oligopoly and monopolistic competition—where there is some degree of monopoly power.

2. Pure monopoly can exist in the long run only if potential competitors find there are *barriers* that prevent their entry into the industry. There are four major **barriers to entry** that can prevent or severely restrict entry into an industry.

    a. *Economies of scale* can reduce production costs in the long run so that one producer can supply a range of output at a minimum total cost. If other producers

try to enter the industry, extensive financing would be required and they may not be able to produce output at a lower cost than the monopolist. The conditions for a *natural monopoly* arise in the extreme case in which the market demand curve cuts the long-run ATC curve where they are still declining. One firm can supply the market demand at a minimum cost.

    b. Government creates legal restrictions through issuing patents and licenses. *Patents* give the inventor the exclusive right to use or allow others to use the invention. *Licenses* give a firm the exclusive right to provide a good or service.

    c. The ownership or control of essential resources can effectively block entry into an industry.

    d. Pricing and other strategic practices, such as price cuts, advertising campaigns, and producing excess capacity, can deter entry into an industry by making entry very costly for a firm.

3. The **demand curve** of the pure monopolist is downsloping because the monopolist is the industry. By contrast, the purely competitive firm has a horizontal (perfectly price-elastic) demand curve because it is only one of many small firms in an industry. There are several implications of the downsloping shape of the monopolist's demand curve.

    a. The monopolist can increase sales only by lowering product price; thus price will exceed marginal revenue ($P > MR$) for every unit of output but the first.

    b. The monopolist will have a pricing policy, and is a *price maker;* the purely competitive firm has no price policy and is a price taker.

    c. The monopolist will avoid setting price in the inelastic segment of its demand curve because total revenue will be decreasing and marginal revenue will be negative; price will be set in the *elastic* portion of the demand curve.

4. The **output and price determination** of the profit-maximizing pure monopolist entails several considerations.

    a. Monopoly power in the sale of a product does not necessarily affect the prices that the monopolist pays for resources or the costs of production; an assumption is made in this chapter that the monopolist hires resources in a competitive market and uses the same technology as competitive firms.

    b. The monopolist produces that output at which marginal cost and marginal revenue are equal ($MR = MC$) and charges a price at which this profit-maximizing output can be sold.

    c. The monopolist has **no supply curve** because there is no unique relationship between price and quantity supplied; price and quantity supplied will change when demand and marginal revenue change. By contrast, a purely competitive firm has a supply curve that is the portion of the marginal cost curve above average variable cost, and there is a unique relationship between price and quantity supplied.

    d. Two popular misconceptions about monopolists are that they charge as high a price as possible and that they seek maximum profit per unit of output.

e. The monopolist is **not guaranteed a profit** and can experience losses because of weak demand for a product or high costs of production.

5. Pure monopoly has significant **economic effects** on the economy when compared to outcomes that would be produced in a purely competitive market.

a. The pure monopolist charges a *higher price* and *produces less output* than would be produced by a purely competitive industry. Pure monopoly is **not productively efficient** because price is greater than the minimum of average cost. It is **not allocatively efficient** because price is greater than marginal cost.

b. Monopoly contributes to income inequality in the economy by transferring income from consumers to stockholders who own the monopoly.

c. A pure monopolist in an industry may produce output at a lower or higher average cost than would be the case for a purely competitive industry producing the same product. The costs of production may differ between the two industries for four reasons.

(1) **Economies of scale** in the production of the product allow the pure monopolist to produce it at a lower long-run average cost than a large number of small pure competitors. In the extreme, a firm may be a **natural monopoly** that can supply the market demand at the lowest average cost. There can also be other factors such as *simultaneous consumption* and *network effects* that create extensive economies of scale for firms, especially those firms involved in information technology.

(2) If a pure monopolist is more susceptible to **X-inefficiency** than firms in a purely competitive industry, then long-run average costs at every level of output are higher than those of purely competitive firms.

(3) **Rent-seeking** expenditures in the form of legal fees, lobbying, and public-relations expenses to obtain or maintain a position as a monopoly add nothing to output, but do increase monopoly costs.

(4) Monopoly is not likely to contribute to technological advance because there is little incentive for the monopolist to produce a more advanced product. The threat of potential competition, however, may stimulate research and technological advance, but the purpose of this effort is often to restrict or block entry into the industry.

d. Monopoly causes problems for an economy because of higher prices and restricted output. Monopoly, however, is relatively rare. Technological advance and the development of substitute products can also undermine a monopoly. The policy options for dealing with the economic inefficiency of monopoly include the use of antitrust laws and the breakup of firms, the regulation of price, output, and profits of the monopolist, and simply ignoring the monopoly because its position cannot be sustained.

6. To increase profits a pure monopolist may engage in **price discrimination** by charging different prices to different buyers of the same product (when the price differences do not represent differences in the costs of producing the product).

a. To discriminate, the seller must have some monopoly power, be capable of separating buyers into groups with different price elasticities of demand, and be able to prevent the resale of the product from one group to another group.

b. Price discrimination is common in the U.S. economy. Airlines charge different fares to different passengers for the same flight. Movie theaters vary prices for the same product based on time of day or age. Discount coupons allow firms to charge different prices to different customers for the purchase of the same product.

c. There are several consequences from **perfect price discrimination,** in which the seller charges each customer the highest price he or she would be willing to pay for the product. It increases the profits, but also increases the output of the monopolist.

7. Monopolies are often **regulated** by government to reduce the misallocation of resources and control prices.

a. A price ceiling determined by the intersection of the marginal-cost and demand schedules is the **socially optimum price** and improves the allocation of resources.

b. This ceiling may force the firm to produce at a loss, and therefore government may set the ceiling at a level determined by the intersection of the average cost and demand schedules to allow the monopolist a **fair return.**

c. The dilemma of regulation is that the socially optimum price may cause losses for the monopolist, and a fair-return price may result in a less efficient allocation of resources.

■ **HINTS AND TIPS**

1. Make sure you understand **how pure monopoly differs from pure competition.** Here are key distinctions: (a) The monopolist's demand curve is downsloping, not horizontal as in pure competition; (b) the monopolist's marginal revenue is less than price (or average revenue) for each level of output except the first, whereas in pure competition marginal revenue equals price; (c) the monopoly firm is a price maker, not a price taker as in pure competition; (d) *the firm is the industry* in monopoly, but not in pure competition; (e) there is the potential for long-run economic profits in pure monopoly, but purely competitive firms will only break even in the long run; and (f) there is no supply curve for a pure monopoly, but there is one for the purely competitive firm.

2. A key similarity between a profit-maximizing pure monopolist and a purely competitive firm is that both types of firms will produce up to that output level at which marginal revenue equals marginal cost (**MR = MC**).

3. Figure 11.3 helps explain why the profit-maximizing monopolist will always want to select some price and quantity combination in the **elastic** and not in the **inelastic** portion of the demand. In the inelastic portion, total revenue declines and marginal revenue is negative.

4. Drawing the marginal revenue curve for a monopolist with a linear demand curve is easy if you remember that the marginal revenue curve will always be a straight line that intersects the quantity axis at half of the level of output as the demand curve. (See Figure 11.3.)

5. Spend extra time studying Figure 11.8 and reading the related discussion. It will help you see how *price discrimination* results in more profits, a greater output, and a higher price for some consumers and lower prices for other consumers.

■ **IMPORTANT TERMS**

pure monopoly
barrier to entry
X-inefficiency
rent-seeking behavior

price discrimination
socially optimal price
fair-return price

SELF-TEST

■ **FILL-IN QUESTIONS**

1. Pure monopoly is an industry in which a single firm is the sole producer of a product for which there are no close (substitutes, complements) _____ and into which entry in the long run is effectively (open, blocked) _____.

2. The closest example of pure monopoly would be government-regulated (nonprofit organizations, public utilities) _____ that provide water, electricity, or natural gas. There are also "near monopolies," such as private businesses that might account for (40, 80) _____% of a particular market, or businesses in a geographic region that are the (multiple, sole) _____ supplier(s) of a good or service.

3. If there are substantial economies of scale in the production of a product, a small-scale firm will find it difficult to enter into and survive in an industry because its average costs will be (greater, less) _____ than those of established firms, and a firm will find it (easy, difficult) _____ to start out on a large scale because it will be nearly impossible to acquire the needed financing.

4. Legal barriers to entry by government include granting an inventor the exclusive right to produce a product for 20 years, or a (license, patent) _____, and limiting entry into an industry or occupation through its issuing of a _____.

5. Other barriers to entry include the ownership of essential (markets, resources) _____ and

strategic changes in product (price, regulation) _____.

6. The demand schedule confronting the pure monopolist is (perfectly elastic, downsloping) _____. This means that marginal revenue is (greater, less) _____ than average revenue (or price) and that both marginal revenue and average revenue (increase, decrease) _____ as output increases.

7. When demand is price elastic, a decrease in price will (increase, decrease) _____ total revenue, but when demand is price inelastic, a decrease in price will _____ total revenue. The demand curve for the purely competitive firm is (horizontal, downsloping) _____, but it is _____ for the monopolist. The profit-maximizing monopolist will want to set price in the price (elastic, inelastic) _____ portion of its demand curve.

8. The supply curve for a purely competitive firm is the portion of the (average-variable-cost, marginal-cost) _____ curve that lies above the _____ curve. The supply curve for the monopolist (is the same, does not exist) _____.

9. When the economic profit of a monopolist is at a maximum, (marginal, average) _____ revenue equals _____ cost and price is (greater, less) _____ than marginal cost.

10. Two common misconceptions about pure monopoly are that it charges the (lowest, highest) _____ price possible and seeks the maximum (normal, per-unit) _____ profit.

11. The pure monopolist (is, is not) _____ guaranteed an economic profit; in fact, the pure monopolist can experience economic losses in the (short run, long run) _____ because of (strong, weak) _____ demand for the monopoly product.

12. The monopolist will typically charge a (lower, higher) _____ price and produce (less, more) _____ output and is (less, more) _____ efficient than if the product was produced in a purely competitive industry.
a. The monopolist is inefficient *productively* because the average (variable, total) _____ cost of producing a product is not at a (maximum, minimum) _____.

b. It is inefficient *allocatively* because (marginal revenue, price) _____ is not equal to (marginal, total) _____ cost.
c. Monopolies seem to result in a greater inequality in the distribution of income because the owners of monopolies are largely in the (upper, lower) _____ income groups.

13. Resources can be said to be more efficiently allocated by pure competition than by pure monopoly only if the purely competitive firms and the monopoly have the same (costs, revenues) _____, and they will not be the same if the monopolist
a. by virtue of being a large firm enjoys (economies, diseconomies) _____ of scale not available to a pure competitor;
b. is more susceptible to X-(efficiency, inefficiency) _____ than pure competitors;
c. may need to make (liability, rent-seeking) _____ expenditures to obtain or maintain monopoly privileges granted by government; and,
d. reduces costs through adopting (higher prices, new technology) _____.

14. The incidence of pure monopoly is relatively (rare, common) _____ because eventually new developments in technology (strengthen, weaken) _____ monopoly power or (substitute, complementary) _____ products are developed.

15. Three general policy options to reduce the economic (losses, inefficiency) _____ of a monopoly are to file charges against it through (liability, antitrust) _____ laws, have government regulate it if it is a (conglomerate, natural monopoly) _____, or ignore it if it is unsustainable.

16. Price discrimination occurs whenever a product is sold at different (markets, prices) _____, and these differences are not equal to the differences in the (revenue from, cost of) _____ producing the product.

17. Price discrimination is possible when the following three conditions exist:
a. _____
b. _____
c. _____

18. The two economic consequences of a monopolist's use of price discrimination are (an increase, a decrease) _____ in profits and _____ in the output.

19. If the monopolist were regulated and a socially optimal price for the product were sought, the price would be set equal to (marginal, average total) _____ cost. Such a legal price would achieve (productive, allocative) _____ efficiency but might result in losses for the monopolist.

20. If a regulated monopolist is allowed to earn a fair return, the ceiling price for the product would be set equal to (marginal, average total) _____ cost. Such a legal price falls short of (allocative, productive) _____ efficiency.

■ **TRUE–FALSE QUESTIONS**

Circle T if the statement is true, F if it is false.

1. The pure monopolist produces a product for which there are no close substitutes. **T F**

2. The weaker the barriers to entry into an industry, the more competition there will be in the industry, other things equal. **T F**

3. In pure monopoly, there are strong barriers to entry. **T F**

4. A monopolist may create an entry barrier by price cutting or substantially increasing the advertising of its product. **T F**

5. The monopolist can increase the sales of its product if it charges a lower price. **T F**

6. As a monopolist increases its output, it finds that its total revenue at first decreases, and that after some output level is reached, its total revenue begins to increase. **T F**

7. A purely competitive firm is a price taker but a monopolist is a price maker. **T F**

8. A monopolist will avoid setting a price in the *inelastic* segment of the demand curve and prefer to set the price in the *elastic* segment. **T F**

9. The monopolist determines the profit-maximizing output by producing that output at which marginal cost and marginal revenue are equal and sets the product price equal to marginal cost and marginal revenue at that output. **T F**

10. The supply curve for a monopolist is the upsloping portion of the marginal cost curve that lies above the average variable cost. **T F**

11. A monopolist will charge the highest price it can get. **T F**

12. A monopolist seeks maximum total profits, not maximum unit profits. **T F**

13. Pure monopoly guarantees economic profits. **T F**

14. Resources are misallocated by monopoly because price is not equal to marginal cost. **T F**

15. One of the economic effects of monopoly is less income inequality. **T F**

16. When there are substantial economies of scale in the production of a product, the monopolist may charge a price that is lower than the price that would prevail if the product were produced by a purely competitive industry. **T F**

17. The purely competitive firm is more likely to be affected by X-inefficiency than a monopolist. **T F**

18. Rent-seeking expenditures that monopolists make to obtain or maintain monopoly privilege have no effect on the firm's costs. **T F**

19. The general view of economists is that a pure monopoly is efficient because it has strong incentives to be technologically progressive. **T F**

20. One general policy option for a monopoly that creates substantial economic inefficiency and is long lasting is to directly regulate its prices and operation. **T F**

21. Price discrimination occurs when a given product is sold at more than one price and these price differences are not justified by cost differences. **T F**

22. A discriminating monopolist will produce a larger output than a nondiscriminating monopolist. **T F**

23. The regulated utility is likely to make an economic profit when price is set to achieve the most efficient allocation of resources ($P = MC$). **T F**

24. A fair-return price for a regulated utility would have price set to equal average total cost. **T F**

25. The dilemma of monopoly regulation is that the production by a monopolist of an output that causes no misallocation of resources may force the monopolist to suffer an economic loss. **T F**

■ MULTIPLE-CHOICE QUESTIONS

Circle the letter that corresponds to the best answer.

1. Which would be defining characteristics of pure monopoly?
   (a) The firm does no advertising and it sells a standardized product.
   (b) No close substitutes for the product exist and there is one seller.
   (c) The firm can easily enter into or exit from the industry and profits are guaranteed.
   (d) The firm holds a patent and is technologically progressive.

2. A barrier to entry that significantly contributes to the establishment of a monopoly would be
   (a) economies of scale
   (b) price-taking behavior
   (c) technological progress
   (d) X-inefficiency

3. The demand curve for the pure monopolist is
   (a) perfectly price elastic
   (b) perfectly price inelastic
   (c) downsloping
   (d) upsloping

4. Which is true with respect to the demand data confronting a monopolist?
   (a) Marginal revenue is greater than average revenue.
   (b) Marginal revenue decreases as average revenue decreases.
   (c) Demand is perfectly price elastic.
   (d) Average revenue (or price) increases as the output of the firm increases.

5. When the monopolist is maximizing total profits or minimizing losses,
   (a) total revenue is greater than total cost
   (b) average revenue is greater than average total cost
   (c) average revenue is greater than marginal cost
   (d) average total cost is less than marginal cost

6. At which combination of price and marginal revenue is the price elasticity of demand less than 1?
   (a) Price equals $102, marginal revenue equals $42.
   (b) Price equals $92, marginal revenue equals $22.
   (c) Price equals $82, marginal revenue equals $2.
   (d) Price equals $72, marginal revenue equals −$18.

7. The region of demand in which the monopolist will choose a price-output combination will be the
   (a) elastic one because total revenue will increase as price declines and output increases
   (b) inelastic one because total revenue will increase as price declines and output increases
   (c) elastic one because total revenue will decrease as price declines and output increases
   (d) inelastic one because total revenue will decrease as price declines and output increases

8. At present output a monopolist determines that its marginal cost is $18 and its marginal revenue is $21. The monopolist will maximize profits or minimize losses by
   (a) increasing price while keeping output constant
   (b) decreasing price and increasing output
   (c) decreasing both price and output
   (d) increasing both price and output

Answer Questions 9, 10, 11, and 12 based on the demand and cost data for a pure monopolist given in the following table.

Output	Price	Total cost
0	$1000	$ 500
1	600	520
2	500	580
3	400	700
4	300	1000
5	200	1500

9. How many units of output will the profit-maximizing monopolist produce?
   (a) 1
   (b) 2
   (c) 3
   (d) 4

10. The profit-maximizing monopolist would set its price at
(a) $120
(b) $200
(c) $233
(d) $400

11. If the monopolist could sell each unit of the product at the maximum price the buyer of that unit would be willing to pay for it, and if the monopolist sold 4 units, total revenue would be
(a) $1200
(b) $1800
(c) $2000
(d) $2800

12. If the monopolist were forced to produce the socially optimal output by the imposition of a ceiling price, the ceiling price would have to be
(a) $200
(b) $300
(c) $400
(d) $500

13. The supply curve for a pure monopolist
(a) is the portion of the marginal cost curve that lies above the average variable cost curve
(b) is perfectly price elastic at the market price
(c) is upsloping
(d) does not exist

14. The analysis of monopoly indicates that the monopolist
(a) will charge the highest price it can get
(b) will seek to maximize total profits
(c) is guaranteed an economic profit
(d) is only interested in normal profit

15. When compared with the purely competitive industry with identical costs of production, a monopolist will charge a
(a) higher price and produce more output
(b) lower price and produce more output
(c) lower price and produce less output
(d) higher price and produce less output

16. At an equilibrium level of output, a monopolist is *not* productively efficient because
(a) the average total cost of producing the product is not at a minimum
(b) the marginal cost of producing the last unit is equal to its price
(c) it is earning a profit
(d) average revenue is less than the cost of producing an extra unit of output

17. Which will tend to increase the inefficiencies of the monopoly producer?
(a) price-taking behavior
(b) rent-seeking behavior
(c) economies of scale
(d) technological progress

18. Which is one of the conditions that must be realized before a seller finds that price discrimination is workable?
(a) The demand for the product is perfectly elastic.
(b) The seller must be able to segment the market.

(c) The buyer must be able to resell the product.
(d) The product must be a service.

19. If a monopolist engages in price discrimination rather than charging all buyers the same price, its
(a) profits and its output are greater
(b) profits and its output are smaller
(c) profits are greater and its output is smaller
(d) profits are smaller and its output is greater

Answer Questions 20, 21, 22, and 23 based on the demand and cost data for a pure monopolist given in the following table.

Quantity demanded	Price	Total cost
0	$700	$ 300
1	650	400
2	600	450
3	550	510
4	500	590
5	450	700
6	400	840
7	350	1020
8	300	1250
9	250	1540
10	200	1900

20. The profit-maximizing output and price for this monopolist would be
(a) 5 units and a $450 price
(b) 6 units and a $400 price
(c) 7 units and a $350 price
(d) 8 units and a $300 price

In answering Questions 21, 22, and 23, assume this monopolist is able to engage in price discrimination and sell each unit of the product at a price equal to the maximum price the buyer of that unit would be willing to pay.

21. The marginal revenue that the price-discriminating monopolist obtains from the sale of an additional unit is equal to
(a) total revenue
(b) average cost
(c) unit cost
(d) price

22. The profit-maximizing output for the price-discriminating monopolist would be
(a) 6 units
(b) 7 units
(c) 8 units
(d) 9 units

23. How much greater would the total economic profits be for the discriminating monopolist than the non-discriminating monopolist?
(a) $720
(b) $830
(c) $990
(d) $1070

Question 24 is based on the following graph.

24. The price and output combination for the unregulated profit-maximizing monopoly compared with the socially optimal price and output combination for the regulated monopoly would be, respectively,

(a) P_4 and Q_1 versus P_3 and Q_2
(b) P_4 and Q_1 versus P_2 and Q_3
(c) P_3 and Q_2 versus P_4 and Q_1
(d) P_2 and Q_3 versus P_3 and Q_2

25. A monopolist who is limited by the imposition of a ceiling price to a fair return sells the product at a price equal to

(a) average total cost
(b) average variable cost
(c) marginal cost
(d) average fixed cost

■ PROBLEMS

1. The demand schedule for the product produced by a monopolist is given in the following table.

Quantity demanded	Price	Total revenue	Marginal revenue	Price elasticity
0	$700	$____		
1	650	____	$____	____
2	600	____	____	____
3	550	____	____	____
4	500	____	____	____
5	450	____	____	____
6	400	____	____	____
7	350	____	____	____
8	300	____	____	____
9	250	____	____	____
10	200	____	____	____
11	150	____	____	____
12	100	____	____	____
13	50	____	____	____
14	0	____	____	____

a. Complete the table by computing total revenue, marginal revenue, and the price elasticity of demand (use midpoints formula).
b. The relationships in the table indicate that
(1) total revenue rises from $0 to a maximum of

$_____ as price falls from $700 to

$_____, and as price falls to $0, total revenue falls from its maximum to $_____;
(2) the relationship between price and total revenue suggests that demand is price (elastic, inelastic)

_____ when quantity demanded is between 0 and 7 units of output, but that demand is

price (elastic, inelastic) _____ when quantity demanded is between 8 units and 14 units;
(3) when demand is price elastic and total revenue rises from $0 to a maximum, marginal revenue is

(negative, positive) _____, but when demand is price inelastic and total revenue falls from

its maximum, marginal revenue is _____.
c. Use the data in the previous table and the graph on page 137 to plot and graph the demand curve and the marginal revenue curve for the monopolist. Indicate the portion of the demand curve that is price elastic and the portion that is price inelastic.

2. The following table shows demand and cost data for a pure monopolist.

Quantity	Price	Total revenue	Marginal revenue	Total cost	Marginal cost
0	$17	$____		$10	
1	16	____	$____	18	$____
2	15	____	____	23	____
3	14	____	____	25	____
4	13	____	____	27	____
5	12	____	____	28	____
6	11	____	____	32	____
7	10	____	____	40	____
8	9	____	____	50	____
9	8	____	____	64	____
10	7	____	____	80	____

a. Complete the table by filling in the columns for total revenue, marginal revenue, and marginal cost.
b. Answer the next three questions using the data you calculated in the table.

(1) What output will the monopolist produce? _____

(2) What price will the monopolist charge? _____
(3) What total profit will the monopolist receive at the

profit-maximizing level of output? _____

3. Now assume that the pure monopolist in problem 2 is able to engage in price discrimination and sell each unit of the product at a price equal to the maximum price the buyer of that unit of the product would be willing to pay.

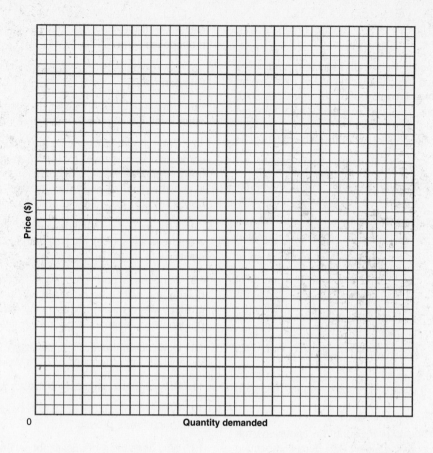

a. Complete the following table by computing total revenue and marginal revenue.

Quantity	Price	Total revenue	Marginal revenue	Total cost	Marginal cost
0	$17	$_____		$10	
1	16	_____	$_____	18	$_____
2	15	_____	_____	23	_____
3	14	_____	_____	25	_____
4	13	_____	_____	27	_____
5	12	_____	_____	28	_____
6	11	_____	_____	32	_____
7	10	_____	_____	40	_____
8	9	_____	_____	50	_____
9	8	_____	_____	64	_____
10	7	_____	_____	80	_____

b. From the table it can be seen that
(1) the marginal revenue that the discriminating monopolist obtains from the sale of an additional unit

is equal to the _____;
(2) using the same table of costs, the discriminating

monopolist would produce _____ units of the product, charge the buyer of the last unit of

product produced a price of $_____, and

obtain a total economic profit of $_____;
(3) If the pure monopolist is able to engage in price discrimination its profits will be (larger, smaller, the

same) _____ and it will produce an out-

put that is (larger, smaller, the same)_____.

4. In the following table are cost and demand data for a pure monopolist.

Quantity demanded	Price	Marginal revenue	Average cost	Marginal cost
0	$17.50			
1	16.00	$16.00	$24.00	$24.00
2	14.50	13.00	15.00	6.00
3	13.00	10.00	11.67	5.00
4	11.50	7.00	10.50	7.00
5	10.00	4.00	10.00	8.00
6	8.50	1.00	9.75	8.50
7	7.00	−2.00	9.64	9.00
8	5.50	−5.00	9.34	9.25
9	4.00	−8.00	9.36	9.50

a. An unregulated monopolist would produce _____

units of this product, sell it at a price of $_____,

and receive a total profit of $_____.
b. If this monopolist were regulated and the maximum price it could charge were set equal to marginal cost,

it would produce _____ units of a product,

sell it at a price of $_____, and receive a

total profit of $_____. Such regulation

would either _____ the firm or require that

the regulating government _____ the firm.

c. If the monopolist were not regulated and were allowed to engage in price discrimination by charging the maximum price it could obtain for each unit sold, it would produce 6 units (because the marginal revenue from the 6th unit and the marginal cost of the 6th unit would both be $8.50). Its total revenue would

be $_____, its total costs would be

$_____, and its total profit would be

$_____.

d. If the monopolist were regulated and allowed to charge a fair-return price, it would produce

_____ units of product, charge a price of

$_____, and receive a profit of

$_____.

e. From which situation—**a, b,** or **d**—does the most efficient allocation of resources result?

_____ From which situation does the least

efficient allocation result? _____ In practice, government would probably select situation

_____.

5. Identify whether the following long-run conditions apply to a firm under pure monopoly (**M**), pure competition (**C**), or both. Put the appropriate letter(s) (**M** or **C**) next to the condition.

a. There is the potential for long-run profits because price is greater than or equal to average total cost.

_____

b. The firm's demand curve is perfectly elastic.

_____

c. The firm maximizes profits at the output level where

MC = MR. _____

d. The firm exhibits productive efficiency because price is equal to the minimum average total cost.

_____

e. Price is greater than marginal revenue for each

output level except the first. _____

f. There is an optimal allocation of resources because

price is equal to marginal cost. _____

■ **SHORT ANSWER AND ESSAY QUESTIONS**

1. What is pure monopoly? Define its characteristics.

2. Give examples of monopoly. How might a professional sports team be considered a monopoly when there are other such teams in the nation?

3. Why are the economies of scale a barrier to entry?

4. Why are most natural monopolies also public utilities? What does government hope to achieve by granting exclusive franchises to and regulating such natural monopolies?

5. How do patents and licenses create barriers to entry? Cite examples.

6. How can the monopolist use changes in price and other strategic actions to maintain a monopoly position?

7. Compare the pure monopolist and the individual pure competitor with respect to: (a) the demand schedule; (b) the marginal-revenue schedule; (c) the relationship between marginal revenue and average revenue; (d) price policy, and (e) the ability to administer (or set) price.

8. Explain why marginal revenue is always less than average revenue (price) when demand is less than perfectly elastic.

9. Suppose a pure monopolist discovered it was producing and selling an output at which the demand for its product was inelastic. Explain why a decrease in its output would increase its economic profits.

10. How does the profit-maximizing monopolist determine what output to produce? What price will it charge?

11. Why is there no supply curve for a monopoly?

12. Why does the monopolist not charge the highest possible price for its product?

13. Why does the monopolist not set the price for its product in such a way that average profit is a maximum?

14. Why are some monopolies unprofitable? Explain what will happen to the firm in the short run and the long run in this situation.

15. In what sense is resource allocation and production more efficient under conditions of pure competition than under monopoly conditions?

16. How do monopolies allegedly affect the distribution of income in the economy and why do monopolies seemingly have this effect on income distribution in the U.S. economy?

17. What are some reasons why costs might differ between a monopoly and purely competitive firms operating in the same industry? Give at least four possible reasons.

18. Explain how economies of scale offset some of the economic inefficiencies of a monopoly. Evaluate the importance of this factor in reducing a monopolist's cost.

19. What is X-inefficiency? How does it affect the cost of production for the monopolist?

20. A monopolist will often engage in rent-seeking behavior. Explain what this means and how it changes a monopolist's cost.

21. Evaluate this statement from an economic perspective: "A pure monopoly has great incentive to discover and use new technology."

22. What is meant by price discrimination? What conditions must be realized before it is workable?

23. Explain how a monopolist who perfectly discriminates would determine what price to charge for each unit of the product sold (or to charge each group of buyers).

24. How does price discrimination affect the profits and the output of the monopolist? How does it affect consumers?

25. Explain what public utility regulatory agencies attempt to do to eliminate the misallocation of resources that results from monopoly. Describe the dilemma of regulation for these agencies, and explain why a fair-return policy only reduces but does not eliminate misallocation.

ANSWERS

Chapter 11   Pure Monopoly

FILL-IN QUESTIONS

1. substitutes, blocked
2. public utilities, 80, sole
3. greater, difficult
4. patent, license
5. resources, price
6. downsloping, less, decrease
7. increase, decrease, horizontal, downsloping, elastic
8. marginal-cost, average-variable-cost, does not exist
9. marginal, marginal, greater
10. highest, per-unit
11. is not, short run, weak
12. higher, less, less; *a.* total, minimum; *b.* price, marginal; *c.* upper
13. costs; *a.* economies; *b.* inefficiency; *c.* rent-seeking; *d.* new technology
14. rare, weaken, substitute
15. inefficiency, antitrust, natural monopoly
16. prices, cost of
17. *a.* the seller has some monopoly power; *b.* the seller is able to separate buyers into groups that have different elasticities of demand for the product; *c.* the original buyers cannot resell the product
18. an increase, an increase
19. marginal, allocative
20. average total, allocative

TRUE–FALSE QUESTIONS

1. T, p. 194	10. F, pp. 201–202	19. F, p. 206
2. T, p. 195	11. F, p. 202	20. T, p. 207
3. T, p. 195	12. T, p. 202	21. T, p. 208
4. T, p. 197	13. F, pp. 202–203	22. T, p. 209
5. T, pp. 197–199	14. T, pp. 203–204	23. F, pp. 210–211
6. F, pp. 197–199	15. F, p. 204	24. T, p. 211
7. T, p. 199	16. T, pp. 204–205	25. T, p. 211
8. T, pp. 199–200	17. F, pp. 205–206	
9. F, pp. 200–201	18. F, p. 206	

MULTIPLE-CHOICE QUESTIONS

1. b, p. 194	10. d, pp. 200–202	19. a, p. 209
2. a, pp. 195–196	11. b, p. 209	20. b, pp. 200–202
3. c, pp. 197–198	12. b, pp. 210–211	21. d, p. 209
4. b, pp. 197–199	13. d, pp. 201–202	22. c, p. 209
5. c, pp. 200–202	14. b, p. 202	23. c, p. 209
6. d, pp. 199–200	15. d, pp. 203–204	24. b, pp. 210–211
7. a, pp. 199–200	16. a, pp. 203–204	25. a, pp. 210–211
8. b, pp. 200–202	17. b, p. 206	
9. c, pp. 200–202	18. b, p. 208	

PROBLEMS

1. *a.* Total revenue: $0, 650, 1200, 1650, 2000, 2250, 2400, 2450, 2400, 2250, 2000, 1650, 1200, 650, 0; Marginal revenue: $650, 550, 450, 350, 250, 150, 50, −50, −150, −250, −350, −450, −550, −650; Price elasticity: 27, 8.33, 4.60, 3.00, 2.11, 1.55, 1.15, .87, .65, .47, .33, .22, .12, .04; *b.* (1) $2450, $350, 0, (2) elastic, inelastic, (3) positive, negative; *c.* see Figure 11.3a in the text as an example

2. *a.* Total revenue: $0, 16, 30, 42, 52, 60, 66, 70, 72, 72, 70; Marginal revenue: $16, 14, 12, 10, 8, 6, 4, 2, 0, −2; Marginal cost: $8, 5, 2, 2, 1, 4, 8, 10, 14, 16; *b.* (1) 6, (2) $11, (3) $34 (TR of $66 minus TC of $32)

3. *a.* Total revenue: $0, 16, 31, 45, 58, 70, 81, 91, 100, 108, 115; Marginal revenue: $16, 15, 14, 13, 12, 11, 10, 9 , 8 , 7; Marginal cost: $8, 5, 2, 2, 1, 4, 8, 10, 14, 16; *b.* (1) price, (2), 7, 10, 51 (TR of $91 minus TC of $40), (3) larger, larger

4. *a.* 4, 11.50, 4.00; *b.* 6, 8.50, −7.50, bankrupt, subsidize; *c.* 73.50, 58.50, 15.00; *d.* 5, 10.00, zero; *e.* b or c, a, d

5. *a.* M; *b.* C; *c.* C, M; *d.* C; *e.* M; *f.* C

SHORT ANSWER AND ESSAY QUESTIONS

1. pp. 194–195	10. pp. 200–202	19. pp. 205–206
2. p. 195	11. p. 201	20. p. 206
3. pp. 195–196	12. p. 202	21. p. 206
4. pp. 195–196	13. p. 202	22. pp. 207–208
5. pp. 196–197	14. pp. 202–203	23. p. 209
6. p. 197	15. pp. 203–204	24. p. 209
7. pp. 197–198	16. p. 204	25. pp. 209–211
8. pp. 197–198	17. pp. 204–206	
9. pp. 199–200	18. pp. 204–205	

CHAPTER 12

Monopolistic Competition and Oligopoly

This chapter examines two market structures, monopolistic competition and oligopoly, that fall between the extremes of pure competition and pure monopoly. Both structures are important because they offer descriptions of firms and industries typically found in the U.S. economy.

Monopolistically competitive firms are prevalent because most retail establishments, such as clothing stores and restaurants, fall into the monopolistically competitive category. In such industries, there are a relatively large number of firms, so no one has a large market share, they sell differentiated products, and each has limited pricing power.

The chapter focuses on the **demand curve** for the monopolistically competitive firm. This demand curve differs from those found in pure competition and pure monopoly. As the individual firm changes the character of its product, or changes product promotion, both the costs of the firm and the demand for its product will change.

The **price-output** analysis of the monopolistic competitor is relatively simple. In the short run, this analysis is identical with the analysis of the price-output decision of a pure monopolist. Only in the long run does the competitive element make itself apparent: The entry of firms forces the price a firm charges to fall. This price, however, is not equal either to minimum average cost or to marginal cost; consequently, monopolistic competition can be said to be less efficient than pure competition.

This chapter also discusses **product variety** under monopolistic competition. A part of the competitive effort of individual firms is devoted to product differentiation, product development, and advertising. Each firm has three things to manipulate—price, product, and advertising—in maximizing profits. Although monopolistic competition has been characterized as inefficient, some of the positive benefits of product variety may offset some of the inefficiencies of this market structure.

The concept of **oligopoly** is fairly easy to grasp: a few firms that are mutually interdependent and that dominate the market for a product. The underlying causes of oligopoly are economies of scale and barriers to entry, subjects you read about earlier. Economists use **concentration ratios** and the **Herfindahl index** to measure the degree of firm dominance of an industry, but these processes have shortcomings.

More difficult to grasp is oligopoly behavior. **Game theory** helps explain *what is meant* by mutual interdependence and *why it exists* in an oligopoly. It also explains why specific conclusions cannot be drawn about the price and output decisions of individual firms. Oligopolists are loath to engage in price competition because of **mutual interdependence,** and frequently resort to **collusion** to set prices and sometimes use nonprice competition to determine market share. Collusion, however, does not give firms complete protection from competition because there are incentives to cheat on collusive agreements.

There is no standard model of oligopoly because of the diversity of markets and the uncertainty caused by mutual interdependence among firms. **Three oligopoly models,** however, cover the range of most market situations. The **kinked-demand curve** explains why, in the absence of collusion, oligopolists will not raise or lower their prices even when their costs change. This model does not explain what price oligopolists will set; it only explains why prices will be relatively inflexible.

The second model examines how oligopolists resort to **collusion** to set price. The collusion can be **overt,** as in a cartel agreement, or the collusion can be **covert,** as in a secret agreement. The OPEC oil cartel is a classic example of covert collusion. Obstacles, such as cheating on price, make collusive agreements difficult to establish and maintain.

The third model of oligopoly is **price leadership.** In some industries a dominant firm serves as the *price leader* for other firms. There is no overt collusion, only tacit understandings about price and competition among firms. This model explains why there are infrequent price changes, why the lead firm makes price and output announcements for other firms to follow, and why low pricing is used to prevent new entry. Such covert collusion, however, can be undermined by price wars.

The next-to-last section of the chapter looks at **advertising** in oligopoly. Product development and advertising are often the means of competition in oligopoly. Drawing conclusions about the effects of advertising, however, is difficult. Reasonable arguments can be made that advertising is both beneficial and costly for consumers and about whether advertising helps or hurts economic efficiency.

Compared with pure competition, oligopoly does not result in allocative or productive efficiency. Nevertheless, the qualifications noted at the end of the chapter may offset some of oligopoly's shortcomings.

■ **CHECKLIST**

When you have studied this chapter you should be able to

☐ Describe monopolistic competition in terms of the number of sellers, type of product, entry and exit conditions, and advertising.

☐ Cite three consequences from having relatively large numbers of sellers in monopolistic competition.

☐ Describe five aspects of differentiated products in monopolistic competition.

☐ Describe the entry and exit conditions in monopolistic competition.

☐ State the role of advertising and nonprice competition in monopolistic competition.

☐ Compare the firm's demand curve under monopolistic competition with a firm's demand curves in pure competition and pure monopoly.

☐ Determine the output of and the price charged by a monopolistic competitor in the short run when given cost and demand data.

☐ Explain why the price charged by a monopolistic competitor will in the long run tend to equal average cost and result in only a normal profit.

☐ Cite two real-world complications that may affect the outcome for monopolistically competitive firms in the long run.

☐ Show graphically how the typical firm in monopolistic competition achieves neither productive nor allocative efficiency and how excess capacity occurs.

☐ Discuss the effects of product variety in monopolistic competition.

☐ Explain why monopolistic competition is more complex in practice.

☐ Define oligopoly in terms of the number of producers, type of product, control over price, and interdependence.

☐ Explain how entry barriers and mergers contribute to the existence of oligopolies.

☐ Define a concentration ratio and cite its shortcomings.

☐ Use the Herfindahl index to assess the distribution of market power among dominant firms in an oligopoly.

☐ Use game theory to explain three characteristics of oligopoly behavior.

☐ Cite two reasons why there is no standard model of oligopoly.

☐ Use the kinked-demand theory to explain the tendency for prices to be inflexible in a noncollusive model oligopoly.

☐ Describe the price and output conditions for a cartel or collusive pricing model of oligopoly.

☐ Give real examples of overt and covert collusion.

☐ State six obstacles to collusion.

☐ Describe the price leadership model of oligopoly and its outcomes.

☐ Explain why advertising is often heavily used in oligopoly.

☐ Cite the potential positive and negative effects of advertising.

☐ Compare economic efficiency in oligopoly to other market structures.

■ **CHAPTER OUTLINE**

1. *Monopolistic competition* has several defining characteristics.

   a. The *relatively large number of sellers* means that each has a small market share, there is no collusion, and firms take actions that are independent of each other.

   b. Monopolistic competition exhibits **product differentiation.** This differentiation occurs through: differences in attributes or features of products; services to customers; location and accessibility; brand names and packaging; and some control over price.

   c. *Entry* into the industry or *exit* is relatively easy.

   d. There is **nonprice competition** in the form of product differentiation and advertising.

   e. Monopolistically competitive firms are common, and examples include clothing stores, restaurants, and grocery stores.

2. Given the products produced in a monopolistically competitive industry and the amounts of promotional activity, it is possible to analyze the **price and output decisions** of a firm.

   a. The **demand curve** confronting each firm will be highly but not perfectly price elastic because each firm has many competitors who produce close but not perfect substitutes for the product it produces.

   (1) Comparing the demand curve for the monopolistic competitor to other market structures suggests that it is not perfectly elastic, as is the case with the pure competitor, but it is also more elastic than the demand curve of the pure monopolist.

   (2) The degree of elasticity, however, for each monopolistic competitor will depend on the number of rivals and the extent of product differentiation.

   b. In the **short run** the individual firm will produce the output at which marginal cost and marginal revenue are equal and charge the price at which the output can be sold; either economic profits or losses may result in the short run.

   c. In the **long run** the entry and exodus of firms will tend to change the demand for the product of the individual firm in such a way that economic profits are eliminated and there are only normal profits. (Price and average costs are made equal to each other.)

3. Monopolistic competition among firms producing a given product and engaged in a given amount of promotional activity results in **less economic efficiency and more excess capacity** than does pure competition.

   a. The average cost of each firm is equal in the long run to its price. The industry **does not realize allocative efficiency** because output is smaller than the output at which marginal cost and price are equal. The industry **does not realize productive efficiency** because the output is less than the output at which average cost is a minimum.

   b. **Excess capacity** results because firms produce less output than at the minimum of average total cost. In monopolistic competition, many firms operate below optimal capacity.

4. Each monopolistically competitive firm attempts to differentiate its product and advertise it to increase the firm's profit. These activities give rise to **nonprice competition** among firms.

a. The benefit of product variety is that firms offer consumers a wide range of types, styles, brands, and quality variants of a product. Products can also be improved. The expanded range of consumer choice from product differentiation and improvement may offset some of the economic inefficiency (excess capacity problem) of monopolistic competition.

b. Monopolistic competition is more complex than the simple model presented in the chapter because the firm must constantly juggle three factors—price, product characteristics, and advertising—in seeking to maximize profits.

5. **Oligopoly** is frequently encountered in the U.S. economy.

a. It is composed of a few firms that dominate an industry.

b. It may produce homogeneous or differentiated products.

c. Firms have control over price, and thus are price makers. **Mutual interdependence** exists because firms must consider the reaction of rivals to any change in price, output, product characteristic, or advertising.

d. Barriers to entry, such as economies of scale or ownership, control over raw materials, patents, and pricing strategies, can explain the existence of oligopoly.

e. Some industries have become oligopolistic not from internal growth but from external factors such as mergers.

f. The concentration in an industry among a few large producers can be measured in several ways.

(1) A **concentration ratio** gives the percentage of an industry's total sales provided by the largest firms. If the four largest firms account for 40 percent or more of the industry output, the industry is considered oligopolistic. Shortcomings of this measure include the imprecise definition of the market area and failure to take into account interindustry competition or import competition.

(2) The **Herfindahl index** measures concentration more accurately because it accounts for the market share of each firm. It is the sum of the squared percentage market shares of all firms in the industry.

6. Insight into the pricing behavior of oligopolists can be gained by thinking of the oligopoly as a game of strategy. This **game theory** approach leads to three conclusions.

a. Firms in an oligopolistic industry are mutually interdependent and must consider the actions of rivals when they make price decisions.

b. Oligopoly often leads to overt or covert collusion among the firms to fix prices or to coordinate pricing because competition among oligopolists results in low prices and profits; collusion helps maintain higher prices and profits.

c. Collusion creates incentives to cheat among oligopolists by lowering prices or increasing production to obtain more profit.

7. Economic analysis of oligopoly is difficult because of the diversity among the firms and complications resulting from mutual interdependence. Nevertheless, two important characteristics of oligopoly are inflexible prices and simultaneous price changes by firms. An analysis of three oligopoly models helps explain the pricing practices of oligopolists.

a. In the **kinked-demand model** there is no collusion. Each firm believes that if it lowers its price its rivals will lower their prices, but if it raises its price its rivals *will not* increase their prices. Therefore the firm is reluctant to change its price for fear of reducing its profits. The model has two shortcomings: it does not explain how the going price gets set; prices are not as rigid as the model implies.

b. Mutual interdependence indicates there is *collusion* among oligopoly firms to maintain or increase profits.

(1) Firms that collude tend to set their prices and joint output at the same level a pure monopolist would set them.

(2) **Collusion may be overt,** as in a cartel agreement. The OPEC cartel is an example of effective overt collusion.

(3) **Collusion may be covert** whereby agreements or tacit understandings between firms set price or market share. Examples of such collusion have included bid rigging on milk prices for schools or fixing worldwide prices for a livestock feed additive.

(4) At least six obstacles make it difficult for firms to collude or maintain collusive arrangements: difference in demand and cost among firms, the number of firms in the arrangement, incentives to cheat, changing economic conditions, potential for entry by other firms, and legal restrictions and penalties.

c. **Price leadership** is a form of covert collusion in which one firm initiates price changes and the other firms in the industry follow the lead. Three price leadership tactics have been observed.

(1) Price adjustments tend to be made infrequently, only when cost and demand conditions change to a significant degree.

(2) The price leader announces the price change in various ways, through speeches, announcements, or other such activities.

(3) The price set may not maximize short-run profits for the industry, especially if the industry wants to prevent entry by other firms.

(4) Price leadership can break down and result in a price war. Eventually the wars end, and a price leader reemerges.

8. Oligopolistic firms often avoid price competition but engage in **product development and advertising** for two reasons: Price cuts are easily duplicated, but nonprice competition is more unique; and firms have more financial resources for advertising and product development.

a. The potential positive effects of advertising include providing low-cost information to consumers that reduces search time and monopoly power, thus enhancing economic efficiency.

b. The potential negative effects of advertising include manipulating consumers to pay higher prices, serving as a barrier to entry into an industry, and offsetting campaigns that raise product costs and prices.

9. The *efficiency of oligopoly* is difficult to evaluate.

a. Many economists think that oligopoly price and output characteristics are similar to those of monopoly. Oligopoly firms set output where price exceeds marginal cost and the minimum of average total cost. Oligopoly is allocatively inefficient ($P > MC$) and productively inefficient ($P > $ minimum ATC).

b. This view must be qualified because of increased foreign competition to oligopolistic firms, the use of limit pricing that sets prices at less than the profit-maximizing price, and the technological advances arising from this market structure.

■ **HINTS AND TIPS**

1. Review the four basic market models in Table 10.1 so that you see how monopolistic competition and oligopoly compare with the other market models on five characteristics.

2. The same **MC = MR** rule for maximizing profits or minimizing losses for the firm from previous chapters is now used to determine output and price in monopolistic competition and in certain oligopoly models. If you understood how the rule applied under pure competition and pure monopoly, you should have no trouble applying it here.

3. Make sure you know how to interpret Figure 12.1 because it is an important graph. It illustrates why a representative firm in monopolistic competition just breaks even in the long run, and earns just a normal rather than an economic profit. It also shows how economic inefficiency in monopolistic competition produces excess capacity.

4. Where is the kink in the kinked-demand model? To find out, practice drawing the model. Then use Figure 12.4 to check your answer. Explain to yourself what each line means in the graph.

5. Price and output determinations under collusive oligopoly or a cartel are essentially the same as those for pure monopoly.

■ **IMPORTANT TERMS**

monopolistic competition
product differentiation
nonprice competition
excess capacity

oligopoly
homogeneous oligopoly
differentiated oligopoly
strategic behavior

mutual interdependence
concentration ratio
interindustry competition
import competition
Herfindahl index
game-theory model

collusion
kinked-demand curve
price war
cartel
tacit understandings
price leadership

SELF-TEST

■ **FILL-IN QUESTIONS**

1. In a monopolistically competitive market, there are a relatively (large, small) _____ number of producers who sell (standardized, differentiated) _____ products. Entry into such a market is relatively (difficult, easy) _____. The number of firms means that each one has a (large, small) _____ market share, the firms (do, do not) _____ collude, and they operate in (an independent, a dependent) _____ manner.

2. Identify the different aspects of production differentiation in monopolistic competition:

a. _____
b. _____
c. _____
d. _____
e. _____

3. In the *short run* for a monopolistically competitive firm,
a. the demand curve will be (more, less) _____ elastic than that facing a monopolist and _____ elastic than that facing a pure competitor;
b. the elasticity of this demand curve will depend on
(1) _____ and
(2) _____; and
c. it will produce the output level where marginal cost is (less than, equal to, greater than) _____ marginal revenue.

4. In the long run for a monopolistically competitive industry,
a. the *entry* of new firms will (increase, decrease) _____ the demand for the product produced by each firm in the industry and _____ the elasticity of that demand.
b. the price charged by the individual firm will tend to equal (average, marginal) _____ cost, its economic profits will tend to be (positive, zero)

_____, and its average cost will be (greater, less) _____ than the minimum average cost of producing and promoting the product.

5. Although representative firms in monopolistic competition tend to earn (economic, normal) _____ profits in the long run, there can be complications that may result in firms earning _____ profits in the long run. Some firms may achieve a degree of product differentiation that (can, cannot) _____ be duplicated by other firms. There may be (collusion, barriers to entry) _____ that prevent penetration of the market by other firms.

6. In monopolistic competition, price is (less than, equal to, greater than) _____ marginal cost, and so the market structure (does, does not) _____ yield allocative efficiency. Also, average total cost is (less than, equal to, greater than) _____ the minimum of average total cost, and so the market structure (does, does not) _____ result in (allocative, productive) _____ efficiency.

7. In the long run, the monopolistic competitor tries to earn economic profits by using (price, nonprice) _____ competition in the form of product differentiation and advertising. This results in a tradeoff between a choice of more consumer goods and services and (more, less) _____ economic efficiency.

8. The more complex model of monopolistic competition suggests that in seeking to maximize profits, each firm juggles the factors of (losses, price) _____, changes in (collusion, product) _____, and decisions about (controls, advertising) _____ until the firm feels no further change in the variables will result in greater profit.

9. In an oligopoly (many, a few) _____ large firms produce either a differentiated or a (heterogeneous, homogeneous) _____ product, and entry into such an industry is (easy, difficult) _____. The oligopolistic firm is a price (maker, taker) _____ and there is mutual (independence, interdependence) _____ among firms in an industry. The existence of oligopoly can be explained by (exit, entry) _____ barriers and by (markets, mergers) _____.

10. The percentage of the total industry sales accounted for by the top four firms in an industry is known as a four-firm (Herfindahl index, concentration ratio) _____, whereas summing the squared percentage market shares of each firm in the industry is the way to calculate the _____.

11. The basics of the pricing behavior of oligopolists can be understood from a (game, advertising) _____ theory perspective. Oligopoly consists of a few firms that are mutually (funded, interdependent) _____. This means that when setting the price of its product, each producer (does, does not) _____ consider the reaction of its rivals. The monopolist (does, does not) _____ face this problem because it has no rivals, and the pure competitor, or monopolistic competitor, _____ face the problem because it has many rivals.

12. It is difficult to use formal economic analysis to explain the prices and outputs of oligopolists because oligopoly encompasses (diverse, similar) _____ market situation(s), and when firms are mutually interdependent, each firm is (certain, uncertain) _____ about how its rivals will react when it changes the price of its product. Despite the analytical problems, oligopoly prices tend to be (flexible, inflexible) _____ and oligopolists tend to change their prices (independently, together) _____.

13. The noncolluding oligopolist has a kinked-demand curve that

a. is highly (elastic, inelastic) _____ at prices above the current or going price and tends to be only slightly _____ or (elastic, inelastic) _____ below that price.
b. is drawn on the assumption that if the oligopolist raises its price its rivals (will, will not) _____ raise their prices or if it lowers its price its rivals _____ lower their prices.
c. has an associated marginal-(cost, revenue) _____ curve with a gap, such that small changes in the marginal-_____ curve do not change the price the oligopolist will charge.

14. A situation in which firms in an industry reach an agreement to fix prices, divide up the market, or otherwise restrict competition among them is called (concentration, collusion) _____. In this case, the prices they set and their combined output tend to be the same as that found with pure (competition, monopoly) _____.

15. A formal written agreement among sellers in which the price and the total output of the product and each seller's share of the market are specified is a (cartel, duopoly) _____. It is a form of (covert, overt) _____ collusion, whereas tacit understandings among firms to divide up a market would be _____ collusion.

16. Six obstacles to collusion among oligopolists are

a. _____

b. _____

c. _____

d. _____

e. _____

f. _____

17. When one firm in an oligopoly is almost always the first to change its price and the other firms change their prices after the first firm has changed its price, the oligopoly model is called the (price war, price leadership) _____ model. The tactics of this model include (infrequent, frequent) _____ price changes, announcements of such price changes, and (limit, no limit) _____ pricing. One event that can undermine this practice is (price leadership, price wars) _____.

18. There tends to be very little (price, nonprice) _____ competition among oligopolists and a great deal of _____ competition such as product development and advertising used to determine each firm's share of the market.

a. The positive view of advertising contends that it is (efficient, inefficient) _____ because it provides important information that (increases, reduces) _____ search costs, and information about competing goods _____ monopoly power.

b. The negative view of advertising suggests that it is (inefficient, efficient) _____ because the advertising campaigns are (offsetting, reinforcing) _____, the creation of brand loyalty serves as a barrier to (entry, exit) _____, and consumers are persuaded to pay (lower, higher) _____ prices than they would have paid otherwise.

19. Although it is difficult to evaluate the economic efficiency of oligopoly, when comparisons are made to pure competition, the conclusion drawn is that oligopoly (is, is not) _____ allocatively efficient and (is, is not) _____ productively efficient. The price and output behavior of the oligopolist is more likely to be

similar to that found under (competition, monopoly) _____.

20. The view that oligopoly is inefficient in the short run needs to be qualified because of the effects of (decreased, increased) _____ foreign competition that make pricing more competitive, policies to restrict entry into an industry that keep consumer prices (high, low) _____, and profits that are used to fund (more, less) _____ research and development that produces improved products.

■ **TRUE–FALSE QUESTIONS**

Circle T if the statement is true, F if it is false.

1. Monopolistic competitors have no control over the price of their products. **T F**

2. The firm's reputation for servicing or exchanging its product is a form of product differentiation under monopolistic competition. **T F**

3. Entry is relatively easy in pure competition, but there are significant barriers to entry in monopolistic competition. **T F**

4. The smaller the number of firms in an industry and the greater the extent of product differentiation, the greater will be the elasticity of the individual seller's demand curve. **T F**

5. The demand curve of the monopolistic competitor is likely to be less elastic than the demand curve of the pure monopolist. **T F**

6. In the short run, firms that are monopolistically competitive may earn economic profits or incur losses. **T F**

7. The long-run equilibrium position in monopolistic competition would be where price is equal to marginal cost. **T F**

8. Representative firms in a monopolistically competitive market earn economic profits in the long run. **T F**

9. One reason why monopolistic competition is economically inefficient is that the average cost of producing the product is greater than the minimum average cost at which the product could be produced. **T F**

10. The more product variety offered to consumers by a monopolistically competitive industry, the less excess capacity there will be in that industry. **T F**

11. Successful product improvement by one firm has little or no effect on other firms under monopolistic competition. **T F**

12. The products produced by the firms in an oligopolistic industry may be either homogeneous or differentiated. **T F**

13. Oligopolistic industries contain a few large firms that act independently of one another. **T F**

14. Concentration ratios include adjustments for interindustry competition in measuring concentration in an industry. **T F**

15. The Herfindahl index is the sum of the market shares of all firms in the industry. **T F**

16. Game theory analysis of oligopolist behavior suggests that oligopolists will not find any benefit in collusion. **T F**

17. One shortcoming of kinked-demand analysis is that it does not explain how the going oligopoly price was established in the first place. **T F**

18. Collusion occurs when firms in an industry reach an overt or covert agreement to fix prices, divide or share the market, and in some way restrict competition among the firms. **T F**

19. A cartel is usually a written agreement among firms which sets the price of the product and determines each firm's share of the market. **T F**

20. Secret price concessions and other forms of cheating will strengthen collusion. **T F**

21. The practice of price leadership is almost always based on a formal written or oral agreement. **T F**

22. Limit pricing is the leadership tactic of limiting price increases to a certain percentage of the basic price of a product. **T F**

23. Those contending that advertising contributes to monopoly power argue that the advertising by established firms creates barriers to the entry of new firms into an industry. **T F**

24. Oligopolies are allocatively and productively efficient when compared with the standard set in pure competition. **T F**

25. Increased competition from foreign firms in oligopolistic industries has stimulated more competitive pricing in those industries. **T F**

■ **MULTIPLE-CHOICE QUESTIONS**

Circle the letter that corresponds to the best answer.

1. Which would be most characteristic of monopolistic competition?
  (a) collusion among firms
  (b) firms selling a homogeneous product
  (c) a relatively large number of firms
  (d) difficult entry into and exit from the industry

2. The concern that monopolistically competitive firms express about product attributes, services to customers, or brand names are aspects of
  (a) allocative efficiency in the industry
  (b) collusion in the industry
  (c) product differentiation
  (d) concentration ratios

3. The demand curve a monopolistically competitive firm faces is

(a) perfectly elastic
(b) perfectly inelastic
(c) highly, but not perfectly inelastic
(d) highly, but not perfectly elastic

4. In the short run, a typical monopolistically competitive firm will earn
  (a) only a normal profit
  (b) only an economic profit
  (c) only an economic or normal profit
  (d) an economic or normal profit or suffer an economic loss

5. A monopolistically competitive firm is producing at an output level in the short run where average total cost is $3.50, price is $3.00, marginal revenue is $1.50, and marginal cost is $1.50. This firm is operating
  (a) with an economic loss in the short run
  (b) with an economic profit in the short run
  (c) at the break-even level of output in the short run
  (d) at an inefficient level of output in the short run

6. If firms enter a monopolistically competitive industry, we would expect the typical firm's demand curve to
  (a) increase and the firm's price to increase
  (b) decrease and the firm's price to decrease
  (c) remain the same but the firm's price to increase
  (d) remain the same and the firm's price to remain the same

Answer Questions 7, 8, 9, and 10 on the basis of the following diagram for a monopolistically competitive firm in short-run equilibrium.

7. The firm's profit-maximizing price will be
  (a) $9
  (b) $12
  (c) $15
  (d) $18

8. The equilibrium output for this firm will be
  (a) 50
  (b) 85
  (c) 115
  (d) 135

9. This firm will realize an economic profit of
  (a) $510

(b) $765

(c) $1021

(d) $1170

10. If firms enter this industry in the long run,

(a) demand will decrease

(b) demand will increase

(c) the marginal revenue curve will shift upward

(d) economic profits will increase

11. Given a representative firm in a typical monopolistically competitive industry, in the long run

(a) the firm will produce that output at which marginal cost and price are equal

(b) the elasticity of demand for the firm's product will be less than it was in the short run

(c) the number of competitors the firm faces will be greater than it was in the short run

(d) the economic profits being earned by the firm will tend to equal zero

12. *Productive* efficiency is not realized in monopolistic competition because production occurs where

(a) MR is greater than MC

(b) MR is less than MC

(c) ATC is greater than minimum ATC

(d) ATC is less than MR and greater than MC

13. The *underallocation* of resources in monopolistic competition means that at the profit-maximizing level of output, price is

(a) greater than MC

(b) less than MC

(c) less than MR

(d) greater than minimum ATC

14. Excess capacity occurs in a monopolistically competitive industry because firms

(a) advertise and promote their product

(b) charge a price that is less than marginal cost

(c) produce at an output level short of the least-cost output

(d) have a perfectly elastic demand for the products that they produce

15. Were a monopolistically competitive industry in long-run equilibrium, a firm in that industry might be able to increase its economic profits by

(a) increasing the price of its product

(b) increasing the amounts it spends to advertise its product

(c) decreasing the price of its product

(d) decreasing the output of its product

16. Which would be most characteristic of oligopoly?

(a) easy entry into the industry

(b) a few large producers

(c) product standardization

(d) no control over price

17. Mutual interdependence means that

(a) each firm produces a product similar but not identical to the products produced by its rivals

(b) each firm produces a product identical to the products produced by its rivals

(c) each firm must consider the reactions of its rivals when it determines its price policy

(d) each firm faces a perfectly elastic demand for its product

18. One major problem with concentration ratios is that they fail to take into account

(a) the national market for products

(b) competition from imported products

(c) excess capacity in production

(d) mutual interdependence

19. Industry A is composed of four large firms that hold market shares of 40, 30, 20, and 10. The Herfindahl index for this industry is

(a) 100

(b) 1000

(c) 3000

(d) 4500

Questions 20, 21, and 22 are based on the following payoff matrix for a duopoly in which the numbers indicate the profit in thousands of dollars for a high-price or a low-price strategy.

		Firm A Strategy	
		High price	Low price
Firm B Strategy	**High price**	A = $425 B = $425	A = $525 B = $275
	Low price	A = $275 B = $525	A = $300 B = $300

20. If both firms collude to maximize joint profits, the total profits for the two firms will be

(a) $400,000

(b) $800,000

(c) $850,000

(d) $950,000

21. Assume that Firm B adopts a low-price strategy while Firm A maintains a high-price strategy. Compared to the results from a high-price strategy for both firms, Firm B will now

(a) lose $150,000 in profit and Firm A will gain $150,000 in profit

(b) gain $100,000 in profit and Firm A will lose $150,000 in profit

(c) gain $150,000 in profit and Firm A will lose $100,000 in profit

(d) gain $525,000 in profit and Firm A will lose $275,000 in profit

22. If both firms operate independently and do not collude, the most likely profit is

(a) $300,000 for Firm A and $300,000 for Firm B

(b) $525,000 for Firm A and $275,000 for Firm B

(c) $275,000 for Firm A and $525,000 for Firm B

(d) $425,000 for Firm A and $425,000 for Firm B

23. If an individual oligopolist's demand curve is kinked, it is necessarily

(a) perfectly elastic at the going price

(b) less elastic above the going price than below it

(c) more elastic above the going price than below it

(d) of unitary elasticity at the going price

Use the following diagram to answer Question 24.

24. The profit-maximizing price and output for this oligopolistic firm is

(a) P_5 and Q_2

(b) P_4 and Q_2

(c) P_3 and Q_3

(d) P_2 and Q_4

25. What is the situation called whenever firms in an industry reach an agreement to fix prices, divide up the market, or otherwise restrict competition?

(a) interindustry competition

(b) incentive to cheat

(c) price leadership

(d) collusion

26. When oligopolists collude the results are generally

(a) greater output and higher price

(b) greater output and lower price

(c) smaller output and lower price

(d) smaller output and higher price

27. To be successful, collusion requires that oligopolists be able to

(a) keep prices and profits as low as possible

(b) block or restrict the entry of new producers

(c) reduce legal obstacles that protect market power

(d) keep the domestic economy from experiencing high inflation

28. Which is a typical tactic that has been used by the price leader in the price leadership model of oligopoly?

(a) limit pricing

(b) frequent price changes

(c) starting a price war with competitors

(d) giving no announcement of a price change

29. Market shares in oligopoly are typically determined on the basis of

(a) product development and advertising

(b) covert collusion and cartels

(c) tacit understandings

(d) joint profit maximization

30. Many economists think that relative to pure competition, oligopoly is

(a) allocatively efficient, but not productively efficient

(b) productively efficient, but not allocatively efficient

(c) both allocatively and productively efficient

(d) neither allocatively nor productively efficient

■ **PROBLEMS**

1. Assume that the short-run cost and demand data given in the following table confront a monopolistic competitor selling a given product and engaged in a given amount of product promotion.

Output	Total cost	Marginal cost	Quantity demanded	Price	Marginal revenue
0	$ 50		0	$120	
1	80	$_____	1	110	$_____
2	90	_____	2	100	_____
3	110	_____	3	90	_____
4	140	_____	4	80	_____
5	180	_____	5	70	_____
6	230	_____	6	60	_____
7	290	_____	7	50	_____
8	360	_____	8	40	_____
9	440	_____	9	30	_____
10	530	_____	10	20	_____

a. Compute the marginal cost and marginal revenue of each unit of output and enter these figures in the table.

b. In the short run the firm will (1) produce _____ units of output, (2) sell its output at a price of $_____, and (3) have a total economic profit of $_____.

c. In the long run, (1) the demand for the firm's product will _____, (2) until the price of the product equals _____, and (3) the total economic profits of the firm are _____.

2. Match the descriptions to the six graphs on page 294. Indicate on each graph the area of economic profit or loss or state if the firm is just making normal profits.

a. a purely competitive firm earning economic profits in the short run   Graph _____

b. a purely competitive firm in long-run equilibrium   Graph _____

c. a natural monopoly   Graph _____

d. a monopolistically competitive firm earning economic profits in the short run   Graph _____

e. a monopolistically competitive firm experiencing economic losses in the short run   Graph _____

f. a monopolistically competitive firm in long-run equilibrium   Graph _____

1

2

3

4

5

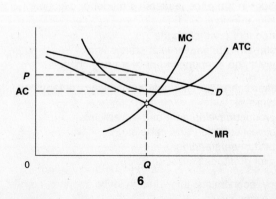

6

3. Consider the following payoff matrix in which the numbers indicate the profit in millions of dollars for a duopoly based on either a high-price or a low-price strategy.

		Firm X Strategy	
		High price	Low price
Firm Y Strategy	High price	X = $200 Y = $200	X = $250 Y = $ 50
	Low price	X = $ 50 Y = $250	X = $ 50 Y = $ 50

a. Situation 1: Each firm chooses a high-price strategy. **Result:** Each firm will earn $_____ million in profit for a total of $_____ million for the two firms.

b. Situation 2: Firm X chooses a low-price strategy while Firm Y maintains a high-price strategy. **Result:**

Firm X will earn $_____ million and Firm Y will earn

$_____ million. Compared to Situation 1, Firm X has an incentive to cut prices because it will earn

$_____ million more in profit and Firm Y will earn

$_____ million less in profit. Together, the firms will

earn $_____ million in profit, which is $_____ million less than in Situation 1.

c. Situation 3: Firm Y chooses a low-price strategy while Firm X maintains a high-price strategy. **Result:** Compared to Situation 1, Firm Y has an incentive

to cut prices because it will earn $_____ million and

Firm X will earn $_____. Compared to Situation 1,

Firm Y will earn $_____ million more in profit and Firm

X will earn $_____ million less in profit. Together,

the firms will earn $_____ million in profit, which is

$_____ less than in Situation 1.

d. Situation 4: Each firm chooses a low-price

strategy. **Result:** Each firm will earn $_____ million

in profit for a total of $_____ million for the two firms.

This total is $_____ less than in Situation 1.

e. Conclusions:

(1) The two firms have a strong incentive to collude and adopt the high-price strategy because there is the

potential for $_____ million more in profit for the two firms than with a low-price strategy (Situation 4), or

the potential for $_____ million more for the two firms than with a mixed-price strategy (Situations 2 or 3).

(2) There is also a strong incentive for each firm to cheat on the agreement and adopt a low-price strategy when the other firm maintains a high-price strategy because this situation will produce

$_____ million more in profit for the cheating firm compared to its honoring a collusive agreement for a high-price strategy.

4. The kinked-demand schedule which an oligopolist believes confronts the firm is presented in the following table.
a. Compute the oligopolist's total revenue at each of the nine prices and enter these figures in the table.
b. Also compute marginal revenue *for each unit* between the nine prices and enter these figures in the table.

Price	Quantity demanded	Total revenue	Marginal revenue per unit
$2.90	100	$_____	
2.80	200	_____	$_____
2.70	300	_____	_____
2.60	400	_____	_____
2.50	500	_____	_____
2.40	525	_____	_____
2.30	550	_____	_____
2.20	575	_____	_____
2.10	600	_____	_____

c. What is the current, or going, price for the oligopolist's product? $_____ How much is it selling? _____

d. On the graph at the top on page 152, plot the oligopolist's demand curve and marginal-revenue curve. Connect the demand points and the marginal-revenue points with as straight a line as possible. (Be sure to plot the marginal-revenue figures at the average of the two quantities involved, that is, at 150, 250, 350, 450, 512.5, 537.5, 562.5, and 587.5.)

e. Assume that the marginal-cost schedule of the oligopolist is given in columns 1 and 2 of the following table. Plot the marginal-cost curve on the graph on which demand and marginal revenue were plotted.

(1) Output	(2) MC	(3) MC′	(4) MC″
150	$1.40	$1.90	$.40
250	1.30	1.80	.30
350	1.40	1.90	.40
450	1.50	2.00	.50
512.5	1.60	2.10	.60
537.5	1.70	2.20	.70
562.5	1.80	2.30	.80
587.5	1.90	2.40	.90

(1) Given demand and marginal cost, what price should the oligopolist charge to maximize profits?

$_____ How many units of product will it

sell at this price? _____
(2) If the marginal-cost schedule changed from that shown in columns 1 and 2 to that shown in columns 1 and 3, what price should it charge?

$_____ What level of output will it pro-

duce? _____ How have profits changed

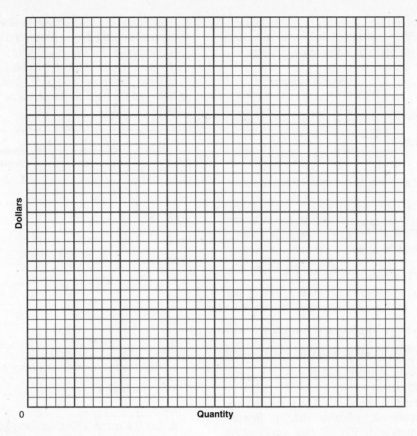

as a result of the change in costs? _____
Plot the new marginal-cost curve on the graph.

(3) If the marginal-cost curve schedule changed from that shown in columns 1 and 2 to that shown in columns 1 and 4, what price should it charge?

$_____ What level of output will it

produce? _____ How have pro-
fits changed as a result of the change in costs?

_____ Plot the new marginal-cost curve
on the graph.

5. An oligopoly producing a homogeneous product is composed of three firms. Assume that these three firms have identical cost schedules. Assume also that if any one of these firms sets a price for the product, the other two

firms charge the same price. As long as the firms all charge the same price they will share the market equally, and the quantity demanded of each will be the same.

Following is the total-cost schedule of one of these firms and the demand schedule that confronts it when the other firms charge the same price as this firm.

a. Complete the marginal-cost and marginal-revenue schedules facing the firm.

b. What price would this firm set if it wished to maximize its profits? $ _____

c. How much would
(1) it sell at this price? _____
(2) its profits be at this price? $ _____

d. What would be the industry's
(1) total output at this price? _____
(2) joint profits at this price? $ _____

Output	Total cost	Marginal cost	Price	Quantity demanded	Marginal revenue
0	$ 0		$140	0	
1	30	$____	130	1	$____
2	50	____	120	2	____
3	80	____	110	3	____
4	120	____	100	4	____
5	170	____	90	5	____
6	230	____	80	6	____
7	300	____	70	7	____
8	380	____	60	8	____

e. Is there any other price this firm can set, assuming that the other two firms charge the same price, that would result in a greater joint profit for them?

_____ If so, what is that price?

$_____

f. If these three firms colluded in order to maximize their joint profit, what price would they charge?

$_____

■ **SHORT ANSWER AND ESSAY QUESTIONS**

1. What are the three characteristics of monopolistic competition?

2. What is meant by product differentiation? By what methods can products be differentiated?

3. How does product differentiation affect the kind of competition and the degree of monopoly in monopolistic competition?

4. Describe the elasticity of the demand curve faced by a monopolistically competitive firm in the short run.

5. Assume that the firm is producing a given product and is engaged in a given amount of promotional activity. What two factors determine how elastic the demand curve will be for a monopolistic competitor?

6. At what level of output will the monopolistic competitor produce in the short run? What price will it charge for its product? Draw a graph to help explain your answer.

7. What determines whether a monopolistically competitive firm will earn economic profits or suffer economic losses in the short run?

8. What will be the level of economic profit that the monopolistic competitor will tend to receive in the long run? What forces economic profits toward this level? Why is this just a *tendency*?

9. What are two complications that would explain why the representative firm may not earn only a normal profit in the long run and may earn economic profits?

10. Use the concepts of allocative and productive efficiency to explain excess capacity and the level of prices under monopolistic competition.

11. Describe the methods, other than price cutting, that a monopolistic competitor can use to protect and increase its economic profits in the long run.

12. Explain how product variety and improvement may offset the economic inefficiency associated with monopolistic competition.

13. What are the essential characteristics of an oligopoly? How does oligopoly differ from pure competition, pure monopoly, and monopolistic competition?

14. Explain how the concentration ratio in a particular industry is computed. What is the relationship between this ratio and fewness? What are the shortcomings of the concentration ratio as a measure of the extent of competition in an industry?

15. What is the Herfindahl index? How can it be used to correct problems with concentration ratios?

16. How can game theory be used to explain strategic behavior under oligopoly? What do mutual interdependence and collusion mean with respect to oligopoly?

17. Why is it difficult to use one standard model to explain the prices charged by and the outputs of oligopolists?

18. How can the kinked-demand curve be used to explain why oligopoly prices are relatively inflexible?

19. Suppose a few firms produce a homogeneous product, have identical cost curves, and charge the same price (act as a cartel). Compare the results in terms of price, combined output, and joint profits with those from a pure monopoly producing the same market output.

20. Why do oligopolists find it advantageous to collude? What are the obstacles to collusion?

21. What is the price leadership model, and what leadership tactics do oligopolistic firms use?

22. Why do oligopolists engage in little price competition and in extensive product development and advertising?

23. How is it possible for consumers to get a lower price on a product with advertising than they would in its absence?

24. Explain how the advertising efforts of firms may be offsetting and lead to higher prices for consumers.

25. Evaluate the economic efficiency of the oligopoly market structure. What qualifications should be noted for the evaluation?

ANSWERS

Chapter 12 Monopolistic Competition and Oligopoly

FILL-IN QUESTIONS

1. large, differentiated, easy, small, do not, an independent
2. *a.* product attributes; *b.* services; *c.* location; *d.* brand names and packaging; *e.* some control over price
3. *a.* more, less; *b.* (1) number of rivals the firm has, (2) the degree of product differentiation; *c.* equal to
4. *a.* decrease, increase; *b.* average, zero, greater
5. normal, economic, cannot, barriers to entry
6. greater than, does not, greater than, does not, productive
7. nonprice, more
8. price, product, advertising
9. a few, homogeneous, difficult, maker, interdependence, entry, mergers
10. concentration ratio, Herfindahl index
11. game, interdependent, does, does not, does not
12. diverse, uncertain, inflexible, together
13. *a.* elastic, elastic, inelastic; *b.* will not, will; *c.* revenue, cost
14. collusion, monopoly
15. cartel, overt, covert

16. *a.* demand and cost differences; *b.* a large number of firms; *c.* cheating (secret price cutting); *d.* a recession; *e.* potential entry; *f.* legal obstacles (antitrust laws) (any order for *a–f*)
17. price leadership, infrequent, limit, price wars
18. price, nonprice; *a.* efficient, reduces, reduces; *b.* inefficient, offsetting, entry, higher
19. is not, is not, monopoly
20. increased, low, more

TRUE–FALSE QUESTIONS

1. F, p. 217
2. T, p. 217
3. F, p. 217
4. F, pp. 218–219
5. F, pp. 218–219
6. T, p. 220
7. F, p. 220
8. F, p. 220
9. T, pp. 220–221
10. F, pp. 220–221
11. F, p. 222
12. T, p. 223
13. F, p. 223
14. F, pp. 224–225
15. F, p. 225
16. F, pp. 225–227
17. T, p. 230
18. T, pp. 230–231
19. T, p. 231
20. F, p. 232
21. F, pp. 232–233
22. F, p. 233
23. T, pp. 234–235
24. F, p. 235
25. T, p. 235

MULTIPLE-CHOICE QUESTIONS

1. c, p. 216
2. c, p. 217
3. d, pp. 218–219
4. d, pp. 219–220
5. a, pp. 219–220
6. b, pp. 219–220
7. d, pp. 219–220
8. b, pp. 219–220
9. a, pp. 219–220
10. a, pp. 219–220
11. d, pp. 219–220
12. c, p. 221
13. a, p. 221
14. c, pp. 221–222
15. b, p. 222
16. b, p. 223
17. c, p. 223
18. b, pp. 224–225
19. c, p. 225
20. c, pp. 225–227
21. b, pp. 225–227
22. a, pp. 225–227
23. c, pp. 227–228
24. b, pp. 227–228
25. d, pp. 230–231
26. d, pp. 230–231
27. b, p. 232
28. a, pp. 232–233
29. a, pp. 233–234
30. d, p. 235

PROBLEMS

1. *a.* Marginal cost: $30, 10, 20, 30, 40, 50, 60, 70, 80, 90; Marginal revenue: $110, 90, 70, 50, 30, 10, −10, −30, −50, −70; *b.* (1) 4, (2) $80, (3) $180; *c.* (1) decrease, (2) average cost, (3) equal to zero
2. *a.* 2; *b.* 5; *c.* 4; *d.* 6; *e.* 3; *f.* 1
3. *a.* 200, 400; *b.* 250, 50, 50, 150, 300, 100; *c.* 250, 50, 50, 150, 300, 100; *d.* 50, 100, 300; *e.* (1) 300, 100, (2) 50
4. *a.* Total revenue: 290, 560, 810, 1040, 1250, 1260, 1265, 1265, 1260; *b.* Marginal revenue: 2.70, 2.50, 2.30, 2.10, 0.40, 0.20, 0, −0.20; *c.* 2.50, 500; *d.* graph; *e.* (1) 2.50, 500, (2) 2.50, 500, they have decreased, (3) 2.50, 500, they have increased
5. *a.* Marginal cost: $30, 20, 30, 40, 50, 60, 70, 80; Marginal revenue: $130, 110, 90, 70, 50, 30, 10, −10; *b.* $90; *c.* (1) 5, (2) $280; *d.* (1) 15, (2) $840; *e.* no; *f.* $90

SHORT ANSWER AND ESSAY QUESTIONS

1. pp. 216–217
2. p. 217
3. p. 217
4. pp. 218–220
5. pp. 218–220
6. pp. 219–220
7. pp. 219–220
8. pp. 219–220
9. p. 220
10. pp. 220–221
11. p. 222
12. p. 222
13. pp. 223–224
14. pp. 224–225
15. p. 225
16. pp. 225–227
17. p. 227
18. pp. 227–229
19. pp. 230–231
20. pp. 230–232
21. pp. 232–233
22. pp. 233–234
23. p. 234
24. pp. 234–235
25. p. 235

CHAPTER 13

Technology, R&D, and Efficiency

A market economy is not static but subject to change over time. One dynamic force affecting an economy and industries is *technological advance.* This advance occurs over a very long time and allows firms to introduce new products and adopt new methods of production.

The chapter begins by discussing the three-step process that constitutes technological advance: *invention, innovation,* and *diffusion.* Here the text describes many real-world examples of how technological change has affected firms and industries. You will also find out that research and development (R&D) expenditures by firms and government play an integral role in directly supporting this technological advance. The traditional view of economists was that technological advance was something external to the economy, but most contemporary economists think that technological advance is integral to capitalism and arises from intense rivalry among firms.

Entrepreneurs and other innovators play a major role in encouraging innovation and technological change. Entrepreneurs typically form small companies—*start-ups*—to create and introduce new products and production techniques. In this activity entrepreneurs assume personal financial risk, but if they are successful, they can be highly rewarded in the marketplace. There are also innovators within existing firms who can use R&D work to develop new products. University and government research can also contribute output that can be useful for fostering technological advance.

A major section of this chapter analyzes how the firm determines the *optimal amount of R&D spending.* The decision is made by equating marginal benefit with marginal cost. The marginal cost is measured by the interest-rate cost of funds that the firm borrows or obtains from other sources to finance its R&D expenditures. The expected rate of return from the last dollar spent on R&D is the measure of marginal benefit. You should remember that the outcomes from R&D spending are only expected, not guaranteed for the firm.

Technological changes can increase a firm's profit in two ways. Recall that profit is simply the difference between total revenue and total cost. *Product innovation* can increase revenues because people buy more products from the innovative firm. These increased revenues will increase profits, assuming that costs stay the same. *Process innovation* can also increase profits by reducing costs. This type of innovation leads to better methods for producing a product and decreases the average total cost for the firm.

One problem with technological advance is that it encourages *imitation.* Successful innovative firms are often emulated by others. This imitation problem can be especially threatening to innovative, smaller firms because the dominant firms in the industry can challenge them. A firm, however, has some advantages in taking the lead in innovation because there are protections and rewards. Legal protections include patents, copyrights, and trademarks; other advantages are early brand-name recognition or the potential for a profitable buyout.

You spent the past three chapters learning about the differences in the four market structures. Now you may be wondering whether one market structure is better suited than another for encouraging technological progress. The answer is clearly mixed because each structure has its strengths and shortcomings. The *inverted-U theory* gives you an even better framework for figuring out the optimal industry structure for R&D.

The chapter ends by returning to the issue of *economic efficiency,* a topic discussed throughout the text. Technological advance has a double benefit because it enhances both productive efficiency and allocative efficiency. Productive efficiency increases from process innovation that reduces production costs. Allocative efficiency increases because product innovation gives consumers more choice and gives society a more desired mix of products. The efficiency results are not automatic, and the outcome may depend on whether innovation strengthens or weakens monopoly power.

■ CHECKLIST

When you have studied this chapter you should be able to

☐ Define technological advance.
☐ Describe each of the three steps in technological advance.
☐ Explain the role of research and development (R&D) in technological advance.
☐ Contrast the traditional with the modern view of technological advance.
☐ Distinguish between entrepreneurs and other innovators and between start-ups and innovation in existing firms.
☐ Explain how innovators are rewarded for anticipating the future.
☐ Describe the role that universities and government play in fostering technological advance.

☐ Identify five means for financing R&D that are available to firms.

☐ Describe and give a rationale for the interest-rate cost-of-funds curve and the expected-rate-of-return curve.

☐ Show graphically with an example how the optimal level of R&D expenditures is determined.

☐ State three important points from the analysis of optimal R&D expenditures.

☐ Explain how product innovation can increase profits by increasing revenues.

☐ Describe how process innovation can increase profits by reducing costs.

☐ Explain the imitation problem for firms.

☐ Identify six protections for or advantages to being the first to develop a new product or process.

☐ Evaluate which of the four market structures is best suited to technological advance.

☐ Explain the inverted-U theory and its implications for technological progress.

☐ Describe how technological advance enhances both productive and allocative efficiency.

☐ Explain how innovation may lead to creative destruction and describe the criticisms of this view.

■ **CHAPTER OUTLINE**

1. **Technological advance** involves the development of new and improved products and new and improved ways of producing and distributing the products. It is a three-step process of invention, innovation, and diffusion.

   a. **Invention** is the most basic part of technological advance and involves the discovery of a product or process. Governments encourage invention by granting the inventor a patent, which is an exclusive right to sell a product.

   b. **Innovation** is the first successful commercial use of a new product or method or the creation of a new form of business. There are two major types: product innovation, which involves new and improved products or services, and process innovation, which involves new and improved production or distribution methods. Innovation is an important factor in competition because it can enable a firm to leapfrog competitors by making their products or methods obsolete.

   c. **Diffusion** is the spread of an innovation through imitation or copying. New and existing firms copy or imitate successful innovation of other firms to profit from new opportunities or to protect their profits.

   d. In business, research and development (R&D) includes work and expenditures directed toward invention, innovation, and diffusion. Government also supports R&D through defense expenditures and the funding of other activities.

   e. The traditional view of technological advance was that it was external to the economy. It was viewed as a random force to which the economy adjusted and it depended on the advance of science. The modern view is that it is internal to capitalism. Intense rivalry among individuals and firms motivates them to seek and exploit new or expand existing opportunities for profit.

Entrepreneurs and other innovators are the drivers of technological advance.

2. The **entrepreneur** is an initiator, innovator, and risk bearer. Other innovators are key people involved in the pursuit of innovation but who do not bear personal financial risk.

   a. Entrepreneurs often form small new companies called **start-ups**, which are firms that create and introduce a new product or production technique.

   b. Innovators are found within existing corporations. R&D work in major corporations has resulted in technological improvements, often by splitting off units to form innovative firms.

   c. Innovators attempt to anticipate future needs. Product innovation and development are creative activities with both nonmonetary and monetary rewards. More resources for further innovation by entrepreneurs often come from past successes. Successful businesses that meet consumer wants are given the opportunity to produce goods and services for the market.

   d. New scientific knowledge is important to technological advance. Entrepreneurs study the scientific results from university and government laboratories to find those with commercial applicability.

3. The **optimal amount of R&D** expenditures for the firm depends on the marginal benefit and marginal cost of R&D activity. To earn the greatest profit, the firm will expand an activity until its marginal benefit equals its marginal cost.

   a. Several sources are available for financing firms' R&D activities: bank loans, bonds, retained earnings, venture capital, or personal savings. A firm's marginal cost of these funds is an interest rate i.

   b. A firm's marginal benefit of R&D is its expected profit (or return) from the last dollar spent on R&D.

   c. The optimal amount of R&D in marginal-cost and marginal-benefit analysis is the point where the **interest-rate cost-of-funds** (marginal-cost) **curve** and the **expected-rate-of-return** (marginal-benefit) **curve** intersect. This analysis leads to three important points. First, R&D expenditures can be justified only if the expected return equals or exceeds the cost of financing the R&D. Second, the firm expects positive outcomes from R&D, but the results are not guaranteed. Third, firms adjust R&D spending when expected rates of return change on various projects.

4. A firm's profit can be increased through **innovation** in two ways.

   a. The firm can increase revenues through **product innovation.** From a utility perspective, consumers will purchase a new product only if it increases total utility from their limited incomes. The purchases of the product by consumers increase the firm's revenues. Note three other points.

   (1) Consumer acceptance of a new product depends on both its marginal utility and price.

   (2) Many new products are not successful, so the firm fails to realize the expected return in these instances.

   (3) Most product innovations are small or incremental improvements to existing products, not major changes.

b. *Process innovation,* the introduction of better ways to make products, is another way to increase profit and obtain a positive return on R&D expenditures. It results in a shift upward in the firm's total product curve and a shift downward in the firm's average total cost curve, which increases the firm's profit.

5. The *imitation problem* is that the rivals of a firm may copy or emulate the firm's product or process and thus decrease the profit from the innovator's R&D effort. When a dominant firm quickly imitates the successful new product of smaller competitors with the goal of becoming the second firm to adopt the innovation, it is using a *fast-second strategy.*

a. Taking the lead in innovation offers the firm several protections and potential advantages from being first to produce a product.

(1) Patents limit imitation and protect profits over time.

(2) Copyrights and trademarks reduce direct copying and increase the incentives for product innovation.

(3) Brand names may provide a major marketing asset.

(4) Trade secrets and learning by doing give firms advantages.

(5) The time lags between innovation and diffusion give innovators time to make substantial economic profits.

(6) There is the potential purchase of the innovating firm by a larger firm at a high price.

6. Certain market structures may foster *technological advance.*

a. Each *market structure* has strengths and limitations.

(1) *Pure competition:* Strong competition gives firms the reason to innovate, but the expected rate of return on R&D may be low or negative for a pure competitor.

(2) *Monopolistic competition:* These firms have a strong profit incentive to develop and differentiate products, but they have limited ability to obtain inexpensive R&D financing. It is also difficult for these firms to extract large profits because the barriers to entry are relatively low.

(3) *Oligopoly:* Although the size of these firms makes them capable of promoting technological progress, there is little reason for them to introduce costly new technology and new products when they earn large economic profits without doing it.

(4) *Pure monopoly:* This type of firm has little incentive to engage in R&D because its high profit is protected by high barriers to entry.

b. *Inverted-U theory* suggests that R&D effort is weak in industries with very low concentration (pure competition) and very high concentration (pure monopoly). The optimal industry structure for R&D is one in which expected returns on R&D spending are high and funds are readily available and inexpensive to finance. This generally occurs in industries with a few firms that are absolutely and relatively large, but the concentration ratio is not so high as to limit strong competition by smaller firms.

c. General support for the inverted-U theory comes from industry studies. The optimal market structure for technological advance appears to be an industry with a mix of large oligopolistic firms (a 40–60% concentration ratio) and several highly innovative smaller firms. The technical characteristics of an industry, however, may be a more important factor influencing R&D and its structure.

7. Technological advance enhances *economic efficiency.*

a. *Process innovation* improves productive efficiency by increasing the productivity of inputs and reducing average total costs.

b. *Product innovation* enhances allocative efficiency by giving society a more preferred mixture of goods and services.

(1) The efficiency gain from innovation, however, can be reduced if patents and the advantages of being first lead to monopoly power.

(2) Monopoly power can be reduced or destroyed by innovation because it provides competition where there was none.

c. Innovation may foster *creative destruction,* whereby the creation of new products and production methods simultaneously destroys the monopoly positions of firms protecting existing products and methods. This view is expressed by Joseph Schumpeter, and there are many examples of it in business history. Another view suggests that creative destruction is not inevitable or automatic. In general, innovation improves economic efficiency, but in some cases it can increase monopoly power.

■ HINTS AND TIPS

1. The section of the chapter on a firm's *optimal amount of R&D* uses marginal-cost and marginal-benefit analysis similar to what you saw in previous chapters. In this case, the interest rate or expected return is graphed on the vertical axis and the amount of R&D spending on the horizontal axis. The only difference from previous MB-MC graphs is that the marginal cost in this example is assumed to be constant at the given interest rate. *It is graphed as a horizontal line.* The expected-rate-of-return curve is downward sloping because there are fewer opportunities for R&D expenditures with higher expected rates of return than at lower expected rates of return.

2. The explanation for how new products gain acceptance by consumers is based on the marginal utility theory that you learned about in Chapter 8. Be sure to review the text discussion of Table 8.1 before reading about the example in Table 13.1.

3. When new processes are developed, they can increase a firm's total product curve and decrease a firm's average total cost curve. Review the section in Chapter 9, "Shifting the Cost Curves," to understand these points.

■ IMPORTANT TERMS

technological advance	venture capital
very long run	interest-rate cost-of-funds curve
invention	expected-rate-of-return curve
patent	optimal amount of R&D
innovation	imitation problem
product innovation	fast-second strategy
process innovation	inverted-U theory of R&D
diffusion	creative destruction
start-ups	

SELF-TEST

■ FILL-IN QUESTIONS

1. Technological advance is a three-step process of

a. _____

b. _____

c. _____

2. The first discovery of a product or process is (innovation, invention) _____, whereas the first commercial introduction of a new product or process is_____; patent protection is available for (invention, innovation) _____ but not _____. The spread of an innovation through imitation or copying is (trademarking, diffusion) _____.

3. The development of new or improved products is (process, product) _____ innovation; the development of new or improved production or distribution methods is _____ innovation.

4. The traditional view of technological advance was that it was (internal, external) _____ to the economy, but the modern view is that technological advance is _____. In the modern view, technological advance arises from (scientific progress, rivalry among firms) _____, but the traditional view holds that it arises from _____ that is largely (internal, external) _____ to the market system.

5. The individual who is an initiator, innovator, and risk bearer who combines resources in unique ways to produce new goods and services is called an (entrepreneur, intrapreneur) _____, but an individual who promotes entrepreneurship within existing corporations is called an _____. Entrepreneurs tend to form (large, small) _____ companies called start-ups, and if they are successful they will receive _____ monetary rewards.

6. Past successes often give entrepreneurs access to (more, less) _____ resources for further innovation because the market economy (punishes, rewards) _____ those businesses that meet consumer wants.

7. To earn the greatest profit from R&D spending, the firm should expand the activity until its marginal benefit is (greater than, less than, equal to) _____ its marginal cost, but a firm should cut back its R&D if its marginal benefit is _____ its marginal cost.

8. Five ways a firm can obtain funding to finance R&D spending are

a. _____

b. _____

c. _____

d. _____

e. _____

9. Product innovation will tend to increase a firm's profit by increasing the (costs, revenues) _____ of the firm; process innovation will tend to increase a firm's profit by reducing the (costs, revenues) _____ of the firm.

10. Consumer acceptance of a new product depends on its marginal utility (and, or) _____ its price. The expected return that motivates product innovation (is, is not) _____ always realized. Most product innovations are (major, minor) _____ improvements to existing products.

11. Process innovation results in a shift (downward, upward) _____ in the firm's total product curve and a shift _____ in the firm's average-total-cost curve, which in turn (increases, decreases) _____ the firm's profit.

12. The imitation problem occurs when the rivals of a firm copy or emulate the firm's product or process and thus (increase, decrease) _____ the innovator's profit from the R&D effort. When a dominant firm quickly imitates the successful new product of smaller competitors with the goal of becoming the second firm to adopt the innovation, it is using a (second-best, fast-second) _____ strategy.

13. An example of legal protection for taking the lead in innovation would be (copyrights, trade secrets)

_____, but a nonlegal advantage might come from (patents, learning by doing) _____.

14. In regard to R&D, purely competitive firms tend to be (less, more) _____ complacent than monopolists, but the expected rate of return for a pure competitor may be (high, low) _____, and they (may, may not) _____ be able to finance R&D.

15. Monopolistically competitive firms have a (weak, strong) _____ profit incentive to develop and differentiate products, but they have (extensive, limited) _____ ability to obtain inexpensive R&D financing, and it is (difficult, easy) _____ for these firms to extract large profits because the barriers to entry are relatively (high, low) _____.

16. The size of oligopolistic firms makes them (capable, incapable) _____ of promoting technological advance, but there is (much, little) _____ reason for them to introduce costly new technology and new products when they earn (small, large) _____ economic profit without doing it.

17. Pure monopoly has a (strong, weak) _____ incentive to engage in R&D because its high profit is protected by (low, high) _____ barriers to entry. This type of firm views R&D spending as (an offensive, a defensive) _____ move to protect the monopoly from new products that would undercut its monopoly position.

18. Inverted-U theory suggests that R&D effort is at best (strong, weak) _____ in industries with very low and very high concentrations. The optimal industry structure for R&D is one in which expected returns on R&D spending are (low, high) _____ and funds are readily available and inexpensive to finance R&D. This generally occurs in industries with (many, a few) _____ firms that are absolutely and relatively large, but the concentration ratio is not so high as to limit strong competition by smaller firms.

19. Technological advance increases the productivity of inputs, and by reducing average total costs it enhances (allocative, productive) _____ efficiency; when it gives society a more preferred mixture of goods and services it enhances _____ efficiency. The efficiency gain from innovation can be (increased, decreased) _____ if patents and the advantages of being first lead to monopoly power, but it can be _____ if innovation provides competition where there was none.

20. Innovation may foster creative destruction, where the (destruction, creation) _____ of new products and production methods simultaneously leads to the _____ of the monopoly positions of firms committed to existing products and methods. Another view, however, suggests that creative destruction (is, is not) _____ automatic. In general, innovation improves economic efficiency, but in some cases it can increase monopoly power.

■ **TRUE–FALSE QUESTIONS**

Circle T if the statement is true, F if it is false.

1. Technological advance consists of new and improved goods and services and new and improved production or distribution processes. **T F**

2. In economists' models, technological advance occurs in the short run, not the long run. **T F**

3. Invention is the first successful commercial introduction of a new product. **T F**

4. Firms channel a majority of their R&D expenditures to innovation and imitation rather than to basic scientific research. **T F**

5. Historically, most economists viewed technological advance as a predictable and internal force to which the economy adjusted. **T F**

6. The modern view of economists is that capitalism is the driving force of technological advance and such advance occurs in response to profit incentives within the economy. **T F**

7. The entrepreneur is an innovator but not a risk bearer. **T F**

8. Start-ups are small companies focused on creating and introducing a new product or using a new production or distribution technique. **T F**

9. The only innovators are entrepreneurs. **T F**

10. The market entrusts the production of goods and services to businesses that have consistently succeeded in fulfilling consumer wants. **T F**

11. Research and development rarely occur outside the labs of major corporations. **T F**

12. When entrepreneurs use personal savings to finance the R&D for a new venture, the marginal cost of financing is zero. **T F**

13. The optimal amount of R&D spending for the firm occurs where its expected return is greater than its interest-rate cost of funds to finance it. **T F**

14. Most firms are guaranteed a profitable outcome when making an R&D expenditure because the decisions are carefully evaluated. **T F**

15. A new product succeeds when it provides consumers with higher marginal utility per dollar spent than do existing products. **T F**

16. Most product innovations consist of major changes to existing products and are not incremental improvements. **T F**

17. Process innovation increases the firm's total product, lowers its average total cost, and increases its profit. **T F**

18. Imitation poses no problems for innovators because there are patent and trademark protections for their innovations. **T F**

19. A fast-second strategy involves letting the dominant firm set the price of the product and then smaller firms quickly undercutting that price. **T F**

20. Pure competition is the best market structure for encouraging R&D and innovation. **T F**

21. One major shortcoming of monopolistic competition in promoting technological progress is its limited ability to secure inexpensive financing for R&D. **T F**

22. The inverted-U theory suggests that R&D effort is strongest in very low-concentration industries and weakest in very high-concentration industries. **T F**

23. The technical and scientific characteristics of an industry may be more important than its structure in determining R&D spending and innovation. **T F**

24. Technological advance enhances productive efficiency but not allocative efficiency. **T F**

25. Creative destruction is the process the inventor goes through in developing new products and innovations. **T F**

■ **MULTIPLE-CHOICE QUESTIONS**

Circle the letter that corresponds to the best answer.

1. The period in which technology can change and in which firms can introduce entirely new products is the
  (a) short run
  (b) very short run
  (c) long run
  (d) very long run

2. Technological progress is a three-step process of
  (a) creation, pricing, and marketing
  (b) invention, innovation, and diffusion
  (c) manufacturing, venturing, and promotion
  (d) start-ups, imitation, and creative destruction

3. The first discovery of a product or process through the use of imagination, ingenious thinking, and experimentation and the first proof that it will work is
  (a) process innovation
  (b) product innovation
  (c) creative destruction
  (d) invention

4. From the time of application, patents have a uniform duration of

  (a) 10 years
  (b) 15 years
  (c) 20 years
  (d) 25 years

5. Innovation is a major factor in competition because it can
  (a) be patented to protect the investment of the developers
  (b) enable firms to make competitors' products obsolete
  (c) guarantee the monopoly position of innovative firms
  (d) reduce research and development costs for firms

6. What idea is best illustrated by the example of McDonald's successfully introducing the fast-food hamburger and then that idea being adopted by other firms such as Burger King and Wendy's?
  (a) start-ups
  (b) diffusion
  (c) invention
  (d) fast-second strategy

7. About what percentage of GDP in the United States is spent on research and development?
  (a) 2.8%
  (b) 7.6%
  (c) 10.6%
  (d) 21.2%

8. The modern view of technological advance is that it is
  (a) rooted in the independent advancement of science
  (b) best stimulated through government R&D spending
  (c) a result of intense rivalry among individuals and firms
  (d) a random outside force to which the economy adjusts

9. The major difference between entrepreneurs and other innovators is
  (a) innovators work in teams, but entrepreneurs do not
  (b) innovators manage start-ups, but entrepreneurs do not
  (c) entrepreneurs bear personal financial risk, but innovators do not
  (d) entrepreneurs invent new products and processes, but innovators do not

10. Past successes in developing products often mean that entrepreneurs and innovative firms
  (a) have access to more private resources for further innovation
  (b) have access to less private resources for further innovation
  (c) have access to more public support for further innovation
  (d) experience no change in the availability of private or public resources for further innovation

Questions 11, 12, and 13 are based on the following table showing the expected rate of return, R&D spending, and interest-rate cost of funds for a hypothetical firm.

Expected rate of return (%)	R&D (millions of $)	Interest-rate cost of funds (%)
15	20	9
13	40	9
11	60	9
9	80	9
7	100	9

11. In a supply and demand graph, the interest-rate cost-of-funds curve would be a(n)
(a) vertical line at 9%
(b) horizontal line at 9%
(c) upward sloping line over the 15 to 7% range
(d) downward sloping line over the 15 to 7% range

12. The optimal amount of R&D would be
(a) $40 million
(b) $60 million
(c) $80 million
(d) $100 million

13. If the interest-rate cost-of-funds curve rose to 13%, the optimal amount of R&D spending would be
(a) $40 million
(b) $60 million
(c) $80 million
(d) $100 million

14. Product innovation tends to increase the profits of firms primarily by
(a) decreasing the firm's average costs
(b) increasing the firm's total revenue
(c) decreasing marginal utility per dollar spent
(d) increasing the success of R&D spending

15. Consumers will buy a new product only if
(a) it has a lower marginal utility per dollar spent than another product
(b) there is a substantial budget for promotion and marketing
(c) it can be sold at a lower price than that for a competing product
(d) it increases the total utility they obtain from their limited income

16. Process innovation produces a(n)
(a) downward shift in the total-product curve and an upward shift in the average-cost curve
(b) upward shift in the total-product curve and a downward shift in the average-cost curve
(c) upward shift in both the total-product and average-cost curves
(d) downward shift in both the total-product and average-cost curves

17. Some dominant firms in an industry use a fast-second strategy that involves
(a) developing two products to compete with rivals
(b) cutting the development time for the introduction of a new product
(c) moving quickly to buy the second largest firm in the industry to gain larger market share
(d) letting smaller firms initiate new products and then quickly imitating the success

18. One legal protection for taking the lead in innovation is
(a) venture capital
(b) trademarks
(c) trade secrets
(d) mergers

19. One major advantage of being the first to develop a product is the
(a) use of the fast-second strategy
(b) increase in retained earnings
(c) lower interest-rate costs of funds
(d) potential for profitable buyouts

20. Which firm has a strong incentive for product development and differentiation?
(a) a monopolistically competitive firm
(b) a purely competitive firm
(c) an oligopolistic firm
(d) a pure monopoly

21. In which market structure is there the least incentive to engage in R&D?
(a) a monopolistically competitive firm
(b) a purely competitive firm
(c) an oligopolistic firm
(d) a pure monopoly

22. The inverted-U theory suggests that R&D effort is at best weak in
(a) low-concentration industries only
(b) high-concentration industries only
(c) low- and high-concentration industries
(d) low- to middle-concentration industries

23. The optimal market structure for technological advance seems to be an industry in which there
(a) are many purely competitive firms
(b) are monopolists closely regulated by government
(c) is a mix of large oligopolistic firms with several small and highly innovative firms
(d) is a mix of monopolistically competitive firms and a few large monopolists in industries with high capital costs

24. Technological advance as embodied in process innovation typically
(a) decreases allocative efficiency
(b) increases allocative efficiency
(c) decreases productive efficiency
(d) increases productive efficiency

25. Why did Joseph Schumpeter view capitalism as a process of "creative destruction"?
(a) Innovation would lead to monopoly power and thus destroy the economy.
(b) The creation of new products and production methods would destroy the market for existing products.
(c) Invention would create new products, but diffusion would destroy many potentially good ideas.
(d) Firms are being creative with learning by doing, but this spirit is destroyed by the inability of firms to finance R&D expenditures.

■ PROBLEMS

1. Match the terms with the phrase using the appropriate number
1. invention   2. innovation   3. diffusion
a. Imitation of the Chrysler Corporation's Jeep Grand Cherokee with sport utility vehicles developed by other auto companies   _____
b. The first working model of the microchip

_____
c. Computers and word processing software that eliminated the need for typewriters   _____
d. Adoption of Alamo's offer of unlimited mileage by other major car rental companies   _____
e. The creation of the first electric light bulb

_____
f. Development of a new brand of carpet by Du Pont

_____

2. Use the following table that shows the rate of return and R&D spending for a hypothetical firm.

Expected rate of return (%)	R&D (millions of $)
24	3
20	6
16	9
12	12
9	15
6	18
3	21

a. Assume the interest-rate cost of funds is 12%. The optimal amount of R&D expenditures will be $_____ million. At this amount, the marginal cost of R&D spending is _____% and the marginal benefit (the expected rate of return) is _____%.
b. Graph the marginal cost and marginal benefit curves of R&D spending in the graph below. Be sure to label the axes.

0

c. Now assume that the interest-rate cost of funds falls to 6%. The optimal amount of spending will be $_____ million. For this amount of R&D spending, the marginal cost of R&D spending is _____% and the marginal benefit (expected rate of return) is _____%.
d. Show on the graph above how the interest-rate cost-of-funds curve changed in the answer that you gave for **b.**

3. Following are two average-total-cost schedules for a firm. The first schedule (ATC$_1$) shows the cost of producing the product at five levels of output before a new innovation. The second schedule (ATC$_2$) shows the average total cost at the five output levels after the innovation.

Output	Before ATC$_1$	After ATC$_2$
10	$30	$27
20	25	18
30	18	14
40	22	19
50	28	26

a. Plot the average-cost curves for the schedules on the graph on the top of page 163.
b. What was the reduction in average total cost at each of the five levels of output as a result of the innovation? 10 _____, 20 _____, 30 _____, 40 _____, 50 _____.
c. If the product price is $20 per unit and the firm was producing at 30 units of output, the profit for the firm before the innovation was $_____. At this level of output, the profit after the innovation was

$ _____.

■ SHORT ANSWER AND ESSAY QUESTIONS

1. Give a definition of technological advance. According to economists, what role does time play in the definition?

2. Explain and give examples of invention. What does government do to protect it?

3. How does innovation differ from invention and diffusion? How does innovation affect competition among firms?

4. Compare and contrast the modern view of technological advance with the traditional view.

5. In what ways do entrepreneurs differ from other innovators? In what types of business does each tend to work? How have the characteristics of entrepreneurs changed over time?

6. What does it mean that "innovators try to anticipate the future"? What are the economic consequences of this effort?

7. Why do entrepreneurs and other innovators actively study the scientific output of universities and government laboratories?

8. What are the many different sources of funding to finance firms' R&D expenditures? If an entrepreneur uses personal funds, is there a cost for financing?

9. Explain how the firm decides on the optimal amount of research and development. Use a marginal-cost and marginal-benefit graph in your explanation.

10. Why might many R&D expenditures be affordable but not worthwhile? Are outcomes from R&D guaranteed?

11. Describe how a firm's revenues and profits are increased through product innovation. Why does consumer acceptance of a new product depend on both its marginal utility and price?

12. Explain how process innovation reduces cost and increases profits. Illustrate the point graphically using a total-product and average-cost curve graph.

13. Describe the fast-second strategy and give an example of it.

14. What is the imitation problem resulting from technological advance?

15. Describe the legal protections and potential advantages of taking the lead in innovation.

16. Compare and contrast the suitability of different market structures for fostering technological advance.

17. Explain the basic conclusions from inverted-U theory. What will be the optimal market structure for technological progress?

18. How does technological advance enhance economic efficiency? Distinguish between its effects on productive efficiency and allocative efficiency.

19. How might innovation create or reduce monopoly power? Why might both effects be possible?

20. Explain the idea of creative destruction as championed by Joseph Schumpeter. What are the objections to that idea?

ANSWERS

Chapter 13 Technology, R&D, and Efficiency

FILL-IN QUESTIONS

1. *a.* invention; *b.* innovation; *c.* diffusion
2. invention, innovation, invention, innovation, diffusion
3. product, process
4. external, internal, rivalry among firms, scientific progress, external
5. entrepreneur, intrapreneur, small, large
6. more, rewards
7. equal to, less than
8. *a.* bank loans; *b.* bonds; *c.* retained earnings; *d.* venture capital; *e.* personal savings (any order *a–e*)
9. revenues, costs
10. and, is not, minor
11. upward, downward, increases

12. decrease, fast-second
13. copyrights, learning by doing
14. less, low, may not
15. strong, limited, difficult, low
16. capable, little, large
17. weak, high, a defensive
18. weak, high, a few
19. productive, allocative, decreased, increased
20. creation, destruction, is not

TRUE–FALSE QUESTIONS

1. T, p. 240
2. F, p. 240
3. F, p. 241
4. T, p. 241
5. F, pp. 241–242
6. T, p. 242
7. F, p. 242
8. T, pp. 242–243
9. F, p. 243
10. T, p. 243
11. F, p. 243
12. F, p. 244
13. F, pp. 244–246
14. F, p. 246
15. T, p. 247
16. F, p. 248
17. T, pp. 248–249
18. F, p. 249
19. F, p. 249
20. F, pp. 251–252
21. T, p. 252
22. F, pp. 252–253
23. T, p. 253
24. F, pp. 253–255
25. F, pp. 255–256

MULTIPLE-CHOICE QUESTIONS

1. d, p. 240
2. b, p. 240
3. d, p. 241
4. c, p. 241
5. b, p. 241
6. b, p. 241
7. a, p. 241
8. c, pp. 241–242
9. c, p. 242
10. a, p. 243
11. b, pp. 244–246
12. c, pp. 244–246
13. a, pp. 244–246
14. b, p. 247
15. d, p. 247
16. b, pp. 248–249
17. d, p. 249
18. b, p. 249
19. d, p. 250
20. a, pp. 251–252
21. d, pp. 251–252
22. c, pp. 252–253
23. c, p. 253
24. d, pp. 253–254
25. b, pp. 255–256

PROBLEMS

1. *a.* 3; *b.* 1; *c.* 2; *d.* 3; *e.* 1; *f.* 2
2. *a.* 12, 12, 12; *b.* similar to Figure 13.5 in the text; *c.* 18, 6, 6; *d.* horizontal interest-rate cost-of-funds curve will drop from 12 to 6%
3. *a.* Put output on the horizontal axis, and put average cost on the vertical axis. Plot the set of points. Connect the set with lines; *b.* 3, 7, 4, 3, 2; *c.* Before: TR is $600 (30 × $20), TC is $540 (30 x $18), profit is $60; After: TR is $600, TC is $420 (30 × $14), profit is $180

SHORT ANSWER AND ESSAY QUESTIONS

1. p. 240
2. p. 241
3. p. 241
4. pp. 241–242
5. pp. 242–243
6. p. 243
7. p. 243
8. p. 244
9. pp. 244–246
10. p. 246
11. p. 247
12. pp. 248–249
13. p. 249
14. p. 249
15. pp. 249–250
16. pp. 251–252
17. pp. 252–253
18. pp. 253–255
19. pp. 255–256
20. pp. 255–256

CHAPTER 14

The Demand for Resources

This chapter is the first of three that examine the market for resources. In resource markets the demanders are the employers of the resources and the suppliers are the owners of the resources. As you already know, the demand for and the supply of a resource will determine the resource price and the quantities in a competitive market.

Chapter 14 focuses on the demand or employer side of the resource market. It offers a general explanation of what determines demand for any resource. Chapters 15 and 16 discuss the characteristics of the market for particular resources—labor, capital, land, or entrepreneurial ability—and present the supply side of the resource market.

The **resource market is important** for several reasons, as you will learn in the first section of the chapter. Resource prices determine what resource owners (or households) receive in exchange for supplying their resources, and thus it determines the incomes of households. Prices allocate resources to their most efficient uses and encourage the least costly methods of production in our economy. Many public policy issues also involve resource pricing, such as setting a minimum wage.

The next section of the chapter focuses on the **marginal productivity theory of resource demand.** When a firm wishes to maximize its profits, it produces that output at which marginal revenue and marginal cost are equal. But how much of each resource does the firm hire if it wishes to maximize its profits? You will learn that the firm hires that amount of each resource up to the point that the marginal revenue product and the marginal resource cost of that resource are equal (**MRP = MPC**).

There is another similarity between the output and the resource markets for the firm. Recall that the competitive firm's supply curve is a portion of its marginal-cost curve. The purely competitive firm's demand curve for a resource is a portion of its marginal-revenue-product curve. Just as cost is the important determinant of supply, the revenue derived from the use of a resource is the important factor determining the demand for that resource in a competitive market for resources.

The next major section of the chapter presents the **determinants of resource demand.** Three major ones are discussed—changes in product demand, productivity, and the prices of other resources. The last one is the most complicated because you must consider whether the other resources are substitutes or complements and also the underlying factors affecting them.

This chapter has a section on the **elasticity of resource demand,** which is no different from the elasticity concept you learned about in Chapter 7. In this case,

it is the relation of the percentage change in quantity demanded of the resource to a percentage change in the price of the resource. As you will discover, the three factors that affect elasticity are the availability of other substitute resources, the elasticity of product demand, and the ratio of resource cost to total cost.

Most of the chapter examines the situation in which there is only one variable resource. The next-to-last section of the chapter, however, offers a general perspective on the **combination of resources** the firm will choose to use when multiple inputs are used and all inputs are variable. Two rules are presented. The *least-cost rule* states that the firm will minimize costs when the last dollar spent on each resource results in the same marginal product. The *profit-maximizing rule* means that in a competitive market the firm will maximize its profits when each resource is used so that its marginal product is equal to its price. The second rule is equally important because a firm that employs the quantity of resources that maximizes its profits also produces the output that maximizes its profits and is thus producing at the least cost.

The marginal productivity theory of resource demand is not without criticism, as you will learn in the last section of the chapter. If resource prices reflect marginal productivity, then this relationship can produce income inequality in society. In addition, market imperfection may skew the distribution of income.

■ CHECKLIST

When you have studied this chapter you should be able to

☐ Present four reasons for studying resource pricing.
☐ Explain why the demand for an economic resource is a derived demand.
☐ Define the marginal revenue product and relate it to the productivity and price of a resource.
☐ Determine the marginal-revenue-product schedule of a resource for a product sold in a purely competitive market, when given the data.
☐ Define the marginal resource cost.
☐ State the rule used by a profit-maximizing firm to determine how much of a resource it will employ.
☐ Apply the **MRP = MRC** rule to determine the quantity of a resource a firm will hire, when you are given the necessary data.
☐ Explain why the marginal-revenue-product schedule of a resource is the firm's demand for the resource.

☐ Find the marginal-revenue-product schedule of a resource for a product sold in an imperfectly competitive market, when given the data.

☐ Derive the market demand for a resource.

☐ List the three factors which would change a firm's demand for a resource.

☐ Predict the effect on resource demand of an increase or decrease in one of its three determinants.

☐ Give trends on the occupations with the fastest growth in jobs both in percentage terms and in absolute numbers.

☐ State three determinants of the price elasticity of resource demand.

☐ Describe how a change in each determinant would change the price elasticity of demand for a resource.

☐ State the rule used by a firm for determining the least-cost combination of resources.

☐ Use the least-cost rule to find the least-cost combination of resources for production, when given data.

☐ State the rule used by a profit-maximizing firm to determine the quantity of each of several resources to employ.

☐ Apply the profit-maximizing rule to determine the quantity of each resource a firm will hire, when given the data.

☐ Explain the marginal productivity theory of income distribution.

☐ Give two criticisms of the marginal productivity theory of income distribution.

■ **CHAPTER OUTLINE**

1. The study of what determines the prices of resources *is important* because resource prices influence the size of individual incomes and the resulting distribution of income. They allocate scarce resources and affect the way in which firms combine resources in production. Resource pricing also raises ethical questions about income distribution.

2. The *demand* for a single resource depends on (or is derived from) the demand for the goods and services it can produce.

   a. Because resource demand is a *derived demand,* it depends on the marginal productivity of the resource and the market price of the good or service it is used to produce.

   b. *Marginal revenue product* (*MRP*) is the change in total revenue divided by a one-unit change in resource quantity. It combines two factors—the marginal product of a resource and the market price of the product it produces—into a single useful tool.

   c. *Marginal resource cost* (*MRC*) is the change in total resource cost divided by a one-unit change in resource quantity. A firm will hire resources until the marginal revenue product of the resource is equal to its marginal resource cost (*MRP = MRC*).

   d. The firm's marginal-revenue-product schedule for a resource is that firm's demand schedule for the resource.

   e. If a firm sells its output in an *imperfectly competitive market,* the more the firm sells, the lower the price of the product becomes. This causes the firm's marginal-revenue-product (resource demand) schedule to be less elastic than it would be if the firm sold its output in a purely competitive market.

   f. The market (or total) demand for a resource is the horizontal summation of the demand schedules of all firms using the resource.

3. The *determinants of resource demand* are changes in the demand for the product produced, changes in the productivity of the resource, and changes in the prices of other resources.

   a. A change in the demand for a product produced by a resource will change the demand of a firm for labor in the same direction.

   b. A change in the productivity of a resource will change the demand of a firm for the resource in the same direction.

   c. A change in the price of a

   (1) *substitute resource* will change the demand for a resource in the same direction if the substitution effect outweighs the output effect and in the opposite direction if the output effect outweighs the substitution effect;

   (2) *complementary resource* will change the demand for a resource in the opposite direction.

   d. Changes in the demand for labor have significant effects on employment growth in occupations, both in percentage and absolute terms. Projections (1998–2008) are reported for the fastest growing occupations (e.g., computer engineers) and the occupations with the greatest absolute job growth (e.g., systems analysts).

4. The *price elasticity of resource demand* measures the sensitivity of producers to changes in resource prices.

   a. Three factors affect the price elasticity of resource demand:

   (1) the ease of substitution of other resources: the more good substitute resources are available, the more elastic the resource demand;

   (2) the elasticity of the demand for the product that the resource produces: the more elastic the product demand, the more elastic the resource demand;

   (3) the ratio of labor cost to total cost: the greater the ratio of labor cost to total cost, the greater the price elasticity of demand for labor.

5. Firms often employ more than one resource in producing a product.

   a. The firm employing resources in purely competitive markets is hiring resources in the least-cost combination when the ratio of the marginal product of a resource to its price is the same for all the resources the firm hires.

   b. The firm is hiring resources in the most profitable combination if it hires resources in a purely competitive market when the marginal revenue product of each resource is equal to the price of that resource.

   c. A numerical example illustrates the least-cost and profit-maximizing rules for a firm that employs resources in purely competitive markets.

6. The marginal productivity theory of *income distribution* seems to result in an equitable distribution of income because each unit of a resource receives a payment equal to its marginal contribution to the firm's revenue. The theory has at least two serious faults.

    a. The distribution of income will be unequal because resources are unequally distributed among individuals in the economy.

    b. The income of those who supply resources will not be based on their marginal productivities if there is monopsony or monopoly in the resource markets of the economy.

■ **HINTS AND TIPS**

1. The list of important terms for Chapter 14 is relatively short, but included in the list are two very important concepts—***marginal revenue product*** and ***marginal resource cost***—which you must grasp if you are to understand how much of a resource a firm will hire. These two concepts are similar to, but not identical with, the marginal-revenue and marginal-cost concepts used in the study of product markets and in the explanation of the quantity of output a firm will produce.

    Marginal revenue and marginal cost are, respectively, the change in the firm's total revenue and the change in the firm's total cost when it produces and sells an additional unit of *output*. Marginal revenue product and marginal resource cost are, respectively, the change in the firm's total revenue and the change in the firm's total cost when it hires an additional unit of *input*. Note that the two new concepts deal with changes in revenue and costs as a consequence of hiring more of a *resource*.

2. The marginal revenue product (MRP) of a resource is simply the marginal product of the resource (MP) times the price of the product that the resource produces (*P*), or MRP = MP × *P*. Under pure competition, MP changes, but *P* is constant as more resources are added to production. Under imperfect competition, both MP and *P* change as more resources are added, and thus each variable (MP and *P*) affects MRP. Compare the data in Tables 14.1 and 14.2 in the textbook to see this difference.

3. Make sure you understand the rule **MRP = MRC**. A firm will hire one more unit of a resource only so long as the resource adds more to the firm's revenues than it does to its costs. If MRP > MRC, the firm will hire more resources. If MRP < MRC, the firm will cut back on resource use.

4. It can be difficult to figure out what outcome will result from a change in the price of a substitute resource (capital) on the demand for another resource (labor). It is easy to understand why the demand for labor might decrease if the price of capital decreases because cheaper capital would be substituted for labor. It is harder to explain why the opposite might be true. That insight requires an understanding of both the ***substitution effect*** and the ***output effect.*** Find out how one effect may offset the other.

5. The ***profit-maximizing rule*** for a combination of resources may seem difficult, but it is relatively simple. Just remember that the price of any resource must be equal to its marginal revenue product, and thus *the ratio must always equal 1.*

■ **IMPORTANT TERMS**

derived demand	output effect
marginal product	elasticity of resource demand
marginal revenue product (MRP)	least-cost combination of resources
marginal resource cost (MRC)	profit-maximizing combination of resources
MRP = MRC rule	marginal productivity theory of income distribution
substitution effect	

SELF-TEST

■ **FILL-IN QUESTIONS**

1. Resource prices allocate (revenues, resources) _____ and are one factor that determines household (incomes, costs) _____ and business _____.

2. The demand for a resource is a (constant, derived) _____ demand that depends on the (productivity, cost) _____ of the resource and the (cost, price) _____ of the product made from the resource.

3. A firm will find it profitable to hire units of a resource up to the quantity at which the marginal revenue (cost, product) _____ equals the marginal resource _____.

4. If the firm hires the resource in a purely competitive market, the marginal resource (cost, product) _____ will be (greater than, less than, equal to) _____ the price of the resource.

5. A firm's demand schedule for a resource is the firm's marginal revenue (cost, product) _____ schedule for that resource because both indicate the quantities of the resource the firm will employ at various resource (costs, prices) _____.

6. A producer in an imperfectly competitive market finds that the more of a resource it employs, the (higher, lower) _____ becomes the price at which it can sell its product. As a consequence, the (supply, demand) _____ schedule for the resource is (more, less) _____ elastic than it would be if the output were sold in a purely competitive market.

7. Adding the quantity demanded for the resource at each and every price for each firm using the resource gives the market (supply, demand) _____ curve for the resource.

8. The demand for a resource will change if the (demand, supply) _____ of the product the resource produces changes, if the (productivity, price) _____ of the resource changes, or if the (price, elasticity) _____ of other resources changes.

9. If the demand for a product increases, then the demand for the resource that produces that product will (increase, decrease) _____. Conversely, if the demand for a product decreases, then the demand for the resource that produces that product will _____.

10. When the productivity of a resource falls, the demand for the resource (rises, falls) _____, but when the productivity of a resource rises, the demand for the resource _____.

11. The output of the firm being constant, a decrease in the price of resource A will induce the firm to hire (more, less) _____ of resource A and _____ of other resources; this is called the (substitution, output) _____ effect. But if the decrease in the price of A results in lower total costs and an increase in output, the firm may hire (more, less) _____ of both resources; this is called the (substitution, output) _____ effect.

12. A decrease in the price of a complementary resource will cause the demand for labor to (increase, decrease) _____, but an increase in the price of a complementary resource will cause the demand for labor to _____.

13. The three determinants of the price elasticity of demand for a resource are the ease with which other resources can be (substitutes, complements) _____ for it, the price elasticity of (supply, demand) _____ for the product the resource produces, and the ratio of resource (demand, cost) _____ to total (demand, cost) _____.

14. If the marginal product of labor declines slowly when added to a fixed stock of capital, the demand curve for labor (MRP) will decline (rapidly, slowly) _____ and will tend to be highly (elastic, inelastic) _____.

15. The larger the number of good substitutes available for a resource, the (greater, less) _____ will be the elasticity of demand for a resource.

16. Suppose a firm employs resources in purely competitive markets. If the firm wishes to produce any given amount of its output in the least costly way, the ratio of the marginal (cost, product) _____ of each resource to its (demand, price) _____ must be the same for all resources.

17. A firm that hires resources in purely competitive markets is employing the combination of resources that will result in maximum profits for the firm when the marginal (revenue product, resource cost) _____ of every resource is equal to its (demand, price) _____.

18. If the marginal revenue product of a resource is equal to the price of that resource, the marginal revenue product divided by its price is equal to (1, infinity) _____.

19. In the marginal productivity theory, the distribution of income is an equitable one because each unit of each resource is paid an amount equal to its (total, marginal) _____ contribution to the firm's (revenues, costs) _____.

20. The marginal productivity theory rests on the assumption of (competitive, imperfect) _____ markets. In the real world, there are many labor markets with imperfections because of employer pricing or monopoly power, so wage rates and other resource prices (do, do not) _____ perfectly measure contributions to domestic output.

■ **TRUE–FALSE QUESTIONS**

Circle T if the statement is true, F if it is false.

1. In the resource markets of the economy, resources are demanded by business firms and supplied by households.　　　　　**T F**

2. The prices of resources are an important factor in the determination of resource allocation.　　　　**T F**

3. The demand for a resource is a derived demand based on the demand for the product it produces.　**T F**

4. A resource that is highly productive will always be in great demand.　　　　**T F**

5. A firm's demand schedule for a resource is the firm's marginal-revenue-product schedule for the resource.　　　　　**T F**

6. It will be profitable for a firm to hire additional units of labor resources up to the point where the marginal revenue product of labor is equal to its marginal resource cost. **T F**

7. A firm with one worker can produce 30 units of a product that sells for $4 a unit, but the same firm with two workers can produce 70 units of that product. The marginal revenue product of the second worker is $400. **T F**

8. The competitive firm's marginal revenue product of labor will fall as output expands because marginal product diminishes and product price falls. **T F**

9. A producer's demand schedule for a resource will be more elastic if the firm sells its product in a purely competitive market than it would be if it sold the product in an imperfectly competitive market. **T F**

10. The market demand for a particular resource is the sum of the individual demands of all firms that employ that resource. **T F**

11. An increase in the price of a resource will cause the demand for the resource to decrease. **T F**

12. The demand curve for labor will increase when the demand for (and price of) the product produced by that labor increases. **T F**

13. There is an inverse relationship between the productivity of labor and the demand for labor. **T F**

14. The demand for a resource will be increased with improvements in its quality. **T F**

15. When two resources are substitutes for each other, both the substitution effect and the output effect of a decrease in the price of one of these resources operate to increase the quantity of the other resource employed by the firm. **T F**

16. The output effect of an increase in the price of a resource increases the quantity demanded of that resource. **T F**

17. If two resources are complementary, an increase in the price of one will reduce the demand for the other. **T F**

18. Price declines for computer equipment have had stronger output effects than substitution effects, increasing the demand for computer software engineers and specialists. **T F**

19. The larger the number of good substitute resources available, the less will be the elasticity of demand for a particular resource. **T F**

20. The greater the elasticity of product demand, the greater the elasticity of resource demand. **T F**

21. The demand for labor will be less elastic when labor is a smaller proportion of the total cost of producing a product. **T F**

Use the following information as the basis for answering Questions 22 and 23. The marginal revenue product and price of resource A are $12 and a constant $2, respectively, and the marginal revenue product and price of resource B are $25 and a constant $5, respectively. The firm sells its product at a constant price of $1.

22. The firm should decrease the amount of A and increase the amount of B it employs if it wishes to decrease its total cost without affecting its total output. **T F**

23. If the firm wishes to maximize its profits, it should increase its employment of both A and B until their marginal revenue products fall to $2 and $5, respectively. **T F**

24. The marginal productivity theory of income distribution results in an equitable distribution if resource markets are competitive. **T F**

25. The marginal productivity theory rests on the assumption of imperfectly competitive markets. **T F**

■ **MULTIPLE-CHOICE QUESTIONS**

Circle the letter that corresponds to the best answer.

1. The prices paid for resources affect
(a) the money incomes of households in the economy
(b) the allocation of resources among different firms and industries in the economy
(c) the quantities of different resources employed to produce a particular product
(d) all of the above

2. In a competitive resource market, the firm employing a resource such as labor is a
(a) price maker
(b) cost maker
(c) wage taker
(d) revenue taker

3. The demand for a resource is *derived* from the
(a) demand for the products it helps produce
(b) price of the resource
(c) supply of the resource
(d) income of the firm selling the resource

4. The law of diminishing returns explains why
(a) the MRP of an input in a purely competitive market decreases as a firm increases the quantity of an employed resource
(b) the MRC of an input in a purely competitive market decreases as a firm increases the quantity of an employed resource
(c) resource demand is a derived demand
(d) there are substitution and output effects for resources

Answer Questions 5, 6, and 7 on the basis of the information in the following table for a purely competitive market.

Number of workers	Total product	Product price ($)
0	0	4
1	16	4
2	26	4
3	34	4
4	40	4
5	44	4

5. At a wage rate of $15, the firm will choose to employ
(a) 2 workers
(b) 3 workers
(c) 4 workers
(d) 5 workers

6. At a wage rate of $30, the firm will choose to employ
(a) 2 workers
(b) 3 workers
(c) 4 workers
(d) 5 workers

7. If the product price increases to a constant $8, then at a wage rate of $30, the firm will choose to employ
(a) 2 workers
(b) 3 workers
(c) 4 workers
(d) 5 workers

Use the following total-product and marginal-product schedules for a resource to answer Questions 8, 9, 10, and 11. Assume that the quantities of other resources the firm employs remain constant.

Units of resource	Total product	Marginal product
0	0	–
1	8	8
2	14	6
3	18	4
4	21	3
5	23	2

8. If the product the firm produces sells for a constant $3 per unit, the marginal revenue product of the fourth unit of the resource is
(a) $3
(b) $6
(c) $9
(d) $12

9. If the firm's product sells for a constant $3 per unit and the price of the resource is a constant $15, the firm will employ how many units of the resource?
(a) 2
(b) 3
(c) 4
(d) 5

10. If the firm can sell 14 units of output at a price of $1 per unit and 18 units of output at a price of $0.90 per unit, the marginal revenue product of the third unit of the resource would be
(a) $4
(b) $3.60
(c) $2.20
(d) $0.40

11. If the firm can sell 8 units at a price of $1.50, 14 units at a price of $1.00, 18 units at a price of $0.90, 21 units at a price of $0.70, and 23 units at a price of $0.50, then the firm is
(a) maximizing profits at a product price of $0.50
(b) minimizing its costs at a product price of $1.00

(c) selling in an imperfectly competitive market
(d) selling in a purely competitive market

12. As a firm that sells its product in an imperfectly competitive market increases the quantity of a resource it employs, the marginal revenue product of that resource falls because
(a) the price paid by the firm for the resource falls
(b) the marginal product of the resource falls
(c) the price at which the firm sells its product falls
(d) both the marginal product and the price at which the firm sells its product fall

13. Which would increase a firm's demand for a particular resource?
(a) an increase in the prices of complementary resources used by the firm
(b) a decrease in the demand for the firm's product
(c) an increase in the productivity of the resource
(d) an increase in the price of the particular resource

14. The substitution effect indicates that a firm will use
(a) more of an input whose relative price has decreased
(b) more of an input whose relative price has increased
(c) less of an input whose relative price has decreased
(d) less of an input whose relative price has remained constant

15. Suppose resource A and resource B are substitutes and the price of A increases. If the output effect is greater than the substitution effect,
(a) the quantity of A employed by the firm will increase and the quantity of B employed will decrease
(b) the quantities of both A and B employed by the firm will decrease
(c) the quantities of both A and B employed by the firm will increase
(d) the quantity of A employed will decrease and the quantity of B employed will increase

16. Two resource inputs, capital and labor, are complementary and used in fixed proportions. A decrease in the price of capital will
(a) increase the demand for labor
(b) decrease the demand for labor
(c) decrease the quantity demanded for labor
(d) have no effect because the relationship is fixed

17. Which would result in an increase in the elasticity of demand for a particular resource?
(a) an increase in the demand for the resource
(b) a decrease in the elasticity of demand for the product that the resource helps to produce
(c) an increase in the percentage of the firm's total costs accounted for by the resource
(d) a decrease in the number of other resources that are good substitutes for the particular resource

18. The demand for labor would most likely become more inelastic as a result of
(a) an increase in the elasticity of the demand for the product that the labor produces

(b) an increase in the time for employers to make technological changes or purchase new equipment
(c) a decrease in the proportion of labor costs to total costs
(d) a decrease in the demand for the product

19. A firm is allocating its expenditures for resources in a way that will result in the least total cost of producing any given output when the
(a) amount the firm spends on each resource is the same
(b) marginal revenue product of each resource is the same
(c) marginal product of each resource is the same
(d) marginal product per dollar spent on the last unit of each resource is the same

20. A business is employing inputs such that the marginal product of labor is 20 and the marginal product of capital is 45. The price of labor is $10 and the price of capital is $15. If the business wants to minimize costs while keeping output constant, then it should
(a) use more labor and less capital
(b) use less labor and less capital
(c) use less labor and more capital
(d) make no change in resource use

21. Assume that a computer disk manufacturer is employing resources so that the MRP of the last unit hired for resource X is $240 and the MRP of the last unit hired for resource Y is $150. The price of resource X is $80 and the price of resource Y is $50. To maximize profit the firm should
(a) hire more of resource X and less of resource Y
(b) hire less of resource X and more of resource Y
(c) hire less of both resource X and resource Y
(d) hire more of both resource X and resource Y

22. Which does not suggest that a firm that hires resources in a purely competitive market is maximizing its profits?
(a) The marginal revenue product of every resource is equal to 1.
(b) The marginal revenue product of every resource is equal to its price.
(c) The ratio of the marginal revenue product of every resource to its price is equal to 1.

(d) The ratio of the price of every resource to its marginal revenue product is equal to 1.

23. Assume that a purely competitive firm uses two resources—labor (L) and capital (C)—to produce a product. In which situation would the firm be maximizing profit?

	MRP_L	MRP_C	P_L	P_C
(a)	10	20	30	40
(b)	10	20	10	20
(c)	15	15	10	10
(d)	30	40	10	5

24. In the marginal productivity theory of income distribution, when all markets are purely competitive, each unit of each resource receives a money payment equal to
(a) its marginal product
(b) its marginal revenue product
(c) the needs of the resource owner
(d) the payments received by each of the units of the other resources in the economy

25. A major criticism of the marginal productivity theory of income distribution is that
(a) labor markets are often subject to imperfect competition
(b) the theory suggests that there eventually will be equality in incomes
(c) purely competitive firms are only interested in profit maximization
(d) the demand for labor resources is price elastic

■ **PROBLEMS**

1. The table below shows the total production a firm will be able to obtain if it employs varying amounts of resource **A** while the amounts of the other resources the firm employs remain constant.
a. Compute the marginal product of each of the seven units of resource **A** and enter these figures in the table.
b. Assume the product the firm produces sells in the market for $1.50 per unit. Compute the total revenue of the firm at each of the eight levels of output and the marginal revenue product of each of the seven units of resource **A.** Enter these figures in the table below.

Quantity of resource A employed	Total product	Marginal product of A	Total revenue	Marginal revenue product of A
0	0		$_____	
1	12	_____	_____	$_____
2	22	_____	_____	_____
3	30	_____	_____	_____
4	36	_____	_____	_____
5	40	_____	_____	_____
6	42	_____	_____	_____
7	43	_____	_____	_____

c. On the basis of your computations, complete the firm's demand schedule for resource **A** by indicating in the following table how many units of resource **A** the firm would employ at the given prices.

Price of A	Quantity of A demanded
$21.00	_____
18.00	_____
15.00	_____
12.00	_____
9.00	_____
6.00	_____
3.00	_____
1.50	_____

2. In the table below are the marginal product data for resource **B**. Assume that the quantities of other resources employed by the firm remain constant.

a. Compute the total product (output) of the firm for each of the seven quantities of resource **B** employed and enter these figures in the table.

b. Assume that the firm sells its output in an imperfectly competitive market and that the prices at which it can sell its product are those given in the table. Compute and enter in the table:

(1) the total revenue for each of the seven quantities of **B** employed.

(2) the marginal revenue product of each of the seven units of resource **B**.

c. How many units of **B** would the firm employ if the market price of **B** were

(1) $25? _____

(2) $20? _____

(3) $15? _____

(4) $9? _____

(5) $5? _____

(6) $1? _____

3. Use the following total-product schedule as a resource to answer questions **a, b,** and **c.** Assume that the quantities of other resources the firm employs remain constant.

Units of resource	Total product
0	0
1	15
2	28
3	38
4	43
5	46

a. If the firm's product sells for a constant $2 per unit, what is the marginal revenue product of the second unit of the resource? _____

b. If the firm's product sells for a constant $2 and the price of the resource is $10, how many units of the resource will the firm employ? _____

c. If the firm can sell 15 units of output at a price of $2.00 and 28 units of output at a price of $1.50, what is the marginal revenue product of the second unit of the resource? _____

4. In the space to the right of each of the following changes, indicate whether the change would tend to increase (+) or decrease (−) a firm's demand for a particular resource.

a. An increase in the demand for the firm's product

_____

b. A decrease in the price of the firm's output _____

c. An increase in the productivity of the resource

_____

d. An increase in the price of a substitute resource when the output effect is greater than the substitution effect _____

e. A decrease in the price of a complementary resource _____

f. A decrease in the price of a substitute resource when the substitution effect is greater than the output effect _____

Quantity of resource B employed	Marginal product of B	Total product	Product price	Total revenue	Marginal revenue product of B
0	−	0		$0.00	−
1	22	_____	$1.00	_____	_____
2	21	_____	.90	_____	_____
3	19	_____	.80	_____	_____
4	16	_____	.70	_____	_____
5	12	_____	.60	_____	_____
6	7	_____	.50	_____	_____
7	1	_____	.40	_____	_____

Quantity of resource C employed	Marginal product of C	Marginal revenue product of C	Quantity of resource D employed	Marginal product of D	Marginal revenue product of D
1	10	$5.00	1	21	$10.50
2	8	4.00	2	18	9.00
3	6	3.00	3	15	7.50
4	5	2.50	4	12	6.00
5	4	2.00	5	9	4.50
6	3	1.50	6	6	3.00
7	2	1.00	7	3	1.50

5. The above table shows the marginal-product and marginal-revenue-product schedules for resource **C** and resource **D**. Both resources are variable and are employed in purely competitive markets. The price of **C** is $2 and the price of **D** is $3. (Assume that the productivity of each resource is independent of the quantity of the other.)

a. The least-cost combination of **C** and **D** that would enable the firm to produce

(1) 64 units of its product is _____ C and _____ D.

(2) 99 units of its product is _____ C and _____ D.

b. The profit-maximizing combination of **C** and **D** is

_____ C and _____ D.

c. When the firm employs the profit-maximizing combination of **C** and **D**, it is also employing **C** and **D** in

the least-cost combination because _____

equals _____.

d. Examination of the figures in the table reveals that

the firm sells its product in a _____ com-

petitive market at a price of $ _____.

e. Employing the profit-maximizing combination of **C** and **D**, the firm's

(1) total output is _____.

(2) total revenue is $ _____.

(3) total cost is $ _____.

(4) total profit is $ _____.

■ **SHORT ANSWER AND ESSAY QUESTIONS**

1. Give four reasons why it is important to study resource pricing.

2. How does the demand for a product differ from the demand for a resource? Explain why the demand for a resource is a derived demand.

3. What two factors determine the strength of the demand for a resource?

4. Explain why firms that wish to maximize their profits follow the MRP = MRC rule.

5. What effects do marginal product and marginal price have on a firm's resource demand curve under pure competition and under imperfect competition?

6. Why is the demand schedule for a resource less elastic when the firm sells its product in an imperfectly competitive market than when it sells it in a purely competitive market?

7. How do you derive the market demand for a resource?

8. Identify and describe three factors that will cause the demand for a resource to increase or decrease. Give examples of how each factor influences changes in demand.

9. What is the difference between the substitution effect and the output effect?

10. If the price of capital falls, what will happen to the demand for labor if capital and labor are substitutes in production? Describe what happens when the substitution effect outweighs the output effect and when the output effect outweighs the substitution effect. What can you conclude?

11. Why does a change in the price of a complementary resource cause the demand for labor to change in the opposite direction?

12. Describe trends in occupational employment data. Give examples of jobs with the greatest projected growth in percentage and absolute terms.

13. What are the three factors that determine the elasticity of demand for a resource?

14. Use an example to explain what happens to elasticity when there are many substitute resources compared to when there are few.

15. How can the ratio of labor cost to the total cost influence how producers react to changes in the price of labor?

16. Assume that a firm employs resources in purely competitive markets. How does the firm know that it is spending money on resources in such a way that it can produce a given output for the least total cost?

17. Why is minimizing cost not sufficient for maximizing profit for a firm?

18. When is a firm that employs resources in purely competitive markets using these resources in amounts that will maximize the profits of the firm?

19. What is the marginal productivity theory of income distribution? What ethical proposition must be accepted if this distribution is to be fair and equitable?

20. What are the two major shortcomings of the marginal productivity theory of income distribution?

ANSWERS

Chapter 14 The Demand for Resources

FILL-IN QUESTIONS

1. resources, incomes, costs
2. derived, productivity, price
3. product, cost
4. cost, equal to
5. product, prices
6. lower, demand, less
7. demand
8. demand, productivity, price
9. increase, decrease
10. falls, rises
11. more, less, substitution, more, output
12. increase, decrease
13. substitutes, demand, cost, cost
14. slowly, elastic
15. greater
16. product, price
17. revenue product, price
18. 1
19. marginal, revenues
20. competitive, do not

TRUE–FALSE QUESTIONS

1. T, p. 260
2. T, p. 260
3. T, p. 261
4. F, pp. 261–262
5. T, pp. 262–263
6. T, pp. 262–263
7. F, p. 262
8. F, pp. 263–264
9. T, pp. 263–264
10. T, p. 264
11. F, pp. 265–266
12. T, p. 265
13. F, pp. 265–266
14. T, pp. 265–266
15. F, pp. 266–267
16. F, pp. 266–267
17. T, pp. 266–267
18. T, p. 268
19. F, p. 269
20. T, p. 269
21. T, p. 269
22. F, pp. 270–272
23. T, pp. 270–272
24. F, pp. 272–273
25. F, pp. 272–273

MULTIPLE-CHOICE QUESTIONS

1. d, pp. 260–261
2. c, p. 261
3. a, p. 261
4. a, pp. 261–262
5. d, pp. 262–263
6. b, pp. 262–263
7. d, pp. 262–263
8. c, pp. 262–263
9. a, pp. 262–263
10. c, pp. 263–264
11. c, pp. 263–264
12. d, pp. 263–264
13. c, pp. 265–267
14. a, pp. 266–267
15. b, pp. 266–267
16. a, pp. 266–267
17. c, p. 269
18. c, p. 269
19. d, p. 270
20. c, p. 270
21. d, pp. 271–272
22. a, pp. 271–272
23. b, pp. 271–272
24. b, pp. 272–273
25. a, pp. 272–273

PROBLEMS

1. *a.* Marginal product of A: 12, 10, 8, 6, 4, 2, 1; *b.* Total revenue: 0, 18.00, 33.00, 45.00, 54.00, 60.00, 63.00, 64.50; Marginal revenue product of A: 18.00, 15.00, 12.00, 9.00, 6.00, 3.00, 1.50; *c.* 0, 1, 2, 3, 4, 5, 6, 7

2. *a.* Total product: 22, 43, 62, 78, 90, 97, 98; *b.* (1) Total revenue: 22.00, 38.70, 49.60, 54.60, 54.00, 48.50, 39.20, (2) Marginal revenue product of B: 22.00, 16.70, 10.90, 5.00, −0.60, −5.50, −9.30; *c.* (1) 0, (2) 1, (3) 2, (4) 3, (5) 4, (6) 4

3. *a.* $26. The second worker increases TP by 13 units (13 × $2 = $26); *b.* 4 units. The marginal product of the fourth resource is 5 units of output (5 × $2 = $10). Thus MRP = $10 and MRC = $10 when the fourth resource is employed; *c.* $12. The total revenue from 1 unit is $30.00 (15 × $2.00). The total revenue with 2 units is $42 (28 × $1.50). The difference is the MR of the second unit.

4. *a.* +; *b.* −; *c.* +; *d.* −; *e.* +; *f.* −

5. *a.* (1) 1, 3, (2) 3, 5; *b.* 5, 6; *c.* the marginal product of **C** divided by its price, the marginal product of **D** divided by its price; *d.* purely, $.50; *e.* (1) 114, (2) 57, (3) 28, (4) 29

SHORT ANSWER AND ESSAY QUESTIONS

1. pp. 260–261
2. pp. 261–262
3. pp. 261–262
4. p. 262
5. pp. 262–264
6. pp. 262–264
7. p. 264
8. pp. 265–267
9. pp. 266–267
10. pp. 266–267
11. pp. 266–267
12. pp. 267–268
13. p. 269
14. p. 269
15. p. 269
16. p. 270
17. pp. 270–271
18. pp. 271–272
19. pp. 272–273
20. pp. 272–273

CHAPTER 15

Wage Determination

The preceding chapter explained the demand for *any* resource in a competitive resource market. Chapter 15 uses demand and supply analysis to describe what determines the quantity of a *particular* resource—*labor*—and the price paid for it—*wages*—in different markets.

The chapter begins by defining terms and briefly discussing the general level of wages in the United States and other advanced economies. You will learn about the role that productivity plays in explaining the long-run growth of real wages and the increased demand for labor over time.

In a product market, the degree of competition significantly influences how prices are determined and what output is produced. In a labor resource market, the degree of competition directly affects the determination of wage rates and the level of employment. The main purpose of the chapter is to explain how wage rates and the quantity of labor are determined in labor markets varying in competitiveness.

Six labor markets are discussed in the chapter: (1) the **purely competitive** market, in which the number of employers is large and labor is nonunionized; (2) the **monopsony** market, in which a single employer hires labor under competitive (nonunion) conditions; (3) a market in which a union controls the supply of labor, the number of employers is large, and the union attempts to increase the total demand for labor; (4) a similar market in which the union attempts to reduce the total supply of labor; (5) another similar market in which the union attempts to obtain a wage rate that is above the competitive-equilibrium level by threatening to strike; and (6) the **bilateral monopoly** market, in which a single employer faces a labor supply controlled by a single union.

What is important for you to learn is how the characteristics of each labor market affect wage rates and employment. In the purely competitive or monopsony labor market, there is no union. The determination of the wage rate and employment will be quite definite, although different for each market. In the next four types of labor markets, **unions** control the supply of labor, and thus the outcomes for wage rates and employment will be less definite. If the demand for labor is competitive, the wage rate and the amount of employment will depend on how successful the union is in increasing the demand for labor, restricting the supply of labor, or setting a wage rate that employers will accept. If there is both a union and one employer (a bilateral monopoly), wages and employment will fall within certain limits, but exactly where will depend on the bargaining power of the union or the employer.

Three other issues are discussed in the last three sections of the chapter. First, for many years the Federal government has set a legal **minimum wage** for labor. The chapter uses supply and demand analysis to make the case for and against the minimum wage and then discusses its real-world effects. Second, wage rates are not homogeneous and differ across workers and occupations. The chapter presents important reasons why these **wage differentials** exist. Third, there is a **principal–agent problem** in most types of employment that may lead to shirking on the job. Different pay schemes have been devised to tie workers' pay to performance in an effort to overcome this problem. Each of these issues should be of direct interest to you and deepen your understanding about how labor markets work.

■ CHECKLIST

When you have studied this chapter you should be able to

☐ Define wages (or the wage rate).
☐ Distinguish between nominal and real wages.
☐ List five reasons for high productivity in the United States and other advanced economies.
☐ Describe the long-run relationship between real wages and productivity in the United States.
☐ Evaluate the importance of the two factors contributing to the secular growth in U.S. real wages.
☐ Define the three characteristics of a purely competitive labor market.
☐ Use demand and supply graphs to explain wage rates and the equilibrium level of employment in a purely competitive labor market.
☐ Define the three characteristics of a labor market monopsony and compare it with a purely competitive labor market.
☐ Explain why the marginal resource cost exceeds the wage rate in monopsony.
☐ Use demand and supply graphs to explain wage rates and the equilibrium level of employment in the monopsony model.
☐ Give examples of monopsony power.
☐ List three types of union models.

☐ Identify three strategies of labor unions to increase the demand for labor and their effects on wage rates and employment.

☐ Explain and illustrate graphically the effects of actions taken by craft unions to decrease the supply of labor on wages and the employment of workers.

☐ Explain and illustrate graphically how the organization of workers by an industrial union in a previously competitive labor market would affect the wage rate and the employment level.

☐ Describe the effect of unions on wage increases and two factors that might reduce the unemployment effect from wage increases.

☐ Use a graph to explain why the equilibrium wage rate and employment level are indeterminate when a labor market is a bilateral monopoly and to predict the range for the wage rate.

☐ Present the case for and the case against a legally established minimum wage.

☐ Use supply and demand analysis to explain wage differentials.

☐ Connect wage differentials to marginal revenue productivity.

☐ Give two reasons why noncompeting groups of workers earn different wages.

☐ Explain why some wage differentials are due to compensatory differences in the nonmonetary aspects of jobs.

☐ Cite four types of labor market imperfections that contribute to wage differentials.

☐ Describe the principal–agent problem in worker pay and performance issues.

☐ Describe four pay schemes employers use to prevent shirking or to tie worker pay to performance.

☐ Explain the negative side effects of pay-for-performance schemes.

■ CHAPTER OUTLINE

1. A *wage* (or the wage rate) is the price paid per unit of time for any type of labor. Earnings are equal to the wage multiplied by the amount of time worked. Wages can be measured either in nominal or real terms. A *real wage* is adjusted for the effects of inflation. It reflects the quantity of goods and services a worker can purchase with a *nominal wage*.

2. The *general level of real wages* in the United States and other advanced economies is high because the demand for labor has been large relative to the supply of labor.

   a. The demand for labor in the United States and advanced economies has been strong because labor is highly productive for several reasons: substantial quantities of capital goods and natural resources; technological advancement; improvements in labor quality; and other intangible factors (management techniques, business environment, and size of the domestic market).

   b. The real hourly wage rate and output per hour of labor are closely and directly related to each other, and real income per worker can increase only at the same rate as output per worker.

   c. Increases in the demand for labor over time have been greater than increases in the supply of labor in the United States, increasing the real wage rate in the long run.

3. In a *purely competitive labor market* many firms compete in hiring a specific type of labor and there are many qualified workers with identical skills who independently supply this labor. Both firms and workers are "wage takers" who do not influence the price of labor.

   a. The market *demand curve* for labor is a horizontal summation of the demand curves for individual firms.

   b. The market *supply curve* slopes upward, indicating that a higher wage will entice more workers to supply their labor.

   c. The *wage rate* for labor in this market is determined by the interaction of the market demand for and the supply of that labor. For the individual firm, the supply of labor is perfectly elastic at this wage rate (so the marginal labor cost is equal to the wage rate). The firm will hire the amount of labor at which its marginal revenue product of labor is equal to its marginal labor cost.

4. In a *monopsony* market for labor, there is only one buyer of a particular kind of labor, the labor is relatively immobile, and the hiring firm is a "wage maker" (the wage rate a firm pays varies with the number of workers it employs).

   a. The supply curve is upsloping and indicates that the firm (the single buyer of labor) must pay higher wages to attract more workers.

   b. A monopsonistic firm's marginal labor costs are greater than the wage rates it must pay to obtain various amounts of labor because once it offers a higher wage to one worker, it must offer the same wage to all workers.

   c. The firm hires the amount of labor at which marginal labor cost and the marginal revenue product of labor are equal. Both the wage rate and the level of employment are less than they would be under purely competitive conditions in labor markets.

   (1) Note that if the firm employs resources in imperfectly competitive markets, it is hiring resources in the least-cost combination when the ratio of the marginal product of a resource to its marginal resource cost is the same for all resources, and

   (2) it is hiring resources in the most profitable combination when the marginal revenue product of each resource is equal to its marginal resource cost.

   d. Monopsony power can be found in such situations as small cities where there are one or two firms that hire most of the workers of a particular type in a region or in professional sports franchises that have exclusive rights to obtain the service of professional athletes.

5. In labor markets in which *labor unions* represent workers, the unions attempt to raise wages in three ways.

   a. The union can increase *the demand for labor* by increasing the demand for the products the union workers produce, by increasing productivity, and by increasing the prices of resources that are substitutes for the labor provided by the members of the union.

b. An *exclusive* or *craft union* will seek to increase wages by reducing the supply of labor. *Occupational licensing* is another means of restricting the supply of a particular type of labor.

c. An *inclusive* or *industrial union* will try to increase wages by forcing employers to pay wages in excess of the equilibrium rate that would prevail in a purely competitive labor market.

d. Labor unions are aware that their actions to increase wage rates may also increase the unemployment of their members, which tends to limit the demands for higher wages. The unemployment effect of higher wages, however, is lessened by increases in, and a relatively inelastic, demand for labor.

6. A *bilateral monopoly* is a labor market with a monopsony (single buyer of labor) and an inclusive union (single seller of labor).

a. In this situation, the wage rate depends, within certain limits, on the relative bargaining power of the union and of the employer.

b. This model may be desirable because the monopoly power on the buy side is offset by the monopoly power on the sell side. The resulting wage rate may be close to levels found in purely competitive markets.

7. The *minimum wage* is a price floor that has been used to set a minimum price for unskilled labor.

a. Critics argue that it increases wage rates and reduces the employment of workers. It is a poor policy for reducing household poverty because the benefits largely go to teenagers who do not need the assistance.

b. Defenders think that in a monopsonistic market, it can increase the wage rate and employment. A minimum wage may also increase productivity, thus increasing the demand for labor and reducing turnover.

c. The evidence is mixed. In theory, a higher wage should reduce employment, but in practice the negative effects on employment may be minor or nil. The minimum wage, however, is not a strong antipoverty policy, despite its popular appeal in this respect.

8. *Wage differentials* are found across many occupations. They are often explained by the forces of demand and supply.

a. The strength of the demand for workers in an occupation, given the supply of workers, is due largely to the productivity of workers and the revenues they generate for the firm (or marginal revenue productivity).

b. One major reason for wage differentials is that workers are not homogeneous and can be thought of as falling into many *noncompeting groups.* The wages for each group differ because of

(1) differences in the abilities or skills possessed by workers, the number of workers in each group, and the demand for those abilities or skills in the labor market, and

(2) *investment in human capital* by workers through education and training.

c. A second reason for wage differentials is that jobs vary in difficulty and attractiveness. Higher wages may be necessary to compensate for less desirable nonmonetary aspects of some jobs.

d. A third reason for wage differentials are market imperfections. These arise from a lack of job information, geographic immobilities, union or government restraints, and discrimination.

9. Wage payments in labor markets are often more complex in practice and are often designed to make a connection between *worker pay and performance.*

a. A principal–agent problem arises when the interests of agents (workers) diverge from the interests of the principals (firms). For example, shirking on the job can occur if workers give less than the desired level of performance for pay received.

b. Firms can try to reduce shirking by monitoring worker activity, but this monitoring is costly; therefore, *incentive pay plans* are adopted by firms to tie worker compensation more closely to performance. Among the various incentive schemes are

(1) piece rate payments, commissions, royalties, bonuses, and profit sharing plans, and

(2) efficiency wages that pay workers above-market wages to get greater effort.

c. Sometimes the "solutions" to principal–agent problems lead to negative results. Commissions may cause employees to pad bills; changes in work rules may demoralize workers.

■ **HINTS AND TIPS**

1. The reason why the market supply curve for labor rises in competitive markets is based on an economic concept from Chapter 2 that you may want to review. To obtain more workers, firms must increase wages to cover the *opportunity cost* of workers' time spent on other alternatives (other employment, household work, or leisure).

2. In monopsony, the marginal resource cost exceeds the wage rate (and the marginal-resource-cost curve lies above the supply curve of labor). The relationship is difficult to understand, so you should pay careful attention to the discussion of Table 15.2 and Figure 15.4.

3. To illustrate the differences in the three union models presented in this chapter, draw supply and demand graphs of each model.

4. The chapter presents the positive economic explanations for the differences in wages between occupations. Remember that whether these wage differentials are "fair" is a normative question. (See Chapter 1 for the positive and normative distinction.)

■ IMPORTANT TERMS

wage rate
nominal wages
real wages
purely competitive labor
   market
monopsony
exclusive unionism
occupational licensing
inclusive unionism

bilateral monopoly
minimum wage
wage differentials
marginal revenue productivity
noncompeting groups
investment in human capital
compensating differences
incentive pay plan

SELF-TEST

■ FILL-IN QUESTIONS

1. The price paid for labor per unit of time is the (piece, wage) _____ rate. The earnings of labor are equal to the _____ rate (divided, multiplied) _____ by the amount of time worked. The amount of money received per hour or day by a worker is the (nominal, real) _____ wage, while the purchasing power of that money is the _____ wage.

2. The general level of wages is high in the United States and other advanced economies because the demand for labor in these economies is (weak, strong) _____ relative to the supply of labor. United States labor tends to be highly productive, among other reasons, because it has access to relatively large amounts of (consumer, capital) _____ goods, abundant (financial, natural) _____ resources, a high-quality (service sector, labor force) _____, and superior (wages, technology) _____. There is a close (short-run, long-run) _____ relationship between output per labor hour and real hourly wages in the United States.

3. In a purely competitive labor market,
   a. the supply curve slopes upward from left to right because it is necessary for employers to pay (higher, lower) _____ wages to attract workers from alternative employment. The market supply curve rises because it is an (average cost, opportunity cost) _____ curve.
   b. the demand is the sum of the marginal (revenue product, resource cost) _____ schedules of all firms hiring this type of labor.
   c. the wage rate will equal the rate at which the total quantity of labor demanded is (less than, equal to, greater than) _____ the total quantity of labor supplied.

4. Insofar as an individual firm hiring labor in a purely competitive market is concerned, the supply of labor is perfectly (elastic, inelastic) _____ because the individual firm is unable to affect the wage rate it must pay. The firm will hire that quantity of labor at which the wage rate, or marginal labor cost, is (less than, equal to, greater than) _____ the marginal revenue product.

5. A monopsonist employing labor in a market that is competitive on the supply side will hire that amount of labor at which the marginal revenue product is (less than, equal to, greater than) _____ marginal labor cost. In such a market, the marginal labor cost is (less, greater) _____ than the wage rate, so the employer will pay a wage rate that is _____ than both the marginal revenue product of labor and the marginal labor cost.

6. A monopsonist facing a competitive supply of labor
   a. is employing the combination of resources that enables it to produce any given output in the least costly way when the marginal product of every resource (divided, multiplied) _____ by its marginal resource cost is the same for all resources.
   b. is employing the combination of resources that maximizes its profits when the marginal revenue product of every resource is (equal to, greater than) _____ its marginal resource cost or when the marginal revenue product of each resource (divided, multiplied) _____ by its marginal resource cost is equal to (infinity, 1) _____.

7. When compared with a competitive labor market, a market dominated by a monopsonist results in (higher, lower) _____ wage rates and in (more, less) _____ employment.

8. The basic objective of labor unions is to increase wages, and they attempt to accomplish this goal either by increasing the (demand for, supply of) _____ labor, restricting the _____ labor, or imposing (a below, an above) _____-equilibrium wage rate on employers.

9. Labor unions can increase the demand for the services of their members by increasing the (demand for, supply of) _____ the products they produce, by increasing the (number, productivity) _____ of their members, and by (increasing, decreasing) _____ the prices of resources that are substitutes for the services supplied by their members.

10. Restricting the supply of labor to increase wages is the general policy of (exclusive, inclusive) _____ unionism, and imposing above-equilibrium wage rates is the strategy used in _____ unionism. An example of exclusive unionism is (an industrial, a craft) _____ union, while an example of inclusive unionism would be _____ union.

11. If unions are successful in increasing wages, employment in the industry will (increase, decrease) _____, but this effect on members may lead unions to _____ their wage demands. Unions, however, will not worry too much about the effect on employment from the higher wage rates if the economy is growing or if the demand for labor is relatively (elastic, inelastic) _____.

12. In a labor market that is a bilateral monopoly, the monopsonist will try to pay a wage (less, greater) _____ than the marginal revenue product of labor; the union will ask for some wage _____ than the competitive and monopsonist equilibrium wage. Within these limits, the (wage rate, elasticity) _____ of labor will depend on the relative bargaining strength of the union and the monopsonist.

13. Critics of the minimum wage contend that in purely competitive labor markets, the effect of imposing such a wage is to (increase, decrease) _____ the wage rate and to _____ employment. Defenders of the minimum wage argue that such labor markets are monopsonistic, so the effect is to (increase, decrease) _____ the wage rate and to _____ employment. The evidence suggests that the employment and antipoverty effects from increasing the minimum wage are (positive, uncertain) _____.

14. Actual wage rates received by different workers tend to differ because workers (are, are not) _____ homogeneous, jobs (vary, do not vary) _____ in attractiveness, and labor markets may be (perfect, imperfect) _____.

15. The total labor force is composed of a number of (competing, noncompeting) _____ groups of workers. Wages differ among these groups as a consequence of differences in (ability, wealth) _____ and because of different investments in (the stock market, human capital) _____.

16. Within each of these noncompeting groups, some workers receive higher wages than others to compensate these workers for the less desirable (monetary, nonmonetary) _____ aspects of a job. These wage differentials are called (monopsony, compensating) _____ differences.

17. Workers performing identical jobs often receive different wages due to market imperfections such as lack of information about (investment, job) _____ opportunities, geographic (mobility, immobility) _____, union or government (subsidies, restraints) _____, and (taxes, discrimination) _____.

18. Firms, or parties, who hire others to achieve their objectives may be regarded as (agents, principals) _____, while workers, or parties, who are hired to advance firms' interests can be regarded as the firms' _____. The objective of a firm is to maximize (wages, profits) _____ and workers are hired to help a firm achieve that objective in return for_____, but when the interests of a firm and the workers diverge, a principal–agent problem is created.

19. An example of this type of problem is a situation in which workers provide less than the agreed amount of work effort on the job, which is called (licensure, shirking)_____. To prevent this situation, firms can closely monitor job (pay, performance) _____, but this is costly; therefore, firms offer different incentive _____ plans.

20. Examples of such pay-for-performance schemes include (efficiency, piece) _____ rate payments, commissions and royalties, bonuses and profit sharing, and _____ wages, which means that workers are paid above equilibrium wages to encourage greater work effort. Such plans must be designed with care because of possible (positive, negative) _____ side effects.

■ **TRUE–FALSE QUESTIONS**

Circle T if the statement is true, F if it is false.

1. If you received a 5% increase in your nominal wage and the price level increased by 3%, then your real wage has increased by 8%. **T F**

2. The general level of wages is high in the United States and other advanced economies because the supply of labor is large relative to the demand for it. **T F**

3. One reason for the high productivity of labor in the United States and other advanced economies is access to large amounts of capital equipment.　**T F**

4. Real hourly compensation per worker can increase only at about the same rate as output per worker.　**T F**

5. In a purely competitive labor market, there are few qualified workers who supply labor and few firms that employ this labor.　**T F**

6. If an individual firm employs labor in a purely competitive market, it finds that its marginal labor cost is equal to the wage rate in that market.　**T F**

7. Given a purely competitive employer's demand for labor, a lower wage will result in more workers being hired.　**T F**

8. Both monopsonists and firms hiring labor in purely competitive markets hire labor up to the quantity at which the marginal revenue product of labor and marginal labor cost are equal.　**T F**

9. Increasing the productivity of labor will tend to increase the demand for labor.　**T F**

10. One strategy unions use to bolster the demand for union workers is to lobby against a higher minimum wage for nonunion workers.　**T F**

11. Restricting the supply of labor is a means of increasing wage rates more commonly used by craft unions than by industrial unions.　**T F**

12. Occupational licensing is a means of increasing the supply of specific kinds of labor.　**T F**

13. Unions that seek to organize all available or potential workers in an industry are called craft unions.　**T F**

14. The imposition of an above-equilibrium wage rate will cause employment to fall off more when the demand for labor is inelastic than it will when the demand is elastic.　**T F**

15. Union members are paid wage rates that on the average are greater by about 15% than the wage rates paid to nonunion members.　**T F**

16. The actions of both exclusive and inclusive unions that raise the wage rates paid to them by competitive employers of labor also cause, other things remaining constant, an increase in the employment of their members.　**T F**

17. In a bilateral monopoly, the negotiated wage will be below the competitive equilibrium wage in that labor market.　**T F**

18. If a labor market is purely competitive, the imposition of an effective minimum wage will increase the wage rate paid and decrease employment in that market.　**T F**

19. If an effective minimum wage is imposed on a monopsonist, the wage rate paid by the firm will increase and the number of workers employed by it may also increase.　**T F**

20. The strength of labor demand differs greatly among occupations due to differences in how much each occupation contributes to its employer's revenue.　**T F**

21. Actual wage rates received in different labor markets tend to differ because the demands for particular types of labor relative to their supplies differ.　**T F**

22. Wage differentials that are used to compensate workers for unpleasant aspects of a job are called efficiency wages.　**T F**

23. Market imperfections that impede workers from moving from lower- to higher-paying jobs help explain wage differentials.　**T F**

24. Shirking is an example of a principal–agent problem.　**T F**

25. There are examples of solutions that have been implemented to solve principal–agent problems that produce negative results.　**T F**

■ **MULTIPLE-CHOICE QUESTIONS**

Circle the letter that corresponds to the best answer.

1. Real wages would decline if the
(a) prices of goods and services rose more rapidly than nominal-wage rates
(b) prices of goods and services rose less rapidly than nominal-wage rates
(c) prices of goods and services and wage rates both rose
(d) prices of goods and services and wage rates both fell

2. The basic explanation for high real wages in the United States and other industrially advanced economies is that the
(a) price levels in these nations have increased at a faster rate than nominal wages
(b) governments in these nations have imposed effective minimum wage laws to improve the conditions of labor
(c) demand for labor in these nations is quite large relative to the supply of labor
(d) supply of labor in these nations is quite large relative to the demand for labor

3. A characteristic of a purely competitive labor market would be
(a) firms hiring different types of labor
(b) workers supplying labor under a union contract
(c) wage taker behavior by the firms
(d) price maker behavior by the firms

4. The supply curve for labor in a purely competitive market is upward sloping because the
(a) opportunity costs are rising
(b) the marginal resource cost is constant
(c) the wage rate paid to workers falls
(d) the marginal revenue product rises

5. The individual firm that hires labor under purely competitive conditions faces a supply curve for labor that
  (a) is perfectly inelastic
  (b) is of unitary elasticity
  (c) is perfectly elastic
  (d) slopes upward from left to right

6. Which is a characteristic of a monopsonist?
  (a) The type of labor is relatively mobile.
  (b) The supply curve is the marginal resource cost curve.
  (c) There are many buyers of a particular kind of labor.
  (d) The wage rate it must pay workers varies directly with the number of workers it employs.

7. A monopsonist pays a wage rate that is
  (a) greater than the marginal revenue product of labor
  (b) equal to the marginal revenue product of labor
  (c) equal to the firm's marginal labor cost
  (d) less than the marginal revenue product of labor

8. If a firm employs resources in imperfectly competitive markets, to maximize its profits the marginal revenue product of each resource must equal
  (a) its marginal product
  (b) its marginal resource cost
  (c) its price
  (d) 1

9. Compared with a purely competitive labor market, a monopsonistic market will result in
  (a) higher wage rates and a higher level of employment
  (b) higher wage rates and a lower level of employment
  (c) lower wage rates and a higher level of employment
  (d) lower wage rates and a lower level of employment

10. The monopsonistic labor market for nurses that would be found in a smaller city with two hospitals would lead to
  (a) lower starting salaries
  (b) higher starting salaries
  (c) more employment opportunities
  (d) greater demand for nursing services

11. Higher wage rates and a higher level of employment are the usual consequences of
  (a) inclusive unionism
  (b) exclusive unionism
  (c) an above-equilibrium wage rate
  (d) an increase in the productivity of labor

12. Which would increase the demand for a particular type of labor?
  (a) a decrease in the wages of that type of labor
  (b) an increase in the prices of those resources that are substitutes for that type of labor
  (c) an increase in the prices of the resources that are complements to that type of labor
  (d) a decrease in the demand for the products produced by that type of labor

13. Occupational licensing laws have the economic effect of
  (a) increasing the demand for labor
  (b) decreasing the supply of labor
  (c) strengthening the bargaining position of an industrial union
  (d) weakening the bargaining position of a craft union

14. Industrial unions typically attempt to increase wage rates by
  (a) imposing an above-equilibrium wage rate on employers
  (b) increasing the demand for labor
  (c) decreasing the supply of labor
  (d) forming a bilateral monopoly

Answer Questions 15, 16, and 17 using the data in the following table.

Wage rate	Quantity of labor supplied	Marginal labor cost	Marginal revenue product of labor
$10	0	—	—
11	100	$11	$17
12	200	13	16
13	300	15	15
14	400	17	14
15	500	19	13
16	600	21	12

15. If the firm employing labor were a monopsonist, the wage rate and the quantity of labor employed would be, respectively,
  (a) $14 and 300
  (b) $13 and 400
  (c) $14 and 400
  (d) $13 and 300

16. But if the market for this labor were purely competitive, the wage rate and the quantity of labor employed would be, respectively,
  (a) $14 and 300
  (b) $13 and 400
  (c) $14 and 400
  (d) $13 and 300

17. If the firm employing labor were a monopsonist and the workers were represented by an industrial union, the wage rate would be
  (a) between $13 and $14
  (b) between $13 and $15
  (c) between $14 and $15
  (d) below $13 or above $15

*Answer Questions 18, 19, 20, and 21 on the basis of the following labor market diagram, where **D** is the demand curve for labor, **S** is the supply curve for labor, and **MRC** is the marginal resource (labor) cost.*

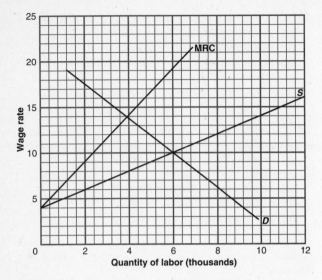

18. If this were a purely competitive labor market, the number of workers hired and the wage rate in equilibrium would be
   (a) 4000 and $14
   (b) 4000 and $8
   (c) 6000 and $10
   (d) 8000 and $12

19. If this were a monopsonistic labor market, the number of workers hired and the wage rate in equilibrium would be
   (a) 4000 and $14
   (b) 4000 and $8
   (c) 6000 and $10
   (d) 8000 and $12

20. Suppose an inclusive union seeks to maximize the employment of workers with the monopsonist. If successful, the number of workers employed and the wage rate would be
   (a) 4000 and $14
   (b) 6000 and $12
   (c) 6000 and $10
   (d) 8000 and $12

21. If the market were characterized as a bilateral monopoly, the number of workers hired and the wage rate in equilibrium would be
   (a) 6000 and $10
   (b) 4000 and $14
   (c) 4000 and $8
   (d) indeterminate

22. The major reason that major league baseball players receive an average salary of over $1 million a year and teachers receive an average salary of about $40,000 a year can best be explained in terms of
   (a) noncompeting labor groups
   (b) compensating differences
   (c) lack of job information
   (d) discrimination

23. The fact that unskilled construction workers typically receive higher wages than bank clerks is best explained in terms of
   (a) noncompeting labor groups
   (b) compensating differences
   (c) geographic immobilities
   (d) union restraints

24. Shirking can be considered to be a principal–agent problem because
   (a) work objectives of the principals (the workers) diverge from the profit objectives of the agent (the firm)
   (b) profit objectives of the principal (the firm) diverge from the work objectives of the agents (the workers)
   (c) the firm is operating in a monopsonistic labor market
   (d) the firm pays efficiency wages to workers in a labor market

25. A firm pays an equilibrium wage of $10 an hour and the workers produce 10 units of output an hour. If the firm adopts an efficiency wage and it is successful, then the wage rate for these workers will
   (a) rise and output will fall
   (b) fall and output will rise
   (c) rise and output will rise
   (d) fall and output will fall

■ **PROBLEMS**

1. Suppose a single firm has for a particular type of labor the marginal-revenue-product schedule given in the following table.

Number of units of labor	MRP of labor
1	$15
2	14
3	13
4	12
5	11
6	10
7	9
8	8

a. Assume there are 100 firms with the same marginal-revenue-product schedules for this particular type of labor. Compute the total or market demand for this labor by completing column 1 in the following table.

(1) Quantity of labor demanded	(2) Wage rate	(3) Quantity of labor supplied
_____	$15	850
_____	14	800
_____	13	750
_____	12	700
_____	11	650
_____	10	600
_____	9	550
_____	8	500

b. Using the supply schedule for labor given in columns 2 and 3,

(1) what will be the equilibrium wage rate? $ _____
(2) what will be the total amount of labor hired in the

market?_____
c. The individual firm will
(1) have a marginal labor cost of $ _____ .

(2) employ _____ units of labor.

(3) pay a wage of $ _____ .
d. On the following graph, plot the market demand and supply curves for labor and indicate the equilibrium wage rate and the total quantity of labor employed.

e. On the following graph, plot the individual firm's demand curve for labor, the supply curve for labor, and the marginal-labor-cost curve which confronts the individual firm, and indicate the quantity of labor the firm will hire and the wage it will pay.
f. The imposition of a $12 minimum wage rate would change the total amount of labor hired in this market

to _____ .

2. In the following table, assume a monopsonist has the marginal-revenue-product schedule for a particular type of labor given in columns 1 and 2 and that the supply schedule for labor is that given in columns 1 and 3.

(1) Number of labor units	(2) MRP of labor	(3) Wage rate	(4) Total labor cost	(5) Marginal labor cost
0		$ 2	$ _____	
1	$36	4	_____	$ _____
2	32	6	_____	_____
3	28	8	_____	_____
4	24	10	_____	_____
5	20	12	_____	_____
6	16	14	_____	_____
7	12	16	_____	_____
8	8	18	_____	_____

a. Compute the firm's total labor costs at each level of employment and the marginal labor cost of each unit of labor, and enter these figures in columns 4 and 5.
b. The firm will

(1) hire _____ units of labor.

(2) pay a wage of $_____ .
(3) have a marginal revenue product for labor of

$ _____ for the last unit of labor employed.
c. Plot the marginal revenue product of labor, the supply curve for labor, and the marginal-labor-cost curve on the following graph and indicate the quantity of labor the firm will employ and the wage it will pay.
d. If this firm's labor market were competitive, there

would be at least _____ units hired at a wage of

at least $_____ .

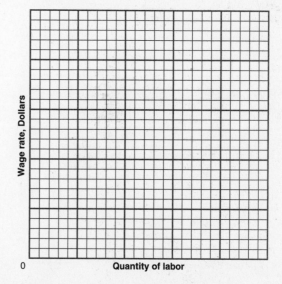

3. Assume that the employees of the monopsonist in problem 2 organize a strong industrial union. The union demands a wage rate of $16 for its members, and the monopsonist decides to pay this wage because a strike would be too costly.

 a. In the following table, compute the supply schedule for labor that now confronts the monopsonist by completing column 2.

(1) Number of labor units	(2) Wage rate	(3) Total labor cost	(4) Marginal labor cost
0	$ ____	$ ____	
1	____	____	$ ____
2	____	____	____
3	____	____	____
4	____	____	____
5	____	____	____
6	____	____	____
7	____	____	____
8	____	____	____

 b. Compute the total labor cost and the marginal labor cost at each level of employment and enter these figures in columns 3 and 4.

 c. The firm will hire _____ units of labor, pay a wage of $ _____, and pay total wages of $ _____.

 d. As a result of unionization, the wage rate has _____, the level of employment has _____, and the earnings of labor have _____.

 e. On the graph below plot the firm's marginal revenue product of labor schedule, the labor supply schedule, and the marginal-labor-cost schedule. Indicate also the wage rate the firm will pay and the number of workers it will hire.

4. Match the following descriptions to the one of the six accompanying graphs on page 185.

 a. A bilateral monopoly   Graph _____
 b. The supply and demand for labor for a purely competitive firm   Graph _____
 c. The labor strategy used by a craft union to raise wages   Graph _____
 d. A monopsonistic labor market   Graph _____
 e. The strategy used by an industrial union to raise wages above a competitive level   Graph _____
 f. A strategy used by a union to get people to buy union-made products   Graph _____

■ SHORT ANSWER AND ESSAY QUESTIONS

1. What is meant by the term "wages"? What is the difference between real wages and nominal wages?

2. How does the level of wages in the United States compare with that in other foreign nations?

3. Explain why the productivity of the U.S. labor force increased in the past to its present high level.

4. Why has the level of real wages continued to increase even though the supply of labor has continually increased?

5. In the competitive model, what determines the market demand for labor and the wage rate? What kind of supply situation do all firms as a group confront? What kind of supply situation does the individual firm confront? Why?

6. In the monopsony model, what determines employment and the wage rate? What kind of supply situation does the monopsonist face? Why? How does the wage rate paid and the level of employment compare with what would result if the market were competitive?

7. In what sense is a worker who is hired by a monopsonist "exploited" and one who is employed in a competitive labor market "justly" rewarded? Why do monopsonists wish to restrict employment?

8. When supply is less than perfectly elastic, marginal labor cost is greater than the wage rate. Why?

9. What basic methods do labor unions use to try to increase the wages their members receive? If these methods are successful in raising wages, what effect do they have on employment?

10. What three methods might labor use to increase the demand for labor? If these methods are successful, what effects do they have on wage rates and employment?

11. When labor unions attempt to restrict the supply of labor to increase wage rates, what devices do they use

1

2

3

4

5

6

to do this for the economy as a whole, and what means do they use to restrict the supply of a given type of worker?

12. How do industrial unions attempt to increase wage rates, and what effect does this method of increasing wages have on employment in the industry affected?

13. Both exclusive and inclusive unions are able to raise the wage rates their members receive. Why might unions limit or temper their demands for higher wages? What two factors determine the extent to which they will or will not reduce their demands for higher wages?

14. What is bilateral monopoly? What determines wage rates in a labor market of this type?

15. Using supply and demand graphs, describe the effect of minimum wage laws on wage rates and employment in (a) purely competitive labor markets and (b) monopsony labor markets.

16. Offer an evaluation of the employment and antipoverty effects of the minimum wage based on past and current evidence.

17. What is meant by the term "noncompeting" groups in a labor market? What two factors tend to explain wage differentials in noncompeting groups?

18. How are wages used to equalize differences in the characteristics of jobs? Give examples.

19. Describe four types of imperfections in labor markets. Discuss how these imperfections contribute to wage differentials.

20. Explain what is meant by the principal–agent problem, and relate it to shirking. What are the different pay incentive plans that correct for shirking on the job? How does profit sharing reduce shirking? What is the reason for efficiency wages?

ANSWERS

Chapter 15 Wage Determination

FILL-IN QUESTIONS

1. wage, wage, multiplied, nominal, real
2. strong, capital, natural, labor force, technology, long-run
3. *a.* higher, opportunity cost; *b.* revenue product; *c.* equal to
4. elastic, equal to
5. equal to, greater, less
6. *a.* divided; *b.* equal to, divided, 1
7. lower, less
8. demand for, supply of, an above
9. demand for, productivity, increasing
10. exclusive, inclusive, a craft, an industrial
11. decrease, decrease, inelastic
12. less, greater, wage rate
13. increase, decrease, increase, increase, uncertain
14. are not, vary, imperfect
15. noncompeting, ability, human capital
16. nonmonetary, compensating
17. job, immobility, restraints, discrimination
18. principals, agents, profits, wages
19. shirking, performance, pay
20. piece, efficiency, negative

TRUE–FALSE QUESTIONS

1. F, pp. 277–278
2. F, p. 278
3. T, p. 278
4. T, p. 279
5. F, p. 280
6. T, p. 280
7. T, pp. 280–281
8. T, pp. 282–283
9. T, p. 285
10. F, p. 285
11. T, p. 285
12. F, p. 286
13. F, pp. 285–286
14. F, p. 287
15. T, p. 287
16. F, pp. 285–287
17. F, pp. 287–288
18. T, pp. 288–289
19. T, pp. 288–289
20. T, p. 290
21. T, p. 290
22. F, pp. 291–292
23. T, pp. 293–294
24. T, p. 293
25. T, p. 295

MULTIPLE-CHOICE QUESTIONS

1. a, pp. 277–278
2. c, p. 278
3. c, p. 280
4. a, p. 280
5. c, pp. 280–281
6. d, p. 282
7. d, pp. 282–283
8. b, pp. 282–283
9. d, pp. 282–283
10. a, p. 284
11. d, p. 285
12. b, p. 285
13. b, p. 286
14. a, pp. 280–281
15. d, pp. 282–283
16. c, pp. 280–281
17. b, pp. 287–288
18. c, pp. 280–281
19. b, pp. 282–283
20. c, pp. 286–287
21. d, pp. 287–288
22. a, pp. 290–291
23. b, pp. 291–292
24. b, p. 293
25. c, p. 294

PROBLEMS

1. *a.* Quantity of labor demanded: 100, 200, 300, 400, 500, 600, 700, 800; *b.* (1) 10.00, (2) 600; *c.* (1) 10.00, (2) 6, (3) 10.00; *d.* graph; *e.* graph; *f.* 400
2. *a.* Total labor cost: 0, 4.00, 12.00, 24.00, 40.00, 60.00, 84.00, 112.00, 144.00, Marginal labor cost: 4.00, 8.00, 12.00, 16.00, 20.00, 24.00, 28.00, 32.00; *b.* (1) 5, (2) 12.00, (3) 20.00; *c.* graph; *d.* 6, 14.00
3. *a.* Wage rate: 16.00, 16.00, 16.00, 16.00, 16.00, 16.00, 16.00, 16.00, 16.00; *b.* Total labor cost: 0, 16.00, 32.00, 48.00, 64.00, 80.00, 96.00, 112.00, 128.00; Marginal labor cost: 16.00, 16.00, 16.00, 16.00, 16.00, 16.00, 16.00, 16.00; *c.* (1) 6, (2) 16.00, (3) 96.00; *d.* increased, increased, increased; *e.* graph (similar to Figure 15.8)
4. *a.* 5; *b.* 3; *c.* 6; *d.* 2; *e.* 4; *f.* 1

SHORT ANSWER AND ESSAY QUESTIONS

1. pp. 277–278
2. pp. 278–279
3. pp. 278–279
4. p. 279
5. pp. 280–282
6. pp. 282–283
7. pp. 282–283
8. pp. 282–283
9. pp. 284–287
10. pp. 284–285
11. pp. 285–286
12. pp. 286–287
13. pp. 286–287
14. pp. 287–288
15. pp. 288–289
16. pp. 288–289
17. pp. 290–291
18. pp. 291–292
19. p. 292
20. pp. 293–294

CHAPTER 16

Rent, Interest, and Profit

Chapter 16 concludes the study of the **prices of resources** by examining rent, interest, and profits. There is nothing difficult about this chapter. By now you should understand that the marginal revenue product of a resource determines the demand for that resource. This understanding can be applied to the demand for land and capital. It will be on the supply side of the land market that you will encounter whatever difficulties there are. The **supply of land** is unique because **it is perfectly inelastic:** Changes in rent do not change the quantity of land that will be supplied. Given the quantity of land available, **demand is the sole determinant of economic rent.** Of course land varies in productivity and can be used for different purposes, but these are merely the factors that explain why the rent on all lands is not the same.

Capital, as the economist defines it, means capital goods. Is the rate of interest, then, the price paid for the use of capital goods? No, not quite. Capital is not one kind of good; it is many different kinds. To be able to talk about the price paid for the use of capital goods, there must be a simple way of adding up different kinds of capital goods. The simple way is to measure the quantity of capital goods in terms of money. **Interest** is the price paid for the use of money (or of financial capital) that in turn is used to purchase **capital goods** (factories, machinery, etc.).

The **demand for and supply of loanable funds** in the economy determines the **interest rate.** In a simplified model, businesses are the primary demanders of loanable funds because they want to use this financial capital to buy capital goods (e.g., equipment, machinery, factories). As with the demand for any good or service, the greater the price of using loanable funds (the interest rate), the smaller the amount of loanable funds that firms will be able and willing to borrow. A business will most likely borrow funds and make an investment in capital goods if the expected rate of return on the investment is greater than the interest rate. Therefore, the lower the interest rate, the greater the opportunities for profitable investments and the greater the amount of loanable funds demanded.

On the supply side, households are the typical suppliers of loanable funds. At a higher rate of interest, households are willing to supply more loanable funds than at lower interest rates because of the weighing of present consumption to future consumption. Most consumers prefer present consumption, but they would be willing to forgo this current use of funds and make them available for loan if there is compensation in the form of interest payments. Thus, the greater the interest rate, the more

saving by households, which in turn creates a greater supply of loanable funds.

The intersection of the demand curve and the supply curve for loanable funds determines the equilibrium rate of interest, or the price of loanable funds, and the equilibrium quantity. This relationship is illustrated in Figure 16.2. The demand and supply curves of loanable funds can also shift due to a variety of factors. For example, there could be an increase in the rates of return on investments, which would increase the demand for loanable funds at each and every interest rate; changes in the tax laws could make savings more attractive and this change would increase the supply of loanable funds. Note too that while in the simplified model businesses are the demanders and households the suppliers of loanable funds, in reality these sectors can operate on both sides of the market.

When it comes to **economic profit,** supply and demand analysis fails the economist. Profits are not merely a wage for a particular type of labor; rather, they are rewards for taking risks and the gains of the monopolist. Such things as "the quantity of risks taken" or "the quantity of effort required to establish a monopoly" simply cannot be measured; consequently, it is impossible to talk about the demand for or the supply of them. Nevertheless, profits are important in the economy. They are largely rewards for doing things that have to be done if the economy is to allocate resources efficiently and to progress and develop; they are the lure or the bait that makes entrepreneurs willing to take the risks that result in efficiency and progress.

The final section of Chapter 16 explains what part of the national income goes to workers and what part goes to capitalists—those who provide the economy with land, capital goods, and entrepreneurial ability. You may be surprised to learn that the lion's share—about 80%—of the national income goes to workers today and went to workers at the beginning of the century, and that only about 20% of national income goes to the capitalists today or went to them in 1900.

■ CHECKLIST

When you have studied this chapter you should be able to

☐ Define economic rent.
☐ Explain why supply of land does not affect economic rent.

□ Illustrate how changes in demand determine economic rent.

□ Explain why land rent is a surplus payment.

□ Give the rationale for a single tax on land proposed by Henry George.

□ State four criticisms of the single tax on land.

□ Illustrate graphically how productivity differences affect land rent.

□ Contrast society's and a firm's perspectives on the alternative uses of land and economic rent.

□ Define interest and state two aspects of it.

□ Describe the loanable funds theory of interest using supply and demand analysis.

□ Show how the equilibrium rate of interest is established in the loanable funds market using supply and demand analysis.

□ Explain why the supply of loanable funds curve has a positive slope.

□ Explain why the demand for loanable funds curve has a negative slope.

□ List factors that change the supply or demand for loanable funds.

□ Distinguish between a change in demand or supply and a change in quantity demanded or supplied as applied to the loanable funds market.

□ Identify the different sides that participants (households, businesses, or government) take in the demand or supply of loanable funds.

□ List five reasons why interest rates differ.

□ Define the pure rate of interest and state how it is measured.

□ Explain how the interest rate affects investment spending, total output, the allocation of capital, and research and development (R&D) spending.

□ Distinguish between nominal and real interest rates.

□ Use graphical analysis to explain the three effects of usury laws.

□ Distinguish between economic and normal profit.

□ Describe the return to the entrepreneurial ability in terms of economic and normal profit.

□ List three sources of economic profit.

□ Explain the relationship between insurable and uninsurable risks and economic profit.

□ Describe how innovation affects economic profit.

□ Discuss the influence of monopoly on economic profit.

□ Identify two functions of profits for the economy.

□ Describe the shares of national income going to labor and capital.

■ **CHAPTER OUTLINE**

1. *Economic rent* is the price paid for the use of land or natural resources whose supply is perfectly inelastic.

   a. The ***supply of land is perfectly inelastic*** because it is virtually fixed in the quantity available. Supply has no influence in determining economic rent.

   b. The demand for land is the active determinant of economic rent. As demand increases or decreases, economic rent will increase or decrease given the perfectly inelastic supply of land.

c. *Economic rent serves no incentive function* given the fixed supply of land. It is not necessary to increase economic rent to bring forth more quantity, as is the case with other natural resources. Economists, therefore, consider economic rent a surplus payment.

d. Socialists have argued that land rent is unearned income and that land should be nationalized.

(1) Henry George, in his 1879 book, *Progress and Poverty*, called for a single tax on land as the sole source of government tax revenue. He based his argument on the grounds of equity and efficiency. Such a tax would not alter the supply of land because economic rent serves no incentive function.

(2) Critics of the single tax cite its inadequacy for meeting government needs, the difficulty of identifying the portion of rent in incomes, the conflicting interpretations of unearned income, and adverse equity effects arising from changes in land ownership.

e. Economic rents on different types of land vary because different plots of land vary in productivity or might have location advantages.

f. From society's perspective, economic rent is a surplus payment, but from a firm's perspective, economic rent is a cost. A firm must pay economic rent to bid the land it wants to use for its production away from alternative uses of the land.

2. *Interest* is the price paid for the use of money. Interest is stated as a percentage. Money is *not* an economic resource because it is not productive. People borrow money at an interest rate and use it to buy capital goods. These capital goods are economic resources that can be used to produce other goods and services.

   a. The ***loanable funds theory of interest*** describes how the interest rate is determined by the demand for and supply of loanable funds. The intersection of the demand for and supply of loanable funds determines the equilibrium interest rate and the quantity of funds loaned.

(1) The ***supply of loanable funds*** is generally provided by households through savings. There is a positive relationship between the interest rate and the quantity of loanable funds supplied. The supply curve, however, may be relatively inelastic and thus not very responsive to changes in the interest rate.

(2) The ***demand for loanable funds*** typically comes from businesses for investment in capital goods. There is an inverse relationship between the interest rate and the quantity of loanable funds demanded. Lower interest rates provide more profitable investment opportunities; higher interest rates reduce investments.

   b. There are some extensions to the simplified model of the loanable funds market.

(1) Financial institutions serve as intermediaries in the supply and demand market for loanable funds.

(2) The supply of funds can change because of changes in factors that affect the thriftiness of households.

(3) The demand for funds can change because of changes in the rate of return on potential investments.

(4) Households and businesses can operate on both sides of the market—as both demanders and suppli-

ers of loanable funds. Government also participates on both sides of the loanable fund market.

c. There is a range of interest rates, although it is convenient to speak as if there were one interest rate. These rates differ because of differences in five factors: risk, maturity, loan size, taxability, and market imperfections.

d. When economists talk about "the interest rate," they are referring to the **pure rate of interest,** which is best measured by the interest paid on long-term and riskless securities, such as 20-year bonds of the U.S. government.

e. The interest rate plays several roles in the economy.

(1) It affects the total output because of the inverse relationship between the interest rate and investment spending; government often tries to influence the interest rate to achieve its policy goals.

(2) It allocates financial and real capital among competing firms and determines the level and composition of the total output of capital goods.

(3) It changes the level and composition of spending on research and development.

(4) These effects are based on changes in the **real interest rate,** which is the rate expressed in inflation-adjusted dollars, not the **nominal interest rate,** which is the rate expressed in current dollars.

f. **Usury laws** specify a maximum interest rate for loans. They were passed to limit borrowing costs, but they can have other effects. First, they may cause a shortage of credit, which is then given only to the most worthy borrowers. Second, borrowers gain from paying less for credit and borrowers lose from receiving less interest income. Third, it creates inefficiency in the economy because funds get directed to less productive investments.

3. **Economic profit** is what remains of the firm's revenue after all its explicit and implicit opportunity costs have been deducted.

a. Economic profit is a payment for entrepreneurial ability. **Normal profit** is the payment necessary to keep the entrepreneur in current work and is thus a cost. Economic profit is the residual payment to the entrepreneur from total revenues after all other costs have been subtracted.

b. Economic profit comes from three basic sources that reflect the dynamic nature of real-world capitalism:

(1) rewards for assuming **uninsurable risk** that arises from changes in economic conditions, the structure of the economy, and government policy;

(2) a return for assuming the uncertainties in innovation; and

(3) surpluses that firms obtain from monopoly power.

c. The expectation of economic profit serves several functions in the economy. Profits encourage businesses to innovate, and this innovation contributes to economic growth. Profits (and losses) guide businesses to produce products and to use resources in the way desired by society.

4. **National income** is distributed among wages, rent, interest, and profit. Using a broad definition, the share of national income going to labor is about 80%. The share going to capitalists is about 20%. These percentages have remained relatively stable since 1900.

■ **HINTS AND TIPS**

1. Although this chapter focuses on three resource payments (rent, interest, and profit), the discussion is much simpler and easier to understand than it was for the one resource payment (wages) in the previous chapter. It will help if you think of this chapter as three minichapters.

2. Use a supply and demand graph for land to explain to yourself why **land rent is surplus payment.** Draw a vertical (perfectly inelastic) supply curve and a downsloping demand curve. Identify the price and quantity combination where the two curves intersect. Then draw a new demand curve showing an increase in demand. What happens to price? (It increases.) What happens to quantity? (No change.) Changes in land rent perform no incentive function for the economy because they bring forth no more supply of land. Land rents are unnecessary (surplus) payments for the economy.

3. The **loanable funds theory of interest** will be easy to understand if you think of it as an application of supply and demand analysis. You need to remember, however, who are the suppliers and who are the demanders of loanable funds. In this simplified model, the suppliers of loanable funds are households who have a different quantity of savings to make available for loans at different interest rates; the higher the interest rate, the greater the quantity of loanable funds supplied. The demanders of loanable funds are businesses that want to borrow a quantity of money at each interest rate; the higher the interest rate, the smaller the quantity of loanable funds demanded for investment purposes.

4. Remember that it is the **expectation of profit,** not the certainty of it, that drives the entrepreneur. The generation of profit involves risk taking by the entrepreneur. You should distinguish, however, between **insurable risks** and those that are not insurable. A major source of profit for the entrepreneur comes from the **uninsurable risks** that the entrepreneur is willing to assume in an uncertain world.

■ **IMPORTANT TERMS**

economic rent

incentive function

single-tax movement

loanable funds theory of interest

pure rate of interest

nominal interest rate

real interest rate

usury laws

explicit costs

implicit costs

economic or pure profit

normal profit

static economy

insurable risks

uninsurable risks

SELF-TEST

■ **FILL-IN QUESTIONS**

1. Economic rent is the price paid for the use of (labor, land) _____ and (capital, natural) _____ resources which are completely (fixed, variable) _____ in supply.

2. The active determinant of economic rent is (demand, supply) _____ and the passive determinant is _____.

3. Economic rent does not bring forth more supply and serves no (profit, incentive) _____ function. Economists consider economic rent a (tax, surplus) _____ payment that is not necessary to ensure that land is available to the economy.

4. Socialists argue that land rents are (earned, unearned) _____ incomes. Henry George called for a single (price, tax) _____ on land to transfer economic rent to government because it would not affect the amount of land. One criticism of George's proposal is that it would not generate enough (revenue, profit) _____.

5. Rents on different pieces of land are not the same because land differs in (price, productivity) _____.

6. From society's perspective, land rent is a (surplus payment, cost) _____, but from a firm's perspective, land rent is a _____ because land (is a free good, has alternative uses) _____.

7. The price paid for the use of money is (profit, interest) _____. It is typically stated as a (price, percentage) _____ of the amount borrowed. Money (is, is not) _____ an economic resource because money _____ productive.

8. Money or financial capital is obtained in the (mutual, loanable) _____ funds market. At the equilibrium rate of interest, the quantity demanded for loanable funds is (greater than, equal to, less than) _____ the quantity supplied of loanable funds.

9. The quantity supplied of loanable funds is (inversely, directly) _____ related to the interest rate while the quantity demanded for loanable funds is _____ related to the interest rate.

10. With a higher interest rate, there are (greater, fewer) _____ opportunities for profitable investment and hence a (larger, smaller) _____ quantity demanded for loanable funds.

11. An increase in the thriftiness of households will result in (an increase, a decrease) _____ in the (supply, demand) _____ of loanable funds. Anything that increases the rate of return on potential investments will (increase, decrease) _____ the (supply, demand) _____ of loanable funds.

12. State five reasons why there is a range of interest rates:

   a. _____

   b. _____

   c. _____

   d. _____

   e. _____

13. Economists often talk of the (loan, pure) _____ rate of interest. It is approximated by the interest paid on (short-term, long-term) _____ U.S. government bonds.

14. A higher equilibrium interest rate often (increases, decreases) _____ business borrowing for investment and thus _____ total spending in the economy, whereas a lower equilibrium interest rate (increases, decreases) _____ business borrowing and thus _____ total spending in the economy.

15. The rate of interest expressed in purchasing power, or inflation-adjusted dollars, is the (real, nominal) _____ interest rate, while the rate of interest expressed in dollars of current value is the _____ interest rate.

16. Laws that state the maximum interest rate at which loans can be made are called (antitrust, usury) _____ laws. These laws cause (market, nonmarket) _____ rationing of credit that favors creditworthy (lenders, borrowers) _____ and leads to (less, more) _____ economic efficiency in the allocation of credit.

17. The difference between total revenue and total cost is (economic, normal) _____ profit. The minimum payment for the entrepreneur to keep him or her in the current line of business is (economic, normal)

_____ profit. The excess of total revenue above total cost is (economic, normal) _____ profit.

18. Economic profit is a reward for either assuming (insurable, uninsurable) _____ risk or for dealing with the uncertainty of (taxation, innovation) _____ .

19. Economic profit over time can also arise from (pure competition, monopoly) _____ , and this source of profit is typically based on (increased, decreased) _____ output, _____ prices above competitive levels, and (increased, decreased) _____ economic efficiency.

20. Defining labor income broadly to include both wages and salaries and proprietors' income, labor's share of national income total is about (20%, 50%, 80%) _____ , while capitalists' share of income is about _____ . The share of income going to capitalists has (increased, decreased, remained stable) _____ since 1900.

■ **TRUE–FALSE QUESTIONS**

Circle T if the statement is true, F if it is false.

1. Rent is the price paid for use of capital resources. **T F**

2. The determination of economic rent for land and other natural resources is based on a demand curve that is perfectly inelastic. **T F**

3. Rent is a surplus payment because it does not perform an incentive function. **T F**

4. Rent is unique because it is not determined by demand and supply. **T F**

5. Henry George argued in _Progress and Poverty_ that the increasing land rents would produce more unearned income for landowners which could then be taxed by government. **T F**

6. Critics of the single tax on land argue that it would bring in too much revenue for the government. **T F**

7. For individual producers, rental payments are surplus payments, but for society they are a cost. **T F**

8. Money is an economic resource and the interest rate is the price paid for this resource. **T F**

9. The quantity of loanable funds demanded is inversely related to the interest rate. **T F**

10. The quantity of loanable funds supplied is directly related to the interest rate. **T F**

11. An increase in the demand for loanable funds would tend to increase the interest rate. **T F**

12. An increase in the rate of return on investments would most likely increase the supply of loanable funds. **T F**

13. Other things equal, long-term loans usually command lower rates of interest than do short-term loans. **T F**

14. The pure rate of interest is best approximated by the interest paid on long-term bonds with very low risk, such as 20-year U.S. Treasury bonds. **T F**

15. A higher equilibrium interest rate discourages business borrowing for investment, reducing investment and total spending. **T F**

16. The interest rate rations the supply of loanable funds to investment projects whose rate of return will be less than the interest rate. **T F**

17. If the nominal rate of interest is 6% and the inflation rate is 3%, the real rate of interest is 9%. **T F**

18. Usury laws result in a shortage of loanable funds and nonmarket rationing in credit markets. **T F**

19. Lenders or banks are the main beneficiaries of usury laws. **T F**

20. If the economists' definition of profit were used, total profit in the economy would be greater than would be the case if the accountants' definition were used. **T F**

21. A normal profit is the minimum payment the entrepreneur must receive to induce him or her to provide entrepreneurial ability for the production of a certain good. **T F**

22. It is the static competitive economy that gives rise to economic profit. **T F**

23. Insurable risk is one of the sources of economic profit. **T F**

24. Economic profit arising from monopoly is more socially desirable than economic profit arising from uncertainty. **T F**

25. Economic profit influences both the level of economic output and the allocation of resources among alternative uses. **T F**

■ **MULTIPLE-CHOICE QUESTIONS**

Circle the letter that corresponds to the best answer.

1. The price paid for a natural resource that is completely fixed in supply is
  (a) profit
  (b) interest
  (c) rent
  (d) a risk payment

2. In total, the supply of land is
  (a) perfectly inelastic
  (b) of unitary elasticity
  (c) perfectly elastic
  (d) elastic but not perfectly elastic

3. The economic rent from land will increase, *ceteris paribus*, whenever the
  (a) price of land decreases
  (b) demand for land increases
  (c) demand for land decreases
  (d) supply curve for land increases

4. Which is a characteristic of the tax proposed by Henry George?
  (a) It would be equal to 20% of all land rent.
  (b) It would be the only tax levied by government.
  (c) It would reduce the supply of land.
  (d) It would reduce rents paid by the amount of the tax.

5. A major criticism of the single tax on land is that it would
  (a) bring in more tax revenues than is necessary to finance all current government spending
  (b) not distinguish between payments for the use of land and those for improvements to land
  (c) take into account the history of ownership of the land in determining the tax
  (d) not tax "unearned" income

6. Which is true?
  (a) The greater the demand for land, the greater the supply of land.
  (b) A windfall profits tax on the increases in the profits of petroleum producers was proposed by Henry George.
  (c) Individual users of land have to pay a rent to its owner because that land has alternative uses.
  (d) The less productive a particular piece of land is, the greater will be the rent its owner is able to earn from it.

7. When the supply curve for a plot of land lies entirely to the right of the demand curve,
  (a) landowners will receive an economic rent
  (b) landowners will not receive an economic rent
  (c) the interest rate on loans for land will increase
  (d) the interest rate on loans for land will decrease

8. Which of the following do economists consider a productive economic resource?
  (a) money
  (b) capital goods
  (c) interest
  (d) profit

9. The upsloping supply of loanable funds is best explained by the idea that most people prefer
  (a) current consumption to future consumption
  (b) future consumption to present consumption
  (c) saving over consumption
  (d) investment over saving

10. Why is the demand for loanable funds downsloping?
  (a) At lower interest rates, fewer investment projects will be profitable to businesses, and hence a small quantity of loanable funds will be demanded.

  (b) At lower interest rates, more investment projects will be profitable to businesses, and hence a small quantity of loanable funds will be demanded.
  (c) At higher interest rates, more investment projects will be profitable to businesses, and hence a large quantity of loanable funds will be demanded.
  (d) At higher interest rates, fewer investment projects will be profitable to businesses, and hence a small quantity of loanable funds will be demanded.

11. In the competitive market for loanable funds, when the quantity of funds demanded exceeds the quantity supplied, then the
  (a) interest rate will decrease
  (b) interest rate will increase
  (c) demand curve will increase
  (d) supply curve will decrease

12. A decrease in the productivity of capital goods will, *ceteris paribus*,
  (a) increase the supply of loanable funds
  (b) decrease the supply of loanable funds
  (c) increase the demand for loanable funds
  (d) decrease the demand for loanable funds

13. Which would tend to result in a lower interest rate for a loan?
  (a) the greater the risk involved
  (b) the shorter the length of the loan
  (c) the smaller the amount of the loan
  (d) the greater the monopoly power of the lender

14. What is the most likely reason why a lender would prefer a high-quality municipal bond that pays a 6% rate of interest rather than a high-quality corporate bond paying 8%?
  (a) The municipal bond is tax-exempt.
  (b) The municipal bond is a long-term investment.
  (c) The corporate bond is safer than the municipal bond.
  (d) The municipal bond is easier to purchase than a corporate bond.

15. The pure rate of interest is best approximated by the interest paid on
  (a) consumer credit cards
  (b) tax-exempt municipal bonds
  (c) 90-day Treasury bills
  (d) 20-year Treasury bonds

16. If the annual rate of interest were 18% and the rate of return a firm expects to earn annually by building a new plant were 20%, the firm would
  (a) not build the new plant
  (b) build the new plant
  (c) have to toss a coin to decide whether to build the new plant
  (d) not be able to determine from these figures whether to build the plant

Questions 17 and 18 refer to the following data.

Expected rate of return	Amount of capital goods investment (in billions)
19%	$220
17	250
15	300
13	360
11	430
9	500

17. If the interest rate is 13%,
(a) $300 billion of investment will be undertaken
(b) $360 billion of investment will be undertaken
(c) $430 billion of investment will be undertaken
(d) $500 billion of investment will be undertaken

18. An increase in the interest rate from 15% to 17% would
(a) increase investment by $40 billion
(b) increase investment by $50 billion
(c) decrease investment by $50 billion
(d) decrease investment by $40 billion

19. Which is the definition of a usury law? It is a law that specifies the
(a) alternative uses of surplus government land
(b) tax rate on interest paid for state and municipal bonds
(c) maximum interest rate at which loans can be made
(d) interest paid on long-term, virtually riskless bonds of the U.S. government

20. Which would be a likely economic effect of a usury law?
(a) There would be an increase in economic efficiency.
(b) There would be a decrease in the rationing of credit.
(c) Creditworthy borrowers would lose and lenders would gain.
(d) Creditworthy borrowers would gain and lenders would lose.

21. Which is the minimum return or payment necessary to retain the entrepreneur in some specific line of production?
(a) normal profit
(b) explicit cost
(c) real interest rate
(d) pure rate of interest

22. Which is an economic cost?
(a) uninsurable risk
(b) normal profit
(c) economic profit
(d) monopoly profit

23. One basic reason why there is economic profit is that
(a) risks are insurable
(b) economies are static
(c) there is innovation
(d) there are purely competitive markets

24. Monopoly profit is typically based on
(a) uncertainty and innovation
(b) insurable and uninsurable risk

(c) productivity and economic efficiency
(d) reduced output and above-competitive prices

25. Since 1900, the share of national income
(a) has increased for capitalists, but decreased for labor
(b) has decreased for capitalists, but increased for labor
(c) has increased for capitalists and for labor
(d) has remained relatively constant for capitalists and labor

■ **PROBLEMS**

1. Assume that the quantity of a certain type of land available is 300,000 acres and the demand for this land is that given in the following table.

Pure land rent, per acre	Land demanded, acres
$350	100,000
300	200,000
250	300,000
200	400,000
150	500,000
100	600,000
50	700,000

a. The pure rent on this land will be $ _____ .

b. The total quantity of land rented will be _____ acres.

c. On the following graph, plot the supply and demand curves for this land and indicate the pure rent for land and the quantity of land rented.

d. If landowners were taxed at a rate of $250 per acre for their land, the pure rent on this land after taxes would be $ _____ but the number of acres rented would be _____ .

2. The following schedule shows interest rates (column 1), the associated quantity demanded of loanable funds (column 2), and the quantity supplied of loanable funds (column 4) in billions of dollars at those interest rates.

Interest rate (1)	Quantity demanded (2)	(3)	Quantity supplied (4)	(5)
12	50	_____	260	_____
10	100	_____	240	_____
8	150	_____	220	_____
6	200	_____	200	_____
4	250	_____	180	_____
2	300	_____	160	_____

a. Plot the demand and supply schedule on the following graph. (The interest rate is measured along the vertical axis and the quantity demanded or supplied is measured on the horizontal axis.)

(1) The equilibrium interest rate is _____%.

The quantity demanded is $ _____ billion and the quantity supplied is $ _____ billion.

(2) At an interest rate of 10%, the quantity demanded of loanable funds is $_____ billion and the quantity supplied of loanable funds is $_____ billion. There is an excess of loanable funds of $_____ billion.

(3) At an interest rate of 4%, the quantity demanded of loanable funds is $_____ billion and the quantity supplied of loanable funds is $_____ billion. There is a shortage of loanable funds of $_____ billion.

b. If technology improves and the demand for loanable funds increases by $70 billion at each interest rate, then the new equilibrium interest rate will be

_____% and the equilibrium quantity of loanable funds will be $_____ billion. Fill in the new demand schedule in column 3 of the table and plot this new demand curve on the graph.

c. Then, because of changes in the tax laws, households become thriftier by $140 at each interest rate. The new equilibrium interest rate will be

_____% and the new equilibrium quantity of loanable funds will be $_____ billion. Fill in the new supply schedule in column 5 of the table, and plot this new supply curve on the graph.

3. Firms make investment decisions based on the rate of return and the interest rate.

a. In each of the following simple cases, calculate the rate of return on an investment.

(1) You invest in a new machine that costs $2000 but which is expected to increase total revenues by $2075

in 1 year. _____

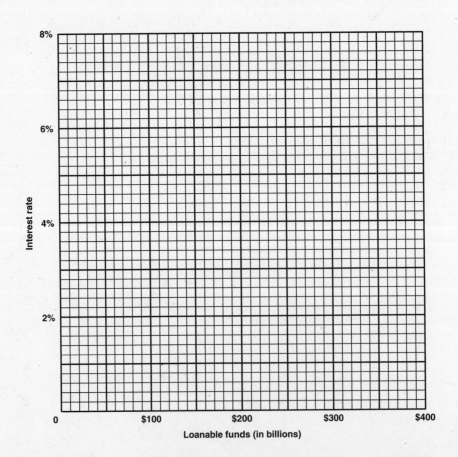

Loanable funds (in billions)

(2) You invest in a new piece of equipment that costs $150,000 but which is expected to increase total revenues in 1 year by $160,000. _____

(3) You invest in a new plant that costs $3 million and which is expected to increase total revenues in 1 year by $3.5 million. _____

b. Given each of the following interest rates, in which situations (1, 2, and 3) would you make an investment?

(1) An interest rate of 5% _____

(2) An interest rate of 8% _____

(3) An interest rate of 15% _____

4. The following table shows estimated wages and salaries, proprietors' income, corporate profits, interest, rent, and the national income of the United States in a recent year.

Wages and salaries	$5,642 billion
Proprietors' income	717 billion
Corporate profits	967 billion
Interest	571 billion
Rent	139 billion
National income	8,036 billion

a. Wages and salaries were _____% of the national income.

b. Labor's share of the national income was _____% and capital's share was _____%.

■ **SHORT ANSWER AND ESSAY QUESTIONS**

1. Explain what determines the economic rent paid for the use of land. What is unique about the supply of land?

2. Why is land rent a surplus payment?

3. What economic difficulties would be encountered if the government adopted Henry George's single tax proposal as a means of confiscating this surplus? What do the critics think of the concept of a single tax on land?

4. Even though land rent is an economic surplus payment, it is also an economic cost for the individual use of land. Why and how can it be both an economic surplus payment and an economic cost?

5. Explain what determines (a) the amount of loanable funds that households are willing to supply, (b) the amount that businesses wish to demand, and (c) how these desires are resolved in the market for loanable funds.

6. How might a change in productivity affect the interest rate? How might a change in the tax laws affect household savings and the interest rate? What are the implications if the supply curve for loanable funds is highly inelastic?

7. What is the connection between the rate of return on a capital goods investment and the interest rate? Give examples of possible investment situations.

8. Why are there actually many different rates in the economy at any given time?

9. What is the pure rate of interest? How is it approximated?

10. What important functions does the rate of interest perform in the economy?

11. What is the difference between the nominal and the real interest rates? How does each one affect investment spending or decisions about research and development?

12. What are usury laws? Explain in terms of demand and supply analysis.

13. What are the effects of usury laws on allocation of credit, borrowers and lenders, and economic efficiency?

14. What is economic profit? In what way is economic profit a return to entrepreneurial ability?

15. Why would there be no economic profit in a purely competitive and static economy?

16. Why is the distinction between insurable and uninsurable risk important from an economic profit perspective? What are three sources that contribute to uninsurable risk?

17. How does economic profit arise from innovation?

18. "The risks that an entrepreneur assumes arise because of uncertainties that are external to the firm and because of uncertainties that are developed by the initiative of the firm itself." Explain.

19. Explain why profit arising from monopoly is not socially desirable, while profit arising from uncertainty is socially desirable.

20. What part of the U.S. national income is labor's share, and what part is the capitalist's share? Have the shares changed much since 1900?

ANSWERS

Chapter 16 Rent, Interest, and Profit

FILL-IN QUESTIONS

1. land, natural, fixed
2. demand, supply
3. incentive, surplus
4. unearned, tax, revenue
5. productivity
6. surplus payment, cost, has alternative uses
7. interest, percentage, is not, is not
8. loanable, equal to
9. directly, inversely
10. fewer, smaller
11. an increase, supply, increase, demand
12. *a.* risk; *b.* length of loan; *c.* amount of loan; *d.* tax status of loan (or investment); *e.* market imperfections (any order for *a–e*)
13. pure, long-term
14. decreases, decreases, increases, increases
15. real, nominal
16. usury, nonmarket, borrowers, less
17. economic, normal, economic
18. uninsurable, innovation
19. monopoly, decreased, increased, decreased
20. 80%, 20%, remained stable

TRUE–FALSE QUESTIONS

1. F, p. 298
2. F, p. 299
3. T, p. 299
4. F, p. 299
5. T, p. 300
6. F, p. 300
7. F, pp. 300–301
8. F, p. 301
9. T, pp. 302–303

10. T, pp. 302–303
11. T, p. 303
12. F, pp. 302–303
13. F, p. 304
14. T, pp. 304–305
15. T, p. 305
16. F, p. 305
17. F, pp. 305–306
18. T, p. 306

19. F, p. 306
20. F, p. 307
21. T, p. 307
22. F, pp. 307–308
23. F, pp. 307–308
24. F, p. 308
25. T, p. 308

MULTIPLE-CHOICE QUESTIONS

1. c, p. 298
2. a, p. 299
3. b, p. 299
4. b, p. 300
5. b, p. 300
6. c, p. 301
7. b, pp. 300–301
8. b, p. 301
9. a, p. 302

10. d, p. 302
11. b, p. 302
12. d, pp. 303–304
13. b, p. 304
14. a, p. 304
15. d, pp. 304–305
16. b, p. 305
17. b, p. 305
18. c, p. 305

19. c, p. 306
20. d, p. 306
21. a, p. 307
22. b, p. 307
23. c, pp. 307–308
24. d, p. 308
25. d, p. 310

PROBLEMS

1. *a.* 250; *b.* 300,000; *c.* graph; *d.* 0, 300,000
2. *a.* (1) 6, 200, 200, (2) 100, 240, 140, (3) 250, 180, 70; *b.* 8, 220; 120, 170, 220, 270, 320, 370; *c.* 4, 320; 400, 380, 360, 340, 320, 300
3. *a.* (1) 3.75; (2) 6.67; (3) 16.67; *b.* (1) 2, 3; (2) 3; (3) 3
4. *a.* 70; *b.* 79, 21

SHORT ANSWER AND ESSAY QUESTIONS

1. pp. 298–299
2. pp. 299–300
3. p. 300
4. pp. 300–301
5. pp. 301–302
6. p. 303
7. p. 303

8. p. 304
9. pp. 304–305
10. p. 305
11. pp. 305–306
12. p. 306
13. p. 306
14. p. 307

15. pp. 307–308
16. pp. 307–308
17. p. 308
18. pp. 307–308
19. p. 308
20. p. 310

CHAPTER 17

Government and Market Failure

This chapter is the first of two on the economic role of government, a topic that was first introduced in Chapter 5. The focus is *market failure* that occurs in our economy. This failure often results in government interventions to provide public goods and services, to address externality problems such as pollution, and to improve the quality and amount of information for buyers and sellers in the private markets.

The chapter first reviews the characteristics of a *public good.* Recall from Chapter 5 that a private good is characterized by rivalry and excludability, but a public good is not. What is new in Chapter 17 is that you are shown how the demand curve and schedule for a public good are constructed and how the optimal allocation of a public good is determined. The demand and supply curves for a public good are related to the collective marginal benefit and cost of providing the good.

Governments sometimes use *cost-benefit analysis* to determine if they should undertake some specific action or project. This analysis requires the government to estimate the marginal costs and the marginal benefits of the project, and it can be used to decide when such projects should be expanded, contracted, or eliminated.

The second topic of the chapter is *externalities,* situations in market transactions that create spillover costs or spillover benefits for parties not involved in the transactions. You learned in Chapter 5 that government can reduce spillover costs to society and increase spillover benefits. This general point is now modified by the *Coase theorem,* which shows that government intervention is not always required because in many cases individual bargaining can settle externality disputes. If this solution is not possible, government action with direct controls or taxes may be used.

Pollution is a prime example of a negative externality. Over the years, the government has developed antipollution policies, but the market-based ones merit your attention in your study of economics. You will discover that the government can create a *market for externality rights,* and that there is a rule for the *optimal reduction of an externality.* You will also learn how supply and demand in the recycling market can reduce landfill demands and the incineration of solid waste.

Another type of market failure you will encounter in the last major section of this chapter is *asymmetric information.* You have probably never thought about the role of information in the functioning of markets, but you will discover how important information is to both buyers and sellers. For example, buyers need some assurance about the measurement standards or quality of products that they purchase, be it gasoline or medical care. The government may intervene in some markets to ensure that this information is made available to buyers.

Inadequate information in markets creates problems for sellers, too. In certain markets, such as insurance, sellers experience a *moral hazard problem* because buyers change their behavior and become less careful, and the change in behavior makes the insurance more costly to sellers. There is also an *adverse selection problem* in the insurance market because those buyers most likely to benefit (higher-risk buyers) are more likely to purchase the insurance; therefore this group imposes higher costs on sellers than if the riskers were more widely spread among the population. Actions of sellers to screen buyers would mean that fewer people will be covered by insurance and create situations that may lead to the provision of social insurance by government. Government may provide better information about workplace safety or enforce safety standards to address these information problems.

You should not finish this chapter with the sole thought that all market failures require government intervention and direct control. Some problems do require a specific government action, but other problems may be handled efficiently or in a more optimal way through individual negotiations, lawsuits, or the use of market incentives. What is important for you to understand is the range of solutions to externality and information problems.

■ CHECKLIST

When you have studied this chapter you should be able to

☐ Compare the characteristics of a public good with a private good.
☐ Calculate the demand for a public good when given tabular data.
☐ Explain how marginal benefit is reflected in the demand for a public good.
☐ Describe the relationship between marginal cost and the supply of a public good.
☐ Identify on a graph where there is an overallocation, an underallocation, and an optimal allocation of a public good.
☐ Use cost-benefit analysis to determine the extent to which government should apply resources to a project or program when you are given the cost and benefit data.

☐ Define and give examples of positive and negative externalities (spillovers).

☐ Use supply and demand graphs to illustrate how spillover costs and spillover benefits affect the allocation of resources.

☐ State the conditions that are necessary for individual bargaining with the Coase theorem and give an example.

☐ Explain how liability rules and lawsuits are used to resolve externality problems.

☐ Discuss two means government uses to achieve allocative efficiency when there are spillover costs.

☐ Identify the four major provisions of the Clean Air Act of 1990.

☐ Describe three government options to correct for the underallocation of resources when spillover benefits are large and diffuse.

☐ Define the "tragedy of the commons."

☐ Determine the price a government agency should charge in a market for externality rights (e.g., air pollution), when given the data for analysis.

☐ Compare the advantages of a market for externality rights with the policy of direct controls.

☐ Explain how pollution rights are traded under the Clean Air Act and the policies of the Environmental Protection Agency (EPA).

☐ Explain and illustrate with a graph a rule for determining the optimal reduction of a negative externality.

☐ Describe the solid waste disposal problem and the reason for interest in recycling.

☐ Explain how a market for recyclable input works using a supply and demand analysis.

☐ Discuss the economics issues involved in global warming policies.

☐ Define the terms "information failure" and "asymmetric information."

☐ Explain how inadequate information about sellers can cause market failure and give two examples of government response.

☐ Define the terms "moral hazard" and "adverse selection."

☐ Describe how inadequate information about buyers can create a moral hazard problem, an adverse selection problem, and a workplace problem, and give examples of how government can respond.

☐ Cite examples of how information failures are overcome without government intervention.

■ CHAPTER OUTLINE

1. Two characteristics of a ***private good*** are rivalry and excludability. Rivalry means that consumption of the product by a buyer eliminates the possibility of consumption of that product by another person. Excludability refers to the ability of the seller to exclude a person from consuming the product if the person does not pay for it. A ***public good,*** such as national defense, is characterized by nonrivalry and nonexcludability. Nonrivalry means that once a public good is consumed by one person, it is still available for consumption by another person. Nonexcludability means that those individuals who do not pay for

the public good can still obtain the benefits from the public good.

  a. The ***demand for a public good*** is determined by summing the prices that people are willing to pay collectively for the last unit of the public good at each possible quantity demanded, whereas the demand for a private good is determined by summing the quantities demanded at each possible price. The demand curve for a public good is downsloping because of the law of diminishing marginal utility.

  b. The ***supply curve of a public good*** is upsloping because of the law of diminishing returns; additional units supplied reflect increasing marginal costs.

  c. The ***optimal allocation*** of a public good is determined by the intersection of the supply and demand curves.

  (1) If the marginal benefit exceeds the marginal cost, there is an underallocation of a public good,

  (2) but if the marginal cost exceeds the marginal benefit there will be an overallocation.

  (3) Only when the marginal benefits equal the marginal costs is there an optimal allocation of public goods.

  d. Government uses ***cost-benefit analysis*** to decide if it should use resources for a project and to determine the total quantity of resources it should devote to a project. The ***marginal cost = marginal benefit rule*** is used to make the decision. Additional resources should be devoted to a project only so long as the marginal benefits to society from the project exceed society's marginal costs. In this case, the total benefits minus the total costs are at a maximum.

2. Market failure can arise from ***externalities,*** or spillovers, whereby a third party bears a portion of the cost associated with the production or consumption of a good or service.

  a. ***Spillover costs*** (negative externalities) result in an ***overallocation*** of resources to the production of a product. All the costs associated with the product are not reflected in the supply curve. The producer's supply curve lies to the right of the full-cost supply curve.

  b. ***Spillover benefits*** (positive externalities) result in an ***underallocation*** of resources to the production of a product. All the benefits from the product are not reflected in the demand curve. The demand curve lies to the left of the full-benefits demand curve.

  c. Individual bargaining can be used to correct negative externalities or to encourage positive externalities. The ***Coase theorem*** suggests that private negotiations rather than government intervention should be the course of action if there is clear ownership of the property, the number of people involved is small, and the cost of bargaining is minimal. When these conditions do not hold, however, it may be necessary for government intervention.

  d. The legal system can be used to resolve disputes arising from externalities. This system defines *property rights* and specifies *liability rules* that can be used for *lawsuits* on externality issues. This method has limita-

tions because of the expense, the length of time to resolve the disputes, and the uncertainty of the outcomes.
e. When there is the potential for severe harm to common resources, such as air or water, and when the situation involves a large number of people, two types of government intervention may be necessary.
(1) **Direct controls** use legislation to ban or limit the activities that produce a negative externality. These actions reduce the supply of the products that create the negative externalities to levels that are allocatively efficient.
(2) **Specific taxes** are also applied to productive activity that creates negative externalities. These taxes increase the cost of production, and thus decrease the supply to levels that are allocatively efficient.
f. With spillover benefits other government actions may be necessary to correct for the underallocation of resources.
(1) The government can give subsidies to buyers to encourage the purchase or consumption of a good or service.
(2) The government can give subsidies to producers to reduce the cost of production and increase output of a good or service.
(3) When spillover benefits are extremely large, government may decide to provide the good or service.
g. There are market-based approaches to spillover problems.
(1) The **tragedy of the commons** refers to situations where common resources such as air, water, or oceans are subject to pollution problems because no individual or organization has a monetary incentive to maintain the quality or purity of the resource.
(2) One solution to the problem has been to create a **market for externality rights** or to internalize the spillover cost in a market.
(3) For example, the government (a pollution-control agency) might set a limit for the amount of pollution permitted in a region. This limit means that the supply curve is perfectly inelastic (vertical) at some level of pollution. The demand curve would reflect the willingness of polluters to pay for the right to pollute at different prices. The price for pollution rights would be determined by the intersection of the demand and supply curves. Given a fixed supply curve, an increase in demand because of economic growth in the region would increase the price of pollution rights.
(4) This market solution has advantages over direct government controls. It is more efficient and thus reduces society's costs. It puts a price on pollution and thus creates a monetary incentive for businesses to not pollute or to reduce their level of pollution.
(5) Real examples of this approach are found in provisions in the Clean Air Act of 1990 and policies of the Environmental Protection Agency (EPA).
h. In most cases, the **optimal reduction of an externality** is not zero from society's perspective.
(1) It occurs where the marginal cost to society from the externality and the marginal benefit of reducing it are equal (**MB = MC**).

(2) Over time, shifts in the marginal-cost and marginal-benefit curves change the optimal level of externality reduction.
i. Solid waste usually has been deposited in garbage dumps or incinerated, but this approach creates negative externalities and is increasingly expensive.
(1) The situation has created a market for recycled items to help reduce this pollution problem.
(2) Government can use either demand or supply incentives to encourage recycling as an alternative to dumps or incineration.
j. Global warming from carbon dioxide and other greenhouse gases may be permanently altering climate patterns and will have economic effects on different regions. In designing government policies, economists stress the use of markets and the need to evaluate the costs and benefits of alternative policies.

3. Economic inefficiency from information failures can occur in markets. These information failures arise from **asymmetric information**—unequal knowledge that is held by parties to a market transaction.
a. When information involving sellers is incomplete, inaccurate, or very costly, there will be market failures. For example, in the market for gasoline, consumers need accurate information about the amount and quality of gasoline they purchase. In the market for medical services, it is important that consumers have some assurances about the credentials of physicians. Government can respond to these information failures by such actions as establishing measurement standards and by testing and licensing.
b. Inadequate information involving buyers creates market failures.
(1) A market may produce less than the optimal amount of goods and services from society's perspective because of a **moral hazard problem,** which results when buyers alter their behavior and increase the costs of sellers. For example, the provision of insurance may cause the insured to be less cautious.
(2) An **adverse selection problem** occurs in many markets. In the case of insurance, the buyers most likely to need or benefit from insurance are the ones most likely to purchase it. These higher-risk buyers impose higher costs on sellers. Sellers then screen out the higher-risk buyers, but this action reduces the population covered by insurance in the private market. In some cases, government may establish a social insurance system that is designed to cover a much broader group of the population than would be covered by the private insurers, such as with Social Security.
(3) Market failures occur in resource markets when there is inadequate information for workers about the health hazards or safety of a workplace. Government can act to correct these problems by publishing health and safety information or by forcing businesses to provide more information. The typical approach to this problem has been the enforcement of standards for health and safety on the job.
c. Government does not always need to intervene in the private market to address information problems.

Businesses can adopt policies to correct these problems, and some firms or other organizations can specialize in providing important market information for buyers or sellers.

■ HINTS AND TIPS

1. Review Chapter 5's discussion of public goods and externalities.

2. Make sure you understand the difference between the demand for public and private goods. The *demand for a private good* is determined by adding the quantities demanded at each possible price. The *demand for a public good* is determined by adding the prices people collectively are willing to pay for the last unit of the public good at each possible quantity demanded.

3. Table 17.3 is important because it summarizes the private actions and government policies taken to correct for spillover costs or benefits. The government can influence the allocation of resources in a private market by taking actions that increase or decrease demand or supply.

4. Problems occur because information in a market is sometimes asymmetric, which means that there is *unequal* information for sellers or buyers about product price, quality, or other product conditions. Use the examples in the text to help you distinguish between the different types of information problems created by sellers or buyers.

■ IMPORTANT TERMS

cost-benefit analysis	market for externality rights
marginal cost = marginal benefit rule	optimal reduction of an externality
externalities (spillovers)	asymmetric information
Coase theorem	moral hazard problem
tragedy of the commons	adverse selection problem

SELF-TEST

■ FILL-IN QUESTIONS

1. Rivalry means that when one person buys and consumes a product, it (is, is not) _____ available for purchase and consumption by another person. Excludability means that the seller (can, cannot) _____ keep people who do not pay for the product from obtaining its benefits. Rivalry and excludability apply to (private, public) _____ goods, but these characteristics do not apply to _____ goods.

2. With a private good, to compute the market demand you add together the (prices, quantities demanded) _____ people are willing to pay for at each

possible (price, quantity demanded) _____. With a public good, to compute the collective demand you add together the (prices, quantities demanded) _____ people are willing to pay for the last unit of the public good at each possible (price, quantity demanded) _____.

3. The demand curve for a public good slopes downward because of the law of diminishing marginal (returns, utility) _____; the supply curve for a public good is upsloping because of the law of diminishing _____. The demand curve for a public good is, in essence, a marginal-(benefit, cost) _____ curve; the supply curve for a public good reflects rising marginal _____. The optimal quantity of a public good will be shown by the intersection of the collective demand and supply curves, which means that marginal (benefit, cost) _____ of the last unit equals that unit's marginal _____.

4. In applying cost-benefit analysis, government should use more resources in the production of public goods if the marginal (cost, benefit) _____ from the additional public goods exceeds the marginal _____ that results from having fewer private goods. This rule will determine which plan from a cost-benefit analysis will result in the (maximum, minimum) _____ net benefit to society.

5. One objective of government is to correct for market failures called spillovers or (internalities, externalities) _____. If there is a cost to an individual or group that is a third party to the market transaction, it is a (positive, negative) _____ externality or a spillover (benefit, cost) _____. If there is a benefit to an individual or group that is a third party to a market transaction, it is a (positive, negative) _____ externality or a spillover (benefit, cost) _____.

6. When there are spillover costs in competitive markets, the result is an (over, under) _____ allocation of resources to the production of the good or service. When there are spillover benefits, the result is an (over, under) _____ allocation of resources to the production of the good or service.

7. The (liability, Coase) _____ theorem suggests that when there are negative or positive externalities in situations in which the ownership of property is (undefined, defined) _____, the number of people involved is (large, small) _____, and the costs of bargaining are (major, minor) _____, then government intervention (is, is not) _____ required.

8. The legal system is also important for settling externality disputes between individuals because laws define (political, property) _____ rights and specify (business, liability) _____ rules that can be used for lawsuits. This method, however, has limitations because of its cost, the length of time, and the (certainty, uncertainty) _____ of the results.

9. Government may use direct controls to reduce spillover (benefits, costs) _____ by passing legislation that restricts business activity. In other cases, the government may (subsidize, tax) _____ a producer.

10. The government may correct for the underallocation of resources where spillover (costs, benefits) _____ are large and diffuse. This objective can be achieved by (taxing, subsidizing) _____ buyers or producers and through government (provision, consumption) _____ of a good or service.

11. When no private individual or institution has a monetary incentive to maintain the purity or quality of resources such as air, water, oceans, or lands, it creates an externality problem that is sometime called the tragedy of the (firm, commons) _____. A policy approach to spillover cost problems is to create a (market, government) _____ for externality rights.

12. Consider how such a market for pollution rights would work.
  a. If the regional government agency sets a limit on the amount of air pollution, the supply curve for the air pollution rights would be perfectly (elastic, inelastic) _____.
  b. The demand curve for air pollution rights would be (up, down) _____ sloping and intersect the supply curve to determine the (quantity, price) _____ for the right to pollute the air.
  c. If the demand for air pollution rights increased over time, then the price would (rise, fall, stay the same) _____, but the quantity supplied would _____.

13. Reducing negative externalities comes at a "price" to society, and therefore society must decide how much of a decrease it wants to (buy, sell) "_____." Further abatement of a negative externality increases

economic efficiency if the marginal cost is (greater than, equal to, less than) _____ the marginal benefit, but it is economically inefficient if the marginal benefit is _____ the marginal cost. The optimal reduction of a negative externality occurs where the society's marginal benefit is (greater than, equal to, less than) _____ society's marginal cost.

14. One way the government can increase the recycling of solid waste is to (decrease, increase) _____ the demand for recycled inputs in the production process or _____ the incentives to supply recycled products.

15. One of the most controversial and continuing problems with air pollution abatement is the issue of global (trade, warming) _____. Over the past few decades, there has been a noticeable (increase, decrease) _____ in the temperature of the earth's surface. Economists stress that in designing policies to address this problem, the benefits of reducing greenhouse-gas emissions problems should be (greater than, less than) _____ the costs. They also note that some adjustment to any climate change will occur naturally because of changes in prices and profits in the (environment, market) _____.

16. Markets can produce failures because of (symmetric, asymmetric) _____ information. When information involving sellers is (complete, incomplete) _____ or obtaining such information is (costless, costly) _____, the market will (under, over) _____ allocate resources to the production of that good or service.

17. To correct such problems in the gasoline market, the government establishes quality (prices, standards) _____. In the medical market, the government protects consumers by (taxing, licensing) _____ physicians.

18. Inadequate information involving buyers can lead to two problems. First, if a market situation arises whereby buyers alter their behavior and increase the cost to sellers, (an adverse selection, a moral hazard) _____ problem is created. Second, if buyers withhold information from sellers that would impose a large cost on sellers, _____ problem is created. The moral hazard problem occurs (at the same time, after) _____ a person makes a purchase, but the adverse selection problem occurs _____ the buyer makes a purchase.

19. Another example of information failure occurs in labor markets in which there is incomplete or inadequate information about (productivity, safety) _____. The government will intervene in these situations to enforce (quotas, standards) _____ or provide (health care, information) _____ related to workplace hazards.

20. Private businesses overcome some information problems about the product reliability or quality through (prices, warranties) _____ for products or the (penalizing, franchising) _____ of businesses that make them more uniform. Some businesses and organizations also collect and publish product information that is useful for (sellers, buyers) _____. Despite these actions, there may still be a need for government actions to correct (wage, information) _____ problems and to promote an efficient allocation of society's scarce resources.

■ **TRUE–FALSE QUESTIONS**

Circle T if the statement is true, F if it is false.

1. Excludability applies to public goods but not to private goods. **T F**

2. When determining the collective demand for a public good, you add the prices people are willing to pay for the last unit of the public good at each possible quantity demanded. **T F**

3. When the marginal benefit of a public good exceeds the marginal cost, there will be an overallocation of resources to that public good use. **T F**

4. The optimal allocation of a public good is determined by the rule that marginal cost (MC) equals marginal revenue (MR). **T F**

5. "Reducing government spending" means the same as "economy in government." **T F**

6. A spillover is a cost or benefit accruing to an individual or group—a third party—which is external to the market transaction. **T F**

7. In a competitive product market and in the absence of spillover costs, the supply curve or schedule reflects the costs of producing the product. **T F**

8. If demand and supply reflected all the benefits and costs of a product, the equilibrium output of a competitive market would be identical with its optimal output. **T F**

9. There is an underallocation of resources to the production of a commodity when negative externalities are present. **T F**

10. The inclusion of the spillover benefits would increase the demand for a product. **T F**

11. When spillover costs are involved in the production of a product, more resources are allocated to the production of that product and more of the product is produced than is optimal or most efficient. **T F**

12. The Coase theorem suggests that government intervention is required whenever there are negative or positive externalities. **T F**

13. Lawsuits and liability rules create externality problems instead of helping resolve them. **T F**

14. Taxes that are imposed on businesses that create an externality will lower the marginal cost of production and increase supply. **T F**

15. Subsidizing the firms producing goods that provide spillover benefits will usually result in a better allocation of resources. **T F**

16. One solution to the negative externalities caused by pollution is to create a market for pollution rights in which the social costs of pollution are turned into private costs. **T F**

17. In a market for pollution rights, if a government agency sets a fixed level for pollution, the supply curve of pollution rights will be perfectly elastic. **T F**

18. If a society has marginal costs of $10 for pollution abatement and the marginal benefit of pollution abatement is $8, to achieve an optimal amount of the pollution the society should increase the amount of pollution abatement. **T F**

19. If the government requires the use of more recycled paper products, then the demand for recycled paper products will increase. **T F**

20. If the government provides a subsidy to producers of recycled paper products, the supply of recycled paper products will increase. **T F**

21. The economic effects of global warming will be uniform across regions of the world. **T F**

22. Asymmetric information is a market failure that occurs when parties to a market transaction possess unequal knowledge. **T F**

23. The inspection of meat products by the Federal government for quality is justified on the grounds that it reduces the costs of obtaining information in the market for meat. **T F**

24. If the provision of government health insurance encourages people to take more health risks, it has created a moral hazard. **T F**

25. Adverse selection problems primarily result when the government begins enforcing standards for safety in the workplace. **T F**

■ MULTIPLE-CHOICE QUESTIONS

Circle the letter that corresponds to the best answer.

1. How do public goods differ from private goods? Public goods are characterized by
(a) rivalry and excludability
(b) rivalry and nonexcludability
(c) nonrivalry and excludability
(d) nonrivalry and nonexcludability

Answer Questions 2, 3, 4, and 5 on the basis of the following information for a public good. P_1 and P_2 represent the prices individuals 1 and 2, the only two people in the society, are willing to pay for the last unit of a public good. P_c represents the price (or collective willingness to pay) for a public good, and Q_s represents the quantity supplied of the public good at those prices.

Q_d	P_1	P_2	P_c	Q_s
1	$4	$5	$9	5
2	3	4	7	4
3	2	3	5	3
4	1	2	3	2
5	0	1	1	1

2. What amount is this society willing to pay for the first unit of the public good?
(a) $10
(b) $9
(c) $8
(d) $7

3. What amount is this society willing to pay for the third unit of the public good?
(a) $5
(b) $6
(c) $7
(d) $8

4. Given the supply curve Q_s, the optimal price and quantity of the public good in this society will be
(a) $9 and 5 units
(b) $5 and 3 units
(c) $5 and 4 units
(d) $3 and 2 units

5. If this good were a private good instead of a public good, the total quantity demanded at the $4 price would be
(a) 3 units
(b) 4 units
(c) 5 units
(d) 6 units

Answer Questions 6, 7, and 8 for a public good on the basis of the following graph.

6. Where the marginal benefits equal the collective marginal costs is represented by point
(a) *b*
(b) *c*
(c) *d*
(d) *e*

7. Which line segment would indicate the amount by which the marginal benefit of this public good is less than the marginal cost?
(a) *ab*
(b) *bc*
(c) *fa*
(d) *gh*

8. If 3 units of this public good are produced, the marginal
(a) cost of $10 is greater than the marginal benefit of $3
(b) cost of $10 is greater than the marginal benefit of $5
(c) benefit of $10 is greater than the marginal cost of $5
(d) benefit of $10 is greater than the marginal cost of $3

9. Assume that a government is considering a new antipollution program and may choose to include in this program any number of four different projects. The marginal cost and the marginal benefits of each of the four projects are given in the table below. What total amount should this government spend on the antipollution program?
(a) $2 million
(b) $5 million
(c) $17 million
(d) $37 million

Project	Marginal cost	Marginal benefit
#1	$ 2 million	$ 5 million
#2	5 million	7 million
#3	10 million	9 million
#4	20 million	15 million

10. When the production and consumption of a product entail spillover costs, a competitive product market results in a(n)
(a) underallocation of resources to the product
(b) overallocation of resources to the product
(c) optimal allocation of resources to the product
(d) higher price for the product

11. A spillover benefit in the production of some product will result in
(a) overproduction
(b) underproduction
(c) the optimal level of production if consumers are price takers
(d) the optimal level of production if consumers are utility maximizers

12. One condition for the Coase theorem to hold is that there be
(a) clear ownership of the property rights
(b) a large number of people involved in the dispute
(c) active government intervention to solve the externality problem
(d) a sizable cost for bargaining to settle the dispute between the private parties

13. The Clean Air Act of 1990
(a) permits the exchange of pollution rights within firms and between firms in an area
(b) sets stricter limits on the dumping of garbage in landfills
(c) funds research on applications of asymmetric information and transaction cost
(d) forces companies to clean up toxic waste dumps

Use the following graph which shows the supply and demand for a product to answer Questions 14, 15, and 16.

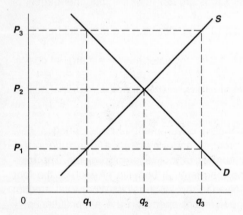

14. If there are neither spillover costs nor spillover benefits, the output that results in the optimal allocation of resources to the production of this product is
(a) q_1
(b) q_2
(c) q_3
(d) 0

15. If the market for a product was in equilibrium at output level q_2 but the optimal level of output for society was at q_1, the government could correct for this

(a) spillover cost with a subsidy to consumers
(b) spillover cost with a subsidy to producers
(c) spillover benefit with a subsidy to producers
(d) spillover cost with a tax on producers

16. If the market for a product was in equilibrium at output level q_2 but the optimal level of output for society was at q_3, the government could correct for this
(a) overallocation of resources by direct controls on consumers
(b) underallocation of resources through taxes on producers
(c) overallocation of resources through a market for externality rights
(d) underallocation of resources through subsidies to producers

17. If government were to sell pollution rights, an increase in the demand for pollution rights would
(a) increase both the quantity of pollutants discharged and the market price of pollution rights
(b) increase the quantity discharged and have no effect on the market price
(c) have no effect on the quantity discharged and increase the market price
(d) have no effect on either the quantity discharged or the market price

Use the following table to answer Questions 18, 19, and 20. The data in the table show the marginal costs and marginal benefits to a city for five different levels of pollution abatement.

Quantity of pollution abatement	Marginal cost	Marginal benefit
500 tons	$500,000	$100,000
400 tons	300,000	150,000
300 tons	200,000	200,000
200 tons	100,000	300,000
100 tons	50,000	400,000

18. If the city seeks an optimal reduction of the externality, it will select how many tons of pollution abatement?
(a) 100
(b) 300
(c) 400
(d) 500

19. If the marginal benefit of pollution abatement increased by $150,000 at each level because of the community's desire to attract more firms, the optimal level of pollution abatement in tons would be
(a) 200
(b) 300
(c) 400
(d) 500

20. What would cause the optimal level of pollution abatement to be 200 tons?
(a) technological improvement in production that decreases marginal costs by $150,000 at each level

(b) an increase in the health risk from this pollution that increases marginal benefits by $200,000 at each level

(c) the need to replace old pollution monitoring equipment with new equipment that increases marginal costs by $200,000 at each level

(d) reduction in the public demand for pollution control that decreases marginal benefits by $100,000 at each level

21. Which would tend to increase the demand for recycled paper?

(a) an increase in the price of regular paper

(b) an increase in taxes on all paper production

(c) a decrease in interest in protecting the environment

(d) a decrease in subsidies for all paper production

22. Inadequate information about sellers and their product can cause market failure in the form of

(a) an increase in the number of market sellers

(b) an increase in the number of market buyers

(c) an overallocation of resources to the product

(d) an underallocation of resources to the product

23. A situation in which one party to a contract alters his or her behavior after signing the contract in ways that can be costly to the other party would be

(a) an adverse selection problem

(b) a moral hazard problem

(c) a tragedy of the commons

(d) a positive externality

24. If Congress adopted an increase in government insurance on bank deposits, this action would create a moral hazard problem because it may

(a) lead to careful screening of depositors and the source of their funds

(b) restrict the amount of deposits made by bank customers

(c) encourage bank officers to make riskier loans

(d) reduce bank investments in real estate

25. Assume that individuals who are most likely to benefit substantially from an insurance policy decide to buy one and the insurance company does not know this information. This situation would be an example of

(a) a free-rider problem

(b) a principal–agent problem

(c) a moral hazard problem

(d) an adverse selection problem

■ PROBLEMS

1. Data on two individuals' preferences for a public good are reflected in the following table. P_1 and P_2 represent the prices individuals 1 and 2, the only two people in the society, are willing to pay for the last unit of the public good.

Quantity	P_1	P_2
1	$6	$6
2	5	5
3	4	4
4	3	3
5	2	2
6	1	1

a. Complete the table below showing the collective demand for the public good in this society.

Q_d	Price	Q_s
1	$ _____	7
2	_____	6
3	_____	5
4	_____	4
5	_____	3
6	_____	2

b. Given the supply schedule for this public good as shown by the Q_s column, the optimal quantity of this public good is _____ units and the optimal price is $ _____.

c. When 3 units of this public good are produced, the perceived marginal benefit is $ _____ and the marginal cost is $ _____; there will be an (overallocation, underallocation) _____ of resources to this public good.

d. When 6 units of this public good are produced, the perceived marginal benefit is $ _____ and the marginal cost is $ _____; there is an (underallocation, overallocation) _____ of resources to this public good.

2. Imagine that a state government is considering constructing a new highway to link its two largest cities. Its estimate of the total costs and the total benefits of building 2-, 4-, 6-, and 8-lane highways between the two cities are shown in the table below. (All figures are in millions of dollars.)

Project	Total cost	Marginal cost	Total benefit	Marginal benefit
No highway	$ 0		$ 0	
2-lane highway	500	$ _____	650	$ _____
4-lane highway	680	_____	750	_____
6-lane highway	760	_____	800	_____
8-lane highway	860	_____	825	_____

a. Compute the marginal cost and the marginal benefit of the 2-, 4-, 6-, and 8-lane highways.

b. Will it benefit the state to allocate resources to construct a highway? _____

c. If the state builds a highway,

(1) it should be a _____-lane highway.

(2) the total cost will be $ _____ million.

(3) the total benefit will be $ _____ million.

(4) the *net* benefit will be $ _____ million.

3. The following graph shows the demand and supply curves for a product bought and sold in a competitive market. Assume that there are no spillover benefits or costs.

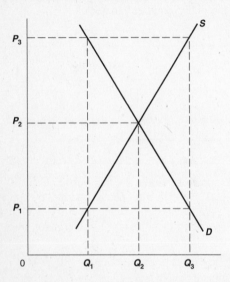

a. Were this market to produce an output of Q_1, there would be an (optimal, under, over) _____ allocation of resources to the production of this product.

b. Were this market to produce Q_3, there would be an _____ allocation of resources to this product.

c. The equilibrium output is _____, and at this output there is an _____ allocation of resources.

4. The two following graphs show product demand and supply curves that do *not* reflect either the spillover costs of producing the product or the spillover benefits obtained from its consumption.

a. On the first graph, draw in another curve that reflects the inclusion of spillover *costs.*

(1) Government might force the (demand for, supply of) _____ the product to reflect the spillover costs of producing it by (taxing, subsidizing) _____ the producers.

(2) The inclusion of spillover costs in the total cost of producing the product (increases, decreases) _____ the output of the product and _____ its price.

b. On the second graph, draw in a demand curve that reflects the inclusion of spillover *benefits.*

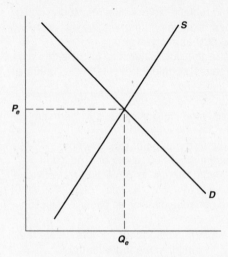

(1) Indicate on the graph the output that is optimal when spillover benefits are included.

(2) To bring about the production of this optimal output, government might (tax, subsidize) _____ the consumers of this product, which would (increase, decrease) _____ the demand for the product.

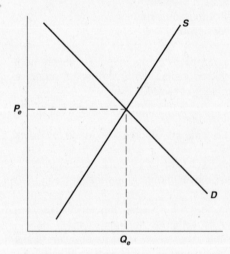

(3) This optimal output is (greater than, less than, equal to) _____ Q_e; and the price of the product is (above, below, equal to) _____ P_e.

5. Assume the atmosphere of Cuyahoga County, Ohio (the Cleveland metropolitan area), is able to reabsorb 1500 tons of pollutants per year. The following schedule shows the price polluters would be willing to pay for the right to dispose of 1 ton of pollutants per year and the total quantity of pollutants they would wish to dispose of at each price.

Price (per ton of pollutant rights)	Total quantity of pollutant rights demanded (tons)
$ 0	4000
1000	3500
2000	3000
3000	2500
4000	2000
5000	1500
6000	1000
7000	500

a. If there were no emission fee, polluters would put _____ tons of pollutants in the air each year, and this quantity of pollutants would exceed the ability of nature to reabsorb them by _____ tons.

b. To reduce pollution to the capacity of the atmosphere to recycle pollutants, an emission fee of $_____ per ton should be set.

c. Were this emission fee set, the total emission fees set would be $_____.

d. Were the quantity of pollution rights demanded at each price to increase by 500 tons, the emission fee could be increased by $_____ and total emission fees collected would increase by $_____.

■ SHORT ANSWER AND ESSAY QUESTIONS

1. What are the basic characteristics of public goods?

2. How do public goods differ from private goods?

3. Contrast how you construct the demand curve for a public good with the procedure for constructing the demand curve for a private good using individual demand schedules.

4. Explain the relationship between the marginal cost and benefit of a public good when there is an underallocation, an overallocation, and an optimal allocation of resources for the provision of the public good.

5. Describe benefit-cost analysis, and state the rules used to make decisions from marginal and total perspectives.

6. Is "economy in government" the same as "reduced government spending"? Explain the distinction.

7. What are externalities and spillovers? Give examples of positive externalities and negative externalities.

8. Under what conditions might it be worthwhile for the government to intervene or not to intervene to settle a spillover problem?

9. Should the government intervene in an externality dispute between two property owners over the use of one party's land? Should government intervene in the case of acid rain?

10. How do lawsuits and liability rules resolve externality problems? How would these actions be justified?

11. What actions can government take to correct for spillover costs in a market?

12. What is the tragedy of the commons? Give examples of it.

13. How do you create a market for externality rights in the case of pollution? What are some advantages and limitations of this approach to the pollution problem?

14. What rule can society use to determine the optimal level of pollution abatement? What is the problem with this approach?

15. Why is solid-waste disposal of national concern? How is recycling a partial alternative to it? How does a market for recyclable items work?

16. Discuss the economic issues involved in global warming.

17. Describe how inadequate information about sellers creates market problems for buyers. Give examples.

18. Explain what is meant by a "moral hazard problem" and describe how it affects sellers. Give some examples of the application of this problem.

19. How can the market for insurance result in an adverse selection problem? What actions might government take to correct this information problem?

20. In what way does workplace safety become an information problem? How might this problem be resolved by government or businesses?

ANSWERS

Chapter 17 Government and Market Failure

FILL-IN QUESTIONS

1. is not, can, private, public
2. quantities demanded, price, prices, quantity demanded
3. utility, returns, benefit, cost, benefit, cost (*either order for last two*)
4. benefit, cost, maximum
5. externalities, negative, cost, positive, benefit
6. over, under
7. Coase, defined, small, minor, is not
8. property, liability, uncertainty
9. costs, tax
10. benefits, subsidizing, provision
11. commons, market
12. *a.* inelastic; *b.* down, price; *c.* rise, stay the same
13. buy, less than, less than, equal to
14. increase, increase
15. warming, increase, greater than, market
16. asymmetric, incomplete, costly, under
17. standards, licensing
18. a moral hazard, an adverse selection, after, at the same time
19. safety, standards, information
20. warranties, franchising, buyers, information

TRUE–FALSE QUESTIONS

1. F, p. 314	**10.** T, pp. 317–318	**19.** T, pp. 325–326
2. T, pp. 315–316	**11.** T, pp. 317–318	**20.** T, p. 326
3. F, pp. 316–318	**12.** F, p. 319	**21.** F, p. 327
4. F, pp. 316–318	**13.** F, pp. 319–320	**22.** T, p. 328
5. F, p. 317	**14.** F, p. 321	**23.** T, p. 329
6. T, p. 318	**15.** T, p. 321	**24.** T, pp. 329–330
7. T, p. 318	**16.** T, pp. 322–323	**25.** F, p. 330
8. T, pp. 317–318	**17.** F, pp. 322–323	
9. F, pp. 317–318	**18.** F, pp. 324–325	

MULTIPLE-CHOICE QUESTIONS

1. d, p. 314	**10.** b, p. 318	**19.** c, pp. 324–325
2. b, pp. 315–316	**11.** b, pp. 318–319	**20.** c, pp. 324–325
3. a, pp. 315–316	**12.** a, p. 319	**21.** a, pp. 325–326
4. b, pp. 315–316	**13.** a, p. 320	**22.** d, pp. 328–329
5. a, pp. 315–316	**14.** b, pp. 318–319	**23.** b, pp. 329–330
6. d, pp. 315–316	**15.** d, pp. 320–321	**24.** c, pp. 329–330
7. b, pp. 315–316	**16.** d, pp. 320–321	**25.** d, pp. 330–331
8. d, pp. 315–316	**17.** c, pp. 322–323	
9. b, pp. 316–317	**18.** b, pp. 324–325	

PROBLEMS

1. *a.* $12, 10, 8, 6, 4, 2; *b.* 4, 6; *c.* 8, 4, underallocation; *d.* 2, 10, overallocation

2. *a.* Marginal cost: $500, $180, $80, $100; Marginal benefit: $650, $100, $50, $25; *b.* yes; *c.* (1) 2, (2) $500, (3) $650, (4) $150

3. *a.* under; *b.* over; *c.* Q_2, optimal

4. *a.* (1) supply of, taxing, (2) decreases, increases; *b.* (1) graph; (2) subsidize, increase, (3) greater than, above

5. *a.* 4000, 2500; *b.* 5000; *c.* 7,500,000; *d.* 1000, 1,500,000

SHORT ANSWER AND ESSAY QUESTIONS

1. p. 314	**8.** pp. 319–320	**15.** pp. 325–326
2. pp. 314–315	**9.** pp. 319–320	**16.** p. 327
3. pp. 315–316	**10.** pp. 319–320	**17.** pp. 328–329
4. pp. 315–316	**11.** pp. 320–321	**18.** pp. 329–330
5. pp. 316–318	**12.** p. 322	**19.** pp. 330–331
6. pp. 317–318	**13.** pp. 322–323	**20.** pp. 330–331
7. pp. 318–319	**14.** pp. 324–325	

CHAPTER 18

Public Choice Theory and the Economics of Taxation

Although both Chapters 17 and 18 analyze the role of government in the economy, they look at government from opposite perspectives. Chapter 17 discussed market failure issues and what actions government takes to correct these market problems. Chapter 18 now examines government failure, or why government makes inefficient use of the scarce resources. For this explanation, you will first be introduced to **public choice theory,** or the economic analysis of public decision making. Later in the chapter you will learn more about the economics of taxation, which includes such topics as tax principles and the economic effects of specific taxes.

Many public decisions are made by **majority voting,** but this decision-making procedure may distort the true preferences of society. In the first section of the chapter you will find out how majority voting may lead to inefficient outcomes in the provision of public goods. In some choices, the benefits of a public good are greater than the costs, but the majority votes against having it. In other choices, the benefits outweigh the costs, but the provision of the public good is supported by the majority vote. Although actions by interest groups and the use of logrolling may tend to reduce inefficiencies created by majority rule, the final result depends on the circumstances of the decision.

Also note that there is a **paradox of voting** from majority voting. Depending on how a vote or election is arranged, it is possible for majority rule to produce choices that are inconsistent with the ranking of preferences among voters. You should spend time working through the example in the textbook so you understand how opposing outcomes can result from majority rule. You should also learn why the median voters strongly influence the result of a vote or an election when there is majority rule. In fact, the **median-voter model** is very useful for explaining why the middle position on issues is often adopted in public decisions.

The second section of Chapter 18 discusses other reasons for *inefficiencies* by government. Here you will learn that (1) the **special-interest effect** and **rent-seeking** impair public decisions; (2) politicians often have a strong incentive to adopt an economic policy that has clear benefits to voters, but hidden or uncertain costs; (3) public choice is more limited and less flexible than private choice because it entails voting for or accepting a "bundle" of programs, some good and some bad; and (4) bureaucratic inefficiencies in the public sector arise from the lack of the economic incentives and competitive pressures found in the private sector.

Chapter 18 then shifts from public choice theory to taxation. In this third section of the chapter you will learn the economic principles used in levying taxes. You also will learn about the **regressive, progressive,** and **proportional** classifications for taxes and how most U.S. taxes fit into this classification scheme.

The **tax incidence** and **efficiency loss of a tax** are described in the fourth section of the chapter. Incidence means "who ends up paying the tax." As you will discover, the *elasticities* of demand and of supply determine how much of the tax will be paid by buyers and how much of it will be paid by sellers. No matter who pays the tax, however, there is an efficiency loss to society from the tax, the size of which is also affected by the elasticities of demand and of supply. With this knowledge, you are now ready to study the probable incidence of five taxes—personal income, corporate income, sales, excise, and property—that are used to raise most of the tax revenue for government in the United States.

■ CHECKLIST

When you have studied this chapter you should be able to

☐ Explain the purpose of public choice theory and the topics it covers.

☐ Illustrate how majority voting procedures can produce inefficient outcomes when the vote is "yes" or the vote is "no."

☐ Describe how interest groups and political logrolling affect the efficiency of outcomes from voting.

☐ Give an example of the paradox of voting.

☐ Describe the median-voter model, its applicability to the real world, and two implications of the model.

☐ Explain the meaning of the phrase "government failure" and cite examples.

☐ Give an example of a special-interest effect and an example of rent-seeking behavior.

☐ Describe the economic problem that arises when a political decision involves clear benefits and hidden costs.

☐ Compare the type of choices consumers make in the private market with the type of choices citizens as voters make.

☐ Contrast the incentives for economic efficiency in private business with those found in public agencies and bureaucracies.

☐ Discuss how government and markets are imperfect in allocating resources.

☐ Distinguish between the ability-to-pay principle of taxation and the benefits-received principle of taxation.

☐ Determine whether a tax is regressive, progressive, or proportional when given the data.

☐ Describe the progressivity or regressivity of the five major taxes used in the United States.

☐ Illustrate the incidence of an excise tax with a supply and demand graph.

☐ Explain how demand and supply elasticities affect tax incidence.

☐ Describe the efficiency loss of a tax with a supply and demand graph.

☐ Explain the effects of demand or supply elasticities on the efficiency loss of a tax.

☐ Evaluate the probable incidence of the personal income, corporate income, sales and excise, and property taxes.

☐ Describe the progressivity of the U.S. tax structure overall and at the Federal, state, and local levels.

■ CHAPTER OUTLINE

1. Most decisions about government activity are made collectively through *majority voting,* but the procedure is not without problems.

　a. Voting outcomes may be economically *inefficient* in cases where voters reject a public good whose total benefits exceed total costs or fail to reject a public good whose total costs are greater than the total benefits. These inefficiencies can be resolved sometimes by

　(1) the formation of special-interest groups that work to overcome inefficient outcomes, or

　(2) the use of *logrolling,* in which votes are traded to secure a favorable and efficient decision,

　(3) but logrolling can also lead to inefficient decisions.

　b. The *paradox of voting* suggests that the public may not be able to make consistent choices that reflect its preferences.

　c. Based on the *median-voter model,* it is suggested that the person or groups holding the middle position on an issue will likely determine the outcome from a majority rule election. Public decisions tend to reflect the median view.

2. Public choice theory suggests that there is *government failure* because the process it uses to make decisions is inherently weak and results in an economically inefficient allocation of resources.

　a. The weakness of the decision-making process in the public sector and the resulting inefficient allocation of resources is often the result of pressures exerted on Congress and the bureaucracy by special interests and other groups.

　(1) There can be a *special-interest effect* in which a small number of people obtain a government program or policy giving them large gains at the expense of a large number of people who individually suffer small losses. This special-interest effect is also present in *pork-barrel politics* where a government program will mostly benefit one constituency.

　(2) *Rent-seeking behavior* is reflected in appeals to government for special benefits or treatment at the taxpayers' or someone else's expense. Government can dispense such rents through laws, rules, hiring, and purchases.

　b. Those seeking election to public office frequently favor programs whose benefits are clear and immediate and whose costs are uncertain and deferred, even when the benefits are less than the costs. Conversely, they frequently oppose programs whose costs are clear and immediate and whose benefits are uncertain and deferred, even when the benefits are greater than the costs.

　c. There are limited and bundle choices in political decisions. When citizens must vote for candidates who represent different but complete programs, the voters are unable to select those parts of a program which they favor and reject the other parts of the program.

　d. It is argued that the public sector (unlike the private sector) is inefficient because those employed there are offered no incentive to be efficient; there is no way to measure efficiency in the public sector; and government bureaucrats can join with the special-interest groups to block budget cuts or lobby for increased funding.

　e. Just as the private or market sector of the economy does not allocate resources perfectly, the public sector does not perform its functions perfectly; the imperfections of both sectors make it difficult to determine which sector will be more efficient in providing a good or service.

3. The financing of public goods and services through taxation also raises an important question about how the *tax burden* is allocated among people.

　a. The *benefits-received principle* and the *ability-to-pay principle* are widely used to determine how the tax bill should be apportioned among the economy's citizens.

　(1) The benefits-received principle suggests that those people who benefit most from public goods should pay for them.

　(2) The ability-to-pay principle states that taxes for the support of public goods should be tied to the incomes and wealth of people or their ability to pay.

　b. Taxes can be classified as *progressive, regressive,* or *proportional* according to the way in which the average tax rate changes as incomes change.

　(1) The average tax rate increases as income increases with a progressive tax, it decreases as income increases with a regressive tax, and it remains the same as income increases with a proportional tax.

　(2) In the United States, the personal income tax tends to be mildly progressive, the corporate income tax is proportional (unless the tax is partially passed to consumers, in which case it is partially regressive), and the payroll, sales, and property taxes are regressive.

4. *Tax incidence* and the *efficiency loss of a tax* are also important in discussion of the economics of taxation.

　a. The price elasticities of demand and supply determine the incidence of a sales or excise tax.

　(1) The imposition of such a tax on a product decreases the supply of the product and increases its

price. The amount of the price increase is the portion of the tax paid by the buyer; the seller pays the rest.

(2) The price elasticities of demand and supply for a product affect the portions paid by buyers and sellers: **(a)** the more *elastic* the demand, the greater the portion paid by the seller; **(b)** the more *inelastic* the demand, the smaller the portion paid by the seller; **(c)** the more *elastic* the supply, the greater the portion paid by the buyer; and **(d)** the more *inelastic* the supply, the smaller the portion paid by the buyer.

b. There is an efficiency loss of a tax. This loss occurs because there is a reduction in output, despite the fact that the marginal benefits of that output are greater than the marginal cost. Thus, the consumption and production of the taxed product have been reduced below the optimal level by the tax.

(1) The degree of the efficiency loss of a sales or an excise tax depends on the elasticities of supply and demand. Other things equal, the *greater* the elasticity of supply and demand, the *greater* the efficiency loss of a sales or an excise tax; consequently, the total tax burden to society may not be equal even though two taxes produce equal tax revenue.

(2) Other tax goals, however, may be more important than minimizing efficiency losses from taxes. These goals may include redistributing income or reducing negative externalities.

c. A tax levied on one person or group of persons may be shifted partially or completely to another person or group; and to the extent that a tax can be shifted or passed on through lower prices paid or higher prices received, its incidence is passed on to others. Table 18.2 in the text summarizes the probable shifting and incidence of the personal income tax, corporate income tax, general sales tax, specific excise taxes, and property taxes.

d. The overall U.S. tax structure is only slightly progressive and has little effect on the distribution of income because progressive taxes are generally offset by regressive taxes; however, estimates of the progressivity of the tax system depend on the assumed incidence of various taxes and transfer payments made by governments to reduce income inequality in the United States.

■ HINTS AND TIPS

1. The first part of the chapter presents **public choice theory,** but this theory has many practical applications to politics. As you read about the reasons for inefficient voting outcomes, the influence of special-interest groups, political logrolling, the median-voter model, rent-seeking behavior, limited and bundled choices, and government failures, see if you can apply the ideas to current public issues at the local, state, or Federal level. Also ask your instructor for current examples of the ideas from public choice theory.

2. Remember that what happens to the **average tax rate** as income increases determines whether a tax is progressive, regressive, or proportional. The average tax rate increases for progressive taxes, decreases for regressive taxes, and remains the same for proportional taxes as income increases.

3. This chapter applies supply, demand, and elasticity concepts to taxation issues. Chapter 7 is worth checking to review your understanding of elasticity. Figure 18.5 and the related discussion in the text are crucially important for understanding the efficiency loss from a tax.

■ IMPORTANT TERMS

public choice theory	benefits-received principle
logrolling	ability-to-pay principle
paradox of voting	progressive tax
median-voter model	regressive tax
government failure	proportional tax
special-interest effect	tax incidence
rent seeking	efficiency loss of a tax

SELF-TEST

■ FILL-IN QUESTIONS

1. Many collective decisions are made on the basis of (minority, majority) _____ voting. One problem with this voting system is that it results in (efficient, inefficient) _____ voting outcomes because it fails to incorporate the strength of (individual, majority) _____ preferences. Voters may defeat a proposal even though the total costs are (less than, greater than) _____ the total benefits, or they might accept a proposal even though the total costs are _____ the total benefits.

2. The voting problem might be resolved or reversed through the influence of (interest, social) _____ groups or through political (primaries, logrolling) _____.

3. Another problem with this voting system occurs in a situation in which the public may not be able to rank its preferences with consistency; this is called the (fallacy, paradox) _____ of voting.

4. There are also insights into majority voting based on the (motor-voter, median-voter) _____ model, whereby the person holding the (lower, middle, upper) _____ position is likely to determine the outcome of an election.

5. When governments use resources to attempt to solve problems and the employment of these resources (does, does not) _____ result in solutions to these problems, there has been (market, government)

_____ failure. This means that there are shortcomings in government that promote economic (efficiency, inefficiency) _____.

6. One reason for this type of failure is that there can be a special-interest effect whereby a (large, small) _____ number of people benefit from a government program at the expense of a _____ number of persons who individually suffer (large, small) _____ losses.

7. Inefficiencies can also be caused by an appeal to government for special benefits at taxpayers' or someone else's expense that is called (revealed preferences, rent-seeking behavior) _____.

8. Another reason for the failure is that the benefits from a government program or project are often (clear, hidden) _____ to citizens or groups, but the costs are frequently _____ when legislation is passed or programs are funded.

9. There can also be inefficiencies in government because voters or elected representatives have to accept political choices that are (limited, unlimited) _____ and (bundled, unbundled) _____, which means government legislation forces voters or elected representatives to take bad programs with the good programs.

10. The incentives for economic efficiency tend to be stronger in the (private, public) _____ sector because there is a profit incentive in the _____ sector but not a similar incentive in the (private, public) _____ sector. As a result, there tends to be (more, less) _____ government bureaucracy and _____ efficient use of scarce resources.

11. Although the public sector can experience (market, government) _____ failure, the private sector can also experience _____ failure, and thus both government and markets can be considered (perfect, imperfect) _____ economic institutions.

12. The tax philosophy that asserts that households and businesses should purchase public goods and services in about the same way as private goods and services are bought is the (ability-to-pay, benefits-received) _____ principle of taxation, but the tax philosophy that the tax burden should be based on a person's wealth or income is the _____ principle of taxation.

13. If the average tax rate remains constant as income increases, the tax is (regressive, progressive, proportional) _____. If the average tax rate decreases as income increases, the tax is _____. If the average tax rate increases as income increases, the tax is (regressive, progressive, proportional) _____.

14. In the United States, the Federal personal income tax is (regressive, progressive, proportional) _____, but sales taxes, property taxes, and payroll taxes are _____. If corporate shareholders bear the burden of the corporate income tax, then it is (regressive, progressive, proportional) _____, but if part of the tax is passed on to consumers in higher prices, then the tax is _____.

15. The person or group who ends up paying a tax is called the tax (avoidance, incidence) _____. When an excise tax is placed on a product, the supply curve will (increase, decrease) _____, or shift to the (right, left) _____. The amount the product price rises as a result of the tax is the portion of the tax burden borne by (buyers, sellers) _____, and the difference between the original price and the after-tax price is the portion of the tax burden borne by _____.

16. The incidence of an excise tax primarily depends on the (price, income) _____ elasticity of demand and of supply. The buyer's portion of the tax is larger the (more, less) _____ elastic the demand and the _____ elastic the supply. The seller's portion of the tax is larger the (more, less) _____ elastic the demand and the _____ elastic the supply.

17. When an excise tax reduces the consumption and production of the taxed product below the level of economic efficiency, there is an efficiency (gain, loss) _____ of the tax. Other things equal, the greater the elasticity of supply and demand, the (greater, less) _____ the efficiency (gain, loss) _____ of the tax.

18. The incidence of the personal income tax is on (individuals, businesses) _____. There is less certainty about the incidence of the corporate income tax because some economists argue that the tax shifts to (businesses, consumers) _____ while other economists argue that it is shifted to _____.

19. The incidence of the sales tax is generally shifted to the (sellers, buyers) _____ of the product, and with excise taxes, if the demand for a product is inelastic, the tax incidence will be shifted to the _____. In the case of the property tax, the incidence of the tax for owner-occupied housing is borne by (owners, government) _____ and with renter-occupied housing it is borne by (owners, renters) _____. In the case of business property, the tax incidence is shifted to (businesses, consumers) _____.

20. The Federal tax system is generally (progressive, regressive, proportional) _____, state and local tax systems are generally _____, and overall the U.S. tax system is slightly _____, but these conditions depend on the incidence of the taxes. The tax system has a relatively (large, small) _____ effect on the distribution of income in the United States, but income inequality is (increased, decreased) _____ by transfer payments made by governments.

■ TRUE–FALSE QUESTIONS

Circle T if the statement is true, F if it is false.

1. Majority voting may produce outcomes that are economically inefficient because it fails to take into account the strength of preferences of the individual voter. **T F**

2. Logrolling will always diminish economic efficiency in government. **T F**

3. The paradox of voting is that majority voting will result in consistent choices that reflect the preferences of the public. **T F**

4. The proposition that the person holding the middle position on an issue will likely determine the outcome of an election is suggested by the median-voter model. **T F**

5. There is a failure in the public sector whenever a governmental program or activity has been expanded to the level at which the marginal social cost exceeds the marginal social benefit. **T F**

6. Those concerned with public choice theory argue that the special-interest effect tends to reduce government sector failures because the pressures exerted on government by one special-interest group are offset by the pressures brought to bear by other special-interest groups. **T F**

7. The appeal to government for special benefits at taxpayers' or someone else's expense is called rent seeking. **T F**

8. When the costs of programs are hidden and the benefits are clear, vote-seeking politicians tend to reject economically justifiable programs. **T F**

9. The limited choice of citizens refers to the inability of individual voters to select the precise bundle of social goods and services that will best satisfy the citizen's wants when he or she must vote for a candidate and the candidate's entire program. **T F**

10. Critics of government contend that there is a tendency for government bureaucracy to justify continued employment by finding new problems to solve. **T F**

11. When comparing government with markets, government is imperfect, whereas markets are perfect in efficiently allocating resources. **T F**

12. The chief difficulty in applying the benefits-received principle of taxation is determining who receives the benefit of many of the goods and services that government supplies. **T F**

13. The state and Federal taxes on gasoline are good examples of taxes levied on the benefits-received principle. **T F**

14. The ability-to-pay principle of taxation states that those with greater incomes should be taxed less, absolutely and relatively, than those with lesser incomes. **T F**

15. A tax is progressive when the average tax rate decreases as income increases. **T F**

16. A general sales tax is considered a proportional tax with respect to income. **T F**

17. A payroll (Social Security) tax is regressive. **T F**

18. When an excise tax is placed on a product bought and sold in a competitive market, the portion of the tax borne by the seller equals the amount of the tax less the rise in the price of product due to the tax. **T F**

19. The more elastic the demand for a good, the greater the portion of an excise tax on the good borne by the seller. **T F**

20. The efficiency loss of an excise tax is the gain in net benefits for the producers from the increase in the price of the product. **T F**

21. The degrees of efficiency loss from an excise tax vary from market to market and depend on the elasticities of supply and demand. **T F**

22. The evidence is certain that in the case of the corporate income tax the incidence is borne by the businesses and not consumers. **T F**

23. The probable incidence of the tax on rented apartment properties is on the landlord, not on the tenant. **T F**

24. The Federal income tax system is progressive. **T F**

25. The state and local tax structures are largely regressive. **T F**

■ **MULTIPLE-CHOICE QUESTIONS**

Circle the letter that corresponds to the best answer.

1. Deficiencies in the processes used to make collective decisions of government and economic inefficiencies caused by government are the primary focus of
   (a) public goods theory
   (b) public choice theory
   (c) the study of tax incidence
   (d) the study of tax shifting

2. The trading of votes to secure favorable outcomes on decisions that otherwise would be adverse is referred to as
   (a) logrolling, and it increases economic efficiency
   (b) logrolling, and it may increase or decrease economic efficiency
   (c) rent-seeking behavior, and it decreases economic efficiency
   (d) rent-seeking behavior, and it may increase or decrease economic efficiency

Answer Questions 3, 4, 5, and 6 on the basis of the following table, which shows the rankings of the public goods by three voters: A, B, and C.

Public good	Voter A	Voter B	Voter C
Dam	1	2	3
School	3	1	2
Road	2	3	1

3. In a choice between a dam and the school,
   (a) a majority of voters favor the dam
   (b) a majority of voters favor the school
   (c) a majority of voters favor both the dam and the school
   (d) there is no majority of votes for either the dam or the school

4. In a choice between a road and a dam,
   (a) a majority of voters favor the dam
   (b) a majority of voters favor the road
   (c) a majority of voters favor both the dam and the road
   (d) there is no majority of votes for either the road or the dam

5. In a choice between a school and a road,
   (a) a majority of voters favor the road
   (b) a majority of voters favor the school
   (c) a majority of voters favor both the road and the school
   (d) there is no majority of votes for either the road or the school

6. What do the rankings in the table indicate about choices made under majority rule? Majority voting in this case
   (a) reflects irrational preferences
   (b) produces inconsistent choices
   (c) produces consistent choices in spite of irrational preferences
   (d) results in economically efficient outcomes because they have been influenced by special interests

7. The idea that the person holding the middle position will in a sense determine the outcome of an election is suggested by the
   (a) rent-seeking behavior
   (b) paradox of voting
   (c) median-voter model
   (d) special-interest effect

8. Actions that groups take to seek government legislation that puts tariffs on foreign products to limit foreign competition or that gives tax breaks to specific corporations would best be an example of
   (a) how the median-voter model works
   (b) how political choices are bundled
   (c) rent-seeking behavior
   (d) the paradox of voting

9. It is difficult to determine whether provision for a particular good or service should be assigned to the private or public sector of the economy because the
   (a) institutions in both sectors function efficiently
   (b) markets function efficiently and the agencies of government perform imperfectly
   (c) markets are faulty and government agencies function with much greater efficiency
   (d) institutions in both sectors are imperfect

10. Which is true of the ability-to-pay principle as applied in the United States?
   (a) It is less widely applied than the benefits-received principle.
   (b) Tax incidence is generally taken as the measure of the ability to pay.
   (c) Gasoline taxes are based on this principle.
   (d) As an individual's income increases, taxes paid increase both absolutely and relatively.

11. Taxing people according to the principle of ability to pay would be most characteristic of
   (a) a payroll tax
   (b) a value-added tax
   (c) a general sales tax
   (d) a progressive income tax

12. With a regressive tax, as income
   (a) increases, the tax rate remains the same
   (b) decreases, the tax rate decreases
   (c) increases, the tax rate increases
   (d) increases, the tax rate decreases

13. Which tends to be a progressive tax in the United States?
   (a) income tax
   (b) property tax
   (c) sales tax
   (d) payroll tax

14. In a competitive market, the portion of an excise tax borne by a buyer is equal to the
   (a) amount the price of the product rises as a result of the tax
   (b) amount of the tax
   (c) amount of the tax less the amount the price of the product rises as a result of the tax

(d) amount of the tax plus the amount the price of the product rises as a result of the tax

15. Which statement is correct?
(a) The more elastic the supply, the greater the portion of an excise tax borne by the seller.
(b) The more elastic the demand, the greater the portion of an excise tax borne by the seller.
(c) The more inelastic the supply, the greater the portion of an excise tax borne by the buyer.
(d) The more inelastic the demand, the greater the portion of an excise tax borne by the seller.

Answer Questions 16, 17, 18, and 19 based on the following graph of an excise tax imposed by government.

16. What is the amount of the excise tax paid by the seller in terms of price per unit sold?
(a) $1
(b) $2
(c) $3
(d) $4

17. The amount of the excise tax paid by consumers is
(a) $2
(b) $6
(c) $12
(d) $16

18. The tax revenue for government is represented by area
(a) *abde*
(b) *abgf*
(c) *fgde*
(d) *abcde*

19. The efficiency loss of the tax is represented by area
(a) *bgc*
(b) *bdc*
(c) *abcf*
(d) *hbci*

20. The efficiency loss of an excise tax is
(a) greater, the greater the elasticity of supply and demand

(b) greater, the less the elasticity of supply and demand
(c) less, the greater the elasticity of supply and demand
(d) not affected by the elasticity of supply and demand

21. If government imposes a tax on wine to shift the market supply to reduce the amount of resources allocated to wine, then the primary purpose of this tax is to
(a) redistribute income
(b) improve tax progressivity
(c) reduce negative externalities
(d) minimize efficiency losses

22. The probable incidence of a sales tax is borne by
(a) government units that collect the tax
(b) businesses that make the product
(c) businesses that sell the product
(d) consumers who buy the product

23. Which tax is the most difficult to shift to others?
(a) personal income tax
(b) corporate income tax
(c) specific excise taxes
(d) business property taxes

24. Which of the following is most likely to pay the incidence of a property tax on a business property that sells a consumer product?
(a) consumers of the product
(b) the business that produces the product
(c) government that taxes the property
(d) resource suppliers to the business

25. The Federal tax system is
(a) proportional, while state and local tax structures are largely progressive
(b) progressive, while state and local tax structures are largely regressive
(c) regressive, while state and local tax structures are largely proportional
(d) proportional, while state and local tax structures are largely regressive

■ **PROBLEMS**

1. The following table shows the demand and supply schedules for copra in the New Hebrides Islands.

Quantity demanded (pounds)	Price (per pound)	Before-tax quantity supplied (pounds)	After-tax quantity supplied (pounds)
150	$4.60	900	____
200	4.40	800	____
250	4.20	700	____
300	4.00	600	____
350	3.80	500	____
400	3.60	400	____
450	3.40	300	0
500	3.20	200	0
550	3.00	100	0

a. Before a tax is imposed on copra, its equilibrium price is $_____.

b. The government of New Hebrides now imposes an excise tax of $.60 per pound on copra. Complete the after-tax supply schedule in the right-hand column of the table.

c. After the imposition of the tax, the equilibrium price of copra is $_____.

d. Of the $.60 tax, the amount borne by

(1) the buyer is $_____ or _____%.

(2) the seller is $_____ or _____%.

2. On the following graph, draw a perfectly elastic demand curve and a normal upsloping supply curve for a product. Now impose an excise tax on the product, and draw the new supply curve that would result.

0

0

a. As a consequence of the tax, the price of the product has _____.

b. It can be concluded that when demand is perfectly elastic, the buyer bears _____ of the tax and the seller bears _____ of the tax.

c. Thus the *more* elastic the demand, the _____ is the portion of the tax borne by the buyer and the _____ is the portion borne by the seller.

d. But the *less* elastic the demand, the _____ is the portion borne by the buyer and the _____ is the portion borne by the seller.

3. In the graph at the top of the next column, draw a perfectly elastic supply curve and a normal downsloping demand curve. Impose an excise tax on the product, and draw the new supply curve.

a. As a result of the tax, the price of the product has

_____.

b. From this it can be concluded that when supply is perfectly elastic, the buyer bears _____ of the tax and the seller bears _____ of the tax.

c. Thus the *more* elastic the supply, the _____ is the portion of the tax borne by the buyer and the _____ is the portion borne by the seller.

d. But the less elastic the supply, the _____ is the portion borne by the buyer and the _____ is the portion borne by the seller.

4. The table at the top of page 217 shows five levels of taxable income and the amount that would be paid at each of the five levels under three tax laws: *A, B,* and *C.* Compute for each of the three tax laws the average rate of taxation at each of the four remaining income levels. Indicate whether the tax is regressive, proportional, progressive, or some combination thereof.

5. Assume a state government levies a 4% sales tax on all consumption expenditures. Consumption expenditures at six income levels are shown in the following table.

Income	Consumption expenditures	Sales tax paid	Average tax rate, %
$ 5000	$5000	$200	4.0
6000	5800	232	3.9
7000	6600	_____	_____
8000	7400	_____	_____
9000	8200	_____	_____
10,000	9000	_____	_____

a. Compute the sales tax paid at the next four incomes.

b. Compute the average tax rate at these incomes.

c. Using income as the tax base, the sales tax is a _____ tax.

Income	Tax A		Tax B		Tax C	
	Tax paid	Av. tax rate	Tax paid	Av. tax rate	Tax paid	Av. tax rate
$ 1500	45.00	3%	30.00	2%	135.00	9%
3000	90.00	_____	90.00	_____	240.00	_____
5000	150.00	_____	150.00	_____	350.00	_____
7500	225.00	_____	187.50	_____	450.00	_____
10,000	300.00	_____	200.00	_____	500.00	_____
Type of tax:	_____		_____		_____	

■ SHORT ANSWER AND ESSAY QUESTIONS

1. Why has there been dissatisfaction with government decisions and the economic efficiency in government?

2. What is the relationship between majority voting and the efficiency of outcomes from an election? How do special-interest groups or the use of logrolling influence the efficiency of outcomes?

3. Why is there a paradox with majority voting? Do the outcomes from majority voting suggest that voters are irrational in their preferences?

4. Describe how median voters influence the election results and debates over public issues. What are two important implications of the median voter model?

5. Explain what is meant by "government failure." Is it related to market failure and externalities?

6. Public choice theory suggests that there are a number of reasons for government failures. What are the reasons? Explain how each would tend to result in the inefficient allocation of the economy's resources.

7. It is generally agreed that "national defense must lie in the public sector while wheat production can best be accomplished in the private sector." Why is there no agreement on where many other goods or services should be produced?

8. What are the two basic philosophies for apportioning the tax burden in the United States? Explain each one.

9. What are the difficulties encountered in putting the two basic tax philosophies into practice?

10. Explain the difference among progressive, regressive, and proportional taxes. Which types of taxes fall into each of these categories?

11. Explain the effect the imposition of an excise tax has on the supply of a product that is bought and sold in a competitive market.

12. Illustrate with a supply and demand graph what part of an excise tax is passed on to the buyer and what part is borne by the seller. What determines the division of the tax between the buyer and the seller?

13. What is the relationship between the price elasticity of demand for a commodity and the portion of an excise tax on a commodity borne by the buyer and the seller?

14. What is the relationship between the price elasticity of supply and the incidence of an excise tax?

15. How does an excise tax produce an efficiency loss for society? Explain and illustrate with a supply and demand graph.

16. How is the efficiency loss from an excise tax affected by the elasticity of supply or demand? All else equal, shouldn't the total tax burden be equal for two taxes that produce equal revenues?

17. Describe the probable incidence of the personal income tax, the sales tax, and the excise tax.

18. For whom is the tax shifted, and on whom is the tax incidence for the corporate income tax?

19. Explain whether businesses or consumers are likely to bear the incidence of a corporate income tax or a business property tax.

20. What general conclusion can be drawn about the progressivity or regressivity of the Federal tax system, taxation by state and local governments, and the overall U.S. tax system?

ANSWERS

Chapter 18 Public Choice Theory and the Economics of Taxation

FILL-IN QUESTIONS

1. majority, inefficient, individual, less than, greater than
2. interest, logrolling
3. paradox
4. median-voter, middle
5. does not, government, inefficiency
6. small, large, small
7. rent-seeking behavior
8. clear, hidden
9. limited, bundled
10. private, private, public, more, less
11. government, market, imperfect
12. benefits-received, ability-to-pay
13. proportional, regressive, progressive
14. progressive, regressive, proportional, regressive
15. incidence, decrease, left, buyers, sellers
16. price, less, more, more, less
17. loss, greater, loss
18. individuals, businesses, consumers (*either order for last two*)
19. buyers, buyers, owners, renters, consumers
20. progressive, regressive, progressive, small, decreased

TRUE–FALSE QUESTIONS

1. T, pp. 336–338	**10.** T, pp. 341–342	**19.** T, pp. 345–347
2. F, p. 338	**11.** F, p. 342	**20.** F, pp. 346–347
3. F, pp. 338–339	**12.** T, p. 343	**21.** T, pp. 346–347
4. T, p. 339	**13.** T, p. 343	**22.** F, p. 348
5. T, pp. 340–341	**14.** F, p. 343	**23.** F, pp. 348–349
6. F, p. 340	**15.** F, p. 344	**24.** T, p. 349
7. T, pp. 340–341	**16.** F, p. 344	**25.** T, p. 350
8. F, p. 341	**17.** T, p. 344	
9. T, p. 341	**18.** T, pp. 345–347	

MULTIPLE-CHOICE QUESTIONS

1. b, p. 336	**10.** d, p. 343	**19.** b, pp. 346–347
2. b, p. 338	**11.** d, p. 343	**20.** a, pp. 346–347
3. b, pp. 338–339	**12.** d, p. 344	**21.** c, pp. 347–348
4. a, pp. 338–339	**13.** a, pp. 344–345	**22.** d, p. 348
5. a, pp. 338–339	**14.** a, pp. 345–346	**23.** a, pp. 348–349
6. b, p. 339	**15.** b, pp. 345–346	**24.** a, pp. 348–349
7. c, p. 339	**16.** b, pp. 345–346	**25.** b, pp. 349–350
8. c, pp. 340–341	**17.** c, pp. 345–346	
9. d, p. 342	**18.** a, pp. 345–346	

PROBLEMS

1. *a.* $3.60; *b.* (reading down) 600, 500, 400, 300, 200, 100; *c.* $4.00; *d.* (1) $.40, 67, (2) $.20, 33

2. *a.* not changed; *b.* none, all; *c.* smaller, larger; *d.* larger, smaller

3. *a.* increased by the amount of the tax; *b.* all, none; *c.* larger, smaller; *d.* smaller, larger

4. Tax A: 3, 3, 3, 3, proportional; Tax B: 3, 3, 2.5, 2, combination; Tax C: 8, 7, 6, 5, regressive

5. *a.* $264, 296, 328, 360; *b.* 3.8, 3.7, 3.64, 3.6; *c.* regressive

SHORT ANSWER AND ESSAY QUESTIONS

1. p. 336	**8.** p. 343	**15.** pp. 346–347
2. pp. 336–338	**9.** pp. 343–344	**16.** pp. 346–347
3. pp. 338–339	**10.** pp. 344–345	**17.** p. 348
4. pp. 339–340	**11.** pp. 345–346	**18.** p. 348
5. pp. 340–341	**12.** pp. 345–346	**19.** pp. 348–349
6. pp. 340–341	**13.** pp. 345–346	**20.** pp. 349–350
7. pp. 341–342	**14.** pp. 345–346	

CHAPTER 19

Antitrust Policy and Regulation

Chapter 19 examines issues related to antitrust policy and the regulation of markets and society. These issues are important for you to study because they affect prices, economic efficiency, and economic welfare.

Over the years the Federal government has taken action to curb or limit the growth of monopolies in the United States through the passage of **antitrust laws** and the establishment of regulatory agencies. The *Sherman Act* of 1890 was the first major antitrust law. It was followed by other antitrust legislation and the creation of regulatory agencies and commissions.

The chapter discusses major antitrust issues and evaluates the effectiveness of **antitrust policy.** Several issues of interpretation address whether businesses should be judged for antitrust violations on the basis of monopoly behavior or structure and what should be the definition of the market. You will learn about the two conflicting perspectives on the enforcement of antitrust laws—activist and laissez-faire. The effectiveness of antitrust policy is also evaluated in the chapter based on such factors as the degree of the monopoly control, mergers, price fixing, price discrimination, and tying contracts.

Industrial regulation focuses on the control of natural monopolies so that they produce economic outcomes that benefit society. It is based on the public interest theory of regulation. This regulation by agencies and commissions has several problems of which you should be aware. One problem is that some of the regulated industries may not be natural monopolies at all and would be competitive industries if they were left unregulated. From this problem comes the legal cartel theory of regulation: Many industries want to be regulated so that competition among the firms will be reduced and the profits will increase.

Beginning in the 1970s, many industries in the United States underwent **deregulation.** These included the airline, trucking, banking, railroad, natural gas, television broadcasting, and telecommunications industries. The results generally show that this deregulation was beneficial for consumers and the efficiency of the economy. A more recent experience with deregulation occurred in the market for electricity. The outcomes from this experiment in deregulation have been less certain because of pricing problems in California.

Beginning in the early 1960s, new agencies and commissions began to engage in **social regulation** that differed from the regulation of the prices, services, and output provided by specific industries. This regulation focused on production conditions, product attributes, and production effects on society. This regulation increases product prices and indirectly reduces worker productivity, but supporters argue that the social benefits over time will exceed the costs. Critics contend that it is costly, often poorly conceived, and has negative secondary effects. The debate over the optimal level of social regulation is not easily resolved because the costs and benefits are difficult to measure. You should spend time understanding both sides of the issue.

■ CHECKLIST

When you have studied this chapter you should be able to

☐ State the purpose of antitrust policy.

☐ Discuss the historical background and rationale for antitrust laws and regulatory agencies.

☐ Describe the purpose and major provisions of the Sherman Act, Clayton Act, Federal Trade Commission Act, Wheeler-Lea Act, and Celler-Kefauver Act.

☐ Contrast the monopoly behavior view of the antitrust laws with the monopoly structure view using two landmark Supreme Court decisions.

☐ Explain the importance of market definition in the interpretation of antitrust laws.

☐ Compare and contrast the active antitrust perspective with the laissez-faire perspective.

☐ Describe the application of antitrust laws to monopoly.

☐ Distinguish among a horizontal, vertical, and conglomerate merger.

☐ Explain the concept of the Herfindahl index and its application to merger guidelines.

☐ Describe antitrust policy toward price fixing and price discrimination.

☐ Discuss the antitrust issue in tying contracts.

☐ Define a natural monopoly and cite two ways government controls natural monopolies.

☐ Explain the public interest theory of regulation.

☐ Describe two problems with industrial regulation by government agencies and commissions.

☐ Explain the legal cartel theory of regulation.

☐ Discuss the outcomes from deregulation of selected U.S. industries since the 1970s.

☐ State three distinguishing features of social regulation.

☐ Make a case for social regulation in terms of benefits and costs.

☐ Present a case against social regulation in terms of benefits and costs.

☐ Offer two economic reminders about social regulation.

■ CHAPTER OUTLINE

1. The basic purposes of **antitrust policy** are to restrict monopoly power, promote competition, and achieve allocative efficiency.

   a. Following the Civil War, the expansion of the U.S. economy brought with it the creation of trusts (or monopolies) in many industries. The economic problem with monopolies is that they produce less output and charge higher prices than would be the case if their industries were more competitive. To control them, government has passed antitrust laws and created regulatory agencies.

   b. The **Sherman Act** of 1890 was the first antitrust legislation. It made restraint of trade and monopolization criminal offenses.

   c. The **Clayton Act** of 1914 outlawed price discrimination not based on cost, **tying contracts,** mergers that lessened competition, and **interlocking directorates.**

   d. The **Federal Trade Commission Act** of 1914 established the **Federal Trade Commission (FTC)** to investigate unfair practices that might lead to the development of monopoly power. In 1938 this act was amended by the **Wheeler-Lea Act** to prohibit deceptive practices (including false and misleading advertising and misrepresentation of products).

   e. The **Celler-Kefauver Act** of 1950 plugged a loophole in the Clayton Act and prohibited mergers that might lead to a substantial reduction in competition.

2. The effectiveness of antitrust laws in preventing monopoly and maintaining competition has depended on judicial interpretation of the laws and enforcement of these laws by Federal agencies.

   a. Two issues arise in the judicial interpretation of the antitrust laws.

   (1) Should a firm be judged on the basis of its monopoly structure or behavior? The **U.S. Steel case** of 1920, which came before the Supreme Court, applied the **rule of reason** and said that a firm should be judged on the basis of its behavior. The **Alcoa case** of 1945 judged a firm on the basis of its structure (large control of a market). The courts and most economists now use the rule of reason that bases antitrust action on market behavior, not structure.

   (2) Should a broad or narrow definition of the market in which firms sell their products be used to judge monopoly power? In the 1956 **DuPont cellophane case,** the Court ruled that DuPont did not monopolize the industry because there were other types of packaging materials that could be used.

   b. There are differences in political philosophies about whether antitrust enforcement should be more or less strictly enforced. The active antitrust perspective calls for enforcement of antitrust laws to stop illegal business activity, prevent anticompetitive mergers, and counter monopoly practices. The laissez-faire perspective contends that enforcement is largely unnecessary because market forces will control monopoly behavior and undermine monopoly positions.

   c. A question can be raised about whether the antitrust laws have been effective regarding monopoly, mergers, price fixing, price discrimination, and tying contracts.

   (1) For existing market structures, enforcement of antitrust laws has been lenient in general if the expansion of market share by a firm is reasonable. The Sherman Act, however, has still been invoked in several high profile cases in which anticompetitive practices were alleged (1982 AT&T and 2000 Microsoft cases).

   (2) For **horizontal, vertical,** or **conglomerate mergers,** the application of the laws usually varies by the type of merger and the particulars of a case. Merger guidelines are based on the Herfindahl index (the sum of the squared values of market shares within an industry), but other factors, such as economies of scale, degree of foreign competition, and ease of entry, are considered.

   (3) Prohibitions against price fixing are strictly enforced. These activities are viewed as **per se violations,** so even the attempt, and not the actual outcome, will bring legal action and penalties.

   (4) Price discrimination is rarely challenged on antitrust grounds because in most cases it benefits consumers, but the practice can be challenged if the purpose is to reduce competition or block entry into a business.

   (5) The laws against tying contracts that require a buyer to purchase other products or take certain actions as a condition of a sale have been strictly enforced.

   (6) Overall, antitrust laws have not been very effective in breaking up monopolies or in preventing the growth of large oligopolies that have developed legally and because of market conditions. The laws have been effective against abusive or predatory monopolies. They have also been effective in blocking anticompetitive mergers, preventing price fixing, and restricting the use of tying contracts.

3. **Industrial regulation** occurs in some industries for economic reasons.

   a. A **natural monopoly** exists if a single producer can provide a good or service for the entire market at a lower average cost (because of economies of scale) than several producers, making competition uneconomical. To achieve better economic outcomes from this situation, government may opt for public ownership of the business or public (industrial) regulation. The latter option is based on the **public interest theory of regulation** that calls for controlling the economic decisions of the monopoly producers to achieve lower costs and greater output benefits for the public.

   b. The effectiveness of the regulation of business firms by regulatory agencies has been criticized for two main reasons.

   (1) Regulation increases costs and leads to an inefficient allocation of resources and higher prices.

   (2) Regulated monopolies get perpetuated over time and would be more competitive firms if they were not

regulated. Regulatory agencies contribute to the problem by protecting these industries, and these actions hurt the public and consumers.

c. The *legal cartel theory of regulation* holds that potentially competitive industries often want and support the regulation of their industries to increase their profits by limiting competition among firms. The government regulatory agency in essence creates a government-sponsored cartel in an industry.

4. Since the 1970s there has been *deregulation* of many industries in the United States: airline, trucking, banking, railroad, natural gas, electricity, television broadcasting, and communications. The overall evidence, however, shows that deregulation has been clearly positive because it has resulted in lower prices, lower costs of production, and increased output. It has also allowed for greater technological advances in many industries. There is less certainty about the positive outcomes from deregulation in electricity markets because of pricing problems in California and illegal manipulations of electricity supplies by some business firms.

5. *Social regulation* has developed since the 1960s and resulted in the creation of additional regulatory agencies that focus on production conditions, product qualities, and production effects on society.

a. Social regulation differs in three ways from industrial regulation: broader coverage of industries; more intrusion into the day-to-day production process; and rapid expansion into many areas.

b. Discussions about social regulation involve deciding whether there is an optimal level of such regulation. The costs and benefits are difficult to measure, so ideology often influences the debate over the proper amount of this regulation.

c. Supporters of social regulation contend it is needed to fight serious problems such as job and auto safety, environment pollution, product defects, and discrimination. Although such regulation is costly, the social benefits would exceed the costs over time, if they could be easily measured. Defenders point to many specific benefits resulting from such regulation.

d. Critics argue that this social regulation is inefficient because the regulations are poorly drawn and targeted. The rules and regulations are also often made based on limited and inadequate information. In addition, there are unintended secondary effects from the regulation that boost product costs. Regulatory agencies tend to attract "overzealous" workers who dislike the market system and advocate government intervention as the only solution.

e. Two reminders are needed in the debate over social regulation.

(1) Supporters need to remember that there is no "free lunch," and that social regulation increases product prices, may slow product innovation, and may lessen competition.

(2) Defenders need to remember that the market system has flaws that sometimes need to be addressed by government through social regulation and that by doing so, government creates continuing support of the operation of the market system.

■ HINTS AND TIPS

1. The first section of the chapter discusses several Federal antitrust laws. After looking at this section, many students ask, "Am I expected to know these laws?" Yes, you should have an understanding of these laws. A related question asked is, "Why should I know them?" To examine a current economic issue, you need to know how the problem arose, what actions have been taken over time to solve it, and what the outcomes are. Many of these major antitrust laws are enforced to some degree today and may affect a business for which you may work.

2. The *Herfindahl index* was first introduced in Chapter 12. Reread that material if you cannot remember what the index is. In Chapter 19 you will learn how the index is used for merger guidelines.

3. This chapter discusses controversies about many topics—antitrust policy, industrial regulation, deregulation, and social regulation. To help understand these controversies, make a table showing the pro and con positions for each issue. See problem 4 for an example.

■ IMPORTANT TERMS

antitrust policy	rule of reason
industrial regulation	Alcoa case
social regulation	DuPont cellophane case
Sherman Act	horizontal merger
Clayton Act	vertical merger
tying contracts	conglomerate merger
interlocking directorate	per se violations
Federal Trade Commission Act	natural monopoly
cease-and-desist order	public interest theory of regulation
Wheeler-Lea Act	legal cartel theory of regulation
Celler-Kefauver Act	
U.S. Steel case	

SELF-TEST

■ FILL-IN QUESTIONS

1. Laws and government actions designed to prevent monopoly and promote competition are referred to as (industrial regulation, antitrust policy) _____. Actions taken to control a firm's prices within selected industries are referred to as (social, industrial) _____ regulation whereas establishing the conditions under which goods are produced, monitoring the physical characteristics of products, and reducing the negative effects of production fall under the category of _____ regulation.

2. The two techniques of Federal control that have been adopted as substitutes for, or to maintain competition in, markets are

   a. _____

   b. _____

3. Antitrust legislation in 1890 that made it illegal to monopolize or restrain trade between the states or between nations was the (Clayton, Sherman) _____ Act. Legislation passed in 1914 that prohibited such practices as price discrimination, acquisition of the stock of corporations to reduce competition, tying contracts, and interlocking directorates was the (Clayton, Sherman) _____ Act.

4. The 1914 act that had set up an agency to investigate unfair competitive practices, hold public hearings on such complaints, and issue cease-and-desist orders was the (Clayton, Federal Trade Commission) _____ Act.

5. The 1938 antitrust act that had the effect of prohibiting false and misleading advertising was the (Celler-Kefauver, Wheeler-Lea) _____ Act, while the act that plugged a loophole in the Clayton Act by banning the acquisition of assets of one firm by another when it would lessen competition was the _____ Act.

6. When the judicial courts used the rule of reason to evaluate industrial concentration by U.S. Steel in 1920, they were judging the firm on the basis of its market (behavior, structure) _____, but when the courts made a decision to break up Alcoa in 1945, they were judging the firm on the basis of its market _____. Since 1945, the courts have returned to evaluating a firm on the basis of its market (behavior, structure) _____.

7. One major issue of interpretation in antitrust law is the definition of a market. The firm's market share will appear small if the courts define a market (narrowly, broadly) _____, but the firm's market share will appear large if the courts define a market share _____. In 1956, the courts ruled that although DuPont sold nearly all the cellophane produced in the United States, it (did, did not) _____ dominate the market for flexible packaging materials.

8. The active antitrust perspective is that antitrust laws need to be (strictly, loosely) _____ enforced to promote (monopoly, competition) _____ in business. The laissez-faire perspective contends that enforcement is largely (necessary, unnecessary) _____ because monopoly power and control can be countered by (government, markets) _____.

9. A merger between two competitors selling similar products in the same market is a (vertical, horizontal, conglomerate) _____ merger; a _____ merger occurs among firms at different stages in the production process of the same industry; a _____ merger results when a firm in one industry is purchased by a firm in an unrelated industry.

10. The (Sherman, Herfindahl) _____ index is used as a guideline for mergers. An industry of only four firms, each with a 25 percent market share, has an index score of (2500, 10,000) _____ but if the industry was a pure monopoly with only one firm its index score would be _____.

11. If a firm attempts to fix prices, even if the attempt were not effective, it would be an example of a (tying contract, per se violation) _____ under antitrust laws; if a producer will only sell a desired product on condition that the buyer acquire other products, it would be an example of a _____ under antitrust laws. In both cases, the laws are (loosely, strictly) _____ enforced.

12. Most economists conclude that, overall, U.S. antitrust policy (has, has not) _____ been effective in achieving its goal of promoting competition and efficiency and that the application of antitrust laws _____ been effective against predatory and abusive monopoly.

13. A natural monopoly exists when a single firm is able to supply the entire market at a (higher, lower) _____ average cost than a number of competing firms. In the United States, many of these natural monopolies are controlled by (business cartels, regulatory commissions) _____.

14. The two major criticisms of regulation of industries by a government agency or commission are
   a. The regulated firms have no incentive to lower their costs because the commission will then require them to (raise, lower) _____ their prices, and because the prices they are allowed to charge are based on the value of their capital equipment, firms tend to make uneconomical substitutions of (labor, capital) _____ for _____.
   b. Regulation has been applied to industries that (are, are not) _____ natural monopolies, which in the absence of regulation would be more competitive.

15. The public interest theory of regulation assumes that the objective of regulating an industry is to (encourage, discourage) _____ the abuses of monopoly power. An alternative theory assumes firms wish to be regulated because it enables them to form, and the regulatory commission helps them to create, a profitable and legal (conglomerate, cartel) _____.

16. The available evidence indicates that deregulation of many industries that began in the 1970s generally resulted in (decreased, increased) _____ prices because _____ competition among firms led to _____ costs and _____ output.

17. The Food and Drug Administration would be an example of a Federal regulatory commission engaged in (social, industrial) _____ regulation and the Federal Communications Commission would be an example of an agency engaged in _____ regulation.

18. Compared with industrial regulation, social regulation applies to (more, fewer) _____ firms, affects day-to-day production to a (greater, lesser) _____ extent, and has expanded more (rapidly, slowly) _____.

19. It should be remembered by supporters of social regulation that there is "no free lunch" because it can (increase, decrease) _____ product prices and _____ worker productivity, and it also may _____ the rate of innovation.

20. It should be remembered by critics of social regulation that it can be (anti-, pro-) _____ capitalist because when social problems in the market are addressed, the public support for the market system is (increased, decreased) _____.

■ **TRUE–FALSE QUESTIONS**

Circle T if the statement is true, F if it is false.

1. The basic purposes of antitrust policy are to prevent monopolization, promote competition, and achieve allocative efficiency.   **T F**

2. The issue of antitrust arose from the emergence of trusts and monopolies in the U.S. economy in the two decades *before* the U.S. Civil War.   **T F**

3. The economic problem with monopolists is that they charge a lower price and produce more output than if their industries were competitive.   **T F**

4. The Clayton Act declares that price discrimination, tying contracts, stock acquisitions between corporations, and interlocking directorates are illegal when their effect is to reduce competition.   **T F**

5. The Federal Trade Commission is in charge of stimulating more international trade between domestic and foreign producers.   **T F**

6. The Celler-Kefauver Act of 1950 prohibits one firm from acquiring the assets of another firm when the result is to lessen competition.   **T F**

7. In 1920 the courts applied the rule of reason to the U.S. Steel Corporation and decided that the corporation possessed monopoly power and had unreasonably restrained trade.   **T F**

8. Those who believe an industry should be judged on the basis of its structure contend that any industry with a monopolistic structure must behave like a monopolist.   **T F**

9. The courts broadly defined the market for cellophane in the DuPont cellophane case of 1956.   **T F**

10. There is only one perspective on the enforcement of antitrust laws, and it calls for strict enforcement of all laws.   **T F**

11. A horizontal merger is a merger between firms at different stages of the production process.   **T F**

12. The Herfindahl index is the sum of the squared values of the market shares within an industry.   **T F**

13. To gain a conviction under *per se violations,* the party making the charge must show that the conspiracy to fix prices actually succeeded or caused damage.   **T F**

14. There is substantial evidence that antitrust policy has *not* been effective in identifying and prosecuting price fixing by businesses.   **T F**

15. Industrial regulation consists of regulation of the conditions under which products are made, the impact of products on society, and the physical qualities of the products.   **T F**

16. Public ownership rather than public regulation has been the primary means used in the United States to ensure that the behavior of natural monopolists is socially acceptable.   **T F**

17. The rationale underlying the public interest theory of regulation of natural monopolies is to allow the consumers of their goods or services to benefit from the economies of scale.   **T F**

18. Regulated firms, because the prices they are allowed to charge enable them to earn a "fair" return over their costs, have a strong incentive to reduce their costs.   **T F**

19. From the perspective of the legal cartel theory of regulation, some industries want to be regulated by government.   **T F**

20. Deregulation of industries since the 1970s has resulted in large gains in economic efficiency for the U.S. economy.   **T F**

21. The marginal costs and benefits of social regulation are easy to measure for determining the optimal level of such regulation.   **T F**

22. Those who favor social regulation believe that the expenditures on it are needed to obtain a hospitable, sustainable, and just society.   **T F**

23. Critics of social regulation argue that its marginal costs exceed its marginal benefits.   **T F**

24. The likely effect of social regulation is that it lowers product prices, raises worker productivity, and increases product innovation.   **T F**

25. Social regulation can contribute to public support for a market system by addressing production and consumption problems arising from the system.   **T F**

■ **MULTIPLE-CHOICE QUESTIONS**

Circle the letter that corresponds to the best answer.

1. Which term describes the laws and government actions designed to prevent monopoly and promote competition?
  (a) industrial regulation
  (b) social regulation
  (c) legal cartel policy
  (d) antitrust policy

2. Which law stated that contracts and conspiracies in restraint of trade, monopolies, attempts to monopolize, and conspiracies to monopolize are illegal?
  (a) Sherman Act
  (b) Clayton Act
  (c) Federal Trade Commission Act
  (d) Wheeler-Lea Act

3. Which act specifically outlawed tying contracts and interlocking directorates?
  (a) Sherman Act
  (b) Clayton Act
  (c) Federal Trade Commission Act
  (d) Wheeler-Lea Act

4. Which act has given the Federal Trade Commission the task of preventing false and misleading advertising and the misrepresentation of products?
  (a) Sherman Act
  (b) Clayton Act
  (c) Federal Trade Commission Act
  (d) Wheeler-Lea Act

5. Which act banned the acquisition of a firm's assets by a competing firm when the acquisition would tend to reduce competition?
  (a) Celler-Kefauver Act
  (b) Wheeler-Lea Act
  (c) Clayton Act
  (d) Federal Trade Commission Act

6. The argument that an industry that is highly concentrated will behave like a monopolist and the Alcoa court case of 1945 would both be support for the case that the application of antitrust laws should be based on industry
  (a) behavior
  (b) structure
  (c) efficiency
  (d) rule of reason

7. If the market is defined broadly to include a wide range of somewhat similar products, then
  (a) firms in the industry will be able to behave as monopolists
  (b) firms in the industry will follow the rule of reason
  (c) a firm's market share will appear large
  (d) a firm's market share will appear small

8. Which perspective holds that the enforcement of antitrust laws is largely unnecessary, especially as related to monopoly, because market forces will counter monopoly?
  (a) concentration perspective
  (b) active antitrust perspective
  (c) relevant market perspective
  (d) laissez-faire perspective

9. The merger of a firm in one industry with a firm in an unrelated industry is called a
  (a) horizontal merger
  (b) vertical merger
  (c) secondary merger
  (d) conglomerate merger

10. Which is most likely to be the focus of antitrust law scrutiny and enforcement?
  (a) a publicly regulated utility
  (b) a conglomerate merger
  (c) a vertical merger
  (d) a horizontal merger

11. An industry has four firms, each with a market share of 25%. There is no foreign competition, entry into the industry is difficult, and no firm is on the verge of bankruptcy. If two of the firms in the industry sought to merge, this action would most likely be opposed by the government because the new Herfindahl index for the industry would be
  (a) 2000 and the merger would increase the index by 1000
  (b) 2500 and the merger would increase the index by 1000
  (c) 3750 and the merger would increase the index by 1250
  (d) 5000 and the merger would increase the index by 1250

12. When the government or another party making a charge can show that there was a conspiracy to fix prices, even if the conspiracy did not succeed, this would be an example of
  (a) a tying contract
  (b) a per se violation
  (c) the rule of reason
  (d) the legal cartel theory

13. Antitrust laws have been most effective in
  (a) breaking up monopolies
  (b) prosecuting price fixing in business
  (c) expanding industrial concentration
  (d) blocking entry of foreign competition in domestic markets

14. If a movie distributor forced theaters to "buy" projection rights to a full package of films as a condition of

showing a blockbuster movie, then this would be an example of
- **(a)** price fixing
- **(b)** a tying contract
- **(c)** a per se violation
- **(d)** an interlocking directorate

15. An example of a government organization involved primarily in industrial regulation would be the
- **(a)** Federal Communications Commission
- **(b)** Food and Drug Administration
- **(c)** Occupational Safety and Health Administration
- **(d)** Environmental Protection Agency

16. Legislation designed to regulate natural monopolies would be based on which theory of regulation?
- **(a)** cartel
- **(b)** public interest
- **(c)** rule of reason
- **(d)** public ownership

17. Those who oppose the regulation of industry by regulatory agencies contend that
- **(a)** many of the regulated industries are natural monopolies
- **(b)** the regulatory agencies may favor industry because they are often staffed by former industry executives
- **(c)** regulation contributes to an increase in the number of mergers in industries
- **(d)** regulation helps moderate costs and improves efficiency in the production of a good or service produced by the regulated industry

18. The legal cartel theory of regulation
- **(a)** would allow the forces of demand and supply to determine the rates (prices) of the good or service
- **(b)** would attempt to protect the public from abuses of monopoly power
- **(c)** assumes that the regulated industry wishes to be regulated
- **(d)** assumes that both the demand for and supply of the good or service produced by the regulated industry are perfectly inelastic

19. Deregulation of previously regulated industries in the United States has resulted in
- **(a)** higher prices, higher costs, and decreased output
- **(b)** higher prices and costs, but increased output
- **(c)** lower prices and costs, but decreased output
- **(d)** lower prices, lower costs, and increased output

20. Which is a concern of social regulation?
- **(a)** the prices charged for goods
- **(b)** the service provided to the public
- **(c)** the conditions under which goods are manufactured
- **(d)** the impact on business profits from the production of goods

21. A major difference between industrial regulation and social regulation is that social regulation
- **(a)** covers fewer industries across the economy

- **(b)** has expanded slowly and waned in recent years
- **(c)** is targeted at the prices charged, the costs of production, and amount of profit
- **(d)** focuses on product design, employment conditions, and the production process

22. Which government organization is primarily engaged in social regulation?
- **(a)** the Federal Trade Commission
- **(b)** the Interstate Commerce Commission
- **(c)** the Environmental Protection Agency
- **(d)** the Federal Energy Regulatory Commission

23. Supporters of social regulation contend that
- **(a)** there is a pressing need to reduce the number of mergers in U.S. business
- **(b)** the presence of natural monopoly requires strong regulatory action by government
- **(c)** the social benefits will exceed the social costs
- **(d)** there are no social costs associated with it

24. A criticism of social regulation by its opponents is that it
- **(a)** is a strong procapitalist force
- **(b)** will decrease the rate of innovation in the economy
- **(c)** will increase the amount of price fixing among businesses
- **(d)** will require too long a time to achieve its objectives

25. The captions for two reminders for proponents and opponents of social regulation are
- **(a)** "there is no free lunch" and "less government is not always better than more"
- **(b)** "the rule of reason will prevail" and "restraint of trade will not be tolerated by government"
- **(c)** "the public interest will win over the powerful" and the "legal cartel will be broken by government"
- **(d)** "demand the lowest price" and "protect the greatest number"

■ **PROBLEMS**

1. Following is a list of Federal laws. Next is a series of provisions found in Federal laws. Match each law with the appropriate provision by placing the appropriate capital letter after each provision.
- **A.** Sherman Act
- **B.** Clayton Act
- **C.** Federal Trade Commission Act
- **D.** Wheeler-Lea Act
- **E.** Celler-Kefauver Act

a. Established a commission to investigate and prevent unfair methods of competition _____

b. Made monopoly and restraint of trade illegal and criminal _____

c. Prohibited the acquisition of the assets of a firm by another firm when such an acquisition would lessen competition _____

d. Had the effect of prohibiting false and misleading advertising and the misrepresentation of products

_____

e. Clarified the Sherman Act and outlawed specific techniques or devices used to create monopolies and restrain trade _____

2. Indicate with the letter **L** for leniently and the letter **S** for strictly how the antitrust laws tend to be applied to each of the following.

a. Vertical mergers in which each of the merging firms sells a small portion of the total output of its industry

_____

b. Price fixing by a firm in an industry _____

c. Conglomerate mergers _____

d. Existing market structures in which no firm sells 60% or more of the total output of its industry _____

e. Horizontal mergers in which the merged firms would sell a large portion of the total output of their industry and no firm is on the verge of bankruptcy _____

f. Action by firms in an industry to divide up sales

_____

g. Horizontal mergers where one of the firms is on the verge of bankruptcy _____

3. The following table contains data on five different industries and the market shares for each firm in the industry. Assume that there is no foreign competition, entry into the industry is difficult, and that no firm in each industry is on the verge of bankruptcy.

	Market share of firms in industry						Herfindahl index
Industry	1	2	3	4	5	6	
A	35	25	15	11	10	4	_____
B	30	25	25	20	—	—	_____
C	20	20	20	15	15	10	_____
D	60	25	15	—	—	—	_____
E	22	21	20	18	12	7	_____

a. In the last column, calculate the Herfindahl index.
b. The industry with the most concentration is Industry _____, and the industry with the least monopoly power is Industry _____.
c. If the *sixth* firm in Industry A sought to merge with the *fifth* firm in that industry, then the government (would, would not) _____ be likely to challenge the merger. The Herfindahl index for this industry is _____, which is higher than the merger guideline of _____ points used by the government, but the merger increases the index by only _____ points.

d. If the *fourth* firm in Industry B sought to merge with the *third* firm in that industry, then the government (would, would not) _____ be likely to challenge the merger. The Herfindahl index for this industry is _____, which is higher than the merger guideline of the government, and the merger increases the index by _____ points.
e. A *conglomerate* merger between the *fourth* firm in Industry C and the *fourth* firm in Industry E (would, would not) _____ likely be challenged by the government. The Herfindahl index would (increase, remain the same) _____ with this merger.
f. If a *vertical* merger between the *first* firm in Industry B with the *first* firm in Industry D lessened competition in each industry, then the merger (would, would not) _____ likely be challenged by the government, but the merger _____ likely be challenged if it did not lessen competition in each industry.

4. Social regulation has had its critics and defenders. In the blank spaces in the following table, indicate the effect that critics and defenders thought social regulation would have on each characteristic. Mark an **I** for increase and **D** for decrease. If the text states nothing about this effect, mark an **N**.

	Critics	Defenders
a. Prices	_____	_____
b. Output	_____	_____
c. Competition	_____	_____
d. Product innovation	_____	_____
e. Net benefits to society	_____	_____

■ **SHORT ANSWER AND ESSAY QUESTIONS**

1. Explain the basic differences between antitrust policy, industrial regulation, and social regulation.

2. What are the historical background to and the main provisions of the Sherman Act?

3. The Clayton Act and the Federal Trade Commission Act amended or elaborated on the provisions of the Sherman Act, and both aimed at preventing rather than punishing monopoly. What were the chief provisions of each act, and how did they attempt to prevent monopoly? In what two ways is the FTC Act important?

4. What loophole in the Clayton Act did the Celler-Kefauver Act plug in 1950, and how did it alter the coverage of the antitrust laws with respect to mergers?

5. Contrast the two different approaches to court interpretation of antitrust laws that are illustrated by the decisions of the courts in the U.S. Steel and Alcoa cases.

6. Why is defining the market an important issue in the application of the antitrust laws? How did the courts define the market in the case brought against DuPont for monopolizing the market for cellophane?

7. Discuss two perspectives on strict enforcement of antitrust laws.

8. How have the antitrust laws been applied in the past and in recent years to monopoly? Give examples.

9. Explain the difference between horizontal, vertical, and conglomerate mergers. Give an example of each type.

10. What is the Herfindahl index and how is it used as a guideline for mergers?

11. What are per se violations? Give examples of recent price-fixing investigations and court cases.

12. What is a natural monopoly? What two alternative ways can a natural monopoly be used to ensure that it behaves in a socially acceptable fashion?

13. Explain how public interest regulation can lead to increased costs and economic inefficiency as it is practiced by U.S. commissions and agencies.

14. Discuss the issue involved in regulation that perpetuates a natural monopoly after the conditions for it have evaporated. Give examples.

15. What is the legal cartel theory of regulation? Contrast it with the public interest theory of regulation.

16. Why were a number of industries in the U.S. economy deregulated beginning in the 1970s? What have been the economic effects of deregulation?

17. How does social regulation differ from industrial (or public) regulation? Describe three major differences.

18. Can the optimal level of social regulation be determined? Explain.

19. What are the major arguments for social regulation?

20. What are the major criticisms of social regulation?

ANSWERS

Chapter 19 Antitrust Policy and Regulation

FILL-IN QUESTIONS

1. antitrust policy, industrial, social
2. *a.* establishing regulatory agencies; *b.* passing antitrust laws (either order for *a* and *b*)
3. Sherman, Clayton
4. Federal Trade Commission
5. Wheeler-Lea, Celler-Kefauver
6. behavior, structure, behavior
7. broadly, narrowly, did not
8. strictly, competition, unnecessary, markets
9. horizontal, vertical, conglomerate
10. Herfindahl, 2500, 10,000
11. per se violation, tying contract, strictly
12. has, has
13. lower, regulatory commissions
14. *a.* lower, capital, labor; *b.* are not
15. discourage, cartel
16. decreased, increased, decreased, increased
17. social, industrial
18. more, greater, rapidly
19. increase, decrease, decrease
20. pro-, increased

TRUE–FALSE QUESTIONS

1. T, p. 354	**10.** F, p. 357	**19.** T, p. 362
2. F, p. 354	**11.** F, p. 359	**20.** T, p. 363
3. F, pp. 354–355	**12.** T, p. 359	**21.** F, p. 364
4. T, p. 355	**13.** F, p. 359	**22.** T, pp. 364–365
5. F, p. 356	**14.** F, p. 360	**23.** T, p. 365
6. T, p. 356	**15.** F, pp. 360–361	**24.** F, pp. 365–366
7. F, p. 356	**16.** F, p. 361	**25.** T, pp. 365–366
8. T, pp. 356–357	**17.** T, p. 361	
9. T, p. 357	**18.** F, pp. 361–362	

MULTIPLE-CHOICE QUESTIONS

1. d, pp. 354–355	**10.** d, p. 359	**19.** d, p. 363
2. a, p. 355	**11.** c, p. 359	**20.** c, pp. 363–364
3. b, p. 355	**12.** b, p. 359	**21.** d, pp. 363–364
4. d, p. 356	**13.** b, pp. 359–360	**22.** c, p. 364
5. a, p. 356	**14.** b, p. 360	**23.** c, pp. 364–365
6. b, pp. 356–357	**15.** a, p. 361	**24.** b, p. 365
7. d, p. 357	**16.** b, p. 361	**25.** a, pp. 365–366
8. d, p. 357	**17.** b, pp. 361–362	
9. d, p. 359	**18.** c, p. 362	

PROBLEMS

1. *a.* C; *b.* A; *c.* E; *d.* D; *e.* B
2. *a.* L; *b.* S; *c.* L; *d.* L; *e.* S; *f.* S; *g.* L
3. *a.* 2312, 2550, 1750, 4450, 1842; *b.* D, C; *c.* would not, 2312, 1800, 80; *d.* would, 2550, 1000; *e.* would not, remain the same; *f.* would, would not
4. *a.* I, N; *b.* D, N; *c.* D, N; *d.* D, N; *e.* D, I

SHORT ANSWER AND ESSAY QUESTIONS

1. pp. 354–355	**8.** p. 358	**15.** p. 362
2. pp. 354–355	**9.** pp. 358–359	**16.** pp. 362–363
3. pp. 355–356	**10.** p. 359	**17.** pp. 363–364
4. pp. 355–356	**11.** p. 359	**18.** p. 364
5. pp. 356–357	**12.** pp. 360–361	**19.** pp. 364–365
6. p. 357	**13.** p. 361	**20.** p. 365
7. pp. 357–358	**14.** pp. 361–362	

CHAPTER 20

Agriculture: Economics and Policy

Agriculture is a large and vital part of the U.S. and world economies, and so it merits the special attention it receives in Chapter 20. As you will learn, the economics of agriculture and farm policies of the Federal government are of concern not only to those directly engaged in farming, but also to U.S. consumers and businesses who purchase farm products and to U.S. taxpayers who subsidize farm incomes. Agriculture is also important in the world economy because each nation must find a way to feed its population, and domestic farm policies designed to enhance farm incomes often lead to distortions in world trade and economic inefficiency in world agricultural production.

The chapter begins by examining both the **short-run farm problem** and the **long-run farm problem** in U.S. agriculture. The short-run problem is that farm prices and incomes have fluctuated sharply from year to year. The long-run problem is that agriculture is a declining industry, and as a consequence, farm incomes have fallen over time. To understand the causes of each problem, you will have to use the concept of inelastic demand and your knowledge of how demand and supply determine price in a competitive market. The effort you have put into the study of these tools in previous chapters will now pay a dividend: an understanding of the causes of a real-world problem and the policies designed to solve the problem.

The agricultural policies of the Federal government have been directed at enhancing and stabilizing farm incomes by supporting farm prices. In connection with the support of farm prices, you are introduced to the **parity concept.** Once you understand parity and recognize that the parity price in the past has been above what the competitive price would have been, you will come to some important conclusions. Consumers paid higher prices for and consumed smaller quantities of the various farm products, and at the prices supported by the Federal government, there were surpluses of these products. The Federal government bought these surpluses to keep the price above the competitive market price. The purchases of the surpluses were financed by U.S. taxpayers. To eliminate these surpluses, government looked for ways to increase the demand for or to decrease the supply of these commodities. Programs to increase demand and decrease supply were put into effect, but they failed to eliminate the annual surpluses.

Over the past 60 years, farm policies have not worked well and the price-support system has been criticized for several reasons. First, the policies confuse the *symptoms* of the problem (low farm prices and incomes) with the

causes of the problem (resource allocation). Second, the costly farm subsidies are also misguided because they tend to benefit the high-income instead of the low-income farmer. Third, some policies of the Federal government contradict or offset other policies to help farmers.

The politics of farm policy can also be studied from the public choice perspective first presented in Chapter 18. In this chapter you will learn how the special-interest effect and rent-seeking behavior related to farm policies result in costly programs that have been supported by political leaders and subsidized by the Federal government for so many years. Nevertheless, the political backing for farm price supports is declining because of a reduction in the farm population. There is also international pressure to reduce farm price supports in all nations to eliminate distortions in world trade and improve worldwide economic efficiency.

The chapter concludes with a discussion of the recent reform of agricultural policy in the United States. The **Freedom to Farm Act** of 1996 was an attempt to eliminate price supports and acreage allotments for many major agricultural products. In return, U.S. farmers were to receive income payments through 2002 to help them make the transition to working in a more competitive market. The deterioration in economic conditions before the end of the act led to emergency aid payments to farmers. The **Farm Act of 2002** was passed by Congress to help stabilize crop prices and incomes for farmers, but as you will learn, this new legislation continued the policy of providing expensive price-support subsidies to agriculture.

■ CHECKLIST

When you have studied this chapter you should be able to

☐ Give several reasons why it is important to study the economics of U.S. agriculture.

☐ List three causes of the short-run problem in agriculture.

☐ Explain why the demand for agricultural products is price inelastic.

☐ Cite a reason for the fluctuations in agricultural output.

☐ Discuss the fluctuations in domestic demand for agricultural products.

☐ Describe the stability of foreign demand for agricultural products.

☐ Identify the two major factors contributing to the long-run problem in U.S. agriculture.

☐ Describe how technological change affects the long-run supply of agricultural products.

☐ Give two reasons why increases in demand lag increases in supply over time in U.S. agriculture.

☐ Use a supply and demand graph to illustrate the long-run problem in U.S. agriculture.

☐ Explain the consequences of the long-run problem in agriculture for industry structure, crop prices, and income.

☐ List the six features of the "farm program."

☐ Give cost estimates of the size of U.S. farm subsidies in recent years.

☐ Present several arguments in support of Federal assistance to agriculture.

☐ Define the parity ratio and explain its significance to agricultural policy.

☐ Use a supply and demand graph to identify the economic effects of price supports for agricultural products on output, farm income, consumer and taxpayer expenditures, economic efficiency, the environment, and international trade.

☐ Give examples of how the Federal government restricts supply and bolsters demand for farm products.

☐ Present three criticisms of the price-support system in agriculture.

☐ Use insights from public choice theory to discuss the politics of agricultural legislation and expenditures by the Federal government for farm programs.

☐ Give two reasons, one domestic and one international, to explain the change in the politics of farm subsidies.

☐ Describe the major features of the Freedom to Farm Act of 1996.

☐ Explain the elements of the Farm Act of 2002 and how it affects crop prices, farm incomes, and subsidies in agriculture.

■ **CHAPTER OUTLINE**

1. The economic analysis of U.S. agriculture is important for several reasons: It is one of the nation's largest industries and is a real-world example of the purely competitive model; it illustrates the economic effects of government intervention in markets; it illustrates the special-interest effect and rent-seeking behavior; and it reflects changes in global markets.

2. There is both a **short-run** and a **long-run farm problem:** The short-run problem is the frequent sharp changes in the incomes of farmers from one year to the next; the long-run problem is the tendency for farm prices and incomes to lag behind the upward trend of prices and incomes in the rest of the economy.

   a. The causes of the **short-run problem** (income instability) are the inelastic demand for farm products, fluctuations in the output of agricultural products, fluctuations in the demand, both domestic and foreign. These factors result in relatively large changes in agricultural prices and farm incomes.

   b. The causes of the **long-run problem** (low farm incomes and farm prices) stem from two basic factors:

(1) the supply of agricultural products increased significantly over most of this century because of technological advances in agriculture, and

(2) the demand for agricultural products failed to match the large increase in supply even though there were large increases in income (and population) because the demand for agricultural products is *income* inelastic (that is, increases in income lead to less than proportionate increases in expenditures on farm products).

3. Since the 1930s, farmers have been able to obtain various forms of public aid, but the primary purposes of the Federal **government subsidies** have been to enhance and stabilize farm prices and incomes.

   a. Several arguments are used to justify these expenditures, such as the poor incomes of farmers, the importance of the family farm, the hazards of farming, and market power problems.

   b. The cornerstone of the Federal policy to raise farm prices is the concept of **parity** (or the parity price), which would give the farmer year after year the same real income per unit of output.

   c. Historically, farm policy supported farm prices at some percentage of the parity price. But because the supported price was almost always above the market price, government had to support the price by purchasing and accumulating surpluses of agricultural products; while farmers gained from this policy, there were losses for consumers and society, and problems were created in the environment and international sectors.

   d. To reduce the annual and accumulated surpluses, government attempted to

(1) reduce the output (or supply) of farm products by acreage allotment and soil bank programs and

(2) expand the demand for farm products by finding new uses for farm products, expanding domestic demand, and increasing the foreign demand for agricultural commodities.

4. Agricultural policies designed to stabilize farm incomes and prices have not worked well over the past 60 years. The policies have been subject to **criticisms** and **political debate.**

   a. There are three basic criticisms of **price-support programs.**

(1) Price-support programs have confused the *symptoms* of the problem (low farm products and low farm incomes) with the *causes* of the problem (resource allocation) and have encouraged people to stay in agriculture.

(2) The major benefits from price-support programs are *misguided* because low-income farmers often receive small government subsidies while high-income farmers often receive large government subsidies; price supports also affect land values and become a subsidy for owners of farmland who rent their land and do not farm.

(3) The various farm programs of the Federal government have often *offset* or contradicted each other.

Price-support programs have tried to stabilize prices, while other programs have increased supply, thus putting downward pressure on prices.

b. The ***politics of agricultural policy*** explain why costly and extensive subsidies have persisted in the United States.

(1) Four insights from public choice theory serve to explain this development: rent-seeking behavior by farm groups, the special-interest effect that impairs public decision making, political logrolling to turn negative outcomes into positive outcomes, and the clear benefits and hidden costs of farm programs.

(2) Changing politics also explains why there has been a reduction in the political support for agricultural subsidies. There has been a decline in the farm population and its political power. The United States also is committed to reducing agricultural subsidies worldwide because they distort world trade. This U.S. support for freer trade makes it harder to support domestic farm subsidies.

5. Since the mid-1990s there have been several attempts to reform farm policy to make the farm sector more market-oriented and less dependent on government subsidies, but they have met with mixed success.

a. The ***Freedom to Farm Act*** of 1996 tried to change 60 years of U.S. farm policy. The law ended price supports and acreage allotments for eight agricultural commodities. In return for accepting more risk, income payments were made to farmers through the year 2002 to help them make the transition to operating in a more competitive market. The change was expected to increase agricultural output, crop diversity, and risk management by farmers. The decline in several farm commodity prices in recent years created pressure to change the Freedom to Farm Act. The U.S. government responded to the problem by increasing subsidies to farmers with emergency aid, but it was only a temporary solution to both a short-run and a long-run farm problem.

b. The ***Farm Act of 2002*** is a six-year bill costing some $118 billion. It continues the policy of giving farmers freedom to plant and provides constant direct payments to farmers based on past crop production levels. There are also countercyclical payments that cover any gap if the market price of a commodity falls below the target price. In addition, marketing loans can provide additional subsidies. The legislation makes it clear that agriculture will continue to receive large government subsidies in spite of the excess production and market distortion arising from these subsidies.

■ **HINTS AND TIPS**

1. This chapter applies several economic ideas—supply and demand, elasticity, price controls, and public choice theory—that you learned about in previous chapters. If your understanding of these ideas is weak, review supply and demand in Chapter 3, elasticity and price controls in Chapter 7, and public choice theory in Chapter 18.

2. There are short-run and long-run problems in agriculture. Make sure you understand the distinction. The short-run problem involves the year-to-year changes in the prices of farm products and farm incomes. The long-run problem is that changes in supply and demand over time have made agriculture a declining industry in the U.S. economy.

3. Figure 20.7 and the related discussion are very important to your study. The figure illustrates the economic effects that agricultural price supports have on different groups and the overall economy.

■ **IMPORTANT TERMS**

short-run farm problem	acreage allotments
long-run farm problem	Freedom to Farm Act
agribusiness	Farm Act of 2002
parity concept	direct payments
parity ratio	countercyclical payments (CCP)
price supports	

SELF-TEST

■ **FILL-IN QUESTIONS**

1. It is important to study the economics of U.S. agriculture for many reasons; it is one of the (largest, smallest) _____ industries in the nation; it provides a real-world example of pure (monopoly, competition) _____; it demonstrates the intended and unintended effects of (consumer, government) _____ policies that interfere with forces of supply and demand; it reflects the (decreased, increased) _____ globalization of agricultural markets; and it illustrates aspects of (public, private) _____ choice theory.

2. The basic cause of the short-run problems in agriculture is the (elastic, inelastic) _____ demand for farm products. This demand occurs because farm products have few good (complements, substitutes) _____ and because of rapidly diminishing marginal (product, utility) _____.

3. The elasticity of demand for farm products contributes to unstable farm prices and incomes because relatively (large, small) _____ changes in the output of farm products result in relatively _____ changes in prices and incomes and because relatively _____ changes in domestic or foreign demand result in relatively _____ changes in prices and incomes.

4. From a long-run perspective, the (demand for, supply of) _____ agricultural products increased rapidly over the past 60 years because of technological progress, but the _____ agricultural products did not increase as fast, in large part because food demand is income (elastic, inelastic) _____ and because the rate of population increase has not matched the increase in production.

5. Four arguments used to justify expenditures for farm subsidies are: the (inelastic, low) _____ income of farmers, the (cost, value) _____ of the family farm as a U.S. institution; the (rent-seeking, hazards) _____ of farming from many natural disasters, and the fact that the farmers sell their output in (purely, imperfectly) _____ competitive markets and purchase their inputs in _____ competitive markets.

6. If farmers were to receive a parity price for a product, year after year a given output would enable them to acquire a (fixed, increased) _____ amount of goods and services.

7. If the government supports farm prices at an above-equilibrium level, the results will be (shortages, surpluses) _____ that the government must (buy, sell) _____ to maintain prices at their support level.

8. With price-support programs, farmers (benefit, are hurt) _____ and consumers _____. The incomes of farmers (increase, decrease) _____, while the prices consumers pay for products _____ and the quantities of the agricultural product that they purchase _____.

9. Society also is hurt by farm price support programs because they encourage economic (efficiency, inefficiency) _____, an (over, under) _____ allocation of resources to agriculture, and a (small, large) _____ government bureaucracy for agriculture.

10. Agricultural price supports have (increased, decreased) _____ domestic agricultural production and _____ the use of inputs such as pesticides and fertilizers, resulting in (positive, negative) _____ effects on the environment.

11. The above-equilibrium price supports make U.S. agricultural markets (more, less) _____ attractive to foreign producers who try to sell _____ of their agricultural products in the United States. This activity is likely to (increase, decrease)

_____ trade barriers, and _____ the efficiency of U.S. agriculture. The trade barriers will have a (negative, positive) _____ effect on developing nations, which are often dependent on worldwide agricultural markets.

12. To bring the equilibrium level of prices in the market up to their support level, government has attempted to (increase, decrease) _____ the demand for and to _____ the supply of farm products.

13. To decrease supply, the Federal government has used (acreage allotment, rent-seeking) _____ programs. To increase demand, the Federal government has encouraged (new, old) _____ uses for agricultural products and sought to increase domestic and foreign (supply, demand) _____ for agricultural products through the domestic food stamps program or the foreign Food for Peace program.

14. The policies of government to support agricultural prices and income (have, have not) _____ worked well over the past 60 years because they have confused the symptoms of the farm problem, which are (high, low) _____ prices and incomes, with the root cause of the problem, which is (efficient, inefficient) _____ allocation of resources.

15. There are two other criticisms. Much of the benefits from farm price supports go to (high, low) _____-income farmers instead of _____-income farmers. The effects of price-support programs of the Federal government are (reinforced, offset) _____ by other government programs.

16. Despite these criticisms, farm policies have received strong support in Congress over the years; the result of this can be explained by insights from (monopoly, public choice) _____ theory. When farm groups lobby for Federal programs that transfer income to them, they are exhibiting (parity, rent-seeking) _____ behavior. There is also a special-interest effect because the costs to individual taxpayers are (large, small) _____ but the benefits to farmers are _____ from farm programs.

17. In addition, when agricultural groups or farm-state politicians trade votes to turn negative into positive outcomes, they are using political (allotments, logrolling) _____. Another public choice problem with farm subsidies is that the benefits of farm programs are (clear, hidden) _____, while much of the costs are _____ in the form of higher consumer prices for agricultural products.

18. There are also world (aid, trade) _____ considerations from agricultural subsidies. The effects of supports for the prices of agricultural products in the United States and European Union (EU) have been to (increase, decrease) _____ domestic production in these nations, _____ export subsidies for farm products in these nations, and _____ world prices for agricultural products, thus distorting worldwide trade in agricultural products.

19. Calls for reforms of farm policy in the United States led in 1996 to the Freedom to (Trade, Farm) _____ Act that sought to (expand, eliminate) _____ price supports for eight farm crops in return for giving farmers freedom to (plant, export) _____ crops. To make the transition from price-supported agriculture to market-oriented agriculture, farmers received transition (licenses, payments) _____, but the fall in several crop prices later in the decade led to emergency measures to (increase, decrease) _____ farm subsidies.

20. The Farm Act of 2002 continues the policy of freedom to (export, plant) _____, and provides income support for farmers in the form of direct (insurance, payments) _____. In addition, there are price-support subsidies in the form of countercyclical (insurance, payments) _____ and marketing (campaigns, loans) _____. As a result of the act, the government's subsidy for agriculture has (increased, decreased) _____, which in turn contributes to _____ crop production and low crop price. This resulting condition then leads to demands for (more, less) _____ farm subsidies.

■ **TRUE–FALSE QUESTIONS**

Circle T if the statement is true, F if it is false.

1. The short-run farm problem is the sharp year-to-year fluctuations in farm prices and farm incomes that frequently occur. **T F**

2. The demand for farm products is price elastic. **T F**

3. The quantities of agricultural commodities produced tend to be fairly *insensitive* to changes in agricultural prices because a large percentage of farmers' total costs are variable. **T F**

4. The foreign demand for farm products is relatively stable. **T F**

5. Appreciation of the dollar will tend to increase the demand for farm products. **T F**

6. The supply of agricultural products has tended to increase more rapidly than the demand for these products in the United States. **T F**

7. Most of the recent technological advances in agriculture have been initiated by farmers. **T F**

8. The demand for farm products is income elastic. **T F**

9. The long-run farm problem is that the incomes of farmers have been low relative to incomes in the economy as a whole. **T F**

10. The consequences over time of supply and demand conditions in agriculture are that minimum efficient scale has increased. **T F**

11. The size of the farm population in the United States has declined in both relative and absolute terms since about 1930. **T F**

12. The major aim of agricultural policy in the United States for the past 70 years was to support agricultural prices and incomes. **T F**

13. If the prices paid by farmers were 500% higher than in the base year and the price received by farmers were 400% higher than in the base year, the parity ratio would be 125%. **T F**

14. Application of the parity concept to farm prices causes farm prices to decline and results in agricultural surpluses. **T F**

15. When government supports farm prices at above-equilibrium levels, it can reduce the annual surpluses of agricultural commodities either by increasing the supply or by decreasing the demand for them. **T F**

16. The acreage allotment program was designed to decrease the supply of farm products. **T F**

17. Restricting the number of acres that farmers use to grow agricultural products has been only a partially successful method of reducing surpluses because farmers tend to cultivate their land more intensively when the acreage is reduced. **T F**

18. Public policy has been effective in alleviating the resource allocation problem in U.S. agriculture, not just the symptoms. **T F**

19. The price-income support programs for agriculture have given the most benefit to those farmers with the least need for the government assistance. **T F**

20. A political action committee organized by a group of sugar beet farmers to lobby Congress for subsidies for sugar beets is an example of political logrolling. **T F**

21. The reason that farmers, who are a small proportion of the population, can impose a large cost to taxpayers in the form of agricultural subsidies is because the cost imposed on each individual taxpayer is small and not given much attention by each taxpayer. **T F**

22. One hidden cost of agricultural price support programs is the higher prices that consumers pay for the product.　　　　　　　　　　　　　　　**T F**

23. The decline in farm population and in the related political representation in rural areas is one reason why political support for farm subsidies has increased.　**T F**

24. Domestic farm subsidies distort world trade and contribute to the inefficiencies in the international allocation of agricultural resources.　　　　　　　**T F**

25. Although the Farm Act of 2002 helped reduce the risk for farmers and raised farm incomes, it continues the Federal government policy of subsidizing agricultural production.　　　　　　　　　　　　　　　　**T F**

■ **MULTIPLE-CHOICE QUESTIONS**

Circle the letter that corresponds to the best answer.

1. The inelasticity of demand for agricultural products can be explained by
   (a) the parity ratio
   (b) economies of scale
   (c) rent-seeking behavior
   (d) diminishing marginal utility

2. The inelastic demand for agricultural products means that a relatively small increase in output will result in a relatively
   (a) small increase in farm prices and incomes
   (b) large decrease in farm prices and incomes
   (c) small decrease in farm prices and a relatively large increase in farm incomes
   (d) large increase in farm prices and a relatively small decrease in farm incomes

3. The reason that large declines in farm prices do not significantly reduce farm production in the short run is that farmers'
   (a) fixed costs are high relative to their variable costs
   (b) variable costs are high relative to their fixed costs
   (c) prices received are greater than prices paid for agricultural products
   (d) prices paid are greater than prices received for agricultural products

4. One reason for the year-to-year instability of agricultural product prices is
   (a) stable production of domestic agricultural products
   (b) stable production of foreign agricultural products
   (c) fluctuations in incomes received for agricultural products
   (d) fluctuations in the foreign demand for agricultural products

5. If, over time, the increases in the supply of an agricultural product are much greater than the increases in demand for it, the supply and demand model would suggest that the product price
   (a) and quantity will both increase
   (b) and quantity will both decrease
   (c) will increase, but the quantity will decrease
   (d) will decrease, but the quantity will increase

6. Which is a significant reason why increases in demand for agricultural products have been small relative to increases in supply?
   (a) Increases in the population of the United States have been greater than increases in the productivity of agriculture.
   (b) Increases in the population of the United States have been greater than decreases in the productivity of agriculture.
   (c) Increases in the incomes of U.S. consumers result in less than proportionate increases in their spending on agricultural products.
   (d) Increases in the incomes of U.S. consumers result in more than proportionate increases in their spending on agricultural products.

7. Given an inelastic demand for farm products, a more rapid increase in the
   (a) demand for such products relative to the supply creates a persistent downward pressure on farm incomes
   (b) supply for such products relative to the demand creates a persistent upward pressure on farm incomes
   (c) supply for such products relative to the demand creates a persistent downward pressure on farm incomes
   (d) demand for such products relative to the supply creates a persistent downward pressure on agricultural product prices

8. As a consequence of the migration out of farming over the years, agricultural income per farm household
   (a) has decreased relative to nonfarm incomes
   (b) has increased relative to nonfarm incomes
   (c) is now significantly greater than nonfarm income
   (d) is now significantly less than nonfarm income

9. The consequences of the long-run supply and demand conditions in agriculture are that minimum efficient scale has
   (a) increased and crop prices have decreased
   (b) increased and crop prices have increased
   (c) decreased and crop prices have increased
   (d) decreased and crop prices have decreased

10. Which is a major rationale for public aid for agriculture in the United States?
   (a) Farmers are more affected by competition from foreign producers than other parts of the economy.
   (b) Farmers sell their products in highly competitive markets and buy resources in highly imperfect markets.
   (c) Technological progress in farming has greatly increased the demand for farm products.
   (d) The demand for farm products is income elastic.

11. Farm parity means that over time,
   (a) the real income of the farmer remains constant
   (b) a given output will furnish the farmer with a constant amount of real income
   (c) the purchasing power of the farmer's nominal income remains constant
   (d) the nominal income of the farmer will buy a constant amount of goods and services

12. If the index of prices paid by farmers were 1000 and the prices received by farmers were 600, then the parity ratio would be

(a) 2.1 (or 210%)

(b) 1.7 (or 170%)

(c) 0.6 (or 60%)

(d) 0.4 (or 40%)

13. The necessary consequence of the government's support of agricultural prices at an above-equilibrium level is

(a) a surplus of agricultural products

(b) increased consumption of agricultural products

(c) reduced production of agricultural products

(d) the destruction of agricultural products

14. Another consequence of having government support farm prices at an above-equilibrium level is that consumers pay higher prices for farm products and

(a) consume more of these products and pay higher taxes

(b) consume less of these products and pay higher taxes

(c) consume more of these products and pay lower taxes

(d) consume less of these products and pay lower taxes

Use the graph below to answer Questions 15, 16, and 17. D is the demand for and S is the supply of a certain product.

15. If the Federal government supported the price of this product at P_3, the total amount it would have to spend to purchase the surplus of the product would be

(a) $0Q_3AP_3$

(b) Q_1Q_3AB

(c) P_1CAP_3

(d) $0Q_1BP_3$

16. With a support price of P_3, the total income of producers of the product will be

(a) $0Q_3AP_3$

(b) $0Q_1BP_3$

(c) $0Q_3CP_1$

(d) $0Q_2DP_2$

17. With a support price of P_3, the amount spent by consumers will be

(a) $0Q_3AP_3$

(b) $0Q_1BP_3$

(c) $0Q_2DP_2$

(d) Q_1Q_3AB

Answer Questions 18, 19, and 20 on the basis of the demand and supply schedules for agricultural product Z as shown below.

Pounds of Z demanded	Price	Pounds of Z supplied
850	$1.30	1150
900	1.20	1100
950	1.10	1050
1000	1.00	1000
1050	.90	950
1100	.80	900
1150	.70	850

18. If the Federal government supports the price of Z at $1.30 a pound, then at this price, there is

(a) a surplus of 200 pounds of Z

(b) a surplus of 300 pounds of Z

(c) a surplus of 400 pounds of Z

(d) a shortage of 400 pounds of Z

19. With a Federal price support of $1.30 a pound, consumers spend

(a) $1040, the Federal government spends $410, and farmers receive income from product Z of $1450

(b) $1105, the Federal government spends $390, and farmers receive income from product Z of $1495

(c) $1296, the Federal government spends $240, and farmers receive income from product Z of $1320

(d) $1045, the Federal government spends $110, and farmers receive income from product Z of $1155

20. If, instead of supporting the price, the Federal government took actions to increase demand by 150 units at each price and to decrease supply by 150 units at each price, then the equilibrium price would be

(a) $1.00 and the income of farmers would be $1000

(b) $1.10 and the income of farmers would be $1320

(c) $1.20 and the income of farmers would be $1260

(d) $1.30 and the income of farmers would be $1300

21. To help eliminate the agricultural surpluses created by farm subsidies, the Federal government has tried to

(a) increase supply and demand

(b) decrease supply and demand

(c) increase supply and decrease demand

(d) decrease supply and increase demand

22. Which is a major criticism of agricultural price supports?

(a) Restricting agricultural output increases farm prices but reduces farm incomes when demand is inelastic.

(b) The principal beneficiaries of these supports have been farmers with low incomes who would be better off in another type of work.

(c) They fail to treat the underlying problem of the misallocation of resources between agriculture and the rest of the economy.

(d) They duplicate other economic policies that are designed to increase the prices for agricultural products.

23. When farmers and farm organizations lobby Congress for a larger appropriation for agricultural price and income programs, according to public choice theory this action would be an example of

(a) confusing symptoms with causes

(b) misguided subsidies

(c) rent-seeking behavior

(d) political logrolling

24. Which has been a consequence of protective trade barriers for agricultural products established by the European Union (EU)?

(a) higher prices for U.S. agricultural products

(b) restriction of exports of EU agricultural products

(c) lower worldwide prices for agricultural products

(d) more sales of U.S. agricultural products to the EU

25. A consistent feature in both the Freedom to Farm Act of 1996 and the Farm Act of 2002 was

(a) decreasing crop price-support subsidies for farmers

(b) giving farmers the freedom to plant various agriculture crops

(c) bolstering of the domestic and foreign demand for U.S. agricultural products

(d) improving of the parity ratio so that the prices farmers paid for their inputs were similar to the prices they received for their output

■ **PROBLEMS**

1. The following table is a demand schedule for agricultural product **X**.

(1) Price	(2) Bushels of X demanded	(3) Bushels of X demanded
$2.00	600	580
1.80	620	600
1.60	640	620
1.40	660	640
1.20	680	660
1.00	700	680
.80	720	700
.60	740	720

a. Based on columns 1 and 2, is demand elastic or inelastic in the price range given?

_____

b. Based on columns 1 and 2, if the amount of **X** produced should increase from 600 to 700 bushels, the income of producers of **X** would

_____ from $_____ to

$_____; an increase of _____%

in the amount of **X** produced would cause income to

_____ by _____ %.

c. If the amount of **X** produced were 700 bushels and the demand for **X** decreased from that shown in columns 1 and 2 to that shown in columns 1 and 3, the price of **X** would _____ from $_____ to $_____; the income of farmers would _____ from $_____ to $_____.

d. Assume that the government supports a price of $1.80, that the demand for **X** is that shown in columns 1 and 2, and that farmers grow 720 bushels of **X**.

(1) At the supported price there will be a surplus of _____ bushels of **X**.

(2) If the government buys this surplus at the support price the cost to the taxpayers of purchasing the surplus is $_____.

(3) The total income of the farmers producing product **X** when they receive the support price of $1.80 per bushel for their entire crop of 720 bushels is $_____.

(4) Had farmers sold the crop of 720 bushels at the free-market price, the price of **X** would be only $_____ per bushel, and the total income of these farmers would be $_____.

(5) The gain to farmers producing **X** from the price-support program is therefore $_____.

(6) In addition to the cost to taxpayers of purchasing the surplus, consumers pay a price that is $_____ greater than the free-market price and receive a quantity of **X** that is _____ bushels less than they would have received in a free market.

2. The following table gives the index of prices farmers paid in three different years. The price farmers received in year 1, the base year, for a certain agricultural product was $3.50 per bushel.

Year	Index of prices paid	Parity price	Price received	Parity ratio
1	100	$3.50	$3.50	100%
2	120	_____	3.78	_____%
3	200	_____	5.25	_____%

a. Compute the parity price of the product in years 2 and 3 and enter them in the table.

b. The prices received for the product in each year are also shown in the table. Complete the table by computing the parity *ratio* in years 2 and 3. (*Hint:* It is *not* necessary to construct an index of prices received in order to compute the parity ratio. This ratio can be computed by dividing the price received by the parity price.)

3. The demand schedule for agricultural product **Y** is given in columns 1 and 2 of the following table.

| (1) | (2) | (3) |
Price	Bales of Y demanded	Bales of Y demanded
$5.00	40,000	41,000
4.75	40,200	41,200
4.50	40,400	41,400
4.25	40,600	41,600
4.00	40,800	41,800
3.75	41,000	42,000
3.50	41,200	42,200

a. If farmers were persuaded by the government to reduce the size of their crop from 41,000 to 40,000 bales,

the income of farmers would _____ from

$_____ to $_____.

b. If the crop remained constant at 41,000 bales and the demand for **Y** increased to that shown in columns

1 and 3, the income of farmers would _____

from $_____ to $_____.

4. Suppose the demand for sow jowls during a certain period of time was that shown in the table below and the Federal government wished to support the price of sow jowls at $.70 a pound.

Price (per pound)	Quantity demanded (pounds)
$1.00	1000
.90	1020
.80	1040
.70	1060
.60	1080
.50	1100
.40	1120

a. If the output of sow jowls were 1100 pounds during that period of time, the market price of sow jowls would

be $_____ and the Federal government

would (buy, sell) _____ (how many)

_____ pounds of sow jowls.

b. But if the output were 1000 pounds during that period of time, the market price of sow jowls would be

$_____ and the Federal government would not have to intervene.

■ SHORT ANSWER AND ESSAY QUESTIONS

1. Why are the economics of agriculture and agricultural policy important topics for study?

2. What is the short-run farm problem and what are its causes?

3. Why does the demand for agricultural products tend to be inelastic? What are the implications for agriculture?

4. What have been the specific causes of the large increases in the supply of agricultural products over time?

5. Why has the demand for agricultural products failed to increase at the same rate as the supply of these products?

6. What have been the consequences of long-run supply and demand conditions in agriculture?

7. What is meant by "the farm program"? What particular aspect of the farm program has traditionally received the major attention of farmers and their representatives in Congress?

8. Why do agricultural interests claim that farmers have a special right to aid from the Federal government?

9. Explain the concept of parity and the parity ratio.

10. Why is the result of government-supported prices invariably a surplus of farm commodities?

11. What are the effects of farm price-support programs on farmers, consumers, and resource allocation in the economy?

12. Identify and describe three ways that society at large loses from farm price-support programs.

13. Explain how U.S. farm policy may cause environmental problems.

14. Discuss the effects of farm price-support programs on international trade and developing nations.

15. What programs has the government used to try to restrict farm production? Why have these programs been relatively unsuccessful in limiting agricultural production?

16. How has the Federal government tried to increase the demand for farm products?

17. Explain the three major criticisms of agricultural price supports.

18. How can public choice theory explain the persistence of Federal government support for farm subsidies for so many decades? Discuss the application of rent-seeking behavior, the special-interest effect, political logrolling, and hidden costs to subsidies for agriculture.

19. What domestic and international factors are contributing to the reduction in political support for agricultural subsidies?

20. What are the key features of the Freedom to Farm Act of 1996 and the Farm Act of 2002? In what ways are the two acts similar and how are they different in terms of government intervention in agriculture, the provision of agricultural price supports, and income payments to farmers?

ANSWERS

Chapter 20 Agriculture: Economics and Policy

FILL-IN QUESTIONS

1. largest, competition, government, increased, public
2. inelastic, substitutes, utility
3. small, large, small, large

4. supply of, demand for, inelastic
5. low, value, hazards, purely, imperfectly
6. fixed
7. surpluses, buy
8. benefit, are hurt, increase, increase, decrease
9. inefficiency, over, large
10. increased, increased, negative
11. more, more, increase, decrease, negative
12. increase, decrease
13. acreage-allotment, new, demand
14. have not, low, inefficient
15. high, low, offset
16. public choice, rent-seeking, small, large
17. logrolling, clear, hidden
18. trade, increase, increase, decrease
19. Farm, eliminate, plant, payments, increase
20. plant, payments, payments, loans, increased, increased, more

TRUE–FALSE QUESTIONS

1. T, pp. 370–371	10. T, p. 374	19. T, p. 380
2. F, pp. 370–371	11. T, p. 375	20. F, p. 381
3. F, p. 372	12. T, p. 376	21. T, p. 381
4. F, p. 373	13. F, pp. 376–377	22. T, p. 381
5. F, p. 373	14. F, pp. 376–377	23. F, pp. 381–382
6. T, pp. 373–374	15. F, p. 378	24. T, p. 382
7. F, p. 374	16. T, p. 379	25. T, pp. 382–383
8. F, p. 374	17. T, p. 379	
9. T, p. 374	18. F, p. 380	

MULTIPLE-CHOICE QUESTIONS

1. d, p. 371	10. b, p. 376	19. b, p. 378
2. b, pp. 371–372	11. b, pp. 376–377	20. d, pp. 378–380
3. a, p. 372	12. c, pp. 376–377	21. d, pp. 378–380
4. d, pp. 372–373	13. a, p. 378	22. c, p. 380
5. d, pp. 373–375	14. b, p. 378	23. c, p. 381
6. c, p. 374	15. b, p. 378	24. c, p. 382
7. c, pp. 374–375	16. a, p. 378	25. b, pp. 382–383
8. b, p. 375	17. b, p. 378	
9. a, pp. 374–375	18. b, p. 378	

PROBLEMS

1. *a.* inelastic; *b.* decrease, 1200.00, 700.00, 16.67, decrease, 41.67; *c.* fall, 1.00, 0.80, fall, 700.00, 560.00; *d.* (1) 100, (2) 180, (3) 1296, (4) 0.80, 576, (5) 720, (6) 1.00, 100
2. *a.* 4.20, 7.00; *b.* 90, 75
3. *a.* increase, 153,750.00, 200,000.00; *b.* increase, 153,750.00, 205,000.00
4. *a.* .50, buy, 40; *b.* 1.00

SHORT ANSWER AND ESSAY QUESTIONS

1. p. 370	8. p. 376	15. pp. 379–380
2. pp. 370–371	9. pp. 376–377	16. pp. 379–380
3. pp. 370–372	10. p. 378	17. pp. 380–381
4. p. 374	11. p. 378	18. p. 381
5. pp. 373–374	12. pp. 378–379	19. p. 382
6. pp. 374–375	13. p. 379	20. pp. 382–383
7. p. 376	14. p. 379	

CHAPTER 21

Income Inequality and Poverty

Chapter 21 examines another current problem in the economy of the United States: the unequal distribution of income and poverty. Recall from Chapter 5 that the market system does not produce an equal distribution of income, so one economic function of government is to redistribute income. Now you will learn about the income distribution problem and specific actions government takes to address it.

The chapter begins with a look at the facts of *income inequality.* You will discover that there is substantial income inequality in the United States and learn how it is measured with the *Lorenz curve* and *Gini ratio.* You should also note that the degree of income inequality for individuals and families will be less over time because of income mobility and because government taxes and transfer payments will also reduce the amount of income inequality.

The chapter discusses the multiple factors that contribute to income inequality. The seven causes that are described should indicate to you that there is no simple explanation for why some people have more income than others. It is not the result of some grand conspiracy; it can be attributed to ability differences, education and training, discrimination, preferences for jobs and risk, wealth, market power, and luck.

Over time there have been changes in the relative distribution of income that indicate income inequality in the United States is increasing. In this section of the chapter you will learn about the probable reasons for this growing income inequality that include shifts in the demand for skilled labor, changes in the demographics of the workforce, and other factors.

A case can be made for both income equality and income inequality. Few people, however, would advocate that there should be an absolutely equal distribution of income. The question to be decided is not one of inequality or equality but of how much or how little inequality there should be. A major insight from the chapter is that there is a fundamental *tradeoff between equality and efficiency* in the economy. If the society wants more equality, it will have to give up some economic efficiency in the form of less output and employment.

The reason for the focus on income distribution is ultimately the concern about *poverty.* In the later sections of the chapter you will learn about the extent of the poverty problem, whom poverty affects, and the actions government has taken to alleviate it. Poverty and other income problems are addressed through the Federal government's income-maintenance system. This system consists of *social insurance programs,* such as Social Security, and *public assistance programs,* or welfare. You will discover how these programs are designed to meet the needs of different groups, either those who are poor or those who require more stability in their incomes.

The reform of the public assistance programs in the United States has been a major topic of debate. You will learn that it is not possible to design a perfect program because of conflicting goals. Criticism of the welfare system led to the passage of the Personal Responsibility Act of 1996. Here the Federal government ended its long-standing policy of guaranteeing cash assistance for the poor and established Temporary Assistance to Needy Families (TANF) funds. The years of eligibility for these funds were limited and people were required to work after receiving benefits for a period of time. As you might expect, this reform has been subject to both praise and criticism in the nation's ongoing debate on public assistance.

■ CHECKLIST

When you have studied this chapter you should be able to

☐ Describe income inequality in the United States based on the percentage of families in a series of income categories.

☐ Discuss income inequality in the United States based on the percentage of personal income received by families in income quintiles.

☐ Explain the Lorenz curve by defining each axis, the diagonal line, and the meaning of the curve.

☐ Use a Lorenz curve to describe the degree of income inequality in the United States.

☐ Use a Gini ratio to measure income inequality.

☐ Explain the effects of time on income mobility and the distribution of U.S. income.

☐ Discuss the effects of government redistribution on income equality in the United States and illustrate the effects using a Lorenz curve.

☐ Explain the seven causes of income inequality in the United States.

☐ Describe the changes in the relative distribution of personal income in the United States over time based on three time periods since 1929.

☐ Identify three probable causes of growing income inequality in the United States over the past three decades.

☐ Present a case for income inequality based on the maximization of total utility.

☐ Make the case for income inequality based on incentives and efficiency.

☐ Explain the tradeoff between equality and efficiency in the debate over how much income inequality there should be.

☐ Give a definition of poverty based on U.S. government standards.

☐ Identify the demographic groups affected by poverty in the United States.

☐ Describe the trends in the poverty rate in the United States since 1960.

☐ Give three reasons why poverty tends to be invisible.

☐ Identify the two basic kinds of programs in the U.S. system for income maintenance.

☐ Describe the characteristics of major social insurance programs.

☐ Explain the purposes of the major public assistance programs.

☐ Discuss the common features and conflicts in three hypothetical plans for public assistance.

☐ State the major criticisms that led to reform of the welfare system.

☐ Describe the major features and offer an economic assessment of Temporary Assistance to Needy Families (TANF).

■ **CHAPTER OUTLINE**

1. There is considerable *income inequality* in the United States.

   a. One way to show this inequality is with a table showing the personal distribution of income of families. In 2001, about 21% of all families had annual before-tax incomes of less than $25,000, but 18% had annual incomes of $100,000 or more.

   b. A table of the personal distribution of income by families in quintiles is a second way to show the inequality. In 2001, the 20% of families with the lowest incomes accounted for 4.2% of personal income while the 20% of families with the highest incomes accounted for 47.7% of personal income.

   c. The degree of income inequality can be shown with a *Lorenz curve.* The percentage of families is plotted on the horizontal axis and the percentage of income is plotted on the vertical axis. The diagonal line between the two axes represents a perfectly equal distribution of income. A Lorenz curve that is bowed to the right from the diagonal shows income inequality. If the actual income distribution were perfectly equal, the Lorenz curve and the diagonal would coincide. The visual measurement of income inequality described by the Lorenz curve can be converted to a *Gini ratio,* which is the area between the Lorenz curve and the diagonal divided by the total area below the diagonal. As the income inequality increases, the Gini ratio will increase.

   d. Looking at income data over a longer time period rather than in a single year shows that there is considerably *less* income inequality. In fact, there is significant *income mobility* for individuals and families in income over time. The longer the time period considered for individuals and families, the more equal the distribution of income.

   e. Government redistribution has had a significant effect on income distribution. The distribution of income can be examined after taxes and transfer payments. When this adjustment is made, the distribution of income is more equal. Transfer payments account for most of the reduction in income inequality. The change can be shown by a shift in the Lorenz curve toward more equality.

2. The market system is impersonal and does not necessarily result in a fair distribution of income. At least seven factors explain *why income inequality exists:*

   a. The distribution of abilities and skills differs greatly among people that influences what work they can do and their pay.

   b. There are differences in education and training that affect wages and salaries.

   c. Discrimination in education, hiring, training, and promotion will affect incomes.

   d. People have different preferences for certain types of jobs, for their willingness to accept risk on the job, and also for the amount of leisure that will be earned through their work.

   e. Wealth can provide a source of income in the form of rents, interest, and dividends, and since there are inequalities in the distribution of wealth, it will contribute to income inequalities.

   f. Some individuals have a degree of market power in either resource or product markets that create higher incomes.

   g. Other factors, such as luck, personal connections, and misfortunes, can play a role in contributing to income inequality.

3. Income inequality in the United States has changed over time.

   a. From 1929–1947, the relative distribution of personal income showed a decrease in income inequality. From 1947–1969 there was a slight increase in income inequality. From 1969–2001, the distribution of income became more unequal.

   b. Among the factors that explain the growing income inequality in the United States over the past three decades are:

   (1) increases in the demand for highly skilled workers compared with the demand for less-skilled workers;

   (2) changes in labor demographics from the influx of less-skilled baby boomers into the labor force, the increase in dual incomes among high-wage households, and more single-parent households earning less income; and

   (3) decreases in wages for less-skilled workers and less job security because of more import competition, the influx of less-skilled immigrants into the labor force, and a decline in unionism.

4. An important question to answer for an economy is not whether there will be income inequality, but what is an acceptable amount of inequality.

a. Those who argue for *equality* contend that it leads to the maximum satisfaction of consumer wants (utility) in the economy.

b. Those who argue for *inequality* contend that equality would reduce the incentives to work, save, invest, and take risks, and that these incentives are needed if the economy is to be efficient to produce as large an output (and income) as it is possible for it to produce from its available resources.

c. In the United States there is a *tradeoff between economic equality and efficiency.* A more nearly equal distribution of income results in less economic efficiency (a smaller domestic output) and greater economic efficiency leads to a more unequal distribution of income. The debate over the right amount of inequality depends on how much output society is willing to sacrifice to reduce income inequality.

5. Aside from inequality in the distribution of income, there is a great concern today with the problem of *poverty* in the United States.

a. Using the generally accepted definition of poverty, 11.7% of the population in the United States lived in poverty in 2001.

b. The poor tend to be concentrated among certain groups, such as blacks, Hispanics, female-headed families, and children.

c. The poverty rate has varied over time, as shown in Figure 21.4 of the text. It fell significantly from 1959–1969 and has ranged from about 11% to 15% since 1969.

d. Poverty in the United States tends to be invisible because the pool of poor people changes, the poor are isolated in large cities, and the poor do not have a political voice.

6. The *income-maintenance system* of the United States is intended to reduce poverty and includes both social insurance and public assistance (welfare) programs.

a. The principal *social insurance programs* are OASDHI (Old Age, Survivors and Disability Health Insurance, also known as Social Security) and Medicare. They are financed by taxes levied on employers and employees. The unemployment insurance programs, maintained by the states and financed by taxes on employers, are also a social insurance program in the United States.

b. The *public assistance programs* include SSI (Supplemental Security Income), TANF (Temporary Assistance for Needy Families), food stamps, and Medicaid. The EITC (earned income tax credit) is for low-income working families, with or without children. Other public assistance programs provide noncash transfers for education, job training, and housing assistance.

7. The *ideal public assistance program* has three basic goals: getting people out of poverty, providing incentives to work, and having a reasonable cost. These goals can conflict as illustrated by three hypothetical public assistance plans.

a. In any plan, a family would be guaranteed a minimum income and the subsidy to a family would decrease as its earned income increased. But a comparison of three alternative plans reveals that the guaranteed income, the (benefit-reduction) rate at which the subsidy declines as earned income increases, and the (break-even) income at which the subsidy is no longer paid, may differ.

b. The comparison of the plans also indicates there is a conflict among the goals of taking families out of poverty, maintaining incentives to work, and keeping the costs of the plan at a reasonable level, and that a tradeoff among the three goals is necessary because no one plan can achieve all three goals.

8. The public assistance system has been reformed in recent years under the Personal Responsibility Act of 1996. The reform arose in large part because of problems with the Aid to Families with Dependent Children (AFDC) program: administrative inefficiency, a negative effect on work incentives, and fostering a dependency on welfare.

a. The reform eliminated the Federal government's guarantee of cash assistance for poor families. In its place, states operated their own programs using lump-sum payments called TANF (Temporary Assistance for Needy Families). The reform limited the number of years (5) that a person could receive TANF benefits, and required able-bodied adults to work after 2 years of help. Other work requirements and restrictive provisions were added for those receiving public assistance. New legal immigrants could receive public assistance only after a 5-year waiting period.

b. Supporters contend that the law ended the "culture of poverty." The percentage of the population on welfare rolls dropped from 4.8% of the population in 1996 to 2% of the population in 2002, which was partly due to the reform. Critics argue that the reforms hurt children and penalize the poor. The true test of the reforms may come from an economic downturn that increases the number of people seeking public assistance.

■ HINTS AND TIPS

1. The distribution of income often raises issues of *normative economics.* For example, some people may say that "no person should be allowed to make that much money" when a high salary is reported in the media for a sports star or business executive. This chapter focuses on *positive economics* and offers explanations for why there are wide differences in the distribution of income and why there is poverty.

2. The *Lorenz curve* looks more complicated than it really is. The curve shows how the cumulative percentage of income is distributed across the percentage of families. The easiest way to learn about the curve is to use income and family data to construct one. Problem 1 in this chapter will help you with that objective.

3. Public assistance plans differ in two ways because there are two variables that affect the outcomes: the size of the minimum annual income and the difference in the benefit-reduction rate. Problem 2 in this chapter illustrates how those two variables affect the outcomes.

■ IMPORTANT TERMS

income inequality	Medicare
Lorenz curve	poverty
Gini ratio	unemployment compensation
income mobility	public assistance programs
noncash transfers	Supplemental Security Income (SSI)
tradeoff between equality and efficiency	Temporary Assistance for Needy Families (TANF)
poverty rate	food stamp program
entitlement programs	Medicaid
social insurance programs	earned income tax credit (EITC)
Old Age, Survivors, and Disability Health Insurance (OASDHI)	

SELF-TEST

■ FILL-IN QUESTIONS

1. The data on the distribution of personal income by families suggest that there is considerable income (equality, inequality) _____ in the United States. The data show that families with annual incomes of less than $25,000 are about (21, 18) _____% of all families, and families with $100,000 or more in income are about _____% of all families.

2. Income inequality can be portrayed graphically by drawing a (Phillips, Lorenz) _____ curve.
  a. When such a curve is plotted, the cumulative percentage of (income, families) _____ is measured along the horizontal axis, and the cumulative percentage of _____ is measured along the vertical axis.
  b. The curve that would show a completely (perfectly) equal distribution of income is a diagonal line that would run from the (lower, upper) _____ left to the _____ right corner of the graph.
  c. The extent or degree of income inequality is measured by the area that lies between the line of complete equality and the (horizontal axis, Lorenz curve) _____.
  d. The Gini ratio measures the area between the line of equality and the Lorenz curve (multiplied, divided) _____ by the total area below the line of equality.

3. One major limitation with census data on the distribution of income in the United States is that the income-accounting period is too (short, long) _____. There appears to be significant income (mobility, loss) _____ over time. Also, the longer the time period considered, the (more, less) _____ equal is the distribution of income.

4. The tax system and the transfer programs in the U.S. economy significantly (reduce, expand) _____ the degree of inequality in the distribution of income. The distribution of household income is substantially less equal (before, after) _____ taxes and transfers are taken into account and substantially more equal _____ taxes and transfers are taken into account.

5. The important factors that explain (or cause) income inequality are differences in _____, education and _____, labor market _____, differences in job tastes and _____, the unequal distribution of _____, market _____, and _____, connections, and misfortune.

6. From 1929 to 1947, the percentage of total before-tax income received by the top quintile of families (increased, decreased) _____, and the percentages received by the other four quintiles _____. Since 1969, the distribution of income by quintiles has become (more, less) _____ unequal.

7. The causes of the growing inequality of incomes are due to (more, less) _____ demand for highly skilled workers, entrance into the 1970s and 1980s labor force of _____-experienced baby boomers, and _____ families headed by single-wage earners. Other factors include (more, less) _____ international competition that reduced the average wage of low-skilled workers, _____ immigration that increased the number of low-income families, and _____ unionism.

8. Those who argue for the equal distribution of income contend that it results in the maximization of total (income, utility) _____ in the economy, while those who argue for the unequal distribution of income believe it results in a greater total _____.

9. The fundamental tradeoff is between equality and (welfare, efficiency) _____. This means that less income equality leads to a (greater, smaller)

_____ total output, and a larger total output requires (more, less) _____ income inequality.

10. The economic problem for a society that wants more equality is how to (minimize, maximize) _____ the adverse effects on economic efficiency.

11. Using the more or less official definition of poverty for 1999, the poor included any family of four with an income of less than ($18,104; $31,389) _____ and any individual with an income of less than ($9039; $16,354) _____ a year. In 2001, about (4, 12) _____% of the population, or about (33, 54) _____ million people, were poor.

12. Poverty tends to be concentrated among the (young, elderly) _____, among (whites, blacks) _____, and in families headed by (men, women) _____.

13. In the affluent economy of the United States, much of the poverty in the country is (visible, invisible) _____ because the poverty pool (stays the same, changes) _____ from year to year, the poor are often isolated in (small, large) _____ cities, and the poor do not have a political voice.

14. One part of the income-maintenance system in the United States consists of social insurance programs such as (OASDHI, AFDC) _____, (Medicare, Medicaid) _____, and (employment, unemployment) _____ compensation.

15. The other part of the income-maintenance system consists of public assistance or welfare programs such as (OASDHI, SSI) _____, (AFDC, SEC) _____, (Medicare, Medicaid) _____, and the food stamp program.

16. Public assistance programs include state-administered ones such as cash assistance for families with children, (EITC, TANF) _____ and a tax credit program for low-income working families, _____. Other public assistance programs also provide help in the form of (cash, noncash) _____ transfers, such as rent subsidies for housing and education assistance such as Head Start.

17. An ideal public assistance program would try to achieve three goals at the same time: The plan should get individuals and families off or out of (Medicare, poverty) _____, provide work (insurance, incentives) _____, and ensure that the program (benefits, costs) _____ are reasonable. In reality, these goals are (complementary, conflicting) _____.

18. The two common elements of a public assistance plan are a (maximum, minimum) _____ annual income provided by the government if the family earned no income and a (cost-benefit, benefit-reduction) _____ rate that specifies the rate at which the transfer payment would be cut if earned income increases.

19. The criticisms of past welfare programs, such as Aid to Families with Dependent Children, were that it provided little (insurance, improvement) _____ and created a culture of welfare (equality for, dependency on) _____ government.

20. In 1996, the Congress passed a major welfare reform, the (Family Support, Personal Responsibility) _____ Act. It set a lifetime limit of (5, 10) _____ years for receiving TANF payments and required able-bodied adults to work after (2, 4) _____ years of receiving assistance. Supporters of the law contend that it will end the culture of (compensation, welfare) _____, whereas critics think that it places the (responsibility, blame) _____ for poverty on its victims.

■ **TRUE–FALSE QUESTIONS**

Circle T if the statement is true, F if it is false.

1. If you knew the average income in the United States, you would know a great deal about income inequality in the United States. **T F**

2. The data on the distribution of personal income by families in the United States indicates that there is considerable income inequality. **T F**

3. In a Lorenz curve, the percentage of families in each income class is measured along the horizontal axis and the percentage of total income received by those families is measured on the vertical axis. **T F**

4. Income mobility is the movement of individuals or families from one income quintile to another over time. **T F**

5. Income is less equally distributed over a longer time period than a shorter time period. **T F**

6. The distribution of income in the United States _after_ taxes and transfers are taken into account is more equal than it is _before_ taxes and transfers are taken into account. **T F**

7. Differences in preferences for market work relative to nonmarket activities are one reason for income differences in the United States.   **T F**

8. The ownership of wealth is fairly equally distributed across households in the United States.   **T F**

9. Luck or misfortune are not factors contributing to income inequality in the United States.   **T F**

10. From 1969 to 2001, there was an increase in income inequality in the United States.   **T F**

11. A significant contributor to the growing income inequality of the past three decades was the greater demand for highly skilled and highly educated workers.   **T F**

12. Growing income inequality means that the "rich are getting richer" in terms of absolute income.   **T F**

13. The basic argument for an equal distribution of income is that income equality is necessary if consumer satisfaction (utility) is to be maximized.   **T F**

14. Those who favor equality in the distribution of income contend that it will lead to stronger incentives to work, save, and invest and thus to a greater national income and output.   **T F**

15. In the tradeoff between equality and economic efficiency, an increase in equality will lead to an increase in efficiency.   **T F**

16. Using the government definition of poverty, approximately 12% of the population was poor in 2001.   **T F**

17. The incidence of poverty is very high among female-headed families.   **T F**

18. OASDHI, Medicare, and unemployment compensation are public assistance or welfare programs.   **T F**

19. Social insurance programs provide benefits for those who are unable to earn income because of permanent handicaps or who have no or very low income and also have dependent children.   **T F**

20. The benefit-reduction rate is the rate at which government benefits decrease as the earned income of a family increases.   **T F**

21. The lower the benefit-reduction rate, the smaller the incentives to earn additional income.   **T F**

22. In comparing welfare plans, it is possible to achieve simultaneously the three goals of eliminating poverty, maintaining work incentives, and holding down program costs.   **T F**

23. Those who have been critical of welfare contend that it creates dependency on government and reduces the motivation to work.   **T F**

24. The Personal Responsibility Act of 1996 was designed to reduce the dependence of the elderly on social security.   **T F**

25. The Temporary Assistance for Needy Families (TANF) has among its provisions work requirements for those

receiving welfare and a specified limit on the number of years for receiving welfare benefits.   **T F**

■ **MULTIPLE-CHOICE QUESTIONS**

Circle the letter that corresponds to the best answer.

1. Recent data on the personal distribution of income in the United States indicate that
(a) average incomes are falling
(b) average incomes are constant
(c) there is considerable income equality
(d) there is considerable income inequality

2. When a Lorenz curve is drawn, the degree of income inequality in an economy is measured by the
(a) slope of the diagonal that runs from the southwest to the northeast corner of the diagram
(b) slope of the Lorenz curve
(c) area between the Lorenz curve and the axes of the graph
(d) area between the Lorenz curve and the southwest –northeast diagonal

Use the following graph to answer Questions 3, 4, 5, and 6. The graph shows four different Lorenz curves (1, 2, 3, and 4).

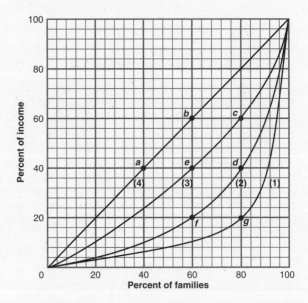

3. The greatest increase in income equality would occur with a shift in a Lorenz curve from
(a) 1 to 2
(b) 1 to 4
(c) 4 to 1
(d) 3 to 1

4. What point indicates that 80% of the families receive only 40% of the income?
(a) *c*
(b) *d*
(c) *e*
(d) *g*

5. The movement from point **b** to point **f** in the graph would indicate that
(a) 60% of families now receive 40% of income instead of 60% of income
(b) 60% of income goes to 20% of families instead of 60% of families
(c) 20% of income goes to 20% of families instead of 60% of families
(d) 60% of families now receive 20% of income instead of 60% of income

6. Which change would indicate that there has been an increase in income inequality and an increase in the Gini ratio? A movement from point
(a) **b** to **a**
(b) **g** to **d**
(c) **g** to **f**
(d) **e** to **d**

7. Suppose that Laura earns $5000 in year 1 and $50,000 in year 2, while Kristin earns $50,000 in year 1 and only $5000 in year 2. Is there income inequality for the two individuals?
(a) Both the annual and the 2-year data indicate equality.
(b) Both the annual and the 2-year data indicate inequality.
(c) The annual data indicate inequality, but the 2-year data indicate equality.
(d) The annual data indicate equality, but the 2-year data indicate inequality.

8. The empirical data indicate that the tax system and the transfer programs of the government
(a) significantly reduce the degree of inequality in the distribution of income
(b) produce only a slight reduction in the degree of inequality in the distribution of income
(c) significantly increase the degree of inequality in the distribution of income
(d) produce only a slight increase in the degree of inequality in the distribution of income

9. Most of the contribution to government redistribution of income comes from
(a) taxes
(b) transfers
(c) income mobility
(d) unemployment insurance

10. Which is one cause of unequal income distribution in the United States?
(a) an equitable distribution of wealth and property
(b) differences in education and training
(c) the high levels of noncash transfers
(d) the low benefit-reduction rate

11. The fact that some individuals are willing to take riskier jobs or assume more risk in their businesses is one major reason why there are differences in
(a) social insurance programs
(b) entitlement programs
(c) welfare
(d) income

12. Inequality in the distribution of wealth contributes to
(a) the same percentage of income received by the highest and lowest percentages of families
(b) a smaller percentage of income received by the highest 20 percentage of families
(c) a greater percentage of income received by the highest 20 percentage of families
(d) a greater percentage of income received by the lowest 20 percentage of families

13. Which would be evidence of a decrease in income inequality over time in the United States?
(a) a decrease in the percentage of total personal income received by the lowest quintile
(b) an increase in the percentage of total personal income received by the highest quintile
(c) an increase in the percentage of total personal income received by the four lowest quintiles
(d) a decrease in the percentage of total personal income received by the four lowest quintiles

14. A factor contributing to the increase in income inequality for the past three decades has been:
(a) less international competition from imports
(b) less demand for highly skilled workers in the labor force
(c) more marriages among men and women with high income potential
(d) more power by unions to obtain wage increases for union workers

15. Suppose Ms. Anne obtains 5 units of utility from the last dollar of income received by her, and Mr. Charles obtains 8 units of utility from the last dollar of his income. Those who favor an equal distribution of income would
(a) advocate redistributing income from Charles to Anne
(b) advocate redistributing income from Anne to Charles
(c) be content with this distribution of income between Anne and Charles
(d) argue that any redistribution of income between them would increase total utility

16. The case for income inequality is primarily made on the basis that income inequality
(a) is reduced by the transfer payment programs for the poor
(b) is necessary to maintain incentives to work and produce output
(c) depends on luck and chance, which cannot be corrected by government action
(d) is created by education and training programs that distort the distribution of income

17. The debate over income redistribution focuses on the tradeoff between equality and
(a) efficiency
(b) unemployment
(c) inflation
(d) economic freedom

18. The pizza slice analogy is used to describe the
(a) welfare reform mess
(b) trends in the poverty rate
(c) economic loss from income redistribution programs
(d) piecemeal approach toward income maintenance programs

19. What was the approximate poverty rate for the U.S. population in 2001?
(a) 2%
(b) 6%
(c) 12%
(d) 25%

20. In 2001, which group had the *smallest* percentage in poverty?
(a) Hispanics
(b) families headed by women
(c) children under 18 years of age
(d) the elderly (65 years and older)

21. An example of a social insurance program would be
(a) Medicare
(b) Medicaid
(c) food stamps
(d) Head Start

22. Which is designed to provide a nationwide minimum income for the aged, the blind, and the disabled?
(a) SSI
(b) FFS
(c) AFDC
(d) OASDHI

23. The purpose of the earned income tax credit (EITC) is to
(a) give a tax credit for spending on education and job training for welfare recipients
(b) give a tax break to businesses if they have low-income workers
(c) substitute the payment of cash for food stamps if people are willing to go to work
(d) offset Social Security taxes paid by low-wage earners so they are not "taxed into poverty"

24. The goals of welfare plans often conflict because it is difficult to construct a plan that
(a) provides reasonable income levels and incentives to work for the poor, but is not too costly
(b) is not subject to substantial administrative costs and bureaucratic red tape
(c) does not discriminate against those individuals with similar circumstances, but who have similar needs
(d) promotes family unity and does not create a "culture of poverty" among the participants in the program

25. The Temporary Assistance for Needy Families (TANF) program is administered by
(a) states and puts a lifetime limit of five years on receiving welfare payments
(b) religious institutions and places people in temporary jobs
(c) businesses and develops skills through education assistance
(d) the Federal government and provides food stamps for the needy

■ **PROBLEMS**

1. The distribution of personal income among families in a hypothetical economy is shown in the table below.
a. Complete the table by computing the
(1) percentage of all families in each income class and all lower classes; enter these figures in column 4.
(2) percentage of total income received by each income class and all lower classes; enter these figures in column 5.
b. From the distribution of income data in columns 4 and 5, it can be seen that
(1) families with less than $15,000 a year income

constitute the lowest _____% of all families

and receive _____% of the total income.
(2) families with incomes of $50,000 a year or more

constitute the highest _____% of all families

and receive _____% of the total income.

(1) Personal income class	(2) Percentage of all families in this class	(3) Percentage of total income received by this class	(4) Percentage of all families in this and all lower classes	(5) Percentage of total income received by this and all lower classes
Under $10,000	18	4	_____	_____
$10,000 – $14,999	12	6	_____	_____
$15,000 – $24,999	14	12	_____	_____
$25,000 – $34,999	17	14	_____	_____
$35,000 – $49,999	19	15	_____	_____
$50,000 – $74,999	11	20	_____	_____
$75,000 and over	9	29	_____	_____

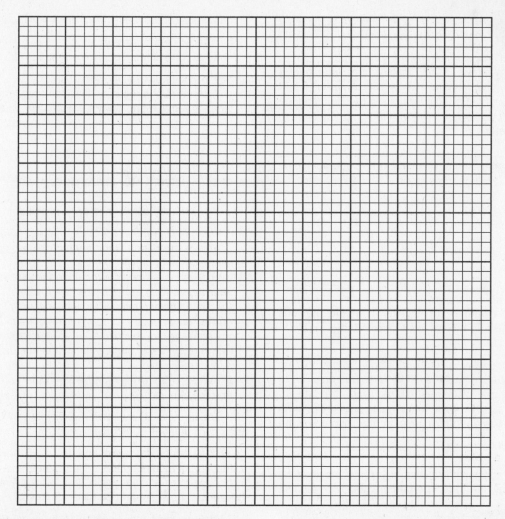

c. Use the figures you entered in columns 4 and 5 to draw a Lorenz curve on the above graph. (Plot the seven points and the zero-zero point and connect them with a smooth curve.) Be sure to label the axes.
(1) Draw a diagonal line that would indicate complete equality in the distribution of income.
(2) Shade the area of the graph that shows the degree of income inequality.

2. The following table contains different possible earned incomes for a family of a certain size.

Earned income	Transfer payment	Total income
$ 0	$ 5000	$ 5000
5000	——	——
10,000	——	——
15,000	——	——
20,000	——	——
25,000	——	——

a. Assume that $5000 is the minimum annual income provided by government for a family of this size and that the benefit-reduction rate is 20%. Enter the transfer payment and the total income at each of the five remaining earned-income levels. (Hint: 20% of $5000 is $1000.)

(1) This program retains strong incentives to work because whenever the family earns an additional $5000 its total income increases by $_____.
(2) But this program is costly because the family receives a subsidy until its earned income, the break-even income, is $_____.
b. To reduce the break-even income, the benefit reduction rate is raised to 50%. Complete the following table.

Earned income	Transfer payment	Total income
$ 0	$ 5000	$ 5000
2500	——	——
5000	——	——
7500	——	——
10,000	——	——

(1) This program is less costly than the previous one because the family only receives a subsidy until it earns the break-even income of $ _____,

(2) but the incentives to work are less because whenever the family earns an additional $5000 its

total income increases by only $_____.

c. Both the previous two welfare programs had a minimum annual income of only $5000. Assume that the minimum annual income is raised to $7500 and the benefit-reduction rate is kept at 50%. Complete the following table.

Earned income	Transfer payment	Total income
$ 0	$ 7500	$ 7500
3000	_____	_____
6000	_____	_____
9000	_____	_____
12,000	_____	_____
15,000	_____	_____

(1) This program is more costly than the previous one because the break-even income has risen to

$_____.

(2) The incentives to earn additional income are no better in this program than in the previous one. But to improve these incentives by reducing the benefit-reduction rate to 40% would raise the break-even income to (divide the minimum annual income by the

benefit-reduction rate) $_____.

d. To summarize:

(1) Given the minimum annual income provided by government, the lower the benefit-reduction rate the

(greater, less) _____ are the incentives to earn additional income and the (greater, less)

_____ are the break-even income and the cost of the welfare program,

(2) and given the benefit-reduction rate, the greater the minimum annual income, the (greater, less)

_____ are the break-even income and the cost of the program,

(3) but to reduce the break-even income and the cost of the program requires either (an increase, a

decrease) _____ in the benefit-reduction

rate or _____ in the minimum annual income.

3. Match the terms with the phrase using the appropriate number.

1. entitlement programs   3. public assistance programs

2. noncash transfers   4. social insurance programs

a. Government programs such as social insurance, food stamps, Medicare, and Medicaid that guarantee particular levels of transfer payments to all who fit the

programs' criteria.   _____

b. Government programs that pay benefits to those who are unable to earn income (because of permanent handicaps or because they have very low incomes

and dependent children).   _____

c. Government transfer payments in the form of goods

and services rather than money.   _____

d. Government programs that replace earnings lost when people retire or are temporarily unemployed.

_____

■ **SHORT ANSWER AND ESSAY QUESTIONS**

1. How much income inequality is there in the U.S. economy? Cite figures to support your conclusion.

2. What is measured along each of the two axes when a Lorenz curve is drawn?

(a) If the distribution of income were completely equal, what would the Lorenz curve look like?

(b) If one family received all of the income of the economy, what would the Lorenz curve look like?

(c) After the Lorenz curve for an economy has been drawn, how is the degree of income inequality in that economy measured?

(d) What is the difference between the Lorenz curve and the Gini ratio?

3. Explain how time affects the distribution of income and interpretations of income trends.

4. What effect do taxes and transfers have on the distribution of income in the United States? How much of this change in the distribution of income is the result of the transfer payments made by government?

5. What seven factors contribute to income inequality in the United States?

6. How has the distribution of income changed in the United States since 1929? What has been the trend in income distribution since 1969?

7. What are three probable explanations for the increase in income inequality in the United States over the past three decades?

8. State the case for equal distribution of income.

9. Explain the advantage to the nation from an unequal distribution of income.

10. What is the fundamental tradeoff involving income inequality? Explain the leaky bucket analogy.

11. What is poverty? What is the minimum income level below which the Federal government defines a person or family as "in poverty"? How many people and what percentage of the U.S. population are "in poverty" using this definition?

12. What characteristics—other than the small amounts of money they have to spend—do the greatest concentrations of the poor families of the nation *tend* to have?

13. What have been the trends in the poverty rate since 1960? What were the trends in the 1980s and 1990s?

14. Why does poverty in the United States tend to be invisible or hidden?

15. Explain the difference between social insurance and public assistance. Which do you think is more important?

16. List and briefly describe three social insurance programs of the income-maintenance system of the United States.

17. Explain the major public assistance programs of the income-maintenance system of the United States.

18. What are the three goals of an ideal welfare program? Explain why there is a conflict among these goals—why all three goals cannot be achieved simultaneously.

19. Explain how poverty and the unequal distribution of income would be reduced by three hypothetical welfare plans. Be sure to include in your explanation the definition of the minimum annual income that would be provided by government, the benefit-reduction rate, and the break-even income.

20. Discuss the Temporary Assistance to Needy Families (TANF) program and explain what supporters and critics say about it.

ANSWERS

Chapter 21 Income Inequality and Poverty

FILL-IN QUESTIONS

1. inequality, 21, 18
2. Lorenz; *a.* families, income; *b.* lower, upper; *c.* Lorenz curve; *d.* divided
3. short, mobility, more
4. reduce, before, after
5. ability, training, discrimination, risks, wealth, power, luck
6. decreased, increased, more
7. more, less, more, more, more, less
8. utility, income
9. efficiency, greater, more
10. minimize
11. $18,104, $9039, 12, 33
12. young, blacks, women
13. invisible, changes, large
14. OASDHI, Medicare, unemployment
15. SSI, AFDC, Medicaid
16. TANF, EITC, noncash
17. poverty, incentives, costs, conflicting
18. minimum, benefit-reduction
19. improvement, dependency on
20. Personal Responsibility, 5, 2, welfare, blame

TRUE–FALSE QUESTIONS

1. F, p. 387	10. T, p. 392	19. F, pp. 398–399
2. T, pp. 387–388	11. T, pp. 392–393	20. T, pp. 400–401
3. T, pp. 388–389	12. F, p. 394	21. F, pp. 400–401
4. T, p. 389	13. T, p. 394	22. F, p. 401
5. F, p. 389	14. F, pp. 394–395	23. T, p. 401
6. T, p. 390	15. F, pp. 395–396	24. F, p. 401
7. T, p. 391	16. T, p. 396	25. T, p. 401
8. F, p. 391	17. T, pp. 396–397	
9. F, p. 392	18. F, pp. 398–399	

MULTIPLE-CHOICE QUESTIONS

1. d, pp. 387–388	10. b, p. 391	19. c, p. 396
2. d, pp. 388–389	11. d, p. 391	20. d, pp. 396–397
3. b, pp. 388–389	12. c, pp. 392–393	21. a, pp. 398–399
4. b, pp. 388–389	13. c, pp. 392–393	22. a, pp. 398–399
5. d, pp. 388–389	14. c, p. 393	23. d, pp. 398–399
6. d, pp. 388–389	15. b, p. 394	24. a, p. 401
7. c, p. 389	16. b, pp. 394–395	25. a, p. 401
8. a, p. 390	17. a, pp. 395–396	
9. b, p. 390	18. c, pp. 395–396	

PROBLEMS

1. *a.* (1) column 4: 18, 30, 44, 61, 80, 91, 100, (2) column 5: 4, 10, 22, 36, 51, 71, 100; *b.* (1) 30, 10, (2) 20, 49 *c.* graph
2. *a.* Transfer payment: 4000, 3000, 2000, 1000, 0; Total income: 9000, 13,000, 17,000, 21,000, 25,000, (1) 4000, (2) 25,000; *b.* Transfer payment: 3750, 2500, 1250, 0; Total income: 6250, 7500, 8750, 10,000, (1) 10,000, (2) 2500; *c.* Transfer payment: 6000, 4500, 3000, 1500, 0; Total income: 9000, 10,500, 12,000, 13,500, 15,000, (1) 15,000, (2) 18,750; *d.* (1) greater, greater, (2) greater, (3) an increase, a decrease
3. *a.* 1; *b.* 3; *c.* 2; *d.* 4

SHORT ANSWER AND ESSAY QUESTIONS

1. pp. 387–388	8. p. 394	15. pp. 398–399
2. pp. 388–389	9. pp. 394–395	16. pp. 398–399
3. p. 389	10. pp. 395–396	17. pp. 398–400
4. p. 390	11. pp. 396–397	18. pp. 400–401
5. pp. 390–392	12. pp. 396–397	19. pp. 400–401
6. pp. 392–393	13. p. 397	20. p. 401
7. pp. 392–394	14. pp. 397–398	

CHAPTER 22

Labor Market Institutions and Issues: Unionism, Discrimination, Immigration

This chapter completes the examination of government and current economic problems by looking at three major issues in labor markets: unionism, discrimination, and immigration. Unions and labor-management relations are frequently in the news because of strikes, new labor legislation, or other issues. Discrimination was cited as a factor contributing to poverty in Chapter 21, but now Chapter 22 extends the discussion by analyzing discrimination in labor markets. Immigration is important because it allows labor resources to move between nations and has economic effects on both the sending and receiving nations.

The **labor union** is an important economic institution in the U.S. economy. Some 16 million workers covering about 13% of the labor force belong to unions. Unions typically focus on specific economic objectives such as improving pay, hours, and working conditions. Union members are more likely to work in government or to be employed in transportation, construction, manufacturing, and mining industries. In spite of its importance, unionism has been on the decline since the mid-1950s, and the explanation for this decline is given in the chapter.

In Chapter 15 you learned how unions directly and indirectly seek to influence wage rates. The impact of the union on its own membership, on employers, and on the economy is more than just a matter of wages; it involves a contract between a union and an employer. This chapter discusses collective bargaining to give you some insights about the union goals and other issues over which employers and employees bargain. Another important idea discussed is that labor-management relations involve more than the periodic signing of a contract; they also involve the day-to-day relations between the union and the employer and the new issues not settled in the contract but which must be resolved under the general provisions of the contract.

The chapter elaborates on the economic effects of unions on the economy. Unions affect their members' wage rates relative to nonunionized workers' wage rates. Unions may also improve the productivity of labor and therefore economic efficiency in the economy. Just how unions affect these economic variables is largely uncertain and debatable. The authors of the text present both sides of the issues and draw conclusions from the empirical evidence.

Discrimination has always been present in labor markets in the form of wage, employment, occupational, or human capital discrimination. This discrimination causes significant costs for individuals who earn lower wages or have fewer work opportunities than would otherwise be the case. There are also costs to society because valuable labor resources are being inefficiently used.

The economic analysis of labor-market discrimination gives you several insights into this significant problem. The taste-for-discrimination model explains the hiring practices of prejudiced employers and the effects on the wages and employment of nonpreferred groups. You will also learn how statistical discrimination, which bases decisions on average characteristics, may disadvantage individuals. The crowding model of occupational discrimination described in the chapter also explains how occupational segregation affects pay and output in an economy.

The government has taken actions and adopted policies to counter discrimination in labor markets. Perhaps the most controversial form of government intervention has been **affirmative action.** You will examine the current debate over affirmative action and learn what supporters and critics have to say about it. You will also learn about recent legal and political developments related to this controversy.

The final major part of the chapter discusses the economics of **immigration,** which moves labor resources from one nation to another. The migration of workers from a poorer nation (such as Mexico) to a richer nation (such as the United States) economically affects wage rates, unemployment, output, and business incomes in the two nations. The method used to analyze the effects of this immigration is similar to the analysis of unions and discrimination you studied earlier in the chapter. The conclusions drawn about immigration using the supply and demand analysis are definite, but as you discover at the end of the chapter, the real world is more complicated, so any conclusions will be modified.

■ **CHECKLIST**

When you have studied this chapter you should be able to

☐ Identify the number and percentage of union members and the major union organizations.
☐ Explain the meaning of business unionism.
☐ Describe the characteristics of workers belonging to unions.
☐ State how unions have declined since the mid-1950s.
☐ Present two hypotheses to explain unionism's decline.

☐ Explain the four basic areas covered by work agreements in collective bargaining.

☐ Describe the bargaining process and major labor relations law.

☐ Draw conclusions about the effects of unions on the wages of workers.

☐ Identify three negative effects unions might have on productivity and efficiency.

☐ Use a supply and demand model to show how a union might lead to a misallocation of labor resources and reduced output.

☐ List three positive effects unions might have on productivity and efficiency.

☐ Describe four types of labor market discrimination.

☐ Illustrate the cost of discrimination with a production possibilities curve.

☐ Use a wage equation to explain the taste-for-discrimination model in labor markets.

☐ Use a supply and demand graph to illustrate the taste-for-discrimination model in labor markets.

☐ Explain and give an example of statistical discrimination.

☐ Use the crowding model of occupational discrimination to explain differences in wages among groups and efficiency effects.

☐ Identify three types of antidiscrimination policies.

☐ Discuss the arguments for and against affirmative action.

☐ Describe recent legal and political developments in affirmative action.

☐ Give estimates of the number of legal and illegal immigrants entering the United States in recent years.

☐ Use a supply and demand model to explain the effects of worker migration from a poor to a rich nation on wage rates, output, and incomes in both nations.

☐ Explain how four complicating factors modify the effects of migration on the two economies.

☐ Describe two contrasting views of the effects of immigration on the United States.

■ **CHAPTER OUTLINE**

1. About 16 million workers in the United States belong to *unions,* and they account for only about 13% of wage and salary workers. Most union workers are members of the *American Federation of Labor and Congress of Industrial Organizations* (AFL-CIO).

　　a. Most unions have adopted a philosophy of *business unionism* that focuses on the economic objectives of higher pay, shorter work hours, and improved working conditions.

　　b. Occupation and industry are important factors that explain who belongs to unions. The rate of unionization is high in government and in the transportation, construction, manufacturing, and mining industries. Men, blacks, and those living in urban areas are more likely to be union members.

　　c. Union membership has declined since the mid-1950s, when about 25% of the workforce was unionized. Two complementary hypotheses explain the decline.

　　(1) The *structural-change hypothesis* is that changes in the structure of the economy and the labor force have limited the expansion of union membership.

　　(2) The *managerial-opposition hypothesis* is that the opposition of management to unions increased because union firms were thought to be less profitable than nonunion firms. The policies management used against unions decreased union membership.

2. *Collective bargaining* between labor and management results in work agreements.

　　a. These agreements take many different forms, but usually cover four basic areas: union status *(open, closed, or agency shops)* and managerial prerogatives; wages and hours; seniority and job protection; and grievance procedures.

　　b. This bargaining process on a new contract typically occurs in the 60-day period before the end of the existing contract. After the deadline, a union can strike, or there can be a lockout by the firm. Most contract agreements are compromises; strikes, lockouts, and violence are rare. The *National Labor Relations Act* specifies legal and illegal practices in collective bargaining, and the *National Labor Relations Board* is authorized to investigate unfair labor practices.

3. Labor unions have *economic effects.*

　　a. While unions have increased the wages of their members relative to the wages of nonunion members, they have had little or no effect on the average level of real wages in the economy.

　　b. Whether unions result in more or less efficiency and an increase or a decrease in the productivity of labor is a two-sided question.

　　(1) The negative view is that unions decrease efficiency by featherbedding and establishing work rules, engaging in strikes, and fostering a misallocation of labor resources.

　　(2) The positive view is that unions increase efficiency by having a shock effect on management performance, reducing worker turnover, and by informally transferring skills from the more- to the less-skilled workers fostered by the seniority system.

　　(3) The empirical evidence is mixed, showing that unions have increased labor productivity in some industries but decreased it in others. There is no generally accepted conclusion as to the effect of unions on the productivity of labor in the economy.

4. *Discrimination* in labor markets occurs when equivalent labor resources that make equally productive contributions are given different pay or treatment. Discrimination affects the earnings of women and minorities in the labor market.

　　a. Labor market discrimination against a group can occur in four ways: lower wages; inferior employment treatment in hiring, promotions, assignments, and working conditions; restrictions or prohibitions that limit entry or mobility in occupations; and less access to opportunities for investments in education and training or other forms of human capital.

b. Discrimination has private and social costs. It transfers income and benefits from one group to another. It also reduces the output and income of the economy by operating as an artificial barrier to competition.

5. The economic analysis of discrimination provides some insights even though the issue is complex and multifaceted.

  a. The **taste-for-discrimination model** explains prejudice using demand theory. The model assumes that a prejudiced employer is willing to pay a "price" to avoid interactions with a nonpreferred group.

  (1) The **discrimination coefficient** measures in monetary units the cost of the employer's prejudice. An employer will hire nonpreferred workers only if their wage rates are below those of the preferred workers by an amount at least equal to the discrimination coefficient.

  (2) In the supply and demand model for nonpreferred workers, an increase in the prejudice of employers will decrease the demand for this labor, the number of workers, and their wage rate. A decrease in the prejudice of employers will increase the demand for this labor, the number employed, and the wage rate.

  (3) The taste-for-discrimination model suggests that in the very long run, competition will reduce discrimination, but critics question this conclusion, given the insufficient progress in reducing discrimination over time in the United States.

  b. **Statistical discrimination** involves judging people based on the average characteristics of the group to which they belong instead of productivity or personal characteristics. In labor markets, employers may stereotype workers by applying the average characteristics of the group in work assessments of individual members of that group. The practice may be profitable and on average it may produce correct decisions, but it fails to take into account the individual skills and capabilities and limits opportunities for workers.

  c. The practice of **occupational segregation** suggests that women and minorities are crowded into a small number of occupations. In this crowding model, the supply of these workers is large relative to the demand for them, and thus their wage rates and incomes are lower in these crowded occupations. Eliminating occupational segregation would raise wage rates and incomes for these workers and also increase the economy's output.

6. The government can try to correct the discrimination problem by promoting a growing economy, improving the education and training of women and minorities, and creating policies that restrict or eliminate discriminatory practices.

  a. **Affirmative action** involves special efforts by employers to increase employment and promotion opportunities for groups that have experienced and continue to experience discrimination.

  (1) Arguments for affirmative action include the need to close the pay and socioeconomic gap for women and minorities and the need to counter long-lasting prejudice and discriminatory employment practices. Eliminating discrimination will also improve economic efficiency and economic growth.

  (2) The opposing view is that economic efficiency is reduced because employers are forced to hire less qualified workers. Hiring quotas and preferential treatment are considered a form of reverse discrimination. Some opponents suggest that affirmative action increases hostility and resentment in the workplace and mistakenly leads people to attribute work success not to their personal contributions but to their protected status.

  b. Affirmative action has been subject to legal and political attacks in recent years. The Supreme Court declared some affirmative action programs illegal because they promote reverse discrimination. The courts have also limited the application of race-based preferences in Federal programs. Congress has debated the issue, and the Clinton administration halted some minority programs that gave contracting preferences to minorities.

7. The **immigration** of workers into the United States is a controversial issue because this international movement of labor has had economic effects on the U.S. economy.

  a. During the 1990s, about 850,000 **legal immigrants** and 100,000 **illegal immigrants** entered the United States each year. About one-third of the recent population growth is from immigration.

  b. The economic effects of immigration can be shown in a two-nation model, one poorer and one richer.

  (1) The movement of workers from a poorer economy raises the average wages of workers in the poorer nation and lowers the average wage rates in the richer nation. Domestic output in the poorer nation will decline and domestic output in the richer nation will expand, but the net effect from a world perspective is an increase in output and economic efficiency.

  (2) The incomes of businesses in the richer nation will increase but decrease in the poorer nation; the richer nation gains "cheap" labor and the poorer nation loses "cheap" labor.

  c. These conclusions must be modified to take into account other factors.

  (1) There is a cost to migration for workers that will reduce the world gain in output.

  (2) Remittances reduce the gains for the richer nation. If immigrant workers remit some of their increased wages to relatives in the poorer nation, then some gain for the domestic economy is lost. The return of immigrants to the poorer nation (backflows) alters gains and losses.

  (3) The model assumes full employment in both nations. If there is unemployment or underemployment in the poorer nation, it can increase domestic output when the surplus workers emigrate.

  (4) Immigration can affect tax revenues and government spending. If immigrants take advantage of welfare benefits in the richer nation, it imposes an additional cost on the richer nation.

d. The positive view of immigration considers it a source of economic progress for a nation, but the negative view is that it causes socioeconomic problems that hinder a nation.

■ HINTS AND TIPS

1. This chapter deals with three issues—unions, discrimination, and immigration—that can provoke emotional reactions. Make sure you remember the distinction between *positive* and *normative* economics made in Chapter 1. The purpose of the chapter is to analyze and explain the economics of unions, discrimination, and immigration (*what is*), and not the ideal world (*what ought to be*).

2. The effects of discrimination are illustrated by the production possibilities curve you first learned about in Chapter 2. In this model discrimination is similar to unemployment in the economy.

3. Although three different issues are discussed in this chapter, the supply and demand graphs comparing the gains and losses of different groups are quite similar (Figures 22.2, 22.5, and 22.6). In each graph, the wage rate is plotted on the vertical axis and the quantity of labor is on the horizontal axis. Each graph shows how segmentation of a labor market affects the wage rate, employment, and domestic output. Problems 3, 4, and 5 in this chapter will help you master this material.

■ IMPORTANT TERMS

American Federation of Labor-Congress of Industrial Organizations (AFL-CIO)

independent unions

business unionism

structural-change hypothesis

managerial-opposition hypothesis

collective bargaining

closed shop

union shop

agency shop

right-to-work laws

open shop

cost-of-living adjustment (COLA)

strike

lockout

National Labor Relations Act (NLRA)

National Labor Relations Board (NLRB)

exit mechanism

voice mechanism

labor market discrimination

wage discrimination

employment discrimination

occupational discrimination

human-capital discrimination

taste-for-discrimination model

discrimination coefficient

statistical discrimination

occupational segregation

affirmative action

reverse discrimination

legal immigrants

illegal immigrants

SELF-TEST

■ FILL-IN QUESTIONS

1. About (16, 32) _____ million workers belong to labor unions in the United States. This number represents about (13, 28) _____% of wage and salary workers.

2. The rate of unionization is relatively (low, high) _____ among workers in government, transportation, construction, and manufacturing, and it is _____ among protective service workers, machine operators, and craft workers. Men are (more, less) _____ likely to be union members than women; blacks are _____ likely to be union members than whites; and those in urban areas are _____ likely to be union members than those workers in other locations.

3. Since the mid-1950s, union membership as a percentage of the labor force has (increased, decreased) _____ and, since 1980, the number of unionized workers has _____.

4. Two complementary hypotheses can be used to explain the changes in the size of union membership. The (structural-change, managerial-opposition) _____ hypothesis suggests that conditions unfavorable to the expansion of unions have occurred in the economy and labor; the _____ hypothesis suggests that union growth has been deterred by the policies of firms to limit or dissuade workers from joining unions.

5. A typical work agreement between a union and an employer covers the following four basic areas:

a. _____

b. _____

c. _____

d. _____

6. Unionization of workers in the U.S. economy has tended to (increase, decrease, have no effect on) _____ the wage rates of union members, _____ the wage rates of nonunion workers, and _____ the average level of real wage rates received by all workers.

7. Unions have a negative effect on productivity and efficiency in the economy to the extent that they engage in (collective bargaining, featherbedding) _____ and impose (a shock effect, work rules) _____ on their employers, participate in (training with, strikes against) _____ their employers, or impose (above, below) _____-equilibrium wage rates on employers that lead to misallocation of labor resources.

8. Unions have a positive effect on productivity and efficiency in the economy when the increased wage rate can have (an income, a shock) _____ effect that induces employers to substitute capital for labor and hasten their search for technologies that (increase, decrease) _____ the costs of production. Unions can also (increase, decrease) _____ labor turnover, and the seniority system can _____ informal training of younger workers by older workers.

9. Discrimination relating to the labor market occurs when women or minorities having (the same, inferior) _____ abilities, education, training, and experience as men or white workers are given _____ treatment with respect to hiring, occupational choice, education and training, promotion, and wage rates. Studies of the differences in earnings between men and women and blacks and whites find that (half, three-fourths) _____ can be explained by factors such as age, education, and training, but about _____ (one-fourth, half) are unexplained and due largely to discrimination.

10. The four principal kinds of economic discrimination are

a. _____

b. _____

c. _____

d. _____

11. Discrimination (increases, decreases) _____ the wages of workers in the nonpreferred group and _____ the wages of workers in the preferred group; it _____ economic efficiency and _____ total output in the economy.

12. In the taste-for-discrimination model, the discrimination coefficient *d* measures the (utility, disutility) _____ that prejudiced employers experience when they must interact with those they are biased against. This coefficient is measured in monetary units and becomes part of the (benefit, cost) _____ of hiring nonpreferred workers. The prejudiced employer will hire nonpreferred workers only if their wage rate is (above, below) _____ that of the preferred workers by at least the amount of the discrimination coefficient.

13. An increase in the prejudice of employers against nonpreferred workers will (increase, decrease) _____ their wage rate and the number employed; a decrease in the prejudice of employers against nonpreferred workers will (increase, decrease) _____ their wage rate and the number employed.

14. When employers base employment decisions about individuals on the average characteristics of groups of workers, this is (reverse, statistical) _____ discrimination. The decisions that firms make based on this type of discrimination may be (irrational, rational) _____ and profitable, on average, but hurt individuals to whom the averages (do, do not) _____ apply.

15. The occupational discrimination that pushes women and blacks into a small number of occupations in which the supply of labor is large relative to the demand is explained by the (managerial-opposition, crowding) _____ model. Because supply is large relative to demand, wages and incomes in these occupations are (high, low) _____. The reduction or elimination of this occupational discrimination would result in a (more, less) _____ efficient allocation of the labor resources of the economy and (an expansion, a contraction) _____ in the domestic output.

16. Those who support affirmative action say that (equal, preferential) _____ treatment is needed to help women and minorities compensate for decades of discrimination. They also argue that affirmative action (increases, decreases) _____ economic efficiency, but opponents argue that it _____ economic efficiency and causes (statistical, reverse) _____ discrimination.

17. The annual number of legal immigrants to the United States in the 1990s was about (450, 850) _____ thousand. About one-(tenth, third) _____ of the population growth in the United States can be attributed to immigration.

18. In the rich nation, the movement of workers from a poor nation to the rich nation tends to (increase, decrease) _____ domestic output, to _____ wage rates, and to (increase, decrease) _____ business incomes; in the poor nation it tends to _____ domestic output, to (increase, decrease) _____ wage rates, and to _____ business incomes; in the world it tends to (increase, decrease) _____ the real output of goods and services.

19. List the four complications that may modify the conclusions reached in question 18.

a. _____

b. _____

c. _____

d. _____

20. Supporters of immigration argue that immigrant workers (increase, decrease) _____ the supply of products with their labor and _____ the demand for products with their incomes, but opponents of immigration contend that immigrants (increase, decrease) _____ the burden of welfare and _____ the wages of domestic workers. These views, however, are too (complex, simplistic) _____ because assessing the net benefits of immigration depends on the number of immigrants, their education, skills, work ethics, and other factors.

■ **TRUE–FALSE QUESTIONS**

Circle T if the statement is true, F if it is false.

1. Most union members in the United States belong to independent unions not affiliated with the AFL-CIO.   **T F**

2. The rate of unionization is high in transportation, construction, and manufacturing industries.   **T F**

3. Union membership as a percentage of the labor force has been rising since the 1950s.   **T F**

4. The managerial-opposition hypothesis argues that structural changes in the economy have limited management opposition to unions.   **T F**

5. Collective bargaining between labor and management means no more than deciding on the wage rates employees will receive during the life of the contract.   **T F**

6. The wages of union members exceed the wages of nonunion members on the average by more than 40%.   **T F**

7. Strikes in the U.S. economy result in little lost work time and reductions in total output.   **T F**

8. The loss of output in the U.S. economy resulting from increases in wage rates imposed by unions on employers is relatively large.   **T F**

9. The seniority system, its advocates argue, expands the informal training of less-skilled, younger workers and improves the productivity of a firm's workforce.   **T F**

10. It is generally agreed that unions decrease the productivity of labor in the U.S. economy.   **T F**

11. Labor market discrimination occurs when equivalent labor resources are paid or treated differently even though their productive contributions are equal.   **T F**

12. Almost all the differences in the earnings between men and women and blacks and whites can be explained by discrimination.   **T F**

13. Sexual and racial harassment would be considered part of human-capital discrimination.   **T F**

14. Discrimination redistributes income and reduces the economy's output.   **T F**

15. In the taste-for-discrimination model, employer preference for discrimination is measured in dollars by discrimination coefficient *d*. These employers will hire nonpreferred workers only if their wages are at least *d* dollars below the wages of preferred workers.   **T F**

16. In the taste-for-discrimination model, a decline in the prejudice of employers will decrease the demand for black workers and lower the black wage rate and the ratio of black to white wages.   **T F**

17. Statistical discrimination occurs when employers base employment decisions about individuals on the average characteristics of groups of workers.   **T F**

18. The crowding model of occupational segregation shows how white males earn higher earnings at the expense of women and minorities, who are restricted to a limited number of occupations.   **T F**

19. Tight labor markets tend to increase discrimination and stereotyping rather than reduce them.   **T F**

20. More than 10 million immigrants enter the United States each year, about half of whom are legal and the other half illegal.   **T F**

21. Supply and demand analysis suggests that the movement of workers from a poor to a rich country decreases domestic output in the rich country and increases domestic output in the poor country.   **T F**

22. An increase in the mobility of labor from one nation to other nations tends to increase the world's output of goods and services.   **T F**

23. Mexican workers who have migrated to the United States and send remittances to their families in Mexico increase the gain to domestic output in the United States and reduce it in Mexico.   **T F**

24. When unemployed or underemployed laborers from a poor nation migrate to a rich nation, the poor nation suffers a loss in domestic output because it loses workers.   **T F**

25. Immigration will always harm a nation because it reduces the wages of workers in the domestic economy and thus reduces national income.   **T F**

■ MULTIPLE-CHOICE QUESTIONS

Circle the letter that corresponds to the best answer.

1. About what percent of employed wage and salary workers in the United States belong to unions?
(a) 7%
(b) 13%
(c) 21%
(d) 35%

2. The rate of unionization is highest in
(a) services
(b) retail trade
(c) government
(d) manufacturing

3. The decline in union membership in the United States in recent years can be explained by the
(a) managerial-growth hypothesis
(b) structural-change hypothesis
(c) relative-income hypothesis
(d) complementary-expansion hypothesis

4. If workers at the time they are hired have a choice of joining the union and paying dues or of not joining the union and paying no dues, there exists
(a) a union shop
(b) an open shop
(c) a nonunion shop
(d) a closed shop

5. A major responsibility of the National Labor Relations Board is to
(a) enforce right-to-work laws
(b) keep unions from becoming politically active
(c) investigate unfair labor practices under labor law
(d) maintain labor peace between the AFL and CIO

6. Unionization has tended to
(a) increase the wages of union workers and decrease the wages of some nonunion workers
(b) increase the wages of some nonunion workers and decrease the wages of union workers
(c) increase the wages of both union and nonunion workers
(d) increase the average level of real wages in the economy

7. The higher wages imposed on employers in a unionized labor market tend to result in
(a) lower wage rates in nonunionized labor markets and a decline in domestic output
(b) lower wage rates in nonunionized labor markets and an expansion in domestic output
(c) higher wage rates in nonunionized labor markets and a decline in domestic output
(d) higher wage rates in nonunionized labor markets and an expansion in domestic output

8. Which tends to decrease (to have a negative effect on) productivity and efficiency in the economy?
(a) the seniority system
(b) reduced labor turnover
(c) featherbedding and union-imposed work rules
(d) the shock effect of higher union-imposed wage rates

9. The reallocation of a unit of labor from employment where its MRP is $50,000 to employment where its MRP is $40,000 will
(a) increase the output of the economy by $10,000
(b) increase the output of the economy by $90,000
(c) decrease the output of the economy by $10,000
(d) decrease the output of the economy by $90,000

10. Which tends to increase (have a positive effect on) productivity and efficiency in the economy?
(a) strikes
(b) reduced labor turnover
(c) featherbedding and union-imposed work rules
(d) a decrease in the training programs for workers

11. A wage increase imposed by unions on employers has a shock effect if it induces employers to
(a) decrease the substitution of capital for labor
(b) slow their search for productivity-increasing technologies
(c) speed their employment of productive techniques that reduce their costs
(d) lockout workers to encourage bargaining

12. Unions tend to reduce labor turnover by providing workers with all but one of the following. Which one?
(a) an exit mechanism
(b) a voice mechanism
(c) a collective voice
(d) a wage advantage

13. What form of discrimination is indicated by a report from the U.S. Department of Labor that states the unemployment rate for blacks is double that for whites?
(a) occupational discrimination
(b) employment discrimination
(c) human-capital discrimination
(d) wage discrimination

14. A study by a labor economist finds that 12% of blacks and 22% of whites have completed 4 or more years of college. These data are evidence of
(a) occupational discrimination
(b) employment discrimination
(c) human-capital discrimination
(d) wage discrimination

15. In the production possibilities model, the effect of discrimination can be illustrated by a
(a) point outside the frontier
(b) point inside the frontier
(c) point on the frontier
(d) shift out from the frontier

16. In a supply and demand model of the labor market for nonpreferred workers, an increase in employer prejudice will
(a) increase supply, raise the wage rate, and decrease the employment of these workers

(b) decrease supply, lower the wage rate, and decrease employment of these workers

(c) decrease demand, lower the wage rate, and decrease the employment of these workers

(d) increase demand, raise the wage rate, and increase the employment of these workers

17. Suppose the market wage rate for a preferred worker is $12 and the monetary value of disutility the employer attaches to hiring a nonpreferred worker is $3. The employer will be indifferent between either type of worker when the wage rate for nonpreferred workers is

    (a) $15

    (b) $12

    (c) $9

    (d) $3

18. When people are judged on the basis of the average characteristics of the group to which they belong rather than on their own personal characteristics or productivity, this is

    (a) human-capital discrimination

    (b) occupational discrimination

    (c) employment discrimination

    (d) statistical discrimination

19. The crowding of women and minorities into certain occupations results in

    (a) higher wages and more efficient allocation of labor resources

    (b) lower wages and less efficient allocation of labor resources

    (c) lower wages, but more efficient allocation of labor resources

    (d) lower wages, but no effect on the efficient allocation of labor resources

20. Supporters of affirmative action believe that

    (a) improved social equity is worth the price society must pay in the form of a lowered domestic output

    (b) preferential treatment is necessary to eliminate bias and is a good strategy for increasing economic efficiency

    (c) it decreases human-capital discrimination but increases statistical discrimination

    (d) it decreases occupational discrimination but increases wage discrimination

21. About what percentage of recent population growth in the United States can be attributed to immigration?

    (a) 10%

    (b) 33%

    (c) 67%

    (d) 90%

22. The elimination of barriers to the international flow of labor tends to

    (a) lower the wage rates for all labor

    (b) raise the wage rates for all labor

    (c) increase worldwide efficiency

    (d) decrease worldwide efficiency

23. If there is full employment in both nations, the effect of the migration of workers from a poor to a rich nation is to increase the

    (a) average wage rate in the rich nation

    (b) domestic output in the rich nation

    (c) business incomes in the poor nation

    (d) domestic output in the poor nation

24. Which would increase the gains realized in the world from the migration of workers?

    (a) the explicit and implicit costs of migration

    (b) the remittances of workers to their native countries

    (c) the migration of unemployed workers to nations in which they find employment

    (d) the migration of employed workers to nations in which the taxes they pay are less than the welfare benefits they receive

25. From a strictly economic perspective, nations seeking to maximize net benefits from immigration should

    (a) expand immigration because it benefits society with a greater supply of products and increased demand for them

    (b) contract immigration because the benefits are minor and it reduces the wage rates of domestic workers

    (c) expand immigration until its marginal benefits equal its marginal costs

    (d) contract immigration until the extra welfare cost for taxpayers is zero

■ **PROBLEMS**

1. Match the union term with the phrase using the appropriate number.

    1. lockout   **5.** open shop

    2. union shop   **6.** agency shop

    3. closed shop   **7.** National Labor Relations Act

    4. right-to-work laws **8.** collective bargaining

    a. Employer can hire union or nonunion workers. _____

    b. Acts by states to make compulsory union membership, or the union shop, illegal. _____

    c. A worker must be a member of the union before he or she is eligible for employment in the firm. _____

    d. First passed as the Wagner Act of 1935 and sets forth the dos and don'ts of union and management-labor practices. _____

    e. Requires a worker to pay union dues or donate an equivalent amount to charity. _____

    f. A firm forbids its workers from returning to work until a new contract is signed. _____

    g. Permits the employer to hire nonunion workers, but provides that these workers must join the union within a specified period or relinquish their jobs. _____

    h. The negotiations of labor contracts. _____

2. Suppose there are two identical labor markets in the economy. The supply of workers and the demand for workers in each of these markets are shown in the following table.

Quantity of labor demanded	Wage rate (MRP of labor)	Quantity of labor supplied
1	$100	7
2	90	6
3	80	5
4	70	4
5	60	3
6	50	2
7	40	1

a. In each of the two labor markets the equilibrium wage rate in a competitive labor market would be

$_____ and employment would be

_____ workers.

b. Now suppose that in the first of these labor markets workers form a union and the union imposes an above-equilibrium wage rate of $90 on employers.

(1) Employment in the unionized labor market will

(rise, fall) _____ to _____ workers; and

(2) the output produced by workers employed by the firms in the unionized labor market will (expand,

contract) _____ by $_____.

c. If the workers displaced by the unionization of the first labor market all enter and find employment in the second labor market, which remains nonunionized and competitive,

(1) the wage rate in the second labor market will (rise,

fall) _____ to $_____.

(2) the output produced by the workers employed by firms in the second labor market will (expand, contract)

_____ by $_____.

d. While the total employment of labor in the two labor markets has remained constant, the total output produced by the employers in the two labor markets

has (expanded, contracted) _____ by

$_____.

3. Match the discrimination terms with the phrase using the appropriate number.

1. statistical discrimination

5. reverse discrimination

2. human-capital discrimination

6. wage discrimination

3. employment discrimination

7. occupational discrimination

4. affirmative action

8. occupational segregation

a. The crowding of women, blacks, and certain ethnic groups into less desirable, lower-paying occupations.

_____

b. The payment of a lower wage to members of particular groups than to white males for the same work.

_____

c. Inferior treatment in hiring, promotions, and work assignments for a particular group of workers. _____

d. Judging an individual on the basis of the average characteristics of the group to which the individual belongs rather than the individual's characteristics.

_____

e. The view that preferential treatment associated with affirmative action efforts constitutes discrimination

against other groups. _____

f. The denial of equal access to productivity-enhancing education and training to members of particular

groups. _____

g. Policies and programs that establish targets of increased employment and promotion for women and

minorities. _____

h. The arbitrary restriction of particular groups from entering more desirable higher-paying occupations.

_____

4. Suppose there are only three labor markets in the economy and each market is perfectly competitive. The following table contains the demand (or marginal-revenue-product) schedule for labor in each of these three markets.

Wage rate (marginal revenue product of labor per hour)	Quantity of labor (millions per hour)
$11	4
10	5
9	6
8	7
7	8
6	9
5	10
4	11
3	12

a. Assume there are 24 million homogeneous workers in the economy and that 12 million of these workers are male and 12 million are female.

(1) If the 12 million female workers can be employed only in the labor market Z, for them all to find employment the hourly wage rate must be

$_____.

(2) If of the 12 million male workers 6 million are employed in labor market X and 6 million are employed in labor market Y, the hourly wage rate in labor mar-

kets X and Y will be $_____.

b. Imagine now that the impediment to the employment of females in labor markets X and Y is removed and that as a result (and because the demand and marginal revenue product of labor is the same in all three markets) 8 million workers find employment in each labor market.

(1) In labor market Z (in which only females had previously been employed)

(a) the hourly wage rate will rise to $_____.

(b) the *decrease* in national output that results from the decrease in employment from 12 million to 8 million workers is equal to the loss of the marginal revenue products of the workers no longer employed, and it totals $_____.

(2) In labor market X and in labor market Y (in each of which only males had previously been employed)

(a) the hourly wage rate will fall to $_____.

(b) the *increase* in national output that results from the increase in employment from 6 million to 8 million workers is equal to the marginal revenue products of the additional workers employed; the gain in each of these markets is $_____ million, and the total gain in the two markets is $_____.

(c) the *net* gain to society from the reallocation of female workers is $_____ million.

5. The following two tables show the demands for labor and the levels of domestic output that can be produced at each level of employment in two countries, *A* and *B.*

Country A		
Wage rate	Quantity of labor demanded	Real output
$20	95	$1900
18	100	1990
16	105	2070
14	110	2140
12	115	2200
10	120	2250
8	125	2290

Country B		
Wage rate	Quantity of labor demanded	Real output
$20	10	$200
18	15	290
16	20	370
14	25	440
12	30	500
10	35	550
8	40	590

a. If there were full employment in both countries and if
(1) the labor force in Country *A* were 110, the wage rate in Country *A* would be $_____.
(2) the labor force in Country *B* were 40, the wage rate in Country *B* would be $_____.
b. With these labor forces and wage rates

(1) total wages paid in *A* would be $_____ and the incomes of businesses (capitalists) in *A* would be $_____. (*Hint:* Subtract total wages paid from the real output.)

(2) total wages paid in *B* would be $_____ and business incomes in *B* would be $_____.
c. Assume the difference between the wage rates in the two countries induces 5 workers to migrate from *B* to

A. So long as both countries maintain full employment,
(1) the wage rate in *A* would (rise, fall) _____ to $_____,
(2) and the wage rate in *B* would _____ to $_____.

d. The movement of workers from *B* to *A* would

(1) (increase, decrease) _____ the output of *A* by $_____,

(2) (increase, decrease) _____ the output of *B* by $_____, and

(3) (increase, decrease) _____ their combined (and the world's) output by $_____.

e. This movement of workers from *B* to *A* also (increased, decreased) _____ business incomes in *A* by $_____ and (increased, decreased) _____ business incomes in *B* by $_____.

■ **SHORT ANSWER AND ESSAY QUESTIONS**

1. Describe the current status of unions in the United States and the major union organization.

2. What is the philosophy of business unionism in the United States? How does it differ from the European approach to unions?

3. Who belongs to unions? Answer in terms of the types of industries and occupations and the personal characteristics of workers.

4. What evidence is there that the labor movement in the United States has declined? What are two possible causes of this decline?

5. What are the four basic areas usually covered in collective-bargaining agreements between management and labor?

6. What four arguments does labor (management) use in demanding (resisting) higher wages? Why are these arguments two-edged?

7. How large is the union wage advantage in the United States? How has the unionization of many labor markets affected the average level of real wages in the U.S. economy?

8. By what basic means do unions have a positive and a negative effect on economic efficiency in the economy? What appears to have been the overall effect of unions on economic efficiency in the U.S. economy?

9. What effect does the unionization of a particular labor market have on the wage rate in that market, wage rates in other labor markets, and the total output of the economy?

10. Explain how unions reduce labor turnover and improve the skills of younger workers.

11. Define labor market discrimination. How much of the differences in the earning of workers is explained by discrimination?

12. Describe the four types of labor market discrimination, and give an example of each type.

13. Describe the cost of discrimination to society. Illustrate the cost using a production possibilities curve.

14. How can discrimination be viewed as resulting from a preference or taste for which the prejudiced employer is willing to pay? What will determine whether the prejudiced employer hires nonpreferred workers in this model?

15. How do changes in employer prejudice affect wage rates for nonpreferred workers and the ratio of wages between preferred and nonpreferred workers?

16. Explain the concept of statistical discrimination and give an example of it. How can it lead to discrimination even in the absence of prejudice?

17. Describe the economic effects of occupational segregation on the wages of women and minorities. How does this type of segregation affect the domestic output of the economy?

18. What three types of antidiscrimination policies have been used in the United States? Distinguish between direct and indirect policies.

19. Explain the arguments for and against affirmative action. Does affirmative action increase or decrease economic efficiency?

20. How has the Supreme Court viewed affirmative action in recent years? What views have been expressed by Congress and the president?

21. Describe the number of legal and illegal immigrants who entered the United States annually during the 1990s. What has been the effect of this immigration on population growth?

22. Construct a supply and demand model to explain the effects of the migration of labor from a poorer nation to a richer nation. Give your answer in terms of the effects on wage rate, domestic output, and business incomes in the two nations.

23. What four complications make it necessary to modify the conclusions that you reached in question 22? Explain how each of these complications alters your conclusion.

24. Why would the elimination of international barriers to the mobility of labor increase worldwide efficiency?

25. Contrast the positive view with the negative view of immigration. Why are these two views too simplistic?

ANSWERS

Chapter 22 Labor Market Institutions and Issues: Unionism, Discrimination, Immigration

FILL-IN QUESTIONS

1. 16, 13
2. high, high, more, more, more
3. decreased, decreased
4. structural-change, managerial-opposition
5. *a.* the degree of recognition and status accorded the union and the prerogatives of management; *b.* wages and hours; *c.* seniority and job opportunities; *d.* a procedure for settling grievances (any order for *a–d*)
6. increase, decrease, have no effect on
7. featherbedding, work rules, strikes against, above
8. a shock, decrease, decrease, increase
9. the same, inferior, half, half
10. *a.* wage discrimination; *b.* employment discrimination; *c.* human-capital discrimination; *d.* occupational discrimination (any order for *a–d*)
11. decreases, increases, decreases, decreases
12. disutility, cost, below
13. decrease, increase
14. statistical, rational, do not
15. crowding, low, more, an expansion
16. preferential, increases, decreases, reverse
17. 850, third
18. increase, decrease, increase, decrease, increase, decrease, increase
19. *a.* including the costs of migration; *b.* remittances and backflows; *c.* the amounts of unemployment in the two nations; *d.* the fiscal aspects of welfare in the country receiving the immigrants (any order *a–d*)
20. increase, increase, increase, decrease, simplistic

TRUE–FALSE QUESTIONS

1. F, p. 406	10. F, p. 413	19. F, p. 419
2. T, p. 407	11. T, p. 413	20. F, p. 421
3. F, pp. 407–408	12. F, pp. 413–415	21. F, pp. 421–422
4. F, p. 408	13. F, pp. 413–414	22. T, p. 422
5. F, pp. 408–409	14. T, p. 415	23. F, pp. 422–423
6. F, p. 410	15. T, pp. 415–416	24. F, p. 423
7. T, p. 411	16. F, pp. 415–416	25. F, p. 423
8. F, pp. 411–412	17. T, p. 417	
9. T, p. 413	18. T, pp. 417–418	

MULTIPLE-CHOICE QUESTIONS

1. b, p. 406	10. b, pp. 412–413	19. b, pp. 417–418
2. c, p. 407	11. c, p. 412	20. b, p. 420
3. b, pp. 407–408	12. a, p. 412	21. b, p. 421
4. b, p. 409	13. b, pp. 413–414	22. c, pp. 421–423
5. c, p. 410	14. c, pp. 413–414	23. b, pp. 421–423
6. a, p. 410	15. b, p. 415	24. c, pp. 421–423
7. a, p. 410	16. c, pp. 415–416	25. c, p. 423
8. c, pp. 410–411	17. c, pp. 415–416	
9. c, pp. 411–412	18. d, p. 417	

PROBLEMS

1. *a.* 5; *b.* 4; *c.* 3; *d.* 7; *e.* 6; *f.* 1; *g.* 2; *h.* 8

2. *a.* 70, 4; *b.* (1) fall, 2, (2) contract, 150; *c.* (1) fall, 50, (2) expand, 110; *d.* contracted, 40

3. *a.* 8; *b.* 6; *c.* 3; *d.* 1; *e.* 5; *f.* 2; *g.* 4; *h.* 7

4. *a.* (1) 3, (2) 9; *b.* (1) (*a*) 7, (*b*) 18, (2) (*a*) 7, (*b*) 15, 30, (*c*) 12

5. *a.* (1) 14, (2) 8; *b.* (1) 1540, 600, (2) 320, 270; *c.* (1) fall, 12, (2) rise, 10; *d.* (1) increase, 60, (2) decrease, 40, (3) increase, 20; *e.* increased, 220, decreased, 70

SHORT ANSWER AND ESSAY QUESTIONS

1. p. 406
2. pp. 406–407
3. p. 407
4. pp. 407–408
5. pp. 408–409
6. pp. 409–410
7. p. 410
8. pp. 410–413
9. pp. 411–412
10. pp. 412–413
11. p. 413
12. pp. 413–414
13. p. 415
14. pp. 415–416
15. pp. 416–417
16. p. 417
17. pp. 417–418
18. p. 419
19. p. 420
20. p. 420
21. p. 421
22. pp. 421–422
23. pp. 422–423
24. pp. 421–423
25. p. 423

CHAPTER 23

The Economics of Health Care

Health care has been a topic of major national debate. One reason is that health care costs have risen. Another reason is that fewer people in the United States are being covered by the health care system or many have only limited access to health care. The first four sections of the chapter discuss the rising costs and limited access problems of the U.S. health care system. The economics you learned in previous chapters will now be put to good use in analyzing these twin problems of health care.

The explanations for the first problem—the rapid rise in *cost*—rely on your prior knowledge of supply and demand. Before you can appreciate the demand and supply factors that influence health care costs, however, you need to recognize the *peculiar features* of the market for health care that make it different from the other markets with which you are familiar. Society is reluctant to ration health care based solely on price or income, as is the case with most products. The market is also subject to asymmetric information between the buyer (patient) and seller (health care provider), with the seller making most of the decisions about the amount of services to be consumed and the prices to be paid. Medical care generates spillover benefits that may lead to underproduction in the private market and require some government intervention to achieve efficient allocation of resources. The system of third-party payments reduces the price to buyers and distorts the traditional price signals of the marketplace.

With this background in mind, you are ready to read about the **demand** for health care. The demand factors have significantly increased the cost of health care. Health care is relatively price insensitive, so increases in price result in little reduction in the quantity consumed. The demand for health care has increased as per capita incomes increased because health care is a normal good. Adding to the demand pressures are an aging population, unhealthy lifestyles, and the practices of physicians that are influenced by medical ethics and a fee-for-payment system. The medical insurance system also contributes to increased demand by reducing the costs to the consumer, as does the Federal government with its tax subsidy of employer-financed health insurance.

Supply has not increased at the same rate as demand in health care. Although the supply of physicians has increased, it has had little effect on reducing health care costs. Health care is also an area of slow productivity growth because of the personal attention required for services. Also, the development and use of new medical technology have increased cost pressures in health care rather than reduced them.

The **reforms** for the health care system that you will read about in the last section of the chapter focus on achieving universal coverage and cost containment. A number of schemes have been proposed to increase coverage. These include play-or-pay insurance programs for businesses, tax credits and vouchers, and a national health insurance system. Suggestions for cost containment call for increased uses of incentives, such as increased deductibles and copayments for medical services, the adoption of more managed care such as is found in health maintenance organizations, and tighter controls over Medicare payments based on specific classifications of treatments. The reform section concludes with a brief discussion of recent health care legislation.

■ **CHECKLIST**

When you have studied this chapter you should be able to

☐ Describe the major characteristics of the health care industry.
☐ State the twin problems with the health care system.
☐ Cite data on the dimensions of cost increases in health in absolute and relative terms.
☐ Discuss the quality of medical care in the United States.
☐ Give three economic implications of rising health care expenditures.
☐ Explain the basic problem with rising health care expenditures.
☐ Identify the reasons why people are medically uninsured and the consequences of this limited access.
☐ List four peculiarities of the market for health care.
☐ Discuss the demand factors that have increased health care costs over time.
☐ Explain how health insurance affects health care costs.
☐ Use supply and demand analysis to explain the rapid rise in health care expenditures.
☐ Identify the supply factors affecting the costs of health care.
☐ Evaluate the relative importance of the demand and supply factors affecting health care.
☐ Discuss proposals to reform the health care system so that there can be universal access.
☐ Cite arguments for and against national health insurance.
☐ Explain how incentives can be used to help contain health care costs.
☐ Describe six recent health care laws or proposals.

■ CHAPTER OUTLINE

1. The **health care industry** in the United States covers a broad range of services provided by doctors, hospitals, dentists, nursing homes, and medical laboratories. It employs about 9 million people, about 700,000 of whom are physicians. There are about 5800 hospitals. Americans make some 824 million visits to physicians each year.

2. Two major problems face the health care system. The **costs** of health care are high and growing rapidly. Some U.S. citizens do not have **access** to health care or adequate coverage by the system.

3. **Health care costs** are rising for many reasons.
   a. Costs have risen in absolute and relative terms.
   (1) Total health care spending pays for many items and is obtained from many sources, as shown in text Figure 23.1.
   (2) Expenditures were about 14% of domestic output in 2001 and may rise to about 16% by the year 2008.
   (3) The highest per capita health care expenditures in the world are in the United States.
   b. There is general agreement that medical care in the United States is probably the best in the world, which is a consequence of its high expenditures for health care. That does not mean, however, that the United States is the healthiest nation. In fact, it ranks low internationally on many health indicators.
   c. Rising health care expenditures and costs have negative economic effects that include
   (1) reduced access and coverage for workers and others;
   (2) labor market problems in the form of slower wage growth, less labor mobility, and more use of part-time or temporary workers; and
   (3) added demands to budgets at all levels of government.
   d. The basic problem is that there is an *overallocation* of resources to health care and *less* economic efficiency in the use of the nation's resources.

4. A problem with health care is **limited access.** A large percentage of the population (about 15% in 2001) has no medical coverage. Those medically uninsured are generally the poor, although some young adults with good health choose not to buy insurance. Low-income workers and those employed in smaller businesses are less likely to be covered, or have limited coverage, because of the higher costs of health care for smaller firms.

5. There are many reasons for the **rapid rise in health care costs.**
   a. The market for health care is different from other markets because of ethical and equity considerations, asymmetric information, spillover benefits, and third-party insurance.
   b. Several demand factors have increased health care costs over time.
   (1) Health care is a normal good with an income elasticity of about +1.0, so that spending on it will rise in proportion to per capita income. Health care is also

price *inelastic,* which means that total health care spending will increase even as the price of health care rises.
   (2) The aging population of the United States increases the demand for health care.
   (3) Unhealthy lifestyles because of alcohol, tobacco, or drug abuse increase the demand for and spending on health care.
   (4) Doctors can add to costs because there is asymmetric information—the provider knows more than the buyer—and thus there is supplier-induced demand. Doctors have no strong incentive to reduce costs for the buyer and perhaps an economic interest in increasing them because they are paid on a **fee-for-service** basis. Two other doctor practices may contribute to increased costs: **defensive medicine** may be used to prevent possible lawsuits, and medical ethics require the best (and often the most expensive) procedures.
   c. Although health insurance plays a positive role in giving people protection against health risks, it contributes to increased costs and demand for health care.
   (1) It creates a moral hazard problem by encouraging some people to be less careful about their health and gives some people incentives to overconsume health care than would be the case without insurance.
   (2) Health insurance financed by employers is exempt from both Federal income and payroll taxation. This **tax subsidy** increases the demand for health care.
   (3) From a supply and demand perspective, health insurance reduces the price to the buyer below the no-insurance equilibrium price. This lower price induces more health care consumption and creates an efficiency or welfare loss for society.
   d. Supply factors affect health care costs.
   (1) Physicians have high incomes that add to medical costs, although it is difficult to identify what specific factors determine the high income levels.
   (2) The productivity growth in health care has been slow.
   (3) Most new medical technology has increased costs, despite the fact that some technological advances in medicine have decreased costs.
   e. Only a relatively minor portion of the increase in health care costs can be attributed to increasing incomes, the aging of the population, or defensive medicine. The most likely explanations for the rise in health care costs are the use of new medical technology and a third-party system of insurance payments with little incentive to control costs.

6. **Reforms** for the health care system call for increased access to health care and cost containment.
   a. There are three basic proposals for increasing universal access.
   (1) **"Play-or-pay"** schemes would require all employers either to fund a basic health insurance program (play) or finance health care through a special payroll tax (pay).
   (2) **Tax credits** and **vouchers** are another option designed to make health insurance more affordable for the poor.

(3) A *national health insurance (NHI)* program would provide universal coverage at no cost or at a low cost and would be financed out of tax revenues. The basic arguments for NHI are its simplicity, its allowing patients their choice of physician, the reduction in administrative costs, the improvement in labor market mobility, and increased government bargaining power to contain costs. Arguments against NHI are the ineffectiveness of price controls, increased waiting for doctors and tests, the inefficiency of the Federal government, and income redistribution problems.

b. To contain health care costs, alternatives that use incentives have been adopted.

(1) Insurance companies have increased deductibles and copayments to provide more incentives for consumers to reduce health expenditures.

(2) Managed care organizations are being more widely used to control health care costs and are of two types. *Preferred provider organizations (PPOs)* offer discounts to insurance companies and consumers who use them. *Health maintenance organizations (HMOs)* are prepaid health plans that closely monitor health care costs because they operate with fixed budgets.

(3) The *diagnosis-related-group (DRG) system* has been used to classify treatments and fix fees in an effort to reduce the costs of Medicare payments, although the DRG systems may also reduce the quality of care.

c. A status report on health care reform shows several recent laws and proposals, and the continuing national debate over the direction of health care policy.

(1) In 1996, the U.S. Congress passed health legislation that allows workers to maintain health insurance when changing jobs or becoming self-employed.

(2) Congress also authorized in the 1996 legislation the trial use of medical savings accounts as a tax-deductible way for selected groups to pay for medical expenses.

(3) Congress has considered a "patients' bill of rights" to regulate HMOs and give legal protection to patients.

(4) There have been congressional efforts to limit the size of medical malpractice awards to contain health care costs.

(5) Congress has debated the coverage of prescription drugs as part of Medicare because of the significant and rising cost of this form of treatment for seniors.

(6) Recent proposals have been made to reform Medicare.

■ HINTS AND TIPS

1. This chapter contains many health care terms (e.g., preferred provider organization) with which you may not be familiar. Make sure you review the meaning of each important term before reading the text chapter and taking the self-test in this chapter.

2. The two economic ideas that are the most difficult to comprehend are asymmetric information and moral hazard. The buyer and seller information problems were discussed extensively in Chapter 17. To remember the meaning of these ideas, associate them with examples from the text or ones that you construct.

3. This chapter uses the concepts of income elasticity and price elasticity of demand to explain the demand for health care. Reread the text discussion of these concepts in Chapter 7 if you cannot recall how these elasticities are defined.

4. The graphical presentation of a market with and without health insurance (Figure 23.3) is a relatively straightforward application of supply and demand. The one difficult concept is efficiency loss. This concept was originally discussed in Chapter 18 as it related to taxation; you will now see it applied to health care.

■ IMPORTANT TERMS

deductibles	national health insurance (NHI)
copayments	preferred provider organization (PPO)
fee for service	
defensive medicine	health maintenance organization (HMO)
tax subsidy	
"play or pay"	diagnosis-related-group (DRG) system

SELF-TEST

■ FILL-IN QUESTIONS

1. The health care industry in the United States employs about (2, 9) _____ million people, about (300, 700) _____ thousand of whom are physicians. There are about (2200, 5800) _____ hospitals.

2. The twin problems facing the health care system are high and rapidly growing (benefits, costs) _____ and the fact that many U.S. citizens (do, do not) _____ have access to health care or adequate coverage by the system.

3. In 1960, health care spending was about (5, 14) _____% of domestic output, but in 2001 it was _____% of domestic output. Compared to other industrialized nations, the United States has the (lowest, highest) _____ level of per capita health care expenditures.

4. The economic effects of rising health care costs are (more, less) _____ access to health care and _____ coverage for workers. There are labor market problems, such as (more, less) _____ wage growth, _____ labor mobility, and (more, less) _____ use of temporary or part-time workers. Health care costs also create _____ demands on the budgets of governments at the Federal, state, and local levels.

5. The basic problem with growing health care expenditures is that there is an (underallocation, overallocation) _____ of resources to health care. The large expenditures for health care mean that at the margin, health care is worth (more, less) _____ than alternative products that could have been produced with the resources.

6. The uninsured represent about (15, 30) _____% of the population. They are concentrated among the poor, many of whom work at (low-wage, high-wage) _____ jobs, (do, do not) _____ qualify for Medicaid, and may work for (small, large) _____ businesses. Others who are uninsured include (older, younger) _____ adults in excellent health and people with (minor, major) _____ health problems.

7. The market for health care is different from other markets because of (technology, ethical–equity) _____ considerations, (symmetric, asymmetric) _____ information, spillover (costs, benefits) _____, and (first-party, third-party) _____ payments.

8. Health care is (an inferior, a normal, a superior) _____ good with an income elasticity of about (0, 1) _____. In this case, a 10% increase in incomes will result in a (1, 10) _____% increase in health care expenditures.

9. Health care is price (inelastic, elastic) _____, with a coefficient estimated to be (0.2, 1.5) _____. The price elasticity of demand for health care means that a 10% increase in price would decrease health care spending by (2, 15) _____%.

10. Other factors increasing the demand for health care include an (older, younger) _____ population and lifestyles that are often (entertaining, unhealthy) _____.

11. The demand for health care is affected by the problem of asymmetric information in the practice of medicine, which means that the (demander, supplier) _____ will decide the types and amount of health care to be consumed. Physicians (have, do not have) _____ an incentive to reduce costs for the buyer and perhaps an economic interest in increasing them because they are paid on a (play-or-pay, fee-for-service) _____ basis.

12. Increased demand and costs can arise from the practice of (offensive, defensive) _____ medicine to limit the possibility of a lawsuit or from medical (insurance, ethics) _____ that require the use of the best medical techniques by doctors.

13. Health insurance increases demand because it creates a moral (dilemma, hazard) _____ problem. It makes people be (more, less) _____ careful about their health and gives people incentives to (underconsume, overconsume) _____ health care more than they otherwise would without health insurance.

14. Health insurance financed by employers is (taxed, tax-exempt) _____ at the Federal level. This (tax, tax subsidy) _____ (increases, decreases) _____ the demand for health care.

15. In a supply and demand analysis, health insurance (raises, lowers) _____ the price to the buyer below the no-insurance equilibrium price. This (higher, lower) _____ price induces (less, more) _____ health care consumption and creates an efficiency (benefit, loss) _____ for society.

16. The supply factors that affect health care costs include the (high, low) _____ cost of physician services, (fast, slow) _____ growth in productivity in health care, and the use of (new, old) _____ medical technology.

17. Increasing access to health care could be achieved by a (fee-for-service, play-or-pay) _____ requirement for all employers either to fund a basic health insurance program or pay a special payroll tax to finance health care for workers. Another option would be the use of tax (levies, credits) _____ and vouchers to make health insurance more affordable for the poor.

18. A program that would provide universal coverage at no cost or at a low cost and would be financed out of tax revenues is (managed care, national health insurance) _____.

   a. Some of its advantages are that it is a simple and (direct, indirect) _____ way to provide universal coverage, it allows patients to choose their own (insurance, physician) _____, it (increases, decreases) _____ administrative costs, it _____ labor market mobility, and (increases, decreases) _____ government bargaining power with medical care providers. **b.** One argument against it is the ineffectiveness of price (ceilings, floors) _____ on physician services. It may also (increase, decrease) _____ waiting for doctors and tests, _____ the inefficiency of the Federal government, and (increase, decrease) _____ redistribution of income.

19. Actions have been taken to contain health care costs. Insurance companies have (increased, decreased) _____ deductibles and copayments to provide incentives for consumers to reduce expenditures, and there has been _____ use of preferred provider organizations (PPOs) to get consumers to use lower-cost health care providers. Businesses and other organizations have formed health maintenance organizations (HMOs) that have prepaid health plans and use a (fee-for-service, managed care) _____ approach to control health costs. Medical treatments have been classified according to a diagnosis-related-group (DRG) system and the government has (fixed, variable) _____ fee payments for each treatment.

20. In recent years, the U.S. Congress has passed laws and considered several types of health care legislation. For example, in 1996 Congress passed a law so that workers with group health insurance can continue their coverage when they change (titles, jobs) _____. Congress also authorized, on a trial basis, the use of (personal, medical) _____ savings. The cost of prescription drug coverage has been considered for inclusion in (managed care, Medicare) _____, and there has been discussion of financial limits to be placed on awards for medical (research, malpractice) _____.

■ **TRUE–FALSE QUESTIONS**

Circle T if the statement is true, F if it is false.

1. The twin problems of health care are the rapidly rising cost of health care and the general decline in the quality of health care. **T F**

2. Medicaid is the nationwide Federal health care program available to Social Security beneficiaries and the disabled. **T F**

3. Per capita expenditures on health care are high in the United States but even higher in Japan and Britain. **T F**

4. Rising health care costs reduce workers' access to health care. **T F**

5. Increasing health care expenditures cause problems for the budgets of Federal, state, and local governments. **T F**

6. Aggregate consumption of health care is so great that at the margin it is worth more than the alternative goods and services these resources could otherwise have produced. **T F**

7. About 40% of the population of the United States had no health insurance for the entire year. **T F**

8. Minimum-wage workers have health insurance because their insurance premiums are covered by the Federal government. **T F**

9. There is asymmetric information in the market for health care because the supplier (doctor) acts as the agent for the buyer (patient) and tells the buyer what health care services should be consumed. **T F**

10. The market for health care is characterized by spillover costs. **T F**

11. Third-party payments are a factor in the health care market because about three-fourths of all health care expenses are paid through public or private insurance. **T F**

12. The demand for health care is price elastic. **T F**

13. There is a strong incentive to underconsume health care because consumers have little information about the costs of medical treatments and doctors are paid on a fee-for-service basis. **T F**

14. "Defensive medicine" refers to the medical practice of physicians using preventive medicine to reduce illness and disease in patients. **T F**

15. Health care insurance is a means by which one pays a relatively small known cost for protection against an uncertain and much larger cost in the future. **T F**

16. A moral hazard problem arises from health insurance because those covered tend to take fewer health risks and consume less health care than would be the case without insurance. **T F**

17. The demand for health care is increased by a Federal tax policy that exempts employer-financed health insurance from taxation. **T F**

18. There is overwhelming evidence that the American Medical Association has purposely kept admissions to medical school artificially low to restrict the supply of doctors. **T F**

19. Productivity growth has been slow in the health care industry. **T F**

20. The development and use of new technology in health care has been a major factor in increasing the costs of health care. **T F**

21. The basic intent of reform proposals calling for tax credits and vouchers to pay for health insurance is to reduce or contain costs. **T F**

22. Proposals for national health insurance would provide a basic package of health care for each citizen at no direct charge or at a low-cost rate and would be financed out of tax revenues rather than health insurance premiums. **T F**

23. A problem with a government-imposed ceiling on the prices for physician services is that physicians can protect their incomes from fixed prices by altering the quantity and quality of care they give a patient. **T F**

24. The diagnostic-related-group (DRG) system is a health maintenance organization that specializes in the diagnoses of illnesses to reduce costs. **T F**

25. The growth of managed care organizations has transformed the medical industry into one dominated by large insurance and health care firms. **T F**

■ MULTIPLE-CHOICE QUESTIONS

Circle the letter that corresponds to the best answer.

1. The two major problems facing the health care system of the United States are
(a) the formation of health alliances and preferred provider organizations
(b) a decline in innovation and the rate of technological changes
(c) increasing supply and decreasing demand for health care
(d) access to health care and rapidly increasing costs

2. The health care industry employs about how many physicians?
(a) 50,000
(b) 100,000
(c) 700,000
(d) 1 million

3. What was total spending for health care as a percentage of GDP in 1960 and in 2001?

	1960	2001
(a)	1	4
(b)	2	6
(c)	5	14
(d)	9	18

4. The contradiction about health care in the United States is that the country's
(a) medical care is the best in the world, but the nation ranks low on many health indicators
(b) expenditures for health care are modest, but its medical care is the best in the world
(c) expenditures for health care are the highest in the world, but its quality of medical care is the worst of all industrial nations
(d) advances in medicine have fallen at a time when its need for better medicine has risen

5. Which is a labor market effect from rapidly rising health care costs?
(a) a decrease in the number of health care workers
(b) an increase in the rate of growth of real wages
(c) an increase in the use of part-time workers
(d) a decrease in the skill of the labor force

6. Which person is most likely to be uninsured or ineligible for health insurance?
(a) a college professor working at a state university
(b) a full-time worker at a big manufacturing plant
(c) an accountant employed by a large corporation
(d) a dishwasher working for minimum wage at a restaurant

7. Which would be considered a peculiarity of the market for health care?
(a) third-party payments
(b) employer mandates
(c) tax credits and vouchers
(d) fee-for-service payments

8. The demand for health care is
(a) price elastic
(b) price inelastic
(c) income elastic
(d) income inelastic

9. From an income perspective, health care is considered
(a) an inferior good
(b) a normal good
(c) a superior good
(d) a supply-induced good

10. Which is a demand factor in the market for health care?
(a) asymmetric information
(b) advance in new medical technology
(c) slow productivity growth in the health care industry
(d) the number of physicians graduating from medical school

11. Asymmetric information causes problems in the health care market because
(a) the buyer, not the supplier, of health care services makes most of the decisions about the amount and type of health care to be provided
(b) the supplier, not the buyer, of health care services makes most of the decisions about the amount and type of health care to be provided
(c) government has less information than the health care providers and can inflate fees
(d) insurance companies, not the health care consumer, control deductibles and copayment policies

12. Most experts attribute a major portion of the relative rise in health care spending to
(a) rising incomes
(b) an aging population
(c) advances in medical technology
(d) an increase in the number of physicians

13. Unhealthy lifestyles may be encouraged by medical insurance because people figure that health insurance

will cover illnesses or accidents. This attitude is characteristic of
(a) asymmetric information
(b) the play-or-pay problem
(c) a moral hazard problem
(d) a reduced access problem

Answer Questions 14, 15, 16, and 17 based on the following demand and supply graph of the market for health care.

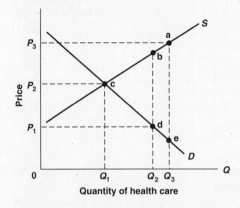

Quantity of health care

14. If there were no health insurance, the equilibrium price and quantity of health care would be
(a) P_1 and Q_2
(b) P_2 and Q_1
(c) P_2 and Q_2
(d) P_3 and Q_3

15. Assume that health insurance pays half the cost of health care. For the consumer, the price and quantity of health care consumed would be
(a) P_1 and Q_2
(b) P_2 and Q_2
(c) P_2 and Q_1
(d) P_3 and Q_3

16. With health insurance paying half the cost of health care, there is allocative
(a) efficiency because at Q_1 the marginal cost to society equals the marginal benefit
(b) efficiency because at Q_2 the marginal cost to society is less than the marginal benefit by the difference between points *b* and *d*
(c) inefficiency because at Q_2 the marginal cost to society exceeds the marginal benefit by the difference between points *b* and *d*
(d) inefficiency because at Q_3 the marginal cost to society exceeds the marginal benefit by the difference between points *a* and *e*

17. The efficiency loss caused by the availability of health insurance is shown by area
(a) $Q_1 caQ_3$
(b) $Q_1 cbQ_2$
(c) *cae*
(d) *cbd*

18. Which is a supply factor in the health care market?
(a) medical technology
(b) an aging population
(c) defensive medicine
(d) growing incomes

19. The play-or-pay proposal for health care reform is intended to
(a) increase access to health care through the use of tax credits and vouchers as part of a national health insurance system
(b) expand health care coverage by requiring all employers to offer a health insurance program for workers or pay a special payroll tax for health care
(c) make states become bigger players in health care reform by having the Federal government match state expenditures for health care and Medicaid
(d) reduce consumption of health care by increasing deductibles and copayments for health insurance

20. Which is primarily designed to increase access to health care rather than contain costs?
(a) national health insurance
(b) diagnosis-related-group system
(c) health maintenance organizations
(d) preferred provider organizations

21. A substantive criticism of national health insurance is that
(a) the Federal government provision of tax credits and vouchers for health care would be inefficient
(b) it would establish a diagnosis-related-group system for the payment of health provider services that is unnecessary and inefficient
(c) it would increase deductibles and copayments that are borne by individuals, making health care more costly
(d) the Federal government does not have a good record of containing the costs of health care programs

22. Insurance companies often have policies that require the insured to pay the fixed portion (e.g., $500) of each year's health costs and a fixed percentage (e.g., 20%) of all additional costs. The expenditures by the insured are
(a) credits and vouchers
(b) deductibles and copayments
(c) fee-for-service payments
(d) diagnosis-related-group expenditures

23. An organization that requires hospitals and physicians to provide discounted prices for their services as a condition for inclusion in the insurance plan is a
(a) health maintenance organization
(b) preferred provider organization
(c) fee-for-service organization
(d) health alliance

24. A portability and accountability act related to health care that the U.S. Congress passed in 1996 was designed to
(a) expand the use of the fee-for-payment system to increase the accountability of health care consumers
(b) make the participation of the employer voluntary in most new health care plans, but employees were required to join

(c) ensure that workers with a group health plan can continue to buy health insurance when they change jobs or become self-employed

(d) limit the number of preferred provider organizations to make health care groups more accountable for costs

25. With medical savings accounts for small business owners, the self-employed, and the uninsured, consumers

(a) make tax-deductible contributions to the accounts and then use the funds to pay for health care expenditures

(b) contract with health maintenance organizations and use the accounts to get medical services at the lowest possible rate

(c) obtain discounted prices for health care services that are provided by the diagnosis-related-group system

(d) deposit money in a bank and receive a certificate of deposit that is indexed to the inflation rate for health care

■ PROBLEMS

1. Following is a table showing a supply and demand schedule for health care. In the left column is the price of health care. The middle column shows the quantity demanded (Q_d) for health care. The right column shows the quantity supplied (Q_s) of health care.

Price ($)	Q_d	Q_s
3000	100	500
2500	200	400
2000	300	300
1500	400	200
1000	500	100

a. Assume that there is no health insurance in this market. At a price of $2000, the quantity demanded

will be _____ units of health care and the

quantity supplied will be _____ units. There will be (a surplus, a shortage, equilibrium)

_____ in this market for health care at

_____ units.

b. Now assume that health insurance cuts the price of health care in half for the consumer. The new price to

the consumer will be $_____ and the

quantity consumed will be _____ units. At this level of quantity, the marginal cost to society of

a unit of health care is $_____ while the

marginal benefit is_____.

c. Draw a supply and demand graph in the following graph based on the data in the preceding table. Make sure to label the axes and identify prices and quantities.

(1) Show the equilibrium point in a market without health insurance and label it as point *a*.

0

(2) Show the price to the consumer and quantity consumed when health insurance covers half of the cost of health care. At this quantity, indicate the marginal cost to society of this unit of health care and label it as point *b*. Also, indicate the marginal benefit to society of this unit of health care and label it as point *c*.

(3) Indicate the area of efficiency loss when health insurance covers half of the cost of health care.

2. In the situations that follow indicate whether the events primarily affect the demand (**D**) for health care or the supply (**S**) of health care. Also, indicate whether it would increase (+) or decrease (−) the demand for or supply of health care.

	D or *S*	+ or −
a. An aging population	_____	_____
b. More use of defensive medicine	_____	_____
c. Healthier lifestyles	_____	_____
d. Less health insurance coverage	_____	_____
e. Increased productivity in health care	_____	_____
f. Newer and more costly medical technology	_____	_____
g. A sharp reduction in the number of physicians	_____	_____
h. A tax subsidy to consumers to cover health care	_____	_____
i. Rising per capita incomes	_____	_____
j. More use of a fee-for-service payment system	_____	_____

3. Match the terms with the phrase using the appropriate number.

1. copayments

2. play-or-pay

3. diagnosis-related-group system

4. preferred provider organization

5. health maintenance organization

6. deductibles

a. A unit set up by insurance companies that requires hospitals and physicians to provide discounted prices for their services as a condition for being included in the insurance plan _____

b. The percentage of cost that an insured individual pays while the insurer pays the remainder _____

c. A health care organization that contracts with employers, insurance companies, and other groups to provide health care for their workers or others who are insured _____

d. The dollar sum of costs that an insured individual must pay before the insurer begins to pay _____

e. An arrangement that gives the hospital a fixed payment for treating each patient with the payments based on hundreds of detailed health categories for patient conditions and needs _____

f. A way to expand health coverage by requiring employers to either provide insurance for their workers or be assessed a special payroll tax to finance insurance for uncovered workers _____

■ **SHORT ANSWER AND ESSAY QUESTIONS**

1. Define and describe the major features of the health care industry.

2. Explain the relationship between the cost of and access to health care.

3. What are the dimensions of the cost increases in health care in absolute and relative terms?

4. How do health care expenditures in the United States compare with those in other industrialized nations?

5. What are the economic implications of rising health care costs?

6. Why is the aggregate consumption of health care in the United States a basic problem?

7. Who are the uninsured in the United States? What are the characteristics of the uninsured?

8. What are four peculiarities of the market for health care?

9. How does income and price elasticity affect the demand for health care?

10. In what ways do an aging population and unhealthy lifestyles influence and shape the demand for health care?

11. Why is there asymmetric information in health care? How does it affect consumption and the cost of health care?

12. What role does health insurance play in affecting health care costs? Explain the advantages and disadvantages of health insurance.

13. Why might physicians' high incomes have nothing to do with supply restrictions?

14. How have changes in medical technology affected health care costs?

15. What is the relative importance of demand and supply factors in affecting the rise in health care costs?

16. How would play-or-pay or tax credit and voucher reforms be used to achieve universal access to health care?

17. Discuss the arguments for and against national health insurance.

18. What actions have insurance companies and the Federal government taken to reduce or contain health care costs?

19. In 1996 Congress passed two health care reforms. Describe and comment on each reform.

20. What is the issue of prescription drug coverage? How does the way it would be provided affect its cost and Medicare reform?

ANSWERS

Chapter 23   The Economics of Health Care

FILL-IN QUESTIONS

1. 9, 700, 5800
2. costs, do not
3. 5, 14, highest
4. less, less, less, less, more, more
5. overallocation, less
6. 15, low-wage, do not, small, younger, major
7. ethical—equity, asymmetric, benefits, third-party
8. a normal, 1, 10
9. inelastic, 0.2, 2
10. older, unhealthy
11. supplier, do not have, fee-for-service
12. defensive, ethics
13. hazard, less, overconsume
14. tax-exempt, tax subsidy, increases
15. lowers, lower, more, loss
16. high, slow, new
17. play-or-pay, credits
18. national health insurance; *a.* direct, physician, decreases, increases, increases; *b.* ceilings, increase, increase, increase
19. increased, increased, managed care, fixed
20. jobs, medical, Medicare, malpractice

TRUE–FALSE QUESTIONS

1. F, pp. 428–429	10. F, p. 433	19. T, p. 437
2. F, p. 430	11. T, p. 433	20. T, p. 437
3. F, p. 430	12. F, p. 433	21. F, p. 439
4. T, p. 431	13. F, pp. 433, 679	22. T, p. 439
5. T, p. 431	14. F, p. 434	23. T, p. 440
6. F, pp. 431–432	15. T, pp. 434–435	24. F, p. 441
7. F, p. 432	16. F, p. 435	25. T, p. 440
8. F, p. 432	17. T, p. 435	
9. T, p. 433	18. F, pp. 436–437	

MULTIPLE-CHOICE QUESTIONS

1. d, pp. 428–429	**10.** a, p. 433	**19.** b, p. 439
2. c, p. 428	**11.** b, pp. 433–434	**20.** a, p. 439
3. c, p. 430	**12.** c, pp. 433–434	**21.** d, p. 439
4. a, pp. 430–431	**13.** c, p. 434	**22.** b, p. 440
5. c, p. 431	**14.** b, pp. 435–436	**23.** b, p. 440
6. d, p. 432	**15.** a, pp. 435–436	**24.** c, p. 441
7. a, p. 433	**16.** c, pp. 435–436	**25.** a, p. 441
8. b, p. 433	**17.** d, pp. 435–436	
9. b, p. 433	**18.** a, p. 437	

PROBLEMS

1. *a.* 300, 300, equilibrium, 300; *b.* 1000, 500, 3000, 1000; *c.* (1) the intersection of price of $2000 and quantity of 300, (2) point *b* is the intersection of $3000 and quantity of 500 units, and point *c* is the intersection of $1000 and quantity of 500 units, (3) the area of efficiency loss is the area in the triangle outlined by points *a*, *b*, and *c*

2. *a.* D, +; *b.* D, +; *c.* D, −; *d.* D, −; *e.* S, +; *f.* S, −; *g.* S, −; *h.* D, +; *i.* D, +; *j.* D, +

3. *a.* 4; *b.* 1; *c.* 5; *d.* 6; *e.* 3; *f.* 2

SHORT ANSWER AND ESSAY QUESTIONS

1. p. 428	**8.** p. 433	**15.** pp. 437–438
2. pp. 428–429	**9.** p. 433	**16.** p. 439
3. pp. 429–430	**10.** pp. 433–434	**17.** pp. 439–440
4. p. 430	**11.** pp. 433–434	**18.** pp. 440–441
5. pp. 430–431	**12.** pp. 434–435	**19.** p. 441
6. pp. 431–432	**13.** pp. 436–437	**20.** p. 441
7. p. 432	**14.** p. 437	

International Trade

In Chapter 6 you learned about the role of the United States in the global economy and the basic principles of international trade. Chapter 24 extends that analysis by giving you a more advanced understanding of comparative advantage. It also uses the tools of supply and demand to explain the equilibrium prices and quantities of imports and exports and the economic effects of tariffs and quotas. It examines the fallacious arguments for trade protectionism and the global efforts to liberalize trade.

After a brief review of the facts of international trade presented in Chapter 6, the text uses graphical analysis to explain why nations trade: to take advantage of the benefits of specialization. Nations specialize in and export those goods and services in the production of which they have a **comparative advantage.** A comparative advantage means that the opportunity cost of producing a particular good or service is lower in that nation than in another nation. These nations will avoid producing and will import the goods and services that other nations have a comparative advantage in producing. In this way all nations are able to obtain products that are produced as inexpensively as possible. Put another way, when nations specialize in those products in which they have a comparative advantage, the world as a whole can obtain more goods and services from its resources; each nation of the world can enjoy a standard of living higher than it would have if it did not specialize and export and import.

The principle of comparative advantage tells us why nations trade, but what determines the equilibrium prices and quantities of the imports and exports resulting from trade? To answer this question, the text uses the **supply and demand analysis,** originally presented in Chapter 3, to explain equilibrium in the world market for a product. A simplified two-nation and one-product model of trade is used to construct export supply curves and import demand curves for each nation. Equilibrium occurs where one nation's export supply curve intersects another nation's import demand curve.

Regardless of the advantages of specialization and trade among nations, people in the United States and throughout the world for well over 200 years have debated whether **free trade or protection** was the better policy for their nation. Economists took part in this debate and, with few exceptions, argued for free trade and against protection. Those who favor free trade contend that free trade benefits both the nation and the world as a whole. "Free traders" argue that tariffs, import quotas, and other barriers to international trade prevent or reduce specialization and decrease both a nation's and the world's production and standard of living.

Despite the case for trade, nations have erected and continue to erect **trade barriers** against other nations. The latter part of this chapter focuses attention on (1) what motivates nations to impose tariffs and to limit the quantities of goods imported from abroad; (2) the economic effects of protection on a nation's own prosperity and on the prosperity of the world economy; (3) the kinds of arguments those who favor protection use to support their position (on what grounds do they base their contention that their nation will benefit from the erection of barriers that reduce imports from foreign nations); and (4) how the nations of the world have responded to trade liberalization through the **World Trade Organization** (WTO).

Whether the direction of the international trade policy in the United States will be toward freer trade or more protectionism is a question that gets debated as each new trade issue is presented to the U.S. public. The decision on each issue may well depend on your understanding of the advantages of free trade and the problems with trade protection for the nation and the world economy.

■ **CHECKLIST**

When you have studied this chapter you should be able to

☐ Cite some key facts about international trade.

☐ State the three economic circumstances that make it desirable for nations to specialize and trade.

☐ Compute the costs of producing two commodities when given the data in a two-nation example.

☐ Determine which nation has the comparative advantage in the production of each commodity using the cost data you computed for the two-nation example.

☐ Calculate the range in which the terms of trade will occur in the two-nation example.

☐ Explain how nations gain from trade and specialization based on the two-nation example.

☐ Discuss how increasing costs affect specialization in the two-nation example.

☐ Restate the case for free trade.

☐ Construct domestic supply and demand curves for two nations that trade a product.

☐ Construct export supply and import demand curves for two nations that trade a product.

☐ Use supply and demand analysis to explain how the equilibrium prices and quantities of exports and imports are determined for two nations that trade a product.

☐ Identify the four principal types of artificial barriers to international trade and the motives for erecting these barriers.

☐ Explain the economic effects of a protective tariff on resource allocation, the price of the commodity, the total production of the commodity, and the outputs of foreign and domestic producers of the commodity.

☐ Analyze the economic effects of an import quota and compare them with the economic effects of a tariff.

☐ Enumerate six arguments used to support the case for protection and find the problems with each argument.

☐ Offer a summation of the arguments for and against trade protection.

☐ Describe the formation, purpose, and issues of the World Trade Organization.

■ **CHAPTER OUTLINE**

1. Some facts on international trade from Chapter 6 are worth reviewing.

    a. About 11% of the total output (GDP) of the United States is accounted for by exports of goods and services, a percentage that has doubled since 1975. The percentage of exports is much higher in other industrially advanced nations (e.g., 62% in the Netherlands, 41% in Canada), but the size of the U.S. economy means that it has the largest volume of imports and exports in the world.

    b. The United States has a trade deficit in goods, a trade surplus in services, and a trade deficit in goods and services.

    c. The major exports of the United States are computers, chemicals, semiconductors, and consumer durables. The major imports are petroleum, automobiles, computers, and household appliances. Most of the trade occurs with other industrially advanced nations. Canada is the largest trading partner for the United States.

    d. The major participants in international trade are the United States, Japan, and the nations of Western Europe. Newer participants include the Asian economies of South Korea, Singapore and Taiwan. Russia, the nations of Eastern Europe, and China have increased their international trade.

    e. International trade and finance is also a focus of economic policy as shown by issues faced by the World Trade Organization (WTO) and International Monetary Fund (IMF).

2. The ***economic basis for trade*** is based on several circumstances. Specialization and trade among nations is advantageous because the world's resources are not evenly distributed and efficient production of different commodities requires different technologies and combinations of resources. Also, products differ in quality and other attributes, so people might prefer imported to domestic goods in some cases.

3. The ***principle of comparative advantage,*** first presented in Chapter 6 to explain the gains from trade, can now be reexamined with the aid of graphical analysis.

    a. Suppose the world is composed of only two nations, each of which is capable of producing two different commodities and in which the production possibilities curves are different straight lines (the nations' opportunity cost ratios are constant but different).

    b. With different domestic opportunity cost ratios, each nation will have a comparative (cost) advantage in the production of one of the two commodities, and if the world is to use its resources economically, each nation must specialize in the commodity in the production of which it has a comparative advantage.

    c. The ratio at which one product is traded for another—the terms of trade—lies between the opportunity cost ratios of the two nations.

    d. Each nation gains from this trade because specialization permits a greater total output from the same resources and a better allocation of the world's resources.

    e. If opportunity cost ratios in the two nations are not constant (if there is increasing cost), specialization may not be complete.

    f. The basic argument for free trade among nations is that it leads to a better allocation of resources and a higher standard of living in the world. Several side benefits from trade are that it increases competition and deters monopoly, and offers consumers a wider array of choices. It also links the interests of nations and can reduce the threat of hostilities or war.

4. ***Supply and demand analysis of exports and imports*** can be used to explain how the equilibrium price and quantity for a product (e.g., aluminum) are determined when there is trade between two nations (e.g., the United States and Canada).

    a. For the United States, there will be *domestic* supply and demand as well as *export* supply and import demand for aluminum.

    (1) The price and quantity of aluminum are determined by the intersection of the domestic demand and supply curves in a world without trade.

    (2) In a world with trade, the export supply curve for the United States shows the amount of aluminum that U.S. producers will export at each world price above the domestic equilibrium price. U.S. exports will increase when the world price rises relative to the domestic price.

    (3) The import demand curve for the United States shows the amount of aluminum that U.S. citizens will import at each world price below the domestic equilibrium price. U.S. imports will increase when world prices fall relative to the domestic price.

    b. For Canada, there will be domestic supply and demand as well as export supply and import demand for aluminum. The description of these supply and demand curves is similar to the account of those of the United States previously described in point **a.**

    c. The equilibrium world price and equilibrium world levels of exports and imports can be determined with further supply and demand analysis. The export supply curves of the two nations can be plotted on one graph. The import demand curves of both nations can be plotted on the same graph. In this two-nation model, equilibrium will be achieved when one nation's import demand curve intersects another nation's export supply curve.

5. Nations limit international trade by erecting *trade barriers.* Tariffs, import quotas, a variety of nontariff barriers, and voluntary export restrictions are the principal barriers to trade.

   a. The imposition of a *tariff* on a good imported from abroad has both direct and indirect effects on an economy.

   (1) The tariff increases the domestic price of the good, reduces its domestic consumption, expands its domestic production, decreases its foreign production, and transfers income from domestic consumers to government.

   (2) It also reduces the income of foreign producers and the ability of foreign nations to purchase goods and services in the nation imposing the tariff, causes the contraction of relatively efficient industries in that nation, decreases world trade, and lowers the real output of goods and services.

   b. The imposition of a *quota* on an imported product has the same direct and indirect effects as that of a tariff on that product, with the exception that a tariff generates revenue for government use whereas an import quota transfers that revenue to foreign producers.

   c. Special-interest groups benefit from protection and persuade their nations to erect trade barriers, but the costs to consumers of this protection exceed the benefits to the economy.

   d. Tariffs and quotas affect the distribution of income. They act like sales or excise taxes on a product, so they are highly regressive for low-income consumers.

6. The arguments for *protectionism* are many, but often of questionable validity.

   a. The military self-sufficiency argument can be challenged because it is difficult to determine which industry is "vital" to national defense and must be protected; it would be more efficient economically to provide a direct subsidy to military producers rather than impose a tariff.

   b. Trade barriers do not necessarily increase domestic employment because

   (1) imports may eliminate some jobs, but create others, so imports may change only the composition of employment, not the overall level of employment;

   (2) the exports of one nation become the imports of another, so tariff barriers can be viewed as "beggar thy neighbor" policies;

   (3) other nations are likely to retaliate against the imposition of trade barriers that will reduce domestic output and employment; and

   (4) in the long run, barriers create a less efficient allocation of resources by shielding protected domestic industries from the rigors of competition.

   c. Using tariff barriers to permit diversification for stability in the economy is not necessary for advanced economies such as the United States, and there may be great economic costs to diversification in developing nations.

   d. It is alleged that infant industries need protection until they are sufficiently large to compete, but the argument may not apply in developed economies: It is difficult to select which industries will prosper; protectionism tends to persist long after it is needed; and direct subsidies may be more economically efficient. For advanced nations, a variant of this argument is *strategic trade policy.* It justifies barriers that protect the investment in high-risk, growth industries for a nation, but the policies often lead to retaliation and similar policies from other trading nations.

   e. Sometimes protection is sought against the "dumping" of excess foreign goods on U.S. markets. Dumping is a legitimate concern and is restricted under U.S. trade law, but to use dumping as an excuse for widespread tariff protection is unjustified, and the number of documented cases is few. If foreign companies are more efficient (low-cost) producers, what may appear to be dumping may actually be comparative advantage at work.

   f. Protection is sometimes sought because of the cheap foreign labor argument; it should be realized that nations gain from trade based on comparative advantage, and without trade, living standards will be lower.

   g. In summary, most protectionist arguments are fallacious or based on half-truths. The only points that have some validity, under certain conditions, are the infant industry and military-sufficiency arguments, but both are subject to abuse. The historical evidence suggests that free trade promotes and protectionism deters prosperity and economic growth in the world.

7. The *World Trade Organization* (WTO) is an international agency with about 145 participating nations that is charged with overseeing a 1994 trade agreement among nations. This agreement sought trade liberalization by: reducing tariffs worldwide; implementing new rules to promote trade in services; cutting domestic subsidies for agricultural products; protecting intellectual property; and phasing out quotas on textiles and apparel. The WTO oversees provisions of the agreement, rules on disputes, and meets on occasion to consider other trade policies. The work of the WTO is not without controversy. Critics wildly claim that it promotes global capitalism at the expense of labor and the environment. Economists argue that trade liberalization increases economic efficiency and output worldwide, and that these benefits can then be used to address domestic concerns.

■ **HINTS AND TIPS**

1. In the discussion of *comparative advantage,* the assumption of a constant-cost ratio means the production possibilities "curves" for each nation can be drawn as straight lines. The slope of the line in each nation is the opportunity cost of one product (wheat) in terms of the other product (coffee). The reciprocal of the slope of each line is the opportunity cost of the other product (coffee) in terms of the first product (wheat).

2. The **export supply and import demand curves** in Figures 24.3 and 24.4 in the text look different from the typical supply and demand curves that you have seen so far, so you should understand how they are constructed. The export supply and import demand curves for a nation do not intersect. Each curve meets at the price point on the *Y* axis showing the equilibrium price for domestic supply and demand. At this point there are no exports or imports.

a. The export supply curve is upsloping from that point because as world prices rise above the domestic equilibrium price, there will be increasing domestic surpluses produced by a nation that can be exported. The export supply curve reflects the positive relationship between rising world prices (above the domestic equilibrium price) and the increasing quantity of exports.

b. The import demand curve is downsloping from the domestic equilibrium price because as world prices fall below the domestic equilibrium price, there will be increasing domestic shortages that need to be covered by increasing imports. The import demand curve reflects the inverse relationship between falling world prices (below the domestic price) and the increasing quantity of imports.

3. One of the most interesting sections of the chapter discusses the arguments for and against trade protection. You have probably heard people give one or more of the arguments for trade protection, but now you have a chance to use your economic reasoning to expose the weaknesses in these arguments. Most are half-truths and special pleadings.

■ IMPORTANT TERMS

labor-intensive goods	equilibrium world price
land-intensive goods	tariff
capital-intensive goods	revenue tariff
cost ratio	protective tariff
principle of comparative advantage	import quota
	nontariff barrier (NTB)
terms of trade	voluntary export restriction (VER)
trading possibilities line	
gains from trade	strategic trade policy
world price	dumping
domestic price	World Trade Organization (WTO)
export supply curve	
import demand curve	

SELF-TEST

■ FILL-IN QUESTIONS

1. Exports of goods and services account for about (11, 22) _____% of total output in the United States and since 1975 this percentage has (doubled, quadrupled)_____.

2. Other industrially advanced nations such as the Netherlands and Canada have a (larger, smaller) _____ percentage of exports than the United States. The United States' volume of exports and imports makes it the world's (largest, smallest) _____ trading nation.

3. Nations tend to trade among themselves because the distribution of economic resources among them is (even, uneven) _____, the efficient production of various goods and services necessitates (the same, different) _____ technologies or combinations of resources, and people prefer (more, less) _____ choices in products.

4. The principle of comparative advantage means total world output will be greatest when each good is produced by that nation having the (highest, lowest) _____ opportunity cost. The nations of the world tend to specialize in the production of those goods in which they (have, do not have) _____ a comparative advantage and then export them, and they import those goods in which they _____ a comparative advantage in production.

5. If the cost ratio in country X is 4 Panama hats equal 1 pound of bananas, while in country Y 3 Panama hats equal 1 pound of bananas, then

a. in country X hats are relatively (expensive, inexpensive) _____ and bananas relatively _____,

b. in country Y hats are relatively (expensive, inexpensive) _____ and bananas relatively _____,

c. X has a comparative advantage and should specialize in the production of (bananas, hats) _____, and Y has a comparative advantage and should specialize in the production of _____.

d. when X and Y specialize and trade, the terms of trade will be somewhere between (1, 2, 3, 4) _____ and _____ hats for each pound of bananas and will depend on world demand and supply for hats and bananas.

e. When the actual terms of trade turn out to be 3 1/2 hats for 1 pound of bananas, the cost of obtaining

(1) 1 Panama hat has been decreased from (2/7, 1/3) _____ to _____ pounds of bananas in Y.

(2) 1 pound of bananas has been decreased from (3 1/2, 4) _____ to _____ Panama hats in X.

f. International specialization will not be complete if the opportunity cost of producing either good (rises, falls) _____ as a nation produces more of it.

6. The basic argument for free trade based on the principle of (bilateral negotiations, comparative advantage) _____ is that it results in a (more, less) _____ efficient allocation of resources and a (lower, higher) _____ standard of living.

7. The world equilibrium price is determined by the interaction of (domestic, world) _____ supply and demand, while the domestic equilibrium price is determined by _____ supply and demand.

8. When the world price of a good falls relative to the domestic price in a nation, the nation will (increase, decrease) _____ its imports, and when the world price rises relative to the domestic price, the nation will _____ its exports.

9. In a two-nation model for a product, the equilibrium price and quantity of imports and exports occur where one nation's import demand intersects another nation's export (supply, demand) _____ curve. In a highly competitive world market, there can be (multiple, only one) _____ price(s) for a standardized product.

10. Excise taxes on imported products are (quotas, tariffs) _____, whereas limits on the maximum amount of a product that can be imported are import _____. Tariffs applied to a product not produced domestically are (protective, revenue) _____ tariffs, but tariffs designed to shield domestic producers from foreign competition are _____ tariffs.

11. There are other types of trade barriers. Imports that are restricted through the use of a licensing requirement or bureaucratic red tape are (tariff, nontariff) _____ barriers. When foreign firms voluntarily limit their exports to another country, it would represent a voluntary (import, export) _____ restraint.

12. Nations erect barriers to international trade to benefit the economic positions of (consumers, domestic producers) _____ even though these barriers (increase, decrease) _____ economic efficiency and trade among nations and the benefits to that nation are (greater, less) _____ than the costs to it.

13. When the United States imposes a tariff on a good that is imported from abroad, the price of that good in the United States will (increase, decrease) _____, the total purchases of the good in the United States will _____, the output of U.S. producers of the good will (increase, decrease) _____, and the output of foreign producers will _____. The ability of foreigners to buy goods and services in the United States will (increase, decrease) _____ and, as a result, output and employment in U.S. industries that sell goods and services abroad will _____.

14. When comparing the effects of a tariff with the effects of a quota to restrict the U.S. imports of a product, the basic difference is that with a (tariff, quota) _____ the U.S. government will receive revenue, but with a _____ foreign producers will receive the revenue.

15. List the six arguments that protectionists use to justify trade barriers.

a. _____

b. _____

c. _____

d. _____

e. _____

f. _____

16. The military self-sufficiency argument can be challenged because it is difficult to determine which industry is (essential, unessential) _____ for national defense and must be protected. Rather than impose a tariff, a direct subsidy to producers would be (more, less) _____ efficient in this case.

17. Trade barriers do not necessarily increase domestic employment because: imports may change only the (level, composition) _____ of employment; trade barriers can be viewed as "beggar thy (customer, neighbor) _____" policies; other nations can (protest, retaliate) _____ against the trade barriers; and in the long run, the barriers create an allocation of resources that is (more, less) _____ efficient by shielding protected domestic industries from competition.

18. Using trade barriers to permit diversification for stability in an economy is not necessary for (advanced, developing) _____ economies such as in the United States, and there may be great economic costs to forcing diversification in _____ nations; it is also alleged that infant industries need protection until they are sufficiently large to compete, an argument that has been modified to strategic trade policy in _____ economies.

19. In sum, most arguments for protectionism are (strong, weak) _____ and are designed to benefit (consumers, domestic producers) _____. If these protectionism arguments were followed, it would create (losses, gains) _____ for protected industries and their workers at the expense of _____ for the economy.

20. The World Trade Organization is charged with overseeing trade (specialization, liberalization) _____. This approach to trade seeks to (increase, decrease) _____ tariffs, _____ agriculture subsidies distorting global trade, and _____ quotas on textiles and apparel. Other areas considered in this agenda are new rules to promote trade in (steel, services) _____ and (more, less) _____ protection of intellectual property rights.

■ TRUE–FALSE QUESTIONS

Circle T if the statement is true, F if it is false.

1. The bulk of U.S. export and import trade is with other industrially advanced nations. **T F**

2. A factor that serves as the economic basis for world trade is the even distribution of resources among nations. **T F**

3. People trade because they seek products of different quality and other nonprice attributes. **T F**

4. Examples of capital-intensive goods would be automobiles, machinery, and chemicals. **T F**

5. The relative efficiency with which a nation can produce specific goods is fixed over time. **T F**

6. Mutually advantageous specialization and trade are possible between any two nations if they have the same domestic opportunity-cost ratios for any two products. **T F**

7. The principle of comparative advantage is that total output will be greatest when each good is produced by that nation which has the higher domestic opportunity cost. **T F**

8. By specializing based on comparative advantage, nations can obtain larger outputs with fixed amounts of resources. **T F**

9. The terms of trade determine how the increase in world output resulting from comparative advantage is shared by trading nations. **T F**

10. Increasing opportunity costs tend to prevent specialization among trading nations from being complete. **T F**

11. Trade among nations tends to bring about a more efficient use of the world's resources and a higher level of material well-being. **T F**

12. Free trade among nations tends to increase monopoly and lessen competition in these nations. **T F**

13. A nation will export a particular product if the world price is less than the domestic price. **T F**

14. In a two-country model, equilibrium in world prices and quantities of exports and imports will occur where one nation's export supply curve intersects the other nation's import demand curve. **T F**

15. A tariff on coffee in the United States is an example of a protective tariff. **T F**

16. The imposition of a tariff on a good imported from abroad will reduce the amount of the imported good that is bought. **T F**

17. A cost of tariffs and quotas imposed by the United States is higher prices that U.S. consumers must pay for the protected product. **T F**

18. The major difference between a tariff and a quota on an imported product is that a quota produces revenue for the government. **T F**

19. To advocate tariffs that would protect domestic producers of goods and materials essential to national defense is to substitute a political-military objective for the economic objectives of efficiently allocating resources. **T F**

20. Tariffs and import quotas meant to increase domestic full employment achieve short-run domestic goals by making trading partners poorer. **T F**

21. One-crop economies may be able to make themselves more stable and diversified by imposing tariffs on goods imported from abroad, but these tariffs are also apt to lower the standard of living in these economies. **T F**

22. Protection against the "dumping" of foreign goods at low prices on the U.S. market is one good reason for widespread, permanent tariffs. **T F**

23. Most arguments for trade protection are special-interest pleas that, if followed, would create gains for protected industries and their workers at the expense of greater losses for the economy. **T F**

24. The only argument for tariffs that has, in the appropriate circumstances, any economic justification is the increase-domestic-employment argument. **T F**

25. The World Trade Organization was established by the United Nations to encourage purchases of products from developing nations. **T F**

■ **MULTIPLE-CHOICE QUESTIONS**

Circle the letter that corresponds to the best answer.

1. Which nation leads the world in the volume of exports and imports?
(a) Japan
(b) Germany
(c) United States
(d) United Kingdom

2. Which group of nations dominates world trade?
(a) Saudi Arabia and other OPEC nations
(b) Singapore, South Korea, and Taiwan
(c) United States, Japan, and the nations of Western Europe
(d) China, Russia, and the nations of Eastern Europe

3. Nations engage in trade because
(a) world resources are evenly distributed among nations
(b) world resources are unevenly distributed among nations
(c) all products are produced from the same technology
(d) all products are produced from the same combinations of resources

Use the following tables to answer Questions 4, 5, 6, and 7.

NEPAL PRODUCTION POSSIBILITIES TABLE

Product	Production alternatives					
	A	B	C	D	E	F
Yak fat	0	4	8	12	16	20
Camel hides	40	32	24	16	8	0

KASHMIR PRODUCTION POSSIBILITIES TABLE

Product	Production alternatives					
	A	B	C	D	E	F
Yak fat	0	3	6	9	12	15
Camel hides	60	48	36	24	12	0

4. The data in the tables show that production in
(a) both Nepal and Kashmir are subject to increasing opportunity costs
(b) both Nepal and Kashmir are subject to constant opportunity costs
(c) Nepal is subject to increasing opportunity costs and Kashmir to constant opportunity costs
(d) Kashmir is subject to increasing opportunity costs and Nepal to constant opportunity costs

5. If Nepal and Kashmir engage in trade, the terms of trade will be
(a) between 2 and 4 camel hides for 1 unit of yak fat
(b) between 1/3 and 1/2 units of yak fat for 1 camel hide
(c) between 3 and 4 units of yak fat for 1 camel hide
(d) between 2 and 4 units of yak fat for 1 camel hide

6. Assume that prior to specialization and trade Nepal and Kashmir both choose production possibility C. Now if each specializes according to its comparative advantage, the resulting gains from specialization and trade will be
(a) 6 units of yak fat
(b) 8 units of yak fat
(c) 6 units of yak fat and 8 camel hides
(d) 8 units of yak fat and 6 camel hides

7. Each nation produced only one product in accordance with its comparative advantage, and the terms of trade were set at 3 camel hides for 1 unit of yak fat. In this case, Nepal could obtain a maximum combination of 8 units of yak fat and
(a) 12 camel hides
(b) 24 camel hides
(c) 36 camel hides
(d) 48 camel hides

8. What happens to a nation's imports or exports of a product when the world price of the product rises above the domestic price?
(a) Imports of the product increase.
(b) Imports of the product stay the same.
(c) Exports of the product increase.
(d) Exports of the product decrease.

9. What happens to a nation's imports or exports of a product when the world price of the product falls below the domestic price?
(a) Imports of the product increase.
(b) Imports of the product decrease.
(c) Exports of the product increase.
(d) Exports of the product stay the same.

10. Which one of the following is characteristic of tariffs?
(a) They prevent the importation of goods from abroad.
(b) They specify the maximum amounts of specific commodities that may be imported during a given period of time.
(c) They often protect domestic producers from foreign competition.
(d) They enable nations to reduce their exports and increase their imports during periods of recession.

11. The motive for barriers to the importation of goods and services from abroad is to
(a) improve economic efficiency in that nation
(b) protect and benefit domestic producers of those goods and services
(c) reduce the prices of the goods and services produced in that nation
(d) expand the export of goods and services to foreign nations

12. When a tariff is imposed on a good imported from abroad,
(a) the demand for the good increases
(b) the demand for the good decreases
(c) the supply of the good increases
(d) the supply of the good decreases

Answer Questions 13, 14, 15, 16, and 17 on the basis of the following diagram, where S_d and D_d are the domestic supply and demand for a product and P_w is the world price of that product.

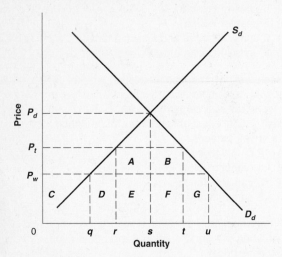

13. In a closed economy (without international trade), the equilibrium price would be
(a) P_d, but in an open economy, the equilibrium price would be P_t
(b) P_d, but in an open economy, the equilibrium price would be P_w
(c) P_w, but in an open economy, the equilibrium price would be P_d
(d) P_w, but in an open economy, the equilibrium price would be P_t

14. If there is free trade in this economy and no tariffs, the total revenue going to the foreign producers is represented by
(a) area C
(b) areas A and B combined
(c) areas A, B, E, and F combined
(d) areas D, E, F, and G combined

15. If a per-unit tariff was imposed in the amount of P_wP_t, then domestic producers would supply
(a) q units and foreign producers would supply qu units
(b) s units and foreign producers would supply su units
(c) r units and foreign producers would supply rt units
(d) t units and foreign producers would supply tu units

16. Given a per-unit tariff in the amount of P_wP_t, the amount of the tariff revenue paid by consumers of this product is represented by
(a) area A
(b) area B
(c) areas A and B combined
(d) areas D, E, F, and G combined

17. Assume that an import quota of rt units is imposed on the foreign nation producing this product. The amount of *total* revenue going to foreign producers is represented by areas

(a) $A + B$
(b) $E + F$
(c) $A + B + E + F$
(d) $D + E + F + G$

18. Tariffs lead to
(a) the contraction of relatively efficient industries
(b) an overallocation of resources to relatively efficient industries
(c) an increase in the foreign demand for domestically produced goods
(d) an underallocation of resources to relatively inefficient industries

19. Tariffs and quotas are costly to consumers because
(a) the price of the imported good rises
(b) the supply of the imported good increases
(c) import competition increases for domestically produced goods
(d) consumers shift purchases away from domestically produced goods

20. Which is a likely result of imposing tariffs to increase domestic employment?
(a) a short-run increase in domestic employment in import industries
(b) a decrease in the tariff rates of foreign nations
(c) a long-run reallocation of workers from export industries to protected domestic industries
(d) a decrease in consumer prices

21. The infant industry argument for tariffs
(a) is especially pertinent for the European Union
(b) generally results in tariffs that are removed after the infant industry has matured
(c) makes it rather easy to determine which infant industries will become mature industries with comparative advantages in producing their goods
(d) might better be replaced by an argument for outright subsidies for infant industries

22. Strategic trade policy is a modified form for advanced economies of which protectionist argument?
(a) the increase-domestic-employment argument
(b) the military self-sufficiency argument
(c) the cheap foreign labor argument
(d) the infant industry argument

23. "The nation needs to protect itself from foreign countries that sell their products in our domestic markets at less than the cost of production." This quotation would be most closely associated with which protectionist argument?
(a) diversification for stability
(b) increase domestic employment
(c) protection against dumping
(d) cheap foreign labor

24. Which is the likely result of the United States using tariffs to protect its high wages and standard of living from cheap foreign labor?
(a) an increase in U.S. exports
(b) a rise in the U.S. real GDP

(c) a decrease in the average productivity of U.S. workers

(d) a decrease in the quantity of labor employed by industries producing the goods on which tariffs have been levied

25. What international agency is charged with overseeing trade liberalization and with resolving disputes among nations?
(a) World Bank
(b) United Nations
(c) World Trade Organization
(d) International Monetary Fund

■ **PROBLEMS**

1. Shown below are the production possibilities curves for two nations: the United States and Chile. Suppose these two nations do not currently engage in international trade or specialization, and suppose that points **A** and **a** show the combinations of wheat and copper they now produce and consume.

a. The straightness of the two curves indicates that the cost ratios in the two nations are (changing, constant) _____.

b. Examination of the two curves reveals that the cost ratio in

(1) the United States is _____ million tons of wheat for _____ thousand pounds of copper.

(2) Chile is _____ million tons of wheat for _____ thousand pounds of copper.

c. If these two nations were to specialize and trade wheat for copper,

(1) The United States would specialize in the production of wheat because _____

_____.

(2) Chile would specialize in the production of copper because_____

_____ .

d. The terms of trade, if specialization and trade occur, will be greater than 2 and less than 4 million tons of wheat for 1000 pounds of copper because _____

_____.

e. Assume the terms of trade turn out to be 3 million tons of wheat for 1000 pounds of copper. Draw in the trading possibilities curve for the United States and Chile.

f. With these trading possibilities curves, suppose the United States decides to consume 5 million tons of wheat and 1000 pounds of copper while Chile decides to consume 3 million tons of wheat and 1000 pounds of copper. The gains from trade to

(1) the United States are _____ million tons of wheat and _____ thousand pounds of copper.

(2) Chile are _____ million tons of wheat and _____ thousand pounds of copper.

2. Following are tables showing the domestic supply and demand schedules and the export supply and import demand schedules for two nations (**A** and **B**).

NATION A

Price	Q_{dd}	Q_{sd}	Q_{di}	Q_{se}
$3.00	100	300	0	200
2.50	150	250	0	100
2.00	200	200	0	0
1.50	250	150	100	0
1.00	300	100	200	0

a. For Nation **A,** the first column of the table is the price of a product. The second column is the quantity demanded domestically (Q_{dd}). The third column is the quantity supplied domestically (Q_{sd}). The fourth column is the quantity demanded for imports (Q_{di}). The fifth column is the quantity of exports supplied (Q_{se}).

(1) At a price of $2.00, there (will, will not) _____ be a surplus or shortage and there _____ be exports or imports.

(2) At a price of $3.00, there will be a domestic (shortage, surplus) _____ of _____ units. This domestic _____ will be eliminated by (exports, imports) _____ of _____ units.

(3) At a price of $1.00, there will be a domestic (shortage, surplus) _____ of _____ units. This domestic _____ will be eliminated by (exports, imports) _____ of _____ units.

NATION B

Price	Q_{dd}	Q_{sd}	Q_{di}	Q_{se}
$2.50	100	300	0	200
2.00	150	250	0	100
1.50	200	200	0	0
1.00	250	150	100	0

b. For Nation **B**, the first column is the price of a product. The second column is the quantity demanded domestically (Q_{dd}). The third column is the quantity supplied domestically (Q_{sd}). The fourth column is the quantity demanded for imports (Q_{di}). The fifth column is the quantity of exports supplied (Q_{se}).

(1) At a price of $1.50, there (will, will not) _____ be a surplus or shortage and there _____ be exports or imports.

(2) At a price of $2.50, there will be a domestic (shortage, surplus) _____ of _____ units. This domestic _____ will be eliminated by (exports, imports) _____ of _____ units.

(3) At a price of $1.00, there will be a domestic (shortage, surplus) _____ of _____ units. This domestic _____ will be eliminated by (exports, imports) _____ of _____ units.

c. The following table shows a schedule of the import demand in Nation **A** and the export supply in Nation **B** at various prices. The first column is the price of the product. The second column is the quantity demanded for imports (Q_{diA}) in Nation **A**. The third column is the quantity of exports supplied (Q_{seB}) in Nation **B**.

Price	Q_{diA}	Q_{seB}
$2.00	0	100
1.75	50	50
1.50	100	0

(1) If the world price is $2.00, then Nation (**A, B**) _____ will want to import _____ units and Nation _____ will want to export _____ units of the product.

(2) If the world price is $1.75, then Nation (**A, B**) _____ will want to import _____ units and Nation _____ will want to export _____ units of the product.

(3) If the world price is $1.50, then Nation (**A, B**) _____ will want to import _____ units and Nation _____ will want to export _____ units of the product.

3. The following table shows the quantities of woolen gloves demanded (**D**) in the United States at several different prices (**P**). Also shown in the table are the quantities of woolen gloves that would be supplied by U.S. producers (S_a) and the quantities that would be supplied by foreign producers (S_f) at the nine different prices.

P	D	S_a	S_f	S_t	S'_f	S'_t
$2.60	450	275	475	_____	_____	_____
2.40	500	250	450	_____	_____	_____
2.20	550	225	425	_____	_____	_____
2.00	600	200	400	_____	_____	_____
1.80	650	175	375	_____	_____	_____
1.60	700	150	350	_____	_____	_____
1.40	750	125	325	_____	_____	_____
1.20	800	0	300	_____	_____	_____
1.00	850	0	0	_____	_____	_____

a. Compute and enter in the table the total quantities that would be supplied (S_t) by U.S. and foreign producers at each of the prices.

b. If the market for woolen gloves in the United States is a competitive one the equilibrium price for woolen gloves is $_____ and the equilibrium quantity is _____.

c. Suppose now that the United States government imposes an 80 cent ($.80) tariff per pair of gloves on all gloves imported into the United States from abroad. Compute and enter into the table the quantities that would be supplied (S'_f) by foreign producers at the nine different prices. [*Hint:* If foreign producers were willing to supply 300 pairs at a price of $1.20 when there was no tariff, they are now willing to supply 300 pairs at

$2.00 (the $.80 per pair tariff plus the $1.20 they will receive for themselves). The quantities supplied at each of the other prices may be found in a similar fashion.]

d. Compute and enter into the table the total quantities that would be supplied (S'_t) by U.S. and foreign producers at each of the nine prices.

e. As a result of the imposition of the tariff the equilibrium price has risen to $_____ and the equilibrium quantity has fallen to _____.

f. The number of pairs sold by

(1) U.S. producers has (increased, decreased) _____ by _____.

(2) foreign producers has (increased, decreased) _____ by _____.

g. The total revenues (after the payment of the tariff) of

(1) U.S. producers—who do not pay the tariff—have (increased, decreased) _____ by $_____.

(2) foreign producers—who do pay the tariff— have (increased, decreased) _____ by $_____.

h. The total amount spent by U.S. buyers of woolen gloves has _____ by $_____.

i. The total number of dollars earned by foreigners has _____ by $_____, and, as a result, the total foreign demand for goods and services produced in the United States has _____ by $_____.

j. The tariff revenue of the United States government has _____ by $_____.

k. If an import quota were imposed that had the same effect as the tariff on price and output, the amount of the tariff revenue, $_____, would now be received as revenue by _____ producers.

■ **SHORT ANSWER AND ESSAY QUESTIONS**

1. Describe the quantity of imports and exports for the United States in absolute and relative terms. How has the quantity of imports and exports changed over time?

2. What are the major imports and exports of the United States? With which nations does the United States trade?

3. What role does the United States play in international trade? Who are the other major players in international trade?

4. What three factors—one dealing with the resource distribution, the second with production, and the third with the variety of product—are the basis of a rationale for trade among nations?

5. Explain
   (a) the theory or principle of comparative advantage;
   (b) what is meant by and what determines the terms of trade; and
   (c) the gains from trade.

6. What is the case for free trade?

7. Explain how the equilibrium prices and quantities of exports and imports are determined.

8. Why will exports in a nation increase when world prices rise relative to domestic prices?

9. What motivates nations to erect barriers to the importation of goods from abroad, and what types of barriers do they erect?

10. Suppose the United States increases the tariff on automobiles imported from Germany (and other foreign countries). What is the effect of this tariff-rate increase on
   (a) the price of automobiles in the United States;
   (b) the total number of cars sold in the United States during a year;
   (c) the number of cars produced by and employment in the German automobile industry;
   (d) production by and employment in the U.S. automobile industry;
   (e) German income obtained by selling cars in the United States;
   (f) the German demand for goods produced in the United States;
   (g) the production of and employment in those U.S. industries that now export goods to Germany;
   (h) the standards of living in the United States and in Germany;
   (i) the allocation of resources in the U.S. economy; and
   (j) the allocation of the world's resources?

11. Explain the economic effects of a tariff and show them in a supply and demand graph.

12. Compare and contrast the economic effects of a tariff with the economic effects of an import quota on a product.

13. Critically evaluate the military self-sufficiency argument for protectionism. What industries should be protected?

14. What are four shortcomings of using tariffs or quotas to increase domestic employment in the United States?

15. What is the basis for the infant industry arguments (including strategic trade policy) for protectionism? How can it be countered?

16. Can a strong case for protectionism be made on the basis of defending against the "dumping" of products? How do you determine if a nation is dumping a product? What are the economic effects of dumping on consumers?

17. Does the economy need to shield domestic workers from competition from "cheap" foreign labor? Explain using the ideas of comparative advantage and standards of living.

18. Offer a summary of the case for protectionism. What does the historical evidence indicate? Give examples.

19. What are the trade liberalization issues that are the focus of the World Trade Organization?

20. What do critics of the World Trade Organization say about its effects on domestic economies and the global economy and what is the response from economists?

ANSWERS

Chapter 24 International Trade

FILL-IN QUESTIONS

1. 11, doubled
2. larger, largest
3. uneven, different, more
4. lowest, have, do not have
5. *a.* inexpensive, expensive; *b.* expensive, inexpensive; *c.* hats, bananas; *d.* 3, 4; *e.* (1) 1/3, 2/7, (2) 4, 3 1/2; *f.* rises
6. comparative advantage, more, higher
7. world, domestic
8. increase, increase
9. supply, only one
10. tariffs, quotas, revenue, protective
11. nontariff, export
12. domestic producers, decrease, less
13. increase, decrease, increase, decrease, decrease, decrease
14. tariff, quota
15. *a.* military self-sufficiency; *b.* support of infant industry; *c.* increase domestic employment; *d.* diversification for stability; *e.* protection against dumping; *f.* cheap foreign labor (any order for *a–f*)
16. essential, more
17. composition, neighbor, retaliate, less
18. advanced, developing, advanced
19. weak, domestic producers, gains, losses
20. liberalization, decrease, decrease, decrease, services, more

TRUE–FALSE QUESTIONS

1. T, p. 446
2. F, p. 447
3. T, pp. 447–448
4. T, p. 447
5. F, p. 448
6. F, pp. 448–449
7. F, p. 449
8. T, pp. 449–450
9. T, p. 450
10. T p. 452
11. T, pp. 452–453
12. F, p. 453
13. F, p. 453
14. T, pp. 455–456
15. F, p. 456
16. T, pp. 457–458
17. T, p. 458
18. F, p. 458
19. T, p. 459
20. T, p. 459
21. T, p. 460
22. F, p. 461
23. T, p. 462
24. F, p. 462
25. F, p. 463

MULTIPLE-CHOICE QUESTIONS

1. c, p. 446
2. c, p. 447
3. b, p. 447
4. b, p. 448
5. a, pp. 449–451
6. a, pp. 449–451
7. c, pp. 449–451
8. c, pp. 453–456
9. a, pp. 453–456
10. c, p. 456
11. b, pp. 456–458
12. d, pp. 457–458
13. b, pp. 457–458
14. d, pp. 457–458
15. c, pp. 457–458
16. c, pp. 457–458
17. c, p. 458
18. a, p. 458
19. a, p. 458
20. c, p. 459
21. d, p. 460
22. d, pp. 460–461
23. c, p. 461
24. c, p. 461
25. c, p. 463

PROBLEMS

1. *a.* constant; *b.* (1) 8, 2, (2) 4, 2; *c.* (1) it has a comparative advantage in producing wheat (its cost of producing wheat is less than Chile's), (2) it has a comparative advantage in producing copper (its cost of producing copper is less than the United States'); *d.* one of the two nations would be unwilling to trade if the terms of trade are outside this range; *f.* (1) 1, 0, (2) 1, 0
2. *a.* (1) will not, will not, (2) surplus, 200, surplus, exports, 200, (3) shortage, 200, shortage, imports, 200; *b.* (1) will not, will not, (2) surplus, 200, surplus, exports, 200, (3) shortage, 100, shortage, imports, 100; *c.* (1) A, 0, B, 100, (2) A, 50, B, 50, (3) A, 100, B, 0
3. *a.* 750, 700, 650, 600, 550, 500, 450, 300, 0; *b.* $2.00, 600; *c.* 375, 350, 325, 300, 0, 0, 0, 0, 0; *d.* 650, 600, 550, 500, 175, 150, 125, 0, 0; *e.* $2.20, 550; *f.* (1) increased, 25, (2) decreased, 75; *g.* (1) increased, $95, (2) decreased, $345; *h.* increased, $10; *i.* decreased, $345, decreased, $345; *j.* increased, $260; *k.* $260, foreign

SHORT ANSWER AND ESSAY QUESTIONS

1. pp. 446–447
2. pp. 446–447
3. pp. 446–447
4. p. 447
5. pp. 448–452
6. pp. 452–453
7. pp. 453–456
8. pp. 453–456
9. pp. 456–457
10. pp. 457–458
11. pp. 457–458
12. pp. 457–458
13. p. 459
14. p. 459
15. pp. 460–461
16. p. 461
17. p. 461
18. p. 462
19. pp. 463–464
20. p. 463

Exchange Rates, the Balance of Payments, and Trade Deficits

In the last chapter you learned *why* nations engage in international trade and *why* they erect barriers to trade with other nations. In Chapter 25 you will learn *how* nations using different currencies are able to trade.

The means nations use to overcome the difficulties that result from the use of different currencies are fairly simple. When the residents of a nation (its consumers, business firms, or governments) wish to buy goods or services or real or financial assets from, make loans or gifts to, or pay interest and dividends to the residents of other nations, they *buy* some of the currency used in that nation. They pay for the foreign money with some of their own currency. In other words, they exchange their own currency for foreign currency.

When the residents of a nation sell goods or services or real or financial assets to, receive loans or gifts from, or are paid dividends or interest by the residents of foreign nations and obtain foreign currencies, they *sell* this foreign currency—often called foreign exchange—in return for some of their own currency. That is, they *exchange* foreign currency for their own currency.

The market in which one currency is sold and is paid for with another currency is called the **foreign exchange market.** The price that is paid (in one currency) for a unit of another currency is called the **foreign exchange rate.** And like most prices, the foreign exchange rate for any foreign currency is determined by the demand for and the supply of that foreign currency.

As you know from Chapter 24, nations buy and sell large quantities of goods and services across national boundaries. But the residents of these nations also buy and sell such financial assets as stocks and bonds and such real assets as land and capital goods in other nations, and the governments and individuals in one nation make gifts (remittances) to other nations. At the end of a year, nations summarize their foreign transactions with the rest of the world. This summary is called the nation's **balance of payments:** a record of how it obtained foreign currency during the year and what it did with this foreign currency.

Of course, all foreign currency obtained was used for some purpose—it did not evaporate—consequently the balance of payments *always* balances. The balance of payments is an extremely important and useful device for understanding the amounts and kinds of international transactions in which the residents of a nation engage. It also allows us to understand the meaning of a balance-of-payments deficit or surplus, the causes of these imbalances, and how to deal with them.

Several difficult sections of this chapter are concerned with how **flexible and fixed exchange-rate systems** handle balance-of-payments deficits and surpluses. A balance-of-payments deficit occurs when the foreign currency receipts are less than foreign currency payments and the nation must reduce its official reserves to balance its payments. Conversely, a balance-of-payments surplus occurs when foreign currency receipts are greater than foreign currency payments, and the nation must expand its official reserves to balance its payments. In these sections pay particular attention to the ways in which a flexible or floating exchange-rate system and a fixed exchange-rate system will correct balance-of-payments deficits and surpluses and the advantages and disadvantages of these two alternative systems for eliminating imbalances in international accounts.

As examples of these two types of exchange-rate systems, the next section of the chapter examines the **gold standard,** the **Bretton Woods system,** and the **managed floating exchange-rate system.** In the first two systems exchange rates are fixed, and in the third system exchange rates are fixed in the short run (to obtain the advantages of fixed exchange rates) and flexible in the long run (to enable nations to correct balance-of-payments deficits and surpluses).

The final section of the chapter examines the U.S. **trade deficits.** As you will learn, these deficits were the result of several factors—differences in national growth rates and a declining saving rate—that contributed to imports rising faster than exports. They also have several implications—increased current consumption at the expense of future consumption and increased U.S. indebtedness to foreigners.

■ CHECKLIST

When you have studied this chapter you should be able to

☐ Explain how U.S. exports create a foreign demand for dollars that in turn generates a supply of foreign currencies.

☐ Describe how U.S. imports create a domestic demand for foreign currencies that in turn generates a supply of dollars.

☐ Give a definition of a nation's balance of payments.

☐ Use the items in the current account to calculate the balance on goods, balance on goods and services, and balance on the current account when given the data.

☐ Describe how balance is achieved in the capital account.

☐ Explain the relationship between the current account, capital account, and official reserves account.

☐ Indicate how the official reserves account is used to determine whether there is a balance-of-payments deficit or surplus.

☐ Use a supply and demand graph to illustrate how a flexible exchange-rate system works to establish the price and quantity of a currency.

☐ Describe the depreciation and appreciation of a nation's currency under a flexible exchange-rate system.

☐ Identify the five principal determinants of the demand for and supply of a particular foreign currency and explain how they alter exchange rates.

☐ Explain how flexible exchange rates eventually eliminate balance-of-payments deficits or surpluses.

☐ List three disadvantages of flexible exchange rates.

☐ Use a supply and demand graph to illustrate how a fixed exchange-rate system functions.

☐ Discuss the objectives and limitations of using official reserves, trade policies, exchange controls, and domestic macroeconomic adjustments to maintain a fixed exchange rate.

☐ Identify three different exchange-rate systems used by the world's nations in recent years.

☐ List three conditions a nation had to fulfill if it was to be on the gold standard.

☐ Explain how the gold standard worked to maintain fixed exchange rates.

☐ Give reasons for the collapse of the gold standard.

☐ Explain how the Bretton Woods system attempted to stabilize exchange rates and to establish orderly changes in exchange rates for correcting balance-of-payments deficits.

☐ State reasons for the demise of the Bretton Woods system.

☐ Describe the current system of managed floating exchange rates.

☐ Discuss the pros and cons of the system of managed floating exchange rates.

☐ Describe the causes of recent trade deficits in the United States.

☐ Explain the economic implications of recent trade deficits in the United States.

■ CHAPTER OUTLINE

1. Trade between two nations differs from domestic trade because the nations use different currencies. This problem is resolved by the existence of *foreign exchange markets,* in which the currency used by one nation can be purchased and paid for with the currency of the other nation.

   a. U.S. exports create a foreign demand for dollars, and the satisfaction of this demand increases the supply of foreign currencies in the foreign exchange market.

   b. U.S. imports create a domestic demand for foreign currencies, and meeting this demand decreases the supplies of foreign currencies in the foreign exchange market.

2. The *balance of payments* for a nation is an annual record of all its transactions with the other nations in the world; it records all the payments received from and made to the rest of the world.

   a. The *current account* section of a nation's balance of payments records its trade in currently produced goods and services. Within this section
   (1) the *balance on goods* of the nation is equal to its exports of goods less its imports of goods;
   (2) the *balance on goods and services* is equal to its exports of goods and services less its imports of goods and services; and
   (3) the *balance on the current account* is equal to its balance on goods and services plus its net investment income (dividends and interest) from other nations and its net private and public transfers to other nations. This balance may be either a surplus or a deficit.

   b. The *capital account* of a nation's balance of payments records foreign purchases of real and financial assets in the United States. This item earns the United States some foreign currencies, so it is entered as a plus (+) in the capital account. U.S. purchases of real and financial assets abroad draw down U.S. holdings of foreign currencies, so this item is entered as a minus (−) in the capital account. The nation has a surplus in its capital account if foreign purchases of U.S. assets are greater than U.S. purchases of assets abroad. The nation has a deficit in its capital account if foreign purchases of U.S. assets are less than U.S. purchases of assets abroad.

   c. The *official reserves* account consists of the foreign currencies owned by the central bank. These reserves *decrease* when they are used to finance a net deficit on the combined current and capital accounts. In this case, the official reserves show as a plus (+) in the balance-of-payments account. The reserves *increase* when a nation has a net surplus on its current and capital account. In this case, they show as a minus (−) in the balance-of-payments account. The three components of the balance of payments— the current account, the capital account, and the official reserves account—must equal zero.

   d. A nation has a *balance-of-payments deficit* when imbalances in the combined current and capital accounts lead to a decrease in official reserves. A *balance-of-payments surplus* arises when imbalances in the combined current and capital accounts result in an increase in official reserves.

3. There are both a flexible or floating exchange system and a fixed exchange-rate system that nations use to correct imbalances in the balance of payments. If nations use a *flexible or floating exchange system,* the demand for and the supply of foreign currencies determine foreign exchange rates. The exchange rate for any foreign

currency is the rate at which the quantity of that currency demanded is equal to the quantity of it supplied.

a. A change in the demand for or the supply of a foreign currency will cause a change in the exchange rate for that currency. When there is an increase in the price paid in dollars for a foreign currency, the dollar has *depreciated* and the foreign currency has *appreciated* in value. Conversely, when there is a decrease in the price paid in dollars for a foreign currency, the dollar has *appreciated* and the foreign currency has *depreciated* in value.

b. Changes in the demand for or supply of a foreign currency are largely the result of changes in tastes, relative incomes, relative price levels, relative interest rates, and speculation.

c. Flexible exchange rates can be used to eliminate a balance-of-payments deficit or surplus.

(1) When a nation has a payment deficit, foreign exchange rates will increase, thus making foreign goods and services more expensive and decreasing imports. These events will make a nation's goods and services less expensive for foreigners to buy, thus increasing exports.

(2) With a payment surplus, the exchange rates will increase, thus making foreign goods and services less expensive and increasing imports. This situation makes a nation's goods and services more expensive for foreigners to buy, thus decreasing exports.

d. Flexible exchange rates have disadvantages because they increase the uncertainties exporters, importers, and investors face, thus reducing international trade. This system also changes the terms of trade and creates instability in domestic economies.

4. If nations use a *fixed exchange-rate system,* the nations fix (or peg) foreign exchange rates. The governments of these nations must intervene in the foreign exchange markets to prevent shortages and surpluses caused by shifts in demand and supply.

a. One way a nation can stabilize foreign exchange rates is for its government to sell its reserves of a foreign currency in exchange for its own currency (or gold) when there is a shortage of the foreign currency. Conversely, a government would buy a foreign currency in exchange for its own currency (or gold) when there is a surplus of the foreign currency; however, currency reserves may be limited and inadequate for handling large and persistent deficits or surpluses, so it may use other means to maintain fixed exchange rates.

b. A nation might adopt trade policies that discourage imports and encourage exports.

c. A nation might impose exchange-rate controls and rationing, but these policies tend to distort trade, lead to government favoritism, restrict consumer choice, and create black markets.

d. Another way a nation can stabilize foreign exchange rates is to use monetary and fiscal policy to reduce its national income and price level and raise interest rates relative to those in other nations. These events would

lead to a decrease in demand for and increase in the supply of different foreign currencies.

5. In their recent history, the nations of the world have used three different exchange-rate systems.

a. Under the **gold standard,** each nation must define its currency in terms of a quantity of gold, maintain a fixed relationship between its gold and its money supply, and allow gold to be imported or exported without restrictions.

(1) The potential gold flows between nations would ensure that exchange rates remained fixed.

(2) Payment deficits and surpluses would be eliminated through macroeconomic adjustments. For example, if a nation had a balance-of-payments deficit and gold flowing out of the country, its money supply would decrease. This event would increase interest rates and decrease total spending, output, employment, and the price level. The opposite would happen in the other country because it would have a payments surplus. The changes in both nations would eliminate any payments deficit or surplus.

(3) During the worldwide depression of the 1930s nations felt that remaining on the gold standard threatened their recoveries, and the policy of devaluing their currencies to boost exports led to the breakdown and abandonment of the gold standard.

b. From the end of World War II until 1971, under the **Bretton Woods system,** nations were committed to the adjustable-peg system of exchange rates. The **International Monetary Fund (IMF)** was created to keep this exchange-rate system feasible and flexible.

(1) The adjustable-peg system required the United States to sell gold to other member nations at a fixed price and the other members of the IMF to define their monetary units in terms of either gold or dollars (which established fixed exchange rates among the currencies of all member nations) and required the other member nations to keep the exchange rates for their currencies from rising by selling foreign currencies, selling gold, or borrowing on a short-term basis from the IMF.

(2) The system also provided for orderly changes in exchange rates to correct a fundamental imbalance (persistent and sizable balance-of-payments deficits) by allowing a nation to devalue its currency (increase its defined gold or dollar equivalent).

(3) The other nations of the world used gold and dollars as their international monetary reserves in the Bretton Woods system. For these reserves to grow, the United States had to continue to have balance-of-payments deficits, but to continue the convertibility of dollars into gold it had to reduce the deficits, and, faced with this dilemma, in 1971 the United States suspended the convertibility of the dollar, brought an end to the Bretton Woods system, and allowed the exchange rates for the dollar and the other currencies to float.

c. Exchange rates today are allowed to float in the long term to correct balance-of-payments deficits and surpluses, but there can be short-term interventions by governments to stabilize and manage currencies. This new system of **managed floating exchange rates** is favored by some and criticized by others.

(1) Its proponents contend that this system has *not* led to any decrease in world trade, and has enabled the world to adjust to severe economic shocks throughout its history.

(2) Its critics argue that it has resulted in volatile exchange rates that can hurt those developing nations that are dependent on exports, has *not* reduced balance-of-payments deficits and surpluses, and is a "nonsystem" that a nation may use to achieve its own domestic economic goals.

6. The United States had large and persistent **trade deficits** in the past decade, and they are likely to continue.

a. These trade deficits were the result of several factors:

(1) more rapid growth in the domestic economy than in the economies of several major trading partners, which caused imports to rise more than exports;

(2) the emergence of large trade deficits with China;

(3) a decline in the rate of saving and a capital account surplus, which allowed U.S. citizens to consume more imported goods.

b. The trade deficits of the United States have had two principal effects: They increased current domestic consumption (allowing the nation to operate outside its production possibilities frontier), and they increased the indebtedness of U.S. citizens to foreigners. A possible negative implication of these persistent trade deficits is that they will lead to permanent debt and more foreign ownership of domestic assets, or lead to large sacrifices of future domestic consumption. But, if the foreign lending increases the U.S. capital stock, then it can contribute to long-term U.S. economic growth.

■ HINTS AND TIPS

1. The chapter is filled with many new terms, some of which are just special words used in international economics to mean things with which you are already familiar. Other terms are new to you, so you must spend time learning them if you are to understand the chapter.

2. The terms **depreciation** and **appreciation** can be confusing when applied to foreign exchange markets.

a. First, know the related terms. "Depreciate" means decrease or fall, whereas "appreciate" means increase or rise.

b. Second, think of depreciation or appreciation in terms of quantities:

(1) what *decreases* when the currency of Country A *depreciates* is the *quantity* of Country B's currency that can be purchased for *1 unit* of Country A's currency;

(2) what *increases* when the currency of Country A *appreciates* is the *quantity* of Country B's currency that can be purchased for *1 unit* of Country A's currency.

c. Third, consider the effect of changes in **exchange rates:**

(1) when the exchange rate for Country B's currency *rises*, this means that Country A's currency has

depreciated in value because 1 unit of Country A's currency will now purchase a smaller quantity of Country B's currency;

(2) when the exchange rate for Country B's currency *falls*, this means that Country A's currency has *appreciated* in value because 1 unit of Country A's currency will now purchase a larger quantity of Country B's currency.

3. The meaning of the balance of payments can also be confusing because of the number of accounts in the balance sheet. Remember that the balance of payments must always balance and sum to zero because one account in the balance of payments can be in surplus, but it will be offset by a deficit in another account. However, when people talk about a balance-of-payments surplus or deficit, they are referring to the sum of the current and capital account balances. If the total is positive, there is a balance-of-payments surplus, but if it is negative, there is a balance-of-payments deficit.

■ IMPORTANT TERMS

balance of payments	fixed exchange-rate system
current account	purchasing-power-parity theory
balance on goods and services	currency interventions
trade deficit	exchange controls
trade surplus	gold standard
balance on current account	devaluation
capital account	Bretton Woods system
balance on the capital account	International Monetary Fund (IMF)
official reserves	managed floating exchange rate
balance-of-payments deficit	
balance-of-payments surplus	
flexible or floating exchange-rate system	

SELF-TEST

■ FILL-IN QUESTIONS

1. The rate of exchange for the European euro is the amount in (euros, dollars) _____ that a U.S. citizen must pay to obtain 1 (euro, dollar) _____. The rate of exchange for the U.S. dollar is the amount in (euros, dollars) _____ that a citizen in the euro zone must pay to obtain 1 (euro, dollar) _____. If the rate of exchange for the euro is (1.05 euros, $0.95) _____, the rate of exchange for the U.S. dollar is _____.

2. U.S. exports create a foreign (demand for, supply of) _____ dollars and generate a

_____ foreign currencies owned by U.S. banks and available to domestic buyers; U.S. imports create a domestic (demand for, supply of) _____ foreign currencies and reduce the _____ foreign currencies held by U.S. banks and available for domestic consumers.

3. The balance of payments of a nation records all payments (domestic, foreign) _____ residents make to and receive from _____ residents. Any transaction that _earns_ foreign exchange for that nation is a (debit, credit) _____, and any transaction that _uses up_ foreign exchange is a _____. A debit is shown with a (+, −) _____ sign, and a credit is shown with a _____ sign.

4. If a nation has a deficit in its balance of goods, its exports of goods are (greater, less) _____ than its imports of goods, and if it has a deficit in its balance on goods and services, its exports of these items are _____ than its imports of them. The current account is equal to the balance on goods and services (plus, minus) _____ net investment income and _____ net transfers.

5. The capital account records the flow of payments from the sale or purchase of real or financial assets. Foreign purchases of real and financial assets in the United States earn foreign currencies, so they are entered as a (plus, minus) _____ in the U.S. capital account, but U.S. purchases of real and financial assets abroad draw down U.S. holding of foreign currencies, so this item is entered as a _____. If foreign purchases of U.S. assets are greater than U.S. purchases of assets abroad, the nation has a (surplus, deficit) _____ in its capital account, but if foreign purchases of U.S. assets are less than U.S. purchases of assets abroad, it has a _____.

6. A nation may finance a current account deficit by (buying, selling) _____ assets or by (borrowing, lending) _____ abroad and may use a current account surplus to (buy, sell) _____ assets or to (borrow, lend) _____ abroad.

7. The official reserves of a nation are the quantities of (foreign currencies, its own money) _____ owned by its central bank. If that nation has a deficit on the current and capital accounts, its official reserves (increase, decrease) _____, but with a surplus on the current and capital accounts, its official

reserves _____. The sum of the current, capital, and official reserves accounts must equal (0, 1) _____.

8. A nation has a balance-of-payments deficit if the sum of its current and capital accounts balances is (positive, negative) _____ and its official reserves (increase, decrease) _____. A nation has a payments surplus when the sum of its current and capital accounts balances is (positive, negative) _____ and its official reserves (increase, decrease) _____.

9. If foreign exchange rates float freely and a nation has a balance-of-payments _deficit,_ that nation's currency in the foreign exchange markets will (appreciate, depreciate) _____ and foreign currencies will _____ compared to it. As a result of these changes in foreign exchange rates, the nation's imports will (increase, decrease) _____, its exports will_____, and the size of its deficit will (increase, decrease) _____.

10. What effect would each of the following have—the appreciation (**A**) or depreciation (**D**) of the euro compared to the U.S. dollar in the foreign exchange market, _ceteris paribus?_

a. The increased preference in the United States for domestic wines over wines produced in Europe:

_____

b. A rise in the U.S. national income: _____

c. An increase in the price level in Europe: _____
d. A rise in real interest rates in the United States:

_____

e. The belief of speculators in Europe that the dollar will appreciate in the foreign exchange market:

_____

11. There are three disadvantages of freely floating foreign exchange rates: the risks and uncertainties associated with flexible rates tend to (expand, diminish) _____ trade between nations; when a nation's currency depreciates, its terms of trade with other nations are (worsened, improved) _____; and fluctuating exports and imports can (stabilize, destabilize) _____ an economy.

12. To fix or peg the rate of exchange for the Mexican peso when the exchange rate for the peso is rising, the United States would (buy, sell) _____ pesos in exchange for dollars, and when the exchange rate for the peso is falling, the United States would _____ pesos in exchange for dollars.

13. Under a fixed exchange-rate system, a nation with a balance-of-payments deficit might attempt to eliminate the deficit by (taxing, subsidizing) _____ imports or by _____ exports. The nation might use exchange controls and ration foreign exchange among those who wish to (export, import) _____ goods and services and require all those who _____ goods and services to sell the foreign exchange they earn to the (businesses, government) _____.

14. If the United States has a payments deficit with Japan and the exchange rate for the Japanese yen is rising, under a fixed exchange-rate system the United States might adopt (expansionary, contractionary) _____ fiscal and monetary policies to reduce the demand for the yen, but this would bring about (inflation, recession) _____ in the United States.

15. When the nations of the world were on the gold standard exchange, rates were relatively (stable, unstable) _____. When a nation had a payments deficit, gold flowed (into, out of) _____ the nation, its money supply (increased, decreased) _____, its interest rates _____, and output, employment, income, and perhaps prices (increased, decreased) _____; thus its payments deficit _____.

16. The Bretton Woods system was established to bring about (flexible, fixed) _____ exchange rates. Under the Bretton Woods system, a member nation defined its monetary unit in terms of (oil, gold) _____ or dollars. Each member nation stabilized the exchange rate for its currency and prevented it from depreciating by (supplying, saving) _____ its official reserves of foreign currency, by (buying, selling) _____ gold, or by (borrowing from, lending to) _____ the International Monetary Fund. A nation with a deeply rooted payments deficit could (devalue, revalue) _____ its currency. The system was designed so that in the short run exchange rates would be (stable, flexible) _____ enough to promote international trade and in the long run they would be _____ enough to correct balance-of-payments imbalances.

17. The role of the dollar as a component of international monetary reserves under Bretton Woods produced a dilemma. For the dollar to remain an acceptable international monetary reserve, the U.S. payments deficits had to be (eliminated, continued) _____, but for international monetary reserves to grow to accommodate world trade, the U.S. payments deficits had to be _____. These deficits caused an acceptability problem because they resulted in (a decrease, an increase) _____ in the foreign holding of U.S. dollars and _____ in the U.S. reserves of gold, which contributed to (a decrease, an increase) _____ in the ability of the United States to convert dollars into gold and the willingness of foreigners to hold dollars as if they were as good as gold. In 1971, the United States essentially ended this system when it (adopted, suspended) _____ the convertibility of dollars into gold and allowed the value of the dollar to be determined by markets.

18. Since then the international monetary system has moved to a system of managed (fixed, floating) _____ exchange rates. This means that exchange rates of nations are (restricted from, free to) _____ find their equilibrium market levels, but nations may occasionally (leave, intervene in) _____ the foreign exchange markets to stabilize or alter market exchange rates.

19. The advantages of the current system are that the growth of trade (was, was not) _____ accommodated and that it has survived much economic (stability, turbulence) _____. Its disadvantages are its (equilibrium, volatility) _____ and the lack of guidelines for nations that make it a (bureaucracy, nonsystem) _____.

20. In recent years, the United States had large trade and current account (surpluses, deficits) _____ that were brought about by the sharp increases in its (exports, imports) _____ and the small increases in its _____. One cause was (stronger, weaker) _____ economic growth in the United States relative to _____ economic growth in Europe and Japan. Another contributing factor was a (rising, falling) _____ saving rate. One effect of the trade deficits of the United States has been (decreased, increased) _____ current domestic consumption that allows the nation to operate outside its production possibility frontier, and another effect was a (rise, fall) _____ in the indebtedness of U.S. citizens to foreigners.

■ TRUE–FALSE QUESTIONS

Circle T if the statement is true, F if it is false.

1. The imports of goods and services by U.S. citizens from abroad create a supply of dollars in the foreign exchange market. **T F**

2. The balance of payments of the United States records all the payments its residents receive from and make to the residents of foreign nations. **T F**

3. Exports are a debit item and are shown with a minus sign (−), and imports are a credit item and are shown with a plus sign (+) in the balance of payments of a nation. **T F**

4. The United States would have a balance-of-payments surplus if the balances on its current and capital accounts were positive. **T F**

5. Any nation with a balance-of-payments deficit in its current and capital accounts must reduce its official reserves. **T F**

6. The sum of a nation's current account balance, its capital account balance, and the change in its official reserves in any year is always equal to zero. **T F**

7. The purchasing-power-parity theory basically explains why there is an inverse relationship between the price of dollars and the quantity demanded. **T F**

8. The expectations of speculators in the United States that the exchange rate for Japanese yen will fall in the future will increase the supply of yen in the foreign exchange market and decrease the exchange rate for the yen. **T F**

9. If a nation has a balance-of-payments deficit and exchange rates are flexible, the price of that nation's currency in the foreign exchange markets will fall; this will reduce its imports and increase its exports. **T F**

10. Were the United States' terms of trade with Nigeria to worsen, Nigeria would obtain a greater quantity of U.S. goods and services for every barrel of oil it exported to the United States. **T F**

11. If a nation wishes to fix (or peg) the foreign exchange rate for the Swiss franc, it must buy Swiss francs with its own currency when the rate of exchange for the Swiss franc rises. **T F**

12. If exchange rates are stable or fixed and a nation has a payments surplus, prices and currency incomes in that nation will tend to rise. **T F**

13. A nation using exchange controls to eliminate a balance-of-payments surplus might depreciate its currency. **T F**

14. If country A defined its currency as worth 100 grains of gold and country B defined its currency as worth 20 grains of gold, then, ignoring packing, insuring, and shipping charges, 5 units of country A's currency would be worth 1 unit of country B's currency. **T F**

15. Under the gold standard, the potential free flow of gold among nations would result in exchange rates that are fixed. **T F**

16. In the Bretton Woods system, a nation could not devalue its currency by more than 10% without the permission of the International Monetary Fund. **T F**

17. In the Bretton Woods system, a nation with persistent balance-of-payments surpluses had an undervalued currency and should have increased the pegged value of its currency. **T F**

18. To accommodate expanding world trade in the Bretton Woods system, the U.S. dollar served as a reserve medium of exchange and the United States ran persistent balance-of-payments deficits. **T F**

19. A basic shortcoming of the Bretton Woods system was its inability to bring about the changes in exchange rates needed to correct persistent payments deficits and surpluses. **T F**

20. Using the managed floating system of exchange rates, a nation with a persistent balance-of-payments surplus should allow the value of its currency in foreign exchange markets to decrease. **T F**

21. Two criticisms of the current managed floating exchange-rate system are its potential for volatility and its lack of clear policy rules or guidelines for nations to manage exchange rates. **T F**

22. The trade deficits of the United States in recent years were caused by sharp increases in U.S. exports and slight increases in U.S. imports. **T F**

23. Improved economic growth in the major economies of the major trading partners of the United States would tend to worsen the trade deficit. **T F**

24. The decline in the saving rate in the United States contributed to the persistent trade deficit of the past decade. **T F**

25. The negative net exports of the United States have increased the indebtedness of U.S. citizens to foreigners. **T F**

■ MULTIPLE-CHOICE QUESTIONS

Circle the letter that corresponds to the best answer.

1. If a U.S. citizen could buy £25,000 for $100,000, the rate of exchange for the pound would be
  (a) $40
  (b) $25
  (c) $4
  (d) $.25

2. U.S. residents demand foreign currencies to
  (a) produce goods and services exported to foreign countries
  (b) pay for goods and services imported from foreign countries
  (c) receive interest payments on investments in the United States
  (d) have foreigners make real and financial investments in the United States

3. Which of the following would be a credit in the current account?
  (a) U.S. imports of goods
  (b) U.S. exports of services

(c) U.S. purchases of assets abroad

(d) U.S. interest payments for foreign capital invested in the United States

4. A nation's balance on the current account is equal to its exports less its imports of
(a) goods and services
(b) goods and services, plus U.S. purchases of assets abroad
(c) goods and services, plus net investment income and net transfers
(d) goods and services, minus foreign purchases of assets in the United States

5. The net investment income of the United States in its international balance of payments is the
(a) interest income it receives from foreign residents
(b) dividends it receives from foreign residents
(c) excess of interest and dividends it receives from foreign residents over what it paid to them
(d) excess of public and private transfer payments it receives from foreign residents over what it paid to them

6. In a flexible- or floating-exchange-rate system, when the U.S. dollar price of a British pound rises, this means that the dollar has
(a) appreciated relative to the pound and the pound has appreciated relative to the dollar
(b) appreciated relative to the pound and the pound has depreciated relative to the dollar
(c) depreciated relative to the pound and the pound has appreciated relative to the dollar
(d) depreciated relative to the pound and the pound has depreciated relative to the dollar

7. Which statement is correct about a factor that causes a nation's currency to appreciate or depreciate in value?
(a) if the supply of a nation's currency decreases, all else equal, that currency will depreciate
(b) if the supply of a nation's currency increases, all else equal, that currency will depreciate
(c) if the demand for a nation's currency increases, all else equal, that currency will depreciate
(d) if the demand for a nation's currency decreases, all else equal, that currency will appreciate

8. Assuming exchange rates are flexible, which of the following should increase the dollar price of the Swedish krona?
(a) a rate of inflation greater in Sweden than in the United States
(b) real interest rate increases greater in Sweden than in the United States
(c) national income increases greater in Sweden than in the United States
(d) the increased preference of Swedish citizens for U.S. automobiles over Swedish automobiles

9. Under a flexible exchange-rate system a nation may be able to correct or eliminate a persistent (long-term) balance-of-payments deficit by
(a) lowering the barriers on imported goods
(b) reducing the international value of its currency

(c) expanding its national income
(d) reducing its official reserves

10. If a nation had a balance-of-payments surplus and exchange rates floated freely, the foreign exchange rate for its currency would
(a) rise, its exports would increase, and its imports would decrease
(b) rise, its exports would decrease, and its imports would increase
(c) fall, its exports would increase, and its imports would decrease
(d) fall, its exports would decrease, and its imports would increase

11. Which would be a result associated with the use of freely floating foreign exchange rates to correct a nation's balance-of-payments surplus?
(a) The nation's terms of trade with other nations would be worsened.
(b) Importers in the nation who had made contracts for the future delivery of goods would find that they had to pay a higher price than expected for the goods.
(c) If the nation were at full employment, the decrease in exports and the increase in imports would be inflationary.
(d) Exporters in the nation would find their sales abroad had decreased.

12. The use of exchange controls to eliminate a nation's balance-of-payments deficit results in decreasing the nation's
(a) imports
(b) exports
(c) price level
(d) income

13. Which of these conditions did a nation have to fulfill if it was to be under the gold standard?
(a) use only gold as a medium of exchange
(b) maintain a flexible relationship between its gold stock and its currency supply
(c) allow gold to be freely exported from and imported into the nation
(d) define its monetary unit in terms of a fixed quantity of dollars

14. If the nations of the world were on the gold standard and one nation had a balance-of-payments surplus,
(a) foreign exchange rates in that nation would rise
(b) gold would tend to be imported into that country
(c) the level of prices in that country would fall
(d) employment and output in that country would fall

15. Which was the principal disadvantage of the gold standard?
(a) unstable foreign exchange rates
(b) persistent payments imbalances
(c) the uncertainties and decreased trade that resulted from the depreciation of gold
(d) the domestic macroeconomic adjustments experienced by a nation with a payments deficit or surplus

16. The objective of the adjustable-peg or Bretton Woods system was exchange rates that were
   (a) adjustable in the short run and fixed in the long run
   (b) adjustable in both the short and the long run
   (c) fixed in both the short and the long run
   (d) fixed in the short run and adjustable in the long run

17. Which is the best definition of international monetary reserves in the Bretton Woods system?
   (a) gold
   (b) dollars
   (c) gold and dollars
   (d) gold, dollars, and British pounds

18. The major dilemma created by the persistent U.S. payments deficits under the Bretton Woods system was that in order to maintain the status of the dollar as an acceptable international monetary reserve, the deficits had to
   (a) decrease, but to expand reserves to accommodate world trade, the deficits had to continue
   (b) continue, but to expand reserves to accommodate world trade, the deficits had to be eliminated
   (c) increase, but to expand reserves to accommodate world trade, the deficits had to be reduced
   (d) decrease, but to expand reserves to accommodate world trade, the deficits had to be eliminated

19. "Floating" the dollar means
   (a) the value of the dollar is determined by the demand for and the supply of the dollar
   (b) the dollar price of gold has been increased
   (c) the price of the dollar has been allowed to crawl upward at the rate of one-fourth of 1% a month
   (d) the IMF decreased the value of the dollar by 10%

20. A system of managed floating exchange rates
   (a) allows nations to stabilize exchange rates in the short term
   (b) requires nations to stabilize exchange rates in the long term
   (c) entails stable exchange rates in both the short and long term
   (d) fixes exchange rates at market levels

21. Floating exchange rates
   (a) tend to correct balance-of-payments imbalances
   (b) reduce the uncertainties and risks associated with international trade
   (c) increase the world's need for international monetary reserves
   (d) tend to have no effect on the volume of trade

22. The trade problem that faced the United States in recent years was a
   (a) deficit in its capital account
   (b) surplus in its balance on goods
   (c) deficit in its current account
   (d) surplus in its current account

23. Which was a cause of the growth of U.S. trade deficits in recent years?
   (a) protective tariffs imposed by the United States
   (b) slower economic growth in the United States
   (c) direct foreign investment in the United States
   (d) a declining saving rate in the United States

24. What would be the effect on U.S. imports and exports when the United States experiences strong economic growth but its major trading partners experience sluggish economic growth?
   (a) U.S. imports will increase more than U.S. exports
   (b) U.S. exports will increase more than U.S. imports
   (c) U.S. imports will decrease but U.S. exports will increase
   (d) there will be no effect on U.S. imports and exports

25. Two major outcomes from the trade deficits of recent years were
   (a) decreased domestic consumption and U.S. indebtedness
   (b) increased domestic consumption and U.S. indebtedness
   (c) increased domestic consumption but decreased U.S. indebtedness
   (d) decreased domestic consumption but increased U.S. indebtedness

■ **PROBLEMS**

1. Assume a U.S. exporter sells $3 million worth of wheat to an importer in Colombia. If the rate of exchange for the Colombian peso is $.02 (2 cents), the wheat has a total value of 150 million pesos.
   a. There are two ways the importer in Colombia may pay for the wheat. It might write a check for 150 million pesos drawn on its bank in Bogotá and send it to the U.S. exporter.
   (1) The American exporter would then sell the check to its bank in New Orleans and its demand deposit there would increase by $_____ million.
   (2) This New Orleans bank now sells the check for 150 million pesos to a correspondent bank (a U.S. commercial bank that keeps an account in the Bogotá bank).
   (a) The New Orleans bank's account in the correspondent bank increases by _____ million (dollars, pesos) _____; and
   (b) the correspondent bank's account in the Bogotá bank increases by _____ million (pesos, dollars) _____.
   b. The second way for the importer to pay for the wheat is to buy from its bank in Bogotá a draft on a U.S. bank for $3 million, pay for this draft by writing a check for 150 million pesos drawn on the Bogotá bank, and send the draft to the U.S. exporter.
   (1) The U.S. exporter would then deposit the draft in its account in the New Orleans bank and its demand deposit account there would increase by $_____ million.

(2) The New Orleans bank collects the amount of the draft from the U.S. bank on which it is drawn through the Federal Reserve Banks.

(a) Its account at the Fed increases by $_____ million; and

(b) the account of the bank on which the draft was drawn decreases by $ _____ million.

c. Regardless of the way used by the Colombian importer to pay for the wheat,

(1) the export of the wheat created a (demand for, supply of) _____ dollars and a _____ pesos.

(2) The number of dollars owned by the U.S. exporter has (increased, decreased) _____ and the number of pesos owned by the Colombian importer has _____.

2. The following table contains hypothetical balance-of-payments data for the United States. All figures are in billions.

Current account

(1) U.S. goods exports	$+150	
(2) U.S. goods imports	−200	
(3) *Balance on goods*		_____
(4) U.S. exports of services	+75	
(5) U.S. imports of services	−60	
(6) *Balance on services*		_____
(7) *Balance on goods and services*		_____
(8) Net investment income	+12	
(9) Net transfers	−7	
(10) *Balance on current account*		_____

Capital account

(11) Foreign purchases of assets in the U.S.	+80	
(12) U.S. purchases of assets abroad	−55	
(13) *Balance on capital account*		_____
(14) *Current and capital account balance*		_____
(15) *Official reserves*		_____
		$ 0

a. Compute with the appropriate sign (+ or −) and enter in the table the seven missing items.

b. The United States had a payments (deficit, surplus) _____ of $ _____.

3. The following table shows supply and demand schedules for the British pound.

Quantity of pounds supplied	Price	Quantity of pounds demanded
400	$5.00	100
360	4.50	200
300	4.00	300
286	3.50	400
267	3.00	500
240	2.50	620
200	2.00	788

a. If the exchange rates are flexible

(1) what will be the rate of exchange for the pound?

$_____

(2) what will be the rate of exchange for the dollar?

£_____

(3) how many pounds will be purchased in the market?

_____

(4) how many dollars will be purchased in the market?

_____

b. If the U.S. government wished to fix or peg the price of the pound at $5.00, it would have to (buy, sell) _____ (how many) _____ pounds for $_____.

c. And if the British government wished to fix the price of the dollar at £ 2/5, it would have to (buy, sell) _____ (how many) _____ pounds for $_____.

■ **SHORT ANSWER AND ESSAY QUESTIONS**

1. What is the foreign exchange rate? Who are the demanders and suppliers of a particular foreign exchange, say, the British pound? Why is a buyer (demander) in the foreign exchange markets also always a seller (supplier)?

2. What is meant when it is said that "A nation's exports pay for its imports"? Do nations pay for all their imports with exports?

3. What is a balance of payments? What are the principal sections in a nation's balance of payments, and what are the principal "balances" to be found in it?

4. How can a nation finance a current account deficit, and what can it do with a current account surplus?

5. How does a nation finance a balance-of-payments deficit, and what does it do with a balance-of-payments surplus?

6. What types of events cause the exchange rate for a foreign currency to appreciate or to depreciate? How will each event affect the exchange rate for a foreign currency and for a nation's own currency?

7. How can flexible foreign exchange rates eliminate balance-of-payments deficits and surpluses? What are the problems associated with this method of correcting payments imbalances?

8. How may a nation use its international monetary reserves to fix or peg foreign exchange rates? Be precise. How does a nation obtain or acquire these monetary reserves?

9. What kinds of trade policies may nations with payments deficits use to eliminate their deficits?

10. How can foreign exchange controls be used to restore international equilibrium? Why do such exchange controls

necessarily involve the rationing of foreign exchange? What effect do these controls have on prices, output, and employment in nations that use them?

11. If foreign exchange rates are fixed, what kind of domestic macroeconomic adjustments are required to eliminate a payments deficit? To eliminate a payments surplus?

12. What is the gold standard? How did the international gold standard correct payments imbalances?

13. What were the disadvantages of the gold standard for eliminating payments deficits and surpluses?

14. What did nations use as international monetary reserves under the Bretton Woods system? Why was the dollar used by nations as international money, and how could they acquire additional dollars?

15. Explain the dilemma created by the need for expanding international monetary reserves and for maintaining the status of the dollar under the Bretton Woods system.

16. Why and how did the United States shatter the Bretton Woods system in 1971?

17. Explain what is meant by a managed floating system of foreign exchange rates. When are exchange rates managed and when are they allowed to float?

18. Explain the arguments of the proponents and the critics of the managed floating system.

19. What were the causes of the trade deficits of the United States in recent years?

20. What were the effects of the trade deficits of recent years on the U.S. economy?

ANSWERS

Chapter 25 Exchange Rates, the Balance of Payments, and Trade Deficits

FILL-IN QUESTIONS

1. dollars, euro, euros, dollar, $0.95, 1.05 euros
2. demand for, supply of, demand for, supply of
3. domestic, foreign, credit, debit, −, +
4. less, less, plus, plus
5. plus, minus, surplus, deficit
6. selling, borrowing, buy, lend
7. foreign currencies, decrease, increase, zero
8. negative, decrease, positive, increase
9. depreciate, appreciate, decrease, increase, decrease
10. *a.* D; *b.* A; *c.* D; *d.* D; *e.* D

11. diminish, worsened, destabilize
12. sell, buy
13. taxing, subsidizing, import, export, government
14. contractionary, recession
15. stable, out of, decreased, increased, decreased, decreased
16. fixed, gold, supplying, selling, borrowing from, devalue, stable, flexible
17. eliminated, continued, an increase, a decrease, a decrease, suspended
18. floating, free to, intervene in
19. was, turbulence, volatility, nonsystem
20. deficits, imports, exports, stronger, weaker, falling, increased, rise

TRUE–FALSE QUESTIONS

1. T, p. 468	10. T, p. 476	19. T, p. 480
2. T, p. 468	11. F, pp. 476–477	20. F, pp. 480–481
3. F, pp. 468–469	12. T, pp. 477–478	21. T, p. 481
4. T, pp. 468–469	13. F, p. 477	22. F, p. 482
5. T, p. 470	14. F, p. 478	23. F, p. 482
6. T, p. 470	15. T, pp. 478–479	24. T, p. 482
7. F, p. 473	16. T, pp. 479–480	25. T, p. 483
8. T, p. 474	17. T, pp. 479–480	
9. T, pp. 474–475	18. T, pp. 479–480	

MULTIPLE-CHOICE QUESTIONS

1. c, pp. 467–468	10. b, p. 475	19. a, p. 480
2. b, pp. 467–468	11. d, p. 476	20. a, pp. 480–481
3. b, pp. 468–469	12. a, p. 477	21. a, pp. 474–475, 481
4. c, pp. 468–469	13. c, p. 478	22. c, p. 482
5. c, p. 469	14. b, pp. 478–479	23. d, p. 482
6. c, p. 471	15. d, p. 479	24. a, p. 482
7. b, pp. 472–473	16. d, pp. 479–480	25. b, p. 483
8. b, p. 474	17. c, pp. 479–480	
9. b, pp. 474–475	18. a, p. 480	

PROBLEMS

1. *a.* (1) 3, (2) (a) 3, dollars, (b) 150, pesos; *b.* (1) 3, (2) (a) 3, (b) 3; *c.* (1) demand for, supply of, (2) increased, decreased
2. *a.* −50, +15, −35, −30, +25, −5, +5; *b.* deficit, 5
3. *a.* (1) 4.00, (2) 1/4, (3) 300, (4) 1200; *b.* buy, 300, 1500; *c.* sell, 380, 950

SHORT ANSWER AND ESSAY QUESTIONS

1. pp. 467–468	8. pp. 476–477	15. p. 480
2. pp. 467–468	9. p. 477	16. p. 480
3. pp. 468–470	10. p. 477	17. pp. 480–481
4. pp. 468–470	11. pp. 477–478	18. p. 481
5. pp. 468–471	12. pp. 478–479	19. p. 482
6. pp. 472–474	13. p. 479	20. p. 483
7. pp. 474–476	14. pp. 479–480	

Transition Economies: Russia and China

Note: The bonus web chapter is available at: www.mcconnell16.com.

In the years following the Russian Revolution of 1917, many people in the United States were convinced that the economic system of the Soviet Union was unworkable and that it would break down sooner or later—proof that Marx and Lenin were unrealistic dreamers—and that the reconversion of the Soviet economy to a market system would follow. Now, some 85 years after the revolution, the Russian economy is being transformed into a market economy and a democracy.

China is also undergoing a rapid transition from a centrally planned economy to a market-based economy, but its experience differs from that of Russia. The transition in China has been longer and more gradual. The economic outcomes have also been very positive, with strong economic growth, rising productivity, and a significantly increased standard of living; however, problems remain because the Communist party retains dictatorial political control and economic development is uneven throughout the country.

This chapter provides insights into the profound turn of events in both Russia and China. The first two sections of the chapter explain the basic ideas behind **Marxian ideology,** which gave rise to these command economies. They also discuss two basic institutional features of the former Soviet Union and prereform China: These economies operated under a system of state ownership of property resources; central planning was used to set prices, restrict consumption, and direct investment to heavy industry and the military.

Although central planning served as a powerful form of economic decision making in the former Soviet Union and prereform China, it had two serious problems, as you will discover in the third section. The first problem was one of **coordination,** which resulted in production bottlenecks and managers and bureaucrats missing production targets. Central planning also created an **incentive problem** because it sent out incorrect and inadequate signals for directing the efficient allocation of an economy's resources and gave workers little reason to work hard. The lack of incentives killed entrepreneurship and stifled innovation and technological advance.

The slowing of economic growth in the Soviet economy in the 1970s and 1980s set the stage for the failure of communism and the **collapse of its command economy.** Certainly other factors contributed to the economy's deterioration, as you will discover in the fourth section of the chapter. Production was of poor quality, and there were inadequate or limited consumer goods to meet consumer demands. The economy was overly burdened by government leaders' desire to support a large military. Agricultural inefficiencies were a drain on resources and restricted investment for other sectors of the economy.

The fifth section of the chapter explains the **five elements of market reform in the Russian economy** and its problems and prospects. The transition has led to the privatization of property resources, the promotion of competition, the decontrol of prices, and better connections to the international economy. The hyperinflation problem was solved by the establishment of a Russian central bank and the adoption of an anti-inflation monetary policy. Other problems continue to plague the economy. Real output, as well as living standards, fell significantly during the transition. Income inequality has grown, and government instability and social unrest have given organized crime the opportunity to flourish. In spite of these problems, Russia is likely to succeed in becoming an advanced market economy, but much work remains to be done.

The **market reform in China** is the focus of the sixth section of the chapter. As already noted, China's reform efforts differed significantly from those of Russia because they started earlier and have been more gradual and experimental. Partial decontrol of land and prices in agriculture unleashed the rural economy and made it more market oriented. State-owned enterprises are being consolidated and forced to become more competitive and operate like corporations. The formation of private businesses has been encouraged. New foreign investment is encouraged to help capital formation and to gain access to advanced technology.

The results from Chinese economic reforms have been impressive, as described in the final section of the chapter. The economy has grown at a 9% annual rate since 1978. The standard of living has risen fourfold and at a much faster rate than population growth. Nevertheless, China's transition to a market economy continues to face significant problems. Property rights are ill-defined. The economy has experienced periods of high inflation and is not well-integrated into the world economy. Economic development across the nation is uneven, and the average income remains low by DVC standards.

The transformations of Russian and Chinese economies into market economies are among the most important economic events of recent decades. The sweeping changes in these economies from centrally planned economies to market economies should deepen your understanding of the principles of economics and how the market system works. These dramatic developments are a fitting topic to conclude your study of economics.

■ **CHECKLIST**

When you have studied this chapter you should be able to

☐ Outline the key elements of Marxian ideology.

☐ Identify two institutional characteristics of the former Soviet Union (prior to collapse) and China (prior to its market reforms).

☐ Make seven generalizations about the central planning goals and techniques in the former Soviet Union and China.

☐ Compare how a market economy coordinates economic activity with how this works in a centrally planned economy.

☐ Explain how a market economy provides incentives and the problems with incentives in a centrally planned economy.

☐ Identify five factors that contributed to the collapse of the Soviet economy.

☐ List five factors that are important for the transition of Russia's economy to a market economy.

☐ Explain the effects of privatization in Russia.

☐ Use a supply and demand graph to discuss the difficulties that price reforms pose in the Russian transition.

☐ Describe the promotion of competition in Russia.

☐ Explain the importance of Russia joining the world economy by making the ruble fully convertible.

☐ Describe the need for price-level stabilization in Russia.

☐ Explain three other major problems the Russian economy has experienced during the transition.

☐ Evaluate the future prospects for Russia's transition to a market economy.

☐ Contrast China's path to market reforms with that of Russia.

☐ Describe agricultural and price reforms in China.

☐ Discuss the reform of urban industries and the use of special economic zones in China.

☐ Describe how the Chinese government has built supporting institutions and transformed state-owned enterprises.

☐ State the positive outcomes from the reform of the Chinese economy.

☐ Identify four significant problems in the Chinese transition to a market economy.

■ **CHAPTER OUTLINE**

1. The centrally planned economies of the former Soviet Union and prereform China were based on **Marxian ideology.** The government was viewed as a dictatorship of the proletariat (or working class) and the peasantry. Especially important was the Marxian concept of a **labor theory of value,** which held that only labor creates value in production and that profits are a **surplus value**

expropriated from workers by capitalists who, because of the institution of private property, were able to control the means of production (capital goods). The purpose of communism was to overthrow capitalism and end this exploitation of workers (and peasants) by eliminating private property and creating a classless society.

2. The two major institutional features of the precollapse Soviet and prereform Chinese economies were **state-owned enterprises** of all property resources and **central economic planning.** The command economy based most economic decisions on bureaucrats' choices rather than relying on market forces to direct economic activity.

   a. The central planning functioned differently in the former Soviet Union and prereform China.

   (1) The former Soviet Union attached great importance to rapid industrialization and military strength, whereas China emphasized rural development.

   (2) Each economy overcommitted its available resources, and often missed planning targets.

   (3) Each economy mobilized resources by increasing the quantity of resources rather than using given resources more productively.

   (4) Directives were used rather than markets and prices to allocate inputs for production in each economy.

   (5) Each government fixed and controlled prices.

   (6) Each economy emphasized self-sufficiency of the nation, viewed capitalist nations as hostile, and restricted trade.

   (7) Each economy passively used monetary and fiscal policies; unemployment was limited or disguised; the price level was controlled through government price fixing.

3. There were two basic problems with a centrally planned economy.

   a. The **coordination problem** involved the difficulty of coordinating the economy's many interdependent segments and avoiding the chain reaction that would result from a bottleneck in any one of the segments. This coordination problem became even more difficult as the economy grew larger and more complex, and more economic decisions had to be made in the production process. There were also inadequate measures of economic performance to determine the degree of success or failure of enterprises or to give clear signals to the economy.

   b. The **incentive problem** arose because in a command economy incentives are ineffective for encouraging economic initiatives and work and for directing the most efficient use of productive resources. In a market economy, profits and losses signal what firms should produce, how they should produce, and how productive resources should be allocated to best meet the wants of a nation. Central planning in the two economies also lacked entrepreneurship and stifled innovation, both of which are important forces for achieving long-term economic growth. Individual workers lacked much motivation to work hard because pay was limited and there were either few consumer goods to buy or they were of low quality.

4. The ***collapse of the Soviet economy*** stemmed largely from the failure of central economic planning.

a. Economic growth declined in the 1970s and 1980s. Real output also fell sharply in the few years before the country's breakup.

b. Technology in manufacturing lagged by western standards, and consumer goods were of poor quality.

c. Consumers received few material benefits from years of sacrifice for rapid industrialization and the military, and consumer goods were in short supply.

d. The large financial burden for military expenditures diverted valuable resources from the production of consumer and capital goods to military production.

e. Agriculture acted as a drag on economic growth and hurt productivity in other sectors of the economy.

5. The ***transition*** of the former Soviet Union, particularly Russia, from a centrally planned to a market economy is occurring in several ways.

a. A market economy relies on private property rights and limited government control of business. Private property rights were established to encourage entrepreneurship, and much government property was transferred to private ownership. This privatization was initially achieved through government distribution of vouchers that could be used to purchase businesses; it is now done through the direct sale of state enterprises. This change stimulated foreign investment and the flow of foreign capital to Russia; however, market reforms in agriculture have been limited.

b. Soviet government controls on prices led to a serious misallocation of resources and poor economic incentives. Most price controls were eliminated, about 90% in 1992, so prices for goods and services were free to change and reflect relative scarcities.

c. For a market economy to work properly, competition must be promoted by splitting up or restructuring large state-owned enterprises to reduce the potential for monopoly power from having one privatized business in an industry. Progress in this area was slow, but joint ventures and foreign investment stimulated more business competition in the Russian economy.

d. The Soviet economy was restricted from actively participating in international trade. Action was taken to open the economy to international trade and finance by making the ruble a convertible currency.

e. The transition to a market economy brought hyperinflation. Contributing factors included price decontrols, the ruble overhang (excess currency saved when there were few consumer goods to purchase), large government budget deficits, and the printing of money to finance the deficits. A Russian central bank was created, and an anti-inflation money policy was adopted to eliminate hyperinflation and keep prices relatively stable.

f. Several other major problems continued to affect the transition, especially during the early years.

(1) Real output and living standards fell during the reforms, although the decline bottomed out in 1992. Inflation, reduced international trade, bankruptcy and the closing of state enterprises, and the massive reallocation of resources and reductions in government and military spending precipitated the decline in output.

(2) Economic inequality and social costs increased during the transition. Market reforms enriched some groups and hurt others. Economic insecurity and instability resulting from the transition raised tensions among workers and other groups, reduced the quality of life and life expectancy, and stimulated the rise of organized crime and "crony" capitalism.

(3) The government has been weak in its enforcement of property rights and laws. It has also been unable or unwilling to collect the taxes necessary to finance basic government services.

g. Russia has "muddled through" its first decade of a transition to a market economy. The fall in real output ended by the late 1990s and economic growth has been robust since 1999. The rate of inflation has fallen to more manageable levels. The government has turned its large budget deficits into budget surpluses, and is providing the economic institutions necessary for an effective market economy. Market reforms have taken hold and the economy is prospering.

6. The path of ***market economic reforms in China*** differed significantly from that in Russia. China's market reforms began earlier and were more gradual and experimental. The Communist Party in China retained dictatorial control, while in Russia the party was replaced with democratic leadership. Russia has privatized much of the economy and sold off state enterprises, whereas China has protected its state enterprises while encouraging competing private enterprises. Russia experienced a significant decline in real output; China's output has continued to grow at high rates.

a. Agricultural reform in China began in 1978 with the leasing of land to individual farmers and permission to sell the output of the farms at competitive rather than government-controlled prices. This decollectivization and price reform provided a market basis for Chinese agriculture and the economy and released labor resources to private rural manufacturing firms (township and village enterprises).

b. Market reforms were also established in urban industries to give ***state-owned enterprises*** (SOEs) more control over production and employment. Enterprises could retain profits and sell more of their output at market prices rather than government-set prices. Urban collectives were formed that operated as private firms jointly owned by managers and workers. The collectives competed strongly with state enterprises and stimulated productivity in the economy.

c. ***Special enterprise zones*** were established that were open to foreign investment, private ownership, and international trade. They attracted foreign capital and increased Chinese exports. These areas undercut the support for central planning.

d. Supporting institutions have been developed to facilitate the transition to a market economy. The Chinese central bank was established to regulate the banking system and control the money supply. The enterprise tax system replaced the profit transfer from state enterprises. Foreign exchange can be swapped as needed between enterprises. A stock market has been established.

e. State-owned enterprises have been transformed; they operate more like corporations and respond to market needs rather than to social directives. The major SOEs have been consolidated into 1000 enterprises. Government plans call for stock to be issued and for the SOEs to become shareholder owned and operate like corporations, with the government retaining control. Other SOEs will be sold or permitted to go bankrupt.

7. There are positive outcomes from China's market-based reforms, but the transition to a market economy is still incomplete.

a. China has an impressive record of growth. It has averaged 9% growth annually since 1978, among the highest percentages on record for such a period. Real output and incomes have quadrupled in less than two decades. Capital formation increased productivity, and labor resources shifted from lower areas of productivity (agriculture) to higher areas of productivity (manufacturing). International trade expanded exports and the imports of critical consumer and capital goods. Foreign investment resulted in access to new technology that can be used to further increase productivity.

b. There are continuing economic problems in China's development.

(1) Property rights are incomplete because the privatization of farmland is opposed by the Communist Party, and such a policy leads to less investment in agriculture.

(2) There have been macroeconomic problems. Until the mid-1990s, China experienced high inflation during the years of rapid economic growth because the financial and monetary control system was weak. (The central bank has been given more control over interest rates and it now has inflation under control.) The financial and banking system is weak because substantial sums are owed by state-owned enterprises to banks. There is considerable unemployment and underemployment, especially in interior regions.

(3) Economic growth is geographically uneven throughout China. Hong Kong is now part of China and has high per capita income. Although people living in enterprise zones and the coastal areas near Hong Kong have experienced substantial growth in incomes and living standards, people in poorer regions still have low incomes. Overall, China is still considered a low-income developing country.

■ **HINTS AND TIPS**

1. This chapter applies your knowledge of economics to explain the transformation of Russia and China from centrally planned to market-oriented economies. Throughout this chapter you will be comparing a market economy with a command economy. Review Chapter 4 before you read this chapter to make sure you have a good understanding of how capitalism works and its major characteristics.

2. View the chapter as a culminating exercise in your study of economics that gives you a chance to *review, apply,* and *integrate* many of the economic concepts and ideas you learned from the text. Only a few terms and concepts will be new to you in this chapter (they apply to Marxian ideology or the reforms in China or Russia).

3. Supply and demand analysis is used to explain price controls in Figure 26W.1 in the text. The figure differs from those you saw in a previous chapter (Chapter 3) because there are two supply curves. One is vertical (perfectly inelastic) because it assumes fixed government control of production and no effect on quantity supplied as price controls are lifted. The upsloping supply curve shows an increase in quantity supplied as price controls are lifted.

■ **IMPORTANT TERMS**

labor theory of value	state-owned enterprises (SOEs)
surplus value	
state ownership	urban collectives
central economic planning	special economic zones (SEZs)
coordination problem	
incentive problem	
township and village enterprises	

SELF-TEST

■ **FILL-IN QUESTIONS**

1. The ideology behind the central planning in the former Soviet Union and prereform China was that the value of any commodity is determined by the amount of

(capital, labor) _____ required to produce it. In capitalist economies, capital was (privately, publicly)

_____ owned, and capitalists exploited workers by paying them a wage that was (greater than, less

than) _____ the value of their production and obtained (shortage, surplus) _____ value at the expense of workers.

2. In a communist economy, capital and other property resources would be (publicly, privately)

_____ owned and society would be (segregated, classless) _____. The Communist Party would serve as the representative of the (capitalists, proletariat) _____ and peasantry and would redistribute the surplus value of workers in the form

of (tax cuts, subsidies) _____ for public and quasi-public goods. In reality, the Communist Party was

(democratic, a dictatorship) _____.

3. One major institution of the former Soviet Union and prereform China was the ownership of property resources by (the state, property owners) _____. Another institutional feature was (central, decentralized) _____ economic planning.

4. Economic planning in the former Soviet Union and prereform China functioned in several ways. In the former Soviet Union, plans sought to achieve rapid (population growth, industrialization) _____ and provision of (civilian, military) _____ goods. In China, emphasis was on (urban, rural) _____ development. In both nations, the planning policies created an (over, under) _____-commitment of the economy's resources and resulted in an _____-production of goods for consumers.

5. Economic growth was achieved by (importing, mobilizing) _____ resources and by reallocating surplus labor from (industry, agriculture) _____ to _____. The government allocated inputs among industries by (prices, directives) _____, and the government set fixed _____ for goods and services and inputs.

6. Each nation also viewed itself as a (capitalist, socialist) _____ nation surrounded by hostile _____ nations, and central plans were designed to achieve economic (freedom, self-sufficiency) _____. Macroeconomic policies were (active, passive) _____.

7. Coordination and decision making in a market economy are (centralized, decentralized) _____, but in the Soviet and prereform Chinese economies it was _____. The market system tends to produce a reasonably (efficient, inefficient) _____ allocation of resources, but in centrally planned economies it was _____ and resulted in production bottlenecks and failures to meet many production targets. Central planning became (more, less) _____ complex and difficult as each economy grew and changed over time. Indicators of economic performance were (adequate, inadequate) _____ for determining the success or failure of economic activities.

8. Another problem with central planning was that economic incentives were (effective, ineffective) _____ for encouraging work or for giving signals to planners for efficient allocation of resources in the economy. The centrally planned system also lacked the (production

targets, entrepreneurship) _____ so important to technological advance. Innovation (fostered, lagged) _____ because there was no competition.

9. A number of factors contributed to the collapse of the Soviet economy. The economy experienced a (rise, decline) _____ in economic growth in the 1970s and 1980s. Consumer goods were of (good, poor) _____ quality, and there were widespread (shortages, surpluses) _____. There was a large (consumer, military) _____ burden on the economy that diverted resources from the production of (consumer, investment) _____ goods. Agriculture was (efficient, inefficient) _____ and (helped, hurt) _____ economic growth and productivity in other sectors of the economy.

10. The Russian transition to a market economy has resulted in major reforms. Property rights have been (revoked, established) _____, and government property has been transferred to (foreign, private) _____ ownership. In Soviet Russia, the prices of goods and services were kept at low levels through price (competition, controls) _____, so the marginal cost of a product (was, was not) _____ equal to its marginal benefit. This pricing policy led to (efficient, inefficient) _____ use of resources to make products and to (surpluses, shortages) _____ of many consumer goods. Today, most prices in Russia are (still fixed, free to vary) _____.

11. Russia is also promoting competition by (forming, dismantling) _____ state-owned enterprises to reduce the potential for (rivalry, monopoly) _____. Russia has (opened, closed) _____ the economy to international trade and finance. One example of this policy is making the ruble a (fixed, convertible) _____ currency on international markets.

12. The Russian transition to a market economy was accompanied by (inflation, deflation) _____. It occurred because of price (controls, decontrols) _____, a ruble (under, over) _____ hang, and government budget (surpluses, deficits) _____. In response to this problem, the nation created an independent central (account, bank) _____ to provide control over (fiscal, monetary) _____ policy.

13. Major problems affected Russia's transition, especially in the early years. There was a (falling, rising) _____ level of real output and a _____ standard of living. Economic inequality also (increased, decreased) _____ and led to _____ economic security and (increased, decreased) _____ corruption and crime. Government provided (strong, weak) _____ enforcement of laws and was _____ in its actions to collect taxes. But in recent years the Russian economy has revived with (strong, weak) _____ levels of economic growth, (higher, lower) _____ levels of inflation, and a more effective government.

14. Compared with Russia, China's market reforms began (later, earlier) _____ and were more (rapid, gradual) _____. China asserts that communist dictatorship and markets are (incompatible, compatible) _____, while Russia views them as _____. China instituted its market reforms and experienced (growth, depression) _____, while Russia experienced _____ in its transition to a market economy. Russia (sold, protected) _____ state enterprises, while China _____ them but encouraged competing private enterprises.

15. Agricultural reform in China began in 1978 with the (selling, leasing) _____ of land to individual farmers and permission for _____ the agriculture products at (market, government) _____ prices. The reform released (capital, labor) _____ resources to private rural manufacturing firms called township and village enterprises.

16. Market reforms were also established in Chinese urban industries to give state-owned enterprises (less, more) _____ decision making about production and employment. Urban (cartels, collectives) _____ were formed that operated as private firms jointly owned by managers and workers. The competition of state and nonstate enterprises (increased, decreased) _____ productivity and innovation in the economy.

17. China created special economic zones that were (open, closed) _____ to foreign investment, private ownership, and international trade. A Chinese central bank was established to regulate the (trading, banking) _____ system and control the (import, money) _____ supply. Profit transfers from state enterprises to the central government were replaced with an enterprise (spending, tax) _____ system. Foreign exchange can be (hoarded, swapped) _____ as needed between enterprises.

18. There has been a transformation of Chinese state-owned enterprises (SOEs). They operate more like (bureaucracies, corporations) _____ and respond to (social directive, the market) _____. Plans call for the major 100 SOEs to issue (money, stock) _____ and operate more like corporations under government control. Other smaller SOEs will be (bought, sold) _____ by the government or permitted to go bankrupt.

19. The transition to a market economy in China shows positive outcomes. Economic growth in China averaged (2, 9) _____% annually since 1978. Real output and income have (doubled, quadrupled) _____ in less than two decades. China's real GDP and real income have grown much (more, less) _____ rapidly than its population.

20. Problems remain with China's transition. Privatization of farmland is (supported, opposed) _____ by the Communist Party, and this policy leads to (more, less) _____ investment in agriculture. Substantial sums are (paid, owed) _____ by state-owned enterprises to the banking system. China (is, is not) _____ fully integrated into the world economy. Economic growth is (even, uneven) _____, and China is still considered a (low, middle) _____-income developing country.

■ **TRUE–FALSE QUESTIONS**

Circle T if the statement is true, F if it is false.

1. The labor theory of value is the Marxian idea that the value of any good is determined solely by the amount of labor required for its production.   **T F**

2. Surplus value in Marxian ideology is the value or price of a commodity at equilibrium in a competitive market.   **T F**

3. The economies of the former Soviet Union and pre-reform China were characterized by state ownership of resources and authoritarian central planning.   **T F**

4. The former Soviet Union was dedicated to the task of rapid industrialization and building economic self-sufficiency.   **T F**

5. Preform China emphasized rural economic development. **T F**

6. Economic resources tended to be undercommitted in both the former Soviet Union and prereform China. **T F**

7. Both the former Soviet Union and prereform China actively used monetary and fiscal policies to manipulate levels of employment, output, and prices. **T F**

8. A centrally planned economy is significantly affected by missed production targets and bottlenecks. **T F**

9. The problems of central planning become easier and less complex as an economy grows over time. **T F**

10. Profit is the key indicator of success and failure in a centrally planned economy. **T F**

11. Central planning provided weak or inaccurate incentives for allocating resources to achieve economic efficiency and encourage hard work. **T F**

12. Centrally planned economies encourage entrepreneurship and technological advance under the directive of the Communist Party. **T F**

13. In the former Soviet Union, greater productivity and technological progress in the civilian sector were often sacrificed or limited by the demands to support a large military. **T F**

14. As part of the transition to a market economy, Russia has taken major steps to privatize its economy and establish property rights. **T F**

15. Price decontrol was a minor problem in the conversion of the Russian economy to capitalism because the prices the Soviet government established over the years were very similar to the economic values established in a competitive market. **T F**

16. The transition to a market economy in Russia has required the breakup of large industries and coordinated actions to promote competition. **T F**

17. A major accomplishment during the Russian transition to a market economy was limited inflation because of balanced budgets and a tight control of the money supply. **T F**

18. Two major problems Russia experienced during its transition to capitalism were a decline in the standard of living and increased economic inequality. **T F**

19. The Chinese economy used a "shock" approach to economic reform to make its transition to a market economy. **T F**

20. Collectivization and price controls were instrumental in strengthening production incentives and moving the Chinese economy toward a market-based agriculture. **T F**

21. The Chinese government has encouraged the formation of nonstate enterprises, called urban collectives, which are jointly owned by workers and managers. **T F**

22. China has created special economic zones that are open to foreign investment, private ownership, and international trade. **T F**

23. A major limitation of Chinese economic reform is the failure to create a stock market for the exchange of shares of newly created corporations. **T F**

24. China's economic growth has declined over the past two decades because of the instability caused by its economic reforms. **T F**

25. One continuing economic problem in China is the uneven regional economic development. **T F**

■ MULTIPLE-CHOICE QUESTIONS

Circle the letter that corresponds to the best answer.

1. Which was an element in Marxian ideology?
  (a) the creation of surplus value by government
  (b) dictatorship over the business class
  (c) the private ownership of property
  (d) the labor theory of value

2. Marxian ideology was highly critical of capitalist societies because in those societies capitalists
  (a) reduced the productivity of workers by not investing their profits in new capital goods
  (b) paid workers a wage that was less than the value of their production
  (c) shared surplus value with the government
  (d) were not taxed as much as the workers

3. The institution that was most characteristic of the former Soviet Union and prereform China was
  (a) private ownership of property
  (b) authoritarian central planning
  (c) a system of markets and prices
  (d) consumer sovereignty

4. Industrialization, rapid economic growth, and military strength in the former Soviet Union and prereform China were primarily achieved by
  (a) mobilizing larger quantities of resources
  (b) joining the international economy
  (c) making currencies convertible
  (d) using an easy-money policy

5. Both the former Soviet Union and prereform China viewed themselves as socialist nations surrounded by hostile capitalist nations, and as a consequence central planning stressed the need for
  (a) hoarding gold
  (b) flexible prices
  (c) consumer sovereignty
  (d) economic self-sufficiency

6. In the former Soviet Union and prereform China, monetary policy
  (a) was active and fiscal policy was passive
  (b) was passive and fiscal policy was active
  (c) and fiscal policy were both passive
  (d) and fiscal policy were both active

7. In the system of central planning, the outputs of some industries became the inputs for other industries, but a failure of one industry to meet its production target would cause
(a) widespread unemployment
(b) inflation in wholesale and retail prices
(c) profit declines and potential bankruptcy of firms
(d) a chain reaction of production problems and bottlenecks

8. What was the major success indicator for Soviet and Chinese state enterprises?
(a) profits
(b) the level of prices
(c) production targets
(d) the enterprise tax

9. The centrally planned system in the former Soviet Union and prereform China lacked
(a) price controls
(b) entrepreneurship
(c) economic growth
(d) allocation by directives

10. In the last year or two before the Soviet economic system collapsed, real output
(a) increased slightly
(b) decreased significantly
(c) remained relatively constant
(d) increased faster than the rate of population growth

11. Which was evidence of the Soviet economy's economic failure?
(a) a tight monetary policy
(b) an oversupply of most products
(c) the poor quality of consumer goods
(d) higher productivity in agriculture than industry

12. What was the size of expenditures for the military as a percentage of domestic output in the former Soviet Union (**SU**) and the United States (**U.S.**)?

	SU %	U.S. %
(a)	26 – 30	18
(b)	21 – 25	12
(c)	15 – 20	6
(d)	10 – 14	3

13. Which was a cause of low productivity in agriculture in the former Soviet Union?
(a) inability to fertilize and weed the abundance of good farmland in the country
(b) failure to construct an effective incentive system for agriculture
(c) increase in the length of the growing season
(d) overuse of certain chemical fertilizers on crops

14. Which helped Russia make a transition to a market economy?
(a) ruble overhang
(b) price controls
(c) privatization
(d) hyperinflation

15. The effect of price controls on most consumer goods in the former Soviet Union was that
(a) surpluses developed because the quantity consumers demanded was greater than the quantity supplied at the price set by government
(b) prices fell because the quantity consumers demanded was greater than the quantity supplied
(c) prices rose because the quantity consumers demanded was less than the quantity supplied
(d) shortages developed because the quantity consumers demanded was greater than the quantity supplied at the price set by government

16. Which set of factors most likely contributed to hyperinflation as Russia made its transition to a market economy?
(a) the breakup of state monopolies, land reform, and the poor quality of consumer goods
(b) increased military spending, investment in new technology, and the convertibility of the ruble
(c) central planning, production targets, and production bottlenecks
(d) government deficits, the ruble overhang, and price decontrols

17. Which two significant problems did Russia encounter in its transition to a market system?
(a) rising taxes and increasing life expectancies
(b) a loose monetary policy and a strict fiscal policy
(c) falling real output and declining living standards
(d) greater military spending and more environmental pollution

18. Compared with Russia, market reforms in China
(a) occurred over a longer time and were more gradual
(b) focused primarily on industry rather than agriculture
(c) relied more on monetary policy than fiscal policy
(d) were less successful and more disruptive

19. The key elements of the 1978–1984 rural economic reforms in China were
(a) passive macroeconomic policies
(b) formations of special economic zones
(c) foreign investment and loans to state-owned enterprises
(d) decollectivization and creation of a two-track price system

20. Privately owned rural manufacturing firms in China are called
(a) township and village enterprises
(b) special economic zones
(c) incentive collectives
(d) farm cooperatives

21. Chinese enterprises in urban areas that are jointly owned by their managers and workers are
(a) industrial unions
(b) urban collectives
(c) business operating units
(d) manufacturing cooperatives

22. Which would be a supporting institution for market reform in China?

(a) a price control authority
(b) a profit transfer system
(c) a farm collective
(d) a central bank

23. Since market reforms began, real output and real income in China have

(a) doubled
(b) tripled
(c) quadrupled
(d) quintupled

24. The shift of employment from agriculture toward rural and urban manufacturing in China has increased

(a) inflation
(b) productivity
(c) bankruptcies
(d) unemployment

25. One significant problem China faces in its transition to a market economy is

(a) establishing a stock market
(b) establishing a central bank
(c) incomplete privatization of land
(d) creation of special economic zones

■ **PROBLEMS**

1. In the following table are several major institutions and characteristics of a capitalistic economy, such as that in the United States, and a centrally planned economy, such as that in the former Soviet Union or prereform China. In the appropriate space, name the corresponding institution or characteristic of the other economy.

Capitalist institution or characteristic	Socialist institution or characteristic
a. _____	labor theory of value
b. _____	surplus value
c. private ownership of economic resources	_____
d. a market economy	_____
e. _____	state-owned enterprises
f. privately owned farms	_____
g. _____	government price controls
h. _____	passive macroeconomic policies
i. representative democracy	_____

2. Answer the following set of questions based on the table in the next column. The columns show the price, quantity demanded Q_d by consumers, and a fixed quantity supplied by government Q_{s1} for a product in the former Soviet Union. The column for Q_{s2} shows the supply curve

for the product after privatization in the industry producing the product.

Price (in rubles)	Q_d	Q_{s1}	Q_{s2}
90	25	25	55
80	30	25	50
70	35	25	45
60	40	25	40
50	45	25	35
40	50	25	30
30	55	25	25

a. When only the government supplies the product as shown in the Q_{s1} schedule, the equilibrium price will be _____ rubles and the equilibrium quantity will be _____ units.

b. If the government tries to make the product more accessible to lower-income consumers by setting the price at 30 rubles, then the quantity demanded will be _____ units and the quantity supplied will be _____ units, producing a shortage of _____ units.

c. If the government decontrolled prices but did not privatize industry, then prices would rise to _____ rubles and the government would still produce _____ units.

d. With privatization, there will be a new quantity supplied schedule (Q_{s2}). The equilibrium price will be _____ rubles and the equilibrium quantity will be _____ units. The equilibrium price has risen by _____ rubles and the equilibrium quantity by _____ units.

3. Match the terms from China's economic reform with the phrase using the appropriate number.

1. special economic zone   4. town and village enterprises
2. urban collective   5. enterprise tax system
3. two-track price system   6. state-owned enterprise

a. Privately-owned rural manufacturing firms _____

b. Replaced the system of profit transfers from state enterprises to the central government _____

c. Areas in coastal regions that are open to foreign investment, private ownership, and international trade

_____

d. Nonstate enterprises jointly owned by managers and their work forces in urban areas _____

e. Gives farmers ability to sell output at market-determined prices _____

f. Enterprises that are controlled by the government

_____

■ SHORT ANSWER AND ESSAY QUESTIONS

1. What are the essential features of Marxian ideology on which the Soviet Union's command economy was based?

2. What were the two principal economic institutions of the prereform and precollapse economies of China and Russia? How do these institutions compare with those in the United States?

3. Describe how central planning functioned in the former Soviet Union and prereform China. What generalizations can you make about resource use, directives, prices, self-sufficiency, and macroeconomic policies?

4. Why does central planning result in a coordination problem? Compare the operation of central planning with the use of markets and prices for economic decision making.

5. How does central economic planning produce a significant incentive problem? What types of economic incentives for business, workers, and consumers exist in a market economy? How are those incentives different in a centrally planned economy?

6. Discuss the five factors that help explain or contributed to the collapse of the Soviet economy.

7. What action has Russia taken to privatize the economy?

8. Why was there a need for price reform in Russia in its transition to a market economy? What has been the *general* effect of this change? Use a supply and demand graph to explain the effect of the price decontrol on a specific product.

9. Discuss what is being done in Russia to promote competition. To what extent are public monopolies a problem?

10. What major problem is confronting Russia as it seeks to join the world economy?

11. How have high rates of inflation affected Russia's transition to a market economy? What has been the shift in macroeconomic policy?

12. What other major problems has Russia encountered in its transition to a market economy?

13. Evaluate the prospects for the transformation of Russia into a market economy.

14. How did China's approach to market reforms differ from that in Russia?

15. Describe how China has tried to transform agriculture and rural production.

16. What market-based changes has the Chinese government made in urban industries?

17. What actions has the Chinese government taken to encourage foreign investment and establish institutions that support a market-based economy?

18. Describe the economic transformation of state-owned enterprises in China.

19. What are the positive outcomes of China's economic reform?

20. Discuss four significant economic problems that China continues to face in its transition to a market economy.

ANSWERS

Chapter 26 Web: Transition Economies: Russia and China

FILL-IN QUESTIONS

1. labor, privately, less than, surplus
2. publicly, classless, proletariat, subsidies, a dictatorship
3. the state, central
4. industrialization, military, rural, over, under
5. mobilizing, agriculture, industry, directives, prices
6. socialist, capitalist, self-sufficiency, passive
7. decentralized, centralized, efficient, inefficient, more, inadequate
8. ineffective, entrepreneurship, lagged
9. decline, poor, shortages, military, consumer, inefficient, hurt
10. established, private, controls, was not, inefficient, shortages, free to vary
11. dismantling, monopoly, opened, convertible
12. inflation, decontrols, over, deficits, bank, monetary
13. falling, falling, increased, decreased, increased, weak, weak, strong, lower
14. earlier, gradual, compatible, incompatible, growth, depression, sold, protected
15. leasing, selling, market, labor
16. more, collectives, increased
17. open, banking, money, tax, swapped
18. corporations, the market, stock, sold
19. 9, quadrupled, more
20. opposed, less, owed, is not, uneven, low

Note: Page numbers for True–False, Multiple Choice, and Short Answer and Essay Questions refer to Bonus Web Chapter 26.

TRUE–FALSE QUESTIONS

1. T, pp. 1–2	10. F, pp. 4–5	19. F, p. 10
2. F, p. 2	11. T, pp. 4–5	20. F, pp. 10–11
3. T, p. 2	12. F, p. 5	21. T, p. 11
4. T, pp. 2–3	13. T, p. 6	22. T, p. 11
5. T, pp. 2–3	14. T, pp. 6–7	23. F, pp. 12–13
6. F, p. 3	15. F, p. 7	24. F, p. 12
7. F, p. 3	16. T, p. 8	25. T, p. 13
8. T, p. 4	17. F, p. 8	
9. F, p. 4	18. T, p. 9	

MULTIPLE-CHOICE QUESTIONS

1. d, p. 2	10. b, p. 6	19. d, pp. 10–11
2. b, p. 2	11. c, p. 6	20. a, p. 10
3. b, p. 2	12. c, p. 6	21. b, pp. 10–11
4. a, p. 3	13. b, p. 6	22. d, p. 11
5. d, p. 3	14. c, pp. 6–7	23. c, p. 12
6. c, p. 3	15. d, p. 7	24. b, p. 12
7. d, p. 4	16. d, p. 8	25. c, pp. 12–13
8. c, pp. 4–5	17. c, p. 9	
9. b, pp. 4–5	18. a, p. 10	

PROBLEMS

1. *a.* supply and demand; *b.* profit; *c.* state ownership of resources; *d.* command or centrally planned economy; *e.* corporations; *f.* collective farms or agricultural cooperatives; *g.* competitive markets and flexible prices; *h.* active or discretionary macroeconomic policies; *i.* dictatorship by the Communist Party
2. *a.* 90, 25; *b.* 55, 25, 30; *c.* 90, 25; *d.* 60, 40, 30, 15
3. *a.* 4; *b.* 5; *c.* 1; *d.* 2; *e.* 3; *f.* 6

SHORT ANSWER AND ESSAY QUESTIONS

1. pp. 1–2
2. p. 2
3. pp. 2–3
4. p. 4
5. pp. 4–5
6. pp. 5–6
7. pp. 6–7
8. pp. 7–8
9. p. 8
10. p. 8
11. p. 8
12. p. 9
13. pp. 9–12
14. p. 10
15. pp. 10–11
16. pp. 10–11
17. p. 11
18. p. 11
19. pp. 11–12
20. pp. 12–13

Glossary

Note: Terms set in *italic* type are defined separately in this glossary.

ability-to-pay principle   The idea that those who have greater *income* (or *wealth*) should pay a greater proportion of it as taxes than those who have less income (or wealth).

abstraction   Elimination of irrelevant and noneconomic facts to obtain an *economic principle*.

acreage allotment program   A pre-1996 government program that determined the total number of acres to be used in producing (reduced amounts of) various food and fiber products and allocated these acres among individual farmers. These farmers had to limit their plantings to the allotted number of acres to obtain *price supports* for their crops.

adjustable pegs   The device used in the *Bretton Woods system* to alter *exchange rates* in an orderly way to eliminate persistent payments deficits and surpluses. Each nation defined its monetary unit in terms of (pegged it to) gold or the dollar, kept the *rate of exchange* for its money stable in the short run, and adjusted its rate in the long run when faced with international payments disequilibrium.

adverse selection problem   A problem arising when information known to one party to a contract or agreement is not known to the other party, causing the latter to incur major costs. Example: Individuals who have the poorest health are most likely to buy health insurance.

advertising   A seller's activities in communicating its message about its product to potential buyers.

affirmative action   Policies and programs that establish targets of increased employment and promotion for women and minorities.

AFL-CIO   An acronym for the American Federation of Labor– Congress of Industrial Organizations; the largest federation of *labor unions* in the United States.

agency shop   A place of employment where the employer may hire either *labor union* members or nonmembers but where those who do not join the union must either pay union dues or donate an equivalent amount of money to a charity.

Alcoa case   A 1945 case in which the courts ruled that the possession of monopoly power, no matter how reasonably that power had been used, was a violation of the antitrust laws; temporarily overturned the *rule of reason* applied in the *U.S. Steel case*.

allocative efficiency   The apportionment of resources among firms and industries to obtain the production of the products most wanted by society (consumers); the output of each product at which its *marginal cost* and *price* or *marginal benefit* are equal.

antitrust laws   Legislation (including the *Sherman Act* and *Clayton Act*) that prohibits anticompetitive business activities such as *price fixing,* bid rigging, monopolization, and *tying contracts*.

antitrust policy   The use of the *antitrust laws* to promote *competition* and economic efficiency.

appreciation (of the dollar)   An increase in the value of the dollar relative to the currency of another nation, so a dollar buys a larger amount of the foreign currency and thus of foreign goods.

asset   Anything of monetary value owned by a firm or individual.

asymmetric information   A situation where one party to a market transaction has much more information about a product or service than the other. The result may be an under- or overallocation of resources.

average fixed cost   A firm's total *fixed cost* divided by output (the quantity of product produced).

average product   The total output produced per unit of a resource employed (*total product* divided by the quantity of that employed resource).

average revenue   Total revenue from the sale of a product divided by the quantity of the product sold (demanded); equal to the price at which the product is sold when all units of the product are sold at the same price.

average tax rate   Total tax paid divided by total (taxable) income, as a percentage.

average total cost   A firm's *total cost* divided by output (the quantity of product produced); equal to *average fixed cost* plus *average variable cost*.

average variable cost   A firm's total *variable cost* divided by output (the quantity of product produced).

backflows   The return of workers to the countries from which they originally migrated.

balance of payments   (See *international balance of payments*.)

balance-of-payments deficit   The amount by which the sum of the *balance on current account* and the *balance on capital account* is negative in a year.

balance-of-payments surplus   The amount by which the sum of the *balance on current account* and the *balance on capital account* is positive in a year.

balance on capital account   The foreign purchases of assets in the United States less American purchases of assets abroad in a year.

balance on current account   The exports of goods and services of a nation less its imports of goods and services plus its *net investment income* and *net transfers* in a year.

balance on goods and services   The exports of goods and services of a nation less its imports of goods and services in a year.

barrier to entry   Anything that artificially prevents the entry of firms into an industry.

barter   The exchange of one good or service for another good or service.

benefit-reduction rate   The percentage by which subsidy benefits in a *public assistance program* are reduced as earned income rises.

benefits-received principle   The idea that those who receive the benefits of goods and services provided by government should pay the taxes required to finance them.

bilateral monopoly   A market in which there is a single seller *(monopoly)* and a single buyer *(monopsony)*.

bond   A financial device through which a borrower (a firm or government) is obligated to pay the principal and interest on a loan at a specific date in the future.

break-even income   The level of *disposable income* at which *households* plan to consume (spend) all their income and to save none of it; also, in an income transfer program, the level of earned income at which subsidy payments become zero.

break-even output   Any output at which a (competitive) firm's *total cost* and *total revenue* are equal; an output at which a firm has neither an *economic profit* nor a loss, at which it earns only a normal profit.

Bretton Woods system   The international monetary system developed after the Second World War in which *adjustable pegs* were employed, the *International Monetary Fund* helped stabilize foreign exchange rates, and gold and the dollar were used as *international monetary reserves.*

budget constraint   The limit that the size of a consumer's income (and the prices that must be paid for goods and services) imposes on the ability of that consumer to obtain goods and services.

budget line   A line that shows the different combinations of two products a consumer can purchase with a specific money income, given the products' prices.

business firm   (See *firm*.)

business unionism   Labor unionism that concerns itself with such practical and short-run objectives as higher wages, shorter hours, and improved working conditions.

capital   Human-made resources (buildings, machinery, and equipment) used to produce goods and services; goods that do not directly satisfy human wants; also called capital goods.

capital account   The section of a nation's *international balance-of-payments* statement that records the foreign purchases of assets in the United States (creating monetary inflows) and U.S. purchases of assets abroad (creating monetary outflows).

capital account deficit   A negative *balance on capital account.*

capital account surplus   A positive *balance on capital account.*

capital gain   The gain realized when securities or properties are sold for a price greater than the price paid for them.

capital goods   (See *capital*.)

capital-intensive commodity   A product that requires a relatively large amount of *capital* to be produced.

capitalism   An economic system in which property resources are privately owned and markets and prices are used to direct and coordinate economic activities.

capital stock   The total available *capital* in a nation.

cartel   A formal agreement among firms (or countries) in an industry to set the price of a product and establish the outputs of the individual firms (or countries) or to divide the market for the product geographically.

causation   A relationship in which the occurrence of one or more events brings about another event.

cease-and-desist order   An order from a court or government agency to a corporation or individual to stop engaging in a specified practice.

ceiling price   (See *price ceiling*.)

Celler-Kefauver Act   The Federal act of 1950 that amended the *Clayton Act* by prohibiting the acquisition of the assets of one firm by another firm when the effect would be less competition.

central economic planning   Government determination of the objectives of the economy and how resources will be directed to attain those goals.

ceteris paribus assumption   (See *other-things-equal assumption*.)

change in demand   A change in the *quantity demanded* of a good or service at every price; a shift of the *demand curve* to the left or right.

change in supply   A change in the *quantity supplied* of a good or service at every price; a shift of the *supply curve* to the left or right.

circular flow model   The flow of resources from *households* to *firms* and of products from firms to households. These flows are accompanied by reverse flows of money from firms to households and from households to firms.

Civil Rights Act of 1964   Federal law that, in Title VII, outlaws *discrimination* based on race, color, religion, gender, or national origin in hiring, promoting, and compensating workers.

Clayton Act   The Federal antitrust act of 1914 that strengthened the *Sherman Act* by making it illegal for firms to engage in certain specified practices.

closed economy   An economy that neither exports nor imports goods and services.

closed shop   A place of employment where only workers who are already members of a labor union may be hired.

Coase theorem   The idea, first stated by economist Ronald Coase, that *spillover* problems may be resolved through private negotiations of the affected parties.

coincidence of wants   A situation in which the good or service that one trader desires to obtain is the same as that which another trader desires to give up and an item that the second trader wishes to acquire is the same as that which the first trader desires to surrender.

COLA   (See *cost-of-living adjustment*.)

collective bargaining The negotiation of labor contracts between *labor unions* and *firms* or government entities.

collective voice The function a *labor union* performs for its members as a group when it communicates their problems and grievances to management and presses management for a satisfactory resolution.

collusion A situation in which firms act together and in agreement (collude) to fix prices, divide a market, or otherwise restrict competition.

command system A method of organizing an economy in which property resources are publicly owned and government uses *central economic planning* to direct and coordinate economic activities; command economy.

communism (See *command system*.)

comparative advantage A lower relative or comparative cost than that of another producer.

compensating differences Differences in the *wages* received by workers in different jobs to compensate for nonmonetary differences in the jobs.

compensation to employees *Wages* and salaries plus *wage and salary supplements* paid by employers to workers.

competition The presence in a market of independent buyers and sellers competing with one another and the freedom of buyers and sellers to enter and leave the market.

competitive industry's short-run supply curve The horizontal summation of the short-run supply curves of the *firms* in a purely competitive industry (see *pure competition*); a curve that shows the total quantities offered for sale at various prices by the firms in an industry in the short run.

competitive labor market A resource market in which a large number of (noncolluding) firms demand a particular type of labor supplied by a large number of nonunion workers.

complementary goods Products and services that are used together. When the price of one falls, the demand for the other increases (and conversely).

concentration ratio The percentage of the total sales of an industry made by the four (or some other number) largest sellers in the industry.

conglomerate merger The merger of a *firm* in one *industry* with a firm in another industry (with a firm that is neither a supplier, customer, nor competitor).

conglomerates Firms that produce goods and services in two or more separate industries.

constant-cost industry An industry in which expansion by the entry of new firms has no effect on the prices firms in the industry must pay for resources and thus no effect on production costs.

consumer goods Products and services that satisfy human wants directly.

consumer sovereignty Determination by consumers of the types and quantities of goods and services that will be produced with the scarce resources of the economy; consumers' direction of production through their dollar votes.

consumer surplus The difference between the maximum price a consumer is (or consumers are) willing to pay for an additional unit of a product and its market price; the triangular area below the demand curve and above the market price.

copayment The percentage of (say, health care) costs that an insured individual pays while the insurer pays the remainder.

copyright A legal protection provided to developers and publishers of books, computer software, videos, and musical compositions against the copying of their works by others.

corporate income tax A tax levied on the net income (accounting profit) of corporations.

corporation A legal entity ("person") chartered by a state or the Federal government that is distinct and separate from the individuals who own it.

correlation A systematic and dependable association between two sets of data (two kinds of events); does not necessarily indicate causation.

cost-benefit analysis A comparison of the *marginal costs* of a government project or program with the *marginal benefits* to decide whether or not to employ resources in that project or program and to what extent.

cost-of-living adjustment (COLA) An automatic increase in the incomes (wages) of workers when inflation occurs; guaranteed by a collective bargaining contract between firms and workers.

cost ratio An equality showing the number of units of two products that can be produced with the same resources; the cost ratio 1 corn $\equiv$ 3 olives shows that the resources required to produce 3 units of olives must be shifted to corn production to produce a unit of corn.

craft union A labor union that limits its membership to workers with a particular skill (craft).

creative destruction The hypothesis that the creation of new products and production methods simultaneously destroys the market power of existing monopolies.

credit An accounting item that increases the value of an asset (such as the foreign money owned by the residents of a nation).

cross elasticity of demand The ratio of the percentage change in *quantity demanded* of one good to the percentage change in the price of some other good. A positive coefficient indicates the two products are *substitute goods;* a negative coefficient indicates they are *complementary goods*.

crowding model of occupational discrimination A model of labor markets suggesting that *occupational discrimination* has kept many women and minorities out of high-paying occupations and forced them into a limited number of low-paying occupations.

currency appreciation (See *exchange-rate appreciation*.)

currency depreciation (See *exchange-rate depreciation*.)

currency intervention A government's buying and selling of its own currency or foreign currencies to alter international exchange rates.

current account The section in a nation's *international balance of payments* that records its exports and imports of goods and services, its *net investment income,* and its *net transfers*.

debit An accounting item that decreases the value of an asset (such as the foreign money owned by the residents of a nation).

declining industry An industry in which *economic profits* are negative (losses are incurred) and that will, therefore, decrease its output as firms leave it.

decreasing-cost industry An industry in which expansion through the entry of firms lowers the prices that firms in the industry must pay for resources and therefore decreases their production costs.

deductible The dollar sum of (for example, health care) costs that an insured individual must pay before the insurer begins to pay.

demand A schedule showing the amounts of a good or service that buyers (or a buyer) wish to purchase at various prices during some time period.

demand curve A curve illustrating *demand*.

dependent variable A variable that changes as a consequence of a change in some other (independent) variable; the "effect" or outcome.

depository institutions Firms that accept deposits of *money* from the public (businesses and persons); *commercial banks, savings and loan associations, mutual savings banks,* and *credit unions.*

depreciation (See *consumption of fixed capital.*)

depreciation (of the dollar) A decrease in the value of the dollar relative to another currency, so a dollar buys a smaller amount of the foreign currency and therefore of foreign goods.

derived demand The demand for a resource that depends on the demand for the products it helps to produce.

determinants of demand Factors other than price that determine the quantities demanded of a good or service.

determinants of supply Factors other than price that determine the quantities supplied of a good or service.

devaluation A decrease in the governmentally defined value of a currency.

developing countries Many countries of Africa, Asia, and Latin America that are characterized by lack of capital goods, use of nonadvanced technologies, low literacy rates, high unemployment, rapid population growth, and labor forces heavily committed to agriculture.

differentiated oligopoly An *oligopoly* in which the firms produce a *differentiated product.*

differentiated product A product that differs physically or in some other way from the similar products produced by other firms; a product such that buyers are not indifferent to the seller when the price charged by all sellers is the same.

diffusion The spread of an *innovation* through its widespread imitation.

dilemma of regulation The tradeoff faced by a *regulatory agency* in setting the maximum legal price a monopolist may charge: The *socially optimal price* is below *average total cost* (and either bankrupts the *firm* or requires that it be subsidized), while the higher, *fair-return price* does not produce *allocative efficiency.*

diminishing marginal returns (See *law of diminishing returns.*)

direct foreign investment (Web chapter) The building of new factories (or the purchase of existing capital) in a particular nation by corporations of other nations.

direct payments Cash subsidies paid to farmers based on past production levels; unaffected by current crop prices and current production.

direct relationship The relationship between two variables that change in the same direction, for example, product price and quantity supplied.

discrimination The practice of according individuals or groups inferior treatment in hiring, occupational access, education and training, promotion, wage rates, or working conditions even though they have the same abilities, education and skills, and work experience as other workers.

discrimination coefficient A measure of the cost or disutility of prejudice; the monetary amount an employer is willing to pay to hire a preferred worker rather than a nonpreferred worker.

diseconomies of scale Increases in the *average total cost* of producing a product as the *firm* expands the size of its *plant* (its output) in the *long run.*

disposable income *Personal income* less personal taxes; income available for *personal consumption expenditures* and *personal saving.*

dividends Payments by a corporation of all or part of its profit to its stockholders (the corporate owners).

division of labor The separation of the work required to produce a product into a number of different tasks that are performed by different workers; *specialization* of workers.

Doha Round The latest, uncompleted (as of 2003) sequence of trade negotiations by members of the *World Trade Organization;* named after Doha, Qatar, where the set of negotiations began.

dollar votes The "votes" that consumers and entrepreneurs cast for the production of consumer and capital goods, respectively, when they purchase those goods in product and resource markets.

domestic capital formation The process of adding to a nation's stock of *capital* by saving and investing part of its own domestic output.

domestic price The price of a good or service within a country, determined by domestic demand and supply.

double taxation The taxation of both corporate net income (profits) and the *dividends* paid from this net income when they become the personal income of households.

dumping The sale of products below cost in a foreign country or below the prices charged at home.

DuPont cellophane case The antitrust case brought against DuPont in which the U.S. Supreme Court ruled (in 1956) that while DuPont had a monopoly in the narrowly defined market for cellophane, it did not monopolize the more broadly defined market for flexible packaging materials. It was thus not guilty of violating the *Sherman Act.*

durable good A consumer good with an expected life (use) of 3 or more years.

earned-income tax credit A refundable Federal tax credit for low-income working people designed to reduce poverty and encourage labor-force participation.

earnings The money income received by a worker; equal to the *wage* (rate) multiplied by the amount of time worked.

economic analysis The process of deriving *economic principles* from relevant economic facts.

economic concentration A description or measure of the degree to which an industry is dominated by one or a handful of firms or is characterized by many firms. (See *concentration ratio*.)

economic cost A payment that must be made to obtain and retain the services of a *resource;* the income a firm must provide to a resource supplier to attract the resource away from an alternative use; equal to the quantity of other products that cannot be produced when resources are instead used to make a particular product.

economic efficiency The use of the minimum necessary resources to obtain the socially optimal amounts of goods and services; entails both *productive efficiency* and *allocative efficiency.*

economic growth (1) An outward shift in the *production possibilities curve* that results from an increase in resource supplies or quality or an improvement in *technology;* (2) an increase of real output *(gross domestic product)* or real output per capita.

economic law An *economic principle* that has been tested and retested and has stood the test of time.

economic model A simplified picture of economic reality; an abstract generalization.

economic perspective A viewpoint that envisions individuals and institutions making rational decisions by comparing the marginal benefits and marginal costs associated with their actions.

economic policy A course of action intended to correct or avoid a problem.

economic principle A widely accepted generalization about the economic behavior of individuals or institutions.

economic profit The *total revenue* of a firm less its *economic costs* (which include both *explicit costs* and *implicit costs*); also called "pure profit" and "above-normal profit."

economic regulation (See *industrial regulation* and *social regulation*.)

economic rent The price paid for the use of land and other natural resources, the supply of which is fixed *(perfectly inelastic).*

economic resources The *land, labor, capital,* and *entrepreneurial ability* that are used in the production of goods and services; productive agents; factors of production.

economics The social science dealing with the use of scarce resources to obtain the maximum satisfaction of society's virtually unlimited economic wants.

economic system A particular set of institutional arrangements and a coordinating mechanism for solving the economizing problem; a method of organizing an economy, of which the *market system* and the *command system* are the two general types.

economic theory A statement of a cause-effect relationship; when accepted by all economists, an *economic principle.*

economies of scale Reductions in the *average total cost* of producing a product as the firm expands the size of plant (its output) in the *long run;* the economies of mass production.

economizing problem The choices necessitated because society's economic wants for goods and services are unlimited but the *resources* available to satisfy these wants are limited (scarce).

efficiency loss (Web chapter) Reductions in combined consumer and producer surplus caused by an underallocation or overallocation of resources to the production of a good or service.

efficiency loss of a tax The loss of net benefits to society because a tax reduces the production and consumption of a taxed good below the level of allocative efficiency.

efficiency wage A wage that minimizes wage costs per unit of output by encouraging greater effort or reducing turnover.

efficient allocation of resources That allocation of an economy's resources among the production of different products that leads to the maximum satisfaction of consumers' wants, thus producing the socially optimal mix of output with society's scarce resources.

elastic demand Product or resource demand whose *price elasticity* is greater than 1. This means the resulting change in *quantity demanded* is greater than the percentage change in *price.*

elasticity coefficient The number obtained when the percentage change in *quantity demanded* (or supplied) is divided by the percentage change in the *price* of the commodity.

elasticity formula (See *price elasticity of demand*.)

elastic supply Product or resource supply whose price elasticity is greater than 1. This means the resulting change in quantity supplied is greater than the percentage change in price.

employment discrimination Inferior treatment in hiring, promotions, work assignments, and such for a particular group of employees.

entitlement programs Government programs such as *social insurance, food stamps, Medicare,* and *Medicaid* that guarantee particular levels of transfer payments or noncash benefits to all who fit the programs' criteria.

entrepreneurial ability The human resource that combines the other resources to produce a product, makes nonroutine decisions, innovates, and bears risks.

equality-versus-efficiency tradeoff The decrease in *economic efficiency* that may accompany a decrease in *income inequality;* the presumption that some income inequality is required to achieve economic efficiency.

Equal Pay Act of 1963 Federal government legislation making it illegal to pay men and women different wage rates if they do equal work on jobs that require equal skill, effort, and responsibility and that are performed under similar working conditions.

equilibrium price The *price* in a competitive market at which the *quantity demanded* and the *quantity supplied* are equal, there is neither a shortage nor a surplus, and there is no tendency for price to rise or fall.

equilibrium quantity (1) The quantity demanded and supplied at the equilibrium price in a competitive market; (2) the profit-maximizing output of a firm.

euro The common currency unit used by 12 European nations (as of 2003) in the Euro zone, which consists of

Austria, Belgium, Finland, France, Germany, Greece, Ireland, Italy, Luxembourg, the Netherlands, Portugal, and Spain.

European Union (EU) An association of 25 European nations (including 10 nations to be added in 2004) that has eliminated tariffs and quotas among them, established common tariffs for imported goods from outside the member nations, eliminated barriers to the free movement of capital, and created other common economic policies.

excess capacity Plant resources that are underused when imperfectly competitive firms produce less output than that associated with achieving minimum average total cost.

exchange control (See *foreign exchange control*.)

exchange rate The *rate of exchange* of one nation's currency for another nation's currency.

exchange-rate appreciation An increase in the value of a nation's currency in foreign exchange markets; an increase in the *rate of exchange* for foreign currencies.

exchange-rate depreciation A decrease in the value of a nation's currency in foreign exchange markets; a decrease in the *rate of exchange* for foreign currencies.

exchange-rate determinant Any factor other than the *rate of exchange* that determines a currency's demand and supply in the *foreign exchange market*.

excise tax A tax levied on the production of a specific product or on the quantity of the product purchased.

exclusive unionism The practice of a *labor union* of restricting the supply of skilled union labor to increase the wages received by union members; the policies typically employed by a *craft union*.

exhaustive expenditure An expenditure by government resulting directly in the employment of *economic resources* and in the absorption by government of the goods and services those resources produce; a *government purchase*.

exit mechanism The process of leaving a job and searching for another one as a means of improving one's working conditions.

expanding industry An industry whose firms earn *economic profits* and for which an increase in output occurs as new firms enter the industry.

expectations The anticipations of consumers, firms, and others about future economic conditions.

expected rate of return The increase in profit a firm anticipates it will obtain by purchasing capital (or engaging in research and development); expressed as a percentage of the total cost of the investment (or R&D) activity.

explicit cost The monetary payment a *firm* must make to an outsider to obtain a *resource*.

exports Goods and services produced in a nation and sold to buyers in other nations.

export subsidies Government payments to domestic producers to enable them to reduce the *price* of a good or service to foreign buyers.

export supply curve An upward-sloping curve that shows the amount of a product that domestic firms will export at each *world price* that is above the *domestic price*.

export transaction A sale of a good or service that increases the amount of foreign currency flowing to a nation's citizens, firms, and government.

external benefit (See *spillover benefit*.)

external cost (See *spillover cost*.)

external debt Private or public debt owed to foreign citizens, firms, and institutions.

externality (See *spillover*.)

factors of production Economic resources: land, capital, labor, and entrepreneurial ability.

fair-return price The price of a product that enables its producer to obtain a *normal profit* and that is equal to the *average total cost* of producing it.

fallacy of composition The false notion that what is true for the individual (or part) is necessarily true for the group (or whole).

Farm Act of 2002 Farm legislation that continued the "freedom to plant" and direct subsidies of the *Freedom to Farm Act* of 1996 but added an automatic, countercyclical system of emergency farm aid.

farm problem The fact that technological advance, coupled with a price-inelastic and relatively constant demand, has made agriculture a *declining industry*; also, the tendency for farm income to fluctuate sharply from year to year.

Federal government The government of the United States, as distinct from the state and local governments.

Federal Trade Commission (FTC) The commission of five members established by the *Federal Trade Commission Act* of 1914 to investigate unfair competitive practices of firms, to hold hearings on the complaints of such practices, and to issue *cease-and-desist orders* when firms were found to engage in such practices.

Federal Trade Commission Act The Federal act of 1914 that established the *Federal Trade Commission*.

financial capital (See *money capital*.)

firm An organization that employs resources to produce a good or service for profit and owns and operates one or more *plants*.

fiscal policy Changes in government spending and tax collections designed to achieve a full-employment and noninflationary domestic output; also called *discretionary fiscal policy*.

fixed cost Any cost that in total does not change when the *firm* changes its output; the cost of *fixed resources*.

fixed exchange rate A *rate of exchange* that is set in some way and therefore prevented from rising or falling with changes in currency supply and demand.

fixed resource Any resource whose quantity cannot be changed by a firm in the *short run*.

flexible exchange rate A *rate of exchange* determined by the international demand for and supply of a nation's money; a rate free to rise or fall (to float).

floating exchange rate (See *flexible exchange rate*.)

food-stamp program A program permitting low-income persons to purchase for less than their retail value, or to obtain without cost, coupons that can be exchanged for food items at retail stores.

foreign competition (See *import competition*.)

foreign exchange control The control a government may exercise over the quantity of foreign currency demanded by its citizens and firms and over the *rates of exchange* in order to limit its *outpayments* to its *inpayments* (to eliminate a *payments deficit*).

foreign exchange market A market in which the money (currency) of one nation can be used to purchase (can be exchanged for) the money of another nation.

foreign exchange rate (See *rate of exchange*.)

Four Fundamental Questions (of economics) The four questions that every economy must answer: what to produce, how to produce it, how to divide the total output, and how to ensure economic flexibility.

freedom of choice The freedom of owners of property resources to employ or dispose of them as they see fit, of workers to enter any line of work for which they are qualified, and of consumers to spend their incomes in a manner that they think is appropriate.

freedom of enterprise The freedom of *firms* to obtain economic resources, to use those resources to produce products of the firm's own choosing, and to sell their products in markets of their choice.

Freedom to Farm Act A law passed in 1996 that revamped 60 years of U.S. farm policy by ending *price supports* and *acreage allotments* for wheat, corn, barley, oats, sorghum, rye, cotton, and rice.

free-rider problem The inability of potential providers of an economically desirable good or service to obtain payment from those who benefit, because of *nonexcludability*.

free trade The absence of artificial (government-imposed) barriers to trade among individuals and firms in different nations.

fringe benefits The rewards other than *wages* that employees receive from their employers and that include pensions, medical and dental insurance, paid vacations, and sick leaves.

full employment (1) The use of all available resources to produce want-satisfying goods and services; (2) the situation in which the *unemployment rate* is equal to the full-employment unemployment rate and there is frictional and structural but no cyclical unemployment (and the real output of the economy equals potential real output).

full production Employment of available resources so that the maximum amount of (or total value of) goods and services is produced; occurs when both *productive efficiency* and *allocative efficiency* are realized.

functional distribution of income The manner in which *national income* is divided among the functions performed to earn it (or the kinds of resources provided to earn it); the division of national income into wages and salaries, proprietors' income, corporate profits, interest, and rent.

gains from trade The extra output that trading partners obtain through specialization of production and exchange of goods and services.

game theory A means of analyzing the pricing behavior of oligopolists that uses the theory of strategy associated with games such as chess and bridge.

GDP (See *gross domestic product*.)

G8 nations A group of eight major nations (Canada, France, Germany, Italy, Japan, Russia, United Kingdom, and United States) whose leaders meet regularly to discuss common economic problems and try to coordinate economic policies.

General Agreement on Tariffs and Trade (GATT) The international agreement reached in 1947 in which 23 nations agreed to give equal and nondiscriminatory treatment to one another, to reduce tariff rates by multinational negotiations, and to eliminate *import quotas*. It now includes most nations and has become the *World Trade Organization*.

generalization Statement of the nature of the relationship between two or more sets of facts.

Gini ratio A numerical measure of the overall dispersion of income among households, families, or individuals; found graphically by dividing the area between the diagonal line and the *Lorenz curve* by the entire area below the diagonal line.

gold standard A historical system of fixed exchange rates in which nations defined their currencies in terms of gold, maintained a fixed relationship between their stocks of gold and their money supplies, and allowed gold to be freely exported and imported.

government failure Inefficiencies in resource allocation caused by problems in the operation of the public sector (government), specifically, rent-seeking pressure by special-interest groups, shortsighted political behavior, limited and bundled choices, and bureaucratic inefficiencies.

government purchases Expenditures by government for goods and services that government consumes in providing public goods and for public (or social) capital that has a long lifetime; the expenditures of all governments in the economy for those final goods and services.

government transfer payment The disbursement of money (or goods and services) by government for which government receives no currently produced good or service in return.

grievance procedure The method used by a *labor union* and a *firm* to settle disputes that arise during the life of the collective bargaining agreement between them.

gross domestic product (GDP) The total market value of all final goods and services produced annually within the boundaries of the United States, whether by U.S. or foreign-supplied resources.

guiding function of prices The ability of price changes to bring about changes in the quantities of products and resources demanded and supplied.

health maintenance organizations (HMOs) Health care providers that contract with employers, insurance companies, labor unions, or government units to provide health care for their workers or others who are insured.

Herfindahl index A measure of the concentration and competitiveness of an industry; calculated as the sum of the squared percentage market shares of the individual firms in the industry.

homogeneous oligopoly An *oligopoly* in which the firms produce a *standardized product*.

horizontal merger The merger into a single *firm* of two firms producing the same product and selling it in the same geographic market.

household An economic unit (of one or more persons) that provides the economy with resources and uses the income received to purchase goods and services that satisfy economic wants.

human capital The accumulation of prior investments in education, training, health, and other factors that increase productivity.

human capital discrimination The denial of equal access to productivity-enhancing education and training to members of particular groups.

human capital investment Any expenditure undertaken to improve the education, skills, health, or mobility of workers, with an expectation of greater productivity and thus a positive return on the investment.

hypothesis A tentative explanation of cause and effect that requires testing.

illegal immigrant A person who enters a country unlawfully for the purpose of residing there.

IMF (See *International Monetary Fund.*)

immobility The inability or unwillingness of a worker to move from one geographic area or occupation to another or from a lower-paying job to a higher-paying job.

imperfect competition All market structures except *pure competition;* includes *monopoly, monopolistic competition,* and *oligopoly.*

implicit cost The monetary income a *firm* sacrifices when it uses a resource it owns rather than supplying the resource in the market; equal to what the resource could have earned in the best-paying alternative employment; includes a *normal profit.*

import competition The competition that domestic firms encounter from the products and services of foreign producers.

import demand curve A downsloping curve showing the amount of a product that an economy will import at each *world price* below the *domestic price.*

import quota A limit imposed by a nation on the quantity (or total value) of a good that may be imported during some period of time.

imports Spending by individuals, *firms,* and governments for goods and services produced in foreign nations.

import transaction The purchase of a good or service that decreases the amount of foreign money held by citizens, firms, and governments of a nation.

incentive function of price The inducement that an increase in the price of a commodity gives to sellers to make more of it available (and conversely for a decrease in price), and the inducement that an increase in price offers to buyers to purchase smaller quantities (and conversely for a decrease in price).

incentive pay plan A compensation structure that ties worker pay directly to performance. Such plans include piece rates, bonuses, *stock options,* commissions, and *profit sharing.*

inclusive unionism The practice of a labor union of including as members all workers employed in an industry.

income A flow of dollars (or purchasing power) per unit of time derived from the use of human or property resources.

income effect A change in the quantity demanded of a product that results from the change in *real income (purchasing power)* caused by a change in the product's price.

income elasticity of demand The ratio of the percentage change in the *quantity demanded* of a good to a percentage change in consumer income; measures the responsiveness of consumer purchases to income changes.

income inequality The unequal distribution of an economy's total income among households or families.

income-maintenance system A group of government programs designed to eliminate poverty and reduce inequality in the distribution of income.

increase in demand An increase in the *quantity demanded* of a good or service at every price; a shift of the *demand curve* to the right.

increase in supply An increase in the *quantity supplied* of a good or service at every price; a shift of the *supply curve* to the right.

increasing-cost industry An *industry* in which expansion through the entry of new firms raises the prices *firms* in the industry must pay for resources and therefore increases their production costs.

increasing marginal returns An increase in the *marginal product* of a resource as successive units of the resource are employed.

increasing returns An increase in a firm's output by a larger percentage than the percentage increase in its inputs.

independent goods Products or services for which there is little or no relationship between the price of one and the demand for the other. When the price of one rises or falls, the demand for the other tends to remain constant.

independent unions U.S. unions that are not affiliated with the *AFL-CIO.*

independent variable The variable causing a change in some other (dependent) variable.

indifference curve A curve showing the different combinations of two products that yield the same satisfaction or *utility* to a consumer.

indifference map A set of *indifference curves,* each representing a different level of *utility,* that together show the preferences of a consumer.

individual demand The demand schedule or *demand curve* of a single buyer.

individual supply The supply schedule or *supply curve* of a single seller.

industrially advanced countries High-income countries such as the United States, Canada, Japan, and the nations of western Europe that have highly developed *market economies* based on large stocks of technologically advanced capital goods and skilled labor forces.

industrial regulation The older and more traditional type of regulation in which government is concerned with the prices charged and the services provided to the public in specific industries, in contrast to *social regulation.*

industrial union A *labor union* that accepts as members all workers employed in a particular industry (or by a particular firm).

industry A group of (one or more) *firms* that produce identical or similar products.

inelastic demand Product or resource demand for which the *price elasticity coefficient* is less than 1. This means the resulting percentage change in *quantity demanded* is less than the percentage change in *price.*

inelastic supply Product or resource supply for which the price elasticity coefficient is less than 1. The percentage change in *quantity supplied* is less than the percentage change in *price.*

inferior good A good or service whose consumption declines as income rises (and conversely), price remaining constant.

inflation A rise in the general level of prices in an economy.

information technology New and more efficient methods of delivering and receiving information through use of computers, fax machines, wireless phones, and the Internet.

infrastructure The capital goods usually provided by the *public sector* for the use of its citizens and firms (for example, highways, bridges, transit systems, wastewater treatment facilities, municipal water systems, and airports).

injunction A court order directing a person or organization not to perform a certain act because the act would do irreparable damage to some other person or persons; a restraining order.

in-kind transfer The distribution by government of goods and services to individuals for which the government receives no currently produced good or service in return; a *government transfer payment* made in goods or services rather than in money; also called a noncash transfer.

innovation The first commercially successful introduction of a new product, the use of a new method of production, or the creation of a new form of business organization.

inpayments The receipts of domestic or foreign money that individuals, firms, and governments of one nation obtain from the sale of goods and services abroad, as investment income and *remittances,* and from foreign purchases of its assets.

insurable risk An event that would result in a loss but whose frequency of occurrence can be estimated with considerable accuracy. Insurance companies are willing to sell insurance against such losses.

interest The payment made for the use of money (of borrowed funds).

interest income Payments of income to those who supply the economy with *capital*.

interest rate The annual rate at which interest is paid; a percentage of the borrowed amount.

interindustry competition The competition for sales between the products of one industry and the products of another industry.

interlocking directorate A situation where one or more members of the board of directors of a *corporation* are also on the board of directors of a competing corporation; illegal under the *Clayton Act*.

international balance of payments A summary of all the transactions that took place between the individuals, firms, and government units of one nation and those of all other nations during a year.

international balance-of-payments deficit (See *balance-of-payments deficit.*)

international balance-of-payments surplus (See *balance-of-payments surplus.*)

international gold standard (See *gold standard.*)

International Monetary Fund (IMF) The international association of nations that was formed after the Second World War to make loans of foreign monies to nations with temporary *payments deficits* and, until the early 1970s, to administer the *adjustable pegs*. It now mainly makes loans to nations facing possible defaults on private and government loans.

international monetary reserves The foreign currencies and other assets such as gold that a nation can use to settle a *balance-of-payments deficit*.

international value of the dollar The price that must be paid in foreign currency (money) to obtain one U.S. dollar.

invention The first discovery of a product or process through the use of imagination, ingenious thinking, and experimentation and the first proof that it will work.

inverse relationship The relationship between two variables that change in opposite directions, for example, product price and quantity demanded.

inverted-U theory A theory saying that, other things equal, *R&D* expenditures as a percentage of sales rise with industry concentration, reach a peak at a four-firm *concentration ratio* of about 50 percent, and then fall as concentration further increases.

investment Spending for the production and accumulation of *capital* and additions to inventories.

investment goods Same as *capital* or capital goods.

investment in human capital (See *human capital investment.*)

invisible hand The tendency of firms and resource suppliers that seek to further their own self-interests in competitive markets to also promote the interest of society.

kinked-demand curve The demand curve for a noncollusive oligopolist, which is based on the assumption that rivals will match a price decrease and will ignore a price increase.

labor People's physical and mental talents and efforts that are used to help produce goods and services.

labor force Persons 16 years of age and older who are not in institutions and who are employed or are unemployed and seeking work.

labor-force participation rate The percentage of the working-age population that is actually in the *labor force*.

labor-intensive commodity A product requiring a relatively large amount of *labor* to be produced.

labor productivity Total output divided by the quantity of labor employed to produce it; the *average product* of labor or output per hour of work.

labor theory of value (Web chapter) The Marxian idea that the economic value of any commodity is determined solely by the amount of labor that is required to produce it.

labor union A group of workers organized to advance the interests of the group (to increase wages, shorten the hours worked, improve working conditions, and so on).

laissez-faire capitalism (See *capitalism.*)

land Natural resources ("free gifts of nature") used to produce goods and services.

land-intensive commodity A product requiring a relatively large amount of land to be produced.

law of demand The principle that, other things equal, an increase in a product's price will reduce the quantity of it demanded, and conversely for a decrease in price.

law of diminishing marginal utility The principle that as a consumer increases the consumption of a good or service, the *marginal utility* obtained from each additional unit of the good or service decreases.

law of diminishing returns The principle that as successive increments of a *variable resource* are added to a *fixed resource,* the *marginal product* of the *variable resource* will eventually decrease.

law of increasing opportunity costs The principle that as the production of a good increases, the *opportunity cost* of producing an additional unit rises.

law of supply The principle that, other things equal, an increase in the price of a product will increase the quantity of it supplied, and conversely for a price decrease.

learning by doing Achieving greater *productivity* and lower *average total cost* through gains in knowledge and skill that accompany repetition of a task; a source of *economies of scale.*

least-cost combination of resources The quantity of each resource a firm must employ in order to produce a particular output at the lowest total cost; the combination at which the ratio of the *marginal product* of a resource to its *marginal resource cost* (to its *price* if the resource is employed in a competitive market) is the same for the last dollar spent on each of the resources employed.

legal cartel theory of regulation The hypothesis that some industries seek regulation or want to maintain regulation so that they may form or maintain a legal *cartel.*

legal immigrant A person who lawfully enters a country for the purpose of residing there.

liability A debt with a monetary value; an amount owed by a firm or an individual.

limited liability Restriction of the maximum loss to a predetermined amount for the owners (stockholders) of a *corporation.* The maximum loss is the amount they paid for their shares of stock.

limited-liability company An unincorporated business whose owners are protected by *limited liability.*

loanable funds *Money* available for lending and borrowing.

loanable funds theory of interest The concept that the supply of and demand for *loanable funds* determine the equilibrium rate of interest.

lockout An action by a firm that forbids workers to return to work until a new collective bargaining contract is signed; a means of imposing costs (lost wages) on union workers in a collective bargaining dispute.

logrolling The trading of votes by legislators to secure favorable outcomes on decisions concerning the provision of *public goods* and *quasi-public goods.*

long run (1) In *microeconomics,* a period of time long enough to enable producers of a product to change the quantities of all the resources they employ; period in which all resources and costs are variable and no resources or costs are fixed. (2) In *macroeconomics,* a period sufficiently long for nominal wages and other input prices to change in response to a change in the nation's price level.

long-run aggregate supply curve The *aggregate supply curve* associated with a time period in which input prices (especially *nominal wages*) are fully responsive to changes in the *price level.*

long-run competitive equilibrium The price at which firms in *pure competition* neither obtain *economic profit* nor suffer losses in the *long run* and the total quantity demanded and supplied are equal; a price equal to the minimum long-run *average total cost* of producing the product.

long-run farm problem The tendency for agriculture to be a declining industry as technological progress increases supply relative to an inelastic and slowly increasing demand.

long-run supply A schedule or curve showing the prices at which a *purely competitive industry* will make various quantities of the product available in the *long run.*

Lorenz curve A curve showing the distribution of income in an economy. The cumulated percentage of families (income receivers) is measured along the horizontal axis and cumulated percentage of income is measured along the vertical axis.

macroeconomics The part of economics concerned with the economy as a whole; with such major aggregates as the household, business, and government sectors; and with measures of the total economy.

managed floating exchange rate An *exchange rate* that is allowed to change (float) as a result of changes in currency supply and demand but at times is altered (managed) by governments via their buying and selling of particular currencies.

managerial-opposition hypothesis An explanation that attributes the relative decline of unionism in the United States to the increased and more aggressive opposition of management to unions.

managerial prerogatives The decisions that management of the firm has the sole right to make; often enumerated in the labor contract (work agreement) between a *labor union* and a *firm.*

marginal analysis The comparison of marginal ("extra" or "additional") benefits and marginal costs, usually for decision making.

marginal benefit The extra (additional) benefit of consuming 1 more unit of some good or service; the change in total benefit when 1 more unit is consumed.

marginal cost The extra (additional) cost of producing 1 more unit of output; equal to the change in *total cost* divided by the change in output (and, in the short run, to the change in total *variable cost* divided by the change in output).

marginal product The additional output produced when 1 additional unit of a resource is employed (the quantity of all other resources employed remaining constant); equal to the change in total product divided by the change in the quantity of a resource employed.

marginal productivity theory of income distribution The contention that the distribution of income is equitable when each unit of each resource receives a money payment equal to its marginal contribution to the firm's revenue (its *marginal revenue product*).

marginal rate of substitution The rate at which a consumer is prepared to substitute one good for another (from a given combination of goods) and remain equally satisfied (have the same *total utility*); equal to the slope of a consumer's *indifference curve* at each point on the curve.

marginal resource cost The amount the total cost of employing a *resource* increases when a firm employs 1 additional unit of the resource (the quantity of all other resources employed remaining constant); equal to the change in the *total cost* of the resource divided by the change in the quantity of the resource employed.

marginal revenue The change in *total revenue* that results from the sale of 1 additional unit of a firm's product; equal to the change in total revenue divided by the change in the quantity of the product sold.

marginal-revenue–marginal-cost approach A method of determining the total output where *economic profit* is a maximum (or losses are a minimum) by comparing the *marginal revenue* and the *marginal cost* of each additional unit of output.

marginal revenue product The change in a firm's *total revenue* when it employs 1 additional unit of a resource (the quantity of all other resources employed remaining constant); equal to the change in total revenue divided by the change in the quantity of the resource employed.

marginal tax rate The tax rate paid on each additional dollar of income.

marginal utility The extra *utility* a consumer obtains from the consumption of 1 additional unit of a good or service; equal to the change in total utility divided by the change in the quantity consumed.

market Any institution or mechanism that brings together buyers (demanders) and sellers (suppliers) of a particular good or service.

market demand (See *total demand*.)

market economy An economy in which only the private decisions of consumers, resource suppliers, and firms determine how resources are allocated; the *market system*.

market failure The inability of a market to bring about the allocation of resources that best satisfies the wants of society; in particular, the overallocation or underallocation of resources to the production of a particular good or service because of *spillovers* or informational problems or because markets do not provide desired *public goods*.

market for externality rights A market in which firms can buy rights to discharge pollutants. The price of such rights is determined by the demand for the right to discharge pollutants and a *perfectly inelastic supply* of such rights (the latter determined by the quantity of discharges that the environment can assimilate).

market period A period in which producers of a product are unable to change the quantity produced in response to a change in its price and in which there is a *perfectly inelastic supply*.

market system All the product and resource markets of a *market economy* and the relationships among them; a method that allows the prices determined in those markets to allocate the economy's scarce resources and to communicate and coordinate the decisions made by consumers, firms, and resource suppliers.

median-voter model The theory that under majority rule the median (middle) voter will be in the dominant position to determine the outcome of an election.

Medicaid A Federal program that helps finance the medical expenses of individuals covered by the *Supplemental Security Income (SSI)* and *Temporary Assistance for Needy Families (TANF)* programs.

Medicare A Federal program that is financed by *payroll taxes* and provides for (1) compulsory hospital insurance for senior citizens and (2) low-cost voluntary insurance to help older Americans pay physicians' fees.

medium of exchange Any item sellers generally accept and buyers generally use to pay for a good or service; *money;* a convenient means of exchanging goods and services without engaging in *barter.*

merger The combination of two (or more) firms into a single firm.

microeconomics The part of economics concerned with such individual units as *industries, firms,* and *households* and with individual markets, specific goods and services, and product and resource prices.

Microsoft case A 2002 antitrust case in which Microsoft was found guilty of violating the *Sherman Act* by engaging in a series of unlawful activities designed to maintain its monopoly in operating systems for personal computers. As a remedy the company was prohibited from engaging in a set of specific anticompetitive business practices.

minimum efficient scale The lowest level of output at which a firm can minimize long-run *average total cost*.

minimum wage The lowest *wage* employers may legally pay for an hour of work.

monetary policy A central bank's changing of the *money supply* to influence interest rates and assist the economy in achieving price stability, full employment, and economic growth.

money Any item that is generally acceptable to sellers in exchange for goods and services.

money capital Money available to purchase *capital;* simply *money,* as defined by economists.

money income (See *nominal income*.)

monopolistic competition A market structure in which many firms sell a *differentiated product,* into which entry is relatively easy, in which the firm has some control over its product price, and in which there is considerable *nonprice competition*.

monopoly A market structure in which the number of sellers is so small that each seller is able to influence the total supply and the price of the good or service. (Also see *pure monopoly*.)

monopsony A market structure in which there is only a single buyer of a good, service, or resource.

moral hazard problem The possibility that individuals or institutions will change their behavior as the result of a contract or agreement. Example: A bank whose deposits are insured against loss may make riskier loans and investments.

most-favored-nation (MFN) status An agreement by the United States to allow some other nation's *exports* into the United States at the lowest tariff level levied by the United States, then or at any later time.

MR = MC rule The principle that a firm will maximize its profit (or minimize its losses) by producing the output at which *marginal revenue* and *marginal cost* are equal, provided product price is equal to or greater than *average variable cost*.

MRP = MRC rule The principle that to maximize profit (or minimize losses), a firm should employ the quantity of a resource at which its *marginal revenue product* (MRP) is equal to its *marginal resource cost* (MRC), the latter being the wage rate in pure competition.

multinational corporations Firms that own production facilities in two or more countries and produce and sell their products globally.

mutual interdependence A situation in which a change in price strategy (or in some other strategy) by one firm will affect the sales and profits of another firm (or other firms). Any firm that makes such a change can expect the other rivals to react to the change.

national health insurance (NHI) A proposed program in which the Federal government would provide a basic package of health care to all citizens at no direct charge or at a low cost-sharing level. Financing would be out of general tax revenues.

National Labor Relations Act (Wagner Act of 1935) As amended, the basic labor-relations law in the United States; defines the legal rights of unions and management and identifies unfair union and management labor practices; established the *National Labor Relations Board*.

National Labor Relations Board (NLRB) The board established by the *National Labor Relations Act* of 1935 to investigate unfair labor practices, issue *cease-and-desist orders,* and conduct elections among employees to determine if they wish to be represented by a *labor union*.

natural monopoly An industry in which *economies of scale* are so great that a single firm can produce the product at a lower average total cost than would be possible if more than one firm produced the product.

negative relationship (See *inverse relationship*.)

net exports *Exports* minus *imports*.

net foreign factor income Payments by a nation of resource income to the rest of the world minus receipts of resource income from the rest of the world.

net investment income The interest and dividend income received by the residents of a nation from residents of other nations less the interest and dividend payments made by the residents of that nation to the residents of other nations.

net transfers The personal and government transfer payments made by one nation to residents of foreign nations less the personal and government transfer payments received from residents of foreign nations.

network effects Increases in the value of a product to each user, including existing users, as the total number of users rises.

net worth The total *assets* less the total *liabilities* of a firm or an individual; for a firm, the claims of the owners against the firm's total assets; for an individual, his or her wealth.

New Economy The label attached by some economists and the popular press to the U.S. economy since 1995. The main characteristics are accelerated *productivity growth* and *economic growth,* caused by rapid technological advance and the emergence of the global economy.

NLRB (See *National Labor Relations Board*.)

nominal wage The amount of money received by a worker per unit of time (hour, day, etc.); money wage.

noncash transfer A *government transfer payment* in the form of goods and services rather than money, for example, food stamps, housing assistance, and job training; also called in-kind transfers.

noncollusive oligopoly An *oligopoly* in which the firms do not act together and in agreement to determine the price of the product and the output that each firm will produce.

noncompeting groups Collections of workers in the economy who do not compete with each other for employment because the skill and training of the workers in one group are substantially different from those of the workers in other groups.

nondurable good A *consumer good* with an expected life (use) of less than 3 years.

nonexcludability The inability to keep nonpayers (free riders) from obtaining benefits from a certain good; a *public good* characteristic.

nonexhaustive expenditure An expenditure by government that does not result directly in the employment of economic resources or the production of goods and services; see *government transfer payment*.

nonprice competition Competition based on distinguishing one's product by means of *product differentiation* and then *advertising* the distinguished product to consumers.

nonpriced goods (Web chapter) Goods or resources that are not priced in markets because they are owned in common by society and available for the taking on public lands.

nonrivalry The idea that one person's benefit from a certain good does not reduce the benefit available to others; a *public good* characteristic.

nontariff barriers All barriers other than *protective tariffs* that nations erect to impede international trade, including *import quotas,* licensing requirements, unreasonable product-quality standards, unnecessary bureaucratic detail in customs procedures, and so on.

normal good A good or service whose consumption increases when income increases and falls when income decreases, price remaining constant.

normal profit The payment made by a firm to obtain and retain *entrepreneurial ability;* the minimum income entrepreneurial ability must receive to induce it to perform entrepreneurial functions for a firm.

normative economics The part of economics involving value judgments about what the economy should be like; focused on which economic goals and policies should be implemented; policy economics.

North American Free Trade Agreement (NAFTA) A 1993 agreement establishing, over a 15-year period, a free-trade zone composed of Canada, Mexico, and the United States.

OASDHI (See *Old Age, Survivors, and Disability Health Insurance*.)

occupational discrimination The arbitrary restriction of particular groups from entering the more desirable, higher-paying occupations.

occupational licensure The laws of state or local governments that require that a worker satisfy certain specified requirements and obtain a license from a licensing board before engaging in a particular occupation.

occupational segregation The crowding of women or minorities into less desirable, lower-paying occupations.

official reserves Foreign currencies owned by the central bank of a nation.

Old Age, Survivors, and Disability Health Insurance (OASDHI) The social program in the United States financed by Federal *payroll taxes* on employers and employees and designed to replace the *earnings* lost when workers retire, die, or become unable to work.

oligopoly A market structure in which a few firms sell either a *standardized* or *differentiated product,* into which entry is difficult, in which the firm has limited control over product price because of *mutual interdependence* (except when there is collusion among firms), and in which there is typically *nonprice competition.*

OPEC (See *Organization of Petroleum Exporting Countries.*)

open economy An economy that exports and imports goods and services.

open-market operations The buying and selling of U.S. government securities by the *Federal Reserve Banks* for purposes of carrying out *monetary policy.*

open shop A place of employment in which the employer may hire nonunion workers and the workers need not become members of a *labor union.*

opportunity cost The amount of other products that must be forgone or sacrificed to produce a unit of a product.

Organization of Petroleum Exporting Countries (OPEC) A cartel of 11 oil-producing countries (Algeria, Indonesia, Iran, Iraq, Kuwait, Libya, Nigeria, Qatar, Saudi Arabia, Venezuela, and the UAE) that controls the quantity and price of crude oil exported by its members and that accounts for 60 percent of the world's export of oil.

other-things-equal assumption The assumption that factors other than those being considered are held constant.

outpayments The expenditures of domestic or foreign currency that the individuals, firms, and governments of one nation make to purchase goods and services, for *remittances,* to pay investment income, and for purchases of foreign assets.

output effect The situation in which an increase in the price of one input will increase a firm's production costs and reduce its level of output, thus reducing the demand for other inputs; conversely for a decrease in the price of the input.

paradox of voting A situation where paired-choice voting by majority rule fails to provide a consistent ranking of society's preferences for *public goods* or services.

parity concept The idea that year after year a specific output of a farm product should enable a farmer to acquire a constant amount of nonagricultural goods and services.

parity ratio The ratio of the price received by farmers from the sale of an agricultural commodity to the prices of other goods paid by them; usually expressed as a percentage; used as a rationale for *price supports.*

partnership An unincorporated firm owned and operated by two or more persons.

patent An exclusive right given to inventors to produce and sell a new product or machine for 20 years from the time of patent application.

payments deficit (See *balance-of-payments deficit.*)

payments surplus (See *balance-of-payments surplus.*)

payroll tax A tax levied on employers of labor equal to a percentage of all or part of the wages and salaries paid by them and on employees equal to a percentage of all or part of the wages and salaries received by them.

$P = MC$ rule The principle that a purely competitive firm will maximize its profit or minimize its loss by producing that output at which the *price* of the product is equal to *marginal cost,* provided that price is equal to or greater than *average variable cost* in the short run and equal to or greater than *average total cost* in the long run.

per capita GDP *Gross domestic product* (GDP) per person; the average GDP of a population.

per capita income A nation's total income per person; the average income of a population.

perfectly elastic demand Product or resource demand in which *quantity demanded* can be of any amount at a particular product *price;* graphs as a horizontal *demand curve.*

perfectly elastic supply Product or resource supply in which *quantity supplied* can be of any amount at a particular product or resource *price;* graphs as a horizontal *supply curve.*

perfectly inelastic demand Product or resource demand in which *price* can be of any amount at a particular quantity of the product or resource demanded; *quantity demanded* does not respond to a change in price; graphs as a vertical *demand curve.*

perfectly inelastic supply Product or resource supply in which *price* can be of any amount at a particular quantity of the product or resource demanded; *quantity supplied* does not respond to a change in price; graphs as a vertical *supply curve.*

per se violations Collusive actions, such as attempts by firms to fix prices or divide a market, that are violations of the *antitrust laws,* even if the actions themselves are unsuccessful.

personal consumption expenditures The expenditures of *households* for *durable* and *nondurable consumer goods* and *services.*

personal distribution of income The manner in which the economy's *personal* or *disposable income* is divided among different income classes or different households or families.

personal income The earned and unearned income available to resource suppliers and others before the payment of *personal taxes.*

personal income tax A tax levied on the *taxable income* of individuals, households, and unincorporated firms.

Personal Responsibility Act A 1996 law that eliminated the Federal government's six-decade-long guarantee of cash assistance for poor families, whether adults in the family work or not; sets a limit of 5 years on receiving *Temporary Assistance for Needy Families (TANF)* benefits and requires that able-bodied adults work after 2 years to continue to receive public assistance.

personal saving The *personal income* of households less *personal taxes* and *personal consumption expenditures; disposable income* not spent for *consumer goods.*

per-unit production cost The average production cost of a particular level of output; total input cost divided by units of output.

plant A physical establishment that performs one or more functions in the production, fabrication, and distribution of goods and services.

"play or pay" A means of expanding health insurance coverage by requiring that employers either provide insurance for their workers or pay a special *payroll tax* to finance insurance for noncovered workers.

policy economics The formulation of courses of action to bring about desired economic outcomes or to prevent undesired occurrences.

positive economics The analysis of facts or data to establish scientific generalizations about economic behavior.

positive relationship A direct relationship between two variables.

post hoc, ergo propter hoc **fallacy** The false belief that when one event precedes another, the first event must have caused the second event.

potential competition The new competitors that may be induced to enter an industry if firms now in that industry are receiving large *economic profits.*

poverty A situation in which the basic needs of an individual or family exceed the means to satisfy them.

poverty rate The percentage of the population with incomes below the official poverty income levels that are established by the Federal government.

preferred provider organization (PPO) An arrangement in which doctors and hospitals agree to provide health care to insured individuals at rates negotiated with an insurer.

price The amount of money needed to buy a particular good, service, or resource.

price ceiling A legally established maximum price for a good or service.

price discrimination The selling of a product to different buyers at different prices when the price differences are not justified by differences in cost.

price elasticity of demand The ratio of the percentage change in *quantity demanded* of a product or resource to the percentage change in its *price;* a measure of the responsiveness of buyers to a change in the price of a product or resource.

price elasticity of supply The ratio of the percentage change in *quantity supplied* of a product or resource to the percentage change in its *price;* a measure of the responsiveness of producers to a change in the price of a product or resource.

price fixing The conspiring by two or more firms to set the price of their products; an illegal practice under the *Sherman Act.*

price floor A legally determined price above the *equilibrium price.*

price leadership An informal method that firms in an *oligopoly* may employ to set the price of their product: One firm (the leader) is the first to announce a change in price, and the other firms (the followers) soon announce identical or similar changes.

price-level stability A steadiness of the price level from one period to the next; zero or low annual inflation; also called "price stability."

price maker A seller (or buyer) of a product or resource that is able to affect the product or resource price by changing the amount it sells (or buys).

price support A minimum price that government allows sellers to receive for a good or service; a legally established or maintained minimum price.

price taker A seller (or buyer) of a product or resource that is unable to affect the price at which a product or resource sells by changing the amount it sells (or buys).

price war Successive and continued decreases in the prices charged by firms in an oligopolistic industry. Each firm lowers its price below rivals' prices, hoping to increase its sales and revenues at its rivals' expense.

principal-agent problem A conflict of interest that occurs when agents (workers or managers) pursue their own objectives to the detriment of the principals' (stockholders') goals.

private good A good or service that is individually consumed and that can be profitably provided by privately owned firms because they can exclude nonpayers from receiving the benefits.

private property The right of private persons and firms to obtain, own, control, employ, dispose of, and bequeath *land, capital,* and other property.

private sector The *households* and business *firms* of the economy.

process innovation The development and use of new or improved production or distribution methods.

producer surplus (Web chapter) The difference between the actual price a producer receives (or producers receive) and the minimum acceptable price; the triangular area above the supply curve and below the market price.

product differentiation A strategy in which one firm's product is distinguished from competing products by means of its design, related services, quality, location, or other attributes (except price).

product innovation The development and sale of a new or improved product (or service).

production possibilities curve A curve showing the different combinations of two goods or services that can be produced in a *full-employment, full-production* economy where the available supplies of resources and technology are fixed.

productive efficiency The production of a good in the least costly way; occurs when production takes place at the output at which *average total cost* is a minimum and *marginal product* per dollar's worth of input is the same for all inputs.

productivity A measure of average output or real output per unit of input. For example, the productivity of labor is determined by dividing real output by hours of work.

productivity growth The percentage change in *productivity* from one period to another.

product market A market in which products are sold by *firms* and bought by *households.*

profit The return to the resource *entrepreneurial ability* (see *normal profit*); *total revenue* minus *total cost* (see *economic profit*).

profit-maximizing combination of resources The quantity of each resource a firm must employ to maximize its profit or minimize its loss; the combination in which the *marginal revenue product* of each resource is equal to its *marginal resource cost* (to its *price* if the resource is employed in a competitive market).

profit-sharing plan A compensation device through which workers receive part of their pay in the form of a share of their employer's profit (if any).

progressive tax A tax whose *average tax rate* increases as the taxpayer's income increases and decreases as the taxpayer's income decreases.

property tax A tax on the value of property (*capital, land, stocks* and *bonds,* and other *assets*) owned by *firms* and *households.*

proportional tax A tax whose *average tax rate* remains constant as the taxpayer's income increases or decreases.

proprietor's income The net income of the owners of unincorporated firms (proprietorships and partnerships).

protective tariff A *tariff* designed to shield domestic producers of a good or service from the competition of foreign producers.

public assistance programs Government programs that pay benefits to those who are unable to earn income (because of permanent disabilities or because they have very low income and dependent children); financed by general tax revenues and viewed as public charity (rather than earned rights).

public choice theory The economic analysis of government decision making, politics, and elections.

public good A good or service characterized by *nonrivalry* and *nonexcludability;* a good or service with these characteristics provided by government.

public interest theory of regulation The presumption that the purpose of the regulation of an *industry* is to protect the public (consumers) from abuse of the power possessed by *natural monopolies.*

public sector The part of the economy that contains all government entities; government.

public utility A firm that produces an essential good or service, has obtained from a government the right to be the sole supplier of the good or service in the area, and is regulated by that government to prevent the abuse of its monopoly power.

purchasing power The amount of goods and services that a monetary unit of income can buy.

purchasing power parity The idea that exchange rates between nations equate the purchasing power of various currencies. Exchange rates between any two nations adjust to reflect the price-level differences between the countries.

pure competition A market structure in which a very large number of firms sells a *standardized product,* into which entry is very easy, in which the individual seller has no control over the product price, and in which there is no nonprice competition; a market characterized by a very large number of buyers and sellers.

pure monopoly A market structure in which one firm sells a unique product, into which entry is blocked, in which the single firm has considerable control over product price, and in which *nonprice competition* may or may not be found.

pure profit (See *economic profit.*)

pure rate of interest An essentially risk-free, long-term interest rate that is free of the influence of market imperfections.

quantity demanded The amount of a good or service that buyers (or a buyer) desire to purchase at a particular price during some period.

quantity supplied The amount of a good or service that producers (or a producer) offer to sell at a particular price during some period.

quasi-public good A good or service to which excludability could apply but that has such a large *spillover benefit* that government sponsors its production to prevent an underallocation of resources.

R&D Research and development activities undertaken to bring about technological progress.

rate of exchange The price paid in one's own money to acquire 1 unit of a foreign currency; the rate at which the money of one nation is exchanged for the money of another nation.

rate of return The gain in net revenue divided by the cost of an investment or an *R&D* expenditure; expressed as a percentage.

rational behavior Human behavior based on comparison of marginal costs and marginal benefits; behavior designed to maximize total utility.

rationing function of prices The ability of market forces in competitive markets to equalize *quantity demanded* and *quantity supplied* and to eliminate shortages and surpluses via changes in prices.

real capital (See *capital.*)

real GDP (See *real gross domestic product.*)

real gross domestic product (GDP) *Gross domestic product* adjusted for inflation; gross domestic product in a year divided by the GDP *price index* for that year, expressed as a decimal.

real income The amount of goods and services that can be purchased with *nominal income* during some period of time; nominal income adjusted for inflation.

real interest rate The interest rate expressed in dollars of constant value (adjusted for *inflation*) and equal to the *nominal interest rate* less the expected rate of inflation.

real wage The amount of goods and services a worker can purchase with his or her *nominal wage;* the purchasing power of the nominal wage.

recession A period of declining real GDP, accompanied by lower real income and higher unemployment.

Reciprocal Trade Agreements Act A 1934 Federal law that authorized the president to negotiate up to 50 percent lower tariffs with foreign nations that agreed to reduce their tariffs on U.S. goods. (Such agreements incorporated the *most-favored-nation* clause.)

regressive tax   A tax whose *average tax rate* decreases as the taxpayer's income increases and increases as the taxpayer's income decreases.

regulatory agency   An agency, commission, or board established by the Federal government or a state government to control the prices charged and the services offered by a *natural monopoly*.

rental income   The payments (income) received by those who supply *land* to the economy.

rent-seeking behavior   The actions by persons, firms, or unions to gain special benefits from government at the taxpayers' or someone else's expense.

resource   A natural, human, or manufactured item that helps produce goods and services; a productive agent or factor of production.

resource market   A market in which *households* sell and *firms* buy resources or the services of resources.

revenue tariff   A *tariff* designed to produce income for the Federal government.

reverse discrimination   The view that the preferential treatment associated with *affirmative action* efforts constitutes discrimination against other groups.

right-to-work law   A state law (in about 22 states) that makes it illegal to require that a worker join a *labor union* in order to retain his or her job; laws that make *union shops* and *agency shops* illegal.

roundabout production   The construction and use of *capital* to aid in the production of *consumer goods*.

rule of reason   The rule stated and applied in the *U.S. Steel case* that only combinations and contracts unreasonably restraining trade are subject to actions under the antitrust laws and that size and possession of monopoly power are not illegal.

rule of 70   A method for determining the number of years it will take for some measure to double, given its annual percentage increase. Example: To determine the number of years it will take for the price level to double, divide 70 by the annual rate of *inflation*.

sales tax   A tax levied on the cost (at retail) of a broad group of products.

saving   Disposable income not spent for consumer goods; equal to *disposable income* minus *personal consumption expenditures*.

scarce resources   The limited quantities of *land, capital, labor,* and *entrepreneurial ability* that are never sufficient to satisfy people's virtually unlimited economic wants.

scientific method   The procedure for the systematic pursuit of knowledge involving the observation of facts and the formulation and testing of hypotheses to obtain theories, principles, and laws.

seasonal variations   Increases and decreases in the level of economic activity within a single year, caused by a change in the season.

self-interest   That which each firm, property owner, worker, and consumer believes is best for itself and seeks to obtain.

seniority   The length of time a worker has been employed absolutely or relative to other workers; may be used to determine which workers will be laid off when there is

insufficient work for them all and who will be rehired when more work becomes available.

separation of ownership and control   The fact that different groups of people own a *corporation* (the stockholders) and manage it (the directors and officers).

service   An (intangible) act or use for which a consumer, firm, or government is willing to pay.

Sherman Act   The Federal antitrust act of 1890 that made monopoly and conspiracies to restrain trade criminal offenses.

shirking   Workers' neglecting or evading work to increase their *utility* or well-being.

shortage   The amount by which the *quantity demanded* of a product exceeds the *quantity supplied* at a particular (below-equilibrium) price.

short run   (1) In microeconomics, a period of time in which producers are able to change the quantities of some but not all of the resources they employ; a period in which some resources (usually plant) are fixed and some are variable. (2) In macroeconomics, a period in which nominal wages and other input prices do not change in response to a change in the price level.

short-run competitive equilibrium   The price at which the total quantity of a product supplied in the *short run* in a purely competitive industry equals the total quantity of the product demanded and that is equal to or greater than *average variable cost*.

short-run farm problem   The sharp year-to-year changes in the prices of agricultural products and in the incomes of farmers.

short-run supply curve   A supply curve that shows the quantity of a product a firm in a purely competitive industry will offer to sell at various prices in the *short run;* the portion of the firm's short-run marginal cost curve that lies above its *average-variable-cost* curve.

shutdown case   The circumstance in which a firm would experience a loss greater than its total *fixed cost* if it were to produce any output greater than zero; alternatively, a situation in which a firm would cease to operate when the *price* at which it can sell its product is less than its *average variable cost*.

slope of a line   The ratio of the vertical change (the rise or fall) to the horizontal change (the run) between any two points on a line. The slope of an upward-sloping line is positive, reflecting a direct relationship between two variables; the slope of a downward-sloping line is negative, reflecting an inverse relationship between two variables.

Smoot-Hawley Tariff Act   Legislation passed in 1930 that established very high tariffs. Its objective was to reduce imports and stimulate the domestic economy, but it resulted only in retaliatory tariffs by other nations.

social insurance programs   Programs that replace the earnings lost when people retire or are temporarily unemployed, that are financed by payroll taxes, and that are viewed as earned rights (rather than charity).

socially optimal price   The price of a product that results in the most efficient allocation of an economy's resources and that is equal to the *marginal cost* of the product.

social regulation   Regulation in which government is concerned with the conditions under which goods and services are produced, their physical characteristics, and the impact of their production on society; in contrast to *industrial regulation*.

Social Security program (See *Old Age, Survivors, and Disability Health Insurance*.)

sole proprietorship An unincorporated *firm* owned and operated by one person.

special economic zones (Web chapter) Regions of China open to foreign investment, private ownership, and relatively free international trade.

special-interest effect Any result of government promotion of the interests (goals) of a small group at the expense of a much larger group.

specialization The use of the resources of an individual, a firm, a region, or a nation to concentrate production on one or a small number of goods and services.

speculation The activity of buying or selling with the motive of later reselling or rebuying for profit.

spillover A benefit or cost from production or consumption, accruing without compensation to nonbuyers and nonsellers of the product (see *spillover benefit* and *spillover cost*).

spillover benefit A benefit obtained without compensation by third parties from the production or consumption of sellers or buyers. Example: A beekeeper benefits when a neighboring farmer plants clover.

spillover cost A cost imposed without compensation on third parties by the production or consumption of sellers or buyers. Example: A manufacturer dumps toxic chemicals into a river, killing the fish sought by sport fishers.

SSI (See *Supplemental Security Income*.)

standardized product A product whose buyers are indifferent to the seller from whom they purchase it as long as the price charged by all sellers is the same; a product all units of which are identical and thus are perfect substitutes for each other.

Standard Oil case A 1911 antitrust case in which Standard Oil was found guilty of violating the *Sherman Act* by illegally monopolizing the petroleum industry. As a remedy the company was divided into several competing firms.

startup (firm) A new firm focused on creating and introducing a particular new product or employing a specific new production or distribution method.

state-owned enterprises (Web chapter) Businesses that are owned by the government; the major type of enterprises in Russia and China before their transitions to the market system.

statistical discrimination The practice of judging an individual on the basis of the average characteristic of the group to which he or she belongs rather than on his or her own personal characteristics.

stock (corporate) An ownership share in a corporation.

stock options Contracts that enable executives or other key employees to buy shares of their employers' stock at fixed, lower prices when the stock prices rise.

strategic behavior Self-interested economic actions that take into account the expected reactions of others.

strategic trade policy The use of trade barriers to reduce the risk inherent in product development by domestic firms, particularly that involving advanced technology.

strike The withholding of labor services by an organized group of workers (a *labor union*).

structural-change hypothesis The explanation that ascribes the decline of unionism in the United States to changes in the structure of the economy and of the labor force.

subsidy A payment of funds (or goods and services) by a government, firm, or household for which it receives no good or service in return. When made by a government, it is a *government transfer payment*.

substitute goods Products or services that can be used in place of each other. When the price of one falls, the demand for the other product falls; conversely, when the price of one product rises, the demand for the other product rises.

substitution effect (1) A change in the quantity demanded of a *consumer good* that results from a change in its relative expensiveness caused by a change in the product's price; (2) the effect of a change in the price of a *resource* on the quantity of the resource employed by a firm, assuming no change in its output.

sunk cost A cost that has been incurred and cannot be recovered.

Supplemental Security Income (SSI) A federally financed and administered program that provides a uniform nationwide minimum income for the aged, blind, and disabled who do not qualify for benefits under the *Old Age, Survivors, and Disability Health Insurance* or *unemployment insurance* program in the United States.

supply A schedule showing the amounts of a good or service that sellers (or a seller) will offer at various prices during some period.

supply curve A curve illustrating *supply*.

surplus The amount by which the *quantity supplied* of a product exceeds the *quantity demanded* at a specific (above-equilibrium) price.

surplus payment A payment to a resource that is not required to ensure its availability in the production process; for example, land rent.

surplus value (Web chapter) The amount by which a worker's daily output in dollar terms exceeds his daily wage; the amount of the worker's output appropriated by capitalists as profit; a Marxian term.

tacit collusion Any method used by an oligopolist to set prices and outputs that does not involve outright (or overt) *collusion*. *Price leadership* is a frequent example.

TANF (See *Temporary Assistance for Needy Families*.)

tariff A tax imposed by a nation on an imported good.

taste-for-discrimination model A theory that views discrimination as a preference for which an employer is willing to pay.

tax An involuntary payment of money (or goods and services) to a government by a *household* or *firm* for which the household or firm receives no good or service directly in return.

tax incidence The person or group that ends up paying a tax.

tax subsidy A grant in the form of reduced taxes through favorable tax treatment. For example, employer-paid health insurance is exempt from Federal income and payroll taxes.

technological advance   New and better goods and services and new and better ways of producing or distributing them.

technology   The body of knowledge and techniques that can be used to combine *economic resources* to produce goods and services.

Temporary Assistance for Needy Families (TANF)   A state-administered and partly federally funded program in the United States that provides financial aid to poor families; the basic welfare program for low-income families in the United States; contains time limits and work requirements.

terms of trade   The rate at which units of one product can be exchanged for units of another product; the price of a good or service; the amount of one good or service that must be given up to obtain 1 unit of another good or service.

theoretical economics   The process of deriving and applying economic theories and principles.

theory of human capital   The generalization that *wage differentials* are the result of differences in the amount of *human capital investment* and that the incomes of lower-paid workers are raised by increasing the amount of such investment.

total cost   The sum of *fixed cost* and *variable cost*.

total demand   The demand schedule or the *demand curve* of all buyers of a good or service; also called market demand.

total product   The total output of a particular good or service produced by a firm (or a group of firms or the entire economy).

total revenue   The total number of dollars received by a firm (or firms) from the sale of a product; equal to the total expenditures for the product produced by the firm (or firms); equal to the quantity sold (demanded) multiplied by the price at which it is sold.

total-revenue test   A test to determine elasticity of *demand* between any two prices: Demand is elastic if *total revenue* moves in the opposite direction from price; it is inelastic when it moves in the same direction as price; and it is of unitary elasticity when it does not change when price changes.

total spending   The total amount that buyers of goods and services spend or plan to spend; also called *aggregate expenditures*.

total supply   The supply schedule or the *supply curve* of all sellers of a good or service; also called market supply.

total utility   The total amount of satisfaction derived from the consumption of a single product or a combination of products.

township and village enterprises   (Web chapter) Privately owned rural manufacturing firms in China.

trade balance   The export of goods (or goods and services) of a nation less its imports of goods (or goods and services).

trade bloc   A group of nations that lower or abolish trade barriers among members. Examples include the *European Union* and the nations of the *North American Free Trade Agreement*.

trade controls   *Tariffs, export subsidies, import quotas,* and other means a nation may employ to reduce *imports* and expand *exports*.

trade deficit   The amount by which a nation's *imports* of goods (or goods and services) exceed its *exports* of goods (or goods and services).

trademark   A legal protection that gives the originators of a product an exclusive right to use the brand name.

tradeoff   The sacrifice of some or all of one economic goal, good, or service to achieve some other goal, good, or service.

trade surplus   The amount by which a nation's *exports* of goods (or goods and services) exceed its *imports* of goods (or goods and services).

trading possibilities line   A line that shows the different combinations of two products that an economy is able to obtain (consume) when it specializes in the production of one product and trades (exports) it to obtain the other product.

transfer payment   A payment of *money* (or goods and services) by a government to a *household* or *firm* for which the payer receives no good or service directly in return.

tying contract   A requirement imposed by a seller that a buyer purchase another (or other) of its products as a condition for buying a desired product; a practice forbidden by the *Clayton Act*.

underemployment   (1) The failure to produce the maximum amount of goods and services that can be produced from the resources employed; the failure to achieve *full production;* (2) a situation in which workers are employed in positions requiring less education and skill than they have.

undistributed corporate profits   After-tax corporate profits not distributed as dividends to stockholders; corporate or business saving; also called retained earnings.

unemployment   The failure to use all available *economic resources* to produce desired goods and services; the failure of the economy to fully employ its *labor force*.

unemployment compensation   (See *unemployment insurance*).

unemployment insurance   The social insurance program that in the United States is financed by state *payroll taxes* on employers and makes income available to workers who become unemployed and are unable to find jobs.

unemployment rate   The percentage of the *labor force* unemployed at any time.

uninsurable risk   An event that would result in a loss and whose occurrence is uncontrollable and unpredictable. Insurance companies are not willing to sell insurance against such a loss.

union shop   A place of employment where the employer may hire either *labor union* members or nonmembers but where nonmembers must become members within a specified period of time or lose their jobs.

unit elasticity   Demand or supply for which the *elasticity coefficient* is equal to 1; means that the percentage change in the quantity demanded or supplied is equal to the percentage change in price.

unit labor cost   Labor cost per unit of output; total labor cost divided by total output; also equal to the *nominal wage* rate divided by the *average product* of labor.

unlimited liability   Absence of any limits on the maximum amount that an individual (usually a business owner) may become legally required to pay.

unlimited wants   The insatiable desire of consumers for goods and services that will give them satisfaction or *utility*.

urban collectives   (Web chapter) Chinese enterprises jointly owned by their managers and their workforces and located in urban areas.

Uruguay Round   A 1995 trade agreement (to be fully implemented by 2005) that established the *World Trade Organization (WTO)*, liberalized trade in goods and services, provided added protection to intellectual property (for example, *patents* and *copyrights*), and reduced farm subsidies.

U.S. Steel case   The antitrust action brought by the Federal government against the U.S. Steel Corporation in which the courts ruled (in 1920) that only unreasonable restraints of trade were illegal and that size and the possession of monopoly power were not violations of the antitrust laws.

usury laws   State laws that specify the maximum legal interest rate at which loans can be made.

utility   The want-satisfying power of a good or service; the satisfaction or pleasure a consumer obtains from the consumption of a good or service (or from the consumption of a collection of goods and services).

utility-maximizing rule   The principle that to obtain the greatest *utility* the consumer should allocate *money income* so that the last dollar spent on each good or service yields the same marginal utility.

value-added tax   A tax imposed on the difference between the value of the product sold by a firm and the value of the goods purchased from other firms to produce the product; used in several European countries.

value judgment   Opinion of what is desirable or undesirable; belief regarding what ought or ought not to be (regarding what is right or just and wrong or unjust).

variable cost   A cost that in total increases when the firm increases its output and decreases when the firm reduces its output.

VAT   (See *value-added tax.*)

vertical integration   A group of *plants* engaged in different stages of the production of a final product and owned by a single *firm*.

vertical intercept   The point at which a line meets the vertical axis of a graph.

vertical merger   The merger of one or more *firms* engaged in different stages of the production of a final product.

very long run   A period in which *technology* can change and in which *firms* can introduce new products.

voice mechanism   Communication by workers through their union to resolve grievances with an employer.

voluntary export restrictions   Voluntary limitations by countries or firms of their exports to a particular foreign nation to avoid enactment of formal trade barriers by that nation.

wage   The price paid for the use or services of *labor* per unit of time (per hour, per day, and so on).

wage differential   The difference between the *wage* received by one worker or group of workers and that received by another worker or group of workers.

wage discrimination   The payment of a lower wage to members of a less preferred group than that paid to members of a more preferred group for the same work.

wage rate   (See *wage.*)

wages   The income of those who supply the economy with *labor*.

wealth   Anything that has value because it produces income or could produce income. Wealth is a stock; income is a flow. Assets less liabilities; net worth.

welfare programs   (See *public assistance programs.*)

Wheeler-Lea Act   The Federal act of 1938 that amended the *Federal Trade Commission Act* by prohibiting and giving the commission power to investigate unfair and deceptive acts or practices of commerce (such as false and misleading advertising and the misrepresentation of products).

world price   The international market price of a good or service, determined by world demand and supply.

World Trade Organization (WTO)   An organization of 145 nations (as of 2003) that oversees the provisions of the current world trade agreement, resolves trade disputes stemming from it, and holds forums for further rounds of trade negotiations.

WTO   (See *World Trade Organization.*)

X-inefficiency   The failure to produce any specific output at the lowest average (and total) cost possible.

Answers to Key Questions

CHAPTER 1

1-4 Use the economic perspective to explain why someone who is normally a light eater at a standard restaurant may become somewhat of a glutton at a buffet-style restaurant which charges a single price for all you can eat.

This behavior can be explained in terms of marginal costs and marginal benefits. At a standard restaurant, items are priced individually—they have a positive marginal cost. If you order more, it will cost you more. You order until the marginal benefit from the extra food no longer exceeds the marginal cost. At a buffet you pay a flat fee no matter how much you eat. Once the fee is paid, additional food items have a zero marginal cost. You therefore continue to eat until your marginal benefit becomes zero.

1-8 Explain in detail the interrelationships between economic facts, theory, and policy. Critically evaluate this statement: "The trouble with economic theory is that it is not practical. It is detached from the real world."

Economic theory consists of factually supported generalizations about economic behavior that can be used to formulate economic policies. Economic theory enables policymakers to formulate economic policies that are relevant to real-world goals and problems that are based upon carefully observed facts.

1-10 Indicate whether each of the following statements applies to microeconomics or macroeconomics:

(a), (d), and (f) are macro; (b), (c), and (e) are micro.

1-11 Identify each of the following as either a positive or a normative statement:
a. The high temperature today was 89 degrees.
b. It was too hot today.
c. Other things being equal, higher interest rates reduce the total amount of borrowing.
d. Interest rates are too high.

(a) and (c) are positive; (b) and (d) are normative.

1-12 Explain and give an illustration of (a) the fallacy of composition; and (b) the "after this, therefore because of this" fallacy. Why are cause-and-effect relationships difficult to isolate in the social sciences?

(a) The fallacy of composition is the mistake of believing that something true for an individual part is necessarily true for the whole. Example: A single auto producer can increase its profits by lowering its price and taking business away from its competitors. But matched price cuts by all auto manufacturers will not necessarily yield higher industry profits.
(b) The "after this, therefore because of this" fallacy is incorrectly reasoning that when one event precedes another, the first event necessarily caused the second. Example: Interest rates rise, followed by an increase in the rate of inflation, leading to the erroneous conclusion that the rise in interest rates caused the inflation. Actually higher interest rates slow inflation.

Cause-and-effect relationships are difficult to isolate because "other things" are continually changing.

CHAPTER 1 APPENDIX

1-2 Indicate how each of the following might affect the data shown in Table 2 and Figure 2 of this appendix:
a. GSU's athletic director schedules higher-quality opponents.
b. An NBA team locates in the city where GSU plays.
c. GSU contracts to have all its home games televised.

(a) More tickets are bought at each price; the line shifts to the right.
(b) Fewer tickets are bought at each price; the line shifts to the left.
(c) Fewer tickets are bought at each price; the line shifts to the left.

1-3 The following table contains data on the relationship between saving and income. Rearrange these data into a meaningful order and graph them on the accompanying grid. What is the slope of the line? The vertical intercept? Interpret the meaning of both the slope and the intercept. Write the equation that represents this line. What would you predict saving to be at the $12,500 level of income?

Income (per year)	Saving (per year)
$15,000	$1,000
0	−500
10,000	500
5,000	0
20,000	1,500

Income column: $0; $5,000; $10,000; $15,000; $20,000. Saving column: $−500; 0; $500; $1,000; $1,500. Slope = 0.1 (= $1,000 − $500)/($15,000 − $10,000). Vertical intercept = $−500. The slope shows the amount of saving will increase for every $1 increase in income; the intercept shows the amount of saving (dissaving) occurring when income is zero. Equation: $S = \$-500 + 0.1Y$ (where S is saving and Y is income). Saving will be $750 at the $12,500 income level.

1-7 The accompanying graph shows curve XX and tangents at points A, B, and C. Calculate the slope of the curve at these three points.

Slopes: at $A = +4$; at $B = 0$; at $C = -4$.

CHAPTER 2

2-4 Classify the following Microsoft resources as land, labor, capital, or entrepreneurial ability: code writers for software, Bill Gates, production facility for Windows CD-ROMs, "campus" on which Microsoft buildings sit, grounds crews at Microsoft campus, Microsoft corporate jet.

Land—campus where Microsoft buildings sit. *Labor*—code writers, grounds crews. *Capital*—production facility, corporate jet. *Entrepreneurial ability*—Bill Gates

2-5 Distinguish between full employment and full production as they relate to production possibilities analysis. Distinguish between productive efficiency and allocative efficiency. Give an illustration of achieving productive efficiency, but not allocative efficiency.

Full employment occurs when all available resources are utilized; full production means that all employed resources are used to provide the maximum possible satisfaction of material wants. Both are required for an economy to be producing on the production possibilities curve. An economy that is employing all available resources but which allocates labor to unproductive tasks will operate inside the curve. Likewise, putting resources to their most productive uses but failing to employ all resources will result in an economy producing inside the curve.

Allocative efficiency means that resources are being used to produce the goods and services most wanted by society. The economy is then located at the optimal point on its production possibilities curve where marginal benefit equals marginal cost for each good. Productive efficiency means the least costly production techniques are being used to produce wanted goods and services. Examples: manual typewriters produced using the least-cost techniques but for which there is no demand; cigarettes produced using least-cost techniques but for which there are "bads" created that are not accounted for by the market.

2-6 Here is a production possibilities table for war goods and civilian goods:

Type of production	Production alternatives				
	A	**B**	**C**	**D**	**E**
Automobiles	0	2	4	6	8
Missiles	30	27	21	12	0

a. Show these data graphically. Upon what specific assumptions is this production possibilities curve based?
b. If the economy is at point C, what is the cost of one more automobile? One more missile? Explain how this curve reflects increasing opportunity costs.

c. What must the economy do to operate at some point on the production possibilities curve?

(a) See curve EDCBA. The assumptions are full employment and productive efficiency, fixed supplies of resources, and fixed technology.

Question 2-6

(b) 4.5 rockets; .33 automobiles, as determined from the table. Increasing opportunity costs are reflected in the concave-from-the-origin shape of the curve. This means the economy must give up larger and larger amounts of rockets to get constant added amounts of automobiles—and vice versa.
(c) It must obtain full employment and productive efficiency.

2-11 Referring again to question 6, suppose improvement occurs in the technology of producing missiles but not in the production of automobiles. Draw the new production possibilities curve. Now assume that a technological advance occurs in producing automobiles but not in producing missiles. Draw the new production possibilities curve. Now draw a production possibilities curve that reflects technological improvement in the production of both products.

See the graph for question 2-6. PPC_1 shows improved missile technology. PPC_2 shows improved auto technology. PPC_3 shows improved technology in producing both products.

CHAPTER 3

3-2 What effect will each of the following have on the demand for product B?
a. Product B becomes more fashionable.
b. The price of substitute product C falls.
c. Income declines and product B is an inferior good.
d. Consumers anticipate the price of B will be lower in the near future.
e. The price of complementary product D falls.

Demand increases in (a), (c), and (e); decreases in (b) and (d).

3-5 What effect will each of the following have on the supply of product B?
a. A technological advance in the methods of producing B.
b. A decline in the number of firms in industry B.
c. An increase in the price of resources required in the production of B.
d. The expectation that the equilibrium price of B will be lower in the future than it is currently.
e. A decline in the price of product A, a good whose production requires substantially the same techniques as does the production of B.
f. The levying of a specific sales tax upon B.

g. The granting of a 50-cent per unit subsidy for each unit of B produced.

Supply increases in (a), (d), (e), and (g); decreases in (b), (c), and (f).

3–7 Suppose the total demand for wheat and the total supply of wheat per month in the Kansas City grain market are as follows:

Thousands of bushels demanded	Price per bushel	Thousand of bushels supplied	Surplus (+) or shortage (−)
85	$3.40	72	−13
80	3.70	73	−7
75	4.00	75	0
70	4.30	77	+7
65	4.60	79	+14
60	4.90	81	+21

a. What will be the market or equilibrium price? What is the equilibrium quantity? Fill in the surplus–shortage column and use it to explain why your answers are correct.

b. Graph the demand for wheat and the supply of wheat. Be sure to label the axes of your graph correctly. Label the equilibrium price "P" and the equilibrium quantity "Q."

c. Why will $3.40 not be the equilibrium price in this market? Why not $4.90? "Surpluses drive prices up; shortages drive them down." Do you agree?

Data from top to bottom: −13; −7; 0; +7; +14; and +21.

(a) P_e = $4.00; Q_e = 75,000. Equilibrium occurs where there is neither a shortage nor surplus of wheat. At the immediately lower price of $3.70, there is a shortage of 7,000 bushels. At the immediately higher price of $4.30, there is a surplus of 7,000 bushels. (See graph above.)

(b) Quantity (thousands) of bushels.

(c) Because at $3.40 there will be a 13,000 bushel shortage which will drive the price up. Because at $4.90 there will be a 21,000 bushel surplus which will drive the price down. Quotation is incorrect; just the opposite is true.

3–8 How will each of the following changes in demand and/or supply affect equilibrium price and equilibrium quantity in a competitive market; that is, do price and quantity rise, fall, remain unchanged, or are the answers indeterminate because they depend on the magnitudes of the shifts? Use supply and demand diagrams to verify your answers.

a. Supply decreases and demand is constant.
b. Demand decreases and supply is constant.
c. Supply increases and demand is constant.

d. Demand increases and supply increases.
e. Demand increases and supply is constant.
f. Supply increases and demand decreases.
g. Demand increases and supply decreases.
h. Demand decreases and supply decreases.

(a) Price up; quantity down;
(b) Price down; quantity down;
(c) Price down; quantity up;
(d) Price indeterminate; quantity up;
(e) Price up; quantity up;
(f) Price down; quantity indeterminate;
(g) Price up, quantity indeterminate;
(h) Price indeterminate and quantity down.

3–13 Refer to the table in question 7. Suppose that the government establishes a price ceiling of $3.70 for wheat. What might prompt the government to establish this price ceiling? Explain carefully the main effects. Demonstrate your answer graphically. Next, suppose that the government establishes a price floor of $4.60 for wheat. What will be the main effects of this price floor? Demonstrate your answer graphically.

At a price of $3.70, buyers will wish to purchase 80,000 bushels, but sellers will only offer 73,000 bushels to the market. The result is a shortage of 7,000 bushels. The ceiling prevents the price from rising to encourage greater production, discourage consumption, and relieve the shortage. See the graph below.

Question 3–13 (Price ceiling)

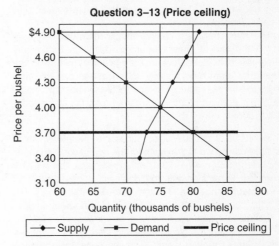

At a price of $4.60, buyers only want to purchase 65,000 bushels, but sellers want to sell 79,000 bushels, resulting in a surplus of 14,000 bushels. The floor prevents the price from falling to eliminate the surplus. See the graph below.

Question 3–13 (Price floor)

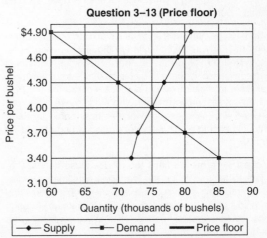

CHAPTER 4

4–7 Assume that a business firm finds that its profits will be at a maximum when it produces $40 worth of product A. Suppose also that each of the three techniques shown in the following table will produce the desired output.

Resource	Price per unit of resource	Resource Units Required		
		Technique No. 1	Technique No. 2	Technique No. 3
Labor	$3	5	2	3
Land	4	2	4	2
Capital	2	2	4	5
Entrepreneurial ability	2	4	2	4

a. With the resource prices shown, which technique will the firm choose? Why? Will production entail profits or losses? Will the industry expand or contract? When is a new equilibrium output achieved?

b. Assume now that a new technique, technique No. 4, is developed. It entails the use of 2 units of labor, 2 of land, 6 of capital, and 3 of entrepreneurial ability. Given the resource prices in the table, will the firm adopt the new technique? Explain your answers.

c. Suppose now that an increase in labor supply causes the price of labor to fall to $1.50 per unit, all other resource prices being unchanged. Which technique will the producer now choose? Explain.

d. "The market system causes the economy to conserve most in the use of those resources which are particularly scarce in supply. Resources that are scarcest relative to the demand for them have the highest prices. As a result, producers use these resources as sparingly as is possible." Evaluate this statement. Does your answer to part c, above, bear out this contention? Explain.

(a) Technique 2 because it produces the output with least cost ($34 compared to $35 each for the other two). Economic profit will be $6 (= 40 − $34), which will cause the industry to expand. Expansion will continue until prices decline to where total revenue is $34 (equal to total cost).

(b) Adopt technique 4 because its cost is now lowest at $32.

(c) Technique 1 because its cost is now lowest at $27.50.

(d) The statement is logical. Increasing scarcity causes prices to rise. Firms ignoring higher resource prices will become high-cost producers and be competed out of business by firms switching to the less expensive inputs. The market system forces producers to conserve on the use of highly scarce resources. Question 8c confirms this: Technique 1 was adopted because labor had become less expensive.

4–10 Some large hardware stores such as Home Depot boast of carrying as many as 20,000 different products in each store. What motivated the producers of those products—everything from screwdrivers to ladders to water heaters—to make them and offer them for sale? How did producers decide on the best combinations of resources to use? Who made these resources available, and why? Who decides whether these particular hardware products should continue to get produced and offered for sale?

The quest for profit led firms to produce these goods. Producers looked for and found the least-cost combination of resources in producing their output. Resource suppliers, seeking income, made these resources available. Consumers, through their dollar votes, ultimately decide on what will continue to be produced.

CHAPTER 5

5–2 Assume that the five residents of Econoville receive incomes of $50, $75, $125, $250, and $500. Present the resulting personal distribution of income as a graph similar to Figure 5.2. Compare the incomes of the lowest and highest fifth of the income receivers.

The distribution of income is quite unequal. The highest 20 percent of the residents receive 10 times more income than the lowest 20 percent.

5–4 What are the three major legal forms of business organization? Which form is the most prevalent in terms of numbers? Why do you think that is so? Which form is dominant in terms of total profits? What major advantages of this form of business organization gave rise to its dominance?

The three legal forms of business organizations are: sole proprietorship, partnership, and corporation.

Proprietorships are the most prevalent. They are easy to start (relatively low cost), often don't require a large customer base to be profitable, and provide maximum freedom for the proprietor to do what she/he thinks best.

Corporations are dominant in terms of total profits. They can access large amounts of money by issuing stocks and bonds; their limited liability is attractive to potential owners; their size and broader ownership base help ensure continuity that helps to build a large customer base and gain cost advantages (a preview for economies of scale).

5–9 What are the two characteristics of public goods? Explain the significance of each for public provision as opposed to private provision. What is the free-rider problem as it relates to public goods? Is the U.S. border patrol a public good or a private good? Why? How about satellite TV? Explain.

Public goods are nonrival (one person's consumption does not prevent consumption by another) and nonexcludable (once the goods are produced nobody—including free riders—can be excluded from the goods' benefits). If goods are nonrival, there is less incentive for private firms to produce them—those purchasing the good could simply allow others to use it without compensation. Similarly, if goods are nonexcludable, private firms are unlikely to produce them as the potential for profit is low. The free-rider problem occurs when people benefit from the public good without contributing to the cost (tax revenue proportionate to the benefit received). The U.S. border patrol is a public good—my use and benefit does not prevent yours. Satellite TV is a private good—if the dish, receiver, and service go to my residence it can't go to my neighbors. The fact that I could invite my neighbor over to watch does not change its status from being a private good.

5–10 Draw a production possibilities curve with public goods on the vertical axis and private goods on the horizontal axis. Assuming the economy is initially operating *on the curve,* indicate how the production of public goods might be increased. How might the output of public goods be increased if the economy is initially operating at a point *inside the curve*?

On the curve, the only way to obtain more public goods is to reduce the production of private goods (from *C* to *B*).

An economy operating inside the curve can expand the production of public goods without sacrificing private goods (say, from *A* to *B*) by making use of unemployed resources.

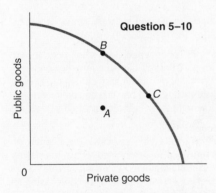

Question 5–10

5–15 Suppose in Fiscalville there is no tax on the first $10,000 of income, but a 20 percent tax on earnings between $10,000 and $20,000 and a 30 percent tax on income between $20,000 and $30,000. Any income above $30,000 is taxed at 40 percent. If your income is $50,000, how much in taxes will you pay? Determine your marginal and average tax rates. Is it a progressive tax? Explain.

Total tax = $13,000; marginal tax rate = 40%; average tax rate = 26%. This is a progressive tax; the average tax rate rises as income goes up.

CHAPTER 6

6–4 The following are production possibilities tables for South Korea and the United States. Assume that before specialization and trade the optimal product-mix for South Korea is alternative B and for the United States alternative U.

Product	South Korea's production possibilities					
	A	B	C	D	E	F
Radios (in 1000s)	30	24	18	12	6	0
Chemicals (in tons)	0	6	12	18	24	30
Product	U.S. production possibilities					
	R	S	T	U	V	W
Radios (in 1000s)	10	8	6	4	2	0
Chemicals (in tons)	0	4	8	12	16	20

a. Are comparative cost conditions such that the two areas should specialize? If so, what product should each produce?

b. What is the total gain in radio and chemical output that results from this specialization?

c. What are the limits of the terms of trade? Suppose actual terms of trade are 1 unit of radios for 1-1/2 units of chemicals and that 4 units of radios are exchanged for 6 units of chemicals. What are the gains from specialization and trade for each area?

d. Can you conclude from this illustration that specialization according to comparative advantage results in more efficient use of world resources? Explain.

(a) Yes, because the opportunity cost of radios is less (1R = 1C) in South Korea than in the United States (1R = 2C). South Korea should produce radios and the United States should produce chemicals.

(b) If they specialize, the United States can produce 20 tons of chemicals and South Korea can produce 30,000 radios. Before specialization South Korea produced alternative B and the United States alternative U for a total of 28,000 radios (24,000 + 4,000) and 18 tons of chemicals (6 tons + 12 tons). The gain is 2,000 radios and 2 tons of chemicals.

(c) The limits of the terms of trade are determined by the comparative cost conditions in each country before trade: 1R = 1C in South Korea and 1R = 2C in the United States. The terms of trade must be somewhere between these two ratios for trade to occur.

If the terms of trade are 1R = 1-1/2C, South Korea would end up with 26,000 radios (= 30,000 − 4,000) and 6 tons of chemicals. The United States would have 4,000 radios and 14 tons of chemicals (= 20 − 6). South Korea has gained 2,000 radios. The United States has gained 2 tons of chemicals.

(d) Yes, the world is obtaining more output from its fixed resources.

6–6 True or false? "U.S. exports create a demand for foreign currencies; foreign imports of U.S. goods generate supplies of foreign currencies." Explain. Would a decline in U.S. consumer income or a weakening of U.S. preferences for foreign products cause the dollar to depreciate or appreciate? Other things equal, what would be the effects of that depreciation or appreciation on U.S. exports and imports?

The first part of this statement is incorrect. U.S. exports create a domestic *supply* of foreign currencies, not a domestic demand for them. The second part of the statement is accurate. The foreign demand for dollars (from US. exports) generates a supply of foreign currencies to the United States.

A decline in U.S. incomes or a weakening of U.S. preferences for foreign goods would reduce U.S. imports, reducing U.S. demand for foreign currencies. These currencies would depreciate (the dollar would appreciate). Dollar appreciation means U.S. exports would decline and U.S. imports would increase.

6–10 Identify and state the significance of each of the following: (a) WTO; (b) EU; (c) euro; and (d) NAFTA. What commonality do they share?

(a) The WTO oversees trade agreements reached by member nations and arbitrates trade disputes among them. (b) The EU is a trading bloc of 25 European countries who have agreed to abolish tariffs and import quotas on most products and have liberalized the movements of labor and capital within the EU. (c) The euro is the common currency that is used by 12 of the original 15 EU countries. (d) NAFTA is a trade bloc made up of the United States, Canada, and Mexico whose purpose is to reduce tariffs and other trade barriers among the three countries.

All of the above have the goals of increasing international trade and a better allocation of the world's resources.

CHAPTER 7

7-2 Graph the accompanying demand data, and then use the midpoint formula for E_d to determine price elasticity of demand for each of the four possible $1 price changes. What can you conclude about the relationship between the slope of a curve and its elasticity? Explain in a nontechnical way why demand is elastic in the northwest segment of the demand curve and inelastic in the southeast segment.

Product price	Quantity demanded
$5	1
4	2
3	3
2	4
1	5

See the graph accompanying the answer to 7-4. Elasticities, top to bottom: 3; 1.4; .714; .333. Slope does not measure elasticity. This demand curve has a constant slope of -1 ($= -1/1$), but elasticity declines as we move down the curve. When the initial price is high and initial quantity is low, a unit change in price is a *low* percentage while a unit change in quantity is a *high* percentage change. The percentage change in quantity exceeds the percentage change in price, making demand elastic. When the initial price is low and initial quantity is high, a unit change in price is a *high* percentage change while a unit change in quantity is a *low* percentage change. The percentage change in quantity is less than the percentage change in price, making demand inelastic.

7-4 Calculate total-revenue data from the demand schedule in question 7-2. Graph total revenue below your demand curve. Generalize about the relationship between price elasticity and total revenue.

See the graph. Total revenue data, top to bottom: $5; $8; $9; $8; $5. When demand is elastic, price and total revenue move in the opposite direction. When demand is inelastic, price and total revenue move in the same direction.

Question 7-4

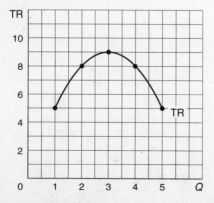

7-5 How would the following changes in price affect total revenue? That is, would total revenue increase, decline, or remain unchanged?
 a. Price falls and demand is inelastic.
 b. Price rises and demand is elastic.
 c. Price rises and supply is elastic.
 d. Price rises and supply is inelastic.
 e. Price rises and demand is inelastic.
 f. Price falls and demand is elastic.
 g. Price falls and demand is of unit elasticity.

Total revenue would increase in (c), (d), (e), and (f); decrease in (a) and (b); and remain the same in (g).

7-6 What are the major determinants of price elasticity of demand? Use those determinants and your own reasoning in judging whether demand for each of the following products is elastic or inelastic:
 (a) bottled water; **(b)** toothpaste; **(c)** Crest toothpaste; **(d)** ketchup; **(e)** diamond bracelets; **(f)** Microsoft Windows operating system.

Substitutability, proportion of income; luxury versus necessity, and time. Elastic: (a), (c), (e). Inelastic: (b), (d), and (f).

7-10 In November 1998, Vincent van Gogh's self-portrait sold at auction for $71.5 million. Portray this sale in a demand and supply diagram and comment on the elasticity of supply. Comedian George Carlin once mused, "If a painting can be forged well enough to fool some experts, why is the original so valuable?" Provide an answer.

The supply is perfectly inelastic—vertical—at a quantity of 1 unit. The $71.5 million price is determined where the downward sloping demand curve intersected this supply curve.

If more than one picture were available (all but one having to be a copy), the demand would likely decrease enormously.

7-12 Suppose the cross elasticity of demand for products A and B is +3.6 and for products C and D is −5.4. What can you conclude about how products A and B are related? Products C and D?

A and B are substitutes; C and D are complements.

7-13 The income elasticities of demand for movies, dental services, and clothing have been estimated to be +3.4, +1.0, and +0.5, respectively. Interpret these coefficients. What does it mean if the income elasticity coefficient is negative?

All are normal goods—income and quantity demanded move in the same direction. These coefficients reveal that a 1 percent increase in income will increase the quantity of movies demanded by 3.4 percent, of dental services by 1.0 percent, and of clothing by 0.5 percent. A negative coefficient indicates an inferior good—income and quantity demanded move in the opposite direction.

CHAPTER 8

8-2 Complete the following table and answer the questions on the next page:

Units consumed	Total utility	Marginal utility
0	0	—
1	10	10
2	—	8
3	25	—
4	30	—
5	—	3
6	34	

a. At which rate is total utility increasing: a constant rate, a decreasing rate, or an increasing rate? How do you know?

b. "A rational consumer will purchase only 1 unit of the product represented by these data, since that amount maximizes marginal utility." Do you agree? Explain why or why not.

c. "It is possible that a rational consumer will not purchase any units of the product represented by these data." Do you agree? Explain why or why not.

Missing total utility data top to bottom: 18; 33. Missing marginal utility data, top to bottom: 7; 5; 1.

(a) A decreasing rate; because marginal utility is declining.

(b) Disagree. The marginal utility of a unit beyond the first may be sufficiently great (relative to product price) to make it a worthwhile purchase. Consumers are interested in maximizing *total* utility, not marginal utility.

(c) Agree. This product's price could be so high relative to the first unit's marginal utility that the consumer would buy none of it.

8-4 Columns 1 through 4 of the accompanying table show the marginal utility, measured in utils, that Ricardo would get by purchasing various amounts of products A, B, C, and D. Column 5 shows the marginal utility Ricardo gets from saving. Assume that the prices of A, B, C, and D are $18, $6, $4, and $24, respectively, and that Ricardo has an income of $106.

Column 1		Column 2		Column 3		Column 4		Column 5	
Units of A	MU	Units of B	MU	Units of C	MU	Units of D	MU	No. of $ saved	MU
1	72	1	24	1	15	1	36	1	5
2	54	2	15	2	12	2	30	2	4
3	45	3	12	3	8	3	24	3	3
4	36	4	9	4	7	4	18	4	2
5	27	5	7	5	5	5	13	5	1
6	18	6	5	6	4	6	7	6	1/2
7	15	7	2	7	3.5	7	4	7	1/4
8	12	8	1	8	3	8	2	8	1/8

a. What quantities of A, B, C, and D will Ricardo purchase in maximizing his utility?

b. How many dollars will Ricardo choose to save?

c. Check your answers by substituting them into the algebraic statement of the utility-maximizing rule.

(a) 4 units of A; 3 units of B; 3 units of C; and 0 units of D.

(b) Save $4.

(c) $36/\$18 = 12/\$6 = 8/\$4 = 2/\$1$. The marginal utility per dollar of the last unit of each product purchased is 2.

8-5 You are choosing between two goods, X and Y, and your marginal utility from each is as shown below. If your income is $9 and the prices of X and Y are $2 and $1, respectively, what quantities of each will you purchase to maximize utility? What total utility will you realize? Assume that, other things remaining unchanged, the price of X falls to $1. What quantities of X and Y will you now purchase? Using the two prices and quantities for X, derive a demand schedule (price-quantity-demanded table) for X.

Units of X	MU_x	Units of Y	MU_y
1	10	1	8
2	8	2	7
3	6	3	6
4	4	4	5
5	3	5	4
6	2	6	3

Buy 2 units of X and 5 units of Y. Marginal utility of last dollar spent will be equal at 4 (= 8/$2 for X and 4/$1 for Y) and the $9 income will be spent. Total utility = 48 (= 10 + 8 for X plus

8 + 7 + 6 + 5 + 4 for Y). When the price of X falls to $1, the quantity of X demanded increases from 2 to 4 (income effect). Total utility is now 58 (= 10 + 8 + 6 + 4 for X plus 8 + 7 + 6 + 5 + 4 for Y).

Demand schedule for X: $P = \$2$; $Q = 2$. $P = \$1$; $Q = 4$.

CHAPTER 8 APPENDIX

8A-3 Using Figure 4, explain why the point of tangency of the budget line with an indifference curve is the consumer's equilibrium position. Explain why any point where the budget line intersects an indifference curve will not be equilibrium. Explain: "The consumer is in equilibrium where MRS = P_B/P_A."

The tangency point places the consumer on the highest attainable indifference curve; it identifies the combination of goods yielding the highest total utility. All intersection points place the consumer on a lower indifference curve. MRS is the slope of the indifference curve; PB/PA is the slope of the budget line. Only at the tangency point are these two slopes equal. If MRS > P_B/P_A or MRS < P_B/P_A, adjustments in the combination of products can be made to increase total utility (get to a higher indifference curve).

CHAPTER 9

9-2 Gomez runs a small pottery firm. He hires one helper at $12,000 per year, pays annual rent of $5,000 for his shop, and spends $20,000 per year on materials. He has $40,000 of his own funds invested in equipment (pottery wheels, kilns, and so forth) that could earn him $4,000 per year if alternatively invested. He has been offered $15,000 per year to work as a potter for a competitor. He estimates his entrepreneurial talents are worth $3,000 per year. Total annual revenue from pottery sales is $72,000. Calculate accounting profits and economic profits for Gomez's pottery.

Explicit costs: $37,000 (= $12,000 for the helper + $5,000 of rent + $20,000 of materials). Implicit costs: $22,000 (= $4,000 of forgone interest + $15,000 of forgone salary + $3,000 of entreprenuership).

Accounting profit = $35,000 (= $72,000 of revenue - $37,000 of explicit costs); Economic profit = $13,000 (= $72,000 - $37,000 of explicit costs - $22,000 of implicit costs).

9-4 Complete the following table by calculating marginal product and average product from the data given. Plot total, marginal, and average product and explain in detail the relationship between each pair of curves. Explain why marginal product first rises, then declines, and ultimately becomes negative. What bearing does the law of diminishing returns have on short-run costs? Be specific. "When marginal product is rising, marginal cost is falling. And when marginal product is diminishing, marginal cost is rising." Illustrate and explain graphically.

Inputs of labor	Total product	Marginal product	Average product
0	0	___	___
1	15	___	___
2	34	___	___
3	51	___	___
4	65	___	___
5	74	___	___
6	80	___	___
7	83	___	___
8	82		

Total product	Total fixed cost	Total variable cost	Total cost	Average fixed cost	Average variable cost	Average total cost	Marginal cost
0	$_____	$ 0	$_____	$_____	$_____	$_____	$_____
1	_____	45	_____	_____	_____	_____	_____
2	_____	85	_____	_____	_____	_____	_____
3	_____	120	_____	_____	_____	_____	_____
4	_____	150	_____	_____	_____	_____	_____
5	_____	185	_____	_____	_____	_____	_____
6	_____	225	_____	_____	_____	_____	_____
7	_____	270	_____	_____	_____	_____	_____
8	_____	325	_____	_____	_____	_____	_____
9	_____	390	_____	_____	_____	_____	_____
10	_____	465	_____	_____	_____	_____	_____

Marginal product data, top to bottom: 15; 19; 17; 14; 9; 6; 3; −1. Average product data, top to bottom: 15; 17; 17; 16.25; 14.8; 13.33; 11.86; 10.25. Your diagram should have the same general characteristics as text Figure 9.2.

MP is the slope—the rate of change—of the TP curve. When TP is rising at an increasing rate, MP is positive and rising. When TP is rising at a diminishing rate, MP is positive but falling. When TP is falling, MP is negative and falling. AP rises when MP is above it; AP falls when MP is below it.

MP first rises because the fixed capital gets used more productively as added workers are employed. Each added worker contributes more to output than the previous worker because the firm is better able to use its fixed plant and equipment. As still more labor is added, the law of diminishing returns takes hold. Labor becomes so abundant relative to the fixed capital that congestion occurs and marginal product falls. At the extreme, the addition of labor so overcrowds the plant that the marginal product of still more labor is negative—total output falls.

Illustrated by Figure 9.6. Because labor is the only variable input and its price (its wage rate) is constant, MC is found by dividing the wage rate by MP. When MP is rising, MC is falling; when MP reaches its maximum, MC is at its minimum; when MP is falling, MC is rising.

9-7 A firm has fixed costs of $60 and variable costs as indicated in the table above. Complete the table. When finished, check your calculations by referring to question 4 at the end of Chapter 10.

a. Graph total fixed cost, total variable cost, and total cost. Explain how the law of diminishing returns influences the shapes of the total-variable-cost and total-cost curves.

b. Graph AFC, AVC, ATC, and MC. Explain the derivation and shape of each of these four curves and their relationships to one another. Specifically, explain in nontechnical terms why the MC curve intersects both the AVC and ATC curves at their minimum points.

c. Explain how the locations of each of the four curves graphed in question 7b would be altered if (1) total fixed cost had been $100 rather than $60, and (2) total variable cost had been $10 less at each level of output.

The total fixed costs are all $60. The total costs are all $60 more than the total variable cost. The other columns are shown in Question 4 in Chapter 10.

(a) See the graph. Over the 0 to 4 range of output, the TVC and TC curves slope upward at a decreasing rate because of increasing marginal returns. The slopes of the curves then increase at an increasing rate as diminishing marginal returns occur.

(b) See the graph. AFC (= TFC/Q) falls continuously since a fixed amount of capital cost is spread over more units of output. The MC (= change in TC/change in Q), AVC (= TVC/Q), and ATC (= TC/Q) curves are U-shaped, reflecting the influence of first increasing and then diminishing returns. The ATC curve sums AFC and AVC vertically. The ATC curve falls when the MC curve is below it; the ATC curve rises when the MC curve is above it. This means the MC curve must intersect the ATC curve at its lowest point. The same logic holds for the minimum point of the AVC curve.

(c1) If TFC had been $100 instead of $60, the AFC and ATC curves would be higher—by an amount equal to $40 divided by the specific output. Example: at 4 units, AVC = $25.00 [= ($60 + $40)/4]; and ATC = $62.50 [= ($210 + $40)/4]. The AVC and MC curves are not affected by changes in fixed costs.

(c2) If TVC had been $10 less at each output, MC would be $10 lower for the first unit of output but remain the same for the remaining output. The AVC and ATC curves would also be lower—by an amount equal to $10 divided by the specific output. Example: at 4 units of output, AVC = $35.00 [= $150 − $10)/4], ATC = $50 [= ($210 − $10)/4]. The AFC curve would not be affected by the change in variable costs.

9–10 Use the concepts of economies and diseconomies of scale to explain the shape of a firm's long-run ATC curve. What is the concept of minimum efficient scale? What bearing may the exact shape of the long-run ATC curve have on the structure of an industry?

The long-run ATC curve is U-shaped. At first, long-run ATC falls as the firm expands and realizes economies of scale from labor and managerial specialization and the use of more efficient capital. The long-run ATC curve later turns upward when the en-larged firm experiences diseconomies of scale, usually resulting from managerial inefficiencies.

The MES (minimum efficient scale) is the smallest level of output needed to attain all economies of scale and minimum long-run ATC.

If long-run ATC drops quickly to its minimum cost, which then extends over a long range of output, the industry will likely be composed of both large and small firms. If long-run ATC descends slowly to its minimum cost over a long range of output, the industry will likely be composed of a few large firms. If long-run ATC drops quickly to its minimum point and then rises abruptly, the industry will likely be composed of many small firms.

CHAPTER 10

10–3 Use the following demand schedule to determine total and marginal revenues for each possible level of sales:

Product price ($)	Quantity demanded	Total revenue ($)	Marginal revenue ($)
2	0	___	___
2	1	___	___
2	2	___	___
2	3	___	___
2	4	___	___
2	5	___	___

a. What can you conclude about the structure of the industry in which this firm is operating? Explain.
b. Graph the demand, total-revenue, and marginal-revenue curves for this firm.
c. Why do the demand and marginal-revenue curves coincide?
d. "Marginal revenue is the change in total revenue associated with additional units of output." Explain verbally and graphically, using the data in the table.

Total revenue, top to bottom: 0; $2; $4; $6; $8; $10. Marginal revenue, top to bottom: $2, throughout.
(a) The industry is purely competitive—this firm is a "price taker." The firm is so small relative to the size of the market that it can change its level of output without affecting the market price.
(b) See graph.
(c) The firm's demand curve is perfectly elastic; MR is con-stant and equal to *P*.

(d) True. Table: When output (quantity demanded) increases by 1 unit, total revenue increases by $2. This $2 increase is the marginal revenue. Figure: The change in TR is measured by the slope of the TR line, 2 (= $2/1 unit).

10–4 Assume the following cost data are for a purely compet-itive producer:

Total product	Average fixed cost	Average variable cost	Average total cost	Marginal cost
0				
1	$60.00	$45.00	$105.00	$45
2	30.00	42.50	72.50	40
3	20.00	40.00	60.00	35
4	15.00	37.50	52.50	30
5	12.00	37.00	49.00	35
6	10.00	37.50	47.50	40
7	8.57	38.57	47.14	45
8	7.50	40.63	48.13	55
9	6.67	43.33	50.00	65
10	6.00	46.50	52.50	75

a. At a product price of $56, will this firm produce in the short run? Why or why not? If it is preferable to produce, what will be the profit-maximizing or loss-minimizing output? Explain. What economic profit or loss will the firm realize per unit of output?
b. Answer the relevant questions of 4a assuming product price is $41.
c. Answer the relevant questions of 4a assuming product price is $32.
d. In the table below, complete the short-run supply sched-ule for the firm (columns 1 and 2) and indicate the profit or loss incurred at each output (column 3).

(1) Price	(2) Quantity supplied, single firm	(3) Profit (+) or loss (l)	(4) Quantity supplied, 1500 firms
$26	___	$___	___
32	___	___	___
38	___	___	___
41	___	___	___
46	___	___	___
56	___	___	___
66	___	___	___

e. Explain: "That segment of a competitive firm's marginal-cost curve which lies above its average-variable-cost curve constitutes the short-run supply curve for the firm." Illustrate graphically.

f. Now assume there are 1500 identical firms in this competitive industry; that is, there are 1500 firms, each of which has the same cost data as shown here. Calculate the industry supply schedule (column 4).

g. Suppose the market demand data for the product are as follows:

Price	Total quantity demanded
$26	17,000
32	15,000
38	13,500
41	12,000
46	10,500
56	9,500
66	8,000

What will be the equilibrium price? What will be the equilibrium output for the industry? For each firm? What will profit or loss be per unit? Per firm? Will this industry expand or contract in the long run?

(a) Yes, $56 exceeds AVC (and ATC) at the profit-maximizing output. Using the MR = MC rule it will produce 8 units. Profits per unit = $7.87 (= $56 − $48.13); total profit = $62.96.
(b) Yes, $41 exceeds AVC at the loss—minimizing output. Using the MR = MC rule it will produce 6 units. Loss per unit of output is $6.50 (= $41 − $47.50). Total loss = $39 (=6 ∞ $6.50), which is less than its total fixed cost of $60.
(c) No, because $32 is always less than AVC. If it did produce according to the MR = MC rule, its output would be 4—found by expanding output until MR no longer exceeds MC. By producing 4 units, it would lose $82 [= 4 ($32 − $52.50)]. By not producing, it would lose only its total fixed cost of $60.
(d) Column (2) data, top to bottom: 0; 0; 5; 6; 7; 8; 9, Column (3) data, top to bottom in dollars: −60; −60; −55; −39; −8; +63; +144.
(e) The firm will not produce if $P <$ AVC. When $P >$ AVC, the firm will produce in the short run at the quantity where P (= MR) is equal to its increasing MC. Therefore, the MC curve above the AVC curve is the firm's short-run supply curve; it shows the quantity of output the firm will supply at each price level. See Figure 10.6 for a graphical illustration.
(f) Column (4) data, top to bottom: 0; 0; 7,500; 9,000; 10,500; 12,000; 13,500.
(g) Equilibrium price = $46; equilibrium output = 10,500. Each firm will produce 7 units. Loss per unit = $1.14, or $8 per firm. The industry will contract in the long run.

10–6 Using diagrams for both the industry and a representative firm, illustrate competitive long-run equilibrium. Assuming constant costs, employ these diagrams to show how (a) an increase and (b) a decrease in market demand will upset that long-run equilibrium. Trace graphically and describe verbally the adjustment processes by which long-run equilibrium is restored. Now rework your analysis for increasing- and decreasing-cost industries and compare the three long-run supply curves.

See Figures 10.8 and 10.9 and their legends. See Figure 10.11 for the supply curve for an increasing cost industry. The supply curve for a decreasing cost industry follows.

Question 10–6

10–7 In long-run equilibrium, P = minimum ATC = MC. Of what significance for economic efficiency is the equality of P and minimum ATC? The equality of P and MC? Distinguish between productive efficiency and allocative efficiency in your answer.

The equality of P and minimum ATC means the firm is achieving *productive efficiency;* it is using the most efficient technology and employing the least costly combination of resources. The equality of P and MC means the firm is achieving *allocative efficiency;* the industry is producing the right product in the right amount based on society's valuation of that product and other products.

CHAPTER 11

11–4 Use the demand schedule that follows to calculate total revenue and marginal revenue at each quantity. Plot the demand, total-revenue, and marginal-revenue curves and explain the relationships between them. Explain why the marginal revenue of the fourth unit of output is $3.50, even though its price is $5.00. Use Chapter 7's total-revenue test for price elasticity to designate the elastic and inelastic segments of your graphed demand curve. What generalization can you make regarding the relationship between marginal revenue and elasticity of demand? Suppose the marginal cost of successive units of output were zero. What output would the profit-seeking firm produce? Finally, use your analysis to explain why a monopolist would never produce in the inelastic region of demand.

Price	Quantity demanded	Price	Quantity demanded
$7.00	0	$4.50	5
6.50	1	4.00	6
6.00	2	3.50	7
5.50	3	3.00	8
5.00	4	2.50	9

Total revenue, in order from Q = 0: 0; $6.50; $12.00; $16.50; $20.00; $22.50; $24.00; $24.50; $24.00; $22.50. Marginal revenue in order from Q = 1: $6.50; $5.50; $4.50; $3.50; $2.50; $1.50; $.50; −$1.50. See the accompanying graph. Because TR is increasing at a diminishing rate, MR is declining. When TR turns downward, MR becomes negative. Marginal revenue is below D because to sell an extra unit, the monopolist must lower the price on the marginal unit as well as on each of the preceding units sold. Four units sell for $5.00 each, but three of these four could have been sold for $5.50 had the monopolist been satisfied to sell only three. Having decided to sell four, the monopolist had to lower the price of the first three from $5.50 to $5.00, sacrificing $.50 on each for a total of $1.50. This "loss" of $1.50 explains the difference between the $5.00 price obtained on the fourth unit of output and its marginal revenue of $3.50. Demand is elastic from P = $6.50 to P =

$3.50, a range where TR is rising. The curve is of unitary elasticity at $P = \$3.50$, where TR is at its maximum. The curve is inelastic from then on as the price continues to decrease and TR is falling. When MR is positive, demand is elastic. When MR is zero, demand is of unitary elasticity. When MR is negative, demand is inelastic. If MC is zero, the monopolist should produce 7 units where MR is also zero. It would never produce where demand is inelastic because MR is negative there while MC is positive.

Quantity
(MR curve approximated)

11–5 Suppose a pure monopolist is faced with the demand schedule shown below and the same cost data as the competitive producer discussed in question 4 at the end of Chapter 10. Calculate the missing total- and marginal-revenue amounts, and determine the profit-maximizing price and profit-earning output for this monopolist. What is the monopolist's profit? Verify your answer graphically and by comparing total revenue and total cost.

Price	Quantity demanded	Total revenue	Marginal revenue
$115	0	$____	$____
100	1	$____	$____
83	2	$____	$____
71	3	$____	$____
63	4	$____	$____
55	5	$____	$____
48	6	$____	$____
42	7	$____	$____
37	8	$____	$____
33	9	$____	$____
29	10	$____	$____

Total revenue data, top to bottom, in dollars: 0; 100; 166; 213; 252; 275; 288; 294; 296; 297; 290. Marginal revenue data, top to bottom, in dollars: 100; 66; 47; 39; 23; 13; 6; 2; 1; −7.

Price = $63; output = 4; profit = $42 [= 4($63 − 52.50)]. Your graph should have the same general appearance as Figure 11.4. At $Q = 4$, TR = $252 and TC = $210 [= 4($52.50)].

11–6 If the firm described in question 5 could engage in perfect price discrimination, what would be the level of output? Of profits? Draw a diagram showing the relevant demand, marginal-revenue, average-total-cost, and marginal-cost curves and the equilibrium price and output for a nondiscriminating monopolist. Use the same diagram to show the equilibrium position of a monopolist that is able to practice perfect price discrimination. Com-

pare equilibrium outputs, total revenues, economic profits, and consumer prices in the two cases. Comment on the economic desirability of price discrimination.

Perfect price discrimination: Output = 6. TR would be $420 (= $100 + $83 + $71 + $63 + $55 + $48). TC would be $285 [= 6(47.50)]. Profit would be $135 (= $420 − $285).

Your single diagram should combine Figures 11.8a and 11.8b in the chapter. The discriminating monopolist faces a demand curve that is also its MR curve. It will sell the first unit at f in Figure 11.8b and then sell each successive unit at lower prices (as shown on the demand curve) as it moves to Q_2 units, where D (= MR) = MC. Discriminating monopolist: Greater output, total revenue, and profits. Some consumers will pay a higher price under discriminating monopoly than with nondiscriminating monopoly; others, a lower price. Good features: greater output and improved allocative efficiency. Bad feature: More income is transferred from consumers to the monopolist.

11–12 It has been proposed that natural monopolists should be allowed to determine their profit-maximizing outputs and prices and then government should tax their profits away and distribute them to consumers in proportion to their purchases from the monopoly. Is this proposal as socially desirable as requiring monopolists to equate price with marginal cost or average total cost?

No, the proposal does not consider that the output of the natural monopolist would still be at the suboptimal level where $P >$ MC. Too little would be produced and there would be an underallocation of resources. Theoretically, it would be more desirable to force the natural monopolist to charge a price equal to marginal cost and subsidize any losses. Even setting price equal to ATC would be an improvement over this proposal. This fair-return pricing would allow for a normal profit and ensure greater production than the proposal would.

CHAPTER 12

12–2 Compare the elasticity of the monopolistic competitor's demand curve with that of a pure competitor and a pure monopolist. Assuming identical long-run costs, compare graphically the prices and output that would result in the long run under pure competition and under monopolistic competition. Contrast the two market structures in terms of productive and allocative efficiency. Explain: "Monopolistically competitive industries are characterized by too many firms, each of which produces too little."

The monopolistic competitor's demand curve is less elastic than a pure competitor's and more elastic than a pure monopolist's. Your graphs should look like Figures 10.12 and 12.1 in the chapters. Price is higher and output lower for the monopolistic competitor. Pure competition: $P =$ MC (allocative efficiency); $P =$ minimum ATC (productive efficiency). Monopolistic competition: $P >$ MC (allocative efficiency) and $P >$ minimum ATC (productive inefficiency). Monopolistic competitors have excess capacity, meaning that fewer firms operating at capacity (where $P =$ minimum ATC) could supply the industry output.

12–7 Answer the following questions, which relate to measures of concentration.
  a. What is the meaning of a four-firm concentration ratio of 60 percent? 90 percent? What are the shortcomings of concentration ratios as measures of monopoly power?
  b. Suppose that the five firms in industry A have annual sales of 30, 30, 20, 10, and 10 percent of total industry sales. For the five firms in industry B, the figures are 60, 25, 5, 5, and 5 percent. Calculate the Herfindahl index for each industry and compare their likely competitiveness.

A four-firm concentration ratio of 60 percent means the largest four firms in the industry account for 60 percent of sales; a four-firm concentration ratio of 90 percent means the largest four firms account for 90 percent of sales. Shortcomings: (1) they pertain to the nation as a whole, although relevant markets may be localized; (2) they do not account for interindustry competition; (3) the data are for U.S. products—imports are excluded; and (4) they don't reveal the dispersion of size among the top four firms.

Herfindahl index for A: 2,400 (= 900 + 900 + 400 + 100 + 100). For B: 4,300 (= 3,600 + 625 + 25 + 25 + 25). We would expect industry A to be more competitive than Industry B, where one firm dominates and two firms control 85 percent of the market.

12–8 Explain the general meaning of the following profit payoff matrix for oligopolists C and D. All profit figures are in thousands.

a. Use the payoff matrix to explain the mutual interdependence that characterizes oligopolistic industries.

b. Assuming no collusion between C and D, what is the likely pricing outcome?

c. In view of your answer to 8b, explain why price collusion is mutually profitable. Why might there be a temptation to cheat on the collusive agreement?

C's possible prices

The matrix shows the four possible profit outcomes for each of two firms, depending on which of the two price strategies each follows. Example: If C sets its price at $35 and D at $40, C's profits will be $59,000 and D's $55,000.

(a) C and D are interdependent because their profits depend not just on their own price, but also on the other firm's price.

(b) Likely outcome: Both firms will set their price at $35. If either charged $40, it would be concerned the other would undercut the price and its profit by charging $35. At $35 for both: C's profit is $55,000, D's, $58,000.

(c) Through price collusion—agreeing to charge $40—each firm would achieve higher profits (C = $57,000; D = $60,000). But once both firms agree on $40, each sees it can increase its profit even more by secretly charging $35 while its rival charges $40.

12–9 What assumptions about a rival's response to price changes underlie the kinked-demand curve for oligopolists? Why is there a gap in the oligopolist's marginal-revenue curve? How does the kinked-demand curve explain price rigidity in oligopoly? What are the shortcomings of the kinked-demand model?

Assumptions: (1) Rivals will match price cuts. (2) Rivals will ignore price increases. The gap in the MR curve results from the abrupt change in the slope of the demand curve at the going price. Firms will not change their price because they fear that if they do their total revenue and profits will fall. Shortcomings of the

model: (1) It does not explain how the going price evolved in the first place; (2) it does not allow for price leadership and other forms of collusion.

12–11 Why is there so much advertising in monopolistic competition and oligopoly? How does such advertising help consumers and promote efficiency? Why might it be excessive at times?

Two ways for monopolistically competitive firms to maintain economic profits are through product development and advertising. Also, advertising will increase the demand for the firm's product. The oligopolist would rather not compete on a basis of price. Oligopolists can increase their market share through advertising that is financed with economic profits from past advertising campaigns. Advertising can operate as a barrier to entry.

Advertising provides information about new products and product improvements to the consumer. Advertising may result in an increase in competition by promoting new products and product improvements. It may also result in increased output for a firm, pushing it down its ATC curve closer to productive efficiency (P = minimum ATC).

Advertising may result in manipulation and persuasion rather than information. An increase in brand loyalty through advertising will increase the producer's monopoly power. Excessive advertising may create barriers to entry into the industry.

CHAPTER 13

13–4 Suppose a firm expects that a $20 million expenditure on R&D will result in a new product that will increase its revenue by a total of $30 million 1 year from now. The firm estimates that the production cost of the new product will be $29 million.

a. What is the expected rate of return on this R&D expenditure?

b. Suppose the firm can get a bank loan at 6 percent interest to finance its $20 million R&D project. Will the firm undertake the project? Explain why or why not.

c. Now suppose the interest-rate cost of borrowing, in effect, falls to 4 percent because the firm decides to use its own retained earnings to finance the R&D. Will this lower interest rate change the firm's R&D decision? Explain.

(a) 5 percent;

(b) No, because the 5 percent rate of return is less than the 6 percent interest rate;

(c) Yes, because the 5 percent rate of return is now greater than the 4 percent interest rate.

13–5 Answer the lettered questions below on the basis of the information in this table:

Amount of R&D, millions	Expected rate of return on R&D, %
$10	16
20	14
30	12
40	10
50	8
60	6

a. If the interest-rate cost of funds is 8 percent, what will be the optimal amount of R&D spending for this firm?

b. Explain why $20 million of R&D spending will not be optimal.

c. Why won't $60 million be optimal either?

(a) $50 million, where the interest-rate cost of funds (i) equals the expected rate of return (r);

(b) at $20 million in R&D, r of 14 percent exceeds i of 8 percent; thus there would be an underallocation of R&D funds;

(c) at $60 million, r of 6 percent is less than i of 8 percent; thus there would be an overallocation of R&D funds.

13–6 Refer to Table 13.1 and suppose the price of new product C is $2 instead of $4. How does this affect the optimal combination of products A, B, and C for the person represented by the data? Explain: "The success of a new product depends not only on its marginal utility but also on its price."

(a) The person would now buy 5 units of product C and zero units of A and B;

(b) The MU/price ratio is what counts; a new product can be successful by having a high MU, a low price, or both relative to existing products.

13–8 Answer the following questions on the basis of this information for a single firm: Total cost of capital = $1,000; price paid for labor = $12 per labor unit; price paid for raw materials = $4 per raw-material unit.

a. Suppose the firm can produce 5,000 units of output by combining its fixed capital with 100 units of labor and 450 units of raw materials. What are the total cost and average total cost of producing the 5,000 units of output?

b. Now assume the firm improves its production process so that it can produce 6,000 units of output by combining its fixed capital with 100 units of labor and 450 units of raw materials. What are the total cost and average cost of producing the 6,000 units of output?

c. Refer to your answers to 8a and 8b and explain how process innovation can improve economic efficiency.

(a) Total cost = $4,000; average total cost = $.80 (= $4,000/5,000 units);

(b) Total cost = $4,000; average total cost = $.667 (= $4,000/6,000 units);

(c) Process innovation can lower the average total cost of producing a particular output, meaning that society uses fewer resources to produce a given amount of output. Resources are freed from this production to produce more of other desirable goods. Society realizes extra output through a gain in efficiency.

CHAPTER 14

14–2 Complete the following labor demand table for a firm that is hiring labor competitively and selling its product in a competitive market.

Units of labor	Total product	Marginal product	Product price	Total revenue	Marginal revenue product
0	0	___	$2	$___	$___
1	17	___	2	___	___
2	31	___	2	___	___
3	43	___	2	___	___
4	53	___	2	___	___
5	60	___	2	___	___
6	65	___	2	___	___

a. How many workers will the firm hire if the going wage rate is $27.95? $19.95? Explain why the firm will not hire a larger or smaller number of units of labor at each of these wage rates.

b. Show in schedule form and graphically the labor demand curve of this firm.

Question 14–2b

Wage rate / Quantity of labor demanded
(plotted at the halfway points along the horizontal axis)

$D_L = MRP_L$

c. Now again determine the firm's demand curve for labor, assuming that it is selling in an imperfectly competitive market and that, although it can sell 17 units at $2.20 per unit, it must lower product price by 5 cents in order to sell the marginal product of each successive labor unit. Compare this demand curve with that derived in question 2b. Which curve is more elastic? Explain.

Marginal product data, top to bottom: 17; 14; 12; 10; 7; 5. Total revenue data, top to bottom: $0; $34; $62; $86; $106; $120; $130. Marginal revenue product data, top to bottom: $34; $28; $24; $20; $14; $10.

(a) Two workers at $27.95 because the MRP of the first worker is $34 and the MRP of the second worker is $28, both exceeding the $27.95 wage. Four workers at $19.95 because workers 1 through 4 have MRPs exceeding the $19.95 wage. The fifth worker's MRP is only $14 so he or she will not be hired.

(b) The demand schedule consists of the first and last columns of the table at the top of the next column.

(c) Reconstruct the table. New product price data, top to bottom: $2.20; $2.15; $2.10; $2.05; $2.00; $1.95. New total revenue data, top to bottom: $0; $37.40; $66.65; $90.30; $108.65; $120.00; $126.75. New marginal revenue product data, top to bottom: $37.40; $29.25; $23.65; $18.35; $11.35; $6.75. The new labor demand is less elastic. Here, MRP falls because of diminishing returns *and* because product price declines as output increases. A decrease in the wage rate will produce less of an increase in the quantity of labor demanded, because the output from the added labor will reduce product price and thus MRP.

14–5 What factors determine the elasticity of resource demand? What effect will each of the following have on the elasticity or location of the demand for resource C, which is being used to produce commodity X? Where there is any uncertainty as to the outcome, specify the causes of the uncertainty.

a. An increase in the demand for product X.

b. An increase in the price of substitute resource D.

c. An increase in the number of resources substitutable for C in producing X.

d. A technological improvement in the capital equipment with which resource C is combined.

e. A fall in the price of complementary resource E.

f. A decline in the elasticity of demand for product X due to a decline in the competitiveness of the product market.

Elasticity of demand for a resource is determined by: (1) ease of resource substitutability; (2) elasticity of product demand; and (3) ratio of resource costs to total costs.

(a) Increase in the demand for resource C.
(b) Uncertainty relative to the change in demand for resource C; answer depends upon which is larger—the substitution effect or the output effect.
(c) Increase in the elasticity of resource C.
(d) Increase in the demand for resource C.
(e) Increase in the demand for resource C.
(f) Decrease in the elasticity of resource C.

14-6 Suppose the productivity of labor and capital are as shown in the accompanying table. The output of these resources sells in a purely competitive market for $1 per unit. Both capital and labor are hired under purely competitive conditions at $3 and $1, respectively.

Units of capital	MP of capital	Units of labor	MP of labor
1	24	1	11
2	21	2	9
3	18	3	8
4	15	4	7
5	9	5	6
6	6	6	4
7	3	7	1
8	1	8	1/2

a. What is the least-cost combination of labor and capital to employ in producing 80 units of output? Explain.
b. What is the profit-maximizing combination of labor and capital the firm should use? Explain. What is the resulting level of output? What is the economic profit? Is this the least costly way of producing the profit-maximizing output?

(a) 2 capital; 4 labor. $MP_L/P_L = 7/1$; $MP_C/P_C = 21/3 = 7/1$. The least-cost combination is found by equating the ratios of the marginal products of each input to their prices.
(b) 7 capital and 7 labor. $MRP_L/P_L = 1$ (= 1/1) = $MRP_C/P_C = 1$(= 3/3). Output is 142 (= 96 from capital + 46 from labor). Economic profit is $114 (= $142 − $28). Yes, least-cost production is part of maximizing profits. The profit-maximizing rule includes the least-cost rule.

14-7 In each of the following four cases, MRP_L and MRP_C refer to the marginal revenue products of labor and capital, respectively, and P_L and P_C refer to their prices. Indicate in each case whether the conditions are consistent with maximum profits for the firm. If not, state which resource(s) should be used in larger amounts and which resource(s) should be used in smaller amounts.
  a. $MRP_L = 8; $P_L = 4; $MRP_C = 8; $P_C = 4
  b. $MRP_L = 10; $P_L = 12; $MRP_C = 14; $P_C = 9.
  c. $MRP_L = 6; $P_L = 6; $MRP_C = 12; $P_C = 12.
  d. $MRP_L = 22; $P_L = 26; $MRP_C = 16; $P_C = 19.

(a) Use more of both;
(b) Use less labor and more capital;
(c) Maximum profits obtained;
(d) Use less of both.

CHAPTER 15

15-3 Describe wage determination in a labor market in which workers are unorganized and many firms actively compete for the services of labor. Show this situation graphically, using W_1 to indicate the equilibrium wage rate and Q_1 to show the number of workers hired by the firms as a group. Show the labor supply curve of the individual firm, and compare it with that of the total market. Why the differences? In the diagram representing the firm, identify total revenue, total wage cost, and revenue available for the payment of nonlabor resources.

The labor market is made up of many firms desiring to purchase a particular labor service and of many workers with that labor service. The market demand curve is downward sloping because of diminishing returns and the market supply curve is upward sloping because a higher wage will be necessary to attract additional workers into the market. Whereas the individual firm's supply curve is perfectly elastic because it can hire any number of workers at the going wage, the market supply curve is upward sloping.
For the graphs, see Figure 15.3 and its legend.

15-4 Complete the following labor supply table for a firm hiring labor competitively.

Units of labor	Wage rate	Total labor cost (wage bill)	Marginal resource (labor) cost
0	$14	$____	$____
1	14	____	____
2	14	____	____
3	14	____	____
4	14	____	____
5	14	____	____
6	14	____	____

a. Show graphically the labor supply and marginal resource (labor) cost curves for this firm. Explain the relationships of these curves to one another.
b. Plot the labor demand data of question 2 in Chapter 14 on the graph in part a above. What are the equilibrium wage rate and level of employment? Explain.

Total labor cost data, top to bottom: $0; $14; $28; $42; $56; $70; $84. Marginal resource cost data: $14, throughout.
(a) The labor supply curve and MRC curve coincide as a single horizontal line at the market wage rate of $14. The firm can employ as much labor as it wants, each unit costing $14; wage rate = MRC because the wage rate is constant to the firm.

(b) Graph: equilibrium is at the intersection of the MRP and MRC curves. Equilibrium wage rate = $14; equilibrium level of employment = 4 units of labor. Explanation: From the tables: MRP exceeds MRC for each of the first four units of labor, but MRP is less than MRC for the fifth unit.

Quantity of labor
(MRP is plotted at the halfway
points on the horizontal axis)

15–6 Assume a firm is a monopsonist that can hire its first worker for $6 but must increase the wage rate by $3 to attract each successive worker. Draw the firm's labor supply and marginal resource cost curves and explain their relationships to one another. On the same graph, plot the labor demand data of question 2 in Chapter 14. What are the equilibrium wage rate and level of employment? What will be the equilibrium wage rate and the level of employment? Why do these differ from your answer to question 4?

The monopsonist faces the market labor supply curve S—it is the only firm hiring this labor. MRC lies above S and rises more rapidly than S because all workers get the higher wage rate that is needed to attract each added worker. Equilibrium wage/rate = $12; equilibrium employment = 3 (where MRP = MRC). The monopsonist can pay a below-competitive wage rate by restricting its employment.

Quantity of labor
(MRP is plotted at the halfway points
on the horizontal axis)

15–7 Assume a monopsonistic employer is paying a wage rate of W_m and hiring Q_m workers, as indicated in Figure 15.8. Now suppose that an industrial union is formed and that it forces the employer to accept a wage rate of W_c. Explain verbally and graph-

ically why in this instance the higher wage rate will be accompanied by an increase in the number of workers hired.

The union wage rate W_c becomes the firm's MRC, which would be shown as a horizontal line to the left of the labor supply curve. Each unit of labor now adds only its own wage rate to the firm's costs. The firm will employ Q_c workers, the quantity of labor where MRP = MRC (= W_c); Q_c is greater than the Q_m workers it would employ if there were no union and if the employer did not have any monopsonistic power, i.e., more workers are willing to offer their labor services when the wage is W_c than W_m.

CHAPTER 16

16–2 Explain why economic rent is a surplus payment when viewed by the economy as a whole but a cost of production from the standpoint of individual firms and industries. Explain: "Rent performs no 'incentive function' for the overall economy."

Land is completely fixed in total supply. As population expands and the demand for land increases, rent first appears and then grows. From society's perspective this rent is a surplus payment unnecessary for ensuring that the land is available to the economy as a whole. If rent declined or disappeared, the same amount of land would be available. If it increased, no more land would be forthcoming. Thus, rent does not function as an incentive for adding land to the economy.

But land does have alternative uses. To get it to its most productive use, individuals and firms compete and the winners are those who pay the highest rent. To the high bidders, rent is a cost of production that must be covered by the revenue gained through the sale of the commodities produced on that land.

16–6 Why is the supply of loanable funds upward sloping? Why is the demand for loanable funds downward sloping? Explain the equilibrium interest rate. List some factors that might cause it to change.

(a) The supply of loanable funds is upward sloping because savers will make more funds available at higher interest rates than lower interest rates.

(b) The demand for loanable funds is downward sloping because there are few investment and R&D projects that yield a high rate of return and many more that will yield a lower rate of return.

(c) The equilibrium interest rate is determined where the interest rate (cost of borrowing the funds) is equal to the expected rate of return (the expected benefit from borrowing the funds and engaging in the investment or R&D project). The supply of loanable funds may change because of a change in households' attitudes about saving (tax policies, macroeconomic conditions) or changes in Federal Reserve policies relative to the money supply. The demand for loanable funds could change as a result of a change in technology or a change in the demand for the final product. If there is either a change in supply of or demand for loanable funds, the interest rate will change.

16–8 Distinguish between nominal and real interest rates. Which is more relevant in making investment and R&D decisions? If the nominal interest rate is 12 percent and the inflation rate is 8 percent, what is the real rate of interest?

The nominal interest rate is the interest rate stated in dollars of current value (unadjusted for inflation). The real interest rate is the nominal interest rate adjusted for inflation (or deflation). The real interest rate is more relevant for making investment decisions—it reflects the true cost of borrowing money. It is compared to the expected return on the investment in the decision process. Real interest rate = 4 percent (= 12 percent − 8 percent).

16–10 How do the concepts of accounting profit and economic profit differ? Why is economic profit smaller than accounting profit? What are the three basic sources of economic profit? Classify each of the following according to those sources:

a. A firm's profit from developing and patenting a new medication that greatly reduces cholesterol and thus diminishes the likelihood of heart disease and stroke.

b. A restaurant's profit that results from construction of a new highway past its door.

c. The profit received by a firm benefiting from an unanticipated change in consumer tastes.

Accounting profit is what remains of a firm's total revenues after it has paid for all the factors of production employed by the firm (its explicit costs) but not for the use of the resources owned by the business itself. Economists also take into consideration implicit costs—the payment the owners could have received by using the resources they own in some other way. The economist adds these implicit costs to the accountant's explicit costs to arrive at total cost. Subtracting the total cost from total revenue results in a smaller profit (the economic profit) than the accountant's profit.

Sources of economic profit: (1) uninsurable risks; (2) innovations; and (3) monopoly.

(a) Profit from assuming the uncertainties of innovation, as well as monopoly profit from the patent.

(b) Monopoly profit arising from its locational advantage.

(c) Profit from bearing the uninsurable risk of a change in demand (the change could have been unfavorable).

CHAPTER 17

17–1 On the basis of the three individual demand schedules below, and assuming these three people are the only ones in the society, determine (a) the market demand schedule on the assumption that the good is a private good, and (b) the collective demand schedule on the assumption that the good is a public good. Explain the differences, if any, in your schedules.

Individual #1		Individual #2		Individual #3	
Price	Q_d	Price	Q_d	Price	Q_d
$8	0	$8	1	$8	0
7	0	7	2	7	0
6	0	6	3	6	1
5	1	5	4	5	2
4	2	4	5	4	3
3	3	3	6	3	4
2	4	2	7	2	5
1	5	1	8	1	6

(a) Private good, top to bottom: P = $8, Q = 1; P = $7, Q = 2; P = $6, Q = 4; P = $5, Q = 7; P = $4, Q = 10; P = $3, Q = 13; P = $2, Q = 16; P = $1, Q = 19. (b) Public good, top to bottom; P = $19, Q = 1; P = $16, Q = 2; P = $13, Q = 3; P = $10, Q = 4; P = $7, Q = 5; P = $4, Q = 6; P = $2, Q = 7; P = $1, Q = 8. The first schedule represents a horizontal summation of the individual demand curves; the second schedule represents a vertical summation of these curves. The market demand curve for the private good will determine—in combination with market supply—an actual price-quantity outcome in the marketplace. Because potential buyers of public goods do not reveal their individual preferences in the market, the collective demand curve for the pub-

lic good is hypothetical or needs to be determined through "willingness to pay" studies.

17–2 Use your demand schedule for a public good determined in question 1 and the following supply schedule to ascertain the optimal quantity of this public good. Why is this the optimal quantity?

Optimal quantity = 4. It is optimal because at 4 units the collective willingness to pay for the final unit of the good (= $10) matches the marginal cost of production (= $10).

P	Q_S
$19	10
16	8
13	6
10	4
7	2
4	0

17–3 The following table shows the total costs and total benefits in billions for four different antipollution programs of increasing scope. Which program should be undertaken? Why?

Program	Total cost	Total benefit
A	$ 3	$ 7
B	7	12
C	12	16
D	18	19

Program B, since the marginal benefit no longer exceeds marginal cost for programs that are larger in scope. Plan B is where net benefits—the excess of total benefits over total costs—are maximized.

17–4 Why are spillover costs and spillover benefits also called negative and positive externalities? Show graphically how a tax can correct for a spillover cost and a subsidy to producers can correct for a spillover benefit. How does a subsidy to consumers differ from a subsidy to producers in correcting for a spillover benefit?

Spillover costs are called negative externalities because they are *external* to the participants in the transaction and *reduce* the utility of affected third parties (thus "negative"). Spillover benefits are called positive externalities because they are *external* to the participants in the transaction and *increase* the utility of affected third parties (thus "positive"). See Figures 17.3 and 17.4. Compare (b) and (c) in Figure 17.4.

17–7 Explain the following statement, using the MB curve in Figure 17.6 to illustrate: "The optimal amount of pollution abatement for some substances, say, water from storm drains, is very low; the optimal amount of abatement for other substances, say, cyanide poison, is close to 100 percent."

Reducing water flow from storm drains has a low marginal benefit, meaning the MB curve would be located far to the left of where it is in the text diagram. It will intersect the MC curve at a low amount of pollution abatement, indicating the optimal amount of pollution abatement (where MB = MC) is low. Any cyanide in public water sources could be deadly. Therefore, the marginal benefit of reducing cyanide is extremely high and the MB curve in the figure would be located to the extreme right where it would intersect the MC curve at or near 100 percent.

17–13 Place an "M" beside items in the following list that describe a moral hazard problem and an "A" beside those that describe an adverse selection problem.

   a. A person with a terminal illness buys several life insurance policies through the mail.

   b. A person drives carelessly because he or she has automobile insurance.

   c. A person who intends to "torch" his warehouse takes out a large fire insurance policy.

   d. A professional athlete who has a guaranteed contract fails to stay in shape during the off-season.

   e. A woman anticipating having a large family takes a job with a firm that offers exceptional child-care benefits.

Moral hazard problem: (b) and (d). Adverse selection problem: (a), (c), and (e).

CHAPTER 18

18–2 Explain the paradox of voting through reference to the accompanying table, which shows the ranking of three public goods by voters Jay, Dave, and Conan.

Public good	Jay	Dave	Conan
Courthouse	2d choice	1st choice	3d choice
School	3d choice	2d choice	1st choice
Park	1st choice	3d choice	2d choice

The paradox is that majority voting does not always provide a clear and consistent picture of the public's preferences. Here the courthouse is preferred to the school and the park is preferred to the courthouse, so we would surmise that the park is preferred to the school. But paired-choice voting would show that the school is preferred to the park.

18–3 Suppose that there are only five people in a society and that each favors one of the five highway construction options shown in Table 17.2 (include no highway construction as one of the options). Explain which of these highway options will be selected using a majority paired-choice vote. Will this option be the optimal size of the project from an economic perspective?

Project B (New 2-lane highway wins) using a paired-choice vote. There is no "paradox of voting" problem here and B is the preference of the median voter. The two voters favoring No new construction and Widening, respectively, will prefer New 2-lane highways—project B—to New 4- or 6-lane highways. The two voters preferring New 4- and 6-lane highways will prefer a New 2-lane highway to Widening or No new construction. The median voter's preference for B will prevail. However, the optimal size of the project from an economic perspective is C—it would provide a greater net benefit to society than B.

18–4 How does the problem of limited and bundled choice in the public sector relate to economic efficiency? Why are public bureaucracies alleged to be less efficient than private enterprises?

The electorate is faced with a small number of candidates, each of whom offers a broad range or "bundle" of proposed policies. Voters are then forced to choose the individual candidate whose bundle of policies most resembles their own. The chances of a perfect identity between a particular candidate's preferences and those of any voter are quite slim. As a result, the voter must purchase some unwanted public goods and services. This represents an inefficient allocation of resources.

Government bureaucracies do not function on the basis of profit, so the incentive for holding down costs is less than in the private sector. Also, because there is no profit-and-loss test of efficiency, it is difficult to determine whether public agencies are operating efficiently. Nor is there entry of competing entities to stimulate efficiency and develop improved public goods and services. Furthermore, wasteful expenditures can be maintained through the self-seeking lobbying of bureaucrats themselves, and the public budgetary process can reward rather than penalize inefficiency.

18–7 Suppose a tax is such that an individual with an income of $10,000 pays $2,000 of tax, a person with an income of $20,000 pays $3,000 of tax, a person with an income of $30,000 pays $4,000 of tax, and so forth. What is each person's average tax rate? Is this tax regressive, proportional, or progressive?

Average tax rates: 20; 15; and 13.3 percent. Regressive.

18–9 What is the incidence of an excise tax when demand is highly inelastic? Elastic? What effect does the elasticity of supply have on the incidence of an excise tax? What is the efficiency loss of a tax, and how does it relate to elasticity of demand and supply?

The incidence of an excise tax is likely to be primarily on consumers when demand is highly inelastic and primarily on producers when demand is elastic. The more elastic the supply, the greater the incidence of an excise tax on consumers and the less on producers.

The efficiency loss of a sales or excise tax is the net benefit society sacrifices because consumption and production of the taxed product are reduced below the level of allocative efficiency which would occur without the tax. Other things equal, the greater the elasticities of demand and supply, the greater the efficiency loss of a particular tax.

CHAPTER 19

19–2 Describe the major provisions of the Sherman and Clayton Acts. What government entities are responsible for enforcing those laws? Are firms permitted to initiate antitrust suits on their own against other firms?

Sherman Act: Section 1 prohibits conspiracies to restrain trade; Section 2 outlaws monopolization. Clayton Act (as amended by Celler-Kefauver Act of 1950): Section 2 outlaws price discrimination; Section 3 forbids tying contracts; Section 7 prohibits mergers which substantially lessen competition; Section 8 prohibits interlocking directorates. The acts are enforced by the Department of Justice, Federal Trade Commission, and state attorneys general. Private firms can bring suit against other firms under these laws.

19–5 How would you expect antitrust authorities to react to (a) a proposed merger of Ford and General Motors; (b) evidence of secret meetings by contractors to rig bids for highway construction projects; (c) a proposed merger of a large shoe manufacturer and a chain of retail shoe stores; (d) a proposed merger of a small life insurance company and a regional candy manufacturer; and (e) an automobile rental firm that charges higher rates for last-minute rentals than for rentals reserved weeks in advance?

(a) They would block this horizontal merger (violation of Section 7 of the Clayton Act). (b) They would charge these firms with price fixing (violation of Section 1 of the Sherman Act). (c) They would allow this vertical merger, unless both firms had very large market shares and the resultant merger substantially lessens competition. (d) They would allow this conglomerate merger. (e) They would not interfere with this price discrimination.

19–10 What types of industries, if any, should be subjected to industrial regulation? What specific problems does industrial regulation entail?

Industries composed of firms with natural monopoly conditions are most likely to be subjected to industrial regulation. Regulation based on "fair-return" prices creates disincentives for firms to minimize costs since cost reductions lead regulators to force firms to charge a lower price. Regulated firms may also use "creative" accounting to boost costs and hide profits. Because regulatory commissions depend on information provided by the firms themselves, and commission members are often recruited from the industry, the agencies may in effect be controlled by the firms they are supposed to oversee. Also, industrial regulation sometimes is applied to industries that are not, or no longer are, natural monopolies. Regulation may lead to the conditions of a cartel, conditions that are illegal in an unregulated industry.

19–12 How does social regulation differ from industrial regulation? What types of benefits and costs are associated with social regulation?

Industrial regulation is concerned with prices, output, and profits in specific industries, whereas social regulation deals with the broader impact of business on consumers, workers, and third parties. Benefits: increased worker and product safety, less environmental damage, reduced economic discrimination. Two types of costs: administrative costs, because regulations must be administered by costly government agencies; compliance costs, because firms must increase spending to comply with regulations.

CHAPTER 20

20–1 Carefully evaluate: "The supply and demand for agricultural products are such that small changes in agricultural supply will result in drastic changes in prices. However, large changes in farm prices have modest effects on agricultural output." (*Hint:* A brief review of the distinction between supply and quantity supplied may be of assistance.) Do exports increase or reduce the instability of demand for farm products? Explain.

First sentence: Shifts in the supply curve of agricultural goods (*changes in supply*) relative to fixed inelastic demand curves produce large changes in equilibrium prices. Second sentence: But these drastic changes in prices produce only small changes in equilibrium outputs (where *quantities demanded* equals *quantities supplied*) because demands are inelastic.

Because exports are volatile from one year to the next, they increase the instability of demand for farm products.

20–3 Explain how each of the following contributes to the farm problem: **(a)** the inelasticity of the demand for farm products, **(b)** the rapid technological progress in farming, **(c)** the modest long-run growth in the demand for farm commodities, and **(d)** the volatility of export demand.

(a) Because the demand for most farm products is inelastic, the frequent fluctuations in supply brought about by weather and other factors have relatively small effects on quantity demanded, but large effects on equilibrium prices of farm products. Farmers' sales revenues and incomes therefore are unstable. (b) Technological innovations have decreased production costs, increased long-run supply for most agricultural goods, and reduced the prices of farm output. These declines in prices have put a downward pressure on farm income. (c) The modest long-run growth in the demand for farm products has not been sufficient to offset the expansion of sup-

ply, resulting in stagnant farm income. (d) Foreign demand has been unpredictable. Any change in demand will affect farm prices but farmers cannot easily adjust production.

20–8 Explain the economic effects of price supports. Explicitly include environmental and global impacts in your answer. On what grounds do economists contend that price supports cause a misallocation of resources?

Price supports benefit farmers, harm consumers, impose costs on society, and contribute to problems in world agriculture. Farmers benefit because the prices they receive and the output they produce both increase, expanding their gross incomes. Consumers lose because the prices they pay for farm products rise and quantities purchased decline. Society as a whole bears several costs. Surpluses of farm products will have to be bought and stored, leading to a greater burden on taxpayers. Domestic economic efficiency is lessened as the artificially high prices of farm products lead to an overallocation of resources to agriculture. The environment suffers: The greater use of pesticides and fertilizers contributes to water pollution; farm policies discourage crop rotation; and price supports encourage farming of environmentally sensitive land. The efficient use of world resources is also distorted because of the import tariffs or quotas that such programs often require. Finally, domestic overproduction leads to supply increases in international markets, decreasing prices and causing a decline in the gross incomes of foreign producers.

CHAPTER 21

21–2 Assume Al, Beth, Carol, David, and Ed receive incomes of $500, $250, $125, $75, and $50, respectively. Construct and interpret a Lorenz curve for this five-person economy. What percentage of total income is received by the richest and by the poorest quintiles?

See the following figure. In this simple economy each person represents a complete income quintile—20 percent of the total population. The richest quintile (Al) receives 50 percent of total income; the poorest quintile (Ed) receives 5 percent.

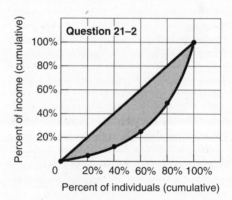

21–5 Briefly discuss the major causes of income inequality. With respect to income inequality, is there any difference between inheriting property and inheriting a high IQ? Explain.

The reasons for income inequality are: differences in abilities and talents among individuals, differences in the amount of education and training an individual obtains, labor market discrimination, differences in tastes and preferences toward work and job attributes, inequality in the distribution of wealth, the ability to use market power to transfer income to oneself, luck, connections, and misfortune.

A high IQ normally does not lead to high income unless it is combined with personal initiative and favorable social circumstances. Inherited property—as long as it is competently managed—provides income irrespective of one's character and personal attributes. Both factors are largely a matter of the luck of being born into a family with good ability genes and/or wealth. What one does with the genes or wealth is up to the recipient.

CHAPTER 22

22-4 What is the estimated size of the union wage advantage? How might this advantage diminish the efficiency with which labor resources are allocated?

Fifteen percent. The higher wages that unions achieve reduce employment, displace workers, and increase the marginal revenue product in the union sector. Labor supply increases in the nonunionized sector, reducing wages and decreasing marginal revenue product there. Because of the lower nonunion marginal revenue product, the workers added in the nonunion sector contribute less to GDP than they would have in the unionized sector. The gain of GDP in the nonunionized sector does not offset the loss of GDP in the unionized sector so there is an overall efficiency loss.

22-7 The labor demand and supply data in the following table relate to a single occupation. Use them to answer the questions that follow. Base your answers on the taste-for-discrimination model.

Quantity of Hispanic labor demanded, thousands	Hispanic wage rate	Quantity of Hispanic labor supplied, thousands
24	$16	52
30	14	44
35	12	35
42	10	28
48	8	20

a. Plot the labor demand and supply curves for Hispanic workers in this occupation.
b. What are the equilibrium Hispanic wage rate and quantity of Hispanic employment?
c. Suppose the white wage rate in this occupation is $16. What is the Hispanic-to-white wage ratio?
d. Suppose a particular employer has a discrimination coefficient, d, of $5 per hour. Will that employer hire Hispanic or white workers at the Hispanic-white wage ratio indicated by part c? Explain.
e. Suppose employers as a group become less prejudiced against Hispanics and demand 14 more units of Hispanic labor at each Hispanic wage rate in the table. What are the new equilibrium Hispanic wage rate and level of Hispanic employment? Does the Hispanic-white wage ratio rise or fall? Explain.
f. Suppose Hispanics as a group increase their labor services in this occupation, collectively offering 14 more units of labor at each Hispanic wage rate. Disregarding the changes indicated in part e, what are the new equilibrium Hispanic wage rate and level of Hispanic employment? Does the Hispanic-white wage ratio rise, or does it fall?

(a)

Question 22–7

Wage

$12

S

D

35

Quantity of Hispanic workers
(thousands)

(b) The equilibrium Hispanic wage rate is $12; the equilibrium quantity of Hispanic employment is 36,000 workers.
(c) The Hispanic-to-white wage ratio is .75 (= $12/$16).
(d) The employer will hire only white workers because the $5 discrimination coefficient exceeds the $4 difference between the wage rates of whites and Hispanics.
(e) The new equilibrium Hispanic wage rate is $14 and the new equilibrium quantity of Hispanic employment is 44,000 workers. The Hispanic-white wage ratio rises to .875 (= $14/$16) because of the increased demand for Hispanic labor in relation to the unchanging supply of Hispanic labor.
(f) The new equilibrium Hispanic wage rate is $10 and the new equilibrium quantity of Hispanic employment is 20,000. This Hispanic-white wage ratio falls to .625 (= $10/$16).

22-9 Use a demand and supply model to explain the impact of occupational segregation or "crowding" on the relative wage rates and earnings of men and women. Who gains and who loses from the elimination of occupational segregation? Is there a net gain or net loss to society? Explain.

See Figure 22.5. Discrimination against women in two of the three occupations will crowd women into the third occupation. Labor supply in the "men's occupations" (X and Y) decreases, making them high-wage occupations. Labor supply in the "women's occupation" (Z) increases, creating a low-wage occupation.

Eliminating occupational segregation would entice women into the high-wage occupations, increasing labor supply there and reducing it in the low-wage occupation. The wage rates in the three occupations would converge to B. Women would gain, men would lose. Society would gain because the increase in output in the expanding occupations would exceed the loss of output in the contracting occupation.

22-12 Use graphical analysis to show the gains and losses resulting from the migration of population from a low-income country to a high-income country. Explain how your conclusions are affected by (a) unemployment, (b) remittances to the home country, (c) backflows of migrants to their home country, and (d) the personal characteristics of the migrants. If the migrants are highly skilled workers, is there any justification for the sending country to levy a "brain drain" tax on emigrants?

See Figure 22.6. Migration of labor from the low- to high-income country increases the labor supply in the high-income country and decreases it in the low-income country. Wages are equalized at W_e. Output and business income increases in the receiving country, declines in the sending country. World output increases: The output gain in the receiving country exceeds the output loss in the sending country.

(a) The gains to the receiving country will not materialize if the migrants are unemployed after they arrive; there may be gains in the low-income country if the immigrant had been unemployed prior to moving. (b) Remittances to the home country will decrease the income gain in the receiving country and reduce the income loss in the sending country. (c) If migrants who return to their home country have enhanced their skills, their temporary departure might be to the long-run advantage of the home country. (d) Young, skilled migrants will increase output and likely be the net taxpayers in the receiving country, but the sending country will experience a "brain drain." Older or less skilled workers who are not so easily assimilated could be net recipients of government services. In view of the sometimes-large investments which sending countries have made in providing education and skills, there is a justification for levying a departure tax on such migrants. But if this tax were too high, it would infringe on a basic human right: the right to emigrate.

CHAPTER 23

23–2 What are the "twin problems" of the health care industry? How are they related?

The "twin problems" are rising prices for all and limited access (lack of insurance) for about 16 percent of the population (41 million). The problems are related since rising costs make insurance unaffordable for many individuals and families, and make it difficult for some businesses to insure their workers.

23–7 What are the estimated income and price elasticities of demand for health care? How does each relate to rising health care costs?

Income elasticity is 1.0, suggesting that health care spending will rise proportionately with income. Some studies indicate that it might be 1.5 in the United States. Price elasticity is only 0.2, meaning higher prices for health care services will increase total health care spending.

23–10 Using the concepts in Chapter 8's discussion of consumer behavior, explain how health care insurance results in an overallocation of resources to the health care industry. Use a demand and supply diagram to specify the resulting efficiency loss.

Health care insurance removes or greatly lessens a person's budget restraint at the time health care is purchased, raising health care utility per dollar spent and causing an overconsumption of health care. In Figure 23.3b, insurance reduces the price of health care at the time of purchase from P_u to P_i, increasing the quantity consumed from Q_u to Q_i. At Q_i the marginal cost of health care is represented by point b and exceeds the marginal benefit represented by c, indicating an overallocation of resources. The efficiency loss is area cab.

CHAPTER 24

24–4 Below are the hypothetical production possibilities tables for New Zealand and Spain.

New Zealand's production possibilities table (millions of bushels)

Product	Production alternatives			
	A	B	C	D
Apples	0	20	40	60
Plums	15	10	5	0

Spain's production possibilities table (millions of bushels)

Product	Production alternatives			
	R	S	T	U
Apples	0	20	40	60
Plums	60	40	20	0

Plot the production possibilities data for each of the two countries separately. Referring to your graphs, answer the following: (a) What is each country's cost ratio of producing plums and apples? (b) Which nation should specialize in which product? (c) Show the trading possibilities lines for each nation if the actual terms of trade are 1 plum for 2 apples. (Plot these lines on your graph.) (d) Suppose the optimum product mixes before specialization and trade were alternative B in New Zealand and S in Spain. What would be gains from specialization and trade?

Question 24–4
New Zealand

Question 24–4
Spain

(a) New Zealand's cost ratio is 1 plum = 4 apples (or 1 apple = 1/4 plum). Spain's cost ratio is 1 plum = 1 apple (or 1 apple = 1 plum). See the graphs.
(b) New Zealand should specialize in apples, Spain in plums.
(c) See the graphs.
(d) Total production before specialization and trade: 40 apples (20 + 20) and 50 plums (10 + 40). After specialization and trade: 60 apples and 60 plums. Gain = 20 apples and 10 plums.

24–6 Refer to Figure 3.5, p. 49 (Chapter 3). Assume that the graph depicts the U.S. domestic market for corn. How many bushels of corn, if any, will the United States export or import at a world price of $1, $2, $3, $4, and $5? Use this information to construct the U.S. export supply curve and import demand curve for corn. Suppose the only other corn-producing nation is France, where the domestic price is $4. Which country will export corn; which will import it?

Question 24–6

At $1: import 15,000. At $2: import 7,000. At $3: no imports or exports. At $4: export 6,000. At $5: export 10,000.

The United States will export corn; France will import it.

24–7 Draw a domestic supply and demand diagram for a product in which the United States does not have a comparative advantage. What impact do foreign imports have on domestic price and quantity? On your diagram show a protective tariff that eliminates approximately one-half the assumed imports. What are the price-quantity effects of this tariff on (a) domestic consumers, (b) domestic producers, and (c) foreign exporters? How would the effects of a quota that creates the same amount of imports differ?

Question 24–7

See the graph. The United States does not have a comparative advantage in this product so the world price P_w is below the U.S. domestic price of P_d. Imports will reduce the domestic price, increasing consumption from nontrade Q_c to Q_e, and decreasing domestic production from Q_c to Q_a. See the graph. A tariff of P_wP_t (a) harms domestic consumers by increasing price from P_w to P_t and decreasing consumption from Q_e to Q_d; (b) aids domestic producers through the increase in price from P_w to P_t and the expansion of domestic production from Q_a to Q_b; (c) harms foreign exporters by decreasing exports from Q_aQ_e to Q_bQ_d.

An import quota of Q_bQ_d would have the same effects as the tariff, but there would be no tariff revenues to government from these imports; this revenue would effectively go to foreign producers.

CHAPTER 25

25–2 Indicate whether each of the following creates a demand for, or a supply of, European euros in foreign exchange markets:

a. A U.S. airline firm purchases several Airbus planes assembled in France.

b. A German automobile firm decides to build an assembly plant in South Carolina.

c. A U.S. college student decides to spend a year studying at the Sorbonne in Paris.

d. An Italian manufacturer ships machinery from one Italian port to another on a Liberian freighter.

e. The United States' economy grows faster than the French economy.

f. A United States government bond held by a Spanish citizen matures, and the loan is paid back to that person.

g. It is widely believed that the euro will depreciate in the near future.

A demand for euros is created in (a),(c),(e), and (f), but see note below for e. A supply of euros is created in (b), (d), and (g).

Note: Answer for (e) assumes U.S. demand for French goods will grow faster than French imports of U.S. goods.

25–3 Alpha's balance-of-payments data for 2003 are shown below. All figures are in billions of dollars. What are (a) the balance of trade, (b) the balance on goods and services, (c) the balance on current account, and (d) the balance on capital account? Does Alpha have a balance-of-payments deficit or surplus? Explain.

Goods exports	+$40	Net transfers	+$10
Goods imports	− 30	Foreign purchases of	+ 10
Service exports	+ 15	U.S. assets	
Service imports	− 10	U.S. purchases of	− 40
Net investment income	− 5	foreign assets	
		Official reserves	+ 10

Balance of trade = $10 billion surplus (= exports of goods of $40 billion minus imports of goods of $30 billion). *Note:* This is goods balance only—uses narrow definition of trade balance. Balance on goods and services = $15 billion surplus (= $55 billion of exports of goods and services minus $40 billion of imports of goods and services). Balance on current account = $20 billion surplus (= credits of $65 billion minus debits of $45 billion). Balance on capital account = $30 billion deficit (= foreign purchases of assets in the United States of $10 billion minus U.S. purchases of assets abroad of $40 billion). Balance of payments = $10 billion deficit. Therefore, U.S. must export official reserves equal to $10 billion.

25–6 Explain why the U.S. demand for Mexican pesos is downward sloping and the supply of pesos to Americans is upward sloping. Assuming a system of flexible exchange rates between Mexico and the United States, indicate whether each of the following would cause the Mexican peso to appreciate or depreciate:

a. The United States unilaterally reduces tariffs on Mexican products.

b. Mexico encounters severe inflation.

c. Deteriorating political relations reduce American tourism in Mexico.

d. The U.S. economy moves into a severe recession.

e. The United States engages in a high interest rate monetary policy.

f. Mexican products become more fashionable to U.S. consumers.

g. The Mexican government encourages U.S. firms to invest in Mexican oil fields.

h. The rate of productivity growth in the United States diminishes sharply.

The U.S. demand for pesos is downward sloping: When the peso depreciates in value (relative to the dollar) the United States finds that Mexican goods and services are less expensive in dollar terms and purchases more of them, demanding a greater quantity of pesos in the process. The supply of pesos to the United States is upward sloping: As the peso appreciates in value (relative to the dollar), U.S. goods and services become cheaper to Mexicans in peso terms. Mexicans buy more dollars to obtain more U.S. goods, supplying a larger quantity of pesos.

The peso appreciates in (a), (f), (g), and (h) and depreciates in (b), (c), (d), and (e).

25–9 Diagram a market in which the equilibrium dollar price of one unit of fictitious currency zee (Z) is $5 (the exchange rate is $5 = Z1). Then show on your diagram a decline in the demand for zees.

a. Referring to your diagram, discuss the adjustment options the United States would have in maintaining the exchange rate at $5 = Z1 under a fixed exchange-rate system.
b. How would the U.S. balance-of-payments surplus that is created (by the decline in demand) get resolved under a system of flexible exchange rates?

See the graph illustrating the market for zees.

Question 25–9

(a) The decrease in demand for zees from D_1 to D_2 will create a surplus (*ab*) of zees at the $5 price. To maintain the $5 to Z1 exchange rate, the United States must undertake policies to shift the demand-for-zees curve rightward or shift the supply-of-zees curve leftward. To increase the demand for zees, the United States could use dollars or gold to buy zees in the foreign exchange market; employ trade policies to increase imports to the United States from Zeeonia; or enact expansionary fiscal and monetary policies to increase U.S. domestic output and income, thus increasing imports from Zeeonia and elsewhere. Expansionary monetary policy could also reduce the *supply* of zees: Zeeons could respond to the lower U.S. interest rates by reducing their investing in the United States. Therefore, they would not supply as many zees to the foreign exchange market.

(b) Under a system of flexible exchange rates, the *ab* surplus of zees (the U.S. balance-of-payments surplus) will cause the zee to depreciate and the dollar to appreciate until the surplus is eliminated (at the $4 = Z1 exchange rate shown in the figure) because the United States would import more from Zeeonia and they would buy less from the United States since zees had lost value.

CHAPTER 26W

26W–5 Use a supply and demand diagram to explain why persistent shortages of many consumer goods occurred under central planning in the Soviet Union and in prereform China. Why were black markets common in each country?

See Figure 26W.1. Because Russia and China set prices and did not allow them to change as supply or demand shifted, prices were below the equilibrium price for most goods and services. When the fixed price, P_f, is below the equilibrium price, P_e, there will be a shortage since the quantity demanded will exceed the quantity supplied.

Black markets are common where prices are fixed below equilibrium levels. People can buy goods at the fixed government prices (or pay off clerks to save such goods to sell to them), and because of the shortages at the low fixed price, resell these goods at a much higher price to those unable to find the goods in government stores at the controlled prices. This reselling is said to occur on the black market.

26W–6 What have been the major components of economic reform in Russia? What is meant when these reforms are described as "shock therapy"? How successful has Russia been thus far in its reforms?

Privatization of state-owned businesses; market-determined prices; promotion of competition; integration with the world economy; and price-level stabilization. These reforms are referred to as shock therapy because they were dramatic and quick rather than phased in over many years. Russia's reform has nominally privatized much of the economy (but property rights are still not clearly defined), establishing market-determined prices, and setting the stage for future prosperity. But the transition has resulted in declining living standards for many and increasing income inequality. Also, the government still does not have a successful program for collecting taxes.

26W–8 Relate each of the following items to the success of market reform in China: (a) leasing farmland, (b) price reform, (c) private rural and urban enterprises, (d) special economic zones, and (e) corporatization of state-owned enterprises.

(a) Leasing of land resulted in individually operated rather than collectivized farms; this greatly increased production incentives and boosted farm output.
(b) Price reform established market-based prices. These higher-than-government prices provided incentives for enterprises to expand output; they also enabled market-determined allocation of resources to replace inefficient central planning.
(c) Private rural and urban enterprises absorbed workers released by greater productivity in China's agricultural sector and established competition for China's state-owned enterprises.
(d) The special economic zones—with their private corporations, free trade, and foreign investment—established the workability and benefits of "near-capitalism."
(e) Corporatization focused the goals of state-owned enterprises on providing high-quality, minimum per-unit cost goods desired by consumers.